Communications
in Computer and Information Science   2013

Rationale

The CCIS series is devoted to the publication of proceedings of computer science conferences. Its aim is to efficiently disseminate original research results in informatics in printed and electronic form. While the focus is on publication of peer-reviewed full papers presenting mature work, inclusion of reviewed short papers reporting on work in progress is welcome, too. Besides globally relevant meetings with internationally representative program committees guaranteeing a strict peer-reviewing and paper selection process, conferences run by societies or of high regional or national relevance are also considered for publication.

Topics

The topical scope of CCIS spans the entire spectrum of informatics ranging from foundational topics in the theory of computing to information and communications science and technology and a broad variety of interdisciplinary application fields.

Information for Volume Editors and Authors

Publication in CCIS is free of charge. No royalties are paid, however, we offer registered conference participants temporary free access to the online version of the conference proceedings on SpringerLink (http://link.springer.com) by means of an http referrer from the conference website and/or a number of complimentary printed copies, as specified in the official acceptance email of the event.

CCIS proceedings can be published in time for distribution at conferences or as post-proceedings, and delivered in the form of printed books and/or electronically as USBs and/or e-content licenses for accessing proceedings at SpringerLink. Furthermore, CCIS proceedings are included in the CCIS electronic book series hosted in the SpringerLink digital library at http://link.springer.com/bookseries/7899. Conferences publishing in CCIS are allowed to use Online Conference Service (OCS) for managing the whole proceedings lifecycle (from submission and reviewing to preparing for publication) free of charge.

Publication process

The language of publication is exclusively English. Authors publishing in CCIS have to sign the Springer CCIS copyright transfer form, however, they are free to use their material published in CCIS for substantially changed, more elaborate subsequent publications elsewhere. For the preparation of the camera-ready papers/files, authors have to strictly adhere to the Springer CCIS Authors' Instructions and are strongly encouraged to use the CCIS LaTeX style files or templates.

Abstracting/Indexing

CCIS is abstracted/indexed in DBLP, Google Scholar, EI-Compendex, Mathematical Reviews, SCImago, Scopus. CCIS volumes are also submitted for the inclusion in ISI Proceedings.

How to start

To start the evaluation of your proposal for inclusion in the CCIS series, please send an e-mail to ccis@springer.com.

Yuqing Sun · Tun Lu · Tong Wang · Hongfei Fan ·
Dongning Liu · Bowen Du
Editors

Computer Supported Cooperative Work and Social Computing

18th CCF Conference, ChineseCSCW 2023
Harbin, China, August 18–20, 2023
Revised Selected Papers, Part II

 Springer

Editors
Yuqing Sun
Shandong University
Jinan, China

Tong Wang
Harbin Engineering University
Harbin, China

Dongning Liu
Guangdong University of Technology
Guangzhou, China

Tun Lu
Fudan University
Shanghai, China

Hongfei Fan
Tongji University
Shanghai, China

Bowen Du
Tongji University
Shanghai, China

ISSN 1865-0929   ISSN 1865-0937 (electronic)
Communications in Computer and Information Science
ISBN 978-981-99-9639-1   ISBN 978-981-99-9640-7 (eBook)
https://doi.org/10.1007/978-981-99-9640-7

This Springer imprint is published by the registered company Springer Nature Singapore Pte Ltd.
The registered company address is: 152 Beach Road, #21-01/04 Gateway East, Singapore 189721, Singapore

Paper in this product is recyclable.

Preface

Welcome to ChineseCSCW 2023, the 18th CCF Conference on Computer Supported Cooperative Work and Social Computing.

ChineseCSCW 2023 was organized by the China Computer Federation (CCF), and co-hosted by the CCF Technical Committee on Cooperative Computing (CCF TCCC) and the Harbin Engineering University, in Harbin, Heilongjiang, China, during 18–20 August 2023. The conference was also supported by HLJ E-LINK Network Co., Ltd., Guangdong Xuanyuan Network Technology Co., Ltd. and SCHOLAT. The theme of the conference was *Human-Centered Collaborative Intelligence*, which reflects the emerging trend of the combination of artificial intelligence, human-system collaboration, and AI-empowered applications.

ChineseCSCW (initially recognized as CCSCW) is a highly reputable conference series on computer supported cooperative work (CSCW) and social computing in China with a long history. It aims at bridging Chinese and overseas CSCW researchers, practitioners and educators, with a particular focus on innovative models, theories, techniques, algorithms and methods, as well as domain-specific applications and systems, from both technical and social aspects in CSCW and social computing. The conference was initially held biennially since 1998, and has been held annually since 2014.

This year, the conference received 221 submissions, and after a rigorous double-blind peer review process, only 54 of them were eventually accepted as full papers to be orally presented, resulting in an acceptance rate of 24%. The program also included 28 short papers, which were presented as posters. In addition, the conference featured 6 keynote speeches, 5 high-level technical seminars, the ChineseCSCW Cup 2023 Collaborative Intelligence Big Data Challenge (Final Round), the Forum for Outstanding Young Scholars, the Forum for Presentations of Top-Venue Papers, and an awards ceremony. We are grateful to the distinguished keynote speakers, *Weimin Zheng* (CAE Member) from *Tsinghua University*, *Yanning Zhang* from *Northwestern Polytechnical University*, *Junzhou Luo* from *Southeast University*, *Nong Xiao* from *Sun Yat-sen University*, *Chunming Hu* from *Beihang University*, and *Zili Zhang* from *Southwest University*.

We hope that you enjoyed ChineseCSCW 2023.

November 2023

Yong Tang
Zhiwen Yu

Organization

Steering Committee

Yong Tang	South China Normal University, China
Weiqing Tang	China Computer Federation, China
Ning Gu	Fudan University, China
Shaozi Li	Xiamen University, China
Bin Hu	Beijing Institute of Technology, China
Yuqing Sun	Shandong University, China
Xiaoping Liu	Hefei University of Technology, China
Zhiwen Yu	Harbin Engineering University, China
Xiangwei Zheng	Shandong Normal University, China
Tun Lu	Fudan University, China

General Chairs

Yong Tang	South China Normal University, China
Zhiwen Yu	Harbin Engineering University, China

Vice Chair

Zheng Dou	Harbin Engineering University, China

Program Committee Chairs

Yuqing Sun	Shandong University, China
Tun Lu	Fudan University, China
Dongning Liu	Guangdong University of Technology, China
Tong Wang	Harbin Engineering University, China

Organization Committee Chairs

Xiaoping Liu	Hefei University of Technology, China
Chunhui Zhao	Harbin Engineering University, China

Publication Chairs

Bin Hu   Beijing Institute of Technology, China
Hailong Sun   Beihang University, China

Proceedings Editors

Yuqing Sun   Shandong University, China
Tun Lu   Fudan University, China
Tong Wang   Harbin Engineering University, China
Hongfei Fan   Tongji University, China
Dongning Liu   Guangdong University of Technology, China
Bowen Du   Tongji University, China

CSCW Cup Competition Chairs

Chaobo He   South China Normal University, China
Lu Wang   Harbin Engineering University, China
Ronghua Lin   South China Normal University, China

Paper Award Chairs

Shaozi Li   Xiamen University, China
Yichuan Jiang   Southeast University, China

Paper Recommendation Chairs

Honghao Gao   Shanghai University, China
Yiming Tang   Hefei University of Technology, China

Publicity Chairs

Xiangwei Zheng   Shandong Normal University, China
Jianguo Li   South China Normal University, China
Zhongjie Wang   Harbin Engineering University, China
Guangsheng Feng   Harbin Engineering University, China

Finance Chairs

Shan Gao	Harbin Engineering University, China
Min Ouyang	Harbin Engineering University, China

Website Chairs

Jianguo Li	South China Normal University, China
Chengzhe Yuan	Guangdong Polytechnic Normal University, China

Program Committee

Tie Bao	Jilin University, China
Zhan Bu	Nanjing University of Finance and Economics, China
Hongming Cai	Shanghai Jiao Tong University, China
Xinye Cai	Nanjing University of Aeronautics and Astronautics, China
Yongming Cai	Guangdong Pharmaceutical University, China
Yuanzheng Cai	Minjiang University, China
Zhicheng Cai	Nanjing University of Science and Technology, China
Buqing Cao	Hunan University of Science and Technology, China
Donglin Cao	Xiamen University, China
Jian Cao	Shanghai Jiao Tong University, China
Jingjing Cao	Wuhan University of Technology, China
Chao Chen	Chongqing University, China
Jianhui Chen	Beijing University of Technology, China
Liangyin Chen	Sichuan University, China
Long Chen	Southeast University, China
Longbiao Chen	Xiamen University, China
Ningjiang Chen	Guangxi University, China
Qingkui Chen	University of Shanghai for Science and Technology, China
Wang Chen	China North Vehicle Research Institute, China
Weineng Chen	South China University of Technology, China
Xin Chen	Taiyuan University of Science and Technology, China
Yang Chen	Fudan University, China

Zhen Chen	Yanshan University, China
Zonggan Chen	South China Normal University, China
Shiwei Cheng	Zhejiang University of Technology, China
Xiaohui Cheng	Guilin University of Technology, China
Yuan Cheng	Wuhan University, China
Lizhen Cui	Shandong University, China
Weihui Dai	Fudan University, China
Wei Dao	Tisson Regaltec Communications Tech. Co., Ltd., China
Xianghua Ding	University of Glasgow, UK
Wanchun Dou	Nanjing University, China
Bowen Du	Tongji University, China
Guodong Du	Yanshan University, China
Hongfei Fan	Tongji University, China
Yili Fang	Zhejiang Gongshang University, China
Lunke Fei	Guangdong University of Technology, China
Liang Feng	Chongqing University, China
Shanshan Feng	Shandong Normal University, China
Honghao Gao	Shanghai University, China
Jing Gao	Guangdong Hengdian Information Technology Co., Ltd., China
Liping Gao	University of Shanghai for Science and Technology, China
Ying Gao	South China University of Technology, China
Yunjun Gao	Zhejiang University, China
Ning Gu	Fudan University, China
Bin Guo	Northwestern Polytechnical University, China
Kun Guo	Fuzhou University, China
Wei Guo	Shandong University, China
Yinzhang Guo	Taiyuan University of Science and Technology, China
Tao Han	Zhejiang Gongshang University, China
Fei Hao	Shaanxi Normal University, China
Fazhi He	Wuhan University, China
Chaobo He	Zhongkai University of Agriculture and Engineering, China
Haiwu He	Chinese Academy of Sciences, China
Bin Hu	Beijing Institute of Technology, China
Daning Hu	Southern University of Science and Technology, China
Wenting Hu	Jiangsu Open University, China
Yanmei Hu	Chengdu University of Technology, China

Changqin Huang	South China Normal University, China
Faliang Huang	Nanning Normal University, China
Yongjian Huang	Guangdong Xuanyuan Network Technology Co., Ltd., China
Lu Jia	China Agricultural University, China
Tao Jia	Southwest University, China
Min Jiang	Xiamen University, China
Bo Jiang	Zhejiang Gongshang University, China
Wenchao Jiang	Guangdong University of Technology, China
Bin Jiang	Hunan University, China
Jiuchuan Jiang	Nanjing University of Finance and Economics, China
Weijin Jiang	Xiangtan University, China
Yichuan Jiang	Southeast University, China
Miaotianzi Jin	Shenzhen Artificial Intelligence and Data Science Institute (Longhua), China
Lanju Kong	Shandong University, China
Yi Lai	Xi'an University of Posts and Telecommunications, China
Chunying Li	Guangdong Polytechnic Normal University, China
Dongsheng Li	Microsoft Research Asia, China
Guoliang Li	Tsinghua University, China
Hengjie Li	Lanzhou University of Arts and Science, China
Jianguo Li	South China Normal University, China
Jingjing Li	South China Normal University, China
Junli Li	Jinzhong University, China
Li Li	Southwest University, China
Pu Li	Zhengzhou University of Light Industry, China
Renfa Li	Hunan University, China
Shaozi Li	Xiamen University, China
Taoshen Li	Guangxi University, China
Weimin Li	Shanghai University, China
Xiaoping Li	Southeast University, China
Yong Li	Tsinghua University, China
Lu Liang	Guangdong University of Technology, China
Hao Liao	Shenzhen University, China
Bing Lin	Fujian Normal University, China
Dazhen Lin	Xiamen University, China
Cong Liu	Shandong University of Technology, China
Dongning Liu	Guangdong University of Technology, China
Hong Liu	Shandong Normal University, China

Jing Liu	Guangzhou Institute of Technology, Xidian University, China
Li Liu	Chongqing University, China
Shijun Liu	Shandong University, China
Shufen Liu	Jilin University, China
Xiaoping Liu	Hefei University of Technology, China
Yupeng Liu	Harbin University of Science and Technology, China
Yuechang Liu	Jiaying University, China
Zhihan Liu	Central South University, China
Tun Lu	Fudan University, China
Dianjie Lu	Shandong Normal University, China
Hong Lu	Shanghai Polytechnic University, China
Huijuan Lu	China Jiliang University, China
Qiang Lu	Hefei University of Technology, China
Haoyu Luo	South China Normal University, China
Zhiming Luo	Xiamen University, China
Chen Lv	Shandong Normal University, China
Jun Lv	Yantai University, China
Mingjie Lv	Zhejiang Lab, China
Peng Lv	Central South University, China
Pin Lv	Guangxi University, China
Xiao Lv	Naval University of Engineering, China
Chaoqing Ma	Yantai University, China
Hui Ma	University of Electronic Science and Technology of China and Zhongshan Institute, China
Keji Mao	Zhejiang University of Technology, China
Chao Min	Nanjing University, China
Li Ni	Anhui University, China
Haiwei Pan	Harbin Engineering University, China
Li Pan	Shandong University, China
Yinghui Pan	Shenzhen University, China
Yijie Peng	Peking University, China
Lianyong Qi	Qufu Normal University, China
Sihang Qiu	National University of Defense Technology, China
Jiaxing Shang	Chongqing University, China
Limin Shen	Yanshan University, China
Yanjun Shi	Dalian University of Science and Technology, China
Yuliang Shi	Shanda Dareway Company Limited, China
Xiaoxia Song	Datong University, China

Kehua Su	Wuhan University, China
Songzhi Su	Xiamen University, China
Hailong Sun	Beihang University, China
Ruizhi Sun	China Agricultural University, China
Yuqing Sun	Shandong University, China
Yuling Sun	East China Normal University, China
Lina Tan	Hunan University of Technology and Business, China
Wen'an Tan	Nanjing University of Aeronautics and Astronautics, China
Yong Tang	South China Normal University, China
Shan Tang	Shanghai Polytechnic University, China
Weiqing Tang	China Computer Federation, China
Xiaoyong Tang	Changsha University of Science and Technology, China
Yan Tang	Hohai University, China
Yiming Tang	Hefei University of Technology, China
Yizheng Tao	China Academy of Engineering Physics, China
Shaohua Teng	Guangdong University of Technology, China
Fengshi Tian	China People's Police University, China
Zhuo Tian	Institute of Software, Chinese Academy of Sciences, China
Jingbin Wang	Fuzhou University, China
Tao Wang	Minjiang University, China
Binhui Wang	Nankai University, China
Dakuo Wang	Northeastern University, USA
Hongbin Wang	Kunming University of Science and Technology, China
Hongjun Wang	Southwest Jiaotong University, China
Hongbo Wang	University of Science and Technology Beijing, China
Lei Wang	Alibaba Group, China
Lei Wang	Dalian University of Technology, China
Tianbo Wang	Beihang University, China
Tong Wang	Harbin Engineering University, China
Wanyuan Wang	Southeast University, China
Xiaogang Wang	Shanghai Dianji University, China
Yijie Wang	National University of Defense Technology, China
Yingjie Wang	Yantai University, China
Zhenxing Wang	Shanghai Polytechnic University, China
Zhiwen Wang	Guangxi University of Science and Technology, China

Zijia Wang	Guangzhou University, China
Yiping Wen	Hunan University of Science and Technology, China
Ling Wu	Fuzhou University, China
Quanwang Wu	Chongqing University, China
Wen Wu	East China Normal University, China
Xiaokun Wu	South China University of Technology, China
Zhengyang Wu	South China Normal University, China
Chunhe Xia	Beihang University, China
Fangxiong Xiao	Jinling Institute of Technology, China
Jing Xiao	South China Normal University, China
Zheng Xiao	Hunan University, China
Xiaolan Xie	Guilin University of Technology, China
Zhiqiang Xie	Harbin University of Science and Technology, China
Yu Xin	Harbin University of Science and Technology, China
Huanliang Xiong	Jiangxi Agricultural University, China
Jianbo Xu	Hunan University of Science and Technology, China
Jiuyun Xu	China University of Petroleum, China
Meng Xu	Shandong Technology and Business University, China
Heyang Xu	Henan University of Technology, China
Yonghui Xu	Shandong University, China
Xiao Xue	Tianjin University, China
Yaling Xun	Taiyuan University of Science and Technology, China
Jiaqi Yan	Nanjing University, China
Xiaohu Yan	Shenzhen Polytechnic, China
Bo Yang	University of Electronic Science and Technology of China, China
Chao Yang	Hunan University, China
Dingyu Yang	Shanghai Dianji University, China
Gang Yang	Northwestern Polytechnical University, China
Jing Yang	Harbin Engineering University, China
Lin Yang	Shanghai Computer Software Technology Development Center, China
Tianruo Yang	Hainan University, China
Xiaochun Yang	Northeastern University, China
Yan Yao	Qilu University of Technology, China
Shanping Yu	Beijing Institute of Technology, China

Xu Yu	Qingdao University of Science and Technology, China
Jianyong Yu	Hunan University of Science and Technology, China
Yang Yu	Zhongshan University, China
Zhengtao Yu	Kunming University of Science and Technology, China
Zhiwen Yu	Northwestern Polytechnical University, China
Zhiyong Yu	Fuzhou University, China
Chengzhe Yuan	Guangdong Engineering and Technology Research Center for Service Computing, China
Junying Yuan	Nanfang College Guangzhou, China
An Zeng	Guangdong Polytechnical University, China
Dajun Zeng	Institute of Automation, Chinese Academy of Sciences, China
Zhihui Zhan	South China University of Technology, China
Changyou Zhang	Chinese Academy of Sciences, China
Chaowei Zhang	Yangzhou University, China
Jia Zhang	Jinan University, China
Jifu Zhang	Taiyuan University of Science and Technology, China
Jing Zhang	Nanjing University of Science and Technology, China
Liang Zhang	Fudan University, China
Libo Zhang	Southwest University, China
Miaohui Zhang	Energy Research Institute of Jiangxi Academy of Sciences, China
Peng Zhang	Fudan University, China
Senyue Zhang	Shenyang Aerospace University, China
Shaohua Zhang	Shanghai Software Technology Development Center, China
Wei Zhang	Guangdong University of Technology, China
Xin Zhang	Jiangnan University, China
Ying Zhang	Northwestern Polytechnical University, China
Zhiqiang Zhang	Harbin Engineering University, China
Zili Zhang	Southwest University, China
Hong Zhao	Xidian University, China
Tianfang Zhao	Jinan University, China
Jiaoling Zheng	Chengdu University of Information Technology, China
Xiangwei Zheng	Shandong Normal University, China
Jinghui Zhong	South China University of Technology, China
Ning Zhong	Beijing University of Technology, China

Yifeng Zhou	Southeast University, China
Huiling Zhu	Jinan University, China
Jia Zhu	South China Normal University, China
Jianhua Zhu	City University of Hong Kong, China
Jie Zhu	Nanjing University of Posts and Telecommunications, China
Nengjun Zhu	Shanghai University, China
Tingshao Zhu	Chinese Academy of Science, China
Xia Zhu	Southeast University, China
Xianjun Zhu	Jinling University of Science and Technology, China
Yanhua Zhu	First Affiliated Hospital of Guangdong Pharmaceutical University, China
Qiaohong Zu	Wuhan University of Technology, China

Contents – Part II

Cooperative Evolutionary Computation and Human-Like Intelligent Collaboration

Domain-Specific Collaborative Applications

Contents – Part I

Social Media and Online Communities

Collaborative Mechanisms, Models, Approaches, Algorithms and Systems

Crowd Intelligence and Crowd Cooperative Computing

Explicit Coordination Based Multi-agent Reinforcement Learning for Intelligent Traffic Signal Control

Yixuan Li[1], Qian Che[1], Yifeng Zhou[2], Wanyuan Wang[1(✉)], and Yichuan Jiang[1]

[1] Southeast University, Nanjing, China
wywang@seu.edu.cn
[2] Nanjing Audit University, Nanjing, China

Abstract. Traffic signal control plays an important role in reducing urban traffic congestion. In complex traffic scenarios, coordinating phase signal control between intersections is a significant challenge. Reinforcement learning is widely used in the field of intelligent traffic signal control because it is good at dealing with sequence decision problems. The current reinforcement learning based approach makes phase decisions through coordinated cooperation. However, existing methods have difficulty with information exchange, because they lack semantic interpretation and explicit quantification of collaborative impact, which results in inefficient or conflicting phase coordination between intersections. Moreover, during the early exploration stage of reinforcement learning training, the phase output of the decision network is unreliable, making it difficult for the model to utilize decision information for self-supervised training. To address these issues, this paper proposes a self-supervised, explicit coordination based multi-agent reinforcement learning approach. Additionally, a phase boosting learning from demonstration method is introduced in the early training stages. Extensive experimental results demonstrate that this method can enhance collaboration among agents, outperforming baseline methods across multiple real-world traffic datasets, while also improving training stability and convergence speed.

Keywords: Traffic Signal Control · Deep Reinforcement Learning · Attention Mechanism · Learning from Demonstration

1 Introduction

Efficient traffic signal control (TSC) plays a crucial role in managing urban intersections and ensuring smooth traffic flow. According to the 2019 INRIX Global Traffic Scorecard [1], American drivers experienced an average loss of 99 h due to traffic congestion, resulting in an economic loss of \$88 billion. Among the various factors to consider in addressing traffic congestion, vehicle queues at signal-controlled urban intersections are one of the most common congestion phenomena and a critical bottleneck to improving urban traffic efficiency.

© The Author(s), under exclusive license to Springer Nature Singapore Pte Ltd. 2024
Y. Sun et al. (Eds.): ChineseCSCW 2023, CCIS 2013, pp. 3–18, 2024.
https://doi.org/10.1007/978-981-99-9640-7_1

Traditional traffic signal control systems often employ pre-determined timing schemes based on fixed cycles at individual intersections. These systems dynamically adjust signal cycles and phase differences at neighboring intersections using historical traffic data and adaptive sensing to accommodate varying traffic flows. Examples of such systems include SCOOT [2] developed by the UK Transport and Road Research Laboratory, SCATS [3] developed by the New South Wales Roads and Traffic Authority in Australia, and ACTRA developed by Siemens in the United States. These traffic signal control systems operate effectively in situations where traffic flow is relatively stable, but they face limitations in terms of global synchronization and are challenging to scale up for controlling large-scale urban traffic networks. They also have limitations in coping with the ongoing growth of urban vehicles. Distributed traffic signal control techniques focus on coordinating the phase differences of traffic signals along main roads to facilitate uninterrupted traffic flow for vehicles traveling upstream and downstream [4]. However, to ensure real-time responsiveness, decision optimization based on local neighboring intersection communication only considers traffic information from adjacent roads, thus falling short of achieving the global optimum for the system and having certain limitations.

Reinforcement learning [5], a data-driven method that learns through trial and error, has exhibited impressive performance in various domains, particularly in decision-making and planning contexts. The proliferation of traffic simulation software and the abundance of traffic data have generated substantial interest in leveraging reinforcement learning to tackle traffic signal control challenges. Among the various methods available, multi-agent reinforcement learning [6], which models each intersection as an agent, has emerged as the most effective approach to tackle these challenges. By enabling agents to share observational information, this method enhances cooperation between agents, making it the preferred research approach for traffic signal control. But how to define an effective information exchange mechanism is the difficulty of these approaches.

Establishing effective communication mechanisms is crucial for enhancing agent cooperation and decision-making. Current methods utilize either neighbor exchange information, where a neighbor's local observations become part of an agent's state [7–10], or information sharing at the hidden layer [11, 12]. However, these approaches merely offer a qualitative characterization of the impact between adjacent intersections and lack a semantic interpretation. Moreover, increasing the exchange of information between neighbors can result in increased complexity in the state representation, making it challenging to train and converge neural networks. Early exploration decisions during the supervised learning stage of the phase prediction module can result in deviations when predicting the impact on the target intersection, impacting the overall convergence speed of the reinforcement learning training.

To address the limitations of existing methods, we propose an explicit coordination-based multi-agent reinforcement learning approach. Our model comprises two components: the upstream network, including traffic and phase prediction networks, which model the influence of neighboring phases and traffic on the local intersection, and the downstream reinforcement learning Q-network, which combines predictions from the upstream network with its own observations to output phase decisions. we also propose a phase boosting learning from demonstration method for self-supervised training. By incorporating the MaxPressure [13] algorithm, which generates phase decisions based on the intersection's traffic flow state, we generate expert actions in the playback record using states explored by the agents. These expert actions serve as labels for phase prediction training, eliminating reliance on real explored decisions.

In conclusion, the contribution of our article can be summarized as follows:

We propose an explicit coordination based multi-agent reinforcement learning approach. This approach models the information exchange of traffic flows from neighboring agents for each agent, enabling information exchange of phase decisions and traffic flow between neighbors to enhance collaborative effectiveness.

We propose an expert-guided method with a self-supervised training framework. This framework involves pre-training the agents by incorporating high-quality expert decisions and adapting the coordination through exploration alongside agent actions. This framework improves training effectiveness and convergence efficiency, enabling the model to adapt to long-term real-time traffic application scenarios.

Extensive experimental results demonstrate that this method can enhance collaboration among agents, outperforming baseline methods across multiple real-world traffic datasets, while also improving training stability and convergence speed.

2 Related Work

The existing traditional methods in the transportation field, such as SOTL [14], use local intersection observation information to generate better decisions. However, these methods do not consider the long-term impact of signal decisions and lack collaboration among multiple intersections. In recent years, reinforcement learning methods have shown good performance in traffic signal control problems. Traffic signal control is a sequential decision-making process, and efficient feedback for training can be obtained based on the short-term traffic changes caused by the current signal decision, with dense reward signals.

In literature [15], a hybrid reward is proposed based on queue length and waiting time information, achieving good training results. However, this method only considers the state-action reward information of single intersections, and the training of the single agent considers the probability transition of its neighbors' possible decisions as the environmental state, resulting in some limitations.

Literature [16] proposes a reward function that allows the decision of a single agent to consider upstream and downstream collaborative information. This reward is derived from the queueing theory proposed in literature [13]. If an intersection greedily selects the phase with the largest flow difference between upstream and downstream traffic, it can avoid the expansion of queued vehicles in the system over long periods of time, maintaining the stable operation of the traffic flow system. Literature [17] further directly incorporates the flow difference into the state representation. Literature [10] introduces the concept of traffic density and uses neighboring agents to assist in decision-making based on lane traffic density information. The agent regards its neighbor's decision as the environment, but as the neighbor's decision iterates, it will lead to biased evaluations of them.

To achieve information sharing between agents, a suitable information exchange mechanism is crucial. Common methods of information sharing include exchanging neighbor observations directly as part of the state, such as in literature [7]. Classic works in this area include MA2C [8] and FMA2C [18]. Another method is to share hidden layer information. Literature [11] uses graph convolutional networks to model and learn the influence weight of neighboring agents' hidden layers using attention mechanisms, achieving good experimental performance on multiple simulation data. Similar ideas can also be found in literature [19]. However, existing methods do not yet accurately and explicitly measure the meaning and information of shared information.

3   Model and Problem Formulation

3.1   Problem Formulation

This section presents the pertinent definitions and concepts of traffic signal control problems, including intersections, road networks, traffic flow, and signal phases. Figure 1 contains illustrations of these defined concepts.

Road network: An intersection is the starting or ending point of a road. A road $R_{i,j} \in \mathcal{R}$ is an edge connecting intersections I_i and I_j. Each road has multiple branching lanes, and each lane represents the direction of traffic flow.

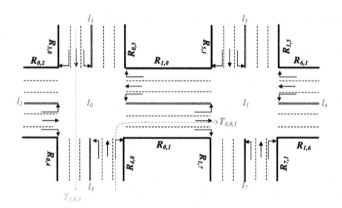

Fig. 1. The symbols in two adjacent intersections indicate.

Traffic movement: $T_{x,i,y}$ is defined as the traffic movement, which represents vehicles traveling from upstream road $R_{x,i}$ passing through intersection I_i and entering downstream road $R_{i,y}$. Typically, an intersection has four upstream roads and four downstream roads, resulting in 12 types of traffic movements. As shown in Fig. 1, $T_{3,0,4}$ and $T_{4,0,1}$ are examples of two traffic movements, where $T_{3,0,4}$ means that the vehicle moves from the upstream road $R_{3,0}$ through junction I_0 to the downstream road $R_{0,4}$. The set of all traffic movements at an intersection is defined as $\mathcal{T}_i = \{T_{x,i,y} | x, y \in \mathcal{I}_i^N, R_{x,i}, R_{i,y} \in \mathcal{R}\}$. We define the vehicle flow on traffic movement $T_{x,i,y}$ as $n_{x,i,y}^t$, which counts all vehicles traveling in direction $R_{x,i}$ and moving in the direction of traffic movement $T_{x,i,y}$.

Signal phase: A signal phase P_i is a set of allowed traffic movements for intersection I_i. Typically, an intersection has eight possible signal phase decisions. A_i represents the set of all phase decisions for the intelligent agent at intersection I_i.

3.2   Traffic Signal Control Model

The problem of multi-agent traffic signal control is defined as a Partially Observed Markov Decision Process (POMDP), which can be represented by a tuple $\langle S, A, P, r, N, \gamma \rangle$. represents the current state of the environment. Suppose there are N agents and each agent $i \in \mathcal{N} := 1, \ldots, N$, chooses an action $a_i \in \mathcal{A}$, and the set of actions for all agents is denoted by $a := [a_i]_{i=1}^{N} \in \mathcal{A}^N$. The transition function $P(s's, a) : S \times \mathcal{A}^N \times S \rightarrow [0, 1]$ transitions from state s to state s'. The environment provides a collective reward defined as the reward function $r(s, a) : S \times \mathcal{A}^N \rightarrow \mathbb{R}$. The ultimate goal of all agents is to maximize the long-term reward of the collective reward, which is defined as $\sum_{i=0}^{\infty} \gamma^i r(s_i, a_i)$, where $\gamma \in [0,1]$ represents the discount factor.

State and Partial Observability: At time step $t \in \mathbb{N}$, agent A_i has partial observation $s_{t,i}$, which includes the average traffic flow $n_{x,i,y}$ of each traffic movement $T_{x,i,y} \in \mathcal{T}_i$ at intersection i, as well as the current traffic signal phase P_i^t. Signal phase P_i^t can control whether traffic movement $T_{x,i,y}$ can pass the intersection i at this moment, which can be denoted as $g_{x,i,y}$. $g_{x,i,y} = 1$ indicates that traffic moving $T_{x,i,y}$ under the current phase P_i^t is passable and $g_{x,i,y} = 0$ indicates that it is not passable.

Action: After receiving partial observation $s_{t,i}$, agent i selects an action from the candidate action set A_i. When an intersection chooses a phase, it will maintain that phase for a duration of Δt. Moreover, when the next effective phase action is different from the current signal phase, the intersection will enter a brief yellow light phase to buffer the traffic flow on the road.

Reward: The goal of the traffic signal control problem is to reduce the average travel time of vehicles. We adopt a globally decomposable reward function $r^t = \sum_{I_i \in \mathcal{I}^R} r_i^t$ that can be linearly decomposed. Here, $r_i^t = -\overline{n_{x,i,y}^{t+1}}$ represents the reciprocal of the average number of vehicles on all lanes entering intersection I_i.

4   Communication Based Dueling Double Deep Q Networks

Since the traffic signal control problem is a partially observed Markov decision process, the purpose of introducing information exchange is to complement the unknown observations of the environment, which in a multi-agent problem is expressed in terms of the decisions that neighbors will take and the potential impact of the decisions on the local agents. This section presents our proposed CommD3QN (Communication based Dueling Double Deep Q Networks). CommD3QN is an explicit framework for exchanging information that enables the influence of neighbors on the local agents to be directly reflected in the rewards of the agents. The model consists of two main parts, the attention based communication prediction part including traffic flow and phase prediction, and the DQN network part with fused phase semantic representation. Figure 2 shows the overview of our model.

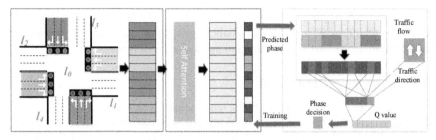

Fig. 2. Overview framework of CommD3QN. CommD3QN predicts the information of neighboring intersections through a self-attentive mechanism. The intersection integrates information to predict the Q value of the phase action to learn the control strategy. The model is a self-supervised learning framework, where the upstream phase prediction network is trained by the phase decisions of the downstream network.

4.1 Explicit Communication Between Agents

We analyze and model the traffic flow between agents for communication. The information that needs to be communicated can be reflected in the reward function. The reward function r^t is defined as the sum of $n_{x,i,y}^{t+1}$, this value can be decomposed into three components:

$$n_{x,i,y}^{t+1} = n_{x,i,y}^t - exit_{x,i,y}^t + in_{x,i,y}^t \tag{1}$$

where $exit_{x,i,y}^t$ is the number of vehicles leaving the traffic movement $T_{x,i,y}$ at time t, and $in_{x,i,y}^t$ is the number of vehicles entering $T_{x,i,y}$. $n_{x,i,y}^t$ can be obtained directly from the local observation of the current intersection, $exit_{x,i,y}^t$ is determined by the number of vehicles in the upstream lane of intersection i and the phase selected by the intersection, so $\sum n_{x,i,y}^t - exit_{x,i,y}^t$ can be introduced by the state information s_i^t of intersection i, noted as a function $f(s_i^t)$. $in_{x,i,y}^t$ is a quantity that is independent of the local observation of intersection i and needs to be obtained by passing exchange information through neighboring intersections. We denote the information passed to it by all neighbor agents of intersection i as c_i^t and denote $in_{x,i,y}^t$ as part of the information c_i^t, so the reward function can be denoted as:

$$r_i^t = f(s_i^t) + c_i^t \tag{2}$$

4.2 Attention Based Prediction Network

Since phases represent the passability of each lane, a 12-dimensional vector $g_{x,i,y}$ can be used to indicate the probability of passing for each lane. $g_{x,i,y}$ is the probability value from 0 to 1. The traffic flow on upstream roads $n_{x,i,y}^t$ can be embedded as a 12-dimensional vector. Since there are a total of 3 driving directions (i.e., straight ahead, left turn, and right turn), the direction is represented by a 3-dimensional one-hot encoding vector, and to obtain better semantic information, the direction one-hot vector is further Embedding into a 2-dimensional vector representation:

$$d_{x,i,y} = Embedding(onehot(d_{x,i,y})) \tag{3}$$

After representing the upstream traffic flow $n^t_{x,i,y}$, the phase $g^t_{x,i,y}$ and the direction vector $d_{x,i,y}$, we obtain the intersection observation vector $h^t_{x,i,y}$. We concatenate the phase vector, the traffic flow vector and the lane movement direction vector to obtain the hidden vector $h^t_{x,i,y}$:

$$h^t_{x,i,y} = linear\left(concat\left(n^t_{x,i,y} + g^t_{x,i,y} + d_{x,i,y}\right)\right) \tag{4}$$

The phase prediction network transforms observation vector $h^t_{x,i,y}$ by attention mechanism and uses the Sigmoid function to generate $g^{t+1}_{x,i,y}$.

$$g^{t+1}_{x,i,y} = Sigmoid\left(Self\_Attention\left(h^t_{x,i,y}\right)\right) \tag{5}$$

Taking intersection 0 as an example, the downstream road 1 is $R_{0,1}$ and $h_{0,1}$ denotes the hidden vector of traffic moving downstream outbound lanes. For downstream road $R_{0,1}$, there are three corresponding upstream lane movement directions, so the result of the product of the hidden vector $h_{x,0,1}$ and $g_{x,0,1}$ for each upstream lane is accumulated to $h_{0,1}$. Since a road contains three branch lanes, the hidden vector $h_{0,1}$ is projected onto each branch lane $l_{0,1,k}$ to calculate the flow in of this lane, which is calculated as:

$$in = linear\left(h_{0,1} + \sum_{x=1}^{3} g_{x,0,1} \times h_{x,0,1}\right) \tag{6}$$

4.3 Downstream DQN Network

By exchanging the *in* information given by the prediction network for neighboring intersections, the intersections are now able to observe the traffic flow on upstream roads $n^t_{x,i,y}$, the traffic flow into the intersection $in_{x,i,y}$ from other intersections, the phase $g_{x,i,y}$ and the lane movement $d_{x,i,y}$. With this observation information, we can design downstream networks to calculate Q values and thus control the behavior of the agents. We first denote the observation vector $o_{x,i,y}$ as the input of the downstream network:

$$o_{x,i,y} = concat\left(add\left(n_{x,i,y}, in_{x,i,y}\right), g_{x,i,y}, d_{x,i,y}\right) \tag{7}$$

Adding the phase of the current moment to the state information can add more observation information to the agent, and concatenate the moving direction vector can also allow the agent to obtain semantic information and enhance the ability to express the state. The obtained observation vector is further characterized as the hidden vector of traffic flow in each moving direction through linear change and ReLu activation function, namely:

$$h_{x,i,y} = ReLu\left(Linear\left(o_{x,i,y}\right)\right) \tag{8}$$

In order to better express the relationship between the decision vector and the hidden vectors of the lanes it affects, the hidden vectors of the passable lanes of each candidate phase decision a are aggregated together, and the average vector of the hidden vectors of the relevant lanes is calculated, that is, for phase a:

$$G = h_{x,i,y} \in h : g^a_{x,i,y} = 1 \tag{9}$$

G represents the hidden vector set of the relevant lane, and the vector average value is linearly transformed to obtain the Q value output of the final decision a:

$$Q_{s,a} = linear(\overline{G}) \tag{10}$$

4.4 Loss Function

We first pre-train the upstream networks by past real phases. The selected phase stored in replay is represented as a 12-dimensional one-hot vector g^r, which indicates whether each lane in the corresponding movement direction of the phase is passable. The g^p is the phase prediction results of the upstream network. We adopt cross-entropy function as the sample loss to optimize the training, which is:

$$L_p = \text{BinaryCrossEntropy}(g^r, g^p) \tag{11}$$

For learning approaching vehicle number, the actual traffic flow of the outflow lane at the next moment is recorded as the label. In order to prevent the training of the flow prediction network from being affected by the training quality of the phase prediction network, the phase vector g^r actually selected in the experience playback is used instead of the predicted vector g^p to perform a cross-product operation to obtain the predicted outflow flow in^r:

$$L_v \leftarrow \text{MeanSquaredError}(Linear(h^r), in^r) \tag{12}$$

5   Expert Experience-Guided Self-Supervised Learning

Our model predicts phase and flow information through the upstream network, which requires reliable phase and flow labels for supervised training. The downstream network relies on the traffic and phase prediction results of the upstream network to make decisions, and through the decision results in turn affects the performance of the upstream network. This section we describe how the model trains the upstream network with the phase output of the downstream network and optimizes the training performance with expert experience (Fig. 3).

5.1   Learning from Demonstration

Learning from demonstration training methods for reinforcement learning have been extensively studied, and one of the most typical works is the DQfD algorithm. This method allows the expert algorithm to interact with the environment to obtain sample data, store it in the experience pool of reinforcement learning.

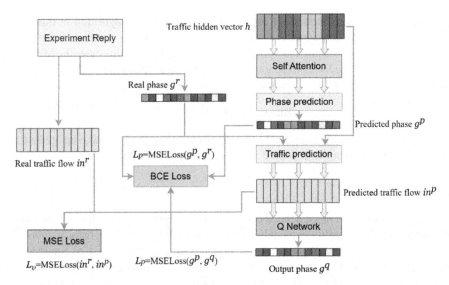

Fig. 3. The framework of expert experience-guided self-supervised learning.

We use the MaxPressure method to interact with the traffic signal control environment to obtain expert experience. Expert optimization exist problem to solve, we propose expert boost technique, the algorithm is mainly trained on expert experience based on the following loss:

$$J(Q) = J_{DQ}(Q) + \lambda_1 J_n(Q) + \lambda_2 J_E(Q) \tag{13}$$

$J_{DQ}(Q)$ is the DQN single-step TD loss:

$$J_{DQ}(Q) = r_t + \gamma Q(s_{t+1}, a) \tag{14}$$

And $J_n(Q)$ is the DQN N-step TD loss:

$$r_t + \gamma r_{t+1} + \ldots + \gamma^{n+1} r_{t+n+1} + \max_a \gamma^n Q(s_{t+n}, a) \tag{15}$$

The use of N-step loss facilitates the propagation of the value of the expert trajectory to the early states, and enables the early decisions of agents to gain expert experience influence in subsequent online learning for better pre-training results. The single-step TD loss with N-step TD loss is based on the Bellman equation, which enables the agents to learn to get a good initial value of the sequence of decision trajectories.

$J_E(Q)$ is a classification loss introduced based on expert experience, which is expressed as:

$$J_E(Q) = \max_{a \in A} \left[Q(s, a) + l(a_E, a) \right] - Q(s, a_E) \tag{16}$$

$l(a_E, a)$ is a marginal function with a constant value greater than zero, which is defined as:

$$l(a_E, a) = \begin{cases} 0, & a_E = a \\ 0.5, & \text{others} \end{cases} \tag{17}$$

Since the upstream network of the reinforcement learning algorithm in this paper contains supervised training tasks for phase prediction and flow prediction, the corresponding supervised learning is required during pre-training. In this case, the MaxPressure expert action to be learned (denoted as g^{MP}) can be used instead of g^r as the sample for phase prediction, and the corresponding cross-entropy loss is calculated as:

$$L_p = \text{BinaryCrossEntropy}\left(g^{MP}, g^p\right) \tag{18}$$

The flow prediction is computed similarly using the product with the upstream flow hidden vector to obtain the flow prediction for the downstream lane.

5.2 Phase Boosting

The use of expert experience actions during the pre-training period helps to learn expert actions, improve the quality of neighboring phase decisions. However, in the exploratory learning phase, the early sample labels are randomly generated or decisions generated by the unconverged Q-network with relatively low decision quality and large differences from the previous expert decision phases, which may lead to the learning effect of pre-training being wasted and increase the learning convergence time of the algorithm.

To address the above problems, this section proposes an expert empirical learning optimization for phase prediction optimization. Since the MaxPressure algorithm is an online planning decision method, the corresponding phase decision can be generated given the traffic flow state of the intersection. Therefore, in the playback record, the corresponding expert actions can be generated based on the states explored by the agents and used as labels for the phase prediction training instead of the explored decisions. The predicted flow is based on the real phase to do the product calculation:

$$in_{i,y} = h_{i,y} + \sum_{x=1}^{3} g^r_{x,i,y} \times h_{x,i,y} \tag{19}$$

Since the calculation of flow prediction is based on the real selected phase rather than the predicted phase, the main influencing factor in the flow training is related to the decision phase selected by the downstream Q-network, which is shown in the updating process of the gradient as

$$\frac{\partial L_y}{\partial h_{x,i,y}} = 0 \ if \ g^r_{x,i,y} = 0 \tag{20}$$

Early in the reinforcement learning training stage, we use MaxPressure's decision phase as a label for supervised training of phase prediction. As the training effect of the agents improves, the real phase of the agents can be used as the label in the subsequent iterations of reinforcement learning training. The phase prediction training loss in this paper is set as

$$L_p = p * \text{BinaryCrossEntropy}\left(g^{MP}, g^p\right) + \\ (1 - p) * \text{BinaryCrossEntropy}\left(g^r, g^p\right) \tag{21}$$

where p is the control coefficient, the initial value is 1, and slowly decreases with the number of training iterations, and is set to decrease to 0 after 15 epochs in the experiment.

6 Experiments

In this section, we aim to validate the effectiveness of the proposed multi-agent reinforcement learning signal control method. The main focus is to examine whether the explicit coordination based multi-agent method can enhance the signal control efficiency. Additionally, we experimentally verify the proposed phase boosting learning form demonstration method through ablation analysis.

6.1 Datasets

In order to simulate the traffic flow in urban road networks, experiments need to be conducted based on a simulation platform. The maximum travel speed of the traffic flow in the experiment is set to 10 m/s. Each vehicle of the traffic network can be described by metazoan (o, t, d), o denotes the starting position, t table the departure time, d is the end position.

Simulation Data: simulation data were generated for four different road network topologies. Among them, large data of 15×15 (i.e., 225 intersections) and 20×20 (400 intersections). Vehicles enter the road network through boundary intersections and follow a uniform arrival rate. The experiments simulate traffic operations with a duration of 3600 s on the traffic road network, and the lane length information H-k-V-l indicates that the lane length within the road network is k m in the horizontal (H) direction and l m in the vertical (V) direction.

Real-world Datasets: traffic datasets collected from three cities [11] were selected to evaluate the performance of the method. The NY dataset is the traffic data of 16 intersections on Eighth Avenue in New York City with one-way traffic on both main and side streets. The JN data is the traffic data collected by roadside cameras from 12 intersections on Dongfeng Street in Jinan, China. The HZ data is the traffic data of 16 intersections on Gudang Street generated from roadside surveillance.

6.2 Evaluation Results

The baseline methods are PressLight [16], LIT [20], MA2C [8], FMA2C [18]. Following existing research [21], we selected average travel time and average waiting time as performance metrics for evaluating signal control methods. In order to calculate waiting time, vehicle speeds are assessed, with vehicles traveling at speeds below a threshold considered as waiting vehicles. In our experiments, we set the speed threshold to 0.1 m/s.

We show the experimental results in Table 1. The experimental results show that, compared to other reinforcement learning methods, the proposed CommD3QN has optimal experimental performance in most scenarios. It can be observed that only PressLight with optimized pressure function as reward performs better among the baseline methods under NY2 data, which prove the effectiveness of the MaxPressure method on this data. On the other datasets, our method performs well on both NY data. And the optimal results on JN, HZ, and SYN_4 show that the introduction of display coordination information allows the agents to efficiently regulate the upstream and downstream traffic flow and improve the traffic operation efficiency under the relatively complex road network.

Table 1. Average travel time

	NY	NY2	JN	HZ	SYN_4
LIT	103.1	295.8	316.4	362.2	184.6
PressLight	106.2	182.4	301.3	365.0	184.8
MA2C	115.4	244.1	306.4	364.1	205.0
FMA2C	120.5	241.2	304.6	361.1	199.6
CommD3QN	**104.8**	**178.6**	**292.3**	**344.8**	**182.2**

Table 2. Average waiting time

	NY	NY2	JN	HZ	SYN_4
LIT	15.9	129.6	52.4	28.6	37.4
PressLight	19.0	**16.2**	78.4	31.4	37.6
MA2C	28.2	77.9	52.4	30.5	57.8
FMA2C	33.3	75.0	37.3	27.5	52.4
CommD3QN	**17.6**	17.4	**42.4**	**11.2**	**35.0**

6.3 Ablation Experiments

The ablation experimental section focuses on the following three approaches: explicitly coordinated multi-agent model without expert experience (NO_LFD), and model with expert experience for pre-training (LFD), and model using expert experience for phase boosting self-supervised learning (LFD + Phase Boost). We conducted experiments on four datasets: JN, HZ, NY, and SYN_4.

Average Traffic Travel Time
On each of the four datasets mentioned above, the reinforcement learning models are trained, and Fig. 4 shows the learning curves of the test datasets. The horizontal coordinate represents the number of training iterations and the vertical coordinate represents the average travel time. Results show that the learning form demonstration in four datasets can make the curve decrease rapidly. In addition, it is observed that the test curve without expert experience still have a "jump" phenomenon after hundreds of epochs, while method with expert experience (LFD and LFD + Phase Boost) results in significantly less oscillatory jumps in the later stages of the curve, demonstrating the expert experience can consolidate the convergence of the model training.

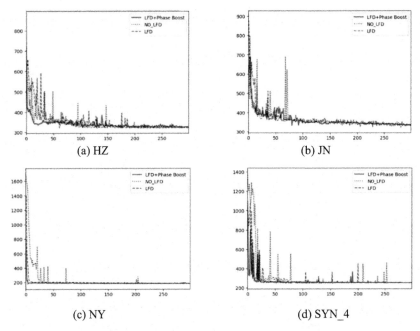

Fig. 4. Training curve of average traffic travel time

Phase Prediction Loss

To observe the performance of different methods on the phase prediction task, the phase prediction loss records after each training were plotted as curves, as shown in Fig. 5. The horizontal coordinate represents the training time and the vertical coordinate represents the binary cross-entropy loss. It is observed that except for the HZ dataset, introducing pre-training on the remaining three datasets all resulted in a faster decrease in phase prediction loss, demonstrating that introducing exemplary learning pre-training can help supervised training to obtain better network parameters at an early stage. The expert phase supervision labels (LFD + Phase Boost) help the agents to obtain extremely low phase prediction loss on some data scenarios, especially on the NY dataset.

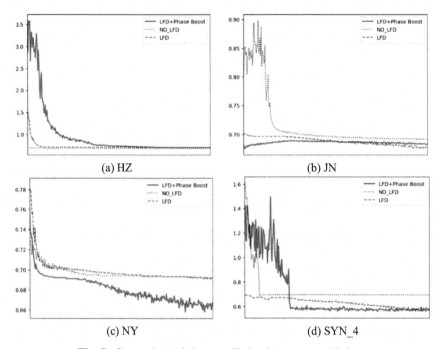

Fig. 5. Comparison of phase prediction loss curves with time

7   Conclusion

Traffic signal control is the key to roadway traffic systems and directly affects roadway flow and traffic stress. The extant approaches are based on implicit learning of information exchange by deep networks, which cannot directly quantify the impact of neighboring intersection decisions on local intersections. Moreover, reinforcement learning requires a large amount of exploration process, and the phase prediction of the agents has the problems of instability and difficulty in convergence. To address the above technical challenges, this paper proposes an explicit coordinated traffic signal control method that predicts neighboring phase and flow information, and designs a phase boosting learning form demonstration method. Since our method needs to be retrained under different traffic road networks and traffic distribution, a promising research direction in the future is to try to improve the generalization migration capability of the model under different road network data, and meta-learning and generative models are solution ideas that can be tried.

Acknowledgement. This research was supported by the National Natural Science Foundation of China (62076060, 62072099, 61932007, 61806053).

References

1. Reed, T.: INRIX global traffic scorecard (2019)

2. Robertson, D.I., Bretherton, R.D.: Optimizing networks of traffic signals in real time-the SCOOT method. IEEE Trans. Veh. Technol. **40**, 11–15 (1991)
3. Lowrie, P.R.: Scats, sydney co-ordinated adaptive traffic system: a traffic responsive method of controlling urban traffic (1990)
4. Ye, B., Weimin, W., Weijie, M.: A two-way arterial signal coordination method with queueing process considered. IEEE Trans. Intell. Transp. Syst. **16**(6), 3440–3452 (2015)
5. Wiering, M.A., Martijn V.O.: Reinforcement Learning. Adaptation, learning, and optimization, p. 729 (2012). https://doi.org/10.1007/978-3-642-27645-3
6. Buşoniu, L., Babuška, R., De Schutter, B.: Multi-agent reinforcement learning: an overview. In: Srinivasan, D., Jain, L.C. (eds.) Innovations in Multi-Agent Systems and Applications - 1, pp. 183–221. Springer, Heidelberg (2010). https://doi.org/10.1007/978-3-642-14435-6_7
7. El-Tantawy, S., Baher, A., Hossam, A.: Multiagent reinforcement learning for integrated network of adaptive traffic signal controllers (MARLIN-ATSC): methodology and large-scale application on downtown Toronto. IEEE Trans. Intell. Transp. Syst. **14**(3), 1140–1150 (2013)
8. Chu, T., Wang, J., Codecà, L., et al.: Multi-agent deep reinforcement learning for large-scale traffic signal control. IEEE Trans. Intell. Transp. Syst. **21**(3), 1086–1095 (2019)
9. Liu, J., Zhang, H., Fu, Z., et al.: Learning scalable multi-agent coordination by spatial differentiation for traffic signal control. Eng. Appl. Artif. Intell. Appl. Artif. Intell. **100**, 104165 (2021)
10. Zhao, W., et al.: IPDALight: Intensity-and phase duration-aware traffic signal control based on reinforcement learning. J. Syst. Architect. **123**, 102374 (2022)
11. Wei, H., et al.: CoLight: learning network-level cooperation for traffic signal control. In: Proceedings of the 28th ACM International Conference on Information and Knowledge Management (2019)
12. Zhu, L., et al.: Meta variationally intrinsic motivated reinforcement learning for decentralized traffic signal control. arXiv preprint arXiv:2101.00746 (2021)
13. Varaiya, P.: Max pressure control of a network of signalized intersections. Trans. Res. C Emerg. Technol. **36**, 177–195 (2013)
14. Cools, S.-B., Gershenson, C., D'Hooghe, B.: Self-organizing traffic lights: a realistic simulation. In: Prokopenko, M. (ed.) Advances in Applied Self-Organizing Systems, pp. 45–55. Springer, London (2013). https://doi.org/10.1007/978-1-4471-5113-5_3
15. Wei, H., et al.: IntelliLight: a reinforcement learning approach for intelligent traffic light control. In: Proceedings of the 24th ACM SIGKDD International Conference on Knowledge Discovery & Data Mining (2018)
16. Wei, H., et al.: PressLight: learning max pressure control to coordinate traffic signals in arterial network. In: Proceedings of the 25th ACM SIGKDD International Conference on Knowledge Discovery & Data Mining (2019)
17. Zhang, L., et al.: Expression might be enough: representing pressure and demand for reinforcement learning based traffic signal control. In: International Conference on Machine Learning. PMLR (2022)
18. Ma, J., Feng, W.: Feudal multi-agent deep reinforcement learning for traffic signal control. In: Proceedings of the 19th International Conference on Autonomous Agents and Multiagent Systems (2020)
19. Zhang, Y., Mehul, D., Guillaume, S.: Multi-agent traffic signal control via distributed RL with spatial and temporal feature extraction. In: Melo, F.S., Fang, F. (eds.) Autonomous Agents and Multiagent Systems. Best and Visionary Papers: AAMAS 2022 Workshops, Springer, Cham (2022). https://doi.org/10.1007/978-3-031-20179-0_7

20. Zheng, G., et al.: Diagnosing reinforcement learning for traffic signal control. arXiv preprint arXiv:1905.04716 (2019)
21. Oroojlooy, A., et al.: AttendLight: universal attention-based reinforcement learning model for traffic signal control. Adv. Neural Inform. Process. Syst. **33**, 4079–4090 (2020)

A Crowdsourcing Task Allocation Mechanism for Hybrid Worker Context Based on Skill Level Updating

Jiuchuan Jiang$^{(\boxtimes)}$ and Jinpeng Wei

School of Information Engineering, Nanjing University of Finance and Economics,
Nanjing 210023, China
jcjiang@nufe.edu.cn

Abstract. Existing crowdsourcing research has traditionally focused on high-skilled workers during the task allocation phase while neglected the potential value and skill enhancement opportunities of workers who are with lower skill levels. Consequently, as the number of completed tasks increases, skill disparities among workers have worsened. This can be primarily attributed to the platform's heavy reliance on high-skilled workers, which makes it difficult for lower-skilled ordinary workers to meet task requirements and limits their chances for skill development. As a result, when a large volume of tasks awaits allocation, the limited number of high-skilled workers falls short of meeting the task demand, resulting in prolonged task completion periods and reduced task allocation success rates. In reality, the majority of tasks on crowdsourcing platforms contain straightforward components that can be handled by ordinary workers. Additionally, collaborative efforts among multiple workers can enhance task execution efficiency and reduce task durations. Building on these practical observations, this paper proposes a task allocation model and simulates the improvement of worker skill levels. In situations where teams take a longer time to complete tasks, the model allows ordinary workers to join the team, thereby assisting professional workers in enhancing work efficiency. Experimental results demonstrate that this model can alleviate worker skill disparities, diminish task durations, and facilitate the development of crowdsourcing platforms.

Keywords: Crowdsourcing · Complex Tasks · Task Allocation · Cooperation of workers · Skill Levels

1 Introduction

In the context of crowdsourcing task allocation, current research primarily focuses on choosing the top workers and teams to carry out tasks [1, 2]. Consequently, most tasks end up being assigned to professional workers, which makes it difficult for ordinary workers to access these tasks. However, task completion plays a crucial role in improving workers' skills [3]. Therefore, the allocation of the majority of tasks to professional workers has widened the skill gap between them and ordinary workers on the platform. This situation poses a potential threat to the platform's long-term sustainability.

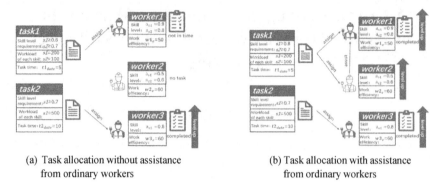

(a) Task allocation without assistance
from ordinary workers

(b) Task allocation with assistance
from ordinary workers

Fig. 1. Task allocation before and after introducing ordinary workers' assistance.

In practical crowdsourcing platforms, we have observed that many complex tasks require high-level expertise but also have simpler components that can be assisted by ordinary workers working together with professionals. For example, in the development of an artificial intelligence project [4], there are several stages involved, such as feasibility assessment, data processing and mining, model construction, model selection, model fusion for enhanced performance, parameter tuning, optimization, testing, and more. Assigning all these tasks to a single professional worker would consume a significant amount of their time. However, if professional workers collaborate with workers who have some knowledge of artificial intelligence models, certain aspects like data processing, parameter adjustments, coding, and testing could be delegated to ordinary workers. This approach allows professional workers to focus on high-level requirements like feasibility assessment, model selection, fusion, and construction, while reducing the wastage of their resources and enhancing their task execution efficiency. Simultaneously, it provides ordinary workers with opportunities to continually improve their skill levels through repeated task engagements.

To address issues such as the shortage of professional workers, heavy workloads, limited opportunities for ordinary workers, and low skill levels within the platform, this paper proposes a collaborative task allocation approach that considers both worker skill improvement and work efficiency. Figure 1 illustrates the scenarios of task allocation and worker skill improvement, including the option for ordinary workers to join the collaboration. The diagram showcases two tasks ($t1$ and $t2$) and three workers ($w1$, $w2$, and $w3$). Before task completion, each worker can only undertake one task. Completing task $t1$ requires workers to possess skills $s1$ (with a skill level of no less than 0.8) and $s2$ (with a skill level of no less than 0.7). The workload for skill s1 is 200, and for s2 is 100. Task $t1$ needs to be completed by workers within 5 days. Completing task $t2$ requires workers to have skill $s1$ (with a skill level of no less than 0.7), and the workload for $s1$ is 500. Task $t2$ needs to be completed by workers within 10 days.

Prior to task completion, each worker can only undertake one task. Task $t1$ requires workers to possess skills $s1$ (with a minimum skill level of 0.8) and $s2$ (with a minimum skill level of 0.7). The workload for skill $s1$ is 200, while for skill $s2$ it is 100. Task $t1$ needs to be completed within 5 days. On the other hand, task $t2$ requires workers to have skill *s1* (with a minimum skill level of 0.7), and the workload for skill *s1* is 500. Task *t2* must be completed within 10 days.

In Fig. 1(a), task *t1* is assigned to worker *w1*, while task *t2* is allocated to worker *w3*. Although worker *w1*'s skill level meets the requirements for task *t1*, their work efficiency is only 50 per day, making it impossible to complete task *t1* within the required 5 days, resulting in the failure of task *t1*. Worker *w2* possesses skills *s1* and *s2*, but due to insufficient skill levels, they remain idle without tasks to perform. Only worker *w3* manages to complete task *t2* in a timely manner, thereby improving their skill level.

Figure 1(b) illustrates the scenario of task allocation and worker skill improvement with the assistance of ordinary workers. Task *t1* involves worker *w2* joining the team of worker *w1* to collaborate on completing the task. This allows task *t1* to be completed on time, and in some cases, even ahead of schedule. Additionally, both worker *w1* and *w2* experience skill level improvements as a result of their collaboration.

This paper introduces a collaborative task allocation approach that enhances the overall work efficiency of professional worker teams by involving ordinary workers with task-specific skills in task completion. In comparison to traditional task allocation methods that overlook ordinary workers, our approach offers several advantages: 1) Improved work efficiency for professional workers, resulting in shorter expected task completion times, enabling them to complete more tasks. 2) Increased opportunities for ordinary workers to complete tasks, thereby raising their skill levels and income. 3) From the platform's perspective, the reduction in expected task completion times enables more tasks to be completed on schedule or even ahead of time, enhancing the mobility of professional workers and alleviating the pressure caused by a shortage of professional workers on the platform. Furthermore, this method can narrow the skill gap between professional and ordinary workers, contributing to the platform's sustainability.

2   Related Work

2.1   Skills Research in Crowdsourcing

In the field of crowdsourcing, there exists a substantial body of research that has focused extensively on worker skills. Previous studies [5, 6] have indicated that workers in crowdsourcing are inherently motivated to enhance their skill levels when selecting tasks. Research on worker skills in crowdsourcing can be broadly categorized into two main types:1) One category of research aims to facilitate worker learning and skill development through crowdsourcing platforms. For instance, a method combining crowdsourcing with learning was proposed by Dontcheva et al. [7]. Research has shown that participants engaged in learning-integrated crowdsourcing tasks exhibit higher enthusiasm, satisfaction, and skill levels. In another study by Dow et al. [8], various management strategies' impacts on work quality in crowdsourcing tasks were investigated. Multiple experiments were designed to evaluate the effectiveness of different management strategies in enhancing crowdsourced work quality. 2) Another category of research focuses on matching tasks with suitable workers based on their skills during the task allocation phase. For example, in the work by Baba et al. [9], an algorithmic framework was designed to match appropriate participants for crowdsourcing contests by considering their skills, experience, and preferences. In the study by Wang et al. [10], a recommendation system for crowdsourced software development projects was proposed, considering skill improvement as a prerequisite. In this work, we consider worker skill level enhancement and find that crowdsourcing platforms primarily allocate tasks to professional workers, thereby overlooking the value of the majority of ordinary workers on the platform.

2.2 Collaboration Among Workers in Crowdsourcing

Collaboration strategies among workers in existing research can be categorized into two main types: 1) Platform-Based Crowdsourcing Worker Recruitment Strategy: The advantage of this approach is that the platform can use worker information effectively to optimize team composition, enhance worker matching, and thereby improve task completion efficiency and quality. However, it also has its limitations, as platform algorithms may exhibit biases and constraints, not fully considering the interpersonal relationships and cooperation among workers. For example, in the work by Samanta et al. [11], a skill-oriented dynamic task assignment method was proposed. It assigns tasks based on skill requirements and candidate skill combinations, also taking into account the preferences of qualified candidates, thus maximizing the platform's net utility. In the study by Yu et al. [12], worker capabilities, task module complexity, and worker activity time were considered to construct optimization objectives. 2) Leader-Based Crowdsourcing Worker Recruitment Strategy: The advantage of this approach lies in the leader's ability to better utilize interpersonal relationships and cooperation among workers, improving teamwork efficiency and quality. However, it also has its drawbacks, as leader capabilities and qualities may vary, potentially affecting the overall team's performance and outcomes. For instance, in the work by Li et al. [13], an efficient algorithm was designed to identify and organize experts in a professional social network. In the study by Anagnostopoulos et al. [14], an online team formation framework was proposed for real-time identification and organization of experts with specific skills and knowledge in social networks to efficiently accomplish tasks. In the work by Hamrouni et al. [15], an algorithm was proposed that utilized team members' knowledge of their social network neighbors to assign a team leader and recruit appropriate teams. These teams not only possessed the required expertise but also had social connections, enabling effective collaboration in task completion.

3 Problem Description

We will introduce the worker skill enhancement mechanism of this paper in Sect. 3.1. In Sect. 3.2, we will present the problem model of this paper.

3.1 Worker Skill Enhancement Mechanism

In real-world scenarios, a worker's skill level tends to improve when they complete tasks within the specified time frame. Additionally, this skill improvement is often related to the task's skill requirements and the worker with the highest skill level in the team. Therefore, to simulate the skill improvement process that occurs when crowdsourcing workers complete tasks in real situations, this paper has devised a mechanism for enhancing worker skill levels. In this mechanism, we initially define the skill level requirements for task t, denoted as $Acc_t(S_t(j))$, the skill levels of worker w_i, denoted as $Acc_{w_i}(S_t(j))$, and the skill level improvement achieved by worker w_i upon completing task t. The specific definition of this mechanism is as follows:

$$Acc_{w_i}(S_t(j)) = Acc_{w_i}(S_t(j)) + \varepsilon_{t \to w_i} \tag{1}$$

where $\varepsilon_{t \to w_i}$ represents the skill level improvement of worker w_i after completing task t, defined as follows:

$$\varepsilon_{t \to w_i} = \left(1 - Acc_{w_i}(S_t(j))\right) \cdot \left[\begin{array}{l} \beta \cdot \left(\max_{w_i \in W} Acc_{w_i}(S_t(j)) - Acc_{w_i}(S_t(j)) \right) + \\ (1 - \beta) \cdot \left| Acc_t(S_t(j)) - Acc_{w_i}(S_t(j)) \right| \end{array} \right] \tag{2}$$

where $Acc_{w_i}(S_t(j))$ represents the skill level of worker w_i in skill $S_t(j)$, and $Acc_t(S_t(j))$ represents the skill level requirement of task t for skill $S_t(j)$. β is a parameter that controls the weight of the influence of the highest-skilled worker in the team and task requirements on the enhancement of worker skill levels, its range is [0, 1.0].

3.2 Problem Model

The current task allocation presents the following issues: platforms often prioritize assigning complex tasks to professional workers, leaving ordinary workers with a lack of tasks and no opportunity to improve their skill levels. Meanwhile, the skill levels of professional workers continue to advance, leading to a gap in the overall skill levels of the worker pool. However, due to the limited number of professional workers and their longer working hours on complex tasks, it becomes increasingly difficult to success-fully allocate these tasks. In order to foster the development of the overall skill level of complex task teams and increase task allocation success rates, we need to address the problem of maximizing the overall skill enhancement of the team while minimizing task completion time. Given the nature of tasks, professional workers can delegate some relatively simple parts to ordinary workers to reduce the workload of professional work-ers, enhance their work efficiency, and enable ordinary workers to improve their skill levels through task participation. Therefore, we need to select a team of members that meet the following criteria: 1) Maximize the overall skill enhancement of team mem-bers after completing tasks; 2) Maximize the efficiency of the team in executing tasks. Therefore, the goal of selecting an appropriate team of members for complex tasks can be formalized as follows:

$$W_t = \arg \max_{W_t \subseteq W} \left(\frac{\sum_{w_i \in W_t} \varepsilon_{t_i \to w_i}}{time_t} \right) \tag{3}$$

$$\text{subject to} : \forall S_t(j) \in S_t, \exists Acc_{w_i}(S_t(j)) \geq Acc_t(S_t(j)) \tag{4}$$

$$\sum_{w_i \in W_t} \gamma_{w_i} \leq b_t \tag{5}$$

$$time_t \leq date_t \tag{6}$$

where $date_t$ represents the completion time requirement for task t, and $time_t$ denotes the expected time for task team W_t to complete the task, expressed as:

$$time_t = \max_{S_t(j) \in S_t} \left\{ \frac{workload_{t_{S_t(j)}}}{efficient_{S_t(j)}^{W_t}} \right\} \tag{7}$$

where $workload_{t_{S_t(j)}}$ represents the workload in task t that requires skill $S_t(j)$, , with a value ranging from [0, 1000]. $efficient_{S_t(j)}^{W_t}$ represents the overall efficiency of workers in task team W_t who possess skill $S_t(j)$, expressed as:

$$
\begin{aligned}
efficient_{S_t(j)}^{W_t} = & \sum_{w_i \in W_t, Acc_{w_i}(S_t(j)) \geq Acc_t(S_t(j))} efficient_{S_t(j)}^{w_i} + \\
\alpha \cdot & \sum_{w_k \in W_t, Acc_{w_k}(S_t(j)) \leq Acc_t(S_t(j))} efficient_{S_t(j)}^{w_k} \cdot Acc_{w_k}(S_t(j))
\end{aligned}
\tag{8}
$$

where $efficient_{S_t(j)}^{w_i}$ represents the efficiency of worker w_i in performing skill $S_t(j)$ tasks in task t. In practice, a worker's efficiency in executing tasks related to different skills is influenced by their skill levels, as indicated below:

$$efficient_{S_t(j)}^{w_i} = efficient_{w_i} \cdot \frac{Acc_{w_i}(s)}{\sum_{s \in S_t \cap S_{w_i}} Acc_{w_i}(s)} \tag{9}$$

where $efficient_{w_i}$ represents the efficiency of the worker, with a value ranging from [0, 100].

4   Task Allocation Model Based on Minimizing Maximum Skill Completion Time Algorithm

This section explores the assignment of tasks to appropriate workers by measuring the cost-effectiveness of workers for the tasks. In the task allocation process of our algorithm in this paper, we divide the worker selection process into two stages: 1) initially selecting professional workers to ensure the team's capability to complete the task; 2) subsequently selecting high-cost-effectiveness workers to reduce the time required for the team to complete the task.

In Sect. 4.1, we introduced the criteria for measuring the cost-effectiveness of workers for tasks in both stages, which are used to determine the priority of workers in task allocation. In Sect. 4.2, we proposed an algorithm based on holistic optimization. The objective of this algorithm is to maximize the overall skill enhancement of the team while minimizing the time taken for the team to execute tasks requiring the longest skill. Through this algorithm, we can better balance the relationship between the overall skill level of the team and task execution efficiency, thereby reducing task cycles and fostering worker skills, laying a solid foundation for subsequent task allocations.

4.1 Worker Cost-Effectiveness

In the first stage, we prioritize professional workers based on their skill levels, the coverage of task skills by workers, and the compensation they require. We also require workers to possess at least one skill that the current team lacks to meet the task requirements, and their skill levels must meet the standards. Additionally, we consider that the higher the skill level of a professional worker, the greater their impact on the skill enhancement of other workers. Therefore, the cost-effectiveness of worker w_i for task t is formally defined as follows:

$$quality_{w_i \to t} = \frac{\sum_{s \in S_t - S_{W_t}} Acc_{w_i}(s)}{\gamma_{w_i}} \tag{10}$$

$$subject\ to : \exists s \in S_t - S_{W_t}, Acc_{w_i}(s) \geq Acc_t(s) \tag{11}$$

Based on the aforementioned definition of cost-effectiveness for professional workers, we can select suitable professional workers to join the team to ensure the team's capability to complete the task. When the task team has the capability to complete the task, the task allocation proceeds to the second stage. In this stage, we screen for workers who possess task skills and high efficiency to assist professional workers in improving work efficiency and reducing the time required to complete the task. Since the task completion time is influenced by the longest time taken for tasks involving various skills, we need to select highly efficient workers who possess the skill $S_t(j)$ requiring the most time within the current team. Additionally, we consider the coverage of workers in other task skills and the potential for skill improvement to maximize the overall skill enhancement of the team. This is formalized as follows:

$$Select_{w_i}^{W_t} = \frac{\left[\begin{array}{c} Acc_{w_i}(S_t(j)) \cdot \left(Acc_t(S_t(j)) - Acc_{w_i}(S_t(j))\right) \\ + \frac{\sum_{s \in S_t \cap S_{w_i} - S_t(j)} Acc_{w_i}(s) \cdot \left(Acc_t(s) - Acc_{w_i}(s)\right)}{|S_t \cap S_{w_i} - S_t(j)|} \end{array} \right]}{\gamma_{w_i}} \cdot efficient_{S_t(j)}^{w_i} \tag{12}$$

4.2 Minimizing Maximum Skill Completion Time Algorithm

Based on the worker value definition provided in Sect. 4.1, we can use the 'Minimizing Maximum Skill Completion Time' method to allocate tasks to teams with the highest value. In Algorithm 1, the task allocation model consists of two main parts: the task allocation process and the task execution process, as detailed below:

1) **Task Allocation Process**: In the first stage, we select suitable professional workers to form the task team based on their 'quality' for the task, denoted as $quality_{w_i \to t}$. We then calculate the completion time for each skill subtask within the team based on the individual work efficiencies $efficient_{w_i}$. In the second stage, we check if the team has the capability to complete the task, i.e., whether the team meets the skill and skill level requirements for the task. We then select appropriate workers to join the team based on the completion time for each skill subtask, aiming to minimize the total task duration until the budget is exhausted or the task duration falls below 1 day. Finally, we verify whether the expected duration of the task completion, denoted as $time_t$, is less than or equal to the task's required duration, denoted as $date_t$.

Algorithm 1: Minimum Maximum Skill-Time Allocation Model (MMT)

Input: Set of tasks T, Set of workers W

Output: Task team W_t

1) Initialize $W_t \leftarrow \emptyset, W_{t_{candidate}} \leftarrow \emptyset, W_{working} \leftarrow \emptyset, task_{num} \leftarrow 0, day \leftarrow 0$

2) For $t \in T$ do

3) $task_{num} += 1$;

4)   If $task_{num} \% day_{task_{num}} == 0$ then

5) $day += 1$;

6)   For $w_i \in W_{working}[1]$ do

7) $Acc_{w_i}(S_t(j)) = Acc_{w_i}(S_t(j)) + \varepsilon_{t \to w_i}$;

8) $W = W \cup \{w_i\}$;

9)   End

10) $W_{working}[1] \leftarrow \emptyset$;

11)   For $time \in W_{working}[time]$ do

12) $W_{working}[time - 1] = W_{working}[time]$;

13)   End

14)   End

15)   For $w_i \in W$

16)   If $S_t(j) \in S_{w_i}$ then

17) $W_{t_{candidate}} = W_{t_{candidate}} \cup \{w_i\}$;

18)   End

19)   End

20)   For $w_i \in W_{t_{candidate}}$ do

21) $quality_{w_i \to t} = \frac{\sum_{s \in S_t - S_{W_t}} Acc_{w_i}(s)}{\gamma_{w_i}}$;

22)   End

23)   While $(b_t > 0) \wedge (S_t - S_{W_t} \neq \emptyset)$ do

24)   Select w_i with the highest $quality_{w_i \to t}$ to add to W_t ;

25)   End

26)   For $w_i \in W_t$ do

27) $efficient_{S_t(j)}^{w_i} = efficient_{w_i} \cdot \frac{Acc_{w_i}(s)}{\sum_{s \in S_t \cap S_{w_i}} Acc_{w_i}(s)}$;

28)   End

29) $efficient_{S_t(j)}^{W_t} = \sum_{w_i \in W_t, Acc_{w_i}(S_t(j)) \geq Acc_t(S_t(j))} efficient_{S_t(j)}^{w_i} +$

      $\alpha \cdot \sum_{w_k \in W_t, Acc_{w_k}(S_t(j)) \leq Acc_t(S_t(j))} efficient_{S_t(j)}^{w_k} \cdot Acc_{w_k}(S_t(j))$;

30)   // Calculate the work efficiency $efficient_{S_t(j)}^{W_t}$ of each skill in task team W_t

31) $time_t = \max_{S_t(j) \in S_t} \{\frac{workload_{S_t(j)}}{efficient_{S_t(j)}^{W_t}}\}$;

32)   While $b_t > 0$ do

33)   Determine the skill $S_t(j)$ with the longest time consumption based on $\frac{workload_{S_t(j)}}{efficient_{S_t(j)}^{W_t}}$;

34)   Select the w_i with the highest value of $Select_{w_i}^{W_t}$ for skill $S_t(j)$ and add them to W_t;

35)   End

36)   For $w_i \in W_t$ do

37) $W_{working}[time_t] = W_{working}[time_t] \cup \{w_i\}$;

38) End

2) Task Execution Process: Workers from the task team are placed in the task execution worker pool. The task progresses by 1 day at a time, moving forward until the expected duration is exhausted. At the end of the task, all team members' skill levels will be improved according to formulas (1) and (2), and all members will be released back into the worker pool, awaiting the next task assignment.

5   Experiment

5.1   Experimental Setting

This experiment utilized a dataset from the crowdsourcing platform Freelancer. In this dataset, worker information includes the skills they possess and their expected compensation, while task information includes the required skills and task budgets.

In this experiment, the distribution ranges for task skill level requirements, denoted as $Acc_t(S_t(j))$, are set from 0.8 to 1.0. The skill workload, represented as $workload_{t_{S_t(j)}}$, ranges from 0 to 1000. Task deadlines, denoted as $date_t$, are distributed within the range of 0 to 20 days. For workers, their skill levels, denoted as $Acc_{w_i}(S_t(j))$, are distributed from 0.1 to 1.0, while their efficiency, denoted as $efficient_{w_i}$, ranges from 0 to 100. The parameter α, controlling the effect of ordinary workers assisting in improving the efficiency of professional workers in $efficient_{S_t(j)}^{W_t}$, is set to 1.0. Parameter β governs the weight of the highest-skilled worker in the team and task requirements on the skill level improvement of workers in $\varepsilon_{t \to w_i}$, is set to 0.5.

5.2   Evaluation and Comparison Methodology

In the experiments, we utilized the worker skill level improvement mechanism proposed in this paper and compared our MMT algorithm with other existing algorithms. As time progressed, we evaluated and compared the task assignment and execution results of the model using seven metrics: the number of successfully assigned tasks, the increase in worker skill levels, the number of workers awaiting assignment, worker participation frequency, the mean and variance of worker skill levels, and task completion time. The specific algorithms for comparison were as follows:

1) **Non-Cooperative MMT Model (NC-MMT)**: In this algorithm, the mechanism for selecting workers to join the team is consistent with MMT, but only workers whose skills exceed the task requirements are allowed to join the team; 2) **Sequentially Assigned Ordinary Workers Model (SC-MMT)**: This algorithm allows ordinary workers to join the team. In the second phase of the model, this algorithm sequentially selects workers from the candidate pool for tasks. If a worker's expected wage is lower than the remaining budget for the current task, the worker is allowed to join the team until the budget is exhausted or all workers have been considered; 3) **Maximize Minimum Team Skill Level Algorithm (max-min)**: This algorithm uses the worker selection mechanism from a previous work [5], which detects the weakest skill in the current team and selects the worker with the highest cost-effectiveness for that skill to join the team, thereby improving the skill level in the weakest area of the team.

To test the performance of the algorithms in different crowdsourcing environments, we conducted comparative experiments in three environments, comparing the performance of the above algorithms under the following conditions: **Environment I**: The task platform releases 200 tasks per day, and worker skill levels are distributed in the range [0.1, 1.0]. **Environment II**: The task platform releases 100 tasks per day, and worker skill levels are distributed in the range [0.1, 1.0]. **Environment III**: The task platform releases 100 tasks per day, and worker skill levels are distributed in the range [0.5, 1.0].

5.3 Experiment Results

5.3.1 Variation in the Number of Successfully Assigned Tasks with Increasing Task Releases

In the context of crowdsourcing task allocation, the number of successfully assigned tasks is a crucial metric for evaluating the effectiveness of crowdsourcing allocation algorithms. To assess the task assignment performance of our proposed algorithm against other methods, we conducted a comparative analysis under different environments. As depicted in Fig. 2, over time, the number of successfully assigned tasks steadily increased across all algorithms and environments. Notably, our proposed algorithm demonstrated an effective enhancement in task assignment success count across all three environmental variations.

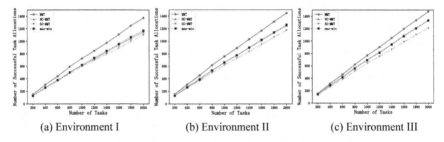

(a) Environment I   (b) Environment II   (c) Environment III

Fig. 2. Changes in the number of successful task assignments with increasing task releases.

Compared to NC-MMT, which exclusively utilizes workers meeting task requirements, our algorithm leverages the involvement of ordinary workers to assist skilled professionals, thereby enabling more tasks to be completed within the designated time frame. When compared to SC-MMT and the max-min algorithm, both of which also incorporate ordinary workers, our algorithm's efficiency-based selection mechanism identifies workers more suitable for both the task and the current team context. In contrast, SC-MMT predominantly accounts for budget constraints and worker sequence, and max-min algorithm places greater emphasis on elevating team skill levels. Consequently, the workers chosen by these algorithms may not necessarily yield the highest efficiency-to-completion ratio for task deadlines.

5.3.2 Variation in Average Expected Task Duration with Increasing Task Quantity

In crowdsourced task allocation, the expected task completion time is a pivotal metric. On one hand, task requesters often impose time constraints on tasks and aspire to have them completed swiftly while ensuring quality. On the other hand, a scarcity of specialized workers on platforms necessitates shorter average task completion times, enhancing the mobility of specialized workers and consequently improving the task allocation success rate. As depicted in Fig. 3, our algorithm consistently outperforms other task allocation algorithms by yielding the shortest average task completion time, significantly reducing task cycles. Furthermore, in the environments of Fig. 3(a) (Environment I) and Fig. 3(b)

(Environment II), our algorithm exhibits a more pronounced advantage in terms of task completion time. In Fig. 3(c) (Environment III), the gap between our algorithm and the other algorithms narrows.

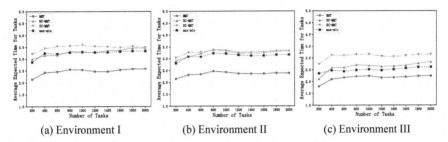

(a) Environment I   (b) Environment II   (c) Environment III

Fig. 3. Changes in average expected task completion time with increasing task releases.

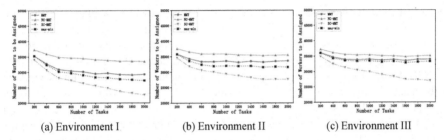

(a) Environment I   (b) Environment II   (c) Environment III

Fig. 4. Changes in the number of workers pending assignment with increasing task releases.

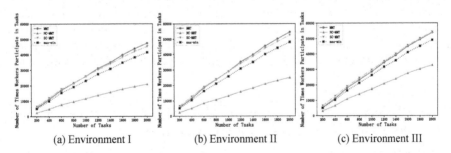

(a) Environment I   (b) Environment II   (c) Environment III

Fig. 5. Changes in the number of worker participation in tasks with increasing task releases.

The reason behind the superior performance of our algorithm lies in its approach during the second phase of worker selection. It simultaneously considers the requirements of the team's longest-duration skill and the need to shorten the duration of other tasks. Our algorithm selects workers with higher skill coverage, which leads to shorter task durations. In contrast, the NC-MMT algorithm is limited by the availability of high-quality workers, performing worse as their numbers diminish. SC-MMT only takes into account the remuneration of ordinary workers, resulting in minimal improvements in team efficiency. The max-min algorithm aims to enhance team efficiency by employing ordinary workers to elevate the team's skill levels but lacks consideration for the skill with the longest duration in the task team.

Additionally, we observed that as we transitioned from Environment I to Environment III, the average task completion times for all algorithms decreased. This phenomenon is attributed to the reduced daily task volume, alleviating the allocation pressure on specialized workers. Task teams find it easier to secure high-quality workers, leading to shortened task durations and early task completion. In the shift from Environment II to Environment III, the distribution of workers' skill levels improved, with more high-quality workers available for selection, resulting in a larger pool of specialized workers. This narrowing gap demonstrates that our algorithm effectively adapts to changing environments.

5.3.3 Variation in the Number of Workers Awaiting Assignment as the Number of Tasks Increases

The number of workers awaiting assignment in a crowdsourcing platform typically impacts the success rate of subsequent task allocations on the platform. In crowdsourcing task allocation, it is essential to select suitable workers to join the teams at a relatively low cost in order to reduce task completion time. As depicted in Fig. 4, compared to the NC-MMT algorithm, our approach involves the inclusion of more ordinary workers in the teams, resulting in a relatively lower number of workers awaiting assignment. In comparison to other allocation methods that also utilize ordinary workers, our approach consistently employs fewer workers in various environments. Combining the insights from Fig. 2 and Fig. 3, it can be observed that our algorithm utilizes fewer workers to reduce task team duration while simultaneously increasing the task allocation success rate. This is because in the second phase, our algorithm selects workers who can significantly reduce task duration and provide the best cost-effectiveness. Each added worker has a substantial impact on shortening task duration. In contrast, the SC-MMT and max-min algorithms prioritize overall cost and skill level improvement, which may not necessarily target the skills associated with the longest duration tasks in the current team.

5.3.4 The Number of Times Workers Participate in Tasks Changing with the Increase in the Number of Task Releases

In crowdsourcing platforms, the number of times workers participate in tasks is often a key indicator reflecting workers' income and platform activity. As shown in Fig. 5, compared to the NC-MMT algorithm, which does not utilize ordinary workers, the allocation method that utilizes ordinary workers significantly increases the number of task participations by workers. As indicated in Fig. 4, we utilize fewer workers in task allocation, so in the early stages of platform task allocation, the number of task participations by our workers may be lower than algorithms that use ordinary workers. However, as Fig. 3 illustrates, our average task completion time is shorter. Therefore, workers under our algorithm can complete tasks earlier and return to the worker pool, awaiting assignment to the next task. Additionally, as shown in Fig. 2, our algorithm can successfully allocate more tasks. Over time, the advantages of our algorithm become more evident, and compared to other allocation methods, workers can participate in tasks more frequently, gaining more income and opportunities to improve their skills.

5.3.5 The Average Skill Level of the Worker Population Changes with the Increase in the Number of Tasks Published

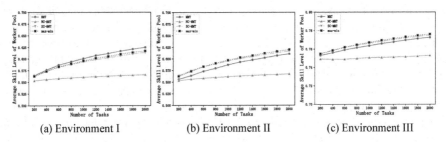

|(a) Environment I | (b) Environment II | (c) Environment III|

Fig. 6. Changes in the mean skill level of the worker population with increasing tasks.

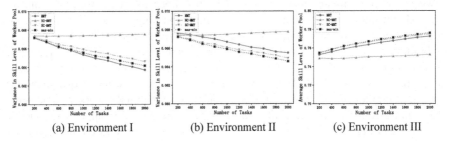

|(a) Environment I | (b) Environment II | (c) Environment III|

Fig. 7. Changes in the variance of worker population skill levels with increasing tasks

In actual crowdsourcing platforms, workers' skill levels usually improve as they complete tasks. As shown in Fig. 6, when the platform publishes a large number of tasks daily (Environment I), our algorithm effectively enhances the skill levels of workers. However, when the daily task volume is lower (Environments II and III), the degree of skill improvement among workers is relatively modest. This is because when a large number of tasks are published daily, it becomes challenging to meet task demands with specialized workers alone. Therefore, our algorithm can efficiently allocate many ordinary workers to enhance the efficiency of specialized workers. Conversely, when the daily task volume is lower, the demand for ordinary workers decreases, resulting in our algorithm utilizing fewer of them. However, as indicated by the results in Fig. 3, our algorithm achieves better task completion times compared to other models. This validates that our model's worker selection mechanism is more reasonable and doesn't require excessive redundant workers. Hence, when the daily task volume is lower, our model utilizes fewer ordinary workers compared to other allocation methods. According to our skill improvement mechanism described in this paper, the skill levels of workers who participate in task completion will all improve. This leads to a slightly lower overall skill level improvement among the worker population in our algorithm compared to other allocation methods.

5.3.6 The Variance in the Skill Levels of the Worker Population as It Changes with the Number of Tasks Released

Within crowdsourcing, workers often see their skill levels improve as they complete tasks. However, relying solely on high-quality workers and neglecting regular workers can lead to an increasing skill gap among workers. This divide further exacerbates the platform's tendency to favor high-quality workers, gradually reducing the opportunities for regular workers to get tasks and hindering their skill improvement. This is unfavorable for the platform's sustainability. As shown in Figs. 7(a) and (b), when there is a significant number of regular workers within the worker pool, not utilizing them, as in the NC-MMT allocation approach, results in an expansion of the skill level variance among workers. In contrast, approaches that involve regular workers significantly reduce the skill level variance. As observed in Fig. 4, our algorithm employs fewer regular workers compared to other algorithms. Consequently, the rate at which the skill level variance decreases is slightly lower than that of other algorithms. However, the difference in variance reduction between our algorithm and others is minimal. This is because our algorithm exhibits a high task allocation success rate, short task completion times, which, in turn, narrows the skill level variance gap caused by differences in the number of workers.

In summary, compared to traditional allocation methods that disregard regular workers, allocation methods involving regular workers can considerably shorten task completion times, enhance task allocation success rates, increase worker participation in tasks, and simultaneously reduce the skill level variance within the worker pool, significantly improving the average skill level. Compared to allocation approaches such as SC-MMT and max-min, which involve regular workers, our proposed algorithm successfully assigns more tasks and selects regular workers who can effectively enhance the efficiency of professional workers in task completion, thereby substantially reducing task cycles.

6 Conclusion

This paper proposes a method that utilizes less skilled ordinary workers to assist professional workers in task execution. The objective is to enhance the efficiency of professional workers, shorten task completion cycles, and promote their mobility. This approach aims to alleviate the shortage of professional workers on crowdsourcing platforms while facilitating the skill improvement of ordinary workers, thereby reducing skill gaps and fostering the sustainable development of task assignments on the platform. Through experimental analysis, we have validated our optimization objectives, which include improving worker skill levels, reducing task cycles, and minimizing skill disparities. The experimental results demonstrate that our model effectively addresses the shortage of professional workers, particularly in environments where there is a high volume of task assignments per unit of time. It outperforms other allocation models in key metrics such as the number of successfully allocated tasks, expected task completion time, worker participation frequency, and the mean and variance of skill level improvements.

Acknowledgments. The work was supported by the National Social Science Funds of China (22BGL261).

References

1. Tong, Y., She, J., Ding, B., et al.: Online mobile micro-task allocation in spatial crowdsourcing. In: 2016 IEEE 32nd International Conference on Data Engineering (ICDE), pp. 49–60. IEEE (2016)
2. Tarable, A., Nordio, A., Leonardi, E., et al.: The importance of being earnest in crowdsourcing systems.In: 2015 IEEE Conference on Computer Communications (INFOCOM), pp. 2821–2829. IEEE (2015)
3. Jiang, L., Wagner, C., Nardi, B.: Not just in it for the money: a qualitative investigation of workers' perceived benefits of micro-task crowdsourcing.In: 2015 48th Hawaii International Conference on System Sciences, pp. 773–782. IEEE (2015)
4. Miller, G.J.: Stakeholder roles in artificial intelligence projects. Proj. Leadersh. Soc. **3**, 100068 (2022)
5. Acar, O.A.: Motivations and solution appropriateness in crowdsourcing challenges for innovation. Res. Policy **48**(8), 103716 (2019)
6. Pee, L.G., Koh, E., Goh, M.: Trait motivations of crowdsourcing and task choice: a distal-proximal perspective. Int. J. Inf. Manage. **40**, 28–41 (2018)
7. Dontcheva, M., Morris, R.R., Brandt, J.R., et al.: Combining crowdsourcing and learning to improve engagement and performance.In: Proceedings of the SIGCHI Conference on Human Factors in Computing Systems, pp. 3379–3388 (2014)
8. Dow, S., Kulkarni, A., Klemmer, S., et al.: Shepherding the crowd yields better work. In: Proceedings of the ACM 2012 Conference on Computer Supported Cooperative Work, pp. 1013–1022 (2012)
9. Baba, Y., Kinoshita, K., Kashima, H.: Participation recommendation system for crowdsourcing contests. Expert Syst. Appl. **58**, 174–183 (2016)
10. Wang, Z., Sun, H., Fu, Y., et al.: Recommending crowdsourced software developers in consideration of skill improvement. In: 2017 32nd IEEE/ACM International Conference on Automated Software Engineering (ASE), pp. 717–722. IEEE (2017)
11. Samanta, R., Ghosh, S.K., Das, S.K.: SWill-TAC: skill-oriented dynamic task allocation with willingness for complex job in crowdsourcing. In: 2021 IEEE Global Communications Conference (GLOBECOM), pp. 1–6. IEEE (2021)
12. Yu, D., Zhou, Z., Wang, Y.: Crowdsourcing software task assignment method for collaborative development. IEEE Access **7**, 35743–35754 (2019)
13. Li, C.T., Shan, M.K.: Team formation for generalized tasks in expertise social networks. In: 2010 IEEE Second International Conference on Social Computing, pp. 9–16. IEEE (2010)
14. Anagnostopoulos, A., Becchetti, L., Castillo, C., et al.: Online team formation in social networks. In: Proceedings of the 21st International Conference on World Wide Web, pp. 839–848 (2012)
15. Hamrouni, A., Ghazzai, H., Alelyani, T., et al.: Optimal team recruitment strategies for collaborative mobile crowdsourcing systems. In: 2020 IEEE Technology & Engineering Management Conference (TEMSCON), pp. 1–6. IEEE (2020)

Blockchain-Based Multi-factor K-Anonymity Group Location Privacy Protection Scheme

Haotian Wang, Shang Wang, Mingzhu Zhao, and Meiju Yu[✉]

School of Computer Science, Inner Mongolia University, Hohhot, China
csymj@imu.edu.cn

Abstract. Nowadays, location privacy issues have become an important problem faced by users of location-based services (LBS). For a long time, most researchers have focused on the location privacy protection of individual users and ignored the location privacy of group users, who will work together to complete an LBS task through collaborative computing. A small number of existing researchers have applied k-anonymity techniques to group location privacy protection, but the single use of k-anonymity techniques still suffers from malicious users providing fake location information, which can lead to the leakage of other users' location information. To solve this problem, this paper proposes a blockchain-based multi-factor k-anonymity group location privacy protection scheme: first, this scheme proposes three factors: entity integrity, location trustworthiness and reputation penalty, fully considers the problem of reputation swing, gives the corresponding calculation scheme, and calculates the user reputation value based on these three factors; second, in the process of k-anonymity zone construction k-anonymous area is constructed by selecting users with high reputation values; finally, this scheme uses blockchain to store users' reputation values and designs reputation calculation contracts to automatically calculate and update users' reputation values. Security and experimental analysis prove that this scheme can effectively reduce the problem of malicious users providing fake location information and reputation swing, and can effectively resist collusion attacks and knowledge background attacks.

Keywords: Blockchain · K-anonymity · Reputation Value Calculation · Group Location Privacy Protection · Reputation Swing

1 Introduction

With the wide popularity of geo-location function and the rapid development of Location Based Service (LBS) applications, more and more users have shown strong demand and heat of using this service [1]. The so-called location-based service is a service that uses geographic information system (GIS) and positioning technology, and users can send location information and query requests to LBS service providers (SPs) through smart portable terminals in order to get the required services. Recent studies have shown that LBS privacy mainly consists of two parts: location privacy and query privacy [2]. And since LBS mainly involves users' location privacy, and these location data are

© The Author(s), under exclusive license to Springer Nature Singapore Pte Ltd. 2024
Y. Sun et al. (Eds.): ChineseCSCW 2023, CCIS 2013, pp. 34–47, 2024.
https://doi.org/10.1007/978-981-99-9640-7_3

easily associated with personal sensitive information (e.g., home address, health status and social relationships, etc.), once a user's location privacy has been compromised, other sensitive information may be exposed as well. Therefore, effective protection and governance are needed.

Existing research solutions are mainly based on the perspective of individual users for location privacy protection, ignoring the fact that in mobile networks, many users will form groups for collaborative LBS publishing, and they hope to achieve location privacy protection and better service results by co-computing with other users [3]. In the group, they can exchange some information with other users in the same group but will not disclose their own location information to accomplish tasks, such as group nearest neighbour (GNN) query [4], group best set location confirmation [3], and group carpooling matching in online car hailing services [5]. Therefore, there is a need to design some location privacy protection schemes from the perspective of user groups. k-anonymous location privacy protection schemes are one of the most popular approaches due to the advantages of easy-to-use implementation and the ability to adapt to different scenario requirements. k-anonymous location privacy protection schemes are based on the idea that when a user sends a query request, it combines the real locations of no less than k-1 participants into an anonymous region and submits the location information of this region to the SP, thus protecting the user's real location information [6].

When designing a privacy protection scheme, the design must be based on a system model, and from the perspective of system architecture, there are two main types: centralised and distributed architectures. Privacy protection schemes with centralised architecture mainly include mobile terminals, central servers and SPs [7]. However, there are several drawbacks of the centralised location privacy protection model: the central server must be trustworthy and reliable, otherwise the user location information collected by the server may be exposed to serious threats; even if the central server is trustworthy, it may still be a performance bottleneck and an attack target in the application; and the introduction of the central server adds additional computation and communication consumption. In order to overcome the drawbacks of centralised architecture, more and more research has turned to distributed architecture models. Distributed architecture models do not require a central server and consist only of mobile terminals and SPs [8]. Blockchain technology contains distributed computing technology and distributed storage technology, which not only prevents information tampering, but also improves the security, reliability and decentralisation of the system. In addition, blockchain can also achieve more complex distributed application scenarios through mechanisms such as smart contracts.

Not all users are trustworthy when the group completes the query task. Malicious users provide false location to construct an anonymous region, i.e., location spoofing. Currently, most research programmes attach a reputation value to each user to determine whether they are honest or not. However, adding reputation values individually can lead to problems, e.g., a malicious user can send a real location to increase the reputation value and then send a false location, i.e., reputation swing. Therefore, more sophisticated reputation calculation schemes are needed to solve these problems.

Therefore, this paper is designed to achieve group location privacy protection of LBS under the support of blockchain technology, which can well solve the above existing problems, the main work of this paper is as follows:

First, this paper proposes three factors: entity integrity, location credibility, and reputation penalty to identify malicious users, which, taken together, can motivate users to provide as much real location information as possible;

Second, this paper proposes a credible de-swinging reputation calculation scheme by combining the above factors, which identifies whether a user can participate in the construction of this anonymous zone by setting a reputation threshold, so that a malicious user can only be forced to provide real location information in the future period of time after submitting false location information once;

Third, this paper designs a reputation value calculation contract based on the smart contract of blockchain, which can automatically calculate and update the user's latest reputation value and store it in the blockchain, making the calculation process decentralised, open and transparent, and guaranteeing that the reputation value will not be tampered with;

Fourth, the security and experimental analysis results show that the scheme proposed in this paper can effectively resist collusion attacks and knowledge background attacks, can effectively inhibit the problem of malicious users providing false location information and reputation swing, and encourages users to honestly submit real location information to build k-anonymity regions.

2 Related Work

To protect location privacy, researchers have proposed several mechanisms. In the literature [9], the authors use differential privacy technique to protect location privacy by randomly interfering with the original data. In addition, in literature [10], another differential privacy scheme using the Laplace mechanism to incorporate noise has been proposed. However, it requires a higher cost in arithmetic. To cope with this problem, literature [11] proposes a personalised k-anonymity authentication algorithm for location services, which uses cryptography to ensure user privacy and applies k-anonymity to sensitive attributes in the location data, thus reducing the risk of personal identification. Meanwhile, literature [12] proposes an approach that incorporates k-anonymity and order-preserving symmetric encryption (OPSE) techniques. However, both approaches suffer from a single point of failure and other centralisation issues, and more and more research is turning to distributed architectures. In this regard, literature [13] classifies the real locations of all users in the network and proposes a distributed k-anonymity privacy preserving scheme based on location labels. In addition, literature [14] proposes a blockchain-based Multi-Attribute Decision Making (MADM) location privacy preservation approach. However, in these above schemes only the location privacy protection of a single user is considered, but in fact there exists another common scenario where multiple users are willing to form a group to cooperate when using LBS to achieve group location privacy protection. For example, a secure group nearest-neighbour query scheme called SecGNN is proposed in the literature [15], which supports GNN querying for n (n $\geq$ 3) LBS users and protects the location privacy of group users. In addition, literature

[3] proposes a location privacy protection method based on k-anonymity technique for distributed architectures, which achieves k-anonymity for each user in a group, showing that the k-anonymity technique is also applicable to group location privacy protection.

Although most location privacy preserving schemes assume that users are honest, in practice users tend to consider their own interests. To address this problem, literature [16] introduces a reputation-based incentive mechanism in distributed k-anonymity schemes. Literature [17] proposes a VANET announcement scheme based on a reputation system for evaluating the reliability of messages. However, both schemes have the risk of tampering with the reputation value. For this reason, blockchain has tamper-proof properties and has been widely used for reputation value storage. For example, literature [14] proposes an algorithm called MADM, which uses blockchain to store reputation values in order to ensure the authenticity and reliability of reputation data and prevent data tampering. Literature [18] proposes a scheme called Trusted Stealth Area Construction (TCAC), which uses reputation values to identify dishonest vehicles while applying blockchain technology to manage reputation data. Literature [19] proposes a distributed IoT device trust mechanism which is based on blockchain technology and quantifies the trust level through canonical trust and risk metrics. A blockchain based reputation management model is proposed in literature [20] which constrains and regulates the behaviour of vehicles through reputation management algorithms. Literature [21] combines blockchain technology and designs a Dirichlet distributed trust management based approach which requires requesters and partners to work only with vehicles they trust.

3   Blockchain-Based Multi-factor K-Anonymous Group Location Privacy Protection Scheme

In this section, the focus is on the system architecture, the multi-factor reputation assessment scheme, and the smart contracts in this scheme.

3.1   System Architecture

In order to better achieve group location privacy protection, the architecture of this system is designed as a peer-to-peer (P2P) network, where the whole process does not require third-party intervention, and consists of four parts: the user, the SP, the blockchain, and the location inspector, as shown in Fig. 1.

Users are the core of building a group, when all users in the group have a common LBS request, the group users will firstly process their precise location information into an area and send it to the blockchain, then calculate an anonymous area containing all qualified users through the smart contract of the blockchain, and finally request services from SP through the location centroid of the anonymous area.

The SP is a server that provides location services to the nodes, such as querying a meeting place that is the smallest distance from all the people in the group, searching for an online car that is the shortest distance from all the customers in a carpooling service, and so on, and the SP queried the results based on the location centroid of the anonymous area and the descriptions of points of interest of the users of the group and returned the

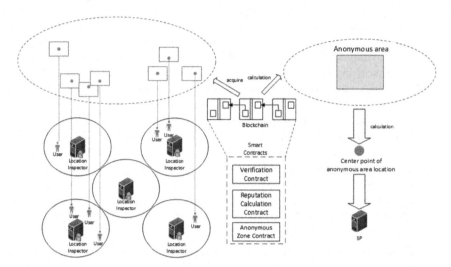

Fig. 1. System architecture diagram.

results to the users of the group, and the returned result may be a single query result or multiple query results for users to choose.

Blockchain is a distributed system, which is mainly used to store user-related information and calculate the user's reputation value in the architecture of this scheme. The information to be stored includes: historical reputation value, service request time, user's reputation swing degree, the number of times the user has provided real location in history and the number of times the user has provided false location, etc., and the contracts involved include authentication contract, anonymity zone contract, and reputation calculation contract.

The location inspector can check whether the location information provided by the user is true and reliable. This scheme is designed to divide a certain region into n small regions, and a location inspector will exist in each small region, due to the division of the region location inspector can easily check the false location information.

3.2 Multi-factor Reputation Assessment Program

The reputation evaluation method proposed in this scheme integrates three factors, namely the user's entity honesty, location trustworthiness and reputation penalty, to calculate the user's reputation value.

Entity Integrity. This scheme calculates the user's entity integrity through the user's historical reputation value $\{R0,R1,R2,....,Rn\}$ and the forgetting function to calculate the user's entity integrity, in the design of the forgetting function by the inspiration of Newton's cooling formula, the degree of time's influence on the user's historical reputation value is taken into account to coordinate the user's historical reputation value through the forgetting function, and the formula of the forgetting function is shown in (1), G_k represents the TimeRk calculated from the current moment of Time to the corresponding moment of updating of the reputation R forgetting function, W is the forgetting period, q_k represents the time decay factor, and the larger the time interval between each historical reputation value and the previous one, the smaller q_k is, as shown in Eq. (2). The closer the time is to the current moment the more the reputation value can reflect the real reputation of the user, so the historical reputation value of the user is given a forgetting function to calculate the entity integrity, as shown in Eq. (3). E_hon represents the entity integrity of the user, and θ is a parameter that will change according to the authenticity of the location data provided by the user.

$$G_k = e^{-q_k \frac{Time - TimeR_k}{W}} \tag{1}$$

$$q_k = a*(TimeR_k - TimeR_{k-1})^{-b} \tag{2}$$

$$E_{hon} = \theta \sum_{k=0}^{n}(G_k * R_k) \tag{3}$$

Location Credibility. The location credibility indicates the credibility degree of the location information provided by the user, and the combined number of times the user provides true location and the number of times the false location is calculated to arrive at the location credibility T. In the design of this scheme, a large area will be divided into n small areas, and there is a location inspector check in each small area to determine whether the location information provided by the user is true or not, if the location information provided by the user is true the user's tru is added 1 operation, and if the location information provided by the user is false the user's fal is calculated by the Formula (4). If the location information provided by the user is true, the tru of the user will be added 1 operation, if the location information provided by the user is false, the fal of the user will be added 1 operation, and the location credibility of the user will be calculated by Formula (4).

$$T = \frac{tru + 1}{tru + fal + 1} \tag{4}$$

Reputation Penalty Degree. In order to punish the reputation swing behaviour of malicious nodes, this scheme stores the reputation swing behaviour in a one-dimensional array A[n], which is used as the basis for calculating the penalty factor. Firstly, the difference between the last two historical reputation values is calculated as shown in Eq. (5). Then the ratio of $\Delta c'$ to the latest historical score is calculated using Eq. (6). Set A[0] according to $\Delta c''$ (different values are assigned according to the degree of change in reputation value), and finally calculate the user's penalty factor Q_pun based on his oscillating behaviour as shown in Eq. (7), where φ and d are parameters.

$$\Delta c' = |R_n - R_{n-1}| \tag{5}$$

$$\Delta c'' = \frac{\Delta c'}{R_n} \tag{6}$$

$$Q_{pun} = e^{\left\{ \sum_{k=0}^{n} \varphi(d^{-k}*A[k]) \right\}} \tag{7}$$

Reputation Value. In the scheme of this paper, the above three factors are taken into account to calculate the reputation value of the user providing location information this time, as shown in Eq. (8), where α denotes the weight of the entity's honesty and X is the penalty coefficient, which is getting bigger and bigger according to the number of times X is provided by the user to provide false location. When a user sends false location information after having a high reputation value, the reputation value decreases rapidly. If a malicious user sends real location information honestly after sending false location information, the reputation value will only increase slowly in the coming period of time because the penalty factor becomes smaller, thus, this scheme can curb the swinging behaviour of malicious users.

$$R_{n+1} = \begin{cases} e^{Q_{pun}} * ln(\alpha E_{hon} + (1 - \alpha)T), \text{ T no change or bigger} \\ e^{Q_{pun}} * ln(\alpha E_{hon} + (1 - \alpha)T) - X, \text{ T get smaller} \end{cases} \qquad (8)$$

3.3 Smart Contract

Blockchain based smart contract, in this section we focus on reputation calculation contract, in this paper we design to calculate user's reputation value by entity integrity, location trustworthiness and reputation penalty, as shown in Algorithm 1.

Algorithm 1: Reputation calculation contract

Input: tru, fal, list of user's historical reputation value {R0,R1 ,......,Rn},user reputation swing list {A0,A1,......,An-1}, user history reputation value time list {TimeR0, TimeR1 ,......, TimeRn};

Output: user reputation value Rn+1;

1 $q = a * (TimeR_k - TimeR_{k-1})^{-b}$;

2 $G_k = e^{-q^{\frac{Time - TimeR_k}{w}}}$;

3 $E_{hon} = \theta(G_0 R_0 + G_1 R_1 + \cdots + G_n R_n)$;

4 $T = (tru+1)/(tru+fal+1)$;

5 $Q_{pun} = exp(_\varphi(d^{-0}A[0] + d^{-(1)}A[1] + \cdots + d^{-(n-1)}A[n-1]))$;

6 If the value of T becomes smaller then

7      $F_{cre} = exp(Q_{pun}) * ln(\alpha E_{hon} + (1 - \alpha)T)$-X;

8 else

9      $F_{cre} = exp(Q_{pun}) * ln(\alpha E_{hon} + (1 - \alpha)T)$;

10 end if

11 $R_{n+1} = F_{cre}$;

---

4 Security Analysis

The security analysis in this paper will focus on how to achieve location privacy protection for group users, preventing tampering of trust data, suppressing malicious behaviours of users, suppressing oscillating behaviours of malicious nodes, preventing collusion attacks, and preventing knowledge context attacks. In order to better analyse the security, this scheme is compared with some typical schemes, as shown in Table 1, and it can be found that this scheme can achieve privacy protection well.

Table 1. Comparison of location privacy protection schemes.

	Literature [3]	Literature [4]	Literature [14]	Our scheme
Prevent tampering of trusted data	×	×	√	√
Suppress malicious behavior of users	×	×	√	√
Suppressing the swinging behavior of malicious nodes	×	×	×	√
Preventing collusive attacks	√	×	×	√
Preventing background knowledge attacks	√	×	×	√
Group location privacy protection	√	√	×	√

4.1 Prevent Tampering of Trust Data

Problem. Attackers may tamper with reputation data, resulting in incorrect reputation values. Malicious nodes can restore the reputation value to a high level at any time and the reputation value of honest nodes is threatened.

Proof. In this paper, we use a blockchain based reputation management scheme. A blockchain typically consists of a linked list in which pointers to previous blocks are replaced with cryptographic hash values to form a hash chain. Each block implicitly verifies the integrity of the entire chain and detects tampering with previous data. Modifying any one block would require reconstruction of all subsequent blocks, making it virtually impossible to tamper with reputable data stored in a block due to the significant cost.

4.2 Suppressing Malicious Behavior of Users

Problem. In location privacy protection, malicious behaviour of users refers to malicious users providing false location information, which leads to the disclosure of honest users' location information, and then leads to the disclosure of users' personal sensitive information.

Proof. In the scheme designed in this paper, a certain area is divided into several small areas, and there is a location inspector in each small area to check whether the location information submitted by users is true or not, and the reputation value is also added in the scheme to inhibit the malicious behaviour of users, through which users can be encouraged to submit true location information to a certain extent, and false location information can be reduced.

4.3 Suppressing the Swinging Behavior of Malicious Nodes

Problem. In the context of having a reputation value, the reputation value of a malicious user can only be minimised after submitting false locations several times, but the malicious user will recover its reputation value in a short period of time.

Proof. In this scheme, an algorithm is designed to inhibit the user's reputation swing, after a malicious user sends false location information once, its reputation value will drop rapidly, and in the future period of time, the malicious user can only send real location information, and the reputation value will only increase horizontally and slowly, and if the malicious user sends false location information continuously again, its reputation value will be lower than the set threshold, and it will be more seriously punished, and it will be more seriously punished. Such a scheme can effectively inhibit the reputation value swinging behaviour of malicious users.

4.4 Prevention of Background Knowledge Attacks

Problem. In the context of location privacy, a malicious user infringes on the privacy information of other users by inferring the user's identity or true location from previously obtained information.

Proof. In the scheme designed in this paper, the location information submitted by a user is a processed location region, and does not submit his or her precise location information to the blockchain, so that a malicious user is unable to determine the user's true location even though he or she knows the user's identity through prior background knowledge. The attacker cannot gain any advantage from the background knowledge attack because it is encrypted during the computation of the zone centroid.

4.5 Prevent Collusion Attacks

Problem. Collusion attack refers to an attack in which attackers co-operate with each other and jointly use multiple location datasets to reveal the user's location privacy.

Proof. In the scheme designed in this paper, the location information submitted by users is processed without submitting the precise location information to the blockchain. Even through collusion, n-1 users can only surmise the region where the user is located rather than the exact location information. Therefore, exposing the identified steganographic region is not considered a threat in itself.

5 Experimental Analysis

In this section, this paper details the advantages of this scheme in suppressing the malicious behaviour of the user by comparing it with literature [22] as well as literature [23]. The necessary parameters of this scheme are designed as shown in Table 2.

5.1 Credibility Value

This paper is compared with literature [22] and literature [23] in terms of trend of reputation value as shown in Fig. 2. The blue, red and green colours in the figure indicate the trend of reputation value for this paper, literature [22] and literature [23] respectively. From the figure, it can be observed that in the first 10 rounds, the user sends authentic messages and both the scheme of this paper and the literature [23] show a gradual increasing trend, and the literature [22] reaches the highest credibility value and stays at the highest level in the ideal case. After the 11th round, the user sends false information

Table 2. Specific settings of credit calculation scheme parameters.

Parameters	Value
a	6.5498
b	1.008
d	6
w	15
φ	2
α	0.62

and in literature [22], the user's reputation value quickly drops to its lowest point and remains available for the next 20 rounds. In literature [23] the user's reputation value decreases partially for each false message sent and after 10 rounds of sending false messages, the user's reputation value decreases to the threshold value. In contrast to the above two literatures, in this scheme the user sends false information only in the 11th round, and the reputation value drops rapidly to near the set threshold, ensuring that the user does not dare to send false information continuously. In the following 20 rounds, the reputation value will only remain at an approximate level despite the fact that the user sends true information, effectively suppressing the oscillating behaviour of the user.

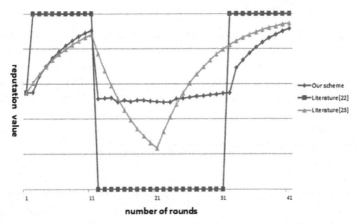

Fig. 2. Comparison of the change in reputation value for the presence of users providing false information.

5.2 Number of Times Users Provide False Information

In order to prove that the scheme proposed in this paper can effectively suppress the number of times the user provides false information, this paper designs the user to submit information a total of 100 times, and the malicious user provides false information as many times as possible. As shown in Fig. 3, the scheme in literature [23] users submit false information up to more than 80 times, and the scheme in literature [23] malicious users submit false information up to 100 times, these schemes can hardly inhibit the malicious behaviour of users effectively, compared with the scheme in this paper in which the malicious users can only submit false information a few times out of the 100 times of information submission.

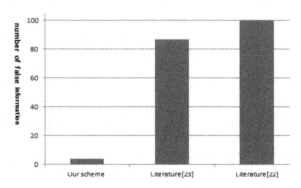

Fig. 3. Comparison chart of false information provided by malicious users.

5.3   Selection of the Weight Value α

In the process of calculating the user's latest reputation value, the selection of appropriate weights for entity integrity and location trustworthiness has a decisive impact on the change of the reputation value, so it is necessary to analyse and compare the selection of weights α. As shown in Fig. 4, when the weight value α is 0.8 or 0.7, the credibility value rises too fast. When the weight value α is 0.6, when the user provides real location information, the user's reputation value at the 1st round will have a downward trend, which is not in line with the scheme of this paper. After many tests, the weight value α of 0.62 meets the trend change of reputation value set in this scheme.

As shown in Fig. 5, when the malicious user sends false location information, the degree of punishment for the malicious user when the weight value α is 0.8 is too short only does not achieve the expected effect, when the weight value α is 0.7, the change in the reputation value of the malicious user from the 20th to 40th rounds rises by a large amount, which is not ideal, and when the weight value α is 0.6 in the 1st round of the user sends the real location information, the reputation value becomes smaller, which is contrary to the scheme Contrary to this scheme. Therefore, after many rounds of testing, the weight value α is 0.62 when the effect is the best, in line with the expected results.

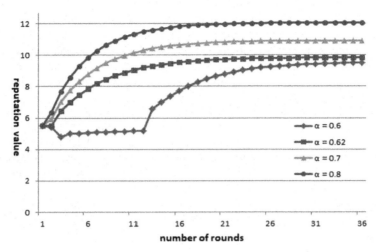

Fig. 4. Effect of the selection of the weight α on the growth of reputation value.

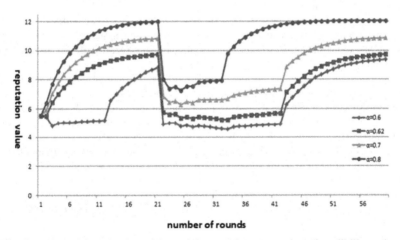

Fig. 5. Effect of the selection of the weight α on the suppression of credibility swing.

6 Conclusion

In this party, in the context of k-anonymous group location privacy protection, this paper designs a multi-factor reputation evaluation scheme for the existence of malicious users providing false location information and reputation swing problem. In the scheme, in order to keep the user's reputation value from being arbitrarily tampered with, the tamper-proof nature of the blockchain is relied upon to store the user's reputation value. Smart contracts of the blockchain are also used to run the reputation algorithm of this scheme as well as to calculate the centroid of the k-anonymity zone location of the group users. The security analysis and simulation results show that the scheme proposed in this paper greatly outperforms existing schemes in several aspects, and is able to withstand malicious attacks, quickly identify malicious nodes, and motivate users to provide as much real location information as possible. In future work, the focus will be on the anonymity zone group location centroid computation, which makes it possible to dynamically adjust the impact of each user's real location on the group centre, and to achieve fine-grained control over the effectiveness of group location privacy protection.

Acknowledgements. This research is supported by the Inner Mongolia Nature Fund project number No. 2023MS06020, the National Natural Science Foundation of China under Grant No. 61862046, the Hohhot Science & Technology Plan under Grant No. 2021-KJXM-TZJW-04, and the Science, the Technology Program of Inner Mongolia Autonomous Region under Grant No. 2020GG0188 and the Inner Mongolia Autonomous Region Science and Technology Achievements Transformation Project under Grant No. CGZH2018124.

References

1. Zhou, A.-Y., Yang, B., Jin, C.-Q., et al.: Location-based services: architecture and progress. Chin. J. Comput. **34**(7), 1155–1171 (2011)
2. Andrés, M.E., Bordenabe, N.E., Chatzikokolakis, K., Palamidessi, C.: Geo-indistinguishability: differential privacy for location-based systems. In: Proceedings of the ACM Conference on Computer and Communications Security, Berlin, 4–8 November 2013, pp. 901–914. ACM Press, New York (2013)
3. Wang, H.J., Yang, Y., et al.: A new group location privacy-preserving method based on distributed architecture in LBS. Secur. Commun. Netw. (2019)
4. Hashem, T., Kulik, L., Zhang, R.: Privacy preserving group nearest neighbor queries. In: Proceedings of the 13th International Conference on Extending Database Technology: Advances in Database Technology (EDBT 2010), vol. 426, pp. 489–500 (2010)
5. Yu, H., Zhang, H., Yu, X., Du, X., Guizani, M.: PGRide: privacy preserving group ridesharing matching in online ride hailing services. IEEE Internet Things J. **8**(7), 5722–5735 (2021)
6. Gruteser, M., Grunwald, D.: Anonymous usage of location-based services through spatial and temporal cloaking. In: Proceedings of the 1st International Conference on Mobile Systems, Applications and Services (MobiSys 2003), pp. 31–42. Association for Computing Machinery, New York (2003)
7. Wang, Y.-H., Zhang, H.-L., Yu, X.-Z.: KAP: location privacy-preserving approach in location services. Tongxin Xuebao/J. Commun. **35**(11), 182–190 (2014)
8. Liu, H., Li, X., Luo, B., Wang, Y., Ren, Y., Ma, J.: Distributed Kanonymity location privacy protection scheme based on blockchain. Chin. J. Comput. **42**(5), 942–960 (2019)
9. Liu, H.L., Di, W.: Application of differential privacy in location trajectory big data. In: 2020 International Conference on Intelligent Transportation, Big Data Smart City (ICITBS), pp. 569–573 (2020)
10. Yin, C., Xi, J., Sun, R., Wang, J.: Location privacy protection based on differential privacy strategy for big data in industrial internet of things. IEEE Trans. Ind. Inform. **14**, 3628–3636 (2018)
11. Ye, Y.-M., Pan, C.-C., Yang, G.-K.: An improved location-based service authentication algorithm with personalized k-anonymity. In: Proceedings of the China Satellite Navigation Conference (CSNC), pp. 257–266. Springer, Singapore (2016). https://doi.org/10.1007/978-981-10-0934-1_23
12. Zhang, S., Choo, K.-K.R., Liu, Q., Wang, G.: Enhancing privacy through uniform grid and caching in location-based services. Futur. Gener. Comput. Syst. **86**, 881–892 (2018)

13. Sun, G., Liao, D., Li, H., Yu, H., Chang, V.: 'L2P2: a location-label based approach for privacy preserving in LBS.' Future Gener. Comput. Syst. **74**, 375–384 (2017)
14. Wang, H., Wang, C., Shen, Z., Liu, K., Liu, P., Lin, D.: A MADM location privacy protection method based on blockchain. IEEE Access **9**, 27802–27812 (2021)
15. Guo, J., Sun, J.: Secure and practical group nearest neighbor query for location-based services in cloud computing. Secur. Commun. Netw. **2021**, 5686506 (2021)
16. Li, X., Miao, M., Liu, H., Ma, J., Li, K.-C.: An incentive mechanism for K-anonymity in LBS privacy protection based on credit mechanism. Soft. Comput. **21**(14), 3907–3917 (2016). https://doi.org/10.1007/s00500-016-2040-2
17. Li, Q., Malip, A., Martin, K.M., Ng, S.L., Zhang, J.: A reputation-based announcement scheme for VANETS. IEEE Trans. Veh. Technol. **61**(9), 4095–4108 (2012)
18. Zhang, J., et al.: A blockchain-based trusted edge platform in edge computing environment. Sensors **21**, 2126 (2021)
19. Li, F., et al.: Wireless communications and mobile computing blockchain-based trust management in distributed internet of things. Wirel. Commun. Mob. Comput. **2020**, 1–12 (2020). https://doi.org/10.1155/2020/8864533
20. Li, B., Liang, R., Zhu, D., Chen, W., Lin, Q.: Blockchain-based trust management model for location privacy preserving in VANET. IEEE Trans. Intell. Transp. Syst. **22**(6), 3765–3775 (2021). https://doi.org/10.1109/TITS.2020.3035869
21. Luo, B., Li, X., Weng, J., Guo, J., Ma, J.: Blockchain enabled trustbased location privacy protection scheme in VANET. IEEE Trans. Veh. Technol. **69**(2), 2034–2048 (2020)
22. Liu, Z., et al.: PPTM: a privacy-preserving trust management scheme for emergency message dissemination in space–air–ground-integrated vehicular networks. IEEE Internet Things J. **9**(8), 5943–5956 (2022). https://doi.org/10.1109/ACCESS.2018.2864189
23. Lu, Z., Liu, W., Wang, Q., Qu, G., Liu, Z.: A privacy-preserving trust model based on blockchain for VANETS. IEEE Access **6**, 45655–45664 (2018)

Context-Aware Automatic Splitting Method for Structured Complex Crowdsourcing Tasks

Yili Fang, Lichuang Jin, Tao Han, Kai Zhang, and Xinyi Ding[✉]

Zhejiang Gongshang University, Hangzhou 310018, Zhejiang, China
{fangyl,hantao,xding}@zjgsu.edu.cn

Abstract. Crowdsourcing as a practical way of ensuring data quality has achieved great success in fields like image annotation, speech recognition, etc. For structured complex tasks like translation which are usually very intensive, one task need to be split first, otherwise workers may feel overwhelmed. However, if we randomly split one task into evenly sized sub tasks, context information may be lost, resulting in low quality data. Take translation as an example, the word 'cookie' could mean cooked snack, or a browser cookie which are text files with small pieces of data. Thus, how to divide one large structured complex task into sub tasks while at the same time maintaining context information becomes a challenge. In this paper, we propose a novel splitting method for structured complex tasks based on minimum cut in graph theory. We design mechanisms to convert one structured complex task into a weighted graph with nodes representing potential sub tasks and weighted edges representing the relationship between sub tasks. Experimental results on real translation tasks demonstrate that using our method could achieve higher scores compared with other methods.

Keywords: Crowdsourcing · Structured Complex Task · Minimum Cut

1 Introduction

Crowdsourcing allows anonymous workers from the Internet participating in tasks that could not be automatically dealt with by computers directly, is an effective way of ensuring data quality [6]. Crowdsourcing has been successfully applied in simple scenarios like image annotation [4,8], sentiment analysis [10], as well as structured complex tasks like translation [15], writing [9], software development [14], etc.

In recent years, researchers start to focus more on structured complex tasks in Crowdsourcing. Haas et al. [7] use secondary crowdsourcing to deal with complex tasks and get high quality aggregation results. Da et al. [2,11] take an iterative approach to optimize the micro writing process. Deng et al. [1,4] utilize the idea similar to Map-Reduce to split one task into sub tasks. Then they combine

Y. Sun et al. (Eds.): ChineseCSCW 2023, CCIS 2013, pp. 48–61, 2024.
https://doi.org/10.1007/978-981-99-9640-7_4

the responses from different workers to form the final result. But their methods ignored the relationship between different sub tasks. These methods have achieved different degrees of success when dealing with complex tasks. However, for tasks like software development or translation that contain complex internal structures, if we randomly divide one task into evenly sized sub tasks, context information may be lost. Take translation as an example, the word 'cookie' could mean cooked snack, or a browser cookie which are text files with small pieces of data. Thus, how to split one large task into almost evenly sized sub tasks, and at the same time preserving the context information becomes a challenge.

Compared with simple tasks like image annotation, it is usually more difficult to deal with structured complex tasks. On one hand, different tasks may have very different internal structures. Some tasks have linear structure while others may have network structure. Thus, there is no unified ways modeling these tasks and their internal architectures. The common way of using task difficulty levels often fail in such complex situations. On the other hand, due to the various types of internal architectures, one task will usually be split, taking similar approach like Map-Reduce [1]. When the relationship among these sub tasks is weak, the quality of the final combined result could be guaranteed. But when there is a strong relationship among these sub tasks and these context information is lost for individual worker, the final combined result is usually not satisfying. Distribute the whole one large task to workers without splitting is also not a good option, since it is very easy for workers to get frustrated [7]. In this study, we propose a novel method for structured complex task modeling and splitting. We first use weighted edges to describe the relationship among different sub tasks. Next, we propose a weighted graph cutting algorithm, converting the structured complex task splitting problem into graph cutting. Furthermore, we provide theoretical analysis about the effectiveness of our method. At last, through extensive experiments, we prove the superior of our cutting algorithm compared with other methods. Overall, our contributions are summarized as follows:

- We first give a formal definition of structured complex task and utilize graph theory to describe the internal architecture, allowing effective modeling of sub tasks and their relationship.
- We propose a novel method that could convert the problem of task splitting into weighted graph cutting. Using our method could effectively divide one large structured complex task into evenly sized sub tasks, while at the same time preserving context information.
- Through extensive experiments, we demonstrate the superior of our method. We also conduct theoretical analysis and computation cost analysis.

The remaining of this paper is organized as follows: In Sect. 2, we discuss the related work. Our proposed method is described in Sect. 3. We discuss the experiment setup and results in Sect. 4. Further discussion and conclusions are presented in Sect. 5 and Sect. 6.

2   Related Work

Crowdsourcing has achieved great success in dealing with both simple and complex tasks. These simple tasks include image annotation [4, 8], sentiment analysis [10], etc. On the other hand, complex tasks like software development [14], micro writing [16], hand written text recognition [3], these tasks usually need to be split into smaller sub tasks before they can be handed out to workers. Yu et el. [14] designed a software development method that could divide the whole project into smaller pieces, since the relationship among these sub tasks is weak, the final combined project could still achieve satisfying results. Reteln et al. [12] utilize the collaborative tool provided by the platform for online software development. Their method is suitable for specific software development like user interface design. However, due to the creation of large number of copies, it is not economic efficiency. Haas et al. [7] recruit a lot of workers for micro writing. They exploit the free mode workflow to finetune different phases of the writing task, e.g. the formulation of the central idea, expanding the paragraph content, polishing of the article, etc. Using their method could obtain high quality result if ignoring the cost. Fang et al. [5] investigated both single character and whole sentence distribution for the task of ancient character recognition and find the later has higher recognition accuracy. They also proposed a partial order based result inference method which could help get high quality data. However, all above mentioned methods simply split one large task into smaller pieces without considering the cost, as well as the relationship among these sub tasks. Thus, such approaches often fail to meet the high quality requirement of requesters.

Different from existing work, the splitting method proposed in this study takes both cost and the context information into consideration. Our method could automatically split one large task into sub tasks based on one task's internal architecture. Thus, the context information is maximally preserved and the quality of the combined result could be guaranteed.

3   Problem Definition and Framework

In this section, we give the formal definition of structured complex task, as well as the problem formulation.

3.1   Problem Definition

The research target of this study is structured complex task which consists of heavily interconnected sub tasks. One structured complex task is usually very large that if published directly to a single worker, it is very easy for this worker to get overwhelmed and the work quality can not be guaranteed. Thus, a common practice is to split one large task into smaller evenly sized sub tasks. The cutting strategy needs to be carefully designed such that the context information is maximally preserved. We first give the formal definition of structured complex task.

Definition 1. *(Structured Complex Crowdsourcing Task–SCT) Let $\mathcal{T}$ = $<V, E>$ be one structured complex crowdsourcing task, where $V_i \in V$ is the set of sub tasks, $fe_{ij} \in E$ is the set of relations between sub tasks v_i and v_j.*

Definition 1 describes the structure of our task. Take translation as an example, an article consists of many sentences and these sentences are interconnected. A good splitting strategy will divide one large task into evenly sized smaller sub tasks while preserving the context information. We formally give the definition of Structured Complex Task Splitting Problem as follows:

Definition 2. *(Structured Complex Task Split Problem SCT-SP) Let $\mathcal{T}$ = $<V, E>$ be a structured complex crowdsourcing task, E is a collection of relationship, $E_i \subseteq \mathcal{T}$ is a collection of association relationships for sub tasks, then the task cutting problem is a cutting strategy $\pi(\mathcal{T}) = \{\mathcal{T}_i | \forall \mathcal{T}_i, \mathcal{T}_j(\mathcal{T}_i, \mathcal{T}_j \subseteq \mathcal{T} \wedge \mathcal{T}_i \neq \mathcal{T}_j \Rightarrow \mathcal{T}_i \cap \mathcal{T}_j = \varnothing)$ and $\bigcup_{i=1}^{n} \mathcal{T}_i = \mathcal{T}\}$, which satisfies the following:*

$$\min(\sum_{e \in E} e - \sum_{\mathcal{T}_i \in \pi(\mathcal{T})} \sum_{e' \in \mathbb{E}_i} e')$$

According to Definition 2, the SCT-SP involves the modeling of the relationship between two sub tasks. For a translation task, the relationship between two sentences are decided by the textual similarity and semantic similarity.

Definition 3. *(Cut Relationship Set CRS). Let $\mathcal{T} = <\mathbb{T}, \mathbb{R}>$ be a structured complex task, $\mathbb{T}_i$ and $\mathbb{T}_j$ are two complex sub tasks of $\mathcal{T}$, $\mathbb{C} = \{(u, v) \in \mathbb{R} | u \in \mathbb{T}_i, v \in \mathbb{T}_j\}$ is a set of cut relationship that connect two sub tasks, one belongs to $\mathbb{T}_i$ and the other belongs to $\mathbb{T}_j$.*

The above defined a set, which is used to store all the relationships cut off when dividing one complex structured task into two sub tasks. When the weights in this set is minimized, we call this set Min Cut Relationship Set (MCRS). We use c to denote the weights in this MCRS.

3.2   Framework

In this section, we give the framework of splitting of structured complex tasks for Crowdsourcing. For structured complex tasks, we convert the problem of task splitting into sub graph cutting in graph theory, as shown in Fig. 1. We aim to divide one large task into smaller sub tasks, within which context information are preserved before submitting to Crowdsourcing platform. Then, we combine the responses from workers into one task. The involved steps are as follows:

1. Roughly split one large task into evenly sized smaller sub tasks. For example, in translation, divide one article into sub sets each of which contains similar number of words.

2. Based on the task description, calculate the relationship among sub tasks. Construct tasks model.
3. Split those sub tasks that have low relationship based on weighted graph of the tasks tree.
4. Publish these sub tasks on Crowdsourcing platform.

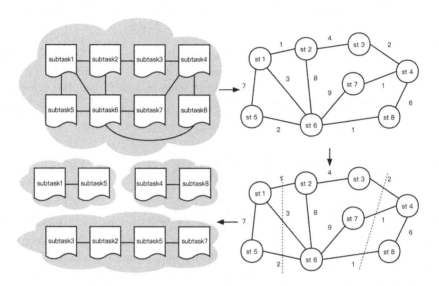

Fig. 1. Transformation of structured complex task splitting into graph cutting

4   Methods

4.1   Context-Aware Splitting Strategy

In this section, we first give a task graph model to describe one structured complex task and a task tree sampling based weighted task graph cutting algorithm (Sect. 4.1). In Sect. 4.2, we provide the detail algorithm implementation.

Let's consider one structured complex task with 8 sub tasks and 11 relationship as shown in Fig. 2. We first convert it into a weighted task graph. We bring in the concept of graph sparsifier to reduce the number of spanning tree in a tree packing.

Definition 4. *(Graph sparsifier) Let $\mathcal{T} = <V, E>$ be one structured complex crowdsourcing task with weight function $w : E \rightarrow \mathbb{E}$, and its corresponding graph sparser $H = <V, E'>$ has the same task set V as $\mathcal{T}$, and whose weight function $w' : E' \rightarrow \mathbb{E}$ has the following properties:*

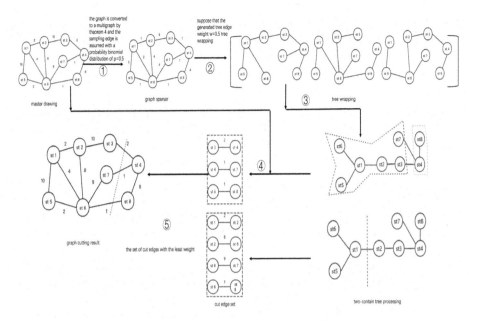

Fig. 2. The framework of structured complex crowdsourcing task cutting method

$$\begin{cases} H \ has \ \widetilde{O}(n) \ edges \\ For \ each \ cut \ edge \ S, \ C_H(S) \in (1 \pm \epsilon)C_G(S) \end{cases}$$

We construct a graph sparsifier with properties described in Definition 4. Firstly, convert weights to the number of edges, thus change the undirected weighted graph to undirected multigraph. Next, sample with binary distribution probability $p = \min(3(d + 2)(\ln n)/(\gamma\epsilon^2 c)/c, 1)$, and the maximum sampled edges is $\lceil(1 + \epsilon^2)12b\rceil$. We use $H = edge\_sample(G)$, and assume the probability of binary distribution sampling $p = 0.5$, resulting in edges reduced undirected multigraph. At last, we convert the number of edges back into weights. Thus, we have the weights reduced graph sparsifier without impacting the minimum cut results.

Definition 5. *(Weighted Task Tree Packing–WTTP) Task tree package P is a set of task spanning trees for structured complex crowdsourcing task $T = <V, E>$. P assigns each edge $e \in E(G)$ to the number of trees containing that edge in T, and $\epsilon e \leq e$, where ϵ represents the task tree package.*

This definition mainly defines the generation method of related weighted task trees that can be generated by structured complex tasks, and provides a phase structure for finding the minimum cut of the graph where structured tasks are located.

Definition 6. *(Second Constrains Task Tree–CST-2) Let T be a task tree of the corresponding structured complex crowdsourced task graph G. If the set of association relations of T has at most 2 identical association relations in the set of min cut relationship set $\mathcal{T}$, the tree is called 2 constrains task tree in this paper.*

Theorem 1. *Let $p = 3(d+2)(\ln n)/(\epsilon^2\gamma c) \leq 1$, where c is the weight of min cut of the unweighted multiplex graph G, $\gamma \leq 1$ and $\gamma = \Theta(1)$. Then, if we sample each relationship of G independently with probability p, the resulting task graph G'' has $1 - 1/n^d$ probability of having the following properties.*

1. *The MCRS size of H is in the $(1+\epsilon)$ factor range of $cp = 3(d+2)(\ln n)/(\gamma\epsilon^2)$, i.e. $O(\epsilon^{-2}\log n)$.*
2. *The cut value of G is equal to a $(1 + \epsilon)$ factor of the expected value of H. In particular, the MCRS in G corresponds to the MCRS of degree $(1 + \epsilon)$ for H.*

Note: The p value calculation formula in Theorem 1. The formula for calculating the probability p is based on the maximum depth d of the task tree, the size n of the task set, the min cut weight c of the unweighted multitask graph G, and the constant γ independent of n and the positive number ϵ less than 1. p represents the probability of sampling each relationship. In general, Theorem 1 provides certain performance guarantees for graph sparsifier and task cutting, and can guide actual task cutting operations, thereby improving the efficiency and accuracy of structured complex crowdsourcing tasks. However, the application of Theorem 1 still needs to be evaluated and verified with the characteristics of specific scenarios and task graphs.

With Theorem 1, it can be shown that sampling the task tree in this tree packing with a probability of $1 - 1/n^d$ will definitely result in a 2 constrains task tree with Definition 6.

We then discuss how to get the MCRS from the WTTP. We first introduce the following theorem, which is first proposed in [13] by Sleator and Tarjan.

Theorem 2. *Given a task tree T, the relationship of T has an order such that the relationship of paths between any two tasks in T consists of the union of up to $2\log n$ continuous subsequences. The order can be found in $O(n)$ times.*

Then we first mark the relations of T in tree-chain decomposition order association $e_1, \ldots, e_{n-1}$ as in Theorem 2. We iteratively look for the best i, j using the order of tree-chain decomposition, then return the found MCRS. To find i, j more effectively, in this study, we use a data structure that allows the following operations on one weighted task tree in $O(logn)$ time complexity.

(1) $Set[e_i]$: A set of cuts containing only one cut edge of T.
(2) $Set[e_i][e_j]$: A set of cuts containing only two cut edges of T.
(3) PathAdd(u,v,x): Find all relationships in $u - v$ *path* of T and add that into $Set[e_i]$.
(4) NonPathAdd(u,v,x): Find all relationships of T that one edge is in $u-v$ *path*, but one edge is not in $u - v$ *path* and add that into $Set[e_i][e_j]$.

(5) QueryMinimum(): Query the minimum weight association sets and weights of $Set[e_i]$ and $Set[e_i][e_j]$.

Using Theorem 2, traverse all the sampled task trees to obtain the cut edge set, and query the cut edge set with the smallest weight and value, which is the minimum cut of the graph.

This section introduces the conversion process of structured complex crowdsourcing tasks, the construction of graph sparsifier, the task tree packing and the definition of 2-constrained task trees, and how to find the MCRS through tree chain decomposition and a special data structure. These concepts and methods provide theoretical support and practical guidance for dealing with structured complex crowdsourcing tasks.

4.2   Algorithm Implementation

Algorithm 1: WTTP algorithm

Input: H
Output: P

1 Initialize $l(e) \leftarrow 0$ for all relationships e of H, $P \leftarrow \emptyset, W \leftarrow 0$;
2 **while** *True* **do**
3   Find a minimum spanning tree T with respect to $l(.)$;
4   **for** $e \in T$ **do**
5          $l(e) \leftarrow l(e) + \epsilon_3^2/(3\ln m)$;
6   **if** $l(e) > 1$ **then**
7   return W,P;
8   **end**
9   **end**
10     $W \leftarrow W + \epsilon_3^2/(3\ln m)$;
11   Add T to P;
12 **end**

In this section, we discuss the implementation details of our proposed cutting algorithm for structured complex tasks. We set a maximum task amount MAX, if the amount of the current task is larger than MAX, it will look for MCRS and split the current task into two sub tasks. We first describe the algorithms looking for MCRS.

The first phase of the algorithm is to get WTTP from structured complex task, then sample $O(logn)$ task trees from WTTP. This task trees set must contains one CST-2. If we uniformly sample the relationship of unweighted multi task graph G with probability p, the probability of the size of MCRS of the resulted simplified task graph H smaller than $(d + 2)(lnn)/\epsilon^2$ is at least $1 - 1/n^{d+2}$. Thus, we set $p_1 = 1 - 1/n^{d+2}$, and use U to represent the maximum estimated value of MCRS of G. We assume the probability of uniformaly sampling the relationship of unweighted mutli task graph G, $p_2 = 3(d + 2)(lnn)/(\gamma\epsilon^2 c) \leq 1$ in Definition 3. Assume $\epsilon_1, \epsilon_2, \epsilon_3 > 0$, then $p_1 = 3/2 - (\frac{2+\epsilon_1}{2-\epsilon_1})(1+\epsilon_2)(1-\epsilon_3)^{-1}$. Thus, the algorithm to get at least $(1-\epsilon_3)c/2$ weighted WTTP from G is shown in Algorithm 1.

We give the function to sample $\lceil -d \ln n / \ln(1 - f) \rceil$ number of tress from WTTP. Our task trees sample algorithms are shown in Algorithm 2.

Algorithm 2: Task Trees sample algorithm

Input: $T, U, p_1, p_2, \epsilon_1, \epsilon_2, \epsilon_3$
Output: Task Trees Set T^{tt}

1 Initialize $c' \leftarrow U$.
2 $G = multigraph(T)$
3 **while** *True* **do**
4    $p = min(p_2, 1)$;
5    $H = edge\_sample(G)$;
6   Run algorithm1 on H;
7   **if** *p=1* **then**
8   Add $tree\_sample(P)$ to T^{tt};
9   break;
10   **else if** $W \geq \frac{1}{2}(1 - \epsilon_3)(1 + \epsilon_2)^{-1}$ **then**
11   Add $tree\_sample(P)$ to T^{tt};
12       $c' = c'/6$;
13   **else**
14       $c' = c'/2$;
15   **end**
16 **end**

At last we use the Algorithm 3 to split task graph. We first get task trees set T^{tt} using Algorithm 2, the rank the relationship edge of T according Theorem 2. Next, we use T to initialize the data structure $PathAdd(u, v, x)$ in Theorem 2. The final result is the minimum cut for each tree.

5   Experiments

In this section, we discuss the experimental setup and results. Current Crowd-sourcing platforms lack a way of automatic splitting of large tasks, thus in this study, we first split these tasks offline before submitting them to the platform. Specifically, we conduct all our experiments on a translation dataset. The goal of this study is to investigate the impact of different splitting methods for the translation quality. We try to answer the following questions: 1) For a translation task, whether putting these sentences that are semantically close to each other could reduce the impact of cutting? 2) Whether splitting using our proposed method SMC could effectively preserve the context information, thus improving the translation results?

Algorithm 3: cut algorithm

Input: $\mathcal{T}$
Output: Subtask $\mathcal{T}_a^S, \mathcal{T}_b^S$
1 get T^{tt} by algorithm2;
2 **for** $T \in T^{tt}$ **do**
3   Arrange the edges of T in the order of Theorem 2, label them $e_1, \ldots, e_{n-1}$;
        Initialize PathAdd(u,v,x), NonPathAdd(u,v,x),QueryMinimum();
4   **for** *(i=1;i<n;i++)* **do**
5   **if** *e_i is on the uv-path* **then**
6   PathAdd(u,v,x);
7   **end**
8   **if** *e_i or e_j is on the uv-path* **then**
9   NonPathAdd(u,v,x);
10   **end**
11   **end**
12   updating weights in QueryMinimum();
13 **end**
14 Return minimum cut in QueryMinimum().

5.1 Datasets and Setup

We use the translation dataset wmt-2018-news commentary zh-en, whose content are crawled from the Internet. Translation is a typical structured complex task, in which some sentences are more semantically close to others, such that we can not simply split the whole article to sub tasks each of which contains the same number of sentences. We must preserve the context information when creating these sub tasks, ensuring the final combined translation quality.

We calculate the correlation between two sentences as follows: 1. We first use the all-MiniLmL6-v2 model trained using sentence-transformers to get the similarity score between two sentences s. 2. We then count the number of sentences between two specific sentences n. 3. We get the correlation r using the formula $r = s$. This study compares the following four methods.

- Google_t, this method uses the Google translation service and translate one sentence at a time.
- Atom, This method considers one sentence as a single task and publish it to the Crowdsourcing platform.
- Combine, this method iteratively merge those sentences that have high correlation score until the number of words in each sub task meets 80 words.
- SMC, This is the proposed minimum cut algorithm in this paper. We treat one structured complex task as a graph and use the minimum cut algorithm to find the minimum cut set. We iteratively split tasks until the number of words in each task is fewer than 80 words.

We randomly select 30 articles from the translation dataset. Using the above mentioned four methods, we split these 30 articles into 2067 sub tasks. After

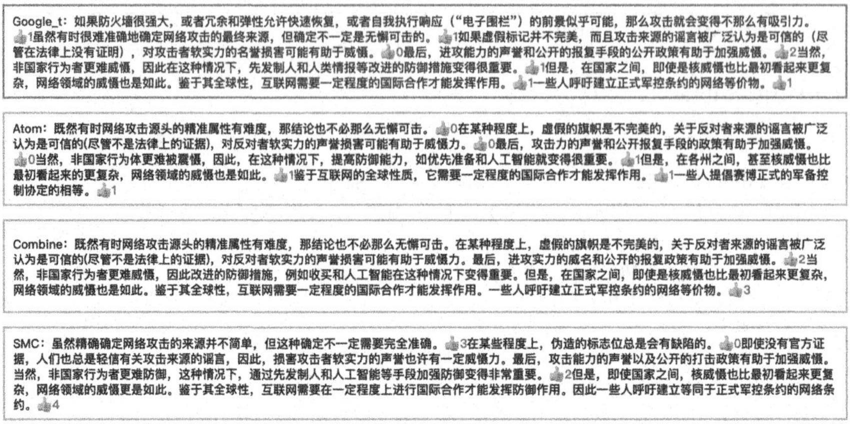

Fig. 3. An example of translation

deleting duplicates, we publish 68 task packages to 68 workers on Crowdsourcing platform. We recruit 10 college students to grade the translation quality. We evaluate the translation results from the following three perspectives. (1) The ratio of likes and score distribution on different methods. (2) Scores from workers (3)Mean scores of different methods from sampling.

Sample Analysis: We believe random splitting may destroy the context information for a translation task, leading to ambiguous results. As shown in Fig. 3, the word 'states' in the sentence 'But, among states...' could mean prefecture or nation, etc. If we publish this single sentence to one worker, without further information, the returned translation may be misleading. In this section, we compare four task splitting methods from different perspectives.

We recruit 10 college students to grade the translations from workers. Figure 4(a) shows the distribution of the scores and likes. As we can see from this figure, the translation tasks using our method SMC has the highest mean score 89.68, with the standard deviation 2.19. The method Combine has the second best performance with the mean score 88.93 and standard deviation 2.28. The method Atom and Google_t perform the worst with low mean scores and large standard deviations. We believe our proposed method SMC could maximally preserve the context information, thus resulting in better performance.

Our grading tool not only allows the graders to give scores for the whole article, but also they can 'like' each sentence. We calculate the like ratio $p = \frac{sum_1}{sum_2}$, where sum_1 is the number of words in all liked sentences and sum_2 is the number of words of the whole article.

5.2 Results

Figure 4(b) shows the distribution of the like ratios using four splitting methods. As we can see from this figure, our method SMC has the best like ration 0.40,

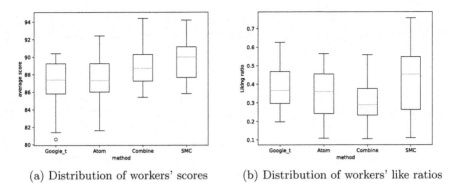

(a) Distribution of workers' scores   (b) Distribution of workers' like ratios

Fig. 4. The distribution of workers' scores and like ratios

with the standard deviation 0.18, the method Google_t has the second best like ration 0.38 and standard deviation 0.11. The method Atom and Combine perform the worst with low like ration and large standard deviations. We believe our proposed method SMC could maximally preserve the context information, thus resulting in better performance.

Figure 5(a) shows the distribution of workers' average scores to these four methods. From this figure, we can tell different worker's preference. The worker with ID 3 tends to give close scores to different methods. Worker with ID 10 did not grade the Google_t method. From the method perspective, there is one worker tends to give high scores to the method Atom, the same for the method Google_t. There are three workers giving high scores for the method Combine and four workers giving high scores to our proposed method SMC.

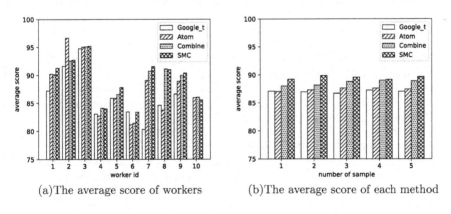

(a)The average score of workers   (b)The average score of each method

Fig. 5. Distribution of average scores

Figure 5(b) demonstrates how sampling may impact the average scores from graders. The x-axis is the number of sampled articles, while the y-axis is the average score. As we can see from this figure, despite the number of sampled articles, our proposed method SMC always has the best performance. The Combine method has the second best performance, while Atom and Google_t perform the worst.

6   Conclusion

In this paper, we propose a novel weighted graph based automatic splitting method for structured complex tasks. We first model the complex internal architecture of one task and the relationship among different sub tasks. We use weighted edges to represent the relationship between two sub tasks, converting the problem of task splitting into weighted graph cutting. We give formal definitions of weighted task tree package and CST-2, proving that there must exist one CST-2 tree with some fixed probability, and provide the way for CST-2 sampling. Then, we propose the automatic splitting method based on CST-2 tree. Through extensive experiments, we demonstrate the effectiveness of our proposed method. Furthermore, we prove such cutting is unique for one weighted graph. We also prove the time complexity of our method is $O(mlog^4 n)$.

Acknowledgement. This research has been supported by the National Nature Foundation of China under grant 61976187, the Natural Science Foundation of Zhejiang Province under grant (LZ22F020008, LQ22F020002, LY20F030002).

References

1. Chen, J., Wang, C., Bai, Y.: CrowdMR: integrating crowdsourcing with mapreduce for AI-hard problems. In: Twenty-Ninth AAAI Conference on Artificial Intelligence (2015)
2. Dai, P., Lin, C.H., Mausam, Weld, D.S.: POMDP-based control of workflows for crowdsourcing. Artif. Intell. **202**, 52–85 (2013)
3. Dai, P., Lin, C.H., Weld, D.S., et al.: POMDP-based control of workflows for crowdsourcing. Artif. Intell. **202**, 52–85 (2013)
4. Deng, J., Dong, W., Socher, R., Li, L.J., Li, K., Fei-Fei, L.: Imagenet: a large-scale hierarchical image database. In: 2009 IEEE Conference on Computer Vision and Pattern Recognition, pp. 248–255. IEEE (2009)
5. Fang, Y., Sun, H., Li, G., Zhang, R., Huai, J.: Context-aware result inference in crowdsourcing. Inf. Sci. **460**, 346–363 (2018)
6. Faradani, S., Hartmann, B., Ipeirotis, P.G.: What's the right price? Pricing tasks for finishing on time. In: Workshops at the Twenty-Fifth AAAI Conference on Artificial Intelligence (2011)
7. Haas, D., Ansel, J., Gu, L., Marcus, A.: Argonaut: macrotask crowdsourcing for complex data processing. Proc. VLDB Endow. **8**(12), 1642–1653 (2015)
8. Korovina, O., Casati, F., Nielek, R., Baez, M., Berestneva, O.: Investigating crowdsourcing as a method to collect emotion labels for images. In: Extended Abstracts of the 2018 CHI Conference on Human Factors in Computing Systems, pp. 1–6 (2018)

9. Kulkarni, A., Can, M., Hartmann, B.: Collaboratively crowdsourcing workflows with turkomatic. In: Proceedings of the ACM 2012 Conference on Computer Supported Cooperative Work, pp. 1003–1012 (2012)

10. Li, G., Wang, J., Zheng, Y., Franklin, M.J.: Crowdsourced data management: a survey. IEEE Trans. Knowl. Data Eng. **28**(9), 2296–2319 (2016)

11. Little, G., Chilton, L.B., Goldman, M., Miller, R.C.: Turkit: tools for iterative tasks on mechanical turk. In: Proceedings of the ACM SIGKDD Workshop on Human Computation, pp. 29–30 (2009)

12. Retelny, D., et al.: Expert crowdsourcing with flash teams. In: Proceedings of the 27th Annual ACM Symposium on User Interface Software and Technology, pp. 75–85 (2014)

13. Tarjan, R.E.: Applications of path compression on balanced trees. J. ACM (JACM) **26**(4), 690–715 (1979)

14. Yu, D., Zhou, Z., Wang, Y.: Crowdsourcing software task assignment method for collaborative development. IEEE Access **7**, 35743–35754 (2019)

15. Zaidan, O., Callison-Burch, C.: Crowdsourcing translation: professional quality from non-professionals. In: Proceedings of the 49th Annual Meeting of the Association for Computational Linguistics: Human Language Technologies, pp. 1220–1229 (2011)

16. Zheng, Q., Wang, W., Yu, Y., Pan, M., Shi, X.: Crowdsourcing complex task automatically by workflow technology. In: Cao, J., Liu, J. (eds.) MIPaC 2016. CCIS, vol. 686, pp. 17–30. Springer, Singapore (2017). https://doi.org/10.1007/978-981-10-3996-6_2

A Method for Security Traffic Patrolling Based on Structural Coordinated Proximal Policy Optimization

Yixuan Li[1], Qian Che[1], Fengchen Wang[1], Huiying Zhang[2], Wanyuan Wang[1(✉)], and Yichuan Jiang[1]

[1] Southeast University, Nanjing, China
wywang@seu.edu.cn
[2] Pujiang Institute, Nanjing Tech University, Nanjing, China

Abstract. Multi-agent patrolling has significant implications for addressing real-world security concerns. In multi-agent systems, the actions of agent directly influence those with whom it interacts. Traditional reinforcement learning-based multi-agent security patrolling methods overlook the role of these localized interactions in coordination among agents, thus failing to enhance the efficiency. To address this issue, this paper introduces a security patrolling approach based on Structured Coordinated Proximal Policy Optimization (PPO). The multi-agent patrolling task is modeled as a finite-time-step distributed partially observable semi-Markov decision process. This method, grounded in the Shapley Value, designs a multi-agent credit allocation function. The efficiency of this function is amplified using the structure of localized interactions. By accurately evaluating the contributions of each agent's selected actions, this function fosters enhanced coordination among agents. Extensive experiments in various scenarios were conducted, and the results demonstrate that our algorithm outperforms benchmark algorithms in terms of convergence speed and patrolling performance.

Keywords: Multi-agent Reinforcement Learning · Security Traffic Patrolling · Structural Coordination

1 Introduction

With the continuous advancement of industrial and technological capabilities in society, multi-agent systems have found extensive applications in numerous scenarios. In the realm of internet security, with the rise of large-scale coordinated attacks, multi-agent systems can be deployed to ensure cybersecurity. During patrolling, they analyze system logs and node traffic of various points in the network to detect potential threats [1, 2]. In the field of traffic safety, multiple agents collaborate to monitor risks on the road network, thereby reducing the likelihood of road accidents [3–5]. Moreover, with their autonomous sensing and decision-making capabilities, agents offer surveillance without blind spots and prolonged security services, which have been widely employed in warehouse security [6, 7].

© The Author(s), under exclusive license to Springer Nature Singapore Pte Ltd. 2024
Y. Sun et al. (Eds.): ChineseCSCW 2023, CCIS 2013, pp. 62–76, 2024.
https://doi.org/10.1007/978-981-99-9640-7_5

Existing algorithms can be categorized into four types: shortest path finding based methods, region partitioning based methods, coordinating based methods and multi-agent reinforcement learning based methods. Algorithms based on the shortest path of traversal graphs initially calculate the shortest path covering all nodes in the graph, subsequently using this path as the patrol route for each agent [8, 9]. The region partitioning-based algorithms transform the patrolling problem into sub-problems of region division and path planning. For instance, a study [10] used an enhanced clustering algorithm to partition the patrolling area, applying a simulated annealing algorithm to find the shortest path within the sub-area. Another study [11] introduced inter-agent communication for self-organized patrol region partitioning. In algorithms leveraging coordination mechanisms, the Heuristic Pathfinder Cognitive Coordinated (HPCC) proposed in [12] has a central coordinator with global information assigning optimal target nodes to each agent. The Conscientious Reactive (CR) approach introduced in [13] designates the adjacent node with the longest idle time (time since its last visit) as the target node for the agent.

The majority of the above strategies assume a known environment model that remains unchanged by the actions of agents, making them unsuitable for unknown or dynamically environments. In contrast, multi-agent reinforcement learning (MARL) algorithms interact with the environment to accumulate experience, which makes them highly adaptable to unknown and changing environments [14]. The DQN [15] has been broadly applied to multi-agent patrolling scenarios. For instance, Luis et al. [16] devised a centralized DQN approach for aquatic patrolling in fully observable environments. Jana et al. [17] designed a reward function and state vector representation, demonstrating satisfactory results under a basic DQN framework. However, these approaches often overlook the role of local interactions in multi-agent coordination, failing to fully bolster their coordination efficiency. Additionally, their experimental settings tend to be simplistic, with limited agent numbers, which aren't always reflective of real-world patrolling.

Considering the limitations of the aforementioned patrolling algorithms, this paper introduces the SCPPO (Structural Coordinated Proximal Policy Optimization) algorithm and applies it to security patrolling scenarios. The main contributions of this paper are:

1. We have designed a reward function based on Shapley value decomposition for multi-agent credit allocation. By incorporating the Shapley value decomposition from game theory [18], we calculate the individual action contributions of agents to the global reward.
2. We Applied the PPO algorithm [19] to complex weighted topological graph patrolling scenarios. In this paper, we account for these edge weights, making corresponding modifications to the PPO algorithm. We model multi-agent security patrolling as Finite Horizon Decentralized Partial Observable Semi Markov Decision Processes (FH-Dec-POSMDP).
3. Comprehensive experiments in various task scenarios were conducted. The results demonstrate that the SCPPO algorithm outshines benchmark algorithms in terms of convergence speed and patrolling performance, achieving higher frequency patrolling of crucial nodes in the patrolling area, and possessing enhanced patrolling efficiency. Furthermore, ablation studies highlight the components of the model.

The structure of this paper is organized as follows: Sect. 2 reviews related work; Sect. 3 introduces the modeling and solution objectives for security patrolling; Sect. 4

presents the PPO algorithm based on structured coordination; Sect. 5 details the simulation experiments and results; and Sect. 6 concludes the paper.

2 Related Works

This section reviews two main areas: the application of multi-agent reinforcement learning (MARL) in security patrolling tasks and the MARL algorithms based on Shapley value decomposition.

2.1 MARL for Security Patrolling

Earlier MARL approaches modeled security patrolling as Markov decision processes, leveraging tabular Q-Learning to update and maintain Q-values for state-action pairs [20, 21]. However, due to the limitations of tabular learning, such methods are suitable only for small-scale problems. For more complex scenarios with vast state-action spaces, deep reinforcement learning algorithms determine agent actions based on neural network outputs, yielding improved practical outcomes. Building on the DQN algorithm [15], Luis et al. [16] developed a centralized DQN for maritime patrolling in fully observable settings, with empirical evidence highlighting its performance and convergence benefits. Jana and colleagues [17] proposed a meticulously crafted reward function and state representation method. While their approach yielded promising results within a basic DQN framework, it didn't address non-stationarities in the environment. Also, their experiments relied on simplified scenarios and fewer agents, assumptions rarely holding in real-world patrolling contexts.

2.2 MARL Algorithms Based on Shapley Value Decomposition

In MARL, attributing precise individual contributions becomes intricate when the global reward is influenced by multiple agent actions. Earlier studies implicitly used neural networks to understand individual contributions to global rewards [22], risking suboptimal solutions [23]. Some researches drew inspiration from cooperative game theory, adopting the Shapley value as an explicit approach for multi-agent credit assignment [18, 24, 25]. Here, an agent's reward is defined as its average marginal contribution to subsets of other agents. Given the computational challenges of precise Shapley value calculation, approximations are often employed. One of this study's contributions is a high-efficiency method for exact Shapley value computation, leveraging the local interaction structure of agent systems, to promote better multi-agent coordination and ensure fairer and more effective reward distribution.

3 Security Patrolling Problem Description

3.1 Patrolling Modeling

The patrolling area is modeled as a weighted undirected topology graph $G = \{V, E, W\}$, Here, $V = \{1, 2, \cdots, n\}$ represents the set of nodes within the region, $E = \{1, 2, \cdots, m\}$ stands for the set of edges connecting adjacent nodes. W is the edge weight matrix. If node I and node j are adjacent, $w_{ij} \in W$ corresponds to the time steps required to move from node i to j. otherwise, $w_{ij} = -1$. Assuming the maximum duration of the patrol task is T, initially, N agents ($N \geq 2$) are randomly placed on nodes in the graph. The security patrolling task is defined as a multi-agent sequential decision problem: within at most T time steps, the system with N agents needs to visit all nodes in the graph as frequently as possible. Upon reaching a target node, they decide on the next target based on inter-agent communication and observed state information until the time limit is reached.

3.2 Evaluation Metrics

To assess the performance of different patrolling algorithms, Machado et al. [26] introduced several metrics based on node idleness (denoted as the time elapsed since the node was last visited, "Idleness"). Common idleness-based metrics include:

Instantaneous Node Idleness (INI): This metric equals the idleness value of node v at time t, represented as $INI(t, v) = t - t_{last}$, where t_{last} is the time step when node v was last visited.

Average Graph Idleness (AGI): It represents the average idleness value of all nodes in the graph after h time steps:

$$AGI^h = \frac{1}{h * n} \sum_{t=0}^{h} \sum_{v=1}^{n} INI(t, v) \tag{1}$$

Max Node Idleness (MNI): It depicts the highest INI value of all nodes within h time steps and is represented as:

$$MNI^h = \max_{t \in [0,h]} \left(\max_{v \in [1,n]} INI(t, v) \right) \tag{2}$$

4   Safe Patrol Method Based on Structured Coordinated PPO

4.1   Distributed Partially Observable Semi-Markov Decision Processes (Dec-POSMDP) Modeling

The multi-agent safe patrol problem is modeled as FH-Dec-POSMDP, described by the tuple $< T, \mathcal{N}, \mathcal{S}, \mathcal{A}, \mathcal{R}, \mathcal{P}, \mathcal{O}, \gamma >$. The meanings of the symbols in the tuple are as follows:

- T is the maximum time step for multi-agent decision-making. This value limits the total duration of agent-environment interactions, confining the problem to a finite time horizon. $\mathcal{N} = \{1, 2, \cdots, N\}$ represents the multi-agent system comprising N agents.
- $\mathcal{S}$ is the finite set of the environment's global state s, which includes the current positions of all agents, instantaneous idleness times of all nodes, average visit idleness times, and maximum node idleness times. However, each agent can only access a s ubset of this global state.

- $\mathcal{A} = A_1 \times \cdots \times A_K$ is the Cartesian product of the action spaces of all agents, with A_i being the action space of agent i. The joint action of all agents is denoted as $\vec{a} = (a_1, a_2, \cdots, a_N)$. In the SMDP, the duration for each agent to perform a single action varies, which distinguishes SMDP from MDP.
- $\mathcal{P}$ is the environment's state transition function. $P(s, \vec{a}, s\prime)$ describes the probability of the environment transitioning from global state s to $s\prime$ given the agents' joint action $\vec{a}$.
- $\mathcal{R}$ is the reward function. Since safe patrolling is a fully cooperative multi-agent scenario, all agents use the same reward function.
- $O \in \mathcal{O}$ represents the joint observation space when all agents observe the environment, with $O = (o_1, o_2, \cdots, o_N)$, where o_i is the information obtained by agent i after observing the environment in state s.
- γ is the discount factor within $[0,1]$. Its magnitude directly correlates with the agent's emphasis on rewards in future time steps.

Then we provide detailed explanations for the action space, observation information, and reward function in the FH-Dec-POSMDP model within the safe patrol scenario.

Action Space: The action space dimension is fixed at d, where d is the maximum degree (number of adjacent nodes) of a node in the topology graph G plus one. If the current node $v\prime$ s degree is less than $d - 1$, actions with indices greater than d^v are considered illegal. At most, d possible legal actions correspond to moving to an adjacent node or remaining at the current one.

Observation Space: The remaining time is appended to the observation vector. During the patrol, agents can only perceive a part of the global state. An individual agent's observation includes the remaining time, node positions of all agents, and idleness times of its adjacent nodes. Assuming that all agents share the position information of the currently visited node, an individual agent's estimate of the graph's idleness matches the actual idleness. Agent i's observation vector at time t, denoted o_t^i, can be expressed by Eq. (3):

$$o_t^i = \left[\bar{t}, v_t^1, \cdots, v_t^N, INI\left(t, n_1^i\right), \cdots, INI\left(t, n_d^i\right) \right] \tag{3}$$

$\bar{t} = 1 - 2(T - t)/T$ denotes the remaining time of normalization, v_t^i denotes the node serial number of the node that the agent i is at moment t (the value is -1 if the agent not currently reached the target node). n_j^k denotes the target access node corresponding to the execution of the action j by the agent i, and if the action j is an illegal action, then the value of $INI\left(t, n_1^i\right)$ is taken as -1.

Reward Function. This section designs a reward function based on Shapley value decomposition. It improves the Shapley value computation based on interactions between multiple agents. The detailed computation process is as follows:

First, the definition of cooperative constraints is given: if the target visit nodes of two agents might overlap in the next moment, there's a cooperative constraint relationship between them. Next, each agent's local interaction set $\mathcal{N}_i^{coor}$ is determined, which consists of agents having cooperative constraints with agent i. This simplifies the entire multi-agent system's cooperative constraint relationships into local cooperative structures of local interacting agent subsets. Lastly, each agent's average Shapley value $\varphi_i^{\vec{a}}$ across all subsets of its local interacting agent set is calculated as its reward.

Considering agents have no contribution to the system outside their local interacting agent set, for agent i, if the joint action of all agents is $\vec{a} = (a_1, \cdots, a_i, \cdots, a_N)$, and $\mathcal{N}_i^{noncoor}$ is the system of agents without local interaction structures with agent i, then its contribution $\phi_i^{\vec{a}}$ when performing action a_i can be calculated using Eq. (4).

$$\phi_i^{\vec{a}} = \frac{1}{N!} \sum_{\mathcal{C} \subseteq \mathcal{N}_i^{coor}} H\left(|\mathcal{C}|, n_i^{irr}\right) \Delta_i^{\vec{a}}(\mathcal{C}) \tag{4}$$

where $\Delta_i^{\vec{a}}(\mathcal{C}) = u(\{i\} + \mathcal{C}) - u(\mathcal{C})$ is the value of the marginal contribution of the agent I to $\mathcal{C}$. $H\left(|\mathcal{C}|, n_i^{irr}\right)$ is a multiplier related only to the number of agents in the subset of locally interacting agents $|\mathcal{C}|$ and n_i^{irr}, and is expressed in Eq. (5) as follows.

$$H\left(|\mathcal{C}|, n_i^{irr}\right) = \sum_{k=0}^{n_i^{irr}} \binom{n_i^{irr}}{k} (|\mathcal{C}| + k)!(N - |\mathcal{C}| - k - 1)! \tag{5}$$

4.2 SCPPO

This section delves into the modifications made to the PPO algorithm within an SMDP setting.

PPO Algorithm in SMDP. One of the salient differences between SMDP and MDP is that the number of time steps required for state transitions depends on the actions performed and is not constant. This feature aligns more closely with many real-world application scenarios. The state transitions in MDP and SMDP, ranging from the local state o_t to the terminal state o_T.

In a similar vein, our method modifies both the Replay Buffer and network update aspects of the PPO algorithm to extend it to the SMDP framework. Firstly, the contents of the interaction trajectory samples in the Replay Buffer are expanded. In addition to the original $< o, a, logprob, r, o\prime, done >$, we now also store the time steps τ taken by the agent to perform action a, resulting in $< o, a, logprob, \tau, r, o\prime, done >$. This additional information regarding the action duration τ becomes vital for subsequent network updates.

Furthermore, when the neural network updating, considering the time steps τ, there is a need to adjust the formulas for calculating the TD-error and the state advantage. As the environment calculates individual rewards only when the agent reaches the target node, the environmental reward received during action execution is zero. Therefore, $\varsigma = \sum_{i=0}^{\tau-1} \gamma^i r_{t+i+1} = \gamma^{\tau-1} r_{t+\tau}$. Consequently, the revised formulas for computing TD-error and state advantage are given in Eqs. (6) and (7):

$$\delta_t = \gamma^{\tau-1} r_{t+\tau} + \gamma^\tau V(o_{t+\tau}) - V(o_t) \tag{6}$$

$$A_t = \delta_t + (\gamma\lambda)^\tau \delta_{t+\tau} + \cdots + (\gamma\lambda)^{T-t+\tau\prime} \delta_{T-\tau\prime} \tag{7}$$

Algorithm Framework. Moreover, agents executing patrolling tasks are homogeneous agents, meaning they share the same state and action spaces. Therefore, a parameter sharing mechanism can enhance sampling efficiency and expedite learning [27]. Compared to each agent training their distinct actor and critic networks, the parameter-sharing PPO algorithm allows multiple agents to retain their individual actor networks while sharing a single critic network. This reduces the total number of networks from 2N to $1 + N$. Agents feed their state observations into the actor network and decide on actions based on its output. Once the number of interactions reaches a predetermined sampling step, both the actor and critic networks are updated. Building on the FH-Dec-POSMDP model and learning methodology described above, this paper introduces the SCPPO algorithm. The comprehensive framework of this algorithm is depicted in Fig. 1.

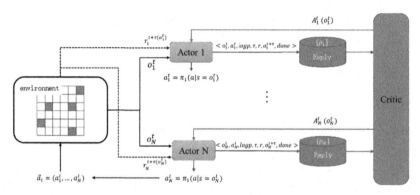

Fig. 1. Algorithm Framework

5 Experimentation

This section will first introduce the design of simulation experiments and then analyze the simulation experiment results for multi-robot patrol and traffic safety patrol scenarios.

5.1 Experimental Settings

This section presents both comparative experiments and ablation experiments, the two types of experiments are detailed as follows: Comparative Experiments. The SCPPO's performance is horizontally compared with other benchmark algorithms in the same safety patrol scenarios. The final outcomes of various algorithms are compared from multiple performance metrics dimensions. Ablation Experiments: Ablation experiments are conducted to validate the theoretical correctness of the FH-Dec-POSMDP model proposed in this chapter. This involves breaking down and analyzing the model's observation information and reward function components. The performance differences before and after ablation are evaluated to assess the effectiveness of each component. Furthermore, to demonstrate the generality of the proposed algorithm, this chapter selects two simulation scenarios: multi-robot patrol and traffic safety patrol. All experiments are conducted on machines with the same configuration: CPU Intel(R) Xeon E-2126G, 3.30 GHz, and 64 GB of memory.

The benchmark methods for comparison include two categories: traditional distributed patrol methods and deep reinforcement learning-based methods. The traditional distributed patrol method is the reactive cooperative method CR. The deep reinforcement learning-based methods include RTD3QN [17] and parameter-sharing-based PSD3QN [27–29]. The observation representation and action space of the latter two methods are consistent with those described in Sect. 4.1, and Q-value updates are also performed according to Eq. (6). Brief introductions to these two methods are provided as follows:

PSD3QN: As the multi-agent system in the experiments of this chapter meets the conditions of homogeneous agents, the parameter-sharing mechanism is combined with the D3QN framework to create the PSD3QN method as a comparative algorithm. In this method, all agents use the same evaluation network and target network as the policy for actions. The reward function for this method is as described in Sect. 4.1.

RTD3QN: In comparison to PSD3QN, the distinction of this method lies in the reward function designed by Jana et al. [17]. In this function, the reward r obtained by an agent at time step t upon reaching node v can be represented using Eq. (8), where p = 1.5.

$$r = \frac{INI(t, v)^p}{\sum_{v \in V} INI(t, v)} \tag{8}$$

The network hyperparameters are set as follows: learning rate 1.5e-4, batch size 256, experience replay pool maximum capacity 1e6, exploration coefficient in the range [0.05,1], exploration coefficient decay rate 1e5, discount factor 0.95, starting training steps 1000, training interval 50, and network exchange steps 64. The exploration coefficient ε decreases gradually as the total training steps increase, and for total training steps k, $\varepsilon(k) = 0.05 + 0.95 * e^{-k/1e5}$. When the number of samples in the experience replay pool exceeds 1000, a network training is conducted every 50 additional samples, and the parameters of the evaluation network and target network are swapped every 64 training iterations.

5.2 Multi-robot Patrol Scenario Experiments

This subsection first introduces the environment settings for the multi-robot patrol scenario, followed by the presentation and analysis of simulation experiment results for multiple topology maps. The average graph idleness (AGI) is selected as the indicator to evaluate algorithm performance, where lower AGI values indicate better performance.

In the multi-robot patrol scenario, multiple robots are deployed on critical nodes within a region. When a robot reaches a node, it can choose to move between neighboring nodes or stay at the current node. During the patrol task, robots have partial environment perception, including time steps since the task began, current positions of all robots, and information about adjacent nodes at the current position. Robots must perform fully cooperative patrol tasks in partially observable environments, continuously monitoring, inspecting, or controlling critical nodes within a given area. The objective is to minimize the average idleness value of all nodes at the end of the patrol task. As described in Sect. 3.1, the patrol area can be modeled as a weighted undirected graph $G = (V, E, W)$. This subsection's simulation experiments include four custom topology maps: GridA, GridB, MapA, and MapB. GridA and MapA have edge weights of 1 each, GridB has edge weights of 10, and MapB's edge weights follow a uniform integer distribution in the range [1, 10].

Comparative Experiments. Comparative experiments are conducted on the four custom topology maps with varying numbers of agents, repeated 10 times to obtain average values. To ensure data stability and reliability, the initial nodes of multiple agents are randomly reset at the start of each experiment.

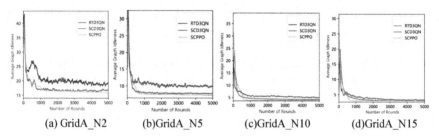

| (a) GridA_N2 | (b)GridA_N5 | (c)GridA_N10 | (d)GridA_N15 |

Fig. 2. AGI training curves in GridA

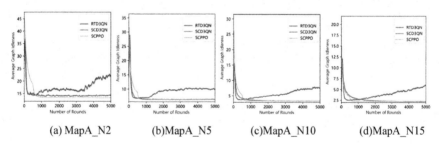

| (a) MapA_N2 | (b)MapA_N5 | (c)MapA_N10 | (d)MapA_N15 |

Fig. 3. AGI training curves in MapA

Algorithm-based on reinforcement learning evaluates the current policy every 10 rounds during the training process and records the average AGI value over 10 rounds. This forms the AGI training curve for each algorithm. The AGI training curves for reinforcement learning-based algorithms on the four topology maps are first compared and analyzed.

For GridA and MapA, with 5000 training rounds and patrol duration T of 100 per round, the AGI training curves for different numbers of agents are shown in Fig. 2 and Fig. 3. The subfigure names, such as GridA_N5, represent curves for 5 agents in topology map GridA, and similar meanings apply to other subfigure names.

Analyzing the training curves in Fig. 2 and Fig. 3 reveals that in GridA, due to its simpler topology, the three reinforcement learning-based algorithms exhibit good convergence. However, in the asymmetric topology of MapA, the RTD3QN algorithm starts to diverge in the later stages of training, while SCPPO and SCD3QN maintain stable convergence. Additionally, comparing the average graph idleness values after convergence, SCPPO and SCD3QN outperform RTD3QN in patrol performance.

Figure 4(a) to 4(c) show that all comparison algorithms exhibit good convergence on the grid-structured topology of GridB. However, SCPPO outperforms the other two algorithms in both convergence stability and AGI indicator. Figure 4(d) to 4(f) show that on the more complex topology of MapB compared to GridB, RTD3QN and SCD3QN converge much slower, while SCPPO maintains a fast convergence rate and achieves lower average graph idleness.

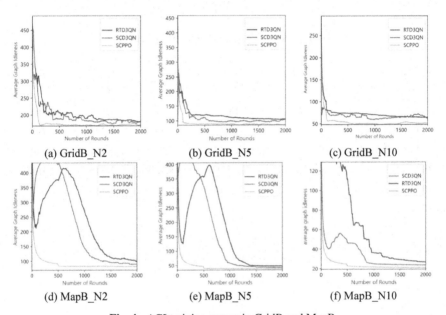

Fig. 4. AGI training curves in GridB and MapB

Furthermore, reinforcement learning-based algorithms dynamically save their best model parameters during training and generate patrol policies based on the best models. After completing training, a final comparison of algorithm performance is made by calculating the average AGI values over 10 test runs. The average AGI values for each compared algorithm are shown in Fig. 5. The data in the figure indicates that across.

Ablation Experiments. Ablation experiments are conducted on the model to analyze two components: remaining time information in the agent's observation representation and the reward function. The algorithms resulting from ablating these two parts are named SCPPO-DECtimeaware and SCPPO-DECshapley. By comparing the performance differences between these ablated algorithms and SCPPO, the effectiveness of the proposed model is validated. In SCPPO-DECshapley, the reward function is replaced with the difference reward mentioned in Sect. 4.1.

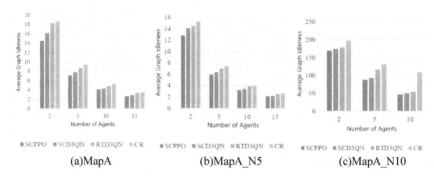

Fig. 5. Comparative average AGI values

Table 1. Ablation results in GridA and MapA

Algorithms	Map	Agent number			
		2	5	10	15
SCPPO	GridA	**14.418**	**7.077**	**4.118**	**2.664**
SCPPO-DECtimeaware		15.139	7.431	4.325	2.797
SCPPO-DECshapley		15.571	7.786	4.736	3.144
SCPPO	MapA	**12.796**	**5.950**	**3.215**	**2.168**
SCPPO-DECtimeaware		13.948	6.486	3.504	2.363
SCPPO-DECshapley		14.332	6.783	3.730	2.558

Table 2. Ablation results in GridB and MapB

Algorithms	Map	Agent number		
		2	5	10
SCPPO	GridB	**169.082**	**87.170**	**46.978**
SCPPO-DECtimeaware		173.321	91.933	49.545
SCPPO-DECshapley		179.578	105.892	55.451
SCPPO	MapB	**77.512**	**37.533**	**22.401**
SCPPO-DECtimeaware		85.007	41.162	24.567
SCPPO-DECshapley		96.083	49.368	30.658

From the data in Tables 1 and 2, it can be observed that across multiple topology maps, SCPPO consistently outperforms SCPPO-DECtimeaware and SCPPO-DECshapley. The SCPPO-DECshapley, which results from ablating the reward function, performs the worst, and this performance gap is more pronounced in complex environments.

5.3 Traffic Safety Patrol Scenario Experiments

Scene Introduction. In the Traffic Safety Patrolling (STP) scenario, multiple agents are deployed to conduct traffic law enforcement patrols on streets to ensure road safety and monitor traffic violations. Ignoring random factors in roads, it is assumed that the likelihood of a traffic accident or violation occurring on each road at each time step, $risk(e, t)$, follows a normal distribution with a mean of 0.15 and a variance of 0.05. At each time step, agents can choose to stay on the current road or move to an adjacent road for enforcement. Their enforcement efficiency on road e at time step t, $eff(e, t)$, is used to measure the historical impact of enforcement on the risk of accidents occurring on that road [30].

In the STP scenario, the historical enforcement records of agents affect their future enforcement efficiency. This characteristic is known as the time halo and distance halo effects [31, 32]. Following Rosenfeld et al. [30], this subsection decomposes $eff(e, t)$ into time efficiency value $eff_{time}(e, t)$ and distance efficiency value $eff_{distance}(e, t)$, representing the effects of time and distance on enforcement efficiency.

The objective in the STP scenario is to coordinate the patrol strategies of these agents to minimize the risk of accidents occurring within T time steps, i.e., $min \sum_{t=1,\cdots,T} \sum_{e \in E} risk(e, t)(1 - eff(e, t))$. The topology structure of the map used in the simulation experiments abstracts from a real road network, containing 284 intersections and 355 roads. Based on this topology map, the cumulative reward $\sum_{t=1,\cdots,T} \sum_{e \in E} risk(e, t)eff(e, t)$ during patrol rounds within T time steps is used as the evaluation metric for algorithm performance. A higher value indicates better algorithm performance.

Comparison Experiments. With a fixed number of agents N as 30 and each patrol round lasting $T = 20$ time steps, training is conducted over 10,000 rounds. For the three reinforcement learning algorithms, policy evaluation is carried out every 10 rounds during training. The training curves of cumulative rewards for each round are depicted in Fig. 6. From the training curves in Fig. 6, it is evident that the SCPPO algorithm achieves the highest cumulative reward during training in the STP scenario, followed by the PSD3QN algorithm, and the RTD3QN algorithm has the lowest cumulative reward. Additionally, RTD3QN exhibits a decreasing trend in cumulative reward in the later stages of training, indicating less stability compared to the other two algorithms.

Moreover, the cumulative rewards of CR and the three trained reinforcement learning algorithms in the STP scenario are compared, as shown in Table 3. It can be observed that due to the structured coordination design, SCPPO and SCD3QN outperform the other two benchmark algorithms, with SCPPO exhibiting superior performance compared to SCD3QN.

Ablation Experiments. With a fixed number of agents N as 30 and each patrol round lasting $T = 20$ time steps, the cumulative rewards of SCPPO-DECtimeaware, SCPPO-DECshapley, and SCPPO are compared.

The cumulative rewards of the three algorithms are presented in Table 4. Analyzing the data in Table 4 reveals that both SCPPO-DECtimeaware and SCPPO-DECshapley exhibit lower cumulative rewards compared to SCPPO. This suggests that

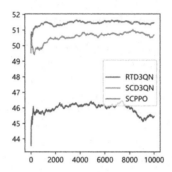

Fig. 6. Round Cumulative Reward Training Curve

Table 3. Round cumulative rewards in STP scenario

Algorithms	Rewards
SCPPO	**53.681**
SCD3QN	50.896
RTD3QN	46.532
CR	40.168

Table 4. Round cumulative rewards in STP scenario

Algorithms	Rewards
SCPPO	**53.681**
SCPPO-DECtimeaware	52.996
SCPPO-DECshapley	50.677

the ablated components contribute positively to the algorithm's performance improvement. The larger reduction in cumulative reward for SCPPO-DECshapley emphasizes the importance of reward function design.

6 Conclusion

Existing multi-agent patrolling algorithms often struggle to effectively leverage local structured coordination and are burdened with idealistic assumptions. In this paper, a structured coordination-based PPO algorithm, SCPPO, is proposed. The paper first models the patrolling environment as a weighted undirected graph. Then, the multi-agent patrolling task is formulated as a distributed partially observable semi-Markov decision process with finite time steps, elaborating on the design of action space, observation information, and reward function in the model. Subsequently, the process and framework of the SCPPO algorithm are outlined. Finally, the proposed algorithm is experimented upon in scenarios involving both multi-robot patrolling and traffic safety patrolling on various topology maps with different numbers of agents, demonstrating its effectiveness. The experimental results affirm that the SCPPO algorithm surpasses the other benchmark algorithms in terms of convergence speed and patrolling performance, showcasing higher efficiency in conducting safe patrols on critical nodes within the patrolling area.

Acknowledgement. This research was supported by the National Natural Science Foundation of China (62076060, 62072099, 61932007, 61806053).

References

1. Ma, X., An, B., Zhao, M., et al.: Randomized security patrolling for link flooding attack detection. IEEE Trans. Depend. Secure Comput. **17**(4), 795–812 (2019)
2. Brázdil, T., Kučera, A., Řehák, V.: Solving patrolling problems in the internet environment. In: Proceedings of the 27th International Joint Conference on Artificial Intelligence, pp. 121–127 (2018)
3. Savkin, A.V., Huang, H.: Asymptotically optimal deployment of drones for surveillance and monitoring. Sensors **19**(9), 2068 (2019)
4. Yang, J., Ding, Z., Wang, L.: The programming model of air-ground cooperative patrol between multi-UAV and police car. IEEE Access **9**, 134503–134517 (2021)
5. Huang, H., Savkin, A.V., Huang, C.: Decentralized autonomous navigation of a UAV network for road traffic monitoring. IEEE Trans. Aerosp. Electron. Syst. **57**(4), 2558–2564 (2021)
6. Gu, H., Zhu, S., Cui, Y., et al.: Application of agent in security platform. In: 2019 IEEE/CIC International Conference on Communications Workshops in China (ICCC Workshops), pp. 233–238. IEEE (2019)
7. Yang, Q., Yindong, L., Wei, X.: Hierarchical planning for multiple AGVs in warehouse based on global vision. Simul. Model. Pract. Theory **104**, 102124 (2020)
8. Elor, Y., Bruckstein, A.M.: Autonomous multi-agent cycle based patrolling. In: Swarm Intelligence: 7th International Conference, ANTS 2010, Brussels, Belgium. Proceedings 7, pp. 119–130. Springer, Heidelberg (2010)
9. Mao, T., Ray, L.: Frequency-based patrolling with heterogeneous agents and limited communication. arXiv preprint arXiv:1402.1757 (2014)
10. Sea, V., Sugiyama, A., Sugawara, T.: Frequency-based multi-agent patrolling model and its area partitioning solution method for balanced workload. In: van Hoeve, W.-J. (ed.) CPAIOR 2018. LNCS, vol. 10848, pp. 530–545. Springer, Cham (2018). https://doi.org/10.1007/978-3-319-93031-2_38
11. Wiandt, B., Simon, V.: Autonomous graph partitioning for multi-agent patrolling problems. In: 2018 Federated Conference on Computer Science and Information Systems (FedCSIS), pp. 261–268. IEEE (2018)
12. Almeida, A., Castro, P., Menezes, T., et al.: Combining idleness and distance to design heuristic agents for the patrolling task. In: II Brazilian Workshop in Games and Digital Entertainment, pp. 33–40 (2003)
13. Machado, A., Almeida, A., Ramalho, G., et al.: Multi-agent movement coordination in patrolling. In: Proceedings of the 3rd International Conference on Computer and Game. pp. 155–170. Springer, Heidelberg (2002). https://doi.org/10.1007/3-540-36483-8_11
14. Sutton, R.S., Barto, A.G.: Reinforcement Learning: An Introduction, 2nd edn. MIT Press (2018)

15. Mnih, V., Kavukcuoglu, K., Silver, D., et al.: Human-level control through deep reinforcement learning. Nature **518**(7540), 529–533 (2015)
16. Luis, S.Y., Reina, D.G., Marín, S.L.T.: A multiagent deep reinforcement learning approach for path planning in autonomous surface vehicles: the Ypacaraí lake patrolling case. IEEE Access **9**, 17084–17099 (2021)
17. Jana, M., Vachhani, L., Sinha, A.: A deep reinforcement learning approach for multi-agent mobile robot patrolling. Int. J. Intell. Robot. Appl. **6**(4), 724–745 (2022)
18. Fatima, S.S., Wooldridge, M., Jennings, N.R.: A linear approximation method for the Shapley value. Artif. Intell. **172**(14) (2008)
19. Schulman, J., Wolski, F., Dhariwal, P., et al.: Proximal policy optimization algorithms. arXiv preprint arXiv:1707.06347 (2017)
20. Santana, H., Ramalho, G., Corruble, V., et al.: Multi-agent patrolling with reinforcement learning. In: International Joint Conference on Autonomous Agents and Multiagent Systems, IEEE Computer Society. vol. 4, pp. 1122–1129 (2004)
21. Lauri, F., Koukam, A.: Robust multi-agent patrolling strategies using reinforcement learning. In: Swarm Intelligence Based Optimization: First International Conference (ICSIBO 2014), Mulhouse, 13–14 May 2014, pp. 157–165, Springer (2014)
22. Rashid, T., Samvelyan, M., De Witt, C.S., et al.: Monotonic value function factorisation for deep multi-agent reinforcement learning. J. Mach. Learn. Res. **21**(1), 7234–7284 (2020)
23. Li, J., Kuang, K., Wang, B., et al.: Shapley counterfactual credits for multi-agent reinforcement learning. In: Proceedings of the 27th ACM SIGKDD Conference on Knowledge Discovery and Data Mining, pp. 934–942 (2021)
24. Han S., Wang H., Su S., et al.: Stable and efficient Shapley value-based reward reallocation for multi-agent reinforcement learning of autonomous vehicles. In: 2022 International Conference on Robotics and Automation (ICRA), pp. 8765–8771. IEEE (2022)
25. Wang, J., Zhang, Y., Kim, T.K., et al.: Shapley Q-value: a local reward approach to solve global reward games. Proc. AAAI Conf. Artif. Intell. **34**(05) 7285–7292 (2020)
26. Machado, A., Ramalho, G., Zucker, J.D., et al.: Multi-agent patrolling: an empirical analysis of alternative architectures. In: Multi-agent-Based Simulation II: Third International Workshop. MABS 2002 Bologna, Italy, pp. 155–170. Springer, Heidelberg (2003)
27. Van Hasselt, H., Guez, A., Silver, D.: Deep reinforcement learning with double q-learning. In: Proceedings of the AAAI Conference on Artificial Intelligence, vol.30, no. 1 (2016)
28. Fatemi, M., Wu, M., Petch, J., et al.: Semi-Markov offline reinforcement learning for healthcare. In: Conference on Health, Inference, and Learning, pp. 119–137. PMLR (2022)
29. Wang, Z., Schaul, T., Hessel, M., et al.: Dueling network architectures for deep reinforcement learning. In: International Conference on Machine Learning, pp. 1995–2003. PMLR (2016)
30. Rosenfeld, A., Maksimov, O., Kraus, S.: When security games hit traffic: a deployed optimal traffic enforcement system. Artif. Intell. **289**, 103381 (2020)
31. Weisburd, S.: Does Police Presence Reduce Car Accidents? Tel Aviv University, Pinhas Sapir Center for Development (2016)
32. Elliott, M.A., Broughton, J.: How Methods and Levels of Policing Affect Road Casualty Rates. TRL Limited, London (2005)

Corwdsourced Task Recommendation via Link Prediction

Song Yu[1,2], Qingxian Pan[2], and Li Li[1(✉)]

[1] School of Computer and Information Science, Southwest University,
Chongqing 400715, China
`lily@swu.edu.cn`
[2] School of Computer and Control Engineering, Yantai University,
Shandong 264005, China

Abstract. Mobile crowdsourcing (MCS) can solve problems that are difficult for computers to solve accurately or efficiently. Current crowdsourcing workers face the challenges of overload, task recommendation is presented to deal with the above issue. The existing MCS task recommendation methods only consider the workers themselves, without taking the potential relationships between workers and workers and tasks, which may fail to grasp the long-term behavioral preferences of workers and cannot solve the cold start problem efficiently. To solve the above problems, this paper proposes a task recommendation method based on heterogeneous graph link prediction. First, we try to obtain the connection relationships between crowdsourcing tasks and workers and build a worker-task heterogeneous graph accordingly. Then, majority voting and DeepWalk are used to generate initial node features of workers. Second, we design two efficient message passing mechanisms to aggregate and update node features between task and worker nodes to explore the potential relationships between nodes. Finally, we obtain attention weights among nodes and use Bi-GRU to capture the long-term behavioral preferences of workers and recommend appropriate tasks to workers based on the similarity between workers and tasks to improve perceptual quality. Evaluations are conducted on seven real datasets. Experimental results show that our method is superior to the state-of-the-art baselines.

Keywords: Mobile Crowdsourcing · task recommendation · heterogeneous graph · link prediction

1 Introduction

Crowdsourcing is a way to harness the power of the group to solve problems. With the rapid development of technology, mobile crowdsourcing (MCS) has emerged as a new solution to monitor the surrounding environment in real-time through sensors in smart devices and constantly moving workers [1]. MCS leverages existing communication technologies such as cellular networks, WiFi, and Bluetooth to efficiently analyze and integrate data from smart devices that are

Y. Sun et al. (Eds.): ChineseCSCW 2023, CCIS 2013, pp. 77–91, 2024.
https://doi.org/10.1007/978-981-99-9640-7_6

distributed across different locations. This form of sensing has great advantages over traditional wireless sensor networks, especially in large-scale sensing tasks, with low sensing costs and high sensing efficiency [3].

With the explosion of information on the Internet, the growth of workers has not kept pace with the growth of tasks on MCS. Although the principle of self-selection allows workers to choose tasks according to their preferences, they still face the challenges of overload. Therefore, an efficient task recommendation mechanism is an important issue for MCS [4], which is crucial for its efficiency and effectiveness [5]. Most of the existing research approaches consider only a single characteristic of workers and ignore the potential connection between workers and workers and tasks [6]. One way to maximize the number of task accomplishments is to assign task to high-quality and appropriate workers. How to model the multidimensional characteristics and connections between workers and tasks and apply them to the task assignment process is one of the urgent problems to be solved.

To maximize the number of task accomplishments, this paper analyzes the potential relationship between perceived tasks and perceived workers and proposes a link prediction method based on heterogeneous graph neural network.

In summary, the main contributions of this paper are summarized as follows:

(1) By analyzing the attributes and features of tasks and workers in MCS, we build an MCS heterogeneous graph to structurally represent the data in MCS and effectively fuse the graph structure features and the association features of tasks and workers.
(2) A heterogeneous graph neural network-based link prediction (HGLP) method is proposed to explore the potential relationship between task nodes and worker nodes and then predict whether there is a link between worker and task.
(3) Improving task assignment efficiency by introducing a Bi-GRU to model workers' long-term preferences.

Our method is applicable to dynamic task recommendation scenarios at coarse-grained time scales. Experimental results show that our method is superior to the state-of-the-art baselines. The advantage of this approach is that it integrates the multidimensional features and potential links between workers and tasks, and uses heterogeneous graph neural networks for link prediction, which can improve the efficiency of the MCS system and increase the number of tasks accomplishments.

2   Related Work

Unlike traditional crowdsourcing, mobile crowdsourcing makes full use of the active crowd and the various sensors they carry with them for mass sensing, and the volume of tasks and data is unmatched by traditional crowdsourcing, which also brings challenges for task assignment.

The literature [7] proposes a fine-grained, batch-based task assignment algorithm that considers nonsmooth settings. This method solves the drawbacks of batch operations and can efficiently complete task assignments in space and adapt to nonsmooth settings as soon as possible. The multi-task assignment problem is very time-consuming as the number of tasks and workers increases. The literature [8] proposes two approaches to reduce the complexity of task assignments that can provide better information quality and ensure timeliness. The literature [9] proposes a predictive algorithm-based cross-regional online task assignment algorithm that accelerates the assignment process through multiple rounds of assignment, combining offline guidance and online assignment strategies in optimizing the process. The literature [10] proposes three impact-aware task assignment algorithms aimed at maximizing the number of assigned tasks and the impact of worker tasks. Such methods work to assign as many tasks as possible in a limited amount of time and ensure the quality of the assignment.

Large-scale perceptual tasks inevitably require recruiting more employees to participate in the task. Considering the varying levels of employees, to ensure task quality, the task assignment algorithm proposed in the literature [11] infers the trust value of workers by calculating their reputation values, which allows assigning tasks to the most trustworthy employees. To ensure sensing quality, the literature [12] proposes a low-complexity heuristic algorithm using submodule optimization properties, called sensing quality-aware task assignment (SQTA), which can improve the average sensing quality of many types of sensors. Such methods aim to infer the workers that meet the task requirements and maximize the quality of task completion.

Due to the flexibility of mobile crowdsourcing, a large number of employees have flocked to crowdsourcing platforms, which offer the possibility of collaboration among employees. The literature [13] allows collaboration between workers and tasks and proposes a multi-agent deep reinforcement learning solution for improving task completion rates and worker profitability. Most of the existing task assignment methods are based on the historical information of workers and tasks for task matching, which cannot guarantee the quality of assignment when the historical behavior of tasks and workers is sparse. The literature [14] proposes a spatio-temporal feature-aware task assignment strategy for when worker and worker historical information is sparse, and experiments show that the strategy can improve task acceptance rates. Such approaches aim to improve worker satisfaction and maximize the rate of task accomplishment.

Large-scale task assignment operations also place higher demands on worker privacy protection. To protect the privacy of workers and tasks, the literature [15] proposes a privacy mechanism based on a planar Laplace distribution and designs a threshold-based online task assignment mechanism. The literature [16] combines blockchain and artificial intelligence to propose a spatial crowdsourcing strategy based on spatio-temporal prediction, which is able to achieve privacy protection while ensuring the efficiency of task assignment. The aim of such approaches is to improve task assignment efficiency as much as possible while ensuring that the privacy of workers and tasks is not compromised. The details of the related work are shown in Table 1.

Table 1. Scheme comparison.

Optimization goal	Method	Scenarios	Article
Allocation efficiency	Based on Multi-armed Bandit	Traveling tasks	6
Task completion rate	Multi-agent based reinforcement learning	Sensing tasks	12
Allocation quality	Based on particle swarm algorithms	Intensive tasks	7
	Based on fuzzy trust and reputation	Comment tasks	10
	Submodule-based optimization algorithm	Traveling tasks	11
Number of allocations	Based on online assignment model	Traveling tasks	8
	Based on data-driven	Check-in tasks	9
	Matrix-based decomposition	Check-in tasks	13
Utility value	Based on Laplace and threshold	Check-in tasks	14
	Based on machine learning	Check-in tasks	15

3   Problem Definition

The method proposed in this paper mainly consists of four parts: constructing heterogeneous graphs, obtaining node representations, graph message passing, and link prediction.

(1) Constructing heterogeneous graphs. We analyze the information of workers and tasks in the crowdsourcing data, mine the correlation between them and build the worker-task graph. In our proposed model, the edges are undirected, so we define the graph as an undirected graph $G = (V, E)$.

(2) Obtaining node representations. We obtain the initial representations of the nodes by majority voting. For those new nodes without ever participation information, we use the DeepWalk algorithm combined with graph topology features to assign node representations to them, which can solve the cold start problem to a certain extent.

(3) Graph message passing. To further explore the potential relationships between workers and tasks, we design two different efficient graph message passing mechanisms for workers and tasks to update node representations. We also use Bi-GRU to capture node long-term preferences.

(4) Link prediction. We build links by computing the similarity between heterogeneous nodes and select workers to complete the perception task.

The overall framework of the model is shown in Fig. 1. The more details of symbol description are summarized in Table 2.

4   Method

In this section, we describe our method in detail.

4.1   Constructing Heterogeneous Graphs

The heterogeneous graph we are going to build consists of two types of nodes, worker nodes, and task nodes. Explicit links can only be generated between nodes of different types.

Table 2. Notation note of symbols.

Symbol	Comments
G	the worker-task graph
V	the set of all nodes
E	the set of all relations
u_i	the worker i
t_j	the task j
V_U	the set of all worker nodes
V_T	the set of all task nodes
$h(u_i)$	the embedding of worker i
$h(t_j)$	the embedding of task j
$h(e_{ij})$	the relation embedding between worker i and task j
l_{ij}	the label assigned to task j by worker i
g_j	the gold label of task j
$J(u_i)$	the set of tasks performed by worker i
$P(t_j)$	the set of workers who perform task j
s_{ij}	the time spent by worker i on task j
a_j	the average time spent by workers performing task j
n	the time step
ϕ	the nonlinear activation function
c	the weight
α, β	the weight of attention
M	the message aggregation function

We establish the MCS heterogeneous graph as shown in Fig. 2 by fully considering the characteristics of MCS platform workers. The blue nodes are task nodes, and each task node has a different id to identify a unique perceptual task. The green nodes are worker nodes, which are distinguished by their ids. Each worker node has three node attributes: label, glabel and time, where label is the label assigned to the task by the worker, glabel is the gold label of the task, and time is the time taken by the worker to perform the task. Attributes are used to calculate the ability value and difficulty of workers and tasks and are the most direct factors affecting the perceived quality.

4.2 Obtaining Node Representations

In the previous subsection, we mined the information between workers and tasks to build heterogeneous graph. In this section, We use majority voting and Deep-Walk to initialize the node representations. For both worker and task nodes u_i, $t_j \in V$, We can compute features by majority voting:

$$h_1(u_i) = \frac{|\{j \in J(u_i)|l_{ij} = g_j\}|}{|J(u_i)|} \tag{1}$$

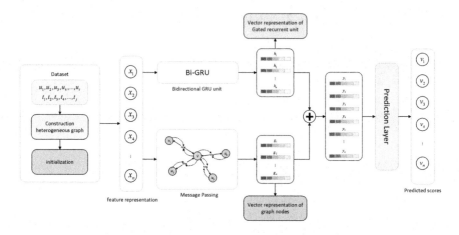

Fig. 1. Overall of our method.

$$h_1(t_j) = 1 - \frac{|\{i \in P(t_j) | l_{ij} = g_j\}|}{|P(t_j)|} \tag{2}$$

Where $J(u_i)$ denotes the set of tasks performed by worker u_i, $P(t_j)$ denotes the set of workers performing task t_j. l_{ij} denotes the label assigned to task t_j by worker u_i, while g_j is the golden label given by majority voting or experts. We consider that the more times a worker gives an answer that agrees with the golden label, the higher his ability is. Similarly, the more label categories workers submit to a task, the more difficult the task is.

The majority voting principle allows an initial estimate of a worker's ability, but the efficiency is also important. Therefore, we additionally consider time information to model another feature for workers and tasks:

$$h_2(u_i) = 1 - \frac{\sum\limits_{j \in J(u_i)} s_{ij}}{\sum\limits_{j \in J(u_i)} a_j} \tag{3}$$

$$h_2(t_j) = \frac{a_j}{|V_T| \times \sum\limits_{j \in V_T} a_j} \tag{4}$$

where s_{ij} denotes the time spent by worker u_i to perform task t_j and a_j is the average time spent by the worker to perform task t_j. We consider that workers with shorter average task execution times are more efficient, and the task with the longest execution time will obviously be more difficult. Finally, we normalize the features and extend them to multiple dimensions.

For those nodes with no historical information, we use DeepWalk [17] to obtain the initial representation of the node. DeepWalk is a graph-structured data mining algorithm that combines random walk and word2vec algorithms. It is a method to learn a network's potential feature vectors of vertices. The algorithm flow is shown in Algorithm 1.

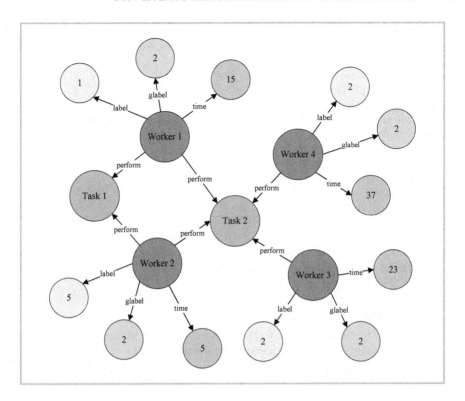

Fig. 2. MCS heterogeneous graph.

4.3   Graph Message Passing

The graph message passing mechanism defines the following node-way and edge-way computations at step $n + 1$, and a typical message passing process is as follows:

$$h^{(n+1)}(u_i) = \phi(c_i h^n(u_i) + (1 - c_i) \sum_{j \in J(u_i)} \alpha_{ij} M_j^i(h^n(u_i), h^n(t_j), h^n(e_{ij}))) \quad (5)$$

where ϕ is the nonlinear activation function, $c_i \in [0, 1]$ is the weight, α_{ij} is the attention weight, M_j^i is the message generation function, and $h^n(u_i)$, $h^n(t_j)$ and $h^n(e_{ij})$ are the embedding of worker u_i, task t_j and edge e_{ij} at step n, respectively. The attention weights are calculated as follows:

$$\alpha_{ij} = \frac{\exp(\mathbf{W}_1(M_j^i(h^n(u_i), h^n(t_j), h^n(e_{ij})) \oplus h^n(u_i) + b_1))}{\sum_{m \in J(u_i)} \exp(\mathbf{W}_1(M_m^i(h^n(u_i), h^n(t_m), h^n(e_{im})) \oplus h^n(u_i) + b_1))} \quad (6)$$

where exp is the exponential function, and $\mathbf{W}_1$ and b_1 are the weight matrix and bias term. In our approach, the interaction between workers and tasks contains not only worker/task node features but also information about crowdsourced

Algorithm 1. DeepWalk

Input: the worker-task graph $G = (V, E)$, window size w, embedding size d, walk per vertex γ, walk length t
Output: matrix of vertex representations $\Omega \in \mathbb{R}^{|V| \times d}$
1: Initialize: Sample Ω from $\Theta^{|V| \times d}$
2: Build a binary Tree T from V
3: **for** $i = 0$ to γ **do**
4:    $O = \text{Shuffle}(V)$
5:    **for each** $v_i \in O$ **do**
6:        $W_{v_i} = RandomWalk(G, v_i, t)$
7:        $\text{SkipGram}(\Omega, W_{v_i}, w)$
8:    **end for**
9: **end for**

---

tags and temporal information. So our message generation function is computed by considering node and edge features as follows:

$$M_j^i(h^n(u_i), h^n(t_j), h^n(e_{ij})) = \phi(\mathbf{W}^u(h^n(t_j) \oplus (\mathbf{W}_e^u h^n(e_{ij})))) \tag{7}$$

where $\mathbf{W}^u$ and $\mathbf{W}_e^u$ are the parameter matrices, and then we pass messages from the workers to the tasks. Similar to the above messaging phase, for each task t_j we receive messages from its connected edges and workers.

$$h^{(n+1)}(t_j) = \phi(c_j h^n(t_j) + (1 - c_j) \sum_{i \in P(t_j)} \beta_{ji} M_i^j(h^n(t_j), h^n(u_i), h^n(e_{ij}))) \tag{8}$$

We use different weight matrices and bias terms $\mathbf{W}_2$ and b_2, and the attention weights for task t_j are calculated as follows:

$$\beta_{ji} = \frac{\exp(\mathbf{W}_2(M_i^j(h^n(t_j), h^n(u_i), h^n(e_{ij})) \oplus h^n(t_j) + b_2))}{\sum\limits_{k \in P(t_j)} \exp(\mathbf{W}_2(M_k^i(h^n(t_j), h^n(u_k), h^n(e_{kj})) \oplus h^n(t_j) + b_2))} \tag{9}$$

Similarly, we use different parameter matrices $\mathbf{W}^t$ and $\mathbf{W}_e^t$ to learn the feature representation.

$$M_i^j(h^n(t_j), h^n(u_i), h^n(e_{ij})) = \phi(\mathbf{W}^t(h^n(u_i) \oplus (\mathbf{W}_e^t h^n(e_{ij})))) \tag{10}$$

We can stack multiple layers of GNNs to get better results, but in our experiments, one layer is sufficient.

To capture the long-term preferences of workers, we use Bi-GRU [18] to model worker interests and capture time and click information in action sequences. Bi-GRU is a sequence processing model consisting of two GRUs, one receiving input forward and the other backward. We transform the worker data into the corresponding embedding vectors in the feature space and feed them into the Bi-GRU. we update our output after stacking multiple layers of Bi-GRU.

After obtaining the vector representation of the output of the Bi-GRU layer, we link it with the output of the GNN layer to obtain our final vector representation.

4.4 Link Prediction

In the previous sections, we introduced the message passing layer between workers and tasks, and the Bi-GRU layer for capturing long-term preferences. We can use the final embeddings to predict the connections between workers and tasks. For a worker u with final embedding h_u^L and a task t with final embedding h_t^L, we predict the connectivity by:

$$y_{u,v} = \phi(h_u^L, h_t^L) \tag{11}$$

In order to train the model, we use a negative sampling technique to obtain negative samples.

Training a link prediction model requires comparing the score between two nodes of a connection and the difference in score between any pair of nodes. For example, for a given link u and v, a good model should be able to get a higher score between u and v than between u and a node u' sampled from a noisy distribution $v' \sim P_n(v)$. We use the margin loss as our loss function:

$$L_{margin} = \sum_{v_i \sim P_n(v)} \max(0, M - y_{u,v} + y_{u,v_i}) \tag{12}$$

where M is the constant hyperparameter, $y_{u,v}$ is the similarity score between positive samples, and y_{u,v_i} is the similarity score between samples obtained by negative sampling. We then represent our algorithm as in Algorithm 2:

Algorithm 2. Link Prediction Model

Input: the worker-task graph $G = (V, E)$, which includes worker nodes and task nodes and edges between them.

Output: the predicted score $y_{u,v}$.

    Initialize the features of worker nodes h_i and task nodes h_j by Equation (1)–(4), DeepWalk algorithm;

2: **while** AUC does not meet requirements **do**

    Update worker features h_i, task features h_j by Equation (5)–(10);

4:    Update worker features h_i, task features h_j by Equation (11)–(14);

    Predict connection score $y_{u,v}$ by Equation (15);

6:    Calculate loss by Equation (16);

    Backpropagation to update model parameters;

8: **end while**

---

5 Experiment

To verify the effectiveness of the proposed method, this paper conducts extensive experiments on publicly available datasets. Our model is implemented based on pytorch1.13 and Deep Graph Library (DGL). The training platform is Intel(R) Xeon(R) Gold 6330 CPU @ 2.00 GHz, RTX 3090 (24 GB), 80 GB RAM, and Ubuntu 20.04.

5.1 Datasets

We conducted experiments on seven widely used real-world datasets.

- **MG**: The Music Genre dataset (MG) is a dataset of 30-second song samples captured from audio data collected by Tzanetakis and Cook.
- **WS**: WS-AMT is a weather mood dataset provided by AMT for the Massive Crowdsourcing Shared Task Challenge.
- **TPD**: Top Personality Dataset, containing information such as worker id, movie id, and worker ratings of movies.
- **APR**: This dataset contains over 568,000 consumer reviews of different Amazon products.
- **WBA**: This dataset has the distribution results of 3 different crowdsourcing tasks started on CrowdFlower, and the associated staff behavior.
- **WINE**: Wine tasting dataset containing 130,000 wine reviews posted to Wine Enthusiast.
- **TOMATO**: Rotten Tomatoes Movie and Critic Reviews Dataset, providing detailed information about movie critic reviews and worker and critic ratings.

For datasets with more than 20,000 data, we randomly grabbed 20,000 data and performed data cleaning operations. The statistics of some datasets are shown in Table 3.

Table 3. Details of datasets.

Dataset	Task	Worker	Relation	Average node degree	Max node degree
MG	700	44	2945	15.833	736
WS	300	110	5995	58.488	544
TPD	6942	1624	19994	9.3364	386
APR	17880	11001	19986	2.7680	64
WBA	772	9	775	3.9693	200
WINE	8182	424	13696	6.3658	2300
TOMATO	8556	3024	19956	6.8933	622

5.2 Evaluation Indicators

In this paper, the Area Under the Curve (AUC) and the precision [19] are used as the main metrics to measure the prediction effectiveness.

- AUC: The AUC value is a metric that evaluates the performance of a model and indicates the probability that the model can correctly distinguish between existing and non-existing links when n independent comparisons are made between them.

$$AUC = \frac{n' + 0.5n''}{n} \qquad (13)$$

- Precision: Based on the ranking of unobserved links, the precision is defined as the ratio of the number of relevant items selected to the number of items selected.

5.3   Comparison Algorithm

We use the following algorithms as the baseline for our comparison:

- **GAT** [20]: The GAT is a graph neural network based on an attention mechanism proposed by Velickovic et al. in 2018.
- **GGNN** [21]: the GGNN is a graph neural network proposed by Li et al. in 2016.
- **GraphSAGE** [22]: GraphSAGE is a graph neural network based on sampled neighbor aggregation proposed by Hamilton et al. in 2017.d nodes to update the features of that node.
- **LowFER** [23]: A factorization bilinear pooling model, which is commonly used for multimodal learning and allows better integration of entities and relations, resulting in an efficient and unconstrained model.
- **MEIM-KGE** [24]: A multi-partitioned embedding interaction model with independent core tensor for integration effects, soft orthogonality for maximum rank mapping, and multi-partitioned embedding.
- **KGA** [25]: A knowledge graph enhancement method that includes text in the embedding model without modifying its loss function.

5.4   Experimental Results

We compare our method with six different baselines and select AUC and precision as evaluation metrics. Due to the limitations of the implementation ideas and conditions, certain algorithms are not able to obtain the precision. The experimental results are shown in Table 4 and Table 5, where our algorithm (HGLP) outperforms the comparison algorithm in most cases.

Table 4. AUC of link prediction on the dataset with different algorithms.

Dataset	GAT [20]	GGNN [21]	GraphSAGE [22]	KGA [25]	LowFER [23]	MEIM-KGE [24]	HGLP
MG	0.752	0.862	0.868	0.890	0.854	0.487	**0.922**
WS	0.711	0.763	0.724	0.710	**0.944**	0.513	0.862
TPD	0.676	0.861	0.984	0.560	0.447	0.684	**0.994**
APR	0.770	0.998	0.869	0.520	0.479	0.640	**0.998**
WBA	0.755	0.941	0.933	0.403	0.700	0.734	**0.943**
WINE	0.864	0.931	0.985	0.501	0.753	0.913	**0.994**
TOMATO	0.743	0.974	0.996	0.530	0.459	0.683	**0.996**

It can be seen that our algorithm performs better on six datasets (MG, TPD, APR, WBA, WINE, TOMATO), and slightly worse on the WS dataset. However, our algorithm has the most stable performance. In the two multi-relationship datasets (MG, WS), our method shows good performance, while in the other five datasets with many entities and few relationships (TPD, APR, WBA, WINE, TOMATO), our method shows superior performance compared to the other methods. We designed our message passing mechanism to better capture the underlying relationships between different classes of nodes. Notice that the performance of comparison algorithms LowFER and KGA degrades severely in datasets with more entities, while comparison algorithm LowFER shows superior performance in the WS dataset with fewer entities and more relationships. We conjecture that the algorithm may be good at capturing dense relational networks but not sparse networks.

Table 5. Precision of link prediction on the dataset with different algorithms.

Dataset	GAT	GGNN	GraphSAGE	KGA	LowFER	MEIM-KGE	HGLP
MG	0.721	0.852	0.886	–	–	–	**0.987**
WS	0.794	0.771	0.744	–	–	–	**0.932**
TPD	0.631	0.766	0.915	–	–	–	**0.953**
APR	0.685	0.977	**0.983**	–	–	–	0.966
WBA	0.808	0.997	0.999	–	–	–	**0.999**
WINE	0.783	0.868	0.956	–	–	–	**0.981**
TOMATO	0.701	0.922	0.971	–	–	–	**0.975**

5.5   Further Exploration

In graph neural networks, the feature dimension of nodes is one of the very important factors that can affect the performance and accuracy of the model. To explore the image of dimensionality on performance, we initialized four different dimensions and conducted experiments on all data sets, as shown in Fig. 3.

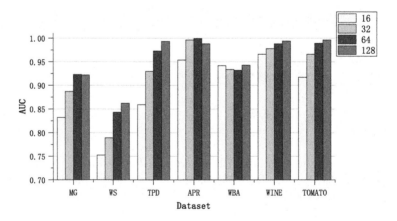

Fig. 3. Dimensional effect.

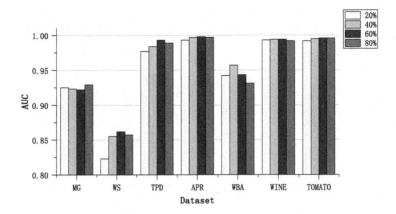

Fig. 4. Training ratio effect.

Fewer feature dimensions degrade the model's performance because the model does not have enough representational power. As the number of dimensions increases, the model performance gradually improves, but around a certain point, it is difficult to further increase the feature dimensions to improve the performance further.

Real-life training data is sometimes difficult to obtain. For models that require large-scale data, acquiring datasets of sufficient size can be even more difficult, especially when the desired dataset domain is more specific. In addition, the cost of acquiring datasets is also a factor to be considered. Therefore, it is important to evaluate the performance of the model on small datasets. To explore how the performance of the model varies on small data, we adjusted the proportion of training data and the experimental results are shown in Fig. 4.

As can be seen from the figure, the AUC increases with the proportion of training data on almost all datasets, but decreasing the proportion of training data does not result in a noticeable decrease in performance, which suggests that our method can achieve reasonably good performance with very little data.

In the similarity comparison phase, given a positive link (u, v), we randomly sample k nodes v' from a noisy distribution, and (u, v') is a link that does not exist as a negative case. k determines the number of negative cases corresponding to each positive case. We investigate the effect of the number of negative samples on the model performance by adjusting the size of k, and the experimental results are shown in Fig. 5.

The experimental results show that the value of k has no significant effect on the model performance. In order to reduce the computational complexity and save time, we fix the value of k to 1 in the training.

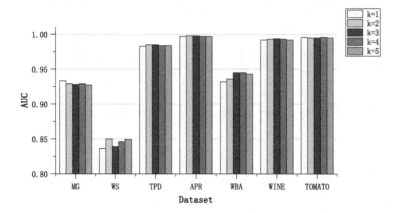

Fig. 5. Negative sampling number effect.

6   Conclusion

In this paper, we analyze the correlation between workers and tasks, build a heterogeneous graph, and use methods such as message aggregation between heterogeneous nodes and Bi-GRU to select workers for perceptual tasks by link prediction. The work is expected to be applied to real-life crowdsourcing scenarios, such as travel tasks.

Our approach still has some shortcomings. For example, our model does not explicitly utilize temporal information and therefore cannot perform time series prediction tasks. In the future, we will create continuous dynamic graphs of workers and tasks.

References

1. Boubiche, D.E., Imran, M., Maqsood, A., Shoaib, M.: Mobile crowd sensing-taxonomy, applications, challenges, and solutions. Comput. Hum. Behav. **101**, 352–370 (2019)
2. Gong, W., Zhang, B., Li, C.: Task assignment in mobile crowdsensing: present and future directions. IEEE Netw. **32**(4), 100–107 (2018)
3. Galinina, O., Mikhaylov, K., Huang, K., Andreev, S., Koucheryavy, Y.: Wirelessly powered urban crowd sensing over wearables: trading energy for data. IEEE Wirel. Commun. **25**(2), 140–149 (2018)
4. Guo, W., Zhu, W., Yu, Z., Wang, J., Guo, B.: A survey of task allocation: contrastive perspectives from wireless sensor networks and mobile crowdsensing. IEEE Access **7**, 78406–78420 (2019)
5. Wang, J., Wang, L., Wang, Y., Zhang, D., Kong, L.: Task allocation in mobile crowd sensing: state-of-the-art and future opportunities. IEEE Internet Things J. **5**(5), 3747–3757 (2018)
6. Tao, D., Cheng, J., Yu, Z., Yue, K., Wang, L.: Domain-weighted majority voting for crowdsourcing. IEEE Trans. Neural Netw. Learn. Syst. **30**(1), 163–174 (2018)

7. Jiao, Y., Lin, Z., Yu, L., Wu, X.: A fine-grain batching-based task allocation algorithm for spatial crowdsourcing. ISPRS Int. J. Geo Inf. **11**(3), 203 (2022)
8. Estrada, R., Valeriano, I., Torres, D.: Multi-task versus consecutive task allocation with tasks clustering for mobile crowd sensing systems. Procedia Comput. Sci. **198**, 67–76 (2022)
9. Zhang, Q., Wang, Y., Cai, Z., Tong, X.: Multi-stage online task assignment driven by offline data under spatio-temporal crowdsourcing. Digital Commun. Netw. **8**(4), 516–530 (2022)
10. Chen, X., Zhao, Y., Zheng, K., Yang, B., Jensen, C.S.: Influence-aware task assignment in spatial crowdsourcing. In: 2022 IEEE 38th International Conference on Data Engineering (ICDE), pp. 2141–2153. IEEE (2022)
11. Rahman, M.M., Abdullah, N.A.: A trustworthiness-aware spatial task allocation using a fuzzy-based trust and reputation system approach. Expert Syst. Appl. **211**, 118592 (2023)
12. Baek, H., Ko, H., Kim, J., Jeon, Y., Pack, S.: Sensing quality-aware task allocation for multi-dimensional vehicular urban sensing. IEEE Internet Things J. **10**, 9989–9998 (2023)
13. Zhao, P., Li, X., Gao, S., Wei, X.: Cooperative task assignment in spatial crowdsourcing via multi-agent deep reinforcement learning. J. Syst. Architect. **128**, 102551 (2022)
14. Tang, T., Cui, L., Yin, Z., Hu, S., Fu, L.: Spatiotemporal characteristic aware task allocation strategy using sparse worker data in mobile crowdsensing. Wirel. Netw. **29**(1), 459–474 (2023)
15. Wang, H., Wang, E., Yang, Y., Wu, J., Dressler, F.: Privacy-preserving online task assignment in spatial crowdsourcing: a graph-based approach. In: IEEE INFOCOM 2022-IEEE Conference on Computer Communications, pp. 570–579. IEEE (2022)
16. Peng, M., et al.: Spatiotemporal prediction based intelligent task allocation for secure spatial crowdsourcing in industrial IoT. IEEE Trans. Netw. Sci. Eng. **10**, 2853–2863 (2022)
17. Perozzi, B., Al-Rfou, R., Skiena, S.: Deepwalk: online learning of social representations. In: Proceedings of the 20th ACM SIGKDD International Conference on Knowledge Discovery and Data Mining, pp. 701–710 (2014)
18. Chung, J., Gulcehre, C., Cho, K., Bengio, Y.: Empirical evaluation of gated recurrent neural networks on sequence modeling. arXiv preprint arXiv:1412.3555 (2014)
19. Lü, L., Zhou, T.: Link prediction in complex networks: a survey. Phys. A **390**(6), 1150–1170 (2011)
20. Veličković, P., Cucurull, G., Casanova, A., Romero, A., Lio, P., Bengio, Y.: Graph attention networks. arXiv preprint arXiv:1710.10903 (2017)
21. Li, Y., Tarlow, D., Brockschmidt, M., Zemel, R.: Gated graph sequence neural networks. arXiv preprint arXiv:1511.05493 (2015)
22. Hamilton, W., Ying, Z., Leskovec, J.: Inductive representation learning on large graphs. Adv. Neural Inf. Process. Syst. **30**, 1–11 (2017)
23. Amin, S., Varanasi, S., Dunfield, K.A., Neumann, G.: Lowfer: low-rank bilinear pooling for link prediction. In: International Conference on Machine Learning, pp. 257–268. PMLR (2020)
24. Tran, H.N., Takasu, A.: Meim: multi-partition embedding interaction beyond block term format for efficient and expressive link prediction. arXiv preprint arXiv:2209.15597 (2022)
25. Wang, J., Ilievski, F., Szekely, P., Yao, K.-T.: Augmenting knowledge graphs for better link prediction. arXiv preprint arXiv:2203.13965 (2022)

Research on Multi-UAV Target Allocation Based on Improved Auction Algorithm

Tong Wang[1], Yicong Li[1], Dandi Yang[2], Wei Song[1(✉)], Liyue Fu[1], Min Ouyang[1], and Shan Gao[1]

[1] Harbin Engineering University, Harbin 150000, China
13703939198@163.com
[2] Beijing Electro-Mechanical Engineering Institute, Beijing 100074, China

Abstract. In this paper, for the modern multi-UAV combat scenario with multiple types of weapons, we propose an improved WTA model that removes the weapon platform constraint and sets the average flight distance of the weapon as the second optimization objective. In response to such problems, this paper proposes an improved multi-objective auction algorithm, which is based on the traditional auction algorithm and the non-dominated sorting strategy, improves the setting of the quotation threshold parameters by introducing the distance factor, and designs an adaptive operator strategy using the number of quotation times initiated by the UAV to the same target. At the same time, a multi-stage auction process is proposed to adapt to the scenario of a larger group of UAVs attacking a smaller group of targets. Finally, this algorithm is compared with MOABC and MOACO in the optimization results of two objective functions and the operation efficiency of the algorithm. Through the simulation experiments of different scale weapons against targets, the effectiveness of the improved strategy and the improved auction algorithm is proved.

Keywords: Weapon target assignment · Auction algorithm · Multi-objective optimization · Undominated sort

1 Introduction

In modern warfare, in the face of dynamic and complex environment, unpredictable potential dangers and diversified missions, multi-UAV cooperative combat has become a new development trend. Compared with a single UAV, multi-UAV has stronger robustness, communication capability, maneuverability, flexibility and higher operational efficiency [1]. Reasonable and efficient collaborative task planning scheme can greatly improve the success rate and efficiency of task execution, reduce risk and cost, and is the basis of task execution. Multi-UAV cooperative target assignment helps to make mission execution plan for the target within a certain decision time, so as to obtain the maximum mission benefit with the minimum system cost. The optimal task allocation scheme conforming to the constraints can not only obtain higher benefits, but also reduce the waste of resources.

© The Author(s), under exclusive license to Springer Nature Singapore Pte Ltd. 2024
Y. Sun et al. (Eds.): ChineseCSCW 2023, CCIS 2013, pp. 92–107, 2024.
https://doi.org/10.1007/978-981-99-9640-7_7

Common models for Target Assignment problems include Vehicle Routing Problem (VRP), Multiple Traveling Salesmen Problem (MTSP) and Weapon-Target Assignment (WTA) model. Weapon target assignment problem is a typical constrained combinatorial optimization problem in the military field, which was first proposed by Manne [2] in 1958 and proved to be NP-Complete problem in 1986 [3]. Its solution time increases exponentially with the increase in the number of weapons and targets, which means that in the scenario of large-scale weapons, traditional mathematical optimization algorithms [4] represented by branch-and-bound method and approximate dynamic programming will face huge challenges in terms of computation. Too much computation time may bungle the chance of winning a battle. Based on this, heuristic optimization algorithms represented by Genetic Algorithm (GA) [5], Differential Evolution (DE) [6], Particle Swarm Optimization (PSO) [7], and distributed algorithms represented by contract network algorithm [8] and auction algorithm [9] have become common technical means for researchers to solve WTA problems. Alexander G [10] et al. proposed a heuristic algorithm for the problem of static weapon target assignment, which can generate optimal solutions for both large and small scale problems. Hamed Shorakaei [11] et al. proposed a parallel genetic algorithm introducing a new genetic operator to solve the WTA problem, which takes mutual collision avoidance among UAVs as a constraint. Yin Gey [12] et al. proposed a multi-objective artificial bee colony algorithm based on non-dominated sorting, and proved its high efficiency and high performance in experiments. The intelligent algorithm has a great solving speed on large-scale problems, but it also has some problems such as difficult to guarantee convergence and insufficient diversity. The auction algorithm based on market mechanism not only has the advantages of low computational complexity and high operational efficiency [13], but also has good adaptability and dynamic change ability in complex and uncertain environment. This is because it relies on mutual negotiation between systems to complete the optimization process. Kanghua Bao [14] et al. improved the applicability of the algorithm by developing a new auction mechanism to solve the objective allocation problems such as one-to-one, many-to-one, and many-to-many. Xuheng Li [15] et al. proposed a compensation mechanism to improve the auction algorithm and improve the efficiency of the algorithm for multi-agent confrontation in attack scenarios. However, most of the above auction algorithms only take the maximum damage to the enemy target as a single objective function in the process of generating the allocation scheme, and do not consider the constraints of the UAV's own capability.

Based on the traditional WTA model, this paper proposed a Vehicle Routing-Weapon-Target Assignment (VR-WTA) model which is more suitable for the multi-type heterogeneous weapon target assignment scenario of modern UAV group operations. At the same time, based on the traditional Auction Algorithm, this paper proposed Improved Multi -stage Auction Algorithm (IMSAA) which resets the bidding parameters and auction process. In order to adapt to the scenario of large-scale UAV attacking small-scale targets, a multi-stage auction process was proposed. The effectiveness of the improved strategy and the improved auction algorithm is proved by the simulation experiments of different scale weapons attacking targets.

2 System Model

When multiple UAVs carry out multi-target allocation, it is necessary to consider the impact of target allocation comprehensively, not only to consider the maximization of UAV's own benefits, but also to maximize the overall benefits. It is necessary to ensure that the UAV can complete the task and control the cost of the UAV. The objective assignment of UAVs is essentially a multi-objective optimization problem. Reasonable construction of objective function, constraint conditions and convergence mode is the key point of constructing mathematical model.

2.1 VR-WTA Model

Common task assignment models include TSP model, VPR model, WTA model and so on. In these models, The success rate of TSP and VRP is 100% by default. They study the shortest path optimization problem. The task execution success rate in WTA is set according to the actual problem, with the expected return as the objective function. In the real battlefield environment, the strike probability of a weapon is never 100%, so this paper chooses to design a WTA model with different damage probabilities for different weapons and targets. In order to solve the problem of only one objective function in WTA, the path distance in VRP is introduced.

The conventional WTA model is as follows: Assume that the defender has M types of weapon resources, which are distributed over W weapon platforms. The attacking side has N targets, and the probability that the defending side's Class i weapon will hit and damage the enemy's j target is p_{ij}, x_{ij} is a Boolean variable used to indicate whether the Target J is allocated, $x_{ij} = 1$ indicates that it is allocated, and $x_{ij} = 0$ indicates that it is not allocated. The objective is to maximize the overall damage probability of the target, then the objective function is as follows.

$$\min f = \sum_{j=1}^{N} V_j \left(1 - \prod_{i=1}^{M} \left(1 - p_{ij} \right)^{x_{ij}} \right) \tag{1}$$

The constraint condition is that the number of weapons used in each class does not exceed the total number of weapons in the class; the number of weapons in each weapon platform cannot exceed the limit; x_{ij} is a non-negative integer.

It can be seen that the application scope of the conventional WTA model is relatively limited. Firstly, it requires the types of weapons and the platforms on which they are distributed. These constraints can increase the complexity of the model and greatly exacerbate the computational burden. Secondly, it only takes the damage probability to the target population as the optimization objective, but does not consider the flight distance of the weapon, energy consumption, weapon damage and other factors during combat, which does not meet the actual needs of the combat environment. Therefore, based on the traditional WTA model, this study introduces the distance objective function in VRP, and constructs a VR-WTA model that considers both the expected return and the total path cost.

First, the concept of weapon platform is eliminated, and the location and attack capability of each weapon are directly considered in the calculation. In this way, the two constraints of the usage limit of each type of weapon and the type limit of each weapon platform are eliminated at the same time, and the processing difficulty of the constraints is reduced. Secondly, based on the optimization goal of VRP, which requires the shortest vehicle path, the flight distance of the weapon is included in the objective function, expressed by the objective function F_1. At the same time, the idea of attacking probability in the WTA model is retained, and the expected return is still regarded as an optimization objective F_2 of the model. In multi-objective optimization theory, all objective functions are generally converted into maximization problems or minimization problems. Considering that the larger expected return is better, while the smaller average distance cost is better, the expected return F_2 is transformed into a minimization problem. The processed model is as follows:

$$\min F = (F_1, F_2) \tag{2}$$

$$F_1 = \frac{1}{N} \sum_{i=1}^{M} \sum_{j}^{N} \frac{x_{ij} d_{ij}}{v_i} \tag{3}$$

$$F_2 = Mq - \sum_{j=1}^{N} V_j \left(1 - \prod_{i=1}^{M} (1 - p_{ij})^{x_{ij}} \right) \tag{4}$$

The constraints are as follows:

1) A weapon can only hit one target:

$$\sum_{j=1}^{N} x_{ij} = 1 \tag{5}$$

2) Every target needs to be hit with at least one weapon:

$$\sum_{i=1}^{M} x_{ij} \geq 1 \tag{6}$$

3) X_{ij} indicates whether to assign i weapon to target j, and its value range is:

$$x_{ij} \in \{0, 1\} \tag{7}$$

4) The total revenue cannot exceed the total value of the target, using Q to represent the total value of the enemy target, using V_j to represent the value of each target:

$$Q = \sum_{j=1}^{N} V_j \tag{8}$$

2.2 Target Value Setting

The importance degree of each target in the enemy formation mainly considers two parts: its own value and the target's attack intention and situation.

Objective Advantage Value. Air combat advantage reflects the advantage of one UAV over another in an air combat situation. The greater the air combat advantage, the greater the survival probability of your own drone, and the higher the possibility of enemy drones being destroyed. An air combat advantage of one's own drone over an enemy drone is equivalent to an enemy drone being threatened by one's own drone.

This paper mainly from the speed, height, distance, type of four aspects to judge the objective advantage value of the target. It is worth noting that the distance between the UAV and the target here is not the Euclidean distance in space, but the distance calculated by using the Dubins curve considering the factors of the initial velocity direction and the minimum turning radius of the UAV.

In order to calculate the objective advantage value of the target, firstly, the membership degree function conforming to the change trend is established according to the characteristics of the above four factors. Then a weight value is set for each factor, and the objective factor value of the target is represented by the weighted sum of the membership value of these four factors. The weight vector should satisfy the constraints of Formula (9).

$$\begin{cases} \sum w_i = 1 \\ w_i \in [0, 1] \end{cases} \tag{9}$$

The weight vector is generally determined by the actual task execution environment and the desired strategic goal. In order to facilitate the experiment, the weight vector in this paper is $w = [0.2, 0.25, 0.35, 0.3]$. The objective value of the goal can be calculated as follows, Where U_j is the objective value matrix of target j. $\mu(v_j)$, $\mu(h_j)$, $\mu(L_j)$, $\mu(s_j)$ represent the objective advantage coefficient of the speed, height, distance and type of the target, respectively.

$$A_j = U_j \cdot w = \left[\mu(v_j) \; \mu(h_j) \; \overline{\mu(L_j)} \; \mu(s_j) \right] \begin{bmatrix} w_1 \\ w_2 \\ w_3 \\ w_4 \end{bmatrix} \tag{10}$$

Target Intention Coefficient. This paper mainly uses the relative flight Angle and relative distance between our weapon and the enemy target to evaluate the intended value coefficient of the target.

As shown in Fig. 1, L_{ij} is the linear distance between the target and the UAV; h_{ij} is the vertical distance between the target T_j and the UAV_j; r_{ij} is the short route between the target and our UAV_i, that is, the vertical distance between the target heading projected on the plane where the UAV is located and the UAV heading, which has a certain correlation with the hit and kill probability when the target attacks our drone.

Given the heading Angle of T_j relative to UAV_i:

$$\theta_{ij} = \arcsin \frac{r_{ij}}{\sqrt{L_{ij}^2 - h_{ij}^2}} \tag{11}$$

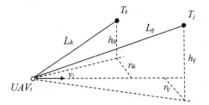

Fig. 1. Schematic diagram of the route shortcut.

The combat intent value of the target to our UAV is calculated by Eq. (12), which is the product of the comprehensive distance function and the relative Angle.

$$V_{ij} = (L_{ij} + h_{ij})\theta_{ij} \tag{12}$$

Substituting Eq. (11) into Eq. (12) can obtain:

$$V_{ij} = (L_{ij} + h_{ij}) \arcsin \frac{r_{ij}}{\sqrt{L_{ij}^2 - h_{ij}^2}} \tag{13}$$

As can be seen from Eq. (13), the smaller the route shortcut is, the larger the intended value function of the target is. This is consistent with the actual strike assignment scenario. Formula (13) only calculates the objective intention value function of T_j for UAV$_i$, and the sum of the intended value function values of a target for all our UAVs constitutes the final intended value of the target. For the target T_j, the formula for calculating the total intention function value is:

$$V_j = \sum_{i=1}^{M} V_{ij} \tag{14}$$

Value Evaluation Scheme. Combining objective advantage value and target intention coefficient of the target, we can get the final evaluation value of the target value by choosing appropriate weight coefficient and coupling them according to the actual battlefield situation. For target j, its value can be calculated as:

$$SV_j = \lambda A_j + (1 - \lambda)V_j \tag{15}$$

In the above formula, λ is the weight factor, which ranges from 0 to 1. If the objective target value is expected to be considered more in the strike task allocation, the larger the value is, the better. If the target intention is to be considered more, the smaller the value, the better.

Suppose our five UAVs need to carry out three strike missions, and now we need to evaluate the value of the three mission targets based on the known information. The position and direction Angle of the UAVs are as follows (Table 1):

Table 1. UAV information

UAV	x/km	y/km	$\theta/°$
UAV1	10	15	52
UAV2	12	26	71
UAV3	23	9	88
UAV4	31	11	38
UAV5	45	14	47

Information about the targets of the three missions is shown in Table 2.

Table 2. Target information

Target	x/km	y/km	h/km	v/Ma	Type
T1	26	29	1.8	0.8	4
T2	32	31	1.4	0.6	1
T3	28	37	1.1	0.7	2

From Formula (10), it can be concluded that the objective advantage value of each target is 0.7624, 0.8595, 0.8113. According to Formula (14), the target intention coefficient of each goal are 0.6334, 0.7129 and 1. Take $\lambda = 0.5$ and plug it into Formula (15) to get the final target values of 0.6979, 0.7862 and 0.9057, respectively. As can be seen, the value ranking of Target 2 and Target 3 changes before and after considering the target intention value. The objective value of the two are close, but the target intention coefficient has a certain gap, which affects the final target value evaluation result. This shows that the value evaluation scheme considering the target intention value proposed in this paper can be combined with the actual battlefield environment to evaluate the target value more comprehensively.

3 Improvement of Algorithm

3.1 Traditional Auction Algorithm

Auction Algorithm is a distributed algorithm for solving allocation problems, first proposed by Bertsekas of MIT's Information and Decision Systems Laboratory. The final result should maximize the interests of all bidders and auction houses as much as possible.

According to the number of bidders N and the number of bidding goods M, it can be mainly divided into the following two categories: 1) When $N \geq M$, it is called a single-assignment problem. 2) When $N < M$, the type of problem is called multiple assignment.

In the auction process, the value of all goods to each person is first displayed. α_{ij} is commonly used to represent the value of the j item to the i individual, and p_j is used to represent the price of the j item. The general flow of the algorithm is as follows:

Step 1 All bidders in turn, according to the principle of self-interest, choose the highest profit among all commodities. The profit is calculated as follows:

$$profit = value - price \tag{16}$$

Step 2 All bidders bid on the selected item. Each quotation is at least ε higher than the original, at most $\varepsilon + \pi$ higher than the original. Call ε the quoted low limit and π the quoted upper limit factor. ε and π set according to the specific situation. The quotation calculation formula is shown in Eq. (17):

$$price_{old} + \varepsilon \leq price_{old} \leq price_{old} + \varepsilon + \pi \tag{17}$$

Step 3 The auction house assigns the highest bidder for each item based on the bids of all bidders. If any bidder is not allocated the goods, repeat Step 1 - Step 2 to make a new round of bidding.

Step 4 If each bidder gets an allocation of goods, or if the maximum return for all items purchased by each person is no greater than 0, the algorithm stops.

3.2 Improved Auction Algorithm

When the auction algorithm is applied to solve the problem of WTA, the UAV is equivalent to the bidder participating in the auction, and the attack target is equivalent to the item being auctioned. The benefits to be gained from attacking a target can be calculated by the distance between the drone and the target, the firepower of the target and the attack intention of each target, which is the target value SV assessed in the previous chapter. However, in the face of the multi-objective WTA model with a large range of weapon and target scale transformation, the traditional auction algorithm will encounter the following problems.

1. The application of the auction algorithm is mainly a single-allocation problem, that is, each bidder has an interest in all the goods and can only win a maximum of one item. When multiple drones attack enemy formations, one drone may be required to attack multiple targets, or each drone may attack at least one target, and no drone can lose the bid. In these cases, the single-allocation model does not solve the problem.
2. In multiple assignment problems, it is difficult to set π and ε parameters, and it is difficult to ensure the convergence of the algorithm.

In order to solve the above problems, this paper introduces distance factor and profit factor into the original quotation formula of classical auction algorithm. The importance of value and distance in the scheme can be changed by adjusting the weight parameters, and the multi-auction method with dynamic change of target value is used to improve the adaptability of the algorithm to the weapon target allocation model, which has strong practical significance.

Quotation Strategy Using Distance Information. In the traditional auction algorithm, the lower limit ε of bidders in each round of bidding is determined only by the number of bidders participating in the auction and the number of items. In this paper, the distance between the UAV and the target is introduced into the method of setting the lower limit parameter ε of the bid price. The farther the distance between the UAV and the target, the weaker the willingness of the UAV to bid on the target, and the smaller the increase of its bid in each round of bidding. On the contrary, the smaller the distance between the two, the greater the increase in the quotation of the UAV.

When UAV_i makes an offer on T_j the lower bound ε for the price increase is calculated as:

$$\varepsilon_{ij} = \frac{\beta}{d_{ij}} + \frac{\alpha}{n} \tag{18}$$

where β is the customized distance weight coefficient of the lower limit of price increase, n is the number of UAVs, and d_{ij} is the distance between the UAV_i and T_j.

An Adaptive Operator Using the Number of Quotes. π determines the maximum price increase of each offer, the greater the π, the greater the price increase of each offer, the faster the price is close to the value of the commodity, the faster the algorithm ends.

Excessive price increase may cause the algorithm to converge too quickly, skip the global optimal solution, and could not get satisfactory income. However, too small π will make the algorithm converge too slowly, increase the computing and communication cost, weaken the influence of the target value on the algorithm, and fall into the meaningless waste of computing resources. This paper presents an adaptive operator μ to control the value of π. Considering that when the same UAV initiates bids for the same target several times, it means that the target is more attractive to the UAV and the UAV could obtain more profits, then the price of the drone is increased to help it bid for the target. The calculation formula of μ is as follows, where $Number_{ij}$ is the number of times that UAV_i initiated bids on T_j up to the current round.

$$\mu = 0.9 - \exp(\frac{1 - Number_{ij}}{C}) \tag{19}$$

$$\pi = \mu(profit_{max} - profit'_{max}) \tag{20}$$

Multi-auction Method with Dynamic Update of Target Value. Since the traditional auction algorithm based on single allocation application is difficult to solve the problem in the war scenario where multiple UAVs attack fewer targets, this paper divides the auction process into multiple auctions. When the number of drones as bidders far exceeds the number of targets as commodities, each target is assigned to the drone and re-enters the auction as a new commodity. Its value is then recalculated based on the damage done to it by the UAV assigned in the previous auction round. The value renewal formula is as follows:

$$Value_{ijnew} = Value_{ijold}(1 - p_{ij}/k) + \lambda A_{jnew}(1 - (k-1)p_{ij}/k)$$

$$= (1 - \lambda)V_{ij}(1 - p_{ij}/k) + \lambda A_{jold}(1 - p_{ij}) \tag{21}$$

A_j is the objective value of *Target$_j$* introduced in the previous chapter, V_{ij} is the target intent parameter of T_j to UAV$_i$, and p_{ij} is the damage probability of UAV$_i$ to T_j. k is a customizable weight coefficient for V_{ij}, requiring k < 1. It can be seen that the part of the target intention coefficient in the target value has a small change value in each update. On the one hand, in order to ensure that the reduction of the target value in the calculation is less than the theoretical value, the conservative calculation method is adopted to make every target get sufficient firepower allocation as far as possible; On the other hand, it is believed that the UAV mainly damages the objective advantage value part of the target value, and has little impact on the target intention. Based on the objective value of the target, set the maximum number of drones that can be assigned to each target.

3.3 Improved Auction Algorithm Flow

With UAVs as bidders and targets as auction objects. The average flight distance of each UAV is taken as objective function F_1. The objective function F_2 is obtained by minimizing the total value obtained by destroying the target. Multi-objective optimization is carried out to determine the target allocation results. The constraint is that at least one UAV is assigned to each target, and each UAV is ultimately assigned one and only one target. The maximum number of UAVs that can be assigned to each target is related to its value, set to WN_{max}. The algorithm flow is shown in Table 3.

4 Experimental Scheme and Simulation Results

4.1 Experimental Parameter Setting

In the model of this experiment, the number of our drones is set as 10, 20, 50, and the take-off point of each drone is randomly assigned. Enemy targets are divided into four categories based on target type, duties and loaded weapons, and target positions are set according to the common formation position distribution. According to the model proposed in Sect. 2.1, the revenue function F_2 is minimized, and the total target value Q minus the actual revenue W is used as the result of the objective function F_2. The processing of model parameters is shown in Table 4.

In terms of experimental parameters, the upper limit of total auction iterations is set at 500, and the upper limit of rounds of each auction is set at 20. In order to reduce the influence of the bidding order on the auction result, the bidding order of bidders in each round of auction is random.

4.2 Analysis of Experimental Results

Simulation experiments were carried out in three cases where the number of our UAVs is 10, 20, and 50 to verify the superiority of the Improved Multi-stage Auction Algorithm (IMSAA) proposed in this paper. Firstly, taking the optimization degree of the two objective functions in the allocation scheme of the algorithm as the index, the effectiveness of the two improved methods of IMSAA under three scales is tested. Secondly,

Table 3. Improved auction algorithm flow

Algorithm: Improved auction algorithm
Input: M, N, α, β, λ, cycle number lo
Output: Pareto optimal solution set, F_1, F_2
1: init Location of UAV swarm and Target swarm, SV, L, Value, p, WN_{max}
2: for lo>0
3: Generate random UAV bidding sequences
4:    while number of unassigned targets > 0
5:       while number of unassigned UAV > 0
6:          Unassigned UAV selects target
7:          if the number of UAVs assigned to the target $\geq WN_{max}$
8:             Select from the remaining targets
9:          end if
10:          Calculate , π, ε according to formula (18),(20)
11:          Each UAV calculates the quote according to formula (17)
12:          Each target assigned to the UAV that makes the highest non-negative bid on it
13:       end while
14:    end while
15:    Store the current allocation scheme and calculate F_1, F_2 by formula (3),(4)
16:    lo-1
17: end for
18: Obtained Pareto solution set by non-dominating ordering of all schemes

Table 4. Model parameters settings.

parameter	Settings
List of target formation values	[50 20 18 15]
Probability of being damaged	[0.08 0.2 0.22 0.26]
Treatment of income	Q- W

IMSAA is compared with the non-dominated MOABC and MOACO, and the evaluation indexes are algorithm efficiency, the overall income F_1 and UAV flight distance F_2 of the distribution scheme.

Effectiveness of the Quotation Strategy Using Distance Information. First, the validity of the quotation strategy using distance information is verified. Keeping the other parameters in the algorithm unchanged, the weight coefficient (α, β) of the price floor parameter ε is set as (1,0), (0.85, 0.15), (0.7, 0.3), (0.5, 0.5) respectively when the weapon scale is 10, 20, 50. The four groups of experiments were recorded as A-D in order, totaling

12 experiments. Each experiment was run independently for 30 times, and the average value of the experimental results was taken, as shown in Fig. 2.

It can be seen that the mean distance cost (F_2) of group B, C, and D is reduced compared to Group A at all weapon sizes. It shows that the strategy of using distance information enhances the optimization degree of the algorithm to the objective of weapon flight distance. However, in Fig. 2(b) and 2(c), the F_1 values of groups B, C and D show an upward trend, indicating that the introduction of the quote floor parameter ε of the overweighted distance operator may have a certain negative effect on other objective functions under certain weapon scales. However, according to the different scale of weapons and emphasis of different objective function, the desired results can be achieved by setting different weight coefficients. Both groups C and D in Fig. 2(a) and B and C in Fig. 2(c) take into account the results of F_1 and F_2 at the same time, showing satisfactory comprehensive performance.

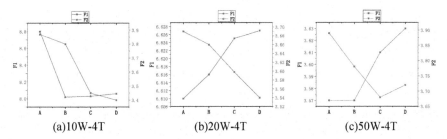

Fig. 2. Experiment results using different quotation floor parameters ε.

Validity of Adaptive Operator Using the Number of Quotes. Under the condition that other conditions remain unchanged (using the results of the experiment in the previous section, the weight coefficient (α, β) of the quote threshold parameter ε is set to (0.7, 0.3)), and the algorithm using the adaptive operator strategy of the quote frequency is carried out when the weapon scales are 10, 20 and 50 respectively. Group A uses the bidding operator π of the classical auction algorithm, and group B uses the bidding parameter π controlled by the adaptive operator μ of the bidding times proposed in this paper. A total of 6 experiments are conducted. Each experiment is also conducted 30 times, and the average value of the experimental results is taken.

The experimental results obtained are shown in Fig. 3, which shows that the performance of the adaptive group B is better than that of group A, which does not use this strategy, at various scales, and better results are obtained in terms of both the average distance cost and the income. It can be seen that the adaptive operator using the number of quotations can reduce the vicious competition in UAV bidding to a certain extent, so as to obtain a distribution scheme that makes all UAV profits greater. To sum up, compared

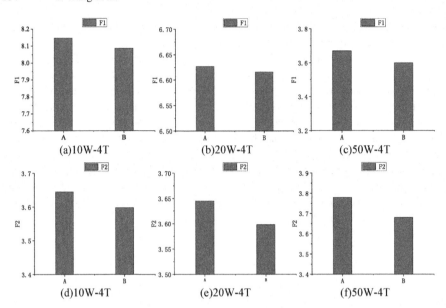

Fig. 3. Experimental results of an adaptive operator using the number of quotes

with the traditional setting method of quotation upper limit parameter π, the adaptive operator strategy of quotation times can solve a higher quality allocation scheme.

Comparative Analysis with Other Multi-objective Optimization Algorithms.
MOABC [16] and MOACO [17], two non-dominated multi-objective optimization algorithms, are selected and compared with IMSAA proposed in this paper. The simulation experiments were carried out under the conditions of weapon size of 10, 20 and 50 respectively, and compared and evaluated from three dimensions: weapon average flight distance, overall program benefit and algorithm running time. For these 9 groups of experiments, each group of experiments was independently conducted 50 times, and the average value of the experimental results was taken. In order to facilitate the comparison of weapon flight distance and incomes of the allocation scheme, the take-off point of the UAV was randomly generated, and the position of the take-off point was not changed in the subsequent experiment. Mark the UAVs assigned to different targets with different colors and connect them with the target.

The experimental results of the comparison of three algorithms at various scales are shown in Fig. 4.

From Fig. 4(a), (d), (g), it can be seen that when the task scale is small, the three algorithms have little difference in the time to complete all tasks. With the increase of task scale, compared with the target allocation algorithms based on MOABC and MOACO, the running time of IMSAA is significantly reduced, showing a strong algorithm efficiency advantage. The run time of MOACO increased dramatically, while IMSAA only increased 20.1% in the scenario of 10 and 50 UAVs. This is because the calculation amount of each iteration of MOACO increases exponentially with the increase of weapon scale, while IMSAA in this paper only needs to increase the rounds

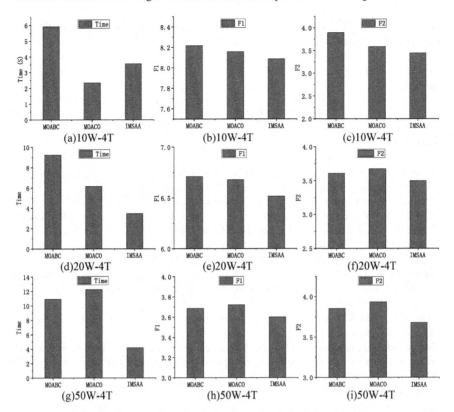

Fig. 4. Comparative experimental results of the three algorithms

of auction. At the same time, in terms of the mean income and the mean distance cost of distribution, IMSAA has better optimization results in the task allocation scheme under various scales.

5   Conclusion

Aiming at the problem of multi-UAV target allocation, this paper proposes a VR-WTA model by introducing the distance factor in VRP model, and the concept of weapon platform is cancelled to reduce the difficulty of constraint processing. At the same time, the Dubins curve is introduced to calculate the actual flight distance of the UAV, and the target intention coefficient is introduced considering the influence of target attack intention when evaluating the value of the target. These measures make the model more suitable to the actual battlefield and more applicable. In terms of algorithm, a multi-stage auction method with dynamic change of target value is proposed to solve the problem that traditional auction algorithm is difficult to adapt to the constraints of WTA model. And through the adaptive quotation strategy based on flight distance and quotation times, the setting of quotation coefficient is improved, which effectively improves the optimization degree of the algorithm for weapon flight distance and target allocation income, and can quickly obtain a low cost and high yield target allocation scheme in the battlefield environment.

Acknowledgement. This article is supported by the National Natural Science Foundation of China (62372131).

References

1. Otto, A., et al.: Optimization approaches for civil applications of unmanned aerial vehicles (UAVs) or aerial drones: a survey. Networks **72**(4), 411–458 (2018)
2. Manne, A.S.: A target-assignment problem. Oper. Res. **6**(3), 346–351 (1958)
3. Lloyd, S.P., Witsenhausen, H.S.: Weapons allocation is NP-complete. In: 1986 Summer Computer Simulation Conference, pp. 1054–1058 (1986)
4. Davis, M.T., Robbins, M.J., Lunday, B.J.: Approximate dynamic programming for missile defense interceptor fire control. Eur. J. Oper. Res. **259**(3), 873–886 (2017)
5. Li, P., Wu, L., Lu, F.: A mutation-based GA for weapon-target allocation problem subject to spatial constraints. In: 2009 International Workshop on Intelligent Systems and Applications, pp. 1–4. IEEE (2009)
6. Wu, W.H., Guo, X.F., Zhou, S.Y., et al.: Improved difference problem. Syst. Eng. Electron. **43**(4), 1012–1021 (2021)
7. Mahmood, M., Mathavan, S., Rahman, M.: A parameter-free discrete particle swarm algorithm and its application to multi-objective pavement maintenance schemes. Swarm Evol. Comput. **43**, 69–87 (2018)
8. Smith Reid, G.: The contract net protocol: high-level communication and control in a distributed problem solver. IEEE Trans. Comput. **29**(12), 1104–1113 (1980)
9. Liu, X., Zhu, R.: An improved market-based auction algorithm for UAVs task assignment problem. Lecture Notes in Electrical Engineering, vol. 211 (2013). https://doi.org/10.1007/978-3-642-34522-7_69
10. Kline, A.G., Ahner, D.K., Lunday, B.J.: Real-time heuristic algorithms for the static weapon target assignment problem. J. Heuristics **25**(3), 377–397 (2019)
11. Shorakaei, H., Vahdani, M., Imani, B., et al.: Optimal cooperative path planning of unmanned aerial vehicles by a parallel genetic algorithm. Robotica (2016)
12. Yin, G.Y., Zhou, S.L., Mo, J.C., et al.: Coordinated multi-task assignment of UAV based on multi-objective particle swarm optimization. Comput. Modern. **08**, 7–11 (2016)
13. Ke, X., et al.: Multi-UAV group task assignment based on distributed auction algorithm. Inf. Control **47**(3), 341–346 (2018)
14. Bao, K., Yi, S., Zhang, H., He, P.: Multi-unmanned aerial vehicle cooperative task allocation algorithm based on improved distributed cooperative auction. In: Fu, W., Gu, M., Niu, Y. (eds.) Proceedings of 2022 International Conference on Autonomous Unmanned Systems (ICAUS 2022), pp. 1535–1543. Springer, Singapore (2023). https://doi.org/10.1007/978-981-99-0479-2_141
15. Li, X., Yu, J., Dong, X., Li, Q., Hua, Y., Ren, Z.: Weapon target assignment based on compensation auction algorithm. In: Yan, L., Duan, H., Deng, Y. (eds.) Advances in Guidance, Navigation and Control: Proceedings of 2022 International Conference on Guidance, Navigation and Control, pp. 4622–4631. Springer, Singapore (2023). https://doi.org/10.1007/978-981-19-6613-2_448

16. Kishor, A., Singh, P.K., Prakash, J.: NSABC: non-dominated sorting based multi-objective artificial bee colony algorithm and its application in data clustering. Neurocomputing **216**, 514–533 (2016)
17. Zhang, Q., Xiong, S.: Routing optimization of emergency grain distribution vehicles using the immune ant colony optimization algorithm. Appl. Soft Comput. **71**, 917–925 (2018)

Enhancement of Cat Breeds Classification Model Based on Meta Loss Correction

Nucharat Khaodee, Wenhao Rao, Hui Qiao, and Songzhi Su[✉]

School of Information, Xiamen University, Xiamen 361005, Fujian, China
ssz@xmu.edu.cn

Abstract. In the area of image recognition, the quality of image label data has a significant impact on the performance of classification models. Therefore, manual annotation has been used as a means to label images. However, manual annotation is laborious and time-consuming and can introduce additional noise. To address these issues, this paper investigates an automatic algorithm for improving a cat breed classification model based on meta loss correction. The proposed algorithm leverages web crawling techniques to obtain unlabeled images of cats, filters them through object recognition, and selects only images containing cats. These images are then fed into the algorithm, which utilizes a pretrained initial model to generate pseudo-labels. These pseudo-labeled data are subsequently refined using a meta loss function, correcting the inaccuracies associated with the pseudo-labels. Finally, the labeled new data is merged with the original dataset, gradually increasing both the quantity and quality of the dataset. Experimental results demonstrate that as the merged dataset expands, the model's error decreases gradually, and its performance improves.

Keywords: Meta Learning · Meta Loss Correction · Label Noise

1 Introduction

Currently, deep learning has achieved remarkable success in various computer vision tasks, most notably in the realm of object detection, image categorization, segmentation, and face recognition. However, the efficacy of these models heavily relies on the availability of substantial label information, particularly vast amounts of high-quality labels. The process of acquiring such clean and extensive datasets is not only time-consuming but also incurs significant costs. Consequently, researchers and practitioners have begun exploring alternative approaches to mitigate these challenges, such as utilizing web crawlers or automated tagging methods [12] AutoML systems were required to deliver predictions, which offer the advantages of expediency and cost-effectiveness. Nevertheless, these alternative methods introduce a notable predicament: the presence of label noise within the obtained data. This label noise can lead to erroneous or incomplete labeling, thereby compromising the overall performance levels of the

Y. Sun et al. (Eds.): ChineseCSCW 2023, CCIS 2013, pp. 108–118, 2024.
https://doi.org/10.1007/978-981-99-9640-7_8

deep learning models. Given this context, our primary objective revolves around enhancing the experience of our models. In other words, we aim to develop strategies and techniques that ameliorate the impact of label noise, thereby elevating the performance and accuracy of our deep learning models in computer vision tasks.

In order to train our model effectively, we have developed a comprehensive dataset. Our dataset comprises images of 10 distinct cat species, each belonging to a separate class. A notable advantage of manual data labeling is the capacity to generate original datasets characterized by precise and meticulous labeling. This meticulous labeling process significantly contributes to improved classification performance.

However, it is important to acknowledge a significant drawback associated with manual data labeling, namely its time-consuming nature. The process of meticulously compiling and labeling the images demanded substantial time and effort. To expand our dataset further, we adopted a Meta Loss Correction (MLC) process, enhancing our model's performance. While the initial labeling of the images was performed manually by our team, the labels associated with the images obtained from the web crawler were automatically generated utilizing our model's auto-labeling capabilities. These auto-generated labels were subsequently refined and rectified through the MLC process, ensuring accurate labeling outcomes.

The approach known as Loss Correction (LC) [3] introduced the concept of MetaCorrection, a technique aimed at enhancing unsupervised domain adaptation in semantic segmentation by rectifying the loss function through meta-learning. [4] proposed MetaLabelNet the method is based on a meta-learning framework that trains the model to learn how to generate soft-labels by observing multiple noisy-labels for the same data point. [4, 5, 7, 8, 13] proposed Meta-Label for Learning with Noisy Labels by training model on the noisy label this method correction label. [9–11, 14] proposed Self-Training method used teacher-student algorithm to enhance classification model. [15] proposed iterative learning approach aims to alleviate the influence of feature-dependent label noise on model training. The algorithm can assess the probability of mislabeling for each example.

Training Noise-Robust Deep Neural Networks via Meta-Learning [1] to learn a noise transition matrix T that can correct the predictions. The model undergoes a learning process wherein it acquires the ability to discern the type and magnitude of noise present in the data, subsequently adjusting its parameters accordingly to mitigate the adverse effects induced by such noise. After training, the model can be used to classify new data that may be affected by noise. This is achieved through alternating optimization of T and the weights θ of the main (backbone) network. The objective of this method is to acquire the optimal T value that can be effectively utilized to enhance the performance of noise prevention measures.

2 Method

The primary objective of this research endeavor is to augment the accuracy of the current cat classification model by integrating crawler technology with the MLC method. By employing exclusively cat images as the training data for Meta Learning, we aim to enhance the learning process. Our research involves training the Cat10 dataset (our dataset) using Meta Learning and continuously gathering clean cat species images through crawler technology to expand the trained model and improve its accuracy. In order to further mitigate the presence of noise in the dataset, we utilize the MLC method to train a noise transfer matrix. This matrix is employed to correct the pseudo-labels obtained from unlabeled images collected through the crawler. Subsequently, we augment the corrected images and labels to the original dataset and proceed to retrain the model. This iterative process aims to enhance the accuracy and robustness of the model in the task of cat classification.

In this study, we applied the MLC technique, which is a meta-learning optimization approach [1]. In contrast to using the noise transition matrix T and the θ encoded backbone network, our approach directly derives the MLC strategy from the available data. The MLC approach consists of three main steps: Pre-Train, Meta-Train, and Actual-Train. During the Pre-Train step, we optimized θ in the presence of noisy data. In the Meta-Train step, we optimized the meta parameter T based on the validation set loss, while fixing the θ parameters. Finally, during the Actual-Train step, we optimized the unfolded θ parameters with the updated T on the noisy training set. This approach enabled us to learn the best T, leading to effective noise reduction and less overfitting.

Pre-Train. is a preparatory stage in the MLC strategy that helps us estimate the model parameters before deployment in the Meta-Train stage. In this stage, we optimize the backbone network θ^t to obtain θ^{t+1} with a constant T^t optimized in the previous iteration. We use a revised loss function in the noisy training set D_{noise} to train the backbone network, but it does not really migrate to θ^{t+1} because it is a virtual step. We optimize the network weights θ^t and modify T^t them in mini-batches to compute the loss function at step t, which is given by the following equation:

$$l_{pre-train} = -\frac{1}{n}\sum_{i=1}^{n} y_i log(T^t f(x_i; \theta^t)) \tag{1}$$

Here, n is the batch size in the training set. Next, we optimize the "virtual" model weights at one-step-forward θ^{t+1} using a gradient descent method with a learning rate α:

$$\widehat{\theta}^{t+1}(T^t) = \widehat{\theta}^t - \alpha\nabla_{\theta^t} l_{pre-train} \tag{2}$$

This sets the stage for the subsequent Meta-Train stage, in which we optimize the noise transition matrix T. This optimization process is guided by the meta-learning optimization strategy and involves leveraging the loss computed on the validation set.

Meta-Train. is a crucial stage of our approach to optimizing the backbone network, and the transition matrix T. In this stage, we hold the optimized $\widehat{\theta}^{t+1}$ constant and update T^{t+1} to minimize the CrossEntropy loss on a small validation set D_{val}. Since D_{val} is noise-free, it provides an excellent control signal for guiding the optimization of T^{t+1}. To enhance T^{t+1} optimization on the validation set, we use the one-step-forward backbone network (fixed $\widehat{\theta}^{t+1}$) as follows:

$$l_{meta-train} = \frac{1}{M} \sum_{i=1}^{M} y_i log f(x_i; \theta^t) \tag{3}$$

Due to the computational complexity of the previous equation, it can be computationally expensive and memory-intensive to compute. To address this issue, we approximate the equation using a mini-batch of the validation set. This approximation helps to save both time and memory while maintaining reasonable accuracy.

$$l_{meta-train} = -\frac{1}{m} \sum_{i=1}^{m} y_i log f(x_i; \theta^t) \tag{4}$$

In this equation, m represents the size of the mini-batch, and the learning rate β is employed to update the noise transition matrix T using the gradient descent method:

$$r^{t+1} = T^t - \beta \nabla_{T^t} l_{meta-train} \tag{5}$$

Use the chain rule to resolve Eq. (5):

$$r^{t+1} = T^t - \beta \{ \nabla_{\theta^t} l_{meta-train} (-\alpha \nabla^2_{\theta^t, T^t} l_{pre-train}) \} \tag{6}$$

It is important to note that r^{t+1} represents the raw one-step-forward noise transition matrix, which may not always have negative values or be appropriate for use as the terminal noise transition matrix. To address this, we make r^{t+1} non-negative using the max operator:

$$\widehat{T}^{t+1} = max(\theta : r^{t+1}, 0) \tag{7}$$

The resulting $\widehat{T}^{t+1}$ is normalized for the j-th row, e.g. $\widehat{T}_j^{t+1} = [\ \widehat{T}_{j1}^{t+1}, ..., \widehat{T}_{jc}^{t+1}]$, which represents the total probability moved to class j. Finally, we obtain the final $\widehat{T}^{t+1}$ as:

$$T_j^{t+1} = \frac{\widehat{T}^{t+1}}{\sum \widehat{T}_j^{t+1} + \delta(\widehat{T}_j^{t+1})} \tag{8}$$

by $\delta(z) = 1$, if $z = 0$ and $\delta(z) = 0$, if $z \neq 0$.   here, $\delta(z)$ is used to prevent dividing by zero.

Actual-Train. refers to the process of optimizing the actual backbone network, which is based on an uncertain network weight represented by θ^t. This network weight is adjusted to achieve θ^{t+1} with updated T^{t+1}. Our current focus is on optimizing the 'real' network in the noise training set, while holding T^{t+1} constant after optimizing the 'virtual' network and Meta-Train. To obtain new network weights θ^{t+1} on the D_{noise} dataset, we perform a gradient with a learning rate. This involves calculating θ^{t+1} using the following formula:

$$\theta^{t+1} = \theta^t - \alpha \nabla_{\theta^t}(-\frac{1}{n}\sum_{i=1}^{n}\hat{y}_i log(T^{t+1}f(x_i;\theta^t))) \tag{9}$$

In this formula, α is the learning rate, n is the number of samples in the dataset, $\hat{y}_i$ represents the predicted label, and $f(x_i;\theta^t))$ represents the output of the network given an input x_i and weight θ^t.

To expand the dataset size after passing the MLC model, we repeat the training process. By doing so, we can generate a larger dataset, which has the advantage of improving the accuracy of the resulting data predictions.

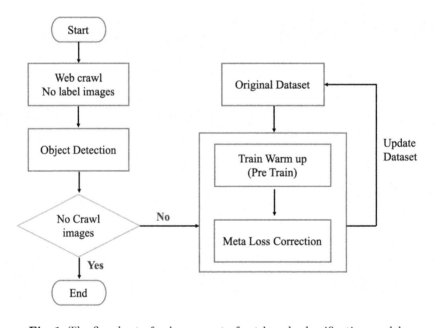

Fig. 1. The flowchart of enhancement of cat breeds classification model

The enhancement of cat breeds classification model involves a flowchart of steps depicted in Fig. 1. The following steps are involved: 1) Train the Cat10 dataset(Our dataset) using meta-learning method to obtain a model that can be used for classification; 2) Crawl a large number of unlabeled cat images from the webpage using crawler technology to expand the data set; 3) Use target detection technology to detect the crawled images one by one and eliminate non-cat images and cat images with poor quality to improve the accuracy of the expanded data set. Since the current model only distinguishes the types of cats, it is important to account for variations in the angle, size, and definition of the cat facing the camera on the webpage; 4) Use the MLC-trained model to classify the crawled and screened, unlabeled cat images and obtain their pseudo-labels; 5) Entails the application of the MLC method to train the noise transfer matrix and correct the classification results. This process serves to enhance the overall quality of the expanded dataset. After obtaining the correct image labels, merge this part of the images into the dataset of 5000 cat images that are manually annotated, and retrain the MLC model to obtain a new model for classification; 6) Repeat steps 2–5 until all crawled images have tags. Through this method, the functions of automatic images acquisition, screening, and automatic label addition can be realized. Furthermore, as a result of the image screening conducted both prior to and after data training, the accuracy of the classification model can be significantly enhanced. In summary, the enhancement of cat breed classification model involves several key steps, including meta-learning, crawler technology, target detection, pseudo-labeling, and MLC. The purpose of these steps is to enhance the accuracy and overall quality of the dataset, thereby laying a foundation for the development of a robust and dependable cat breed classification model.

3   Experiment

3.1   Experimental Setup

We collected our own dataset by labeling images of 10 cat breeds: Abyssinian, Bengal, British Shorthair, Egyptian Mau, Maine Coon, Persian, Ragdoll, Russian Blue, Siamese, and Sphynx. By class1 - class10 in the order, each class within the dataset comprises a total of 500 images, resulting in a cumulative dataset size of 5000 images. These images served as the original dataset used for training our model. We used 4250 images (85%) for training and 750 images (15%) for testing, with a Wide-Resnet model, SGD optimizer with a batch-size of 64, learning rate of 1e–4, momentum of 0.9, and weight decay of 5e–4. We set $\alpha = 1e–3$ and $\beta = 1e–2$ for the training process.

3.2   Experimental Results

In our experiments, we used the original dataset as the initial dataset and manually labeled it. And we downloaded new data by web crawling, which consisted of 200 images per class for a total of 10 classes, without any labels. The newly acquired data was employed to train our Meta Loss Correction (MLC) model, which significantly enhanced the robustness of the images through corrections and predictions derived from the original dataset. The new dataset contained 2000 images, which were divided into 4 models for training. Each round of training used 500 images from the new data. Finally, we get four model which is more and more higher accuracy. The model's accuracy and ROC are show as Table 1.

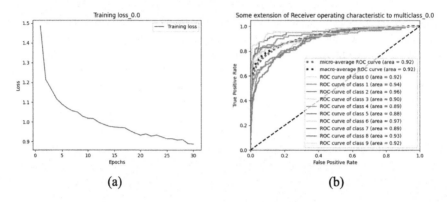

Fig. 2. Our original model includes: (a) Training loss (%), (b) Every classes of ROC (%).

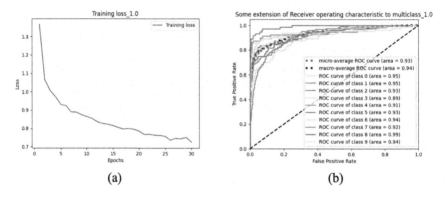

Fig. 3. Results of Our model 1: (a) Training loss (%), (b) Every classes of ROC (%).

From Fig. 2 shows result train with our original model. We added new images to the training set. Each of these models used a dataset divided into 4 parts, which were distributed to the four models. Each model was labeled with the new data, resulting in a fully labeled dataset from the web crawl. Figure 3 is Our Model 1 is added new 500 images, Fig. 4 is Our Model 2 is added new 1000 images, Fig. 5 is Our Model 3 is added new 1500 images and Fig. 6 is Our Model 4 is added new 2000 images, as we added more data to our dataset, the accuracy increased, the loss decreased, and the receiver operating characteristic (ROC) approached 1.

From the Table 2, it can be seen that using the Oxford-IIIT Pet dataset for training and classification, our algorithm has higher classification accuracy, indicating that our method of improving classification accuracy by improving model performance is effective.

We conducted a classification comparison between the Cat10 dataset, which we trained using additional data obtained from our web-crawling, and the standardized Oxford-IIIT Pet dataset. The test results have strengthened our

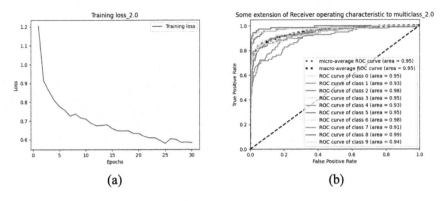

Fig. 4. Results of Our model 2: (a) Training loss (%), (b) Every classes of ROC (%).

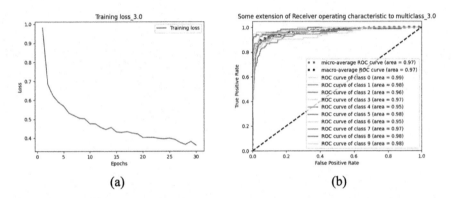

Fig. 5. Results of Our model 3: (a) Training loss (%), (b) Every classes of ROC (%).

Table 1. Compare the performance of each model

Model	Accuracy	Loss	ROC
Original	0.725	0.85	0.96
Model 1	0.775	0.73	0.93
Model 2	0.825	0.58	0.98
Model 3	0.9	0.36	0.96
Model 4	**0.975**	**0.1**	**0.99**

concept, as the web-crawled data contained real-world noise, which we addressed in our methodology to enhance the intelligence of our model. In Fig. 7 is Compare between Oxford-IIIT Pet dataset and Our dataset: Accuracy of Oxford-IIIT Pet is 91.25 (%) and Cat10 dataset train use model 4 is 97.5(%). It can be observed that the accuracy of the original model was 72.5(%), while the accuracy of Model 4 reached 97.5(%). Our model, which was trained using MLC and exposed to more data, achieved superior performance.

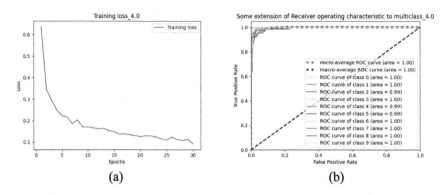

Fig. 6. Results of Our model 4: (a) Training loss (%), (b) Every classes of ROC (%).

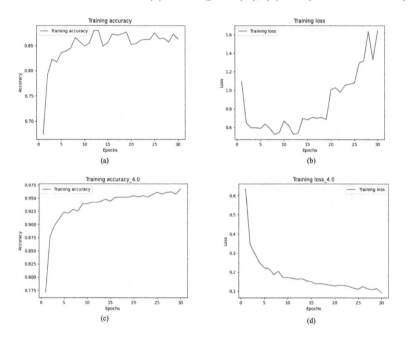

Fig. 7. Compare between Oxford-IIIT Pet dataset and Cat10 dataset (Our dataset): (a) Training accuracy (%) of Oxford-IIIT Pet dataset, (b) Training loss (%) of Oxford-IIIT Pet dataset, (c) Training accuracy (%) of Cat10 dataset and (d) Training loss (%) of Cat10 dataset.

To summarize, our experiments involved training an MLC model using a newly downloaded dataset from web crawling. We divided the dataset into 4 models and added new images to the training set in each round of training. Each model utilized a dataset that was partitioned into four parts, and subsequently, the new data was labeled and incorporated into each part. As a result, a comprehensive and fully labeled dataset was obtained for training purposes. As

Table 2. A comparative experiment is conducted utilizing the Oxford-IIIT Pet dataset, In conjunction with an alternative methodology.

Method	Accuracy
Transfer Learning	0.8999
MobileNet	0.9385
RestNet	0.9141
ResNet50V2	0.9318
Our	**0.9750**

we added more data, the accuracy increased and the loss decreased, demonstrating the effectiveness of our approach in improving the robustness of the MLC model.

4 Conclusion

In this article, we propose a solution to address the problem of poor model performance caused by inadequate datasets. By meticulously organizing the annotations and utilizing the initial dataset of 5000 images as input, we trained our model and successfully developed an initial cat breed classification model. Based on this model, we combined it with a web crawler method to gradually expand the training dataset, and ultimately enhance the effect of the initial model. The model enhancement is divided into two parts. The first part involves using the existing model and MLC's label verification ability to obtain the label results of crawler images, achieving automatic and accurate labeling of images. The second phase involves amalgamating the labeled data obtained from the crawler with the existing dataset. By training the combined dataset, we aim to attain a more robust model, thereby achieving a continuous process of model enhancement. From the experimental results, it can be seen that using our method, The ROC curve approach 1 with the enhancement of the model, and the accuracy also gradually improves.

References

1. Wang, Z., Hu, G., Hu, Q.: Training noise-robust deep neural networks via meta-learning. In: CVPR, pp. 4523–4532 (2020)
2. Deng, W., Zheng, L.: Are labels always necessary for classifier accuracy evaluation? In: CVPR, pp. 15064–15073 (2021)
3. Guo, X., Yang, C., Li, B., Yuan, Y.: MetaCorrection: domain-aware meta loss correction for unsupervised domain adaptation in semantic segmentation. In: CVPR, pp. 3926–3935 (2021)
4. Algan, G., Ulusoy, I.: MetaLabelNet: learning to generate soft-labels from noisy-labels. IEEE Trans. Image Process. **31**, 4352–4362 (2022)

5. Zheng, G., Awadallah, A.H., Dumais, S.: Meta label correction for noisy label learning. arXiv e-prints arXiv1911.03809 (2019)
6. Algan, G., Ulusoy, I.: Image classification with deep learning in the presence of noisy labels: a survey. arXiv preprint arXiv:1912.05170 (2019)
7. Shu, J., Zhao, Q., Xu, Z., Meng, D.: Meta transition adaptation for robust deep learning with noisy labels. arXiv preprint arXiv:2006.05697 (2020)
8. Mao, J., Yu, Q., Yamakata, Y., Aizawa, K.: Noisy annotation refinement for object detection. arXiv preprint arXiv:2110.1045 (2021)
9. Wei, C., Shen, K., Chen, Y., Ma, T.: Theoretical analysis of self-training with deep networks on unlabeled data. arXiv preprint arXiv:2010.03622 (2020)
10. Wang, P., Peng, J., Pedersoli, M., Zhou, Y., Zhang, C., Desrosiers, C.: Self-paced and self-consistent co-training for semi-supervised image segmentation. arXiv preprint arXiv:2011.0032 (2020)
11. Xie, Q., Luong, M. -T., Hovy, E., Le, Q.V.: Self-training with noisy student improves imagenet classification. In: CVPR, pp. 10684–10695 (2020)
12. Feurer, M., Eggensperger, K., Falkner, S., Lindauer, M., Hutter, F.: Auto-Sklearn 2.0: hands-free AutoML via meta-learning. arXiv preprint arXiv:2007.04074 (2020)
13. Kye, S. M., Lee, H. B., Kim, H., Hwang, S.J.: Meta-learned confidence for few-shot learning. arXiv preprint arXiv:2002.12017 (2020)
14. Yi, L., Liu, S., She, Q., McLeod, A.I., Wang, B.: On learning contrastive representations for learning with noisy labels. arXiv preprint arXiv:2203.01785 (2022)
15. Zhang, Y., Zheng, S., Wu, P., Goswami, M., Chen, C.: Learning with feature-dependent label noise: a progressive approach. arXiv preprint arXiv:2103.07756 (2021)
16. Chew, R., Wenger, M., Kery, C., Nance, J., Richards, K., Hadley, E., Baumgartner, P.: SMART: an open source data labeling platform for supervised learning. arXiv preprint arXiv:1812.06591 (2018)

Multi-UAV Cooperative Reconnaissance Task Allocation Based on IEPPSO Algorithm

Xiao Lv[1(✉)], Gang Wang[1], and Junhua Chen[2]

[1] College of Computer Engineering, Naval University of Engineering, Wuhan, China
XiaoLv_nue@163.com
[2] Data Information Office, Hubei Provincial Military Command, Wuhan, China

Abstract. Multi-UAV system can play an important role in reconnaissance mission during a combat. In actual military operations, some targets need to be reconnoitered within a given time. So, time window constraints of targets should be considered in the model. This paper introduces time window constraints into the task allocation model we established before, and presents a multi-UAV cooperative reconnaissance task allocation model with time window constraints (TW-MCRTA). And in order to better solve the TW-MCRTA model, the IEPPSO algorithm is proposed by introduce the probability-based constraint verification initialization strategy and the experience pool updating mechanism into the EPPSO algorithm we proposed before. Finally, The contrast experiment proves that the initialization ability and optimization ability of IEPPSO are better than comparison algorithm.

Keywords: Multi-UAV · Task allocation · Time window · Constraint verification · Updating mechanism

1 Introduction

As we all know, UAVs have been widely used in military reconnaissance [1,2]. Using multiple UAVs to perform tasks together can improve efficiency, but how to allocate tasks is important to cooperation [3]. In task allocation, it is necessary to consider the differences in UAVs and targets, as well as various constraint conditions [4]. There have been many research achievements on this issue [5–8].

In the previous work [9], we established a MCRTAP model, in which the reconnaissance time window constraint of targets were not taken into consideration. In actual military operations, multi-UAV may need to perform reconnaissance in a specified time period so as to cooperate with other combat forces. So, it is necessary to consider the reconnaissance time window constraint of targets when allocating tasks. Therefore, this paper introduces time window constraints into MCRTAP, and presents a multi-UAV cooperative reconnaissance task allocation model with time window constraints (TW-MCRTA).

Y. Sun et al. (Eds.): ChineseCSCW 2023, CCIS 2013, pp. 119–129, 2024.
https://doi.org/10.1007/978-981-99-9640-7_9

Task allocation problems can be divided into offline task allocation and online task allocation. TW-MCRTA model belongs to offline task allocation. The most commonly used algorithms for offline task allocation includes deterministic algorithm and heuristic algorithm. The deterministic algorithm includes integer programming [10–12], graph theory [13] and so on. The heuristic algorithm includes method based on clustering [14], evolutionary algorithm [5,15,16], swarm intelligence algorithm [17–20], tabu search algorithm [21] and so on. The task allocation problem is NP-hard [22], while the deterministic method takes too long to solve. With the deepening of research, more and more scholars use swarm intelligence algorithms to solve problems. Particle swarm optimization and its improved algorithms are often used to solve such problems [23–25].

In the previous work [9], we proposed EPPSO algorithm to allocate tasks in MCRTAP model. However, as time window constraints were introduced, particles in EPPSO algorithm may need to be randomly generated many times in the initialization stage, resulting the long time consuming or initialization failure. In order to better solve TW-MCRTA model, the improved EPPSO algorithm (IEPPSO) is proposed.

The paper is organized as follows: In Sect. 2, TW-MCRTA model is established. In Sect. 3, improvement of IEPPSO than EPPSO is introduced. In Sect. 4, contrast experiments are conducted. Finally, conclusions are drawn in Sect. 5.

2   TW-MCRTA Model

2.1   Background

Assuming that during an island landing operation, multi-UAV need to carry out close reconnaissance on targets. As shown in Fig. 1, the prior information of targets in enemy island has been acquired by satellite, warship and early warning aircraft, etc. Targets need to be allocated according to prior information, so as to accomplish a well cooperation of multiple UAVs.

In actual military operations, UAV needs to establish a circular reconnaissance route around the target to obtain detailed information when conducting reconnaissance. Prior information of targets includes approximate coordinates, radius of circular route. Radius of circular route is depended on the size and threat level of target. As shown in Fig. 2, UAVs set off from ship platforms, and will come back after finish all its tasks.

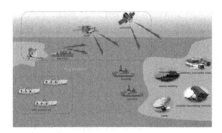

Fig. 1. Acquisition of prior information   **Fig. 2.** Multi-UAV reconnaissance

2.2   Multi-UAV and Targets Model

Multi-UAV System. UAVs are carried by ship platforms before mission begin. Suppose there are N_s ship platforms in our combat formation, $S = \{S_0, S_1, ..., S_{N_s-1}\}$. The information of UAVs carried on platforms is known including cruising speed V_i, maximum range MR_i. UAV set is $U = \{U_0, U_1, ..., U_{N_u-1}\}$, N_u is the quantities of UAVs.

Targets. Suppose there are N_t targets need to be reconnoitered, target set is $T = \{T_0, T_1, ..., T_{N_t-1}\}$. According to prior information, T_j is located at $[X_{T_j}, Y_{T_j}]$, the radius of circular route is R_{T_j}. Some of targets may need to be reconnoitered during a time window, for example $TW_j = [TS_j, TE_j]$ is the time window of T_j.

2.3   Constraint Condition

Range Constraint. The Range of U_i can't exceed its maximum range:

$$Range_i \leq MR_i, \forall i = 0, 1, 2, ..., N_u - 1 \tag{1}$$

Suppose the task list of U_i is $TL_i = \{t_i^1, t_i^2, ..., t_i^{n_i}\}$, Then $Range_i$ can be calculated as follows

$$Range_i = L_{U_i, t_i^1} + \sum_{k=1}^{n_i} 2\pi R_{t_i^k} + \sum_{k=1}^{n_i-1} L_{t_i^k, t_i^{k+1}} + L_{t_i^{n_i}, U_i} \tag{2}$$

In the formula, L_{U_i, t_i^1} is the range from starting point to t_i^1; $2\pi R_{t_i^k}$ is the length of circular route of t_i^k; $L_{t_i^k, t_i^{k+1}}$ is the range from t_i^k to t_i^{k+1}; $L_{t_i^{n_i}, U_i}$ is the range of return voyage.

Reconnaissance Time Constraint. If T_j is restricted by time window, the reconnaissance of T_j must be finished between $TW_j = [TS_j, TE_j]$:

$$ts_i^j \geq TS_j, te_i^j \leq TE_j \tag{3}$$

where, ts_i^j and te_i^j are the moment that U_i start and finish the reconnaissance on T_j. The moment UAV depart from platform is the starting time of timing.

2.4   Objective Function

From the perspective of improving the reconnaissance efficiency and the overall energy consumption, the mission completion time CT and the average flight time AT of UAVs are taken as the optimization objectives [9], and the above two objectives need to be considered simultaneously in the optimization. The *fitness* is used to represent the overall cost of the solution. Considering that there are some constraints in the model, when a solution does not satisfy the constraints, one of the most commonly used methods to punish it is to assign a large value to its fitness when solving the minimization problem [10]. Therefore, this paper establishes the following objective function:

$$\min fitness = \alpha \cdot CT + \beta \cdot AT + \gamma \cdot 10^4 \qquad (4)$$

where, $\alpha, \beta \in [0,1]$ and $\alpha + \beta = 1$, which are used to adjust the proportion of two optimization objectives. In the actual task, α, β can be adjusted according to the needs of the task. Referring to existing literature [8,18], here $\alpha = \beta = 0.5$. And if the solution doesn't satisfy constraints, $\gamma = 1$, otherwise, $\gamma = 0$.

3   IEPPSO Algorithm

3.1   Probability-Based Constraint Verification Initialization Strategy

In EPPSO, every particle will be subject to constraint verification after initialized. And the particles that do not meet the constraints need to be regenerated until all constraints are met. This paper introduces the verification probability P_v into the initialization stage. As shown in Fig. 3, the algorithm perform constraint verification on initialized particles at the probability of P_v.

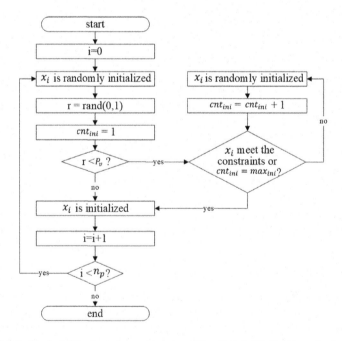

Fig. 3. Probability-based constraint verification initialization strategy

The times of particle random initialization behavior is limit to max_{ini}, that is, if x_i still can't meet constraints after max_{ini} initialization, the last initialization is adopted. Considering that N_{exp} is 20% of the total number of particles N_p [9], to guarantee the quality of experience pool, the verification probability P_v is set to 0.2. This improvement strategy has two main advantages: (1) improve initialization speed. It can effectively reduce the times of particle constraint verification and re-generation, shorten the particle initialization time. (2) increase population diversity. Although some particles may not satisfy with the constraints, the position information contained therein can promote particles search a larger space.

3.2 Experience Pool Updating Mechanism Based on Elite Selection Strategy

In the iteration of EPPSO, particles that do not satisfied with constraints should be reconstructed based on experience pool. However, the particles in experience pool of EPPSO tend to be stable at the later stage. Therefore, the position reconstruction strategy could hardly help particles explore a better position in the later iterations. In order to enhance optimization ability, this paper introduces an experience pool updating mechanism.

Algorithm 1. Experience pool updating mechanism based on elite selection strategy

---

Input: N_u, N_t, N_{exp}, P_l, P_{mu}, gb, $cnt_{unchange}$, $max_{unchange}$, max_{upd}
Output: updated experience pool
  if $cnt_{unchange} \geq max_{unchange}$ **then**
    for t in range N_{exp} **do**
      $tempx = e_t$
      $cnt_{upd} = 0$
      while $cnt_{upd} < max_{upd}$ **do**
        for d in range N_t **do**
          $r = rand(0, 1)$
          if $r \leq P_{mu}$ **then**
            $tempx_d = rand(0, N_u)$
          else if $r \leq P_{mu} + P_l$ **then**
            $tempx_d = gb_d$
          end if
        end for
        if $fitness(tempx) < fitness(e_t)$ **then**
          $e_t = tempx$
          break
        end if
        $cnt_{upd} = cnt_{upd} + 1$
      end while
    end for
    $cnt_{unchange} = 0$
  end if

If there is no better solution is found in the current round of evolution, $cnt_{unchange}$ is accumulated. When $cnt_{unchange}$ exceeds the trigger threshold $max_{unchange}$, we consider that the algorithm may have fallen into local optimal solution, then the experience pool updating mechanism is triggered. In the process of updating, each particle e_t in the experience pool needs to be updated in turn. As shown in formula, updates mainly depends on mutation and learning:

$$e_{t,d} = \begin{cases} rand(0, N_u), & r \leq P_{mu} \\ gb_d, & P_{mu} < r \leq P_{mu} + P_l \\ e_{t,d}, & r > P_{mu} + P_l \end{cases} \quad (5)$$

where, $e_{t,d}$ is the dth dimension of e_t, P_{mu} is the mutation probability, P_l is the learning probability, gb_d is the dth dimension of the global optimal particle, $r = rand(0,1)$.

In updating mechanism, the elite selection strategy is adopted, that is, only when the better particles are generated, the original particles in the experience pool are replaced, otherwise the original particles remain unchanged. The specific method is shown in Algorithm 1. Where, max_{upd} is the maximum update times. The significance of max_{upd} is to prevent the algorithm from taking too long to calculate due to repeated update failures.

After being updated, much different position information will be included in experience pool, and the quality of these position information can be guaranteed under the guidance of the elite selection strategy. In the subsequent algorithm iteration process, these position information would promote particles search more effective space, so as to let particles escape from local optimal position.

4   Performance Analysis

Some simulation experiments are conducted in this section to analysis IEPPSO algorithm. The experiments are based on TW-MCRTAP model. These experiments are implemented in python 3.9 on a computer with AMD Ryzen 5-5600H. Some parameters of IEPPSO algorithm are set as follow: $P_v = 0.2$, $max_{ini} = 50$, $max_{unchange} = 40$, $max_{upd} = 50$, $P_{mu} = 0.2$, $P_l = 0.1$. And the remaining parameters are set according to the EPPSO algorithm [9]. In the hole experiment, the unit of distance is km, the unit of time is s, and the unit of speed is km/s.

4.1   Validation of Effectiveness

The verification experiment is used to verify the effectiveness of IEPPSO. In this experiment, the location of three ship platforms are initialized in $[0, 100] \times [0, 100]$ randomly, and each platform carries two UAVs. Referring to the existing studies [8,9,18], the information of platforms and UAVs are shown in Table 1. The targets are randomly located in $[100, 300] \times [100, 300]$ area, suppose $N_t = 15$,

Table 1. Platforms and UAVs information

Platform	UAV	Cruising speed (V,km/h)	Maximum range (MR,km)
S_0	U_0	0.22	1000
	U_1	0.18	1200
S_1	U_2	0.16	1500
	U_3	0.22	1000
S_2	U_4	0.18	1200
	U_5	0.16	1500

DR_j are the random number within $[1,3]$. In particular, 4 targets are randomly selected to set the time window constraint: $TW_1 = [900, 1400]$, $TW_4 = [1300, 1700]$, $TW_{10} = [800, 1400]$, $TW_{14} = [1100, 1600]$.

The IEPPSO algorithm is used to allocate tasks. The final solution: $plan = [[0, 7, 5, 12], [13, 11], [], [1, 10, 14, 8, 2], [3, 9, 6, 4], []]$. The reconnaissance mission is carried out by 4 of the 6 UAVs. The routes of UAVs and task execution time chart are represented in Fig. 4 and Fig. 5. The lines in Fig. 4 represent the route of dispatched UAVs, and the gantt chart represents the time period that each target is reconnoitered. The actual reconnaissance periods of the targets with time window requirements are $T_1 : [928.4, 1011.2]$, $T_4 : [1596.1, 1678.4]$, $T_{10} : [1094.8, 1149.8]$, $T_{14} : [1477.3, 1529.5]$, which are satisfied with the time window constraint.

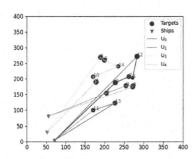

Fig. 4. Routes of UAVs

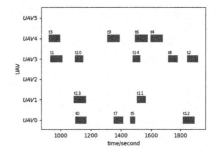

Fig. 5. Task execution time chart

4.2   Initialization Ability Comparison

In order to prove the improvement of initialization ability of IEPPSO, three comparative experiments are conducted, comparison algorithm including PSO [26] and EPPSO [9]. Test 1: $N_t = 15$, $TW_3 = [800, 1100]$, $TW_9 = [1100, 1400]$, $TW_{13} = [1000, 1500]$. Test 2: $N_t = 20$, $TW_2 = [900, 1300]$, $TW_5 = [1100, 1700]$,

$TW_{10} = [900, 1500]$, $TW_{15} = [1000, 1600]$. Test 3: $N_t = 25$, $TW_3 = [800, 1300]$, $TW_6 = [1100, 1700]$, $TW_{10} = [1200, 1700]$, $TW_{16} = [900, 1400]$, $TW_{23} = [1300, 1800]$. The remaining background settings are the same as Sect. 4.1.

Every experiment repeats 10 times. The results are listed in Table 2. Three indicators are compared: initialization failure times cnt_{fail}, average time consumption of initialization T_{ini} and mean value of initialization optimal fitness F_{ini} (Exclude the cases of EPPSO initialization failure).

According to Table 2, EPPSO algorithm may fail in initializing the particles, while the original PSO and IEPPSO algorithm can ensure the smooth initialization. In addition, EPPSO and IEPPSO algorithm can significantly improve the quality of the initial particles.

Table 2. Initialization results

Experiment	Test 1			Test 2			Test 3		
Algorithm	PSO	EPPSO	IEPPSO	PSO	EPPSO	IEPPSO	PSO	EPPSO	IEPPSO
cnt_{fail}	0	3	0	0	4	0	0	4	0
T_{ini}	0.02	2.45	0.10	0.03	101.71	0.16	0.03	45.80	0.19
F_{ini}	3875.3	1966.4	2212.8	11886.3	3167.3	5464.4	10078.5	3177.6	5481.1

4.3 Optimization Ability Comparison

A comparative experiment on optimization ability is conducted in this section. The comparison algorithm includes MDWAP [27], ISAFGA [28], RPSO [29] and EPPSO [9]. In the experiment, $N_t = 20$, $TW_2 = [800, 1300]$, $TW_5 = [1200, 1600]$, $TW_9 = [1100, 1700]$, $TW_{12} = [1000, 1500]$, the remaining background settings are the same as Sect. 4.1. Repeat the experiment 30 times and take the average fitness as results, the result is shown in Fig. 6.

Analysis from the results of Fig. 6, on the one hand, the IEPPSO and EPPSO algorithm can obtain initial particles with lower fitness values. On the other hand, the convergence performance of IEPPSO and EPPSO algorithm is significantly better than other comparative algorithms, and the final fitness value of IEPPSO algorithm is relatively small. Although the initial particles quality of the EPPSO algorithm is better, the IEPPSO algorithm has stronger optimization ability in the subsequent iteration process. This is because the experience pool update mechanism based on elite selection strategy can make the particles of the IEPPSO algorithm have a greater probability to escape from the local optimal position in the later stage of iteration, so as to obtain a better solution.

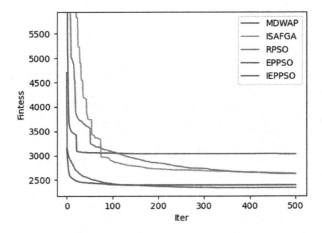

Fig. 6. Average fitness variation

5   Conclusion and Future Work

Based on our previous work, this paper introduce time window constraints into MCRTAP model, and establish the TW-MCRTA model. The maximum range, speed difference of UAVs, size difference of targets and time window constraints are comprehensively taken into consideration in TW-MCRTA model. And an improved EPPSO algorithm is proposed (IEPPSO). On the one hand, by proposing probability-based constraint verification initialization strategy, IEPPSO algorithm effectively shortens time consuming of initialization while guarantees the quality of initial particles. On the other hand, the experience pool update mechanism based on the elite selection strategy is introduced, which makes particles have a greater probability to escape from local optimal position in later stage of evolution, thus improving optimization ability.

Our next work is to study the task reallocation problem during the mission.

References

1. Chen, H.X., Nan, Y., Yang, Y.: Multi-UAV reconnaissance task assignment for heterogeneous targets based on modified symbiotic organisms search algorithm. Sensors (Basel, Switzerland) **19**(3), 734 (2019). https://doi.org/10.3390/s19030734
2. Schwarzrock, J., Zacarias, I., Bazzan, A.L., de Araujo Fernandes, R.Q., Moreira, L.H., de Freitas, E.P.: Solving task allocation problem in multi unmanned aerial vehicles systems using swarm intelligence. Eng. Appl. Artif. Intell. **72**(1), 10–20 (2018). https://doi.org/10.1016/j.engappai.2018.03.008
3. Wang, J.F., Jia, G.W., Lin, J.C., Hou, Z.X.: Cooperative task allocation for heterogeneous multi-UAV using multi-objective optimization algorithm. J. Central South Univ. **27**(2), 432–448 (2020). https://doi.org/10.1007/s11771-020-4307-0
4. Zhang, J., Xing, J.: Cooperative task assignment of multi-UAV system. Chin. J. Aeronaut. **33**(11), 2825–2827 (2020). https://doi.org/10.1016/j.cja.2020.02.009

5. Cao, Y., Wei, W., Bai, Y., Qiao, H.: Multi-base multi-UAV cooperative reconnaissance path planning with genetic algorithm. Clust. Comput. **22**(S3), 5175–5184 (2019). https://doi.org/10.1007/s10586-017-1132-9
6. Wang, T., Zhang, B., Zhang, M., Zhang, S.: Multi-UAV collaborative path planning method based on attention mechanism. Math. Probl. Eng. **2021**(2), 1–8 (2021). https://doi.org/10.1155/2021/6964875
7. Xie, S., Zhang, A., Bi, W., Tang, Y.: Multi-UAV mission allocation under constraint. Appl. Sci. **9**(11), 2184 (2019). https://doi.org/10.3390/app9112184
8. Wang, Z., Liu, L., Long, T., Wen, Y.: Multi-UAV reconnaissance task allocation for heterogeneous targets using an opposition-based genetic algorithm with double-chromosome encoding. Chin. J. Aeronaut. **31**(2), 339–350 (2018). https://doi.org/10.1016/j.cja.2017.09.005
9. Wang, G., Lv, X., Ben, K., Cui, L.: A particle swarm optimization algorithm based on experience pool for multi-UAV cooperative reconnaissance task allocation. In: 2023 26th International Conference on Computer Supported Cooperative Work in Design (CSCWD), pp. 861–866. IEEE (2023)
10. Karaman, S., Frazzoli, E.: Linear temporal logic vehicle routing with applications to multi-UAV mission planning. Int. J. Robust Nonlinear Control **21**(12), 1372–1395 (2011). https://doi.org/10.1002/rnc.1715
11. Schumacher, C., Chandler, P.R., Pachter, M., Pachter, L.S.: Optimization of air vehicles operations using mixed-integer linear programming. J. Oper. Res. Soc. **58**(4), 516–527 (2007)
12. Samiei, A., Ismail, S., Sun, L.: Cluster-based Hungarian approach to task allocation for unmanned aerial vehicles. In: 2019 IEEE National Aerospace and Electronics Conference (NAECON), pp. 148–154 (2019)
13. Deng, Q., Yu, J., Mei, Y.: Deadlock-free consecutive task assignment of multiple heterogeneous unmanned aerial vehicles. J. Aircr. **51**(2), 596–605 (2014). https://doi.org/10.2514/1.C032309
14. Fu, Z., Mao, Y., He, D., Yu, J., Xie, G.: Secure multi-UAV collaborative task allocation. IEEE Access **7**, 35579–35587 (2019). https://doi.org/10.1109/ACCESS.2019.2902221
15. Liu, H., et al.: Multi-UAV optimal mission assignment and path planning for disaster rescue using adaptive genetic algorithm and improved artificial bee colony method. Actuators **11**(1), 4 (2022). https://doi.org/10.3390/act11010004
16. Ye, F., Chen, J., Tian, Y., Jiang, T.: Cooperative task assignment of a heterogeneous multi-UAV system using an adaptive genetic algorithm. Electronics **9**(4), 687 (2020). https://doi.org/10.3390/electronics9040687
17. Gao, S., Wu, J., Ai, J.: Multi-UAV reconnaissance task allocation for heterogeneous targets using grouping ant colony optimization algorithm. Soft. Comput. **25**(10), 7155–7167 (2021). https://doi.org/10.1007/s00500-021-05675-8
18. Perez-Carabaza, S., Besada-Portas, E., Lopez-Orozco, J.A., de La Cruz, J.M.: Ant colony optimization for multi-UAV minimum time search in uncertain domains. Appl. Soft Comput. **62**(4), 789–806 (2018). https://doi.org/10.1016/j.asoc.2017.09.009
19. Alhaqbani, A., Kurdi, H., Youcef-Toumi, K.: Fish-inspired task allocation algorithm for multiple unmanned aerial vehicles in search and rescue missions. Remote Sens. **13**(1), 27 (2021). https://doi.org/10.3390/rs13010027
20. Yan, M., Yuan, H., Xu, J., Yu, Y., Jin, L.: Task allocation and route planning of multiple UAVs in a marine environment based on an improved particle swarm optimization algorithm. EURASIP J. Adv. Signal Process. **2021**(1), 39 (2021). https://doi.org/10.1186/s13634-021-00804-9

21. Alighanbari, M., Kuwata, Y., How, J.: Coordination and control of multiple UAVs with timing constraints and loitering. In: Proceedings of the American Control Conference, vol. 6, pp. 5311–5316 (2003). https://doi.org/10.1109/ACC.2003.1242572

22. Zhen, Z., Wen, L., Wang, B., Hu, Z., Zhang, D.: Improved contract network protocol algorithm based cooperative target allocation of heterogeneous UAV swarm. Aerosp. Sci. Technol. **119**(6), 107054 (2021). https://doi.org/10.1016/j.ast.2021.107054

23. Zhang, A., Han, X., Bi, W., Shuangfei, X.: Adaptive mutant particle swarm optimization based precise cargo airdrop of unmanned aerial vehicles. Appl. Soft Comput. **130**, 109657 (2022)

24. Li, M., Liu, C., Li, K., Liao, X., Li, K.: Multi-task allocation with an optimized quantum particle swarm method. Appl. Soft Comput. **96**(6), 106603 (2020). https://doi.org/10.1016/j.asoc.2020.106603

25. He, W., Qi, X., Liu, L.: A novel hybrid particle swarm optimization for multi-UAV cooperate path planning. Appl. Intell. **51**(10), 7350–7364 (2021). https://doi.org/10.1007/s10489-020-02082-8

26. Kennedy, J., Eberhart, R.: Particle swarm optimization. In: Proceedings of ICNN'95-International Conference on Neural Networks, vol. 4, pp. 1942–1948 (1995)

27. Xu, S., Li, L., Zhou, Z., Mao, Y., Huang, J.: A task allocation strategy of the UAV swarm based on multi-discrete wolf pack algorithm. Appl. Sci. **12**(3), 1331 (2022). https://doi.org/10.3390/app12031331

28. Wu, X., Yin, Y., Xu, L., Wu, X., Meng, F., Zhen, R.: Multi-UAV task allocation based on improved genetic algorithm. IEEE Access **9**, 100369–100379 (2021). https://doi.org/10.1109/ACCESS.2021.3097094

29. Liu, W., Wang, Z., Zeng, N., Yuan, Y., Alsaadi, F.E., Liu, X.: A novel randomised particle swarm optimizer. Int. J. Mach. Learn. Cybern. **12**(2), 529–540 (2021). https://doi.org/10.1007/s13042-020-01186-4

Cooperative Evolutionary Computation and Human-Like Intelligent Collaboration

Group Role Assignment with Trust Between Agents

Meiqiao Pan, Yanyan Fan, Shiyu Wu, and Libo Zhang[⊠]

College of Artificial Intelligence, Southwest University, Chongqing 400715, China
lbzhang@swu.edu.cn

Abstract. As a vital methodology for collaboration problems, Role-Based Collaboration (RBC) consists of three essential stages: agent evaluation, Group Role Assignment (GRA), and role transfer. Among these stages, GRA holds significant importance as a critical step in the process. In Social Sciences, trust between group members in collaboration tends to profoundly impact the final performance. However, existing GRA problems neglected the trust relationship between agents, which plays a decisive role in whether agents can work together. Therefore, this paper discusses the GRA problem with the constraint of trust between agents, aiming to maximize group performance while satisfying the trust constraint. The contributions of this paper include: 1) A new problem of GRA called GRA with trust between agents (GRATA) is formalized; 2) A feasible solution and a theorem are proposed to address the GRATA problem effectively; 3) Comprehensive experiments are conducted to validate the benefits of solving the problem.

Keywords: RBC · GRA · Trust · GRATA

1 Introduction

Role-Based Collaboration (RBC) has been established as a highly effective approach to tackling collaboration challenges [10]. It places great emphasis on the significance of roles and provides an abstract model environment that incorporates Classes, Agents, Roles, Groups, and Objects (E-CARGO) [4]. Role assignment plays a vital role in the RBC process, as the team's overall performance relies on the cumulative performance of each agent in their designated roles [7,9]. Building upon the foundation of RBC, Group Role Assignment (GRA) has been developed to determine the optimal role assignment plan, aiming to maximize the overall group performance [8].

Trust among team members plays a pivotal role in fostering cooperation within a team. Establishing a foundation of trust facilitates effective communication, understanding, collaboration, and coordination among team members, ultimately enhancing team cohesion and efficiency [1]. Trustworthy relationships effectively reduce communication costs and risks while minimizing the occurrence of misunderstandings and conflicts [2]. Mutual trust among team members enables them to better accomplish tasks, overcome difficulties and challenges, and improve the overall quality of their work [3]. Once the trust relationship is strong enough, members can freely share their thoughts and experiences,

© The Author(s), under exclusive license to Springer Nature Singapore Pte Ltd. 2024
Y. Sun et al. (Eds.): ChineseCSCW 2023, CCIS 2013, pp. 133–147, 2024.
https://doi.org/10.1007/978-981-99-9640-7_10

further enhancing collaborative outcomes and team creativity. Therefore, basic trust among members is fundamental in teamwork environments. Having certain demand for trust can avoid potential negative effects on the team and enhance overall performance.

To address the trust-related collaboration problem, this paper proposes an algorithm to obtain the optimal role assignment plan, taking into account the trust constraints. The trust levels between agents are quantified using numerical values, and each role requires a specific level of trust to be fulfilled. Specifically, an agent can only be assigned a role if the trust between the agent and each agent on that role, taken pairwise, exceeds a sufficient level of trust. The effectiveness of the algorithm is further validated through experiments, demonstrating its capability to obtain the optimal assignment plan. By incorporating trust as a crucial factor in the GRA problem, this research contributes to enhancing the understanding and practical application of role-based collaboration in trust-dependent scenarios. The proposed algorithm offers a valuable approach to optimizing role assignments while considering trust thresholds among team members, thus facilitating more effective and reliable collaboration within the group.

The rest of the paper is distributed as follows. Section 2 provides an overview of relevant research papers. Section 3 presents a detailed description of a real-world scenario. Section 4 outlines specific definitions for constructing the GRATA model. Section 5 conducts comprehensive experiments and provides an extensive analysis of the obtained. In Sect. 6, a comprehensive summary is provided, accompanied by a forward-looking perspective on potential future directions.

2   Related Work

Trust is closely intertwined with collaboration and has a notable influence on the ultimate performance outcomes. While the existing literature on GRA does not explicitly cover this specific topic, it has provided a foundational basis for the exploration and investigation of the GRATA problem.

Zhu et al. [13] conducted an extensive investigation into the research requirements for collaboration systems. They reviewed past research achievements, addressed unresolved issues, proposed fundamental research methodologies for studying RBC and E-CRAGO, identified related challenges, and analyzed the connections between these areas and other cutting-edge fields.

Zhu [14] provided clarification on the Group Role Assignment Problem (GRAP) and introduced a General Assignment Problem (GAP), which was used to convert GRA into GAP. Zhu developed a powerful algorithm based on the Kuhn-Munkres (K-M) algorithm to address the problem and conducted simulation experiments to analyze the solution's performance.

Liu et al. [5] put forward a range of methods to address the problem of balancing group role assignment, by utilizing the one clause at a time approach in association rule mining, which is a well-established and logic-based method, we can obtain valuable insights and patterns.

Zhu [17] developed a formalized version of GRA-MC that considers the intricacy of evaluating agents in actual GRA scenarios. Zhu examined three multi-criteria decision algorithms - Simple Weighting (SAW), Multiplicative Exponential Weighting (MEW), and Weighted Distance (WD) - and validated the effectiveness of the GRA-MC approach. Additionally, Zhu discussed the outcomes of applying GRA-MC to the GRA problems.

Zhang [10] explored the development of the training plan and post-training role assignment with the aim of maximizing team performance. By leveraging RBC and its universal model, Zhang proposed solutions and developed optimal training plans to guarantee that selected agents excel in specific roles over their in-service counterparts.

Yu et al. [8] considered the collaborative issues of multiple groups in the context of GRA. They formalized the problem as a multi-group role assignment (MGRA) problem and proposed corresponding algorithms to solve the problem in static scenarios. Furthermore, they demonstrated the effectiveness of the MGRA algorithm in dynamic collaborative settings.

Wu et al. [6] formalized the problem about personal wishes by the GRA with Balance (GRAB). And he proposed an approach that can achieve a state of equilibrium between wishes and performance.

3   A Real-World Scenario

A construction company is preparing to undertake a new project. In an effort to enhance the company's focus on security measures and ensure an effective response to emergencies, including potential fire incidents, the company has made the decision to establish a volunteer fire department. Ann, the Chief Executive Officer (CEO), has tasked Bob, the security department manager, with forming the volunteer fire department. The department is expected to consist of various specialized groups, namely Fire Suppression, Evacuation, Rescue, Equipment, Security, and Driving, each requiring a specific number of members (Table 1). With the project's imminent commencement, Bob is tasked with swiftly and thoughtfully selecting suitable candidates, assigning respective roles to them, to guarantee safe and efficient execution of the mission. Thus, he requests data analysts to evaluate candidates' qualifications for each position (Table 2). There are sixteen candidates with different levels of ability but only fourteen positions to compete.

Bob is fully aware that establishing a sufficient level of trust within each group is crucial for the candidates to fulfill their responsibilities effectively. When

Table 1. Required positions.

Position	Fire Suppression	Evacuation	Rescue	Equipment	Security	Driving
Required Number	3	3	4	1	2	1

Table 2. The qualifications.

	Fire Suppression	Evacuation	Rescue	Equipment	Security	Driving
Amy	0.8	0.5	0.7	0.4	0.5	0.2
Ben	0.5	0.7	0.6	0.4	0.6	0.5
Chris	0.6	0.7	0.7	0.8	0.7	0.5
Dave	0.6	0.5	0.7	0.4	0.5	0.5
Ella	0.5	0.5	0.4	0.4	0.5	0.5
Frank	0.7	0.3	0.4	0.3	0.7	0.5
Gabby	0.6	0.5	0.7	0.4	0.5	0.8
Helen	0.7	0.3	0.4	0.6	0.7	0.5
Irene	0.9	0.8	0.7	0.3	0.4	0.9
Jay	0.3	0.9	0.7	0.9	0.5	0.9
Kevin	0.7	0.8	0.8	0.6	0.4	0.9
Larry	0.8	0.4	0.9	0.4	0.9	0.7
Molly	0.7	0.5	0.7	0.6	0.9	0.4
Nile	0.5	0.5	0.7	0.8	0.7	0.3
Oliver	0.7	0.8	0.7	0.7	0.4	0.3
Peter	0.4	0.4	0.5	0.6	0.4	0.7

faced with life-threatening situations, firefighters must rely on their teammates to make split-second decisions and execute coordinated actions. Therefore, it is essential for the members within the same group to have a minimum level of trust that surpasses a certain threshold. This ensures seamless collaboration and enhances the overall effectiveness of the group's response during critical moments. Therefore, he asks the data analysts to evaluate and provide related materials. Table 3 illustrates the trust thresholds that vary based on the distinct risks and demands associated with each position's tasks. For each pair of agents, there exists a level of trust between them, and the trust relationships among all agents form a network-like structure, which is partly demonstrated in Fig. 1. Table 4 details the trust level between agents, the higher the value, the higher the trust between the two. It is assumed that all agents fully trust themselves, manifested by each individual attributing a trust value of 1 to themselves.

Table 3. Trust threshold.

Position	Fire Suppression	Evacuation	Rescue	Equipment	Security	Driving
Lower Limit of Trust	0.7	0.5	0.6	0	0.3	0

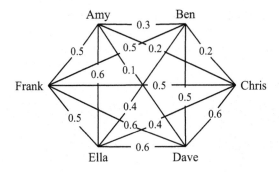

Fig. 1. Trust relationships within a subset of agents in a network topology.

Now, Bob faces the challenge of deciding upon the finalists and assigning appropriate roles to the agents, aiming to maximize team performance while adhering to trust constraints. Considering the complexity of the task, Ann suggests that he utilize the E-CARGO model and the principles of RBC theory to simplify the process.

4   The Proposed Extended E-CARGO Model

In RBC, $\sum$ is a collaborative system represented by sets of E-CARGO components, demonstrated as a 9-tuple $\sum ::= \langle \mathcal{C}, \mathcal{O}, \mathcal{A}, \mathcal{M}, \mathcal{R}, \mathcal{E}, \mathcal{G}, s_0, \mathcal{H} \rangle$, which are sets of E-CARGO components. Here, $\mathcal{C}$ denotes the set of Classes, $\mathcal{O}$ represents the set of objects, $\mathcal{A}$ represents the set of Agents, $\mathcal{M}$ stands for the set of Messages, $\mathcal{R}$ refers to the set of Roles, $\mathcal{E}$ signifies the Environment, $\mathcal{G}$ denotes the

Table 4. The trust matrix.

	Amy	Ben	Chris	Dave	Ella	Frank	Gabby	Helen	Irene	Jay	Kevin	Larry	Molly	Nile	Oliver	Peter
Amy	1.0	0.3	0.2	0.1	0.6	0.5	0.5	0.3	0.1	0.7	0.8	0.8	0.9	0.4	0.1	0.9
Ben	0.3	1.0	0.2	0.5	0.4	0.5	0.2	0.7	0.8	0.5	0.9	0.6	0.6	0.3	0.8	0.4
Chris	0.2	0.2	1.0	0.6	0.4	0.5	0.8	0.4	0.1	0.4	0.7	0.8	0.6	0.4	0.7	0.9
Dave	0.1	0.5	0.6	1.0	0.6	0.6	0.4	0.6	0.9	0.4	0.2	0.6	0.6	0.8	0.2	0.2
Ella	0.6	0.4	0.4	0.6	1.0	0.5	0.3	0.9	0.9	0.2	0.5	0.6	0.3	0.9	0.8	0.2
Frank	0.5	0.5	0.5	0.6	0.5	1.0	0.2	0.6	0.3	0.5	0.7	0.8	0.9	0.8	0.4	0.8
Gabby	0.5	0.2	0.8	0.4	0.3	0.2	1.0	0.8	0.8	0.1	0.8	0.5	0.8	0.3	0.2	0.9
Helen	0.3	0.7	0.4	0.6	0.9	0.6	0.8	1.0	0.5	0.8	0.3	0.2	0.9	0.8	0.3	0.8
Irene	0.1	0.8	0.1	0.9	0.9	0.3	0.8	0.5	1.0	0.3	0.3	0.5	0.7	0.2	0.8	0.4
Jay	0.7	0.5	0.4	0.4	0.2	0.5	0.1	0.8	0.3	1.0	0.8	0.2	0.4	0.3	0.5	0.9
Kevin	0.8	0.9	0.7	0.2	0.5	0.7	0.8	0.3	0.3	0.8	1.0	0.8	0.2	0.3	0.9	0.3
Larry	0.8	0.6	0.8	0.6	0.6	0.8	0.5	0.2	0.5	0.2	0.8	1.0	0.3	0.2	0.9	0.4
Molly	0.9	0.6	0.6	0.6	0.3	0.9	0.8	0.9	0.7	0.4	0.2	0.3	1.0	0.9	0.6	0.8
Nile	0.4	0.3	0.4	0.8	0.9	0.8	0.3	0.8	0.2	0.3	0.3	0.2	0.9	1.0	0.5	0.5
Oliver	0.1	0.8	0.7	0.2	0.8	0.4	0.2	0.3	0.8	0.5	0.9	0.9	0.6	0.5	1.0	0.4
Peter	0.9	0.4	0.9	0.2	0.2	0.8	0.9	0.8	0.4	0.9	0.3	0.4	0.8	0.5	0.4	1.0

set of Groups, s_0 represents the Initial system state, and $\mathcal{H}$ represents the set of human users [11,15,16]. It should be noted that m and n denote the cardinality of sets $\mathcal{A}$ and $\mathcal{R}$ respectively. By leveraging the E-CARGO model, the problem of GRATA can be formalized and solved. To formalize the proposed model, the introduction of certain concepts is necessary.

4.1   Basic Assumptions

We made several logical assumptions when introducing trust into the GRA problem.

Assumption 1: Based on the RBC theory, an individual's capacity in a given role is commensurate with its corresponding qualification value, which represents the explicit manifestation of such capacity.

For example, a student's grades serve as an indicator of their ability.

Assumption 2: During the collaboration, the trust value between the agents will remain stable and will not change.

Collaboration typically occurs during a short-duration project, resulting in a relatively stable trust value during that period. In the case of longer-term projects, the work can be segmented into smaller sub-projects with shorter duration, in which the trust value can also be considered stable.

4.2   The Formulation of the GRATA Problem

According to the assumptions in Sect. 4.1, several definitions are presented to formalize the problem specifically. Due to the extensive research on RBC theory and the E-CARGO extended model, foundational definitions such as role range vector L, and role assignment matrix T can easily be obtained through abundant literature [8,11,12,16]. Therefore, they are not explicitly introduced in this paper.

Definition 1. [11,12,16] Role j is workable if it is assigned to enough personnel, i.e., $\sum_{i=0}^{m-1} T[i,j] \geq L[j]$.

Definition 2. [11,12,16] T is workable if each role j is workable, specifically, the number of agents assigned to each role meets the lower limit, i.e., $\sum_{i=0}^{m-1} T[i,j] \geq L[j](0 \leq j < n)$.

Definition 3. The matrix Q is an $m \times n$ matrix, where $Q[i,j] \in [0,1]$ expresses the qualification value of agent i for role j.

The qualification value expresses the agent's suitability for being assigned a certain role.

For example, $Q[i_1, j_1]$ stands for the qualification of agent i_1 when assigned role j_1. The higher the value of $Q[i_1, j_1]$, the more suitable agent i_1 for role j_1.

Definition 4. The group performance σ is defined as the sum of the assigned agents' qualifications, that is:

$$\sigma = \sum_{i=0}^{m-1} \sum_{j=0}^{n-1} Q[i,j] \times T[i,j]. \tag{1}$$

Definition 5. The matrix Tr is an $m \times m$ matrix, where $Tr[i_1, i_2] \in [0,1](0 \leq i_1 < m, 0 \leq i_2 < m)$ denotes the overall trust between agent i_1 and agent i_2.

The higher the value of $Tr[i_1, i_2]$, the higher the level of trust between the two individuals. When $i_1 = i_2$, $Tr[i_1, i_2]$ indicates an agent's self-trust value, which is set to be 1.

Definition 6. The matrix L_{Tr} is an n-vector, where $L_{Tr}[j] \in [0,1](0 \leq j < n)$ expresses the lower limit of the overall trust.

Definition 6-1. For any two agents i_1 and i_2 in a group of agents assigned the same role j, the overall trust between them, represented by $Tr[i_1, i_2]$, should be equal to or greater than $L_{Tr}[j]$.

$$Tr[i_1, i_2] \geq L_{Tr}[j] \tag{2}$$

(i_1 and i_2 are any two agents assigned role j)

For example, assume that three agents i_1, i_2 and i_3 are assigned the same role j, then $Tr[i_1, i_2]$, $Tr[i_1, i_3]$ and $Tr[i_2, i_3]$ should satisfy the following constraints:

$$Tr[i_1, i_2] \geq L_{Tr}[j], \tag{3}$$
$$Tr[i_1, i_3] \geq L_{Tr}[j], \tag{4}$$
$$Tr[i_2, i_3] \geq L_{Tr}[j]. \tag{5}$$

Definition 7. Given the trust matrix Tr, the qualification matrix Q, and the lower limit matrix L_{Tr}, the assignment matrix T can be achieved.

$$\max \left\{ \sigma = \sum_{i=0}^{m-1} \sum_{j=0}^{n-1} Q[i,j] \times T[i,j] \right\}.$$

s.t.

$$T[i,j] \in \{0,1\} \quad (0 \leq i < m, 0 \leq j < n), \tag{6}$$

$$\sum_{i=0}^{m-1} T[i,j] = L[j] \quad (0 \leq j < n), \tag{7}$$

$$\sum_{j=0}^{n-1} T[i,j] \leq 1 \quad (0 \leq i < m), \tag{8}$$

$$T[i_1, j] * T[i_2, j] * Tr[i_1, i_2] \geq T[i_1, j] * T[i_2, j] * L_{Tr}[j] \quad (0 \leq i_1, i_2 < m), \tag{9}$$

where (6) is an 0-1 constraint, (7) makes group workable, (8) represents that each agent can only be assigned no more than one role, (9) makes any two agents assigned role j meet the trust constraint.

However, the constraint Eq. (9) can not be easily solved in our program, thus we propose a theorem to modify it to a better-solved form.

Theorem 1. *The trust constraint Eq. (9) can be expressed as follows:*

$$(L_{Tr}[j] - \frac{1}{2} * Tr[i_1, i_2]) * (T[i_1, j] + T[i_2, j]) \leq L_{Tr}[j] \quad (0 \leq i_1, i_2 < m, 0 \leq j < n).$$
(10)

Proof. Constraint Eq. (9) can be discussed in three situations:
For agents i_1 and i_2, according to the role assignment matrix T

1) both i_1 and i_2 are assigned role j;
2) only i_1 or i_2 is assigned role j;
3) both i_1 and i_2 are not assigned role j;

Which can be correspondingly expressed as

1) $T[i_1, j] = 1$, $T[i_2, j] = 1$, that is $T[i_1, j] + T[i_2, j] = 2$;
2) $T[i_1, j] = 1$, $T[i_2, j] = 0$ or $T[i_1, j] = 0$, $T[i_2, j] = 1$, that is $T[i_1, j] + T[i_2, j] = 1$;
3) $T[i_1, j] = 0$, $T[i_2, j] = 0$, that is $T[i_1, j] + T[i_2, j] = 0$;

Intuitively, only when agents i_1 and i_2 are assigned the same role j do the trust level between them need to meet the threshold. Taking the sum of $T[i_1, j]$ and $T[i_2, j]$ as a distinction between the three different cases, the trust constraint can be demonstrated as:

$$(1/2) * Tr[i_1, i_2] * (T[i_1, j] + T[i_2, j]) \geq L_{Tr}[j] * ((T[i_1, j] + T[i_2, j]) - 1). \quad (11)$$

According to Eq. (11), when $T[i_1, j] + T[i_2, j] = 2$, the inequality can be simplified as:

$$Tr[i_1, i_2] \geq L_{Tr}[j].$$

As the GRATA problem is abstracted as an optimization problem, we further reduce the above inequality to a less-than-equal inequality for easy computation.

$$(L_{Tr}[j] - \frac{1}{2} * Tr[i_1, i_2]) * (T[i_1, j] + T[i_2, j]) \leq L_{Tr}[j] \quad (0 \leq i_1, i_2 < m, 0 \leq j < n).$$
(12)

Therefore, the trust constraint Eq. (9) in Definition 6-1 and Definition 7 can be expressed as Eq. (12), which will be used to explain the trust constraint in the following part of this paper.

Definition 8. Given the trust matrix Tr, the qualification matrix Q, and the lower limit matrix L_{Tr}, the assignment matrix T can be achieved.

$$\max \left\{ \sigma = \sum_{i=0}^{m-1} \sum_{j=0}^{n-1} Q[i,j] \times T[i,j] \right\}.$$

s.t. (6), (7), (8) and

$$(L_{Tr}[j] - \frac{1}{2} * Tr[i_1, i_2]) * (T[i_1, j] + T[i_2, j]) \leq L_{Tr}[j] \quad (0 \leq i_1, i_2 < m, 0 \leq j < n), \quad (13)$$

where (13) makes any two agents assigned role j meet the trust constraint.

We attain the optimal T matrix, representing the finest solution, by employing the Intlinprog function in MATLAB as the solver, which operates using the branch and bound method to optimize the outcome.

Definition 9. The number of agents in pair on role j that are below the trust threshold is $A^c[j](0 \leq j < n)$. In addition, $A^c[j] = 1$ when $L[j] = 1$.

Definition 10. The total number of agents in pair on role j is $A^a[j](0 \leq j < n)$.

Definition 11. The trust loss rate λ is the rate of agent's qualification loss.

5 Experiment

In this section, simulation experiments are conducted to verify the effectiveness of the proposed method. In Sect. 5.1, we experiment with cases in Sect. 3 and come up with results. In Sect. 5.2, to present the trend of the consumed time, two experiments are carried out. In Sect. 5.3, the correctness and effectiveness of the model are verified by comparing the group performance using GRATA with the group performance using GRA through simulation experiments.

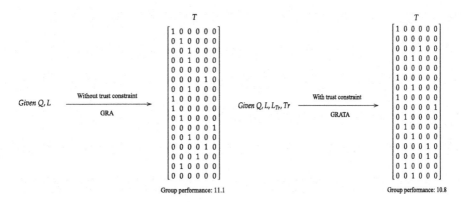

Fig. 2. Solving Real-World Scenarios using GRA.

Fig. 3. Solving Real-World Scenarios using GRATA.

5.1   The Solution to the Real-World

To make the model more convincing, we conduct experiments using the GRATA algorithm based on the case in Sect. 3. Another experiment has been conducted using GRA algorithm for comparison.

Figure 2 is the role assignment matrix by GRA, and Fig. 3 is the role assignment matrix by GRATA. The group performance via GRATA is 10.8, while GRA's is 11.1. The former is calculated to be 97% of the latter, indicating that the GRATA algorithm sacrifices little group performance but brings the role assignment to the trust threshold.

5.2   Performance Experiment

In this part, a trend of increasing consumption time versus problem scale is established through two experiments. In each step, we test for 10 random cases.

We perform time-consuming experiments based on different scales of m and different scales of n respectively. In each case, Q, L, Tr, and L_{Tr} are randomly generated, where

1) $1 \leq L[j] \leq 3$;
2) $0 \leq L_{Tr}[j] \leq 1$.

Figure 4 shows the results of $n = 6$, m varies from 15 to 100 with a step size of 5, and Fig. 5 shows the results of $m = 75$ and n varies from 2 to 15 with a step size of 1.

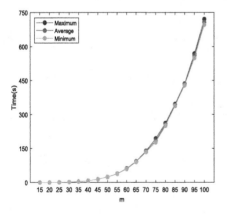

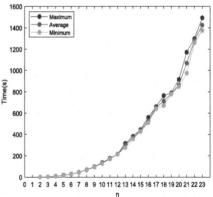

Fig. 4. Time consumption at different m-scales.

Fig. 5. Time consumption at different n-scales.

By analyzing Figs. 4 and 5, The results of the experiment can be summarized as follows:

1) The time consumption of the problem is relevant to m and n, specifically, as m and n increase, the consumed time for obtaining the desired result also increases;

2) The maximum consumption time of experiments based on n at different scales is up to close to 750 s, while the maximum consumption time of experiments based on different scales m is more than 2500 s, which indicates that n has a greater impact on the consumption time of the problem than m, although the scale of the two experiments is not exactly the same;

3) The maximum consumption time, minimum consumption time, and average consumption time are similar, which indicates that the GRATA algorithm is extremely stable.

5.3   Benefits

To further validate the effectiveness of GRATA, two simulation experiments are executed to identify the benefits of GRATA by analyzing the experimental results and drawing corresponding conclusions in comparison with the original GRA model.

Group Performance Comparison of GRA and GRATA. The experiment follows the same configuration as the experiment in Sect. 5.2, where $n = 6$ and m from 15 to 100 at intervals of 5. Figure 6 shows the experimental results, showing the group performance via GRA and the group performance via GRATA, which can be observed that the latter is almost identical to the former, indicating that the threshold of trust is reached with only a small sacrifice of group performance.

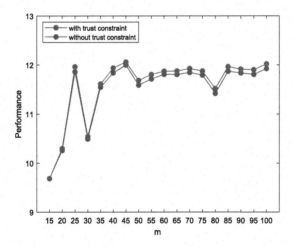

Fig. 6. Group performance with (and without) trust constraint.

Data Analysis of GRA and GRATA. To compare the loss of not considering trust with the benefits of considering that, it is necessary to find the untrusted agents in each role in the assignment plan that without trust constraint. After that, agent qualification can be recalculated values and form Q', where

$$Q' = Q[i,j] * (1 - \lambda * \frac{A^c[j]}{A^a[j]}) \quad (0 \leq i < m, 0 \leq j < n).$$

To demonstrate the different effects of the trust rates, the simulation experiment conducts with λ as the variable, where $m = 50$, $n = 8$, and λ from 10% to 50%, with a step of 10%, the rest of the configuration is the same as the first experiment and is obtained by random values.

For each group, we collect the following data items:

1) σ, the group performance without trust constraints, i.e., GRA;
2) σ_{tr}, the group performance with trust constraints, i.e., GRATA;
3) σ^*, the group performance after recalculation, i.e.,

$$\sigma^* = \sum_{i=0}^{m-1} \sum_{j=0}^{n-1} Q'[i,j] \times T[i,j].$$

Table 5 shows the results of the data analysis. By observing the experiment result, it is evident that considering the trust level between agents obtains benefits. Column σ_{tr}/σ^* reveals group performance considering the trust level between agents doesn't sacrifice much, and column σ/σ^* indicates that without trust constraint has resulted in significant losses in group performance. And when $\lambda > 0.1$, significant benefits are obtained GRATA.

Table 5. The recalculated group performance and comparisons under different λ.

λ	Indicators		
	σ^*	σ_{tr}/σ^*	σ/σ^*
0.05	14.67	0.95	1.03
0.10	14.27	0.98	1.05
0.15	13.89	1.01	1.08
0.20	13.52	1.03	1.11
0.25	13.13	1.06	1.14
0.30	12.67	1.10	1.18
0.35	12.38	1.13	1.21
0.40	12.01	1.16	1.25
0.45	11.63	1.20	1.29
0.50	11.25	1.24	1.34
0.55	10.88	1.29	1.38
0.60	10.50	1.33	1.43
0.65	10.12	1.38	1.48
0.70	9.75	1.44	1.54
0.75	9.37	1.49	1.60
0.80	8.99	1.56	1.67
0.85	8.61	1.63	1.74
0.90	8.23	1.70	1.82
0.95	7.86	1.78	1.91

$*\sigma$ is computed by GRA, its' value is 15.02. σ_{tr} is computed by GRATA, its' value is 13.97. σ^* is the recalculated group performance with the loss of not considering trust between agents.

6   Discussion and Conclusion

This paper focused on addressing the GRA problem with trust between agents, introducing trust as a constraint into GRA. The proposed problem, called GRATA, brings a new perspective to the field of GRA by highlighting the trust relationship between agents and refines the system through augmented reality. The study investigated the impact of trust levels on group performance and proposed a GRATA model to obtain the optimal assignment plan. The correctness and validity of the proposed approach were verified through simulations and experiments.

In this paper, we discuss the basic scenario and application of the GRATA problem. In addition to the findings presented in this paper, there are several promising directions for future research in the field of GRATA:

1) The trust of superiors in juniors and juniors' in superiors have different degrees of influence on the final performance.
2) The GRATA problem in the dynamic scenario, where the trust level and trust threshold may vary over time.

Acknowledgements. This work is supported by the National Nature Science Foundation of China (No. 62106205), Natural Science Foundation of Chongqing (Nos. cstc2021jcyj-msxmX0824 and cstc2021jcyj-msxmX0565), the project of science and technology research program of Chongqing Education Commission of China (Nos. KJQN202100207 and KJZD-K202100203), and the Chongqing Municipal Training Program of Innovation and Entrepreneurship for Undergraduate (Nos. X202310635137 and X202310635236).

References

1. Costa, A.C., Roe, R.A., Taillieu, T.: Trust within teams: the relation with performance effectiveness. Eur. J. Work Organ. Psy. **10**(3), 225–244 (2001)
2. De Jong, B.A., Dirks, K.T., Gillespie, N.: Trust and team performance: a meta-analysis of main effects, moderators, and covariates. J. Appl. Psychol. **101**(8), 1134 (2016)
3. Erdem, F., Ozen, J., Atsan, N.: The relationship between trust and team performance. Work Study **52**(7), 337–340 (2003)
4. Guo, C., Wu, S., Zhu, H., Sheng, Y., Zhang, L.: Adaptive collaboration with a training plan. In: 2022 IEEE 25th International Conference on Computer Supported Cooperative Work in Design (CSCWD), pp. 389–394 (2022)
5. Liu, D., Yuan, Y., Zhu, H., Teng, S., Huang, C.: Balance preferences with performance in group role assignment. IEEE Trans. Cybern. **48**(6), 1800–1813 (2018)
6. Wu, S., Zhu, H., Zeng, Y., Liu, D.: Balance personal wishes with performance via group role assignment. In: 2022 IEEE 25th International Conference on Computer Supported Cooperative Work in Design (CSCWD), pp. 17–22 (2022)
7. Wu, S., Pan, M., Fan, Y., Li, S., Zhang, L.: Group role assignment with a training plan considering the duration in adaptive collaboration. In: 2023 26th International Conference on Computer Supported Cooperative Work in Design (CSCWD), pp. 739–744 (2023)
8. Yu, Z., Yang, R., Liu, X., Zhu, H., Zhang, L.: Multi-group role assignment with constraints in adaptive collaboration. In: 2022 IEEE International Conference on Systems, Man, and Cybernetics (SMC), pp. 748–754 (2022)
9. Zhang, L., Yu, Z., Wu, S., Zhu, H., Sheng, Y.: Adaptive collaboration with training plan considering role correlation. IEEE Trans. Comput. Soc. Syst., 1–13 (2022)
10. Zhang, L., Yu, Z., Zhu, H., Sheng, Y.: Group role assignment with a training plan. In: 2021 IEEE International Conference on Networking, Sensing and Control (ICNSC), vol. 1, pp. 1–6 (2021)
11. Zhu, H.: Avoiding conflicts by group role assignment. IEEE Trans. Syst. Man Cybern. Syst. **46**(4), 535–547 (2016)
12. Zhu, H.: Group multi-role assignment with conflicting roles and agents. IEEE/CAA J. Automatica Sinica **7**(6), 1498–1510 (2020)
13. Zhu, H.: E-cargo and role-based collaboration. In: 2021 IEEE 24th International Conference on Computer Supported Cooperative Work in Design (CSCWD), pp. iii–iii (2021)

14. Zhu, H.: Group Role Assignment (GRA), pp. 141–171 (2022)
15. Zhu, H., Zhou, M.: Role-based collaboration and its kernel mechanisms. IEEE Trans. Syst. Man Cybern. C (Appl. Rev.) **36**(4), 578–589 (2006)
16. Zhu, H., Zhou, M., Alkins, R.: Group role assignment via a Kuhn-Munkres algorithm-based solution. IEEE Trans. Syst. Man Cybern. A Syst. Hum. **42**(3), 739–750 (2011)
17. Zhu, X., Zhou, X., Zhang, M., Zhu, H., He, X.: Group role assignment based on multiple criteria in collaboration systems. In: 2016 IEEE International Conference on Systems, Man, and Cybernetics (SMC), pp. 003175–003180 (2016)

Memetic Algorithm with Exchange Coding for Intelligent Scheduling Optimization

Yiyan Cao, Xin Zhang$^{(\boxtimes)}$, and Pengjiang Qian

Jiangnan University, WuXi 214000, China
zhangxin@jiangnan.edu.cn

Abstract. In response to the limited and fixed scheduling patterns in existing intelligent scheduling technologies, this paper proposes a Memetic algorithm with Exchange Coding (MA-EC) based on flexible and non-uniform work schedules to develop rational scheduling plans that meet the needs of employees and production plans, thereby improving employee satisfaction and enhancing enterprise competitiveness. Firstly, three-dimensional binary coding is used to clearly express population individuals. Secondly, a greedy initialization of population individuals is performed to meet work requirements. Thirdly, the exchange coding method is utilized to update the population and reduce the search space, accelerating the convergence rate of the algorithm. Finally, a local search based on employee preferences is designed to avoid the algorithm from getting trapped in local optima and enhance the global search ability of the algorithm. Experimental results on instances with nine problem scales generated randomly show that compared with competing algorithms, the proposed algorithm has faster convergence speed, higher search efficiency, and can obtain intelligent scheduling plans with higher employee satisfaction.

Keywords: Intelligent scheduling · Memetic algorithm · Exchange coding · Satisfaction

1 Introduction

Intelligent production is an important trend in the development of manufacturing industry. Its core lies in the use of modern information technology means to achieve the intelligence and automation of the production process, so as to improve production efficiency, reduce costs and improve product quality [1–3]. Intelligent production technology has been widely used in manufacturing, service industry, medical industry and other fields, but the intelligent scheduling technology is rarely studied [4–6]. Intelligent scheduling optimization is to improve customer satisfaction and employee satisfaction under the constraints of limited number of employees and complex employee preferences, thus enhancing the competitiveness of the company.

In recent years, more and more researchers have started to use intelligent algorithms to solve scheduling problems, among which the highly applicable and simple particle swarm optimization algorithms are widely used. For example, to solve the nurse scheduling problem, Gao et al. [7] used a traditional particle swarm optimization algorithm to improve nurse satisfaction. After considering soft and hard constraints on the nurse scheduling problem, Chen et al. [8] proposed a particle swarm optimization algorithm combining decision tree method and greedy search algorithm to obtain a better scheduling solution in a short time. To address the university course scheduling problem, Hossain et al. [9] proposed a particle swarm optimization algorithm based on selective search to obtain a reasonable scheduling scheme by designing exchange sequences, selective search and repair mechanisms. To address the aircrew scheduling problem, Zheng et al. [10] proposed an improved discrete particle swarm optimization algorithm with binary coding and XOR-based update rules for updating speed and location to speed up the convergence of the algorithm, considering aircrew cost, workload bias and cooperation bias. The above mentioned literature has effectively solved different scheduling problems using particle swarm optimization algorithms. However, there are problems such as inflexibility of working slots in the problem model, poor adaptability of the proposed algorithm to different constraints and insufficient local search capability. In order to solve the difficulty, this paper designs a scheduling problem model with more complex and variable work slots, and proposes a memetic algorithm with exchange coding(MA-EC) to solve the problem, which is more flexible and incorporates local search strategies. the main novelties and advantages of MA-EC algorithm are summarized as follows.

1) For the three elements of the decision solution within the problem model, a three-dimensional binary encoding scheme is utilized to provide a clearer representation of the population individuals corresponding to the scheduling solutions.
2) In order to satisfy the basic work requirements of the problem model, a greedy initialization of population individuals is performed to enhance the effectiveness of the scheduling process.
3) To address the problem constraints, an exchange encoding approach is employed to update the population, thereby reducing the search space and accelerating the convergence speed of the algorithm.
4) In order to improve the global search capability of the algorithm, a local search algorithm based on employee preferences is designed to prevent the algorithm from getting trapped in local optima.

1.1 Problem Model

The scheduling solution for this problem model consists of three elements: date, time slot, and employee, as shown in Fig. 1. In the model, each date can be divided into multiple variable-length work time slots. It is worth noting that the time slot 1 on date 1 can be different from the time slot 1 on date 2. For example, the data in the third row and fourth column (employees 1 and 2) indicate that employees 1 and 2 are assigned to work during the second time slot on Wednesday to meet the work requirements. Intelligent scheduling optimization aims to find employee scheduling solutions that not only fulfill the work requirements of each time slot but also maximize employee satisfaction, thereby enhancing the competitiveness of the enterprise. The work requirements can be represented as the number of staff assigned to the shift in order to meet customer demands in the current time slot.

	date 1	date 2	date 3	date 4	date 5	date 6	date 7
time slot 1	employee 1,2	employee 3,2	employee 3,2	employee 2,6	employee 3,6	employee 3,2	employee 3,2
time slot 2	employee 2,4	employee 1,3,7	employee 1,2	employee 6,3	employee 6,8	employee 5	employee 1,3
time slot 3	employee 4	employee 8,4	employee 7,2	employee 3,9	employee 3,2	employee 3,9	employee 3,4

Fig. 1. Example of intelligent scheduling solution.

The scheduling solution of the problem model can be represented as whether each employee is on duty during a specific date and time slot, this paper adopts a three dimensional binary encoding. The three dimensions represent the three elements of the scheduling solution, which are date, time slot and employee, respectively. The binary values 0 and 1 indicate whether an employee is on duty. Therefore, the decision variable $x_{i,j,k}$ can be used to represent whether employee k is on duty during the i day and the j time slot. If $x_{i,j,k} = 1$, it indicates that the employee is on duty during that date and time slot; otherwise, it represents that the employee is on break. It can be expressed as:

$$x_{i,j,k} \in \{0,1\}, \forall i \in \{1,2,3,...,X\}, \forall j \in \{1,2,3,...,Y\}, \forall k \in \{1,2,3,...,Z\} \quad (1)$$

Employee preferences can be divided into preferences for working time slots and preferences for rest time slots. In the scheduling problem, let $Pref_{i,j,k} = 1$ represent that employee k prefers to work during time slot j on day i, and $Pref_{i,j,k} = 0$ represent that employee k prefers to have a rest during time slot j on day i. It can be expressed as:

$$Pref_{i,j,k} \in \{0,1\}, \forall i \in \{1,2,3,...,X\}, \forall j \in \{1,2,3,...,Y\}, \forall k \in \{1,2,3,...,Z\} \quad (2)$$

The deviation between actual working time and preferences for employees, denoted as $Dev_{i,j,k}$, can be calculated based on the employee schedule table $x_{i,j,k}$ and the employee preference table $Pref_{i,j,k}$, as follows:

$$Dev_{i,j,k} = Pref_{i,j,k} - x_{i,j,k}, \forall i \in \{1,2,3,...,X\}, \forall j \in \{1,2,3,...,Y\}, \forall k \in \{1,2,3,...,Z\} \quad (3)$$

	Work($x_{i,j,k}$= 1)	Rest($x_{i,j,k}$= 0)
Preferred Work ($Pref_{i,j,k}$= 1)	Category 1 ($Dev_{i,j,k}$= 0)	Category 3 ($Dev_{i,j,k}$= 1)
Preferred Rest ($Pref_{i,j,k}$= 0)	Category 2 ($Dev_{i,j,k}$= -1)	Category 4 ($Dev_{i,j,k}$= 0)

Fig. 2. Employee Work and Preference Classification Chart.

The deviation between actual working time and preference for employees can be classified into four categories, as illustrated in Fig. 2. The four categories are as follows: Category 1) Work time matches preferred work time ($Dev i, j, k = 0$); Category 2) Work time conflicts with preferred rest time ($Dev i, j, k = -1$); Category 3) Rest time conflicts with preferred work time ($Dev i, j, k = 1$); Category 4) Rest time matches preferred rest time ($Dev i, j, k = 0$). Employees in Category 2 represent dissatisfaction.

The objective of this problem model is to maximize the employee satisfaction $Satisf$. It can be calculated as follows:

$$\max Satisf = \frac{\sum_{i=1}^{X}\sum_{j=1}^{Y}\sum_{k=1}^{Z}\left\lceil\frac{1+sign(Dev_{i,j,k})}{2}\right\rceil}{X \times Y \times Z} \times 100\% \qquad (4)$$

This problem model must satisfy the following constraints: each employee can work a maximum of $maxH\_Day$ hours per day, as given by Eq. (5); each employee can work a maximum of $maxH\_Week$ hours per week, as given by Eq. (6); and the workforce allocation must meet the demand, which means that the number of employees assigned to each time slot should equal the predicted staffing requirement, as expressed in Eq. (7). $Dem_{i,j}$ represents the required number of employees for the j time slot on the i day, based on the predicted number of customers.

$$\sum_{j=1}^{Y} x_{i,j,k} \leq maxH\_Day, \forall i \in \{1,2,3,...,X\}, \forall k \in \{1,2,3,...,Z\} \qquad (5)$$

$$\sum_{i=1}^{X}\sum_{j=1}^{Y} x_{i,j,k} \leq maxH\_Week, \forall k \in \{1,2,3,...,Z\} \qquad (6)$$

$$Dem_{i,j} = \sum_{k=1}^{Z} x_{i,j,k}, \forall i \in \{1,2,3,...,X\}, \forall j \in \{1,2,3,...,Y\} \qquad (7)$$

2   Proposed MA-EC Algorithm

The Memetic Algorithm (MA) is an optimization algorithm that combines evolutionary algorithms with local search, providing powerful global and local search capabilities [11]. The basic idea of MA is to achieve the optimization of problem objectives by integrating evolutionary operations and local search operations on individuals. This paper proposes a memetic algorithm with exchange coding (MA-EC) to solve the scheduling problem.

2.1   The General Framework of MA-EC

Algorithm 1. MA-EC

Input: X, Y, Z:the number of dates, time slots and employees; $MaxFEs$:the maximum number of the fitness evaluation; NP:the size of population; $Pref_{i,j,k}$: employee preference table

Output: Global Optimal Individual $\boldsymbol{Gbest}$

1: Initialization $\boldsymbol{pop}$:$\boldsymbol{x}^1$,$\boldsymbol{x}^2$,...,$\boldsymbol{x}^{NP}$ via greedy method;
2: $FEs = 0$;
3: calculate the fitness of population $\boldsymbol{pop}$;
4: Initialize the $\boldsymbol{Pbest}^{ind}$ of each individual;
5: Initialize the $\boldsymbol{Gbest}$ of the population;
6: **while** $FEs < MaxFEs$ **do**
7:     **for all** individual $\boldsymbol{x}^{ind} \in \boldsymbol{pop}$ **do**
8:         update the $\boldsymbol{x}^{ind}$ via the algorithm 2;
9:         calculate the $Satisf_{ind}$ of the $\boldsymbol{x}^{ind}$;
10:        **if** $Satisf_{ind} > Satisf_{Pbest^{ind}}$ **then**
11:            $\boldsymbol{Pbest}^{ind} = \boldsymbol{x}^{ind}$;
12:        **end if**
13:        **if** $Satisf_{Pbest^{ind}} > Satisf_{Gbest}$ **then**
14:            $\boldsymbol{G}_{best} = \boldsymbol{Pbest}^{ind}$;
15:        **end if**
16:        **if** $Satisf_{ind} = Satisf_{Gbest}$ **then**
17:            **if** random()<=0.5 **then**
18:                Use $\boldsymbol{Pref}_{i,j,k}$ to update $\boldsymbol{x}^{ind}$ by local search;
19:            **else**
20:                Random exchange $\boldsymbol{x}^{ind}$ encoding
21:            **end if**
22:        **end if**
23:        $FEs = FEs + 1$;
24:    **end for**
25: **end while**
26: **return** Global Optimal Individual $\boldsymbol{Gbest}$.

The general framework of MA-EC is shown in Algorithm 1. The population $\boldsymbol{pop}$ is initialized using a three-dimensional binary coding method and a greedy method in line 1. The population **pop** consists of NP individuals, where each individual represents a scheduling solution. The fitness of each individual in the population **pop** is computed in line 3. The historical best solution $\boldsymbol{Pbest}^{ind}$ and the global best solution **Gbest** are initialized for each individual in lines 4 and 5. Each individual is updated using the Exchange Coding (EC) algorithm in lines 6–8. After the update, the fitness values of the individuals are calculated, and the historical best solutions $\boldsymbol{Pbest}^{ind}$ and the global best solution **Gbest** are updated for all individuals in lines 9–15. Last, the individual will be updated by localsearch while the fitness value of individual equal the fitness value of **Gbest** in line 16–22. The iteration process continues until the maximum number of iterations $MaxFEs$ is reached. Finally, the global best individual **Gbest** of the population is returned.

2.2 Three-Dimensional Binary Individual Encoding Method and Greedy Initialization

To address the scheduling problem, this paper adopts a three-dimensional binary encoding to clearly represent the three elements of the scheduling model: date, time slot, and employee. Each dimension represents a different element, as shown in Fig. 3.

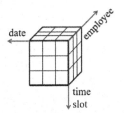

Fig. 3. Example of intelligent scheduling solution.

The population individuals were optimized by changing the position of 0 and 1 in the individual code. In addition, the fulfillment of constraint conditions can be quickly determined by calculating the number of 1 in certain dimensions of the three-dimensional encoding.

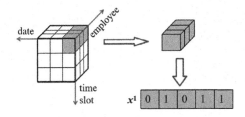

Fig. 4. Data of a dimension in an individual.

This study uses a greedy initialization method to determine the number of 0 and 1 in the employee dimension for each date and time slot, in order to satisfy the employee requirement for each time slot as specified in Eq. (7). As shown in Fig. 4, let's assume that a certain time slot requires 3 employee, and the total number of employees in the company is 5. The 3 number of 1 and 2 number of 0 can be initialized and their positions randomly assigned. For example, {0, 1, 0, 1, 1} indicates that employees 2, 4, and 5 are working in that date's time slot, while employees 1 and 3 are on rest. In the subsequent individual updates, the number of 0 s and 1 s remains unchanged, and only their positions are exchanged. It is worth to be noticed that it is ensured that individuals are searched in the feasible solution space.

2.3   Exchange Coding (EC)

The population is updated by the way of the exchange coding, which is based on the ideas of *Gbest* and *Pbest* in the particle swarm algorithm [12]. *Gbest* and *Pbest* are population awareness and self-awareness, respectively. The differences between individual and **Gbest** and between individual and **Pbest**^{ind} were used to guide the update of the location exchange between individuals. It is worth noting that individuals search in the feasible space and accelerate the convergence of the algorithm. The algorithm2 exchange coding is as follows: the algorithm calculates the position differences between the global best individual **Gbest** and the individual x^{ind}, resulting in **diffG**. Similarly, **diffP** is obtained in lines 1–2. The algorithm merges **diffG** and **diffP** into **diffAll** for subsequent operations in line 3. The algorithm separates the codes representing position 0 (**POS0**) and representing position 1 (**POS1**) from **diffAll** in line 4. If **POS0** and **POS1** are not empty then randomly select one of the positions for the exchange coding operation in lines 5–11.

Algorithm 2. Exchange Coding (EC)

Input: x^{ind}: The individual in the population
Output: x^{ind}: The individual after being exchanged coding
1: **diffG** is composed of the differences between **Gbest** and x^{ind};
2: **diffP** is composed of the differences between **Pbest**^{ind} and x^{ind};
3: **diffAll** is obtained by combining **diffG** and **diffP**;
4: **POS0** and **POS1** are separated from **diffAll**;
5: **if POS0** is not null **then**
6:     $pos0 = $ random(**POS0**);
7: **end if**
8: **if POS1** is not null **then**
9:     $pos1 = $ random(**POS1**);
10: **end if**
11: $x^{ind} = $ Swap($pos0$,$pos1$);
12: **return** x^{ind}.

As shown in Fig. 5, the x^1, *Gbest* and *Pbest*^{ind} are {0, 1, 0, 1, 1}, {1, 0, 1, 0, 1} and {1, 0, 0, 1, 1}, respectively. Comparing *Gbest* and x^1 results in differences at positions 0,1,2,3, where positions 0 and 2 represent 0 and positions 1 and 3 represent 1 can be expressed as 0:{0, 2}, 1:{1, 3}. Similarly, the differences between x^1 and *Pbest*^{ind} are recorded as 0:{0} and 1:{1}.

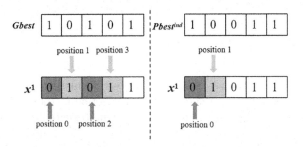

Fig. 5. Example for differences with individual.

After performing the comparison operation, the differences can be merged as follows: 0:{0, 0, 2}, 1:{1, 1, 3}. It is worth noting that the probability of selecting the part of the update process that is different from both *Gbest* and *Pbest*^{ind} is higher, such as the above-mentioned position 0 and position 1 are more likely to be selected to represent 0 and 1, respectively. However, to visualize the process, positions 2 and 3 are assumed to be exchanged to obtain new individual as {0, 1, 1, 0, 1}.

2.4 Local Search (LS)

Upon completion of the exchange coding operation, x^{ind} only moves towards *Gbest*. However, x^{ind} will not be updated, which leads the population into local optimum. Therefore, this paper employs a local search operation based on employee preferences to re-explore the x^{ind}. Similar to the aforementioned exchange coding, the differences between employee preferences and population individuals are calculated to guide the further updates of individuals. In addition, a completely randomized position exchange is used to increase the population diversity so that the algorithm has the ability to jump out of the local optimal solution.

Figure 6.a) is based on the employee preference table is re-updated for x^{ind}. The employee preference table $Pref_{i,j,k}$ guides the position updates of x^{ind} by assigning work to employees with preferred schedules. For example, x^{ind}{1, 0, 1, 0, 1} and $Pref_{i,j,k}${0, 1, 1, 1, 1} indicate that employee 1 has a break in work preference at this time slot, which is used as the basis for position exchanging. Similar to the operation of exchange coding, the difference between x^{ind} and $Pref_{i,j,k}$ is compared, 0:{1, 3},1:{0}. The repetitive exchange coding operation exchanges position 0 representing 1 with position 1 or position 3

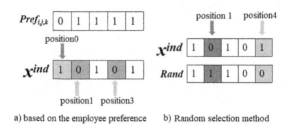

Fig. 6. Two ways of re-exploring x^{ind}.

representing 0. The exchange of the same position in the operation is chosen randomly. Figure 6.*b*) is a completely random selection method, which randomly generates position exchanges to greatly reduce the repeated exchanges between the same positions, in order to increase the diversity of solutions in the population and improve the search ability of the algorithm. For example, $x^{ind}\{1, 0, 1, 0, 1\}$, the random initial velocity is position 1 and position 5 exchange to get $Rand\{1, 1, 1, 0, 0\}$.

3   Experimental Result and Comparisons

3.1   Experimental Setting

The experiment of MA-EC is conducted on nine random instances with different problem scales. Three algorithms are compared, including BPSO [13,16], ImGA [14] and MSFLA [15]. Specifically, The BPSO uses binary encoding for optimization and normalizes all velocities to optimize discrete space constraint problems and possesses strong global search capabilities [13]. The Improved Genetic Algorithm employs optimal preservation strategy, adaptive crossover probability, and mutation probability for optimization design [14]. A new technique Modified Shuffled Frog Leaping algorithm (MSFLA) with GA cross-over is developed and evaluated that combines the benefits of both meme-based Memetic Algorithm (MA) and social behaviour based Particle Swarm Optimization (PSO) [15]. The BPSO algorithm was improved by incorporating a repair operation, enabling control over the number of employee that be referred to as IBPSO. The parameter settings of the comparison algorithms are mostly based on the original references. The MA-EC algorithm affects the parameters of the algorithm only in a

Table 1. Parameter Settings of Comparisons

Algorithm	Parameter Setting
IBPSO	$w/c_1 = [0.9 - 0.4], c_2 = [0.4 - 0.9]$ [13]
ImGA	$NP = 50, CR/MR = adaptive$ [14]
MSFLA	$M = 80, L = 40, G = 50, CR = 0.6$ [15]
MA-EC	$v = random[local(0/1)]$

completely random local search with random initialization of 0 and 1 exchanging positions expressed as $v = \text{random}[\text{local}(0/1)]$. The parameters of compared algorithms are set in Table 1.

For the sake of fairness, the population size is set to 50. Each algorithm is run 30 times independently on each instance and the average fitness value is calculated to represent the final energy consumption of the system obtained by the corresponding algorithm. All algorithms were terminated at a maximum fitness evaluation (FEs) of 10000. Other parameters were set as follows: employee preference table and employee prediction table consisted of survey data, as well as the constrained parameters of daily working hours not exceeding 8 ($maxH\_Day$=8) and weekly working hours not exceeding 40 ($maxH\_Week$=40).

3.2 Comparative Results and Discussions

The results of all algorithms on each instance (Inst.) are shown in Table 2, including the average (Mean) and standard deviation (STD) of satisfaction scores from 30 runs. The last row of the table represents the average value (Avg.) across all instances for each algorithm. Higher values indicate better results in the problem. The data highlighted in bold in the table represents the best result among all algorithms.

Table 2. The Results (Satisfaction Mean(STD)) of All Algorithms

Inst.	X, Y, Z	MA-EC Mean (STD)	IBPSO Mean (STD)	ImGA Mean (STD)	MSFLA Mean (STD)
1	7, 10, 10	**96.57%** **(0.19%)**	89.42% (1.51%)	85.85% (1.45%)	85.71% (1.02%)
2	7, 10, 20	**97.35%** **(0.20%)**	89.50% (1.32%)	85.86% (1.64%)	85.74% (1.42%)
3	7, 10, 30	**98.33%** **(0.16%)**	88.91% (1.71%)	85.79% (1.32%)	85.80% (1.22%)
4	7, 20, 10	**93.87%** **(0.12%)**	85.84% (1.25%)	83.22% (1.23%)	83.31% (1.15%)
5	7, 20, 20	**95.82%** **(0.27%)**	87.14% (1.88%)	82.53% (1.02%)	82.57% (1.06%)
6	7, 20, 30	**96.06%** **(0.24%)**	87.45% (1.36%)	82.54% (1.22%)	82.59% (1.67%)
7	7, 30, 10	**96.12%** **(0.26%)**	87.58% (1.23%)	83.01% (1.17%)	82.58% (1.82%)
8	7, 30, 20	**96.25%** **(0.38%)**	85.84% (1.88%)	82.62% (1.84%)	82.59% (1.94%)
9	7, 30, 30	**96.04%** **(0.45%)**	86.04% (1.98%)	82.57% (1.68%)	82.54% (1.28%)
Avg.		**96.26%**	87.52%	83.77%	83.71%

According to Table 2, the proposed MA-EC algorithm obtains the optimal results in all cases. MA-EC algorithm demonstrates higher stability compared to other algorithms and achieves an improvement of approximately 13%. However, the IBPSO algorithm solely relies on repair operations to constrain the solution space without incorporating problem-specific knowledge, leading to a plateau in performance after a modest improvement of around 4%. The MA-EC is more stable than the comparison algorithm because it combines knowledge of the problem to solve the problem.

It can be seen from the observation in Fig. 7. First, the solution speed of the MA-EC algorithm decreases as the problem size increases, but the performance of the algorithm is still the best. Second, the reason why the proposed MA-EC algorithm is similar to the other compared algorithms in all instances is that for all algorithms a greedy initialization is used, which generates solutions greedily and randomly in a narrow space. In addition, the trends of MA-EC and IBPSO algorithms are similar because both algorithms control the number of zeros and ones in the early stage of the convergence process and thus reduce the solution space. It is important to note that the same results can be achieved even if the updating methods are different. However, the local search method proposed by the MA-EC algorithm in dealing with the local optimum problem can effectively solve this problem and thus enable continuous exploration while IBPSO is stuck in a local optimum solution. Thirdly, the IBPSO algorithm is an optimization of the original algorithm to control the number of employees so that a better

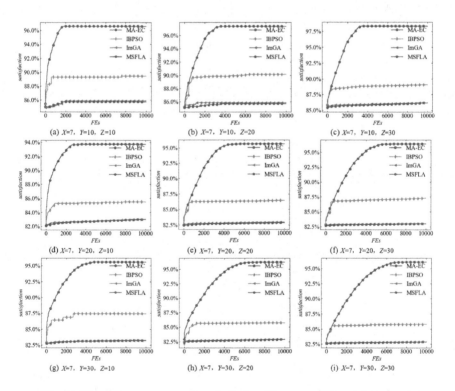

Fig. 7. The convergence graphs of all algorithms on different instances.

solution can be obtained than ImGA and MSFLA by delimiting the solution range. Finally, merely controlling the number does not solve the problem well, so the results are still not better than MA-EC. This result also proves that MA-EC is more competent than other algorithms on the Intelligent Scheduling optimization problem.

3.3 Effectiveness of MA-EC

The effectiveness of MA-EC is only experimented on three different problem scales. MA-EC without greedy initialization is called MA-EC_noGreedy, which still has the function of random initialization. Since the subsequent exchange coding operation is based on greedy initialization, all subsequent operations are invalidated. MA-EC without exchange coding operation called MA-EC_noEC, which still retains the evolutionary approach of global optimization in the MA. MA-EC without local search called MA-EC_noLS, which still has the exchange coding operation, and the convergence of these algorithms are shown in Fig. 8. From the observation in Fig. 8, it can be seen that the proposed MA-EC performs best on three instances, which proves the effectiveness of greedy initialization, EC, and EC-localsearch. Firstly, since without greedy initialization, the MA-EC_noGreedy turns to be the simplest MA and is poor on the problem. Secondly, without EC, the number of 0 and 1 is controlled at the beginning of the MA-EC_noEC, but the advantage is lost during the evolutionary process when the exchange operation is lost, resulting in a large number of individuals that violate the constraints and thus the algorithm is not optimized subsequently. Thirdly, without local search, MA-EC_noLS cannot be optimized after the algorithm falls into a local optimum due to the lack of re-exploration of globally optimal individuals. In addition, the convergence speed of the MA-EC_noLS is better than that of MA-EC because the global search speed of the algorithm is accelerated by eliminating the local search. Therefore, it can be concluded that greedy initialization, EC, and EC-localsearch are significant for the effectiveness of MA-EC.

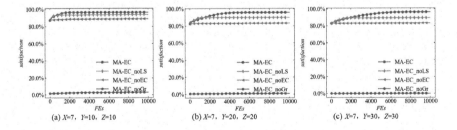

Fig. 8. The results of different versions of MA-EC.

4 Conclusion

In this paper, a MA-EC algorithm is proposed to solve the intelligent scheduling optimization problem. The novelties and advantages of MA-IT algorithm are summarized as follows. Firstly, a three-dimensional binary encoding is used to represent the three elements of the problem model to facilitate the representation of individuals. Secondly, a greedy initialization approach is employed, where the initial population consists of feasible solutions that satisfy the required number of employees. Thirdly, the evolutionary guidelines for the update operation in which the population individuals are exchanged by position codes with the globally optimal individuals and their own historically optimal individuals have accelerated the convergence of the algorithm. Finally, the optimal individual is re-explored by a local search based on employee preferences and a randomized approach, which accelerates the convergence of the algorithm and increases the diversity of solutions, respectively. A set of randomized instances with different scales and three comparison algorithms are used for comparison experiments. The experimental results show that MA-EC outperforms the other comparison algorithms.

References

1. Shi, Z.Q., Cai, R.L., Zhu, X.Q.: Study of business model innovation for intelligent production sharing. China Soft Sci. **6**, 130–139 (2017)
2. Gao, K., Huang, Y., Sadollah, A., Wang, L.: A review of energyefficient scheduling in intelligent production systems. Complex Intell. Syst. **6**, 237–249 (2020)
3. Fu, Y., Hou, Y., Wang, Z., Wu, X., Gao, K., Wang, L.: Distributed scheduling problems in intelligent manufacturing systems. Tsinghua Sci. Technol. **26**(5), 625–645 (2021)
4. Liang, S., Rajora, M., Liu, X., Yue, C., Zou, P., Wang, L.: Intelligent manufacturing systems: a review. Int. J. Mech. Eng. Robot. Res. **7**(3), 324–330 (2018)
5. Cai, X., Geng, S., Wu, D., Cai, J., Chen, J.: A multicloud-modelbased many-objective intelligent algorithm for efficient task scheduling in internet of things. IEEE Internet Things J. **8**(12), 9645–9653 (2020)
6. Lee, D., Seong, N.: Application of artificial intelligence-based technologies in the healthcare industry: opportunities and challenges. Int. J. Environ. Res., 271 (2021)
7. Gao, S., Lin, C.: Particle swarm optimization based nurses' shift scheduling. In: Proceedings of the Institute of Industrial Engineers Asian Conference 2013. Springer Singapore (2013). https://doi.org/10.1007/978-981-4451-98-7_93
8. Chen, P., Zeng, Z.: Developing two heuristic algorithms with metaheuristic algorithms to improve solutions of optimization problems with soft and hard constraints: an application to nurse rostering problems. Appl. Soft Comput. **93**, 106336 (2020)
9. Hossain, S.I., Akhand, M.A.H., Shuvo, M.I.R., Siddique, N., Adeli, H.: Optimization of university course scheduling problem using particle swarm optimization with selective search. Expert Syst. Appl. **127**, 9–24 (2019)
10. Zheng, R.: An improved discrete particle swarm optimization for airline crew rostering problem. In: 2020 IEEE Congress on Evolutionary Computation (CEC). IEEE (2020)

11. Sun, J., Miao, Z., Gong, D., Zeng, X., Li, J., Wang, G.: Interval multiobjective optimization with memetic algorithms. IEEE Trans. Cybern. **50**(8), 3444–3457 (2019)
12. Zhang, X., Du, K.J., Zhan, Z.H., Kwong, S., Gu, T.L., Zhang, J.: Cooperative coevolutionary bare-bones particle swarm optimization with function independent decomposition for large-scale supply chain network design with uncertainties. IEEE Trans. Cybern. **50**(10), 4454–4468 (2020)
13. Lee, J., Lee, H., Nah, W.: Minimizing the number of X/Y capacitors in an autonomous emergency brake system using the BPSO algorithm. IEEE Trans. Power Electron. **37**(2), 1630–1640 (2021)
14. Yang, Y.M., Gao, W.C., Gao, Y.: Mathematical modeling and system design of timetabling problem based on improved GA. In: 2017 13th International Conference on Natural Computation, Fuzzy Systems and Knowledge Discovery (ICNC-FSKD). IEEE (2017)
15. Roy, P.: A new memetic algorithm with GA crossover technique to solve Single Source Shortest Path (SSSP) problem. In: 2014 Annual IEEE India Conference (INDICON). IEEE (2014)
16. Zhou, S., Gao, Y., Wu, Q.P.: UAV cooperative multiple task assignment based on discrete particle swarm optimization. In: 2015 7th International Conference on Intelligent Human-Machine Systems and Cybernetics, vol. 2. IEEE (2015)

A Dimension-Based Elite Learning Particle Swarm Optimizer for Large-Scale Optimization

Shuai Liu[1], Zi-Jia Wang[1(✉)], and Zong-Gan Chen[2]

[1] School of Computer Science and Cyber Engineering, Guangzhou University, Guangzhou 510006, China
zijiawang@gzhu.edu.cn
[2] School of Computer Science, South China Normal University, Guangzhou 510898, China

Abstract. The large-scale optimization problems (LSOPs) have been a hot research in evolutionary computation (EC) community. Although there have been many contributions from researchers in solving LSOPs, the large search space and the numerous local optimal solutions of LSOPs are still two important challenges. In order to alleviate the above challenges, this paper proposes a dimension-based elite learning particle swarm optimizer (DELPSO). In DELPSO, individuals in the population have their unique update probabilities and select specific learning exemplars according to their own properties, making the evolution of the population more efficient. Meanwhile, in the evolutionary process, each individual chooses two different learning exemplars for each dimension, so that each individual can learn from multiple learning exemplars and using the information from multiple individuals to help its own evolution and enhance the diversity. To testify the effectiveness of the proposed algorithm, DELPSO and some large-scale algorithms are experimented on a widely used large-scale benchmark suite IEEE 2013 and the experimental results show that DELPSO outperforms other comparative algorithms in general.

Keywords: large-scale optimization · a dimension-based elite learning particle swarm optimizer (DELPSO) · particle swarm optimization (PSO)

1 Introduction

Large-scale optimization problems (LSOPs) have been a hot research in both of the academic field and real-life applications. Especially in the era of big data, how to improve the accuracy of solutions in LSOPs has become an urgent problem.

This work was supported in part by the National Natural Science Foundations of China (NSFC) under Grants 62106055, in part by the Guangdong Natural Science Foundation under Grants 2022A1515011825, in part by the Guangzhou Science and Technology Planning Project under Grants 2023A04J0388 and 2023A03J0662.

Evolutionary computation (EC) algorithms, including evolutionary algorithm (EA) and swarm intelligence (SI), have achieved promising results in solving optimization problems [22,23]. However, when solving high-dimensional problems, traditional EC algorithms become less effective. The main reason is that high-dimensional problems bring about "the curse of dimensionality" [4,11,27], which is mainly reflected in two aspects. In high-dimensional problems, the scale of the search space rises exponentially, which makes the search space immense and thus makes the search work of EC algorithms become difficulty. At the same time, as the dimensionality rises, the spatial properties change drastically and many local optimal solutions appear, making it easy for EC algorithms to fall into local optimal solutions.

To address the above challenges, researchers have devised many algorithms for LSOPs [7,10]. These algorithms are broadly classified into two categories: 1) EC algorithms based on the cooperative co-evolutionary (CC) framework, referred to as CCECs; 2) non-decomposition EC algorithms.

The main idea of CCECs is to split the original high-dimensional problem into several low-dimensional subproblems, then solve each subproblem separately, and finally integrate the solutions of each subproblem to generate the solution of the original high-dimensional problem. However, interrelated variables affect each other in optimization, and we cannot assume that all variables are uncorrelated with each other in LSOPs. Therefore, a core issue of CCECs is to design decomposition strategies to detect the correlation among variables and divide the correlated variables into the same subproblem while separating the uncorrelated variables into different subproblems.

Although CCECs, including DECC-G [26], MLCC [25] and CCPSO2 [9], have made progress to some degree in solving some types of LSOPs, the effect of CCECs is more sensitive to their decomposition strategies. In addition, the decomposition strategies may not be effective in solving partially separable and fully non-separable problems. At the same time, the detection of correlations among variables usually consumes some additional number of fitness evaluations (FEs) [13,25,26], which results in insufficient evolution of the algorithms.

Unlike CCECs, non-decomposition EC algorithms evolve all variables together, thus avoiding the problems associated with decomposing variables [2,3,18]. In general, researchers improve the effectiveness of the algorithms by designing some novel evolutionary or local search strategies in non-decomposition EC algorithms [2,3,6,18–20]. Through these evolutionary strategies or local search strategies, the exploration and exploitation capabilities of the population are enhanced, which enables the non-decomposition EC algorithms to achieve some promising results in solving LSOPs.

Although the above algorithms have made significant contributions in solving LSOPs, the large search space and the existence of numerous local optimal solutions are still two important challenges. To alleviate the aforementioned challenges, this paper proposes a dimension-based elite learning particle swarm optimizer (DELPSO). The main contributions of this paper are as follows:

1) To improve the convergence of the population, different update probabilities are assigned for each individual. In each generation, the update probabilities

are assigned to individuals based on their fitness ranking. On the one hand, small update probabilities are assigned to superior individuals to increase their chances of directly entering the next generation and thus preserve excellent evolutionary information in the population. On the other hand, large update probabilities are assigned to relatively poor individuals, enabling them to improve themselves as much as possible by learning from exemplars.

2) A learning exemplars selection strategy based on elite sets is proposed. To ensure good diversity, unlike other algorithms where the population shares a single elite set, each individual is assigned a different elite set in this paper. In addition, each individual to be updated selects one highly ranked and one moderately ranked learning exemplar from their unique elite set for learning, balancing the convergence and diversity of the population.

3) To prevent individuals in the population from being excessively attracted and clustered by superior ones, leading to premature convergence. The learning exemplars selection strategy is executed on a dimension-wise level, meaning that each dimension of an individual selects two different learning exemplars for learning. This allows each individual to learn from multiple individuals, thereby avoiding excessive aggregation of the population to some degree and improving the diversity.

By adopting the aforementioned strategy, DELPSO is able to seek promising regions and find high-quality solutions when solving LSOPs. To test the effectiveness of the proposed algorithm, we select some large-scale optimization algorithms as comparisons and conduct experiments on a widely used large-scale test suite, IEEE CEC2013 [8].

The remainder of this paper is organized as follows. In Sect. 2, some large-scale optimization algorithms are introduced, and then in Sect. 3, the details of DELPSO are described. The results of all algorithms on the IEEE CEC2013 test suite are shown to demonstrate the effectiveness of the proposed algorithm in Sect. 4. Finally, the conclusion is given in Sect. 5.

2   Related Work

LSOPs are generally difficult to optimize because of the large search space and the existence of numerous locally optimal solutions. And these challenges seriously affect the efficiency and effectiveness of traditional EC algorithms. Therefore, researchers have designed a series of large-scale optimization algorithms to solve LSOPs. Large-scale optimization algorithms can be broadly classified into two categories, one is CCECs based on the divide-and-conquer method, and the other is non-decomposition EC algorithms.

2.1   CCECs

Initially, the cooperative co-evolutionary (CC) framework is first proposed by Potter et al. [14] and has been used in a variety of classical EC algorithms to solve LSOPs. Bergh and Engelbrecht propose a cooperative co-evolutionary particle swarm optimizer (CCPSO) [1] that decomposes the high-dimensional problem into K subproblems with equal size and then uses PSO [15] to optimize each subproblem. Li and Yao improve CCPSO by proposing CCPSO2 [9], where they design an integer pool to dynamically determine the subproblem size.

In CCECs, the correlation among variables has a significant impact on the effectiveness of the algorithms. Therefore, researchers try to divide interrelated variables into the same subproblem and unrelated variables into different subproblems as much as possible to improve the performance of the algorithms. Yang et al. propose DECC-G [26], which introduces a random grouping-based decomposition strategy into DE. They further propose a multilevel CC framework called MLCC [25], which constructs different decomposers for groups with different sizes. Omidvar et al. propose a method for detecting correlations among variables, called differential grouping (DG) [13], which has improved the performance of solving LSOPs to some degree. However, DG only detects direct correlations among variables and indirect correlations among variables are ignored. To remedy this deficiency, Sun et al. and Mei et al. propose extended DGX (XDG) [16] and global DG (GDG) [12], respectively, so that both direct and indirect correlations among all variables can be detected.

2.2   Non-decomposition EC Algorithms

Different from CCECs, non-decomposition EC algorithms evolve all variables together. To cope with the challenges associated with LSOPs, researchers generally devise some novel evolutionary strategies or local search strategies to enhance the exploration and exploitation abilities of the algorithms. A competitive learning swarm optimizer (CSO) [3] is proposed by Cheng and Jin, and the idea of CSO is to introduce a competitive mechanism into PSO, in which individuals in the population are randomly paired, and the winner in each pair is directly preserved for the next generation, while the loser learns from the winner. At approximately the same time, they propose social learning PSO (SL-PSO) [2], in which each individual is assigned a different update probability and the social information embedded in the population is used to help individuals evolve. Jian and Chen propose SLPSO-ARS [5] based on SL-PSO, which develops a novel adaptive region search (ARS) for further exploitation by the elite individuals in the population. Inspired by CSO, Yang et al. propose a segment-based predominant learning swarm optimizer (SPLSO) [20], which uses a competition mechanism similar to that of CSO to divide all individuals into winner and loser groups. Moreover, SPLSO divides each individual in the loser group into m segments, allowing each segment to randomly select an individual in the winner group as the learning exemplar, enabling segment-based learning. In addition, they propose a level-based learning swarm optimizer (DLLSO) [18], which classifies the population into different levels by individuals' performance, and then improves the exploration and exploitation capabilities of the algorithm by having individuals in the lower levels learn from those in the higher levels. Yang et al. further propose a stochastic dominant learning swarm optimizer (SDLSO) [19]. In SDLSO, they design a stochastic comparison mechanism, which makes each individual update only when it randomly finds two individuals that are not inferior to itself and learns from both of them. Otherwise, the individuals are directly preserved for the next generation. Similar to DLLSO, Wang et al. propose an adaptive granularity learning distributed particle swarm optimizer (AGLDPSO) [17] that also divides the individuals in the population into different groups. In this optimizer, the individuals are randomly assigned to m subpopulations of equal size, and only the worst individual in each subpopulation learns from both the best individual in the current subpopulation and the global best individual, while the other individuals in the subpopulation are directly enter the next generation.

In the above algorithms, researchers have proposed some evolutionary strategies or local search strategies to help the algorithms maintain good convergence and diversity during evolution, so they have good performance in solving LOSPs.

3   Dimension-Based Elite Learning Particle Swarm Optimizer

In LSOPs, it is crucial to maintain good convergence and diversity of the algorithm in order to avoid falling into local optimal solutions and find high-quality solutions in the huge space. Based on this consideration, we propose DELPSO.

In contrast to individual-based evolutionary algorithms, swarm intelligence algorithms not only focus on the evolution of individuals, but also exploit the mutual collaboration among individuals, thus promoting the evolution of the whole population. Different individuals in the population have different properties, and if the exact same rules are used to deal with different individuals, the potential capabilities of each individual may not be realized. Based on the above idea, we design three evolutionary strategies to help the individuals utilize their properties to evolve from different perspectives.

3.1   Update Probability Strategy

The first strategy is that the update probability of each individual is differentiated. Generally, whether an individual is superior or not is judged by its fitness value. The inferior individuals in the population usually have more room for improvement, and updating these individuals can achieve good results, so these individuals should be updated more frequently. On the other hand, the superior individuals in the population, which carry good information, have relatively little room for improvement, updating them may not only make them worse, but also may cause the loss of the excellent information they carried. Therefore, such individuals should be updated more rarely as possible. Inspired by this idea, we set different update probabilities for each individual, as follows:

$$UP = (\frac{i}{NP})^2 \tag{1}$$

where i represents the current ranking of the individual in the population (from better to worse), NP represents the number of individuals in the population. It

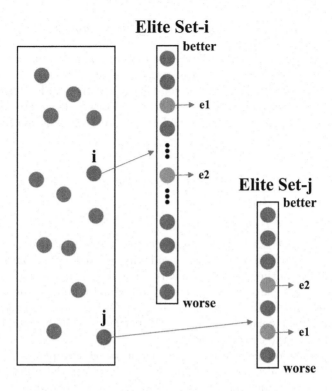

Fig. 1. Schematic diagram of selecting exemplars

is known from (1) that the inferior individuals have large update probabilities. On the contrary, the superior individuals have small update probabilities. Thus, the algorithm will update the inferior individuals as much as possible and update the superior individuals less.

3.2 Learning Exemplars Selection Strategy

The second of the evolutionary strategies is to choose the appropriate learning exemplars for each individual. In many large-scale optimization algorithms, elite individuals have been selected as learning exemplars and have achieved good results [6,21,24]. Drawing on this idea, a learning exemplars selection strategy based on elite individuals is designed in this paper. Unlike the algorithms that share the same elite set with all individuals [6,21,24]. We set up separate elite sets and different learning examples selection rules for each individual. First of all, the elite set is composed of all individuals in the population that are better than the current individual, so that each individual has its own unique elite set. Next, the selection of each individual's learning exemplars is done in their unique elite sets. In the learning exemplars selection, two learning examples are selected, noted as e_1 and e_2. To ensure that the algorithm maintains a balance of convergence and diversity during the evolutionary process, the selection rules for e_1 and e_2 are different.

First, we introduce the selection method of e_1. The individual ranked top_ith in its elite set is selected as e_1, and the reason for selecting the top_ith individual is in order to select an individual that is good enough as the first learning exemplar and thus improve the convergence speed of the algorithm. It is worth noting that top_i is not a fixed value, it varies with different individuals. The specific formulas are as follows:

$$k = random(es) \tag{2}$$

$$top_i = \begin{cases} \lfloor \beta \times k \rfloor & if \ k > \alpha \\ \\ k & otherwise \end{cases} \tag{3}$$

where $\beta=0.1$, $\alpha=0.04 \times NP$, es is the number of individuals in the current individual's elite set, and $random(es)$ is a randomly selected order from the ranking of the individuals in the elite set, which is denoted as k. If k is not greater than the threshold α, it means that the selected individual is good enough to be used as the first learning exemplar e_1. If k is larger, this indicates that the randomly selected individual is relatively worse, so the better individual should be selected as e_1 according to the certain ratio β.

Next, the selection method for the second learning exemplar e_2 is presented. Similar to e_1, e_2 is also selected from the elite set, but the difference is that not only the convergence but also the diversity of the algorithm is taken into account when selecting e_2. The selection idea of e_1 is to select an individual who is good enough to improve the convergence of the algorithm, but this will make the diversity of the algorithm suffer some impact and may cause the algorithm to stagnate prematurely. Therefore, the selection method of e_2 is designed to balance the convergence and diversity of the algorithm as much as possible. In the elite set, the top-ranked individuals generally have better convergent information, while the bottom-ranked individuals may have good diversity information. In order to have a good balance of convergence and diversity, we finally choose the middle-ranked individual, i.e., the $\frac{es}{2}$th-ranked individual, as e_2.

It should be noted that in most cases, the individual's learning exemplar e_1 is better than e_2, as shown by the individual i in Fig. 1. However, for some particularly excellent individuals in the population, the learning exemplar e_2 may be better than e_1, like the individual j shown in Fig. 1. The reason for this design is that for particularly excellent individuals, the elite individuals included in their elite sets are already good enough. Even if we choose an individual with a lower ranking as e_1, it will not affect the convergence of the population and can slightly improve its diversity.

3.3 Dimension-Based Learning Strategy

The third evolutionary strategy is dimension-based learning. In SDLSO [19], the update operation is based on the whole individual. In SPLSO [20], it is based on segments composed of some dimensions in the individual for the update operation. Different from the above two algorithms, the update operation in this paper is dimension-based, i.e., learning exemplars are picked once for each dimension of the individual to be updated, which enables an individual to learn from multiple individuals at the same time and thus can absorb and integrate the information contained in different individuals. The update formulas that are generated by combining all three evolutionary strategies are shown below:

$$v_i^d(t+1) = \omega^d \times v_i^d(t) + r_1^d \times (e_1^d(t) - x_i^d(t)) + \varphi \times r_2^d \times (e_2^d(t) - x_i^d(t)) \quad (4)$$

$$x_i^d(t+1) = x_i^d(t) + v_i^d(t+1) \quad (5)$$

where v_i and x_i represent the velocity and position of the individual, respectively. ω is the inertia weight, which takes the value of a random real number from 0 to 1, t represents the current generation, d represents the current dimension to be updated. r_1 and r_2 are two random numbers uniformly distributed in the range of 0 to 1.

3.4 Dynamic Parameter Adjustment

In (4), φ controls the influence of the second learning exemplar e_2, thus avoiding the individual to move excessively towards the first learning exemplar e_1 during the updating process. In the early stages of the population evolution, individuals should focus more on exploration to find more promising areas. In the later stages of the population evolution, there is a need for rapid convergence, which requires individuals to exploit promising areas vigorously to find a suitable solution. Based on this consideration, we design a dynamic adjustment strategy for φ, which is presented as follows:

$$\varphi = 0.5 - 0.3 * (\frac{NOWFEs - NP}{TOTALFEs - NP}) \quad (6)$$

where $NOWFEs$ is the number of FEs used so far, $TOTALFEs$ is the maximum value of FEs, and NP is the number of individuals in the population. In the early stage of evolution, $NOWFEs$ will be small, making the φ relatively large and close to 0.5. In general, e_2 takes more diversity into account compared to e_1, a large φ is conducive to improving the exploration ability of the population. On the contrary, in the late evolutionary stage, $NOWFEs$ will be large, and the φ will become small and close to 0.2, which can make e_1 play a greater effect and thus improve the exploitation ability of the population.

3.5 Complete Algorithm

In summary, we propose three different evolutionary strategies to improve the convergence and diversity of the algorithm in different aspects, which can help the algorithm achieve good performance in solving LSOPs. The complete pseudo-code of DELPSO is presented in Algorithm 1.

Algorithm 1. DELPSO

Begin

1. $NP = 500; NOWFEs = 0$;

2. Randomly generate NP individuals as the initial population;

3. Evaluate the population;

4. $NOWFEs = NOWFEs + NP$;

5. **While** $NOWFEs \leq TOTALFEs$

6.   Set the influence factor φ of e_2 according to (6);

7.   Sort the individuals according to their fitness and find their elite sets;

8.   **For** $i = NP$ to 1

9.   Calculate the update probability UP of the individual according to (1);

10.   **If** $rand < UP$

11.   **For** $j = 1$ to D

12.   Select learning exemplars e_1 and e_2 from its elite set;

13.   Update the individual according to (4) and (5);

14.   **End For**

15.   Evaluate the individual;

16. $NOWFEs = NOWFEs + 1$;

17.   **End If**

18.   **End For**

19. **End While**

End

In each generation, the influence factor φ is first calculated according to (6), and then all individuals in the population are ranked according to their fitness (from better to worse) and the elite set of each individual is find. Next, for each individual in the population, their update probabilities are calculated to determine which individuals need to be updated. When updating an individual, e_1 and e_2 are first selected from the elite set for each dimension of the individual using the learning exemplars selection strategy, and then it is updated according to (4) and (5). Finally, the program is terminated when the used FEs ($NOWFEs$) exceed the maximum value of the FEs ($TOTALFEs$).

4   Experiments

To verify the effectiveness of the proposed DELPSO, it is tested on a widely used large-scale test suite, IEEE CEC2013. This test suite contains fifteen benchmark functions, namely three fully separable functions $F_1 - F_3$, eight partially separable functions $F_4 - F_{11}$, three overlapping functions $F_{12} - F_{14}$, and one fully non-separable function F_{15}. Five state-of-the-art large-scale optimization algorithms are selected as comparisons to demonstrate the competitiveness of DELPSO. For the sake of fairness, the parameters of all compared algorithms are set as they are recommended in their original papers. In addition, the maximum number of fitness evaluations, i.e., $TOTALFEs$, is set as 3000000. Each algorithm is run 30 times independently, and then the mean and standard deviation of each algorithm are used to measure the performance of the algorithm. To more accurately compare DELPSO with the other comparison algorithms, Wilcoxon's rank-sum test at $\alpha = 0.05$ is used to determine whether DELPSO is significantly better than $(+)$, similar to $(\approx)$, or worse than $(-)$ the comparison algorithms.

4.1 Comparisons with State-of-the-Art Algorithms

To testify the performance of DELPSO, five state-of-the-art large-scale optimization algorithms are selected for comparison, including three non-decomposition EC algorithms, namely SDLSO [19], AGLDPSO [17] and SLPSO-ARS [5]. The remaining two are large-scale optimization algorithms based on the CC framework, namely CCPSO2 [9] and DECC-G [26]. The detailed results of DELPSO and these five compared algorithms are presented in Table 1.

As can be seen from Table 1, DELPSO achieves the best optimization results on seven of the fifteen functions on the IEEE CEC2013 test suite. In contrast, the other comparison algorithms achieved the best optimization results on no more than two functions. DELPSO has a good performance on the fully separable functions $F_1 - F_3$, especially on F_1, achieving the global optimal solution of this function. On the next eight partially separable functions $F_4 - F_{11}$, DELPSO outperforms almost all other comparison algorithms and achieves the best results on F_4, F_7 and F_{11}. DELPSO has an amazing performance on the three overlapping functions $F_{12} - F_{14}$. On these three functions, DELPSO outperforms all other comparison algorithms, and achieves the best results. Moreover, DELPSO outperforms all other algorithms by at least one order of magnitude in the final results. Finally, on the fully non-separable function F_{15}, DELPSO performs second only to AGLDPSO, but the difference between them is very close.

Overall, by analyzing the results of DELPSO and the other five comparison algorithms on the IEEE CEC2013 test suite, DELPSO outperforms the other comparison algorithms. Although DELPSO does not achieve the best results on all fifteen functions, it can be seen that DELPSO stays on the same order of magnitude as the best results on the partially separable functions F_5, F_6, F_8, F_9, F_{10} and the fully non-separable function F_{15} for which DELPSO does not achieve the best results. Only on the fully separable functions F_2 and F_3, DELPSO differs from the best results by less than two orders of magnitude. All this proves its ability to solve LSOPs to some degree.

4.2 Convergence Curves on the IEEE CEC2013 Test Suite

To gain more insight into the evolution process of DELPSO and other comparison algorithms, we plot the convergence curves of these algorithms on the IEEE CEC2013 test suite. For the sake of brevity and convenience, we do not show the convergence curves of all fifteen functions, but select some representative functions in each of the four different groups for display, including F_1 in the fully separable functions, F_7 and F_{11} in the partially separable functions, F_{13} and F_{14} in the overlapping functions, and F_{15} in the fully non-separable function. The specific convergence curves are shown in Fig. 2.

Table 1. Results for 1000 dimensions on the IEEE CEC2013 large-scale benchmark test suite

FUN	DELPSO	SDLSO	AGLDPSO
	Mean±Std	Mean±Std	Mean±Std
F_1	**0.00E+00±0.00E+00**	1.51E-21±1.44E-22(+)	1.46E-21±7.48E-22(+)
F_2	8.59E+02±4.63E+01	6.17E+02±2.55E+01(−)	3.31E+03±2.79E+02(+)
F_3	2.16E+01±6.37E-03	2.17E+01±3.30E-02(+)	2.16E+01±6.19E-03(≈)
F_4	**5.58E+08±9.54E+07**	4.66E+09±8.75E+08(+)	8.91E+08±1.97E+08(+)
F_5	6.16E+05±9.37E+04	**5.68E+05±9.81E+04(−)**	1.10E+06±1.56E+05(+)
F_6	1.06E+06±1.44E+03	1.08E+06±6.08E+03(+)	1.06E+06±9.85E+02(+)
F_7	**1.10E+05±6.22E+04**	2.11E+06±1.10E+06(+)	9.32E+06±9.79E+06(+)
F_8	2.70E+13±1.00E+13	6.79E+13±1.80E+13(+)	**1.41E+13±8.89E+12(−)**
F_9	3.92E+07±5.36E+06	**3.33E+07±4.25E+06(−)**	8.48E+07±1.34E+07(+)
F_{10}	9.40E+07±2.42E+05	9.74E+07±1.30E+06(+)	9.40E+07±2.23E+05(−)
F_{11}	**1.84E+07±7.79E+06**	3.35E+08±1.06E+08(+)	1.30E+08±1.20E+08(+)
F_{12}	**9.40E+02±3.45E+01**	1.05E+03±3.68E+01(+)	1.60E+03±1.26E+02(+)
F_{13}	**7.72E+06±2.50E+06**	6.86E+08±2.15E+08(+)	4.80E+07±4.65E+07(+)
F_{14}	**3.95E+06±3.55E+05**	1.78E+09±1.62E+09(+)	9.87E+07±9.46E+07(+)
F_{15}	3.24E+06±2.36E+05	2.17E+08±2.63E+08(+)	**2.47E+06±2.80E+05(−)**
+(BLPSO is significantly better)		12	11
−(BLPSO is significantly worse)		3	3
≈		0	1
FUN	SLPSO-ARS	CCPSO2	DECC-G
	Mean±Std	Mean±Std	Mean±Std
F_1	6.75E-19±4.73E-20(+)	5.19E+00±1.21E+01(+)	2.41E-12±1.90E-12(+)
F_2	3.96E+03±5.15E+02(+)	**4.37E+00±5.35E+00(−)**	4.95E+01±2.88E+01(−)
F_3	2.03E+01±5.45E-02(−)	**2.00E+01±3.88E-04(−)**	2.01E+01±2.46E-03(−)
F_4	8.59E+09±2.30E+09(+)	7.06E+10±4.31E+10(+)	9.08E+10±3.44E+10(+)
F_5	8.33E+05±1.61E+05(+)	1.50E+07±3.18E+06(+)	8.45E+06±1.58E+06(+)
F_6	**1.03E+06±1.08E+04(−)**	1.05E+06±4.48E+03(−)	1.06E+06±1.66E+03(≈)
F_7	3.54E+06±1.07E+06(+)	3.34E+09±2.20E+09(+)	3.84E+08±2.45E+08(+)
F_8	1.66E+14±3.01E+13(+)	5.14E+15±4.47E+15(+)	2.95E+15±9.28E+14(+)
F_9	4.65E+07±8.18E+06(+)	1.32E+09±3.24E+08(+)	5.82E+08±1.27E+08(+)
F_{10}	**9.24E+07±3.43E+05(−)**	9.36E+07±5.68E+05(−)	9.28E+07±4.39E+05(−)
F_{11}	8.12E+08±1.99E+09(+)	5.01E+11±4.39E+11(+)	5.75E+10±4.10E+10(+)
F_{12}	1.06E+03±9.02E+01(+)	2.00E+03±5.88E+02(+)	3.46E+03±4.50E+02(+)
F_{13}	3.71E+08±2.00E+08(+)	2.71E+10±1.17E+10(+)	5.57E+09±1.98E+09(+)
F_{14}	3.10E+09±3.30E+09(+)	4.47E+11±2.67E+11(+)	7.12E+10±3.52E+10(+)
F_{15}	8.19E+06±7.04E+05(+)	4.05E+11±1.23E+12(+)	6.44E+06±6.34E+06(+)
+	12	11	11
-	3	4	3
≈	0	0	1

As shown in Fig. 2(a), DELPSO converges significantly faster than the other comparison algorithms on the fully separable function F_1 and achieves the optimal result at the end. DELPSO also achieves the best results at the end of the evolution on the partially separable functions F_7 and F_{11}. As shown in Fig. 2(b),

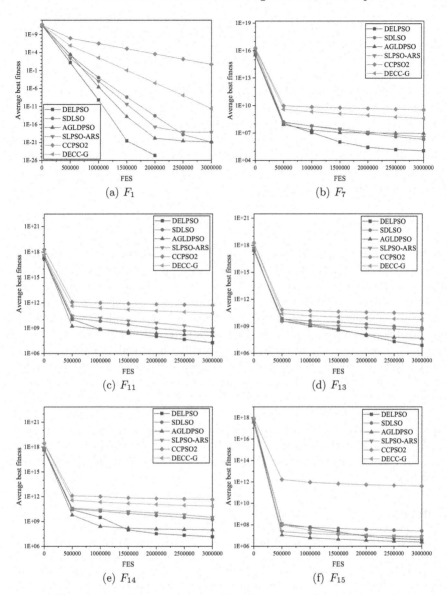

Fig. 2. Convergence curves of DELPSO and other comparison algorithms on six representative functions from IEEE CEC2013.

the convergence speed of DELPSO on F_7 is always the fastest from the beginning to the end of the evolution. As shown in Fig. 2(c), DELPSO outperforms all the other comparison algorithms at the late stage of the evolution, although the convergence performance is slightly inferior to that of AGLDPSO at the early stage of the evolution on F_{11}. Figure 2(d) and Fig. 2(e) show the convergence of the algorithms on the overlap functions F_{13} and F_{14}, respectively. On F_{13}, both

DELPSO and AGLDPSO have good convergence performance, but in the late evolutionary stage, DELPSO obviously outperforms AGLDPSO and achieves the best result. On F_{14}, AGLDPSO has the fastest convergence speed in the early stage of the evolution, but the convergence stagnates in the middle and late stage of the evolution. On the contrary, although the convergence speed of DELPSO in the early stage of the evolution is slightly inferior to AGLDPSO, it keeps converging throughout the evolutionary process and achieves the best result at the end. As shown in Fig. 2(f), on the fully non-separable function F_{15}, although it is AGLDPSO that converges fastest and achieves the best results at the end, DELPSO performs very close to AGLDPSO and is almost identical to AGLDPSO in the final results.

5   Conclusion

In this paper, we design a dimension-based elite learning particle swarm optimizer (DELPSO) for LSOPs. Firstly, we design an update probability strategy that the superior individuals in the population should have a higher probability of being retained, while the inferior individuals in the population should have a higher probability of being updated. Secondly, with the learning exemplars selection strategy, each individual has its unique elite set and chooses the suitable exemplars from the elite set for learning. Finally, the learning of each individual is performed on a dimensional level, which means that each individual can learn from multiple individuals at the same time and make better use of the potential evolutionary information in the population.

To verify the efficiency and effectiveness of the proposed algorithm, we have experimented DELPSO and five state-of-the-art large-scale algorithms on the IEEE CEC2013 test suite, and the results show that DELPSO performs better than the other comparison algorithms, demonstrating the ability of DELPSO to solve LSOPs.

References

1. van den Bergh, F., Engelbrecht, A.: A cooperative approach to particle swarm optimization. IEEE Trans. Evol. Comput. **8**(3), 225–239 (2004). https://doi.org/10.1109/TEVC.2004.826069
2. Cheng, R., Jin, Y.: A social learning particle swarm optimization algorithm for scalable optimization. Inf. Sci. **291**, 43–60 (2015)
3. Cheng, R., Jin, Y.: A competitive swarm optimizer for large scale optimization. IEEE Trans. Cybern. **45**(2), 191–204 (2015). https://doi.org/10.1109/TCYB.2014.2322602
4. Cheng, R., Jin, Y., Olhofer, M., Sendhoff, B.: Test problems for large-scale multiobjective and many-objective optimization. IEEE Trans. Cybern. **47**(12), 4108–4121 (2017). https://doi.org/10.1109/TCYB.2016.2600577
5. Jian, J.R., Chen, Z.G., Zhan, Z.H., Zhang, J.: Region encoding helps evolutionary computation evolve faster: a new solution encoding scheme in particle swarm for large-scale optimization. IEEE Trans. Evol. Comput. **25**(4), 779–793 (2021). https://doi.org/10.1109/TEVC.2021.3065659

6. Lan, R., Zhu, Y., Lu, H., Liu, Z., Luo, X.: A two-phase learning-based swarm optimizer for large-scale optimization. IEEE Trans. Cybern. **51**(12), 6284–6293 (2021). https://doi.org/10.1109/TCYB.2020.2968400
7. LaTorre, A., Muelas, S., Peña, J.M.: A comprehensive comparison of large scale global optimizers. Inf. Sci. **316**, 517–549 (2015)
8. Li, X., Tang, K., Omidvar, M.N., Yang, Z., Qin, K.: Benchmark Functions for the CEC'2013 Special Session and Competition on Large-Scale Global Optimization. Technical report, Evol. Comput. Mach. Learn. Group, RMIT Univ., Melbourne, VIC, Australia (2013)
9. Li, X., Yao, X.: Cooperatively coevolving particle swarms for large scale optimization. IEEE Trans. Evol. Comput. **16**(2), 210–224 (2012). https://doi.org/10.1109/TEVC.2011.2112662
10. Mahdavi, S., Shiri, M.E., Rahnamayan, S.: Metaheuristics in large-scale global continues optimization: a survey. Inf. Sci. **295**, 407–428 (2015)
11. Meerkov, S.M., Ravichandran, M.T.: Combating curse of dimensionality in resilient monitoring systems: conditions for lossless decomposition. IEEE Trans. Cybern. **47**(5), 1263–1272 (2017). https://doi.org/10.1109/TCYB.2016.2543701
12. Mei, Y., Omidvar, M.N., Li, X., Yao, X.: A competitive divide-and-conquer algorithm for unconstrained large-scale black-box optimization. ACM Trans. Math. Softw. **42**(2) (2016). https://doi.org/10.1145/2791291
13. Omidvar, M.N., Li, X., Mei, Y., Yao, X.: Cooperative co-evolution with differential grouping for large scale optimization. IEEE Trans. Evol. Comput. **18**(3), 378–393 (2014). https://doi.org/10.1109/TEVC.2013.2281543
14. Potter, M.A., Jong, K.A.D.: A cooperative coevolutionary approach to function optimization. In: Proceedings of International Conference on Parallel Problem Solving from Nature, pp. 249–257 (1994)
15. Shi, Y., Eberhart, R.: A modified particle swarm optimizer. In: Proceedings of IEEE Congress Evolutionary Computing, pp. 69–73 (1998). https://doi.org/10.1109/ICEC.1998.699146
16. Sun, Y., Kirley, M., Halgamuge, S.K.: Extended differential grouping for large scale global optimization with direct and indirect variable interactions. In: Proceedings of the 2015 Annual Conference on Genetic and Evolutionary Computation, GECCO 2015, pp. 313–320. Association for Computing Machinery, New York (2015). https://doi.org/10.1145/2739480.2754666
17. Wang, Z.J., Zhan, Z.H., Kwong, S., Jin, H., Zhang, J.: Adaptive granularity learning distributed particle swarm optimization for large-scale optimization. IEEE Trans. Cybern. **51**(3), 1175–1188 (2021). https://doi.org/10.1109/TCYB.2020.2977956
18. Yang, Q., Chen, W.N., Deng, J.D., Li, Y., Gu, T., Zhang, J.: A level-based learning swarm optimizer for large-scale optimization. IEEE Trans. Evol. Comput. **22**(4), 578–594 (2018). https://doi.org/10.1109/TEVC.2017.2743016
19. Yang, Q., Chen, W.N., Gu, T., Jin, H., Mao, W., Zhang, J.: An adaptive stochastic dominant learning swarm optimizer for high-dimensional optimization. IEEE Trans. Cybern. **52**(3), 1960–1976 (2022). https://doi.org/10.1109/TCYB.2020.3034427
20. Yang, Q., et al.: Segment-based predominant learning swarm optimizer for large-scale optimization. IEEE Trans. Cybern. **47**(9), 2896–2910 (2017). https://doi.org/10.1109/TCYB.2016.2616170
21. Yang, Q., et al.: A distributed swarm optimizer with adaptive communication for large-scale optimization. IEEE Trans. Cybern. **50**(7), 3393–3408 (2019)

22. Yang, Q., Chen, W.N., Li, Y., Chen, C.P., Xu, X.M., Zhang, J.: Multimodal estimation of distribution algorithms. IEEE Trans. Cybern. **47**(3), 636–650 (2016)
23. Yang, Q., et al.: Adaptive multimodal continuous ant colony optimization. IEEE Trans. Evol. Comput. **21**(2), 191–205 (2016)
24. Yang, Q., et al.: A dimension group-based comprehensive elite learning swarm optimizer for large-scale optimization. Mathematics **10**, 1072 (2022). https://doi.org/10.3390/math10071072
25. Yang, Z., Tang, K., Yao, X.: Multilevel cooperative coevolution for large scale optimization. In: Proceedings of IEEE Congress Evolutionary Computing, pp. 1663–1670 (2008). https://doi.org/10.1109/CEC.2008.4631014
26. Yang, Z., Yao, X., Tang, K.: Large scale evolutionary optimization using cooperative coevolution. Inf. Sci. **178**(15), 2985–2999 (2008)
27. Zhang, Y.F., Chiang, H.D.: A novel consensus-based particle swarm optimization-assisted trust-tech methodology for large-scale global optimization. IEEE Trans. Cybern. **47**(9), 2717–2729 (2017). https://doi.org/10.1109/TCYB.2016.2577587

Compactness and Separateness Driven Fuzzy Clustering Validity Index Called TLW

Yiming Tang[1,2(✉)], Xiang Wang[1], Bing Li[1], Xianghui Hu[1], and Wenjun Xie[1]

[1] Anhui Province Key Laboratory of Affective Computing and Advanced Intelligent Machine,
School of Computer and Information, Hefei University of Technology,
Hefei 230601, Anhui, China
tym608@163.com

[2] Engineering Research Center of Safety Critical Industry Measure and Control Technology,
Ministry of Education, Hefei University of Technology, Hefei 230601, Anhui, China

Abstract. The design of validity index of fuzzy clustering has always been a historical problem in fuzzy clustering field. When the distribution of cluster centers is very close, it is difficult for the existing fuzzy clustering validity indexes to obtain a reasonable cluster number, and the separation mechanism of these indexes is too simple. In order to solve the above problems, we propose a novel fuzzy clustering validity index called TLW (Tang-Li-Wang) index. Firstly, compactness is expressed as the ratio of the membership weighted distance value to the sample variance of the dataset. Secondly, the sum of the maximum distance between cluster centers and the mean distance is used in separateness, and the sample variance of cluster centers is introduced, and the two are multiplied to describe the separateness. Thirdly, on the basis of considering compactness and separateness, the introduction of cluster number can alleviate the phenomenon that the index value may change monotonically with the increase of cluster number. Finally, the classical FCM (Fuzzy C-Mean) algorithm is used to conduct experiments on indexes. Comparative experiments and analyses were carried out on 17 typical datasets and 12 clustering validity indexes. From the experimental results of normal simple datasets and high-dimensional difficult datasets, the proposed index shows some advantages. All in all, these results verify that the proposed TLW index has better accuracy and stronger stability.

Keywords: Fuzzy clustering · clustering validity index · compactness · separateness · fuzzy c-means algorithm

1 Introduction

Clustering is an unsupervised machine learning method [1–4], which has been widely applied and studied in various fields. Cluster verification is an important method to evaluate the quality of clustering [5, 6] and plays a vital role in clustering analysis.

Y. Sun et al. (Eds.): ChineseCSCW 2023, CCIS 2013, pp. 177–190, 2024.
https://doi.org/10.1007/978-981-99-9640-7_13

Clustering validation is a quantitative evaluation of clustering results, which is called clustering validity index (CVI) [7]. The function of CVI is to judge the optimal number of clusters and the optimal partition result. For the results divided by clustering algorithm, we calculate the corresponding index, and analyze the quality of clustering results according to the CVI.

Nowadays, many CVIs [8] have been proposed for various clustering algorithms, but after a lot of research, it is found that there is no effective index for all types of datasets. CVIs mentioned here are mainly internal validity indexes, most of which are based on the fuzzy c-means (FCM) algorithm. For the optimal number of clusters determined by FCM, the Calinski-Harabasz index (CH) [9], partition coefficient (PC) [10], Dunn index (Dunn) [11], standard separation coefficient (NPC) [12], Fuyama-Sugeno index (FSI) [13], Xie-Beni index (XBI) [14], Davis-Bouldin index (DBI) [15], WLI index [16], IMI index [17], and Mittal Saraswat index (SMI) [18] were proposed. The VCVI index [19] was based on the initial center selection method of the density parameter, rather than randomly selecting the initial center. Secondly, Maulik and Bandyopadhyay [20] proposed MB index after comparing the hard clustering algorithm (K-means), the single link algorithm and the simulated annealing algorithm. Some complex CVIs considered the distance between the data objects and the cluster centers, or the distance between the cluster centers, and calculated the average of these distances, such as the CH index and the FSI index, and used them as key components of the CVI formula. However, using these factors as key components leaded to CVIs that only produced better results for specific datasets. There were also some indexes that referred to some combinations of the maximum, median, average and minimum values of the above distances, such as the WLI and IMI indexes. It improved the robustness of the index, but the computation is more complex.

The existing indexes still have problems that cannot be ignored [21]:

1) The basic principle of clustering is that data objects with homogeneous characteristics are grouped into the same cluster, while data objects in different clusters are heterogeneous. This is usually achieved by considering compactness and separateness between clusters. Compactness measures the concentration of data objects within a cluster. The distance between objects with homogeneous features should be relatively small. However, this processing strategy goes wrong when dealing with intensive datasets.
2) The separateness is used to measure the degree of separation between clusters, so that the data with heterogeneous characteristics should be as different as possible. This can be evaluated by calculating the distance between each pair of cluster centers, or by the distance between two heterogeneous objects from two different clusters. The greater the distance, the better the separation effect of clusters. Most of the existing indexes express the degree of separation too simply, leading to inadequate characterization of the dataset. Hence we need a more comprehensive CVI.

Therefore, in this study, a new clustering validity index called the Tang-Li-Wang (TLW) index is proposed based on the above factors.

2 The TLW Index for Fuzzy Clustering

2.1 Compactness Analysis

The TLW index consists of three factors. The first part is the number of clusters K, which can alleviate the phenomenon that the value of the index may change monotonically with the increase of K. In addition, separateness and compactness are described in the other two factors of the index.

The first factor is K, as shown in (1):

$$C_1 = K. \tag{1}$$

In TLW index, we retain the advantages of the WLI index, but also increase the sample variance of the dataset. Therefore, we can have a macro grasp from the compactness of individual clusters to the compactness of the whole dataset. We add new elements to the compactness of TLW index, and also consider the possible drawbacks of traditional indexes in the past. The TLW index reduces the complexity of E_k and effectively reduces the operation time. Finally, the TLW index can get satisfactory results when dealing with complex datasets of different data distributions.

To sum up, we give a new fuzzy compactness expression, as follows:

$$C_2 = \frac{E_k}{E_1}. \tag{2}$$

$$E_k = \sum_{k=1}^{K} \sum_{i=1}^{N} \mu_{ik}^m ||x_i - v_k||^2. \tag{3}$$

Here K is the number of data clustering categories. N is the sum of the samples of the dataset. m is the index of membership matrix and represents the fuzzy weighting index. x_i is a data object in all datasets and its subscript represents the i-th data object. v_k is a cluster center and the subscript represents the k-th cluster center. u_{ik} represents data membership. $\sum_{i=1}^{N} \mu_{ik}^m ||x_i - v_k||^2$ is called the sum of squared errors within the class.

$$E_1 = \frac{\sum_{i=1}^{N} ||x_i - v_0||^2}{N}. \tag{4}$$

$$v_0 = \frac{1}{N} \sum_{i=1}^{N} x_i. \tag{5}$$

2.2 Separateness Analysis

The TLW index uses the maximum distance of cluster centers, the mean distance of cluster centers and the sample variance of cluster centers to represent the separateness. Therefore, the TLW index can better control the separateness of each pair of cluster centers and the separateness of the whole cluster centers, and can achieve almost unbiased evaluation. Adding the mean distance of cluster centers to the separateness can make the index have a better result in evaluating the data cluster with dense cluster centers. The third factor D_k, which measures the maximum degree of separation between the two clusters in all possible cluster pairs, will increase as the value of K increases. This value is the upper bound on the maximum separation between two points in the dataset. This ensures that we do not over-partition data that belongs to a cluster. The experiment also proves that the combination of the minimum distance of cluster centers and the mean distance of cluster centers is worse than the combination of the maximum distance of cluster centers and the mean distance of cluster centers.

Secondly, the index adds the sample variance of the cluster centers. The new separateness measure is obtained as follows:

$$C_3 = (\max_{i \neq j}||v_i - v_j||^2 + \text{mean}_{i \neq j}||v_i - v_j||^2)$$
$$\times \frac{1}{K-1} \sum_{k=1}^{K} ||v_k - \bar{v}||^2. \tag{6}$$

According to the above formula, it can be seen that the third factor of the index considers the maximum distance between cluster centers and the mean distance between cluster centers. It makes TLW index have better results in the evaluation of the dataset with intensive structure, and avoids excessive division of clusters that originally belong to one class.

2.3 Function Expressions

Based on the above, we can get the TLW index, and its formula is as follows:

$$TLW^{(-)} = C_1 \times C_2 \times C_3 \tag{7}$$

The TLW index consists of three factors. The first factor is used to avoid the monotonicity of the index as the number of clusters increases. The second factor is a characterization of compactness and the third factor is the characterization of separateness. The third one restricts and balances each other. Meanwhile, the smaller the index, the better the clustering result.

The evaluation of an CVI is to see whether it can adapt to more kinds of datasets, and try to exclude the influence of clustering algorithms. The TLW index adds the variance of the whole sample dataset and the sample variance of the cluster centers for compactness and separateness, respectively. This increases the grasp of the overall separateness of the data and can better adapt to different structured datasets. At the same time, the TLW index not only considers the compactness and separateness of the whole dataset, but also considers the compactness and separateness of each cluster. The evaluation of the effect of clustering division is more refined.

The following is the calculation process of Table 1, which is the clustering validity index TLW.

Next, we describe the reasons why the TLW index is better than previous indexes. The composition of the index is divided into three factors. The first factor is the number of clusters, which can alleviate the monotonicity of the index caused by the increase of the number of clusters. The second factor is compactness, which consists of the ratio of the weighted distance of cluster membership to the variance of the sample points in the datasets. The advantage of this is that the index can handle datasets with different structures well, and the overall separateness of the dataset can also be included in the consideration of index compactness. The third factor is separateness, which is the sum of the maximum distance of the cluster centers and mean distance of the cluster centers, then multiplied by the sample variance of the cluster centers. The mean distance allows the TLW index to handle intensive datasets and the maximum distance prevents the index from over-partitioning when dealing with datasets that already belong to the same cluster. The sample variance of cluster centers refers to the deviation degree of cluster centers. Therefore, when classifying clusters, the TLW index not only considers the overall separation degree of cluster centers, but also involves the relationship between each pair of cluster centers. Finally, the TLW index not only considers the compactness and separateness of the whole dataset, but also the compactness and separateness of each cluster. All these make the evaluation of the TLW index on the effect of data agglomeration analysis more refined.

Table 1. The calculation process of TLW.

Algorithm 1. The calculation process of TLW. **Input**: Input hyperparameter: Maximum iterations *Iter*, threshold for stopping iteration ε , membership matrix $U = [u_{ij}]$, the minimum number of clusters $K_{\min}$ and the maximum number of clusters $K_{\max}$. **Output**: The index value of TLW under different cluster number.
procedure P1: Set *Iter*, ε and $K_{\max}$; initializes the membership matrix $U = [u_{ij}]$ (satisfy $\sum_{i=1}^{c} u_{ij} = 1$); let the number of initial iterations be 0, $K_{\min} = 2$, $K = K_{\min}$, $m = 2$; P2: Update membership matrix U; P3: Update cluster center V; P4: $k = k + 1$; P5: If $\| V^{(k+1)} - V^{(k)} \| \geq \varepsilon$ and $k < Iter$, return Step2; else, continue; P6: Calculate C_2 using (2); P7: Compute C_3 using (6); P8: Figure out the value of TLW using (7); P9: $K = K + 1$; P10: If $K \leq K_{\max}$, return P2; else, continue; P11: Find the minimum value of TLW(K) and the corresponding number of clusters K (optimization fraction); **end procedure**

3 Experiments and Analysis

We adopted the FCM algorithm for verification. We used Intel(R) Core(TM)i7-8700 CPU @ 3.20 GHz 3.19 GHz, and Windows 10OS. Employed programming software was MATLAB 2018b.

A total of 17 datasets are used in the comparative experiment. Firstly, we run the FCM algorithm with different K values, and get the clustering results on some datasets. Then we calculate the value of the index in each round to find the best value. When the index value obtains the optimal result, the corresponding cluster number is the obtained cluster number. In this experiment, 12 indexes are used for comparative experiment. The specific experimental results and analyses are as follows.

3.1 Datasets and Comparison Indexes

Three types of datasets are used in this experiment, namely the UCI datasets [17], the artificial datasets and the Olivetti face dataset.

Eight UCI datasets are used in the experiment, including six normal datasets and two high-dimensional datasets. Normal UCI datasets include SPECTF-heart, Monk, Hayes-Roth, Seeds, Glass and Zoo. The SPECTF-heart dataset collects diagnostic information from patients' heart scan (SPECT) images, which are divided into two categories: normal and abnormal. The SPECTF-heart dataset contains 267 patients' diagnostic information samples with 44 dimensions, and the number of clusters is 2. The Monk dataset has 432 data samples with a 6-dimensional data dimension, and the number of clusters is 2. The Hayes-Roth dataset has 132 data samples with a 5-dimensional data dimension, and the number of clusters is 3. The Seeds dataset has 210 samples with a 7-dimensional data dimension, and the number of clusters is 3. The Glass dataset has 214 data samples with 9 dimensions, and the number of clusters is 6. The Zoo dataset has 101 data samples with a 16-dimensional data dimension, and the number of clusters is 7. The other two high-dimensional datasets are Libras and Letter. The Libras dataset has 360 data samples with a 90-dimensional data dimension, and the number of clusters is 15. The Letter dataset has 20000 data samples with 16 dimensions, and the number of clusters is 26.

While real datasets can make our conclusions more convincing, real datasets are too homogeneous. In order to avoid this problem, we should select other types of datasets to enhance the strength of experimental persuasion. Eight artificial datasets are used in the experiment, including six normal datasets and two high-dimensional datasets. Normal artificial datasets include Data_60, Data_11, E6, X8D5K, Fc1 and Sn. The Data_60 dataset has 60 data samples with a 2-dimensional data dimension, and the number of clusters is 3. The Data_11 dataset has 150 data samples with a 2-dimensional structure, and the number of clusters is 3. The E6 dataset has 8537 data samples with 2 dimensions, and the number of clusters is 4. The X8D5K dataset has 1000 data samples with a 8-dimensional data dimension, and the number of clusters is 5. The Fc1 dataset has 1035 data samples with 2 dimensions, and the number of clusters is 5. The Sn dataset has 513 data samples with 2 dimensions, and the number of clusters is 5. The other two high-dimensional datasets are Dim_128 and Dim_256. The Dim_128 dataset has 1024 data samples with 128 dimensions, and the number of clusters is 16. The Dim_256 dataset has

1024 data samples with a 256-dimensional data dimension, and the number of clusters is 16.

In addition, 12 indexes are selected for comparative experiment. Some indexes have the best clustering result with maximum values, such as CH, PC, Dunn, NPC and MB. While others have the best clustering result with minimum values, such as FS, XBI, DB, WLI, VCVI, IMI and SMI.

3.2 Experiments

In our experiments, the optimal number of clusters in some datasets is less than 10. We repeat the datasets for 10 rounds, with the number of clusters in each round ranging from 2 to 10. For other datasets, the optimal cluster number is greater than 10. These datasets are run for 30 rounds, with the number of clusters per round ranging from 2 to 30. At the end of each round, each index will have a maximum or minimum value, and then the optimal index value of each round is calculated. In this case, the number of clusters corresponding to the most optimal index values is the number of optimal clusters we seek. We make use of CVI^+ to denote a larger-the-better index, and CVI^- to stand for a smaller-the-better one. The experimental results on the high-dimensional and normal datasets of UCI datasets are shown in Table 2.

Table 2. Results of experiments on the UCI datasets.

	Spectf-heart	Monk	Hayes-Roth	Seeds	Glass	Zoo	Letter	Libras
CH$^+$	$2^3 3^6 4^1$	10^{10}	2^{10}	2^{10}	2^{10}	2^{10}	$2^{18} 3^{11} 9^1$	30^{30}
PC$^+$	2^{10}	2^{10}	2^{10}	2^{10}	2^{10}	2^{10}	2^{30}	2^{30}
Dunn$^+$	2^{10}	2^{10}	2^{10}	2^{10}	2^{10}	$2^2 3^8$	$2^{20} 3^5 4^5$	2^{30}
NPC$^+$	2^{10}	2^{10}	2^{10}	2^{10}	2^{10}	2^{10}	2^{30}	2^{30}
FSI$^-$	10^{10}	2^{10}	10^{10}	3^{10}	4^{10}	10^{10}	30^{30}	30^{30}
XBI$^-$	$2^7 3^3$	$8^2 9^8$	3^{10}	3^{10}	$2^4 6^6$	$2^9 8^1$	$2^6 24^5 26^{19}$	$5^1 14^2 15^9 19^{12} 28^4 30^2$
DB$^-$	$2^4 3^4 4^2$	$2^7 3^3$	2^{10}	2^{10}	2^{10}	4^{10}	$2^{12} 3^9 4^6 5^3$	2^{30}
WLI$^-$	$2^7 3^3$	$8^2 9^8$	4^{10}	3^{10}	$3^8 6^2$	$3^4 7^6$	$2^4 24^2 26^{22} 28^2$	$3^3 15^{18} 27^4 20^2$
VCVI$^-$	$5^2 6^5 8^3$	2^{10}	$3^6 4^4$	3^{10}	$2^4 6^6$	2^{10}	$2^6 7^4 9^5 14^7 18^8$	$7^6 9^4 10^5 11^4 15^7 18^4$
IMI$^-$	$2^5 4^5$	$8^8 9^2$	$2^2 3^7 4^1$	3^{10}	$2^9 6^1$	$2^4 3^6$	$8^5 23^{13} 26^5 30^7$	$4^5 15^{15} 17^5 18^3 20^1 21^1$
MB$^+$	$2^9 9^1$	$2^7 9^3$	$3^9 10^1$	3^{10}	$6^5 10^5$	$7^6 10^4$	$26^{19} 30^{11}$	$15^{21} 29^9$
SMI$^-$	2^{10}	2^{10}	$3^8 9^2$	3^{10}	2^{10}	$2^2 3^8$	$2^{16} 7^7 8^7$	2^{30}
TLW$^-$	2^{10}	2^{10}	$3^9 4^1$	3^{10}	$6^8 7^2$	$6^3 7^7$	$20^{11} 26^{19}$	$11^5 15^{25}$

In Table 2, for the Zoo dataset, the optimal cluster number of CH after 10 rounds is 2, so the optimal cluster number determined by CH is 2. In fact, the result is wrong. The WLI index produced two results after 10 rounds, which were 3 and 7. Among them, 3 appeared 4 times, and 7 appeared 6 times, so the index finally determined that the best cluster number was 7. It can be seen that the WLI index get the correct result. The meanings of other indexes in the table are the same as those described above.

K is taken as the optimal cluster number when the index obtains the most times, as shown in Table 3, in which * indicates that the obtained result is inconsistent with the correct result.

Table 3. The optimal value of the index on the UCI datasets.

	Spectf-heart	Monk	Hayes-Roth	Seeds	Glass	Zoo	Letter	Libras
Best	2	2	3	3	6	7	26	15
CH$^+$	3*	10*	2*	2*	2*	2*	2*	30*
PC$^+$	2	2	2*	2*	2*	2*	2*	2*
Dunn$^+$	2	2	2*	2*	2*	3*	2*	2*
NPC$^+$	2	2	2*	2*	2*	2*	2*	2*
FSI$^-$	10*	2	10*	3	4*	10*	30*	30*
XBI$^-$	2	9*	3*	3	6	2*	26	19*
DB$^-$	2,3*	2	2*	2	2*	4*	2*	2*
WLI$^-$	2	9*	4*	3	3*	7	26	15
VCVI$^-$	5*	2	3	3	6	2*	18*	15
IMI$^-$	2,4*	8*	3	3	2*	3*	23*	15
MB$^+$	2	2	3	3	6,10*	7	26	15
SMI$^-$	2	2	3	3	2*	3*	2*	2*
TLW$^-$	2	2	3	3	6	7	26	15

In the Letter dataset, there are 20000 16-dimensional samples, and the correct number of categories is 26. In Table 2, we can see the results of each index on the Letter dataset. The optimal cluster number of CH obtained for 18 times is 2, and the optimal one for 11 times is 3, and the optimal one for 1 time is 9. The optimal cluster numbers obtained by the PC and NPC after 30 rounds of operation are all 2. The optimal cluster number of Dunn obtained for 20 times is 2, and the optimal one for 5 times is 3, and the optimal one for 5 time is 4. The optimal cluster numbers obtained by FSI after 30 rounds of operation are all 30. The optimal cluster number of XBI obtained for 19 time is 26, and the optimal one for 5 times is 24, and the optimal one for 6 times is 2. The optimal cluster number of DB obtained for 12 times is 2, and the optimal one for 9 times is 3, and the other outcomes are distributed in 4 and 5 classes. The optimal cluster number of WLI obtained for 22 times is 26, and the optimal one for 4 times is 2, and the other outcomes are distributed in 24 and 28 classes. The optimal cluster number of VCVI obtained for 8 times is 18, and the optimal one for 7 times is 14, and the other outcomes are distributed in 2, 7 and 9 classes. The optimal cluster number of IMI obtained for 13 times is 23, and the optimal one for 7 times is 30, and the other outcomes are distributed in 8 and 26 classes. The optimal cluster number of MB obtained for 19 times is 26, and the optimal one for 11 times is 30. The optimal cluster number of SMI obtained for 16 times is 2, and the optimal one for 7 times is 7, and the optimal one for 7 time is 8. The optimal cluster number of TLW index obtained for 19 times is 26, and the optimal one for 11 times is 20. We find that the result of TLW is correct, and the occurrence of correct optimal cluster number is the most frequent and relatively stable. Other indexes are inferior to TLW in terms of occurrence of correct cluster number and stability.

The Best row in the table is the correct number of clusters for the datasets. Taking the Libras dataset as an example, WLI, VCVI, IMI, MB and TLW all obtain correct clustering number. However, CH, PC, Dunn, NPC, FSI, XBI, DB, and SMI do not get clustering number. The changes of the results obtained from K of each index from 2 to 10 on the Libras dataset are shown in Fig. 1. Red marks the optimal number of clusters for each index.

Figure 1 is a line chart of each index function, representing the different index function values corresponding to the change of cluster number K from 2 to 30. When each index in the figure obtains the optimal value, the corresponding number of clusters is not exactly the same. And the convergence direction of each index algorithm is not exactly the same when obtaining the optimal result. In the Fig. 1, we can see that the CH, PC, Dunn, NPC and MB indexes are all the best results when the value of the index reaches the maximum value, while the remaining indexes are the best clustering results when the value of the minimum index. By observing the function value graphs of 13 indexes and their performance on UCI datasets, the newly proposed TLW index has high accuracy and stability.

Table 4 shows the results of the indexes on artificial datasets. We can see the results of each index on the Dim_128 dataset. The optimal cluster number of CH obtained for 25 times is 2, and the optimal one for 3 times is 4, and the optimal one for 2 time is 6. The optimal cluster numbers obtained by the PC, Dunn and NPC indexes after 30 rounds of operation are all 2. The optimal cluster numbers obtained by FSI after 30 rounds of operation are all 30. The optimal cluster number of XBI index obtained for 18 times is 16, and the optimal one for 7 time is 30, and the optimal one for 5 times is 25. The optimal cluster number of DB obtained for 20 times is 2, and the optimal one for 5 time is 4, and the optimal one for 5 times is 7. The optimal cluster number of WLI obtained for 18 times is 16, and the one for 8 time is 15, and the one for 4 times is 24. The optimal cluster number of VCVI obtained for 28 times is 2, and the optimal one for 2 time is 3. The optimal cluster number of IMI obtained for 12 times is 16, and the optimal one for 10 time is 24, and the optimal one for 8 times is 15. The optimal cluster number of MB obtained for 22 times is 16, and the optimal one for 8 time is 9. The optimal one of SMI obtained for 14 times is 6, and the optimal one for 10 time is 2, and the optimal one for 6 times is 8. The optimal one of TLW obtained for 22 times is 16, and the optimal one for 8 time is 13.

We select the number of clusters with the most optimal values as the final result. The performance of all indexes is summarized in Table 5. K^* indicates a case where the evaluation is incorrect.

In Table 5, the FS index gets the correct number of clusters in all normal artificial datasets, but not in high-dimensional artificial datasets. Another index that performed well is the XBI index, which gets correct results in all seven datasets. And our proposed TLW index gets correct results in all datasets. The remaining indexes, such as CH and Dunn, have many errors and even fail to evaluate a dataset correctly.

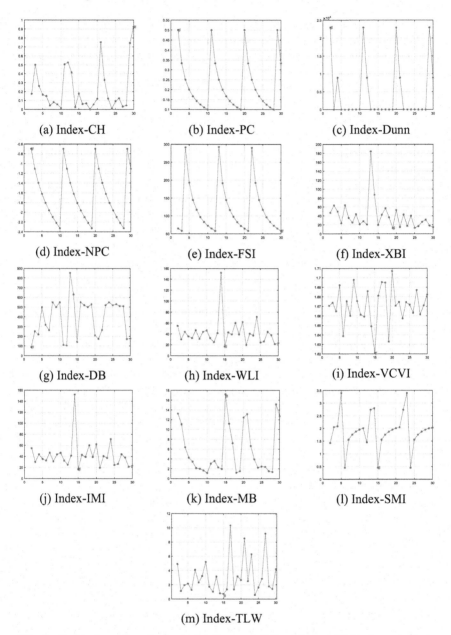

Fig. 1. Comparison of results for each index on the Libras dataset. (Color figure online)

Table 6 shows the clustering results of all indexes on the Olivetti face dataset. The Olivetti face dataset has a total of 40 sets of photos, and each set contains 10 images. These 10 images are from the same person's face information, which is the same person's different expressions and images.

Table 4. Results of experiments on the artificial datasets.

	Data_60	Data_11	E6	Fc1	X8D5K	Sn	Dim_128	Dim_256
CH$^+$	2^{10}	2^{10}	2^{10}	2^{10}	2^{10}	2^{10}	$2^{25}4^36^2$	$2^{24}3^55^1$
PC$^+$	3^{10}	2^{10}	4^{10}	3^{10}	5^{10}	5^{10}	2^{30}	2^{30}
Dunn$^+$	2^{10}	2^{10}	2^{10}	2^{10}	2^{10}	2^{10}	2^{30}	$2^{18}4^56^58^2$
NPC$^+$	3^{10}	2^{10}	4^{10}	3^{10}	5^{10}	5^{10}	2^{30}	2^{30}
FSI$^-$	3^77^3	3^{10}	4^{10}	$4^15^76^2$	5^{10}	5^66^4	30^{30}	30^{30}
XBI$^-$	3^{10}	3^{10}	4^{10}	3^{10}	5^{10}	5^{10}	$16^{18}25^530^7$	$16^{19}25^330^8$
DB$^-$	2^{10}	3^{10}	4^{10}	3^{10}	5^{10}	5^{10}	$2^{20}4^57^5$	$2^{16}4^56^57^29^2$
WLI$^-$	2^{10}	2^{10}	3^44^6	3^{10}	4^25^8	3^{10}	$15^816^{18}24^4$	$9^216^{18}29^530^5$
VCVI$^-$	2^{10}	2^{10}	2^24^8	2^{10}	2^35^7	2^{10}	$2^{28}3^2$	2^{30}
IMI$^-$	2^{10}	3^{10}	2^74^3	$2^23^35^5$	3^25^8	3^65^4	$15^816^{12}24^{10}$	$15^{11}16^629^830^5$
MB$^+$	2^{10}	3^{10}	2^94^1	5^68^4	5^88^2	5^78^3	9^816^{22}	$9^{10}16^{20}$
SMI$^-$	2^{10}	$3^89^110^1$	4^610^4	5^78^3	2^35^7	3^35^7	$2^{10}8^616^{14}$	$2^{14}9^516^{11}$
TLW$^-$	3^{10}	3^{10}	4^{10}	5^89^2	5^{10}	5^{10}	13^816^{22}	$9^712^216^{21}$

Table 5. The optimal value of each index on the artificial datasets.

	Data_60	Data_11	E6	Fc1	X8D5K	Sn	Dim_128	Dim_256
Best	3	3	4	5	5	5	16	16
CH$^+$	2*	2*	2*	2*	2*	2*	2*	2*
PC$^+$	3	2*	4	3*	5	5	2*	2*
Dunn$^+$	2*	2*	2*	2*	2*	2*	2*	2*
NPC$^+$	3	2*	4	3*	5	5	2*	2*
FSI$^-$	3	3	4	5	5	5	30*	30*
XBI$^-$	3	3	4	3*	5	5	16	16
DB$^-$	2*	3	4	3*	5	5	2*	2*
WLI$^-$	2*	2*	4	3*	5	3*	16	16
VCVI$^-$	2*	2*	4	2*	5	2*	2*	2*
IMI$^-$	2*	3	2*	5	5	3*	16	15*
MB$^+$	2*	3	2*	5	5	5	16	16
SMI$^-$	2*	3	4	5	5	5	16	2*
TLW$^-$	3	3	4	5	5	5	16	16

Table 6. Results of experiments on the Olivetti face data set.

	Olivetti face
Best	10
CH^+	30^{30}
PC^+	2^{30}
$Dunn^+$	2^{30}
NPC^+	2^{30}
FSI^-	30^{30}
XBI^-	$10^{20}30^{10}$
DB^-	$2^{13}3^{6}4^{8}12^{3}$
WLI^-	$10^{20}12^{9}27^{1}$
$VCVI^-$	$2^{9}5^{4}10^{17}$
IMI^-	$10^{12}30^{18}$
MB^+	$10^{15}24^{6}30^{9}$
SMI^-	$2^{13}4^{6}10^{11}$
TLW^-	$8^{2}10^{22}12^{6}$

Table 7 provides the number of indexes correctly classified on the three datasets. It can be seen that the number of datasets with correct classification of TLW is the largest. It shows that the TLW index has better stability and correctness.

Table 7. Clustering cases of all CVIs.

	UCI datasets	Artificial datasets	The Olivetti face dataset	Sum total
CH^+	0	0	0	0
PC^+	2	4	0	6
$Dunn^+$	2	0	0	2
NPC^+	2	4	0	6
FSI^-	2	6	0	8
XBI^-	4	7	1	12
DB^-	2	4	0	6
WLI^-	5	4	1	10
$VCVI^-$	5	2	1	8

(*continued*)

Table 7. (*continued*)

	UCI datasets	Artificial datasets	The Olivetti face dataset	Sum total
IMI^-	3	4	1	8
MB^+	7	6	1	14
SMI^-	4	6	1	11
TLW^-	8	8	1	17

4   Summary and Outlook

In this study, we propose a new fuzzy clustering validity index named TLW index. The TLW index takes the good aspects of previous index and improves them. The TLW index have three components. On the basis of separateness and compactness, cluster number K is added to alleviate the problem that the index may change monotonically with the increase of cluster number. The TLW index also improves separateness and compactness. The experiment adopts the classical FCM clustering algorithm, 12 comparative indexes and 17 datasets. The experimental results prove the feasibility and accuracy of the TLW index.

In recent years, granular computing [22, 23] and logical reasoning [24, 25] have highlighted great research value in the field of artificial intelligence. We hope that the proposed TLW index combined with new research theories and directions may bring new breakthroughs.

Acknowledgment. It was subsidized from National Natural Science Foundation of China (62176083, 62176084) and Fundamental Research Funds for Central Universities of China (PA2023GDSK0061).

References

1. Tang, Y.M., Pan, Z.F., Pedrycz, W., Ren, F.J., Song, X.C.: Viewpoint-based kernel fuzzy clustering with weight information granules. IEEE Trans. Emerg. Top. Comput. Intell. 7(2), 342–356 (2023)
2. Tang, Y.M., Ren, F.J., Pedrycz, W.: Fuzzy C-means clustering through SSIM and patch for image segmentation. Appl. Soft Comput. 87, 105928, 1–16 (2020)
3. Tang, Y.M., Li, L., Liu, X.P.: State-of-the-art development of complex systems and their simulation methods. Complex Syst. Model. Simulat. 1(4), 271–290 (2021)
4. Tang, Y.M., Huang, J.J., Pedrycz, W., et al.: A fuzzy cluster validity index induced by triple center relation. IEEE Trans. Cybernet. 53(8), 5024–5036 (2023)
5. Wu, C.H., Ouyang, C.S., Chen, L.W., et al.: A new fuzzy clustering validity index with a median factor for centroid-based clustering. IEEE Trans. Fuzzy Syst. 23(3), 701–718 (2014)
6. Wan, Y.T., Ma, A.L., Zhang, L.P., Zhong, Y.F.: Multiobjective sine cosine algorithm for remote sensing image spatial-spectral clustering. IEEE Trans. Cybernet. 52(10), 11172–11186 (2022)
7. Rathore, P., Ghafoori, Z., Bezdek, J.C., Palaniswami, M., Leckie, C.: Approximating Dunn's cluster validity indices for partitions of big data. IEEE Trans. Cybernet. 49(5), 1629–1641 (2019)

8. Salem, S.A., Nandi, A.K.: Development of assessment criteria for clustering algorithms. Pattern Anal. Appl. **12**(1), 79–98 (2009)
9. Calinski, R.B., Harabasz, J.: A dendrite method for cluster analysis. Commun. Stat. **3**(1), 1–27 (1974)
10. Bezdek, J.C.: Numerical taxonomy with fuzzy sets. J. Math. Biol. **7**(1), 57–71 (1974)
11. Dunn, J.C.: A fuzzy relative of the ISODA TA process and its use in detecting compact well-separated clusters. Cybern. Syst. **3**(3), 32–57 (1973)
12. Roubens, M.: Pattern classification problems and fuzzy sets. Fuzzy Sets Syst. **1**(4), 239–253 (1978)
13. Fukuyama, Y., Sugeno, M.: A new method of choosing the number of cluster for the fuzzy c-means method. In: 5th Fuzzy Systems Symposium Kobe, pp. 247–250 (1989)
14. Xie, X.L., Beni, G.: A validity measure for fuzzy clustering. IEEE Trans. Pattern Anal. Mach. Intell. **13**(8), 841–847 (1991)
15. Davies, D.L., Bouldin, D.W.: A cluster separation measure. IEEE Trans. Pattern Anal. Mach. Intell. **1**(2), 224–227 (1979)
16. Wu, C.H., Ouyang, C.S., Chen, L.W., et al.: A new fuzzy clustering validity index with a median factor for centroid-based clustering. IEEE Trans. Fuzzy Syst. **23**(3), 701–718 (2015)
17. Liu, Y., Jiang, Y., Hou, T., et al.: A new robust fuzzy clustering validity index for imbalanced data sets. Inf. Sci. **547**, 579–591 (2021)
18. Mittal, H., Saraswat, M.: A new fuzzy cluster validity index for hyperellipsoid or hyperspherical shape close clusters with distant centroids. IEEE Trans. Fuzzy Syst. **29**(11), 3249–3258 (2020)
19. Zhu, E., Ma, R.: An effective partitional clustering algorithm based on new clustering validity index. Appl. Soft Comput. **71**, 608–621 (2018)
20. Maulik, U., Bandyopadhyay, S.: Performance evaluation of some clustering algorithms and validity indices. IEEE Trans. Pattern Anal. Mach. Intell. **24**(12), 1650–1654 (2002)
21. Liang, J., Bai, L., Dang, C., et al.: The K-means-type algorithms versus imbalanced data distributions. IEEE Trans. Fuzzy Syst. **20**(4), 728–745 (2012)
22. Tang, Y.M., Ren, F.J.: Fuzzy systems based on universal triple I method and their response functions. Int. J. Inf. Technol. Decis. Mak. **16**(2), 443–471 (2017)
23. Tang, Y.M., Zhang, L., Bao, G.Q., Ren, F.J., Pedrycz, W.: Symmetric implicational algorithm derived from intuitionistic fuzzy entropy. Iranian J. Fuzzy Syst. **19**(4), 27–44 (2022)
24. Tang, Y.M., Pan, Z.H., Hu, X.H., Pedrycz, W., Chen, R.H.: Knowledge-induced multiple kernel fuzzy clustering. IEEE Trans. Pattern Anal. Mach. Intell. (2023). https://doi.org/10.1109/TPAMI.2023.3298629
25. Tang, Y.M., Pedrycz, W.: Oscillation bound estimation of perturbations under Bandler-Kohout subproduct. IEEE Trans. Cybernet. **52**(7), 6269–6282 (2022)

Cross-Lingual Speaker Transfer for Cambodian Based on Feature Disentangler and Time-Frequency Attention Adaptive Normalization

Yuanzhang Yang[1,2], Linqin Wang[1,2], Shengxiang Gao[1,2,3](✉), Zhengtao Yu[1,2,3], and Ling Dong[1,2,3]

[1] Faculty of Information Engineering and Automation, Kunming University of Science and Technology, Kunming 650500, People's Republic of China
gaoshengxiang.yn@foxmail.com
[2] Yunnan Key Laboratory of Artificial Intelligence, Kunming University of Science and Technology, Kunming 650500, People's Republic of China
[3] Yunnan Key Laboratory of Media Convergence, Kunming 650500, People's Republic of China

Abstract. Given the scarcity of a multi-speaker corpus in Cambodian, conventional methods have shown poor performance in Cambodian speaker tranfer. On the other hand, simply using Chinese-English rich resources to expand the training data faces problems in disentangling of linguistic feature and speaker timbre feature. This paper proposes to build a cross-lingual feature disentangler and incorporate Time-Frequency Attention Adaptive Normalization (TFAAN) to effectively transform Cambodian speaker timbre into Chinese-English without altering Cambodian speech content, which enables leveraging speaker timbre features from non-parallel Chinese-English corpus as an augmentation. The experiments show that the synthesized audio achieves a MOS score of 3.81, indicating an effective disentangling and controlled transfer of speaker timbre feature.

Keywords: speaker transfer · cross-lingual non-parallel resource · feature disentangler · Cambodian

1 Introduction

Speaker voice transfer aims to convert the speech of a source speaker into the speech of a target speaker without altering the speech content. This task can be achieved through multiple approaches, such as Text-To-Speech (TTS) and Voice Conversion (VC), both of which aim to separate speaker characteristics from speech and allow arbitrary combinations of timbre and speech content [1]. Synthesizing Cambodian speech with different timbre characteristics plays a crucial role in data augmentation for tasks like speech synthesis and recognition. It also has wide practical applications including personalized intelligent speech customization, dubbing for movies and games, online education, and smart homes.

© The Author(s), under exclusive license to Springer Nature Singapore Pte Ltd. 2024
Y. Sun et al. (Eds.): ChineseCSCW 2023, CCIS 2013, pp. 191–203, 2024.
https://doi.org/10.1007/978-981-99-9640-7_14

However, due to the scarcity of multi-speaker corpus in Cambodian, conventional methods yield poor performance in achieving Cambodian speaker voice conversion. In this paper, we employ the method of voice conversion and leverage Chinese and English rich resources, to transform the speaker timbre characteristics from Cambodian to Chinese and English, thereby achieving speaker transfer in Cambodian.

Cambodian language (formerly known as Khmer) belongs to the Austroasiatic language family, specifically the Mon-Khmer branch. It is primarily based on the Phnom Penh dialect and exhibits complex phonetics. It consists of 33 consonants, 27 vowel symbols, and 12 independent vowels. Consonants are classified into high and low categories, while vowel symbols have different pronunciations depending on the the the accompanying high or low consonants, result in two sets of vowels. Vowels can also be long or short, light or heavy, and can be placed above, below, left, or right of consonants when written. Consonants can form syllables and words independently, and complex consonant clusters are represented by overlapping characters [2]. Due to historical influences, Cambodian pronunciation shares some similarities with Chinese and English [3]. For example, the Cambodian word for "noodles" sounds similar to the Chinese character "媚" and the English word "mel," and the Cambodian word for "duck" sounds similar to the Chinese character "地啊" and the English word "tea." However, due to the differences in language, there are also discrepancies in pronunciation between Cambodian and Chinese or English. Cambodian syllables have faster tonal changes compared to Chinese and English, and in a sentence with the same meaning, Cambodian syllables are more numerous and exhibit richer tonal variations than Chinese and English syllables. The challenge of using Chinese and English to achieve Cambodian speaker voice conversion lies in the difficulty of disentangling speaker timbre characteristics and the potential loss of syllabic information.

In the field of speaker transfer and voice conversion based on Chinese and English, statistical methods such as frequency warping [4] and Gaussian mixture models [5] are commonly used. In recent years, with the rapid development of Deep Learning (DL) techniques, the performance of speaker transfer has significantly improved due to its powerful feature learning and non-linear mapping capabilities [6–9]. The task of voice conversion can be divided into following categories based on the corpus used: 1) Parallel corpus-based methods: Significant research achievements have been made in speaker adaptation and voice conversion using parallel corpora of the source language. The voice conversion task can be treated as a regression problem that maps the source speech to the target speech. Early approaches utilized parallel corpora with time-aligned source and target speech for training [10]. However, collecting such data is extremely challenging in practice, and even with aligned speech data, misaligned segments can affect the quality of transfer. Pre-selection and manual correction are often necessary [11]. 2) Non-parallel corpus-based methods: These methods use non-parallel corpora where the source and target speech content does not match. Inspired by computer vision, CycleGAN-VC was proposed [12], which utilizes non-parallel data and adversarial training with GAN networks. It also incorporate a "cycle" training method to achieve voice conversion. However, the quality of the converted speech is not optimal due to the limited integration of speech features. Subsequent models like CycleGAN-VC2 [13] and CycleGAN-VC3 [14] were proposed to enhance the quality by introducing additional modules and loss functions. However, the addition of new modules in CycleGAN-VC3 increased the model size. MaskCycleGAN-VC [15] introduced a mask mechanism to generate higher-quality converted speech while maintaining the model size. SRD [16] utilized different encoders to encode various speech information such as pitch, tone, timbre, and rhythm, and employed mutual information to further decouple the different parts of speech in a self-supervised manner. These non-parallel corpus based methods have achieved good results in resource-rich languages. However, due to the scarcity of Cambodian language resources, there is no relevant research on voice conversion in Cambodian. It is challenging to obtain sufficient speech data and parallel speech data from different speakers.

In this paper, we explore the similarities and differences in pronunciation between Cambodian and Chinese-English and propose a Cambodian speaker transfer method based on cross-lingual feature disentangler. We leverage the rich resources of Chinese and English to expand the Cambodian multi-speaker dataset. However, we face challenges such as the difficulty of disentangling speaker characteristics and the loss of phonetic information. Therefore, we propose a Cambodian speaker transfer method based on a cross-lingual feature disentangler, using MaskCycleGAN-VC as the baseline model and constructing cross-lingual feature disentangler. Though adversarial learning maximizes the error of the language feature classifier, we aim to effectively disentangle and separate speaker characteristics in Cambodian under the dataset of multi-speaker Chinese and English. Furthermore, due to the richer variations in tone and pitch in Cambodian phonemes, the quality of the converted speech is lower, and there may even be cases of phoneme loss, significantly impacting the fluency and naturalness of the synthesized speech. To address this, we integrate the Time-Frequency Attention Adaptive Normalization (TFAAN) into the generator to prevent information loss in the converted speech and improve the naturalness and fluency of the synthesized speech. The contributions of this paper are as follows:

1. Given the scarcity of multi-speaker Cambodian resources and the unsatisfactory performance of traditional voice conversion methods, we propose a cross-lingual Cambodian voice conversion method. This method leverages abundant Chinese and English corpora to augment Cambodian data and achieve speaker transfer from Cambodian to Chinese-English without altering the linguistic content of Cambodian speech.
2. When using the augmented Chinese and English data, the challenge of disentangling linguistic features and acoustic features arises. We propose a cross-lingual disentangler based on non-parallel corpora, This approach employs adversarial learning to maximize the error of the language feature classifier, effectively disentangling and separating speaker characteristics in Cambodian and Chinese-English multi-speaker datasets. We also integrate TFAAN into the transfer model to mitigate syllables loss in cross-lingual voice conversion, enhancing the naturalness and fluency of synthesized audio.
3. The experimental results demonstrate that the approach in this paper enhances cross-lingual transfer performance for Cambodian speakers, achieving a MOS (Mean Opinion Score) rating of 3.81 for the transformed audio. In comparison to the baseline model, it exhibits superior naturalness and prosody.

2 Methods

2.1 Cross-Linguistic Transfer Methods for Cambodian Speakers

Traditional voice conversion methods based on monolingual non-parallel corpora face challenges in achieving voice conversion for Cambodian language in the current dataset. In this paper, we propose a cross-lingual Cambodian multi-speaker voice conversion method based on MaskCycleGAN-VC. It utilizes a cross-lingual non-parallel corpus and incorporates Language Feature Disentangler and Time-Frequency Attention Normalization module. The overall structure of the model is shown in Fig. 1, consisting of Generator, Discriminator, Language Feature Disentangler, and Time-Frequency Attention Adaptive Normalization module. The specific details are illustrated in Fig. 2. The Generator incorporates TFAAN and the Language Feature Disentangler. Here, x represents Cambodian speech, y represents speech from Chinese or English speakers, y' represents Cambodian speech with the timbre of Chinese or English speakers, and x' represents Cambodian speech after two conversions by:

$$y\prime = G_{X \to Y}(x) \tag{1}$$

$$x\prime = G_{Y \to X}(y\prime) = G_{Y \to X}(G_{X \to Y}(x)) \tag{2}$$

In Formulas (1) and (2), $G_{X \to Y}$ represents the generator for transforming from speaker X to speaker Y, while $G_{Y \to X}$ represents the generator for transforming from speaker Y to speaker X. The identity-consistency loss, adversarial loss, and cycle-consistency loss in Fig. 1 are the losses used in MaskCycleGAN-VC, and the specific details of the loss function can be found in the original paper [15]. During the training stage, all modules are active, and the training is performed using the training scheme X $\to$ Y' $\to$ X' as described in Eq. (3) to ensure the preservation of the input and output speech content. During the inference stage, only the Generator $G_{X \to Y}$ or $G_{Y \to X}$ is used.

$$L_{cyc} = |G_{Y \to X}(G_{X \to Y}(x)) - x| \tag{3}$$

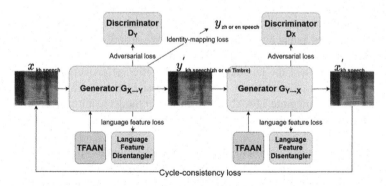

Fig. 1. Cross-Linguistic Transfer Methods for Cambodian Speakers

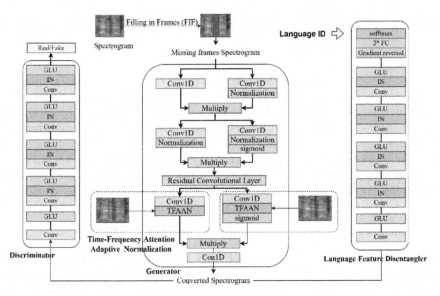

Fig. 2. Model Details

2.2 Language Feature Disentangler Based on Cross-Lingual Non-parallel Corpora

Due to the rapid variation in phonemes and tones in Cambodian speech, as well as the differences between Cambodian and other languages such as Chinese and English, we propose Language Feature Disentangler based on cross-lingual non-parallel corpora. This Disentangler aims to capture the pronunciation differences between different languages, Disentangling the language information of different speakers in cross-lingual voice conversion. By training the Generator with the assistance of the Disentangler, it can explore the hidden voice information between different language varieties, in coordination with the Discriminator, further enhancing the voice conversion capability of the Generator in cross-lingual voice conversion. This approach solves the challenge of disentangling language and acoustic features in the context of cross-lingual non-parallel corpora.

The Disentangler is inspired by domain adversarial learning [17, 18] and utilizes domain adversarial training [19] (Domain Adversarial Training, DAT). It constructs a Language Feature Disentangler and employs gradient reversal during training to maximize the classification error of the language feature classifier. By using the adversarial speaker Language Feature Disentangler, it achieves the disentangling of voice characteristics in cross-lingual voice conversion. The Disentangler consists of five convolutional layers, two fully connected layers, a softmax layer, and a gradient reversal layer. It takes the mel-spectrogram from the Generator output as input. To ensure training stability, gradient clipping is applied to minimize the cross-entropy loss for language disentanglement. The structure details are illustrated in Fig. 2. The capability of the Generator to transform cross-lingual voice characteristics is trained using the language feature loss:

$$\mathcal{L}_{\text{lan}} = CE(C_{lan}(G_{X \to Y}(x)), x_{lan}) + CE(C_{lan}(G_{Y \to X}(y\prime)), y_{lan}) \qquad (4)$$

In the Eq. (4), C_{lan} represents the adversarial speaker Language Feature Disentangler, G represents the Generator, CE represents the cross-entropy loss, x represents the source speech of input, and $y\prime$ represents the speech generated by the Generator $G_{X \to Y}$. x_{lan} and y_{lan} represent the language of the speakers, where in this paper, three languages are used, thus $x_{\text{lan}}, y_{\text{lan}} \in \{0, 1, 2\}$. The Language Feature Disentangler is first pre-trained using 300 Cambodian monolingual speaker data and a total of 3000 Chinese and 3000 English speech data from 10 speakers in the ESD dataset. During the training of the entire model, the learning rate of the Language Feature Disentangler is reduced for fine-tuning.

2.3   Time-Frequency Attention Adaptive Normalization (TFAAN)

During voice conversion, the Generator takes the input mel-spectrogram and performs downsampling feature extraction (mapping high-dimensional features to low-dimensional ones) and then upsampling (mapping low-dimensional features back to high-dimensional ones) to restore the features. However, this model's downsampling feature extraction process can lead to the loss of mel-spectrogram information. The loss of spectrogram information results in the loss of speech content, causing certain phonemes to be incorrectly pronounced. In the context of cross-lingual voice conversion tasks, this information loss becomes more pronounced due to the differences between languages.

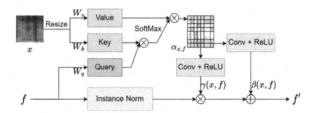

Fig. 3. TFAAN

Based on the aforementioned findings, this paper proposes the application of TFAAN to the upsampling module of the Generator, as illustrated in Fig. 3. The original input mel-spectrogram x is resized and multiplied by W_k and W_v to obtain the Key and Value, respectively. The downsampled feature f is multiplied by W_q to obtain the Query, which represents the correlation features $\alpha_{x,f}$ capturing the relevance between x and f, including speech content, voice characteristics, and language information. This attention module dynamically adjusts x by increasing the emphasis on useful features (such as speech content) while reducing the weight of irrelevant features (such as timbre characteristics), thus focusing on meaningful parts of the original input x and improving the flow of information within the network.

The correlation features $\alpha_{x,f}$ are passed through two convolutional layers to adjust the weights and biases of the feature f. For the downsampled feature f,, TFAAN regularizes it in a manner similar to Instance Normalization (IN) [20]. Then, the feature is modulated using the weight coefficient $\gamma(x,f)$ and the bias $\beta(x,f)$, which are calculated using a CNN from the correlation features $\alpha_{x,f}$. The computation of TFAAN is as follows:

$$f\prime = \gamma(x,f)\frac{f - \mu(f)}{\sigma(f)} + \beta(x,f) \tag{5}$$

$$\gamma(x,f) = Relu(Conv(\alpha_{x,f})), \beta(x,f) = Relu(Conv(\alpha_{x,f})) \tag{6}$$

$$\alpha_{x,f} = softmax\left(\frac{Q^{\top}K}{\sqrt{D_k}}\right)V^{\top}, Q = W_q f, K = W_k x, V = W_v x \tag{7}$$

In the equations, x represents the input source mel-spectrogram, f represents the downsampled feature, $\alpha_{x,f}$ represents the correlation feature vector between f and the original speech x, f' represents the feature output by the TFAAN module, $\mu(f)$ and $\sigma(f)$ represent the mean and variance of the f feature, respectively. $\gamma(x)$ and $\beta(x)$ are the weight coefficient and bias obtained through convolutional calculations from $\alpha_{x,f}$. W_* represents the learnable parameters.

3 Experiment

3.1 Dataset

This paper utilizes a total of 320 recordings of Cambodian female speech. The training set consists of 300 recordings, while the validation and test sets contain 20 recordings. The total duration of the recordings is approximately 1 h, all of which were recorded by a Cambodian female speaker (KH as speak id). For other languages, publicly available datasets were used, including BZNSYP (Chinese female speech, 000 as speak id) and ESD dataset with speakers 010 (Chinese male speech), 014 (English male speech), 015 (English female speech), and 016 (English female speech). Each speaker contributed 300 recordings for training. The goal of the training process is to transform timbre of one Cambodian speaker (Speaker A) to that of another Chinese or English speaker (Speaker B). During training, timbre, and speech content of speakers A and B are completely different.

3.2 Experimental Setup

In this study, Cambodian female speech is used as the source and transformed into Chinese and English speech of different speakers. The performance of the proposed method is compared with baseline models [15], CycleGAN-VC2 [13], CycleGAN-VC3 [14], and SRD [16]. To evaluate the effectiveness of the introduced modules, ablation experiments are also conducted. The quality of the generated speech is evaluated using Mean Opinion Score (MOS) ratings, which provide subjective evaluations by human listeners. Objective evaluations are performed using Mel Cepstral Distortion (MCD)

[10] and Root Mean Square Error (RMSE) of the fundamental frequency (F0). To ensure experimental fairness, all speech data was sampled at a rate of 22.05 kHz. The optimizer employed was Adam, with a batch size set to 1. The learning rate gradually decreased in accordance with the training steps. All experiments were iterated 150,000 steps on an NVIDIA GeForce RTX 3090 to maintain consistency.

3.3   Experimental and Results Analysis

3.3.1   MOS Scores Compared to Other Models

In order to validate the effectiveness of the proposed method, it is compared to five other models, and experiments are conducted with different gender speakers and cross-lingual speaker. The compared models are:

VC2: A voice conversion model based on GAN networks, using mel-cepstrum as input and output.
VC3: This model uses mel-spectrogram as input and output instead of mel-cepstrum. It is an extension of VC2 with the addition of Time-Frequency Normalization module.
MaskVC: An extension of VC2 with a mask mechanism.
SRD: A voice conversion model that utilizes mutual information.
Proposed method: Based on VC, it incorporates speaker Language Feature Disentangler and includes TFAAN.

Table 1. MOS scores for naturalness and similarity of several models

Data	Methods	Naturalness	Similarity	Data	Methods	Naturalness	Similarity
$kh - zh_{(000,fe)}$	VC2	2.32 ± 0.12	2.20 ± 0.22	$en_{(015,fe)} - en_{(014,ma)}$	VC2	2.29 ± 0.20	2.25 ± 0.20
	VC3	3.48 ± 0.15	3.10 ± 0.12		VC3	3.62 ± 0.12	3.32 ± 0.12
	MaskVC	3.51 ± 0.18	3.54 ± 0.16		MaskVC	3.79 ± 0.12	**3.66 ± 0.13**
	SRD	3.49 ± 0.13	3.62 ± 0.13		SRD	3.72 ± 0.13	3.62 ± 0.13
	Our	**3.81 ± 0.12**	**3.68 ± 0.20**		Our	**3.82 ± 0.10**	3.44 ± 0.20
$kh - zh_{(010,ma)}$	VC2	2.05 ± 0.25	2.3 ± 0.20	$en_{(015,fe)} - en_{(016,fe)}$	VC2	2.9 ± 0.19	2.6 ± 0.18
	VC3	3.45 ± 0.18	3.28 ± 0.12		VC3	**3.83 ± 0.12**	3.45 ± 0.17
	MaskVC	3.46 ± 0.12	3.52 ± 0.12		MaskVC	3.80 ± 0.16	3.50 ± 0.12
	SRD	3.61 ± 0.12	3.55 ± 0.13		SRD	3.79 ± 0.13	**3.59 ± 0.20**
	Our	**3.63 ± 0.12**	**3.65 ± 0.20**		Our	3.82 ± 0.10	3.41 ± 0.20
$kh - zh_{(015,fe)}$	VC2	2.52 ± 0.15	2.9 ± 0.15	$zh_{(000,fe)} - en_{(015,fe)}$	VC2	2.48 ± 0.12	2.61 ± 0.16
	VC3	3.48 ± 0.12	3.35 ± 0.18		VC3	3.13 ± 0.15	3.25 ± 0.12
	MaskVC	3.69 ± 0.12	3.32 ± 0.12		MaskVC	3.48 ± 0.12	**3.68 ± 0.15**
	SRD	3.62 ± 0.13	**3.55 ± 0.15**		SRD	3.58 ± 0.13	3.66 ± 0.13
	Our	**3.74 ± 0.12**	3.50 ± 0.15		Our	**3.76 ± 0.10**	3.66 ± 0.20

The speech naturalness and speaker similarity of the converted results from the above five models are evaluated using MOS scores. The experimental results are presented in Table 1. In this paper, "kh" represents Cambodian (Khmer), "zh" represents Chinese, "en" represents English, the number within the parentheses on the right side of each language indicates the speaker's identification, "fe" represents females, and "ma" represents males. Among them, Khmer has only one female speaker.

In the experiment of converting Khmer (female) to Chinese (female 000) using a voice conversion model that incorporates Language Feature Disentangler based on cross-lingual non-parallel corpora and TFAAN, the naturalness and similarity scores reached 3.81 and 3.68, respectively. Compared to the baseline model, there was an improvement of 0.30 and 0.14 in the scores, respectively. Furthermore, based on the evaluation scores of the other two sets of Cambodian cross-lingual voice conversion experiments, the proposed method outperformed the baseline model. Other models had limited performance in cross-lingual voice conversion tasks due to the differences in pronunciation between different languages, which resulted in poorer performance. This fully demonstrates that incorporating Language Feature Disentangler and TFAAN in the model can effectively enhance the ability of cross-lingual voice conversion and improve the quality of synthesized audio.

Additionally, by observing the data from the two sets of same-language conversion experiments, namely English (female 015) to English (male 014) and English (female 015) to English (female 016), it can be observed that the proposed model structure performs similarly to existing models in terms of naturalness and similarity. This is because the Language Feature Disentangler becomes ineffective when training on the same language, but TFAAN still plays a role, allowing the model to maintain a good performance. In terms of cross-gender voice conversion, the experiments involving Khmer (female) to Chinese (male 010) and English (female 015) to English (male 014) showed relatively lower naturalness and similarity scores. This is due to the difference in vocal characteristics between male and female speakers. Furthermore, in cross-lingual voice conversion experiments conducted with Chinese and English, the proposed method achieved higher naturalness and similarity scores compared to existing models, demonstrating its superior performance in cross-lingual voice conversion.

3.3.2   Comparison of Mel Cepstral Distortion (MCD) and Root Mean Square Error (RMSE) Among the Models

Continuing from the previous section, this study objectively evaluates the experimental results by calculating the MCD and RMSE between the synthesized and real speech for the five models mentioned earlier. The RMSE measures the deviation between observed values and true values, calculated using fundamental frequency (F0). The source speech is used as the ground truth, converted to the target speaker using $G_{X \to Y}$, and then converted back to the source speaker using $G_{Y \to X}$ to obtain the predicted values. The MCD and RMSE scores are then calculated. The experimental results are shown in Table 2. The variables described by the term "data" in the table are consistent with Table 1.

In the experiment of Khmer to Chinese (Female 000) conversion, after two conversions, the proposed method achieved an MCD score of 5.85 and an RMSE score

Table 2. MCD and RMSE scores of several models

Data	Methods	MCD	RMSE	Data	Methods	MCD	RMSE
$kh - zh_{(000,fe)}$	VC2	8.19	43.30	$en_{(015,fe)} -$ $en_{(014,ma)}$	VC2	7.78	52.08
	VC3	5.90	30.90		VC3	4.61	43.09
	MaskVC	6.36	37.20		MaskVC	**4.53**	48.93
	SRD	-	-		SRD	5.02	44.06
	Our	**5.85**	**29.88**		Our	4.60	**42.22**
$kh - zh_{(010,ma)}$	VC2	8.42	45.52	$en_{(015,fe)} -$ $en_{(016,fe)}$	VC2	6.45	57.38
	VC3	6.04	32.78		VC3	5.32	42.69
	MaskVC	6.53	38.84		MaskVC	5.59	49.61
	SRD	-	-		SRD	5.52	**38.06**
	Our	**5.80**	**32.04**		Our	**5.38**	42.66
$kh - zh_{(015,fe)}$	VC2	8.41	46.44	$zh_{(000,fe)} -$ $en_{(015,fe)}$	VC2	8.79	55.06
	VC3	6.00	33.69		VC3	6.77	40.41
	MaskVC	6.53	38.64		MaskVC	6.99	50.33
	SRD	–	–		SRD	–	–
	Our	**5.91**	**31.20**		Our	**6.60**	**39.66**

of 29.88. Compared to the baseline model with an MCD score of 6.36 and an RMSE score of 37.20, the proposed method shows a significant improvement in performance. Furthermore, in the experiments of Khmer to Chinese (Male 010), Khmer to English (Female 015), and Chinese (Female) to English (Female 015) cross-language conversions, the proposed method exhibits lower MCD and RMSE scores compared to other models. This indicates that the proposed method further reduces the loss of speech information after two conversions, thus validating its effectiveness. For conversions between speakers of the same language, the proposed method still achieves good results after two conversions compared to other models. This is because the TFAAN module in the Generator incorporates the original audio information during the upsampling stage, thereby preserving the original speech information and minimizing information loss during the conversion process.

3.3.3 Ablation Studies

In this study, we conducted various experiments to explore the optimal method of incorporating different modules to improve the quality of cross-lingual voice conversion. The specific experimental setups are presented in Table 3.

To verify the effectiveness of the proposed Language Feature Disentangler and TFAAN modules based on cross-lingual non-parallel corpora, we conducted ablation experiments as shown in Table 3. The experiments were performed using Cambodian female speech and Chinese female speech. When TFAAN was added to the baseline

Table 3. Ablation Studies $kh - zh_{(000,fe)}$

Methods	Naturalness	Similarity	MCD	RMSE
MaskVC	3.51 ± 0.18	3.54 ± 0.16	6.36	37.20
MaskVC + TFAAN	3.78 ± 0.18	3.56 ± 0.16	5.90	30.90
MaskVC + Disentangler	3.62 ± 0.18	$\mathbf{3.66 \pm 0.16}$	5.99	34.20
MaskVC + TFAAN + Disentangler	$\mathbf{3.81 \pm 0.12}$	3.62 ± 0.20	**5.85**	**29.88**

model, the naturalness score improved by 0.27, from 3.51 to 3.78, and the similarity score improved by 0.02, from 3.54 to 3.56. When the Disentangler was added, there was an improvement of 0.11 in naturalness and 0.12 in similarity. When both modules were added, the naturalness score improved by 0.30 and the similarity score improved by 0.08. Both modules contributed to the improvement of MCD and RMSE scores.

These results indicate that the TFAAN module helps increase the naturalness of the synthesized speech, while the increase in speaker similarity is not significant. This is because the TFAAN module incorporates some characteristics of the source speaker during the upsampling stage in the Generator, preventing the loss of speech content but not completely eliminating the influence of the source speaker. On the other hand, the Disentangler module assists in cross-lingual speaker voice conversion by better separating the language and acoustic features. When both modules are present, the overall performance of the model is significantly improved, providing further evidence for the effectiveness of the proposed method.

3.3.4 Visualization of Spectrograms and Fundamental Frequency Conversion Results

The visualizations of the conversion results are shown in Fig. 4. The red curves in the figures represent the fundamental frequency (F0), and the images behind the curves represent the spectrograms. In samples (a) and (b), as well as (c) and (d), the speech content remains the same. From the figures, it can be observed that when converting the speech from Khmer to Chinese (female 000), there is little difference in the spectrograms. This is because voice conversion aims to preserve the speech content while only transforming the speaker characteristics, and the converted spectrograms in the figures demonstrate the successful transformation of speaker characteristics. On the other hand, there is a noticeable change in the magnitude of the fundamental frequency, but the overall trend of the fundamental frequency remains consistent. This further validates the effectiveness of our proposed method.

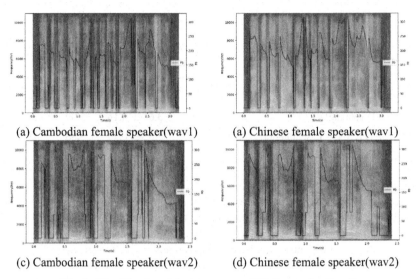

(a) Cambodian female speaker(wav1)   (a) Chinese female speaker(wav1)

(c) Cambodian female speaker(wav2)   (d) Chinese female speaker(wav2)

Fig. 4. Visualization of Spectrogram and F0 Conversion Results

4   Conclusion

In this paper, we solve the challenge of speaker timbre characteristics Disentangling and phoneme loss in cross-lingual Cambodian voice conversion tasks based on a single-speaker Cambodian speech corpus. To overcome these issues, we propose Language Feature Disentangler based on cross-lingual non-parallel corpora, which incorporates Time-Frequency Attention Normalization module. By leveraging speech data from both Chinese and English speakers, we successfully tackle the training difficulties encountered in existing voice conversion methods when dealing with cross-lingual non-parallel resources. Moreover, we resolve the problem of phoneme loss in the converted speech. Our proposed approach enables cross-lingual and multi-speaker transfer of Cambodian voice conversion in the context of rich-resource multilingual corpora in Chinese and English, along with a single-speaker Cambodian speech corpus.

Acknowledgments. The work was supported by National Natural Science Foundation of China (Grant Nos. 61972186, U21B2027), Yunnan high-tech industry development project (Grant No. 201606), Yunnan Provincial Key Research and Development Plan (Grant Nos. 202303AP140008, 202103AA080015), Yunnan Basic Research Project (Grant No. 202001AS070014), and Talents and Platform Program of Science and Technology of Yunnan (Grant No. 202105AC160018).

References

1. Hsu, W.N., et al.: Hierarchical generative modeling for controllable speech synthesis. In: Proceedings of the International Conference on Learning Representations (ICLR), New Orleans (2019)

2. Henderson, E.J.A.: The main features of Cambodian pronunciation. Bull. Sch. Orient. Afr. Stud. **14**(1), 149–174 (1952)
3. McFarland, J.R.: Language Contact and Lexical Changes in Khmer and Teochew in Cambodia and Beyond, pp. 91–128. Sinophone Southeast Asia, Brill (2021)
4. Sundermann, D, Ney, H.: VTLN-based voice conversion. In: Proceedings of the 3rd IEEE International Symposium on Signal Processing and Information Technology (IEEE Cat. No. 03EX795), pp. 556–559. IEEE (2003)
5. Stylianou, Y., Cappé, O., Moulines, E.: Continuous probabilistic transform for voice conversion. IEEE Trans. Speech Audio Process. **6**(2), 131–142 (1998)
6. Desai, S., Raghavendra, E.V., Yegnanarayana, B., Black, A.W., Prahallad, K.: Voice conversion using artificial neural networks. In: 2009 IEEE International Conference on Acoustics, Speech and Signal Processing, pp. 3893–3896. IEEE (2009)
7. Hsu, C.C., Hwang, H.T., Wu, Y.C., et al.: Voice Conversion from Unaligned Corpora Using Variational Autoencoding Wasserstein Generative Adversarial Networks (2017). https://doi.org/10.21437/Interspeech.2017-63
8. Zhang, J.-X., Ling, Z.-H., Liu, L.-J., Jiang, Y., Dai, L.-R.: Sequence-to-sequence acoustic modeling for voice conversion. IEEE/ACM Trans. Audio Speech Lang. Process. **27**(3), 631–644 (2019)
9. Ribeiro, M.S., Roth, J., Comini, G., Huybrechts, G., Gabry's, A., Lorenzo Trueba, J.: Cross-speaker style transfer for text-to-speech using data augmentation. In: ICASSP 2022–2022 IEEE International Conference on Acoustics, Speech and Signal Processing (ICASSP), pp. 6797–6801. IEEE (2022)
10. Toda, T., Black, A.W., Tokuda, K.: Voice conversion based on maximum-likelihood estimation of spectral parameter trajectory. IEEE Trans. Audio Speech Lang. Process. **15**(8), 2222–2235 (2007)
11. Helander, E., Schwarz, J., Nurminen, J., Silen, H., Gabbouj, M.: On the impact of alignment on voice conversion performance. In: Ninth Annual Conference of the International Speech Communication Association (2008)
12. Kaneko, T., Kameoka, H.: Parallel-data-free voice conversion using cycle-consistent adversarial networks (2017). https://doi.org/10.48550/arXiv.1711.11293
13. Kaneko, T., Kameoka, H., Tanaka, K., Hojo, N.: Cyclegan-vc2: improved cyclegan-based non-parallel voice conversion. In: ICASSP 2019–2019 IEEE International Conference on Acoustics, Speech and Signal Processing (ICASSP), pp. 6820–6824. IEEE (2019)
14. Kaneko, T., Kameoka, H., Tanaka, K., Hojo, N.: Cyclegan-vc3: examining and improving cyclegan-vcs for mel-spectrogram conversion. arXiv preprint arXiv:2010.11672 (2020)
15. Kaneko, T., Kameoka, H., Tanaka, K., Hojo, N.: Maskcyclegan-vc: learning non-parallel voice conversion with filling in frames. In: ICASSP 2021–2021 IEEE International Conference on Acoustics, Speech and Signal Processing (ICASSP), pp. 5919–5923. IEEE (2021)
16. Yang, S.C., Tantrawenith, M., Zhuang, H., et al.: Speech representation disentanglement with adversarial mutual information learning for one-shot voice conversion. arXiv preprint arXiv:2208.08757 (2022)
17. Zhang, Y., Weiss, R.J., Zen, H., et al.: Learning to Speak Fluently in a Foreign Language: Multilingual Speech Synthesis and Cross-Language Voice Cloning (2019). https://doi.org/10.21437/Interspeech.2019-2668
18. Terashima, R., et al.: Cross-speaker emotion transfer for low-resource text-to-speech using non-parallel voice conversion with pitch-shift data augmentation. arXiv preprint arXiv:2204.10020 (2022)
19. Nekvinda, T., Duek, O.: One model, many languages: meta-learning for multilingual text-to-speech (2020). https://doi.org/10.48550/arXiv.2008.00768
20. Ulyanov, D., Vedaldi, A., Lempitsky, V.: Instance normalization: the missing ingredient for fast stylization (2016). https://doi.org/10.48550/arXiv.1607.08022

Refining Skeleton-Based Temporal Action Segmentation with Edge Information

Mengzhen Chen⬤, Jixiang Du$^{(\boxtimes)}$⬤, Hongbo Zhang⬤, Qing Lei⬤,
and Chuanmin Zhai

Huaqiao University, Xiamen 361000, China
jxdu@hqu.edu.cn

Abstract. The purpose of temporal action segmentation (TAS) is to identify the actions of each frame in the long untrimmed action sequence and classify multiple actions. Most of the existing methods analyze video data without considering the spatial information of human joints. Although the classification of single-frame action has achieved remarkable results, there are challenges in over-segmentation under high precision. To address this challenge, we propose Local Refining with Spatial-temporal Graph Convolutional Neural Network (LR-GCN). The initial prediction is generated by spatial-temporal graph convolutional. The initial predictions are then fed into two branches, one branch is used to refine the initial prediction and the other uses the Motion Edge Prediction (MEP) module to predict the edges of the action segment. Finally the output from both branches is fed together into a Local Smooth Adjustment (LSA) module, which combines the edge information with the prediction results for a more accurate classification result. Our framework is compared with state-of-the-art methods and experimental results show that our framework effectively mitigates the over-segmentation problem on TAS tasks.

Keywords: Temporal action segmentation · Spatial-temporal convolutional · Skeleton recognition · Action classification · Activity detection

1 Introduction

Human Activity Recognition and Analysis (HAR) is an important area of research in computer vision. Understanding human behaviour is important for real-life applications such as medical rehabilitation [1], human-computer interaction [2] and automated navigation systems [3]. In the past few years, there are many studies using images or video for human activity recognition and analysis. It mainly focuses on the fields of action recognition [4,5], action detection [6,7], and action segmentation [8–10]. Action recognition classifies short sequences of trimmed actions, but real-world actions are usually continuous untrimmed. Methods for recognition of actions in long untrimmed motion capture (MoCap) sequences are action detection and action segmentation. Action segmentation aims to predict and classify the actions that occur in each frame. And action detection is to determine the start time, end time and action label of each action segment. In this paper, we focus on the action segmentation task.

Action segmentation tasks are mostly performed on video. Although video-based action segmentation methods capture long-term temporal patterns, video features are affected by redundant information such as luminance and background, and are less robust to changes in the scene. In contrast, skeleton data encode the trajectory of human joints, which has the advantages of simplicity and efficiency, and is not easily affected by appearance factors, and provides a good representation for describing human activities. To address this limitation, [11] proposed a Multi-Stage Spatial-Temporal Graph Convolutional Neural Network (MS-GCN). It utilizes spatial graph convolution and dilated temporal convolution instead of temporal convolution in the initial stage to better exploit the spatial configuration of joints and their long-term temporal dynamics.

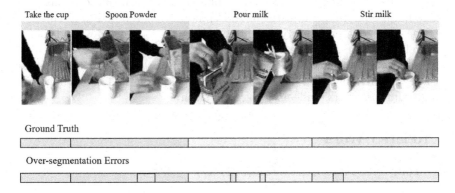

Fig. 1. Examples of excessive segmentation: When analyzing the steps taken in the kitchen video, over-segmentation will result in the detection of additional steps. For example, an action fragment performs only the action of "stir milk", but we recognize other actions from that action fragment, such as "take the cup", which breaks the continuity of the action fragment.

Although MS-GCN achieves relatively good results on several datasets, it does not take into account the influence of edge information of different action segments on adjacent action recognition. Simply classify and recognize the whole sequence, ignoring the role of local information on the whole modeling, easy to excessive segmentation error (see Fig. 1) exists.

To alleviate the over-segmentation problem, we use MS-GCN as Baseline and design Local Refining with Spatial-temporal Graph Convolutional Neural Network (LR-GCN). In the first stage, LR-GCN uses ST-GCN [12] with dilated convolution to learn human skeleton information and generate initial predictions. The second stage inputs the initial prediction into the two branches, one branch is used to refine the initial prediction and the other branch contains

MEP, which is used to predict the probability of each frame being the edge of a action segment. Finally, the outputs of these two branches are converged into LSA to smooth the prediction results, and this network can effectively alleviate the over-segmentation phenomenon.

We evaluate our framework on three challenging datasets: HuGaDB [13], PKU-MMD v2 [14] and LARa [15]. Experimental results demonstrate that our LR-GCN yields a notable performance gain against with the state-of-the-art method. In particular, our method achieves about 6.6% and 3.1% gain in F1@50 for LARa and PKU-MMD v2 dataset, a consistent improvement about 5.9% and 2.9% for LARa and PKU-MMD v2 in Acc. Despite the decrease of 2.9% and 1.4% in Acc and F1@50 of HuGaDB dataset, the performance of our model has improved significantly compared to the increase of other dataset indicators. In summary, our paper makes three main contributions:

- The Motion Edge Prediction (MEP) module is proposed, which uses the edge information of the action segment as supervision to strengthen the consistency within the segment and maintain the difference between the segments.
- The Local Smoothing Adjustment (LSA) module is proposed to calculate the frame level edge probability weighted sum in the local window and mix the initial prediction and edge information flexibly.
- The proposed framework is experimented on three publicly datasets, and the experimental results show that our proposed method can reduce over-segmentation errors while ensuring high accuracy.

2   Related Work

2.1   Temporal Action Detection (TAD)

TAD aims at action localization and classification of MoCap, and the main methods are two-stage methods and single-stage methods. Traditional methods [16,17] use hand-extracted features to model the relationship between action transition probabilities and features. With the development of deep learning, deep learning-based methods have gradually replaced these manual feature methods. [18] proposes a pyramid-structured score distribution framework to locate sequential actions. [19] proposed multi-stage CNNs to improve the efficiency of positioning actions by gradually reducing the local window. [7] uses structured segment networks to improve the performance of action detection. [20] optimizes the generation of action candidate proposals by combining multimodal features and self-complementing mechanisms.

2.2   Temporal Action Segmentation (TAS)

The purpose of TAS is to assign a predefined class label to each frame in MoCap. [10] proposed MS-TCN, which expands temporal modeling capabilities by stacking multiple dilated convolution. [21] proposed a post-processing method of boundary regression to assist the segmentation of action segments. [22] proposed a two-stream action segmentation pipeline to effectively learn short-term dynamic and long-term temporal information to improve the performance of action segmentation. Graph networks have also been applied in TAS, [23] using graph convolutional networks to model the temporal relationship of actions. [11] proposed MS-GCN, this is the first effective framework for action segmentation tasks using skeleton data. Although some work [7,21] considers the use of boundary information to help split the action, our MEP is more efficient than this post-processing approach because it is synchronized with the thinning branch. Traditional work [24–26] uses Gaussian smoothing or other smoothing methods to smooth the results, but these smoothing methods have higher computational complexity, and our LSA can further adjust the action segmentation results more efficiently, and better alleviate the problem of excessive segmentation.

2.3   Skeleton-Based Action Recognition

The skeleton sequence encodes the human joint motion trajectory and spatial information, which can be obtained through RGB images, videos, depth maps or motion capture systems. Earlier work [27–30] used manual feature extraction, mainly joint based method [31] and body part based method [32]. With the development of deep learning, skeleton-based action recognition methods can be divided into graph neural networks and Transformer-based methods. [12] proposed Spatial Temporal Graph Convolution Networks (ST-GCN) treats the human body structure as a topological graph (see Fig. 2), where the vertices on the graph are the joints of the human skeleton and the edges in the graph are regarded as the natural connections between the joints of the human body. [33] proposes a Spatio-temporal Tuples Transformer (STTFormer) method, it divides the skeleton sequence into non-overlapping segments, calculates the attention between multiple joints within the segment to capture joint dependencies, and aggregates the features of different segments for final classification.

Pose Estimation

Input Video   Spatial-temporal Graph

Fig. 2. We obtained skeleton data from the video through the pose estimation algorithm, and the coordinate information and temporal information in the skeleton data helped ST-GCN build a spatial-temporal graph of the human body structure.

3 Method

In this section, we present our Local Refining with Spatial-temporal Graph Convolutional Neural Network (LR-GCN) (see Fig. 3). Section 3.1 describes the application of ST-GCN in the first stage to generate initial predictions. Section 3.2 shows how the refinement branch works in the second stage. Sections 3.3 and 3.4 illustrate the ideas of the Motion Edge Prediction (MEP) and Local Smooth Adjustment (LSA) module, respectively. Section 3.5 explains the implementation details of our network. Given $X = [x_1, \ldots, x_T] \in \mathbb{R}^{T \times N \times C}$ as input to LR-GCN, our goal is to predict the category label for each frame $Y = [Y_1, \ldots, Y_T]$, where T is the length of the skeleton sequence, N is the number of nodes, and C is the number of characteristic channels per node.

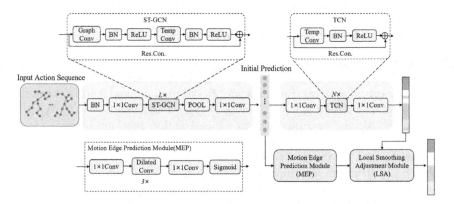

Fig. 3. Illustration of the overall architecture of the proposed model. Given an untrimmed action sequence, we fist fed it into ST-TCN with dilation convolution to generate the initial prediction, then input into the upper branch for refinement and to the lower MEP for edge probability prediction, and finally the two outputs are fed to the LSA for local adjustment to obtain the final result.

3.1 Single Stage ST-GCN

Input skeleton sequence X. In the first stage of the network, we use ST-GCN with the introduction of dilated convolution as the classifier, and first use a 1×1 convolution to adjust the input dimension:

$$X \in \mathbb{R}^{T \times N \times C} \rightarrow \mathbb{R}^{T \times N \times C_0} \tag{1}$$

X is then fed into the ST-GCN block at layer L, with $L = 10$. This 10-layer ST-GCN uses dilated convolution (see Fig. 4) instead of ordinary convolution, which is a convolution operation based on dilation factor, and the dilation rate enables the network to maintain the temporal order of samples while capturing long-term dependencies without increasing the model complexity.

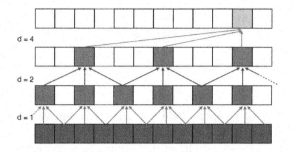

Fig. 4. Visualization of the dilated convolution process. The dilation rate of the first layer is 1. With the increase of the number of network layers, the dilation rate($2^l, l \in \{0, 1, 2, ..\}$) also increases, and l is the index of the number of layers, starting at 0.

By stacking ST-GCN continuously, we can get more advanced semantic information from the graph. Finally, we aggregate the spatial features of human joints through a pooling layer, as well as a 1×1 convolution to output the initial prediction $\hat{Y} \in \mathbb{R}^{T \times K}$, K is the number of classes. $\hat{Y}$ is entered into two branches respectively, one is the refinement branch, consisting of multi-stage SS-TCN [10], and the other is the edge prediction branch that made up of MEP.

3.2   Multi-stage SS-TCN

In the multi-stage SS-TCN, each stage refines the prediction of the previous stage as follows:

$$\hat{Y}^t = \Gamma\left(\hat{Y}^{t-1}\right) \tag{2}$$

where $\hat{Y}^t$ is the output of stage t , Γ is the SS-TCN, and $\hat{Y}^{t-1}$ is the output of the previous stage of stage t. The SS-TCN contains multiple TCN blocks, each consisting of dilated temporal convolution, BN layer and ReLU activation, and residual connectivity, which proceeds as follows:

$$\hat{Y}^t = \delta\left(BN\left(b_0 + W_0 *_l \hat{Y}\right)\right) + \hat{Y} \tag{3}$$

where $\hat{Y}^t$ is the output of the t-th SS-TCN, b_0 is the bias, $*_l$ is the dilation convolution operator, W_0 is the weight of the dilation convolution filter with convolution kernel size k, and δ is the ReLU activation function.

3.3   Motion Edge Prediction (MEP) Module

The MEP takes the initial prediction A of the first stage output as input and evaluates the probability that each frame in the sequence will be at the edge of the action segment, whether it is at the start or end edge of the action segment. The first layer of the module is a 1D convolution with a convolution kernel of size 1:

$$Y_{\text{out}} = b_1 + W_1 * \hat{Y} \tag{4}$$

where Y_{out} is the output after 1D convolution, b_1 is the learnable parameter, and W_1 is the weight. Then, the dilated convolution (dilation rate is 2^l, $l \in \{2, 3, 4\}$) is used to replace the ordinary convolution to expand the receptive field and obtain the long-term time dependence:

$$D_i = D_{i-1} + (k - 1) \times s \tag{5}$$

where D_i is the current receptive field, D_{i-1} is the receptive field of the previous layer, k is the convolution kernel size, and s is the step size. This is followed by a 1D convolution to adjust the output dimension, and a filter with Sigmoid activation is added as a classifier in the last layer to generate an action edge probability for each frame to evaluate the confidence score p_i.

3.4   Local Smooth Adjustment (LSA) Module

For each frame of the action sequence, we estimate the duration of the action segment to which the current frame belongs and set a local window centered on the current frame (see Fig. 5).

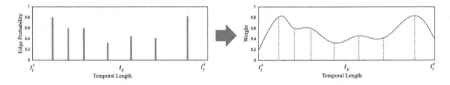

Fig. 5. Visualization of LSA. When an action edge is encountered, the weight corresponding to the current frame has a faster decreasing rate.

Given a window centered on the current frame, the left-centered action segment is $S_l : \lceil t_l^s, t_l^e, c_l \rceil$ and the right-centered action segment is $S_r : \lceil t_r^s, t_r^e, c_r \rceil$, where t^s, t^e denotes the edge of the action segment and $c \in [1, \ldots, K]$ denotes the corresponding action label. The frame in the connected part of these two action segments is the center frame, which can be denoted as $t_b = t_l^e + 1 = t_r^s$. Using the neighborhood parameter $v \in [0, 1]$ and defining the ranges of the left action segment and the right action segment as V_l and V_r, respectively, the window lengths $L = V_l + V_r$, V_l and V_r are defined as follows:

$$\begin{aligned} V_l &= [t_b - (t_b - t_l^s) * v, t_b) \\ V_r &= [t_b, t_b + (t_r^e - t_b) * v) \end{aligned} \tag{6}$$

At the same time, in each local window, this paper uses the following formula to assign the mixed probability and calculate the weight of all frames. The calculation process is as follows:

$$y_{\text{out}} = \frac{\sum_{s \in \{S_l, S_r\}} \sum_{\beta=1}^{L} \hat{y}' \cdot \exp\left(-\alpha \sum_{j=1}^{\beta} p_i\right)}{1 + \sum_{s \in \{S_l, S_r\}} \sum_{\beta=1}^{L} \exp\left(-\alpha \sum_{j=1}^{\beta} p_i\right)} \tag{7}$$

where y_{out} is the output of the local smoothing adjustment module, $\hat{y}'$ is the initial prediction after the introduction of the local window, p_i is the edge confidence, α is used to control the weight decay rate, the local window length is L, and the weighting in the local window is aggregated to the left action segment S_l and the right action segment S_r. By calculating the weighted sum of frame-level edge probability in the local window, the classification confidence score of the current frame can be adjusted smoothly, so that the moving edge information and the initial prediction can be mixed flexibly to generate more accurate classification results and prevent over-segmentation.

3.5   Implementation Details

Loss Function. We use the same loss functions as MS-GCN, the cross-entropy loss (CE) and the mean square error loss (MSE), respectively, with the overall loss being the combination of CE and MSE:

$$L = L_{CE} + \lambda L_{MSE} \tag{8}$$

where L_{CE} is the cross-entropy loss, L_{MSE} is the mean-squared error loss, and λ is the hyperparameter that determines the contribution of the two loss functions.

CE loss is commonly used in classification problems to measure the similarity of ground truth and predicted classification results, which is defined as shown below:

$$L_{CE} = \frac{1}{T} \sum_t -y_{t,l} \log\left(\hat{y}_{t,l}\right) \tag{9}$$

where T is the sequence length, $y_{t,l}$ is the ground truth of label l at frame t, and $\hat{y}_{t,l}$ is the predicted probability of label l at frame t.

MSE loss can evaluate the magnitude of the error between ground truth and prediction results, thus ensuring that adjacent action frames have classification consistency in the segmentation results and thus avoiding over-segmentation:

$$L_{MSE} = \frac{1}{TL} \sum_{t,l} \left(\log\left(\hat{y}_{t,l}\right) - \log\left(\hat{y}_{t-1,l}\right)\right)^2 \tag{10}$$

where L is the number of action categories and the rest of the parameters are the same as those defined earlier.

Hyperparameters of the Model. In this paper, the experimental equipment we use is two GeForce RTX 2080 Ti GPU cards. We choose the same model parameters as MS-GCN for training, specifically, stacking L ST-GCN blocks in a single-stage ST-GCN, with $L = 10$. The number of hidden layers is 256 in MEP. Stacking N TCN blocks in a multi-stage SS-TCN, $N=10$, while multi-stage refers to 3 stages. For the optimizer, we use the Adam optimizer with a learning rate of 0.0005. The hyperparameter λ of the loss function is 0.15.

4   Experiments

4.1   Datasets

HuGaDB. The HuGaDB dataset is a human gait analysis dataset containing 12 action categories with a total of 18 subjects performing typical lower limb activities such as walking, running, and cycling, among others. Its data is collected from a network of body sensors consisting of six wearable inertial sensors located on the left and right thighs, calves and feet.

LARa. The LARa dataset is the first freely accessible logistics dataset for human activity recognition. This dataset recorded two picking and one packing scenes for 14 subjects using OMoCap, IMU and RGB cameras. These operations were performed in different warehouse scenarios.

PKU-MMD. The PKU-MMD dataset is a benchmark dataset for 3D human continuous motion understanding. The data in this dataset, captured by Kinect v2 [34], contains 51 motion categories, a total of 1,076 long video sequences, executed by 66 subjects in three camera views, and contains nearly 20,000 action instances and a total of 5.4 million frames.

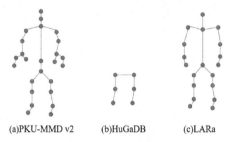

(a)PKU-MMD v2   (b)HuGaDB   (c)LARa

Fig. 6. Skeleton representation diagram for three datasets: (a) PKU-MMD v2, (b) HuGaDB, (c) LARa. The dot is the joint point and the solid line is the natural connection of the joint point.

For each dataset, we have drawn the skeleton representation (see Fig. 6). PKU-MMD v2 is shown with a 25-point structure diagram, HuGaDB is a gait dataset with only 6 nodes in the lower body, and LARa is represented with a 19-point diagram. We also present some information about the three datasets in Table 1.

4.2   Evaluation Metrics

For all datasets, we use the evaluation metrics commonly used for action segmentation: frame-level accuracy (Acc) [10], segment-level F1 score (F1) [8] and segment-level edit score (Edit) [35]. Acc focuses on frame-level classification accuracy, F1 and Edit penalizes over-segmentation errors.

Table 1. Information on the three datasets.

Datasets	Nodes	Classes	Sampling Rates
HuGaDB	6	12	60 Hz
LARa	19	8	50 Hz
PKU-MMD v2	25	52	30 Hz

4.3 Comparison with the State of the Art

Table 2 compares our model with the state of the art on three datasets. Experimental results show that our LR-GCN performs better than other methods on the LARa and PKU-MMD v2 datasets, achieving the most advanced results with 5.9% and 2.9% increases in Acc, respectively. The F1@50 score increased by 6.6% and 3.1%, respectively. However, the performance on HuGaDB datasets is not satisfactory, which may be because our proposed method is unfriendly to small datasets and requires more data for training to improve the performance of the model.

Table 2. Comparison with the state-of-the-art on HuGaDB, LARa, PKU-MMD v2.

Methods	HuGaDB		LARa		PKU-MMD v2	
	Acc	F1@50	Acc	F1@50	Acc	F1@50
Bi-LSTM	86.1	81.5	63.9	32.3	56.5	25.4
ST-GCN	88.7	67.7	67.9	25.8	15.5	64.9
MS-TCN	86.8	89.9	65.8	39.6	65.5	46.3
MS-GCN	**90.4**	**93.0**	65.6	43.6	68.5	51.6
LR-GCN(Ours)	87.5	91.6	**71.5**	**50.2**	**71.4**	**54.7**

The LSTM-based method Bi-LSTM [6] is suitable for modeling time series data, but it does not take spatial information into account. ST-GCN focuses on extracting spatial features but is not suitable to work on multi-classification tasks with long sequences alone. Both MS-TCN and MS-GCN are successful practices of action segmentation tasks, MS-TCN is used to segment video data, and MS-GCN is to work on skeleton-based data. Our work is the same as MS-GCN, and the input is skeleton data. Compared with MS-GCN, our LR-GCN performs better on large datasets.

4.4 Effect of the Window Length in LSA

In order to analyze the influence of different window lengths on the experimental results in LSA, we take LARa as an example to conduct the ablation experiment of local window length (see Fig. 7).

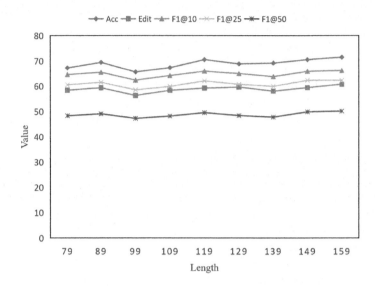

Fig. 7. Effect of window length on the metrics in the LARa dataset.

As we can see from the graph, the window length has no significant impact on performance, although there is a slight increase in the data of the metrics as the window length increases, but the change is not significant. Reducing the window length to 119 or even to 89 still improves the performance, and we can see by the line graph that the experiment works best in the LARa dataset when the window length is taken as 159, probably because the appropriate window length helps to maintain the consistency of actions within action segments while maintaining the inconsistency between different action segments.

4.5   Ablation Study on α

This hyperparameter α defines the decay rate of the weights in the LSA, and the effect of the LSA is controlled by two hyperparameters, α and the window length, Table 3 shows the effect of different values of α on the experimental results on the LARa dataset. It can be observed that when $\alpha = 0$, the weight of edge confidence will be ignored, and the effect is not optimistic at this time, so the prediction refinement should be properly combined with edge confidence and initial prediction. When $\alpha = 0.6$, edge confidence plays a larger role in the final prediction process, and although the effect is improved, it is worse than that when $\alpha = 0.2$. $\alpha = 0.2$ works best, with both edge confidence and initial predictions playing an appropriate role.

Table 3. Ablation studies for α on the LARa dataset in LSA.

Impact of α	Acc	Edit	F1@10,25,50		
LR-GCN (L = 159, α = 0)	66.8	55.9	63.3	59.0	46.0
LR-GCN (L = 159, α = 0.2)	**71.4**	**71.1**	**71.8**	**67.1**	**54.7**
LR-GCN (L = 159, α = 0.4)	64.7	56.9	63.4	58.8	46.6
LR-GCN (L = 159, α = 0.6)	71.3	60.4	65.7	61.5	49.8
LR-GCN (L = 159, α = 0.8)	61.2	53.0	59.2	55.4	45.1
LR-GCN (L = 159, α = 1)	66.38	56.6	62.3	58.3	46.7

4.6 Ablation Study on MEP and LSA

In this paper, we propose two modules to improve the performance of the skeleton-based temporal action segmentation task. Therefore, we do ablation experiments to test the effectiveness of these two parts of the work. Since MEP and LSA are to be used together in combination, we only discuss the case of adding these two modules and not adding these two modules. The experimental results on the three datasets are given in Table 4. The one without two modules is Baseline, and the one with two modules is our method. It can be seen that Acc and Edit on all datasets are improved after the addition of the two modules, which indicates that our proposed LR-GCN can effectively reduce over-segmentation errors while ensuring high accuracy. The overall model performance is improved, except that the F1@50 on the HuGaDB dataset has decreased, but the impact is not significant.

Table 4. Performance of MEP and LSA on the three datasets.

Datasets	MEP	LSA	Acc	Edit	F1@10,25,50		
HuGaDB	×	×	85.1	91.6	94.2	93.4	**92.2**
	✓	✓	**87.5**	**94.1**	**94.7**	**93.8**	91.6
LARa	×	×	64.2	53.7	59.1	54.1	42.3
	✓	✓	**71.5**	**60.7**	**66.2**	**62.3**	**50.2**
PKU-MMD v2	×	×	68.0	65.9	65.7	60.4	47.0
	✓	✓	**71.4**	**71.1**	**71.8**	**67.1**	**54.7**

The paper also visualizes how our LR-GCN compares to Baseline's experimental results on the PKU-MMD v2 dataset (see Fig. 8). Adding MEP and LSA results in a reduction in over-segmentation errors.

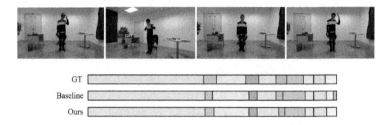

Fig. 8. Visualization of experimental results on the PKU-MMD v2 dataset. The image show that the method proposed in this paper is helpful for smoothing action segments with excessive segmentation errors.

5   Conclusion

Aiming at the problem of over-segmentation in skeleton-based temporal action segmentation task, The paper proposes a framework Local Refining with Spatial-temporal Graph Convolutional Neural Network (LR-GCN) to mitigate this problem. LR-GCN uses MS-GCN as the baseline, and introduces MEP and LSA, which can smooth the fragments with excessive segmentation errors, so as to improve the performance of the model. A large number of experimental results show that our proposed method is effective. The limitation of this study is that it is not friendly to small datasets. It can be known from the experimental results on HuGaDB datasets that it is difficult to present more accurate classification results with insufficient data. Therefore, we will explore better action segmentation methods to make the model suitable for datasets of various sizes in future work.

References

1. Yang, X., Gang, H.: Recognition of human activities based on decision optimization model. In: 2021 4th International Conference on Algorithms, Computing and Artificial Intelligence, pp. 1–8 (2021)
2. Rodomagoulakis, I., et al.: Multimodal human action recognition in assistive human-robot interaction. In: 2016 IEEE International Conference on Acoustics, Speech and Signal Processing (ICASSP), pp. 2702–2706. IEEE (2016)
3. Donahue, J., et al.: Long-term recurrent convolutional networks for visual recognition and description. In: Proceedings of the IEEE Conference on Computer Vision and Pattern Recognition, pp. 2625–2634 (2015)
4. Szegedy, C., et al.: Going deeper with convolutions. In: Proceedings of the IEEE Conference on Computer Vision and Pattern Recognition, pp. 1–9 (2015)
5. Wang, L., Xiong, Y., Wang, Z., Qiao, Yu., Lin, D., Tang, X., Van Gool, L.: Temporal segment networks: towards good practices for deep action recognition. In: Leibe, B., Matas, J., Sebe, N., Welling, M. (eds.) ECCV 2016. LNCS, vol. 9912, pp. 20–36. Springer, Cham (2016). https://doi.org/10.1007/978-3-319-46484-8_2
6. Singh, B., Marks, T.K., Jones, M., Tuzel, O., Shao, M.: A multi-stream bi-directional recurrent neural network for fine-grained action detection. In: Proceedings of the IEEE Conference on Computer Vision and Pattern Recognition, pp. 1961–1970 (2016)

7. Zhao, Y., Xiong, Y., Wang, L., Wu, Z., Tang, X., Lin, D.: Temporal action detection with structured segment networks. In: Proceedings of the IEEE International Conference on Computer Vision, pp. 2914–2923 (2017)
8. Lea, C., Flynn, M.D., Vidal, R., Reiter, A., Hager, G.D.: Temporal convolutional networks for action segmentation and detection. In: Proceedings of the IEEE Conference on Computer Vision and Pattern Recognition, pp. 156–165 (2017)
9. Lei, P., Todorovic, S.: Temporal deformable residual networks for action segmentation in videos. In: Proceedings of the IEEE Conference on Computer Vision and Pattern Recognition, pp. 6742–6751 (2018)
10. Farha, Y.A., Gall, J.: Ms-tcn: multi-stage temporal convolutional network for action segmentation. In: Proceedings of the IEEE/CVF Conference on Computer Vision and Pattern Recognition, pp. 3575–3584 (2019)
11. Filtjens, B., Vanrumste, B., Slaets, P.: Skeleton-based action segmentation with multi-stage spatial-temporal graph convolutional neural networks. IEEE Trans. Emerg. Top. Comput. (2022)
12. Yan, S., Xiong, Y., Lin, D.: Spatial temporal graph convolutional networks for skeleton-based action recognition. In: Proceedings of the AAAI Conference on Artificial Intelligence, vol. 32 (2018)
13. Chereshnev, R., Kertész-Farkas, A.: HuGaDB: human gait database for activity recognition from wearable inertial sensor networks. In: van der Aalst, W.M.P., Ignatov, D.I., Khachay, M., Kuznetsov, S.O., Lempitsky, V., Lomazova, I.A., Loukachevitch, N., Napoli, A., Panchenko, A., Pardalos, P.M., Savchenko, A.V., Wasserman, S. (eds.) AIST 2017. LNCS, vol. 10716, pp. 131–141. Springer, Cham (2018). https://doi.org/10.1007/978-3-319-73013-4_12
14. Liu, C., Hu, Y., Li, Y., Song, S., Liu, J.: Pku-mmd: a large scale benchmark for skeleton-based human action understanding. In: Proceedings of the Workshop on Visual Analysis in Smart and Connected Communities, pp. 1–8 (2017)
15. Niemann, F., et al.: Lara: creating a dataset for human activity recognition in logistics using semantic attributes. Sensors 20(15), 4083 (2020)
16. Maji, S., Bourdev, L., Malik, J.: Action recognition from a distributed representation of pose and appearance. In: CVPR 2011, pp. 3177–3184. IEEE (2011)
17. Weinzaepfel, P., Harchaoui, Z., Schmid, C.: Learning to track for spatio-temporal action localization. In: Proceedings of the IEEE International Conference on Computer Vision, pp. 3164–3172 (2015)
18. Yuan, J., Ni, B., Yang, X., Kassim, A.A.: Temporal action localization with pyramid of score distribution features. In: Proceedings of the IEEE Conference on Computer Vision and Pattern Recognition, pp. 3093–3102 (2016)
19. Shou, Z., Wang, D., Chang, S.F.: Temporal action localization in untrimmed videos via multi-stage cnns. In: Proceedings of the IEEE Conference on Computer Vision and Pattern Recognition, pp. 1049–1058 (2016)
20. Gao, J., Chen, K., Nevatia, R.: Ctap: complementary temporal action proposal generation. In: Proceedings of the European Conference on Computer Vision (ECCV), pp. 68–83 (2018)
21. Ishikawa, Y., Kasai, S., Aoki, Y., Kataoka, H.: Alleviating over-segmentation errors by detecting action boundaries. In: Proceedings of the IEEE/CVF Winter Conference on Applications of Computer Vision, pp. 2322–2331 (2021)
22. Kang, M.S., Park, R.H., Park, H.M.: Efficient two-stream network for online video action segmentation. IEEE Access 10, 90635–90646 (2022)
23. Zeng, R., et al.: Graph convolutional networks for temporal action localization. In: Proceedings of the IEEE/CVF International Conference on Computer Vision, pp. 7094–7103 (2019)

24. Yang, R., Ni, B., Ma, C., Xu, Y., Yang, X.: Video segmentation via multiple granularity analysis. In: Proceedings of the IEEE Conference on Computer Vision and Pattern Recognition, pp. 3010–3019 (2017)
25. Wang, H., Schmid, C.: Action recognition with improved trajectories. In: Proceedings of the IEEE International Conference on Computer Vision, pp. 3551–3558 (2013)
26. Yu, C.P., Le, H., Zelinsky, G., Samaras, D.: Efficient video segmentation using parametric graph partitioning. In: Proceedings of the IEEE International Conference on Computer Vision, pp. 3155–3163 (2015)
27. Du, Y., Wang, W., Wang, L.: Hierarchical recurrent neural network for skeleton based action recognition. In: Proceedings of the IEEE Conference on Computer Vision and Pattern Recognition, pp. 1110–1118 (2015)
28. Shahroudy, A., Liu, J., Ng, T.T., Wang, G.: Ntu rgb+ d: a large scale dataset for 3d human activity analysis. In: Proceedings of the IEEE Conference on Computer Vision and Pattern Recognition, pp. 1010–1019 (2016)
29. Liu, J., Shahroudy, A., Xu, D., Wang, G.: Spatio-temporal LSTM with trust gates for 3D human action recognition. In: Leibe, B., Matas, J., Sebe, N., Welling, M. (eds.) ECCV 2016. LNCS, vol. 9907, pp. 816–833. Springer, Cham (2016). https://doi.org/10.1007/978-3-319-46487-9_50
30. Song, S., Lan, C., Xing, J., Zeng, W., Liu, J.: An end-to-end spatio-temporal attention model for human action recognition from skeleton data. In: Proceedings of the AAAI Conference on Artificial Intelligence, vol. 31 (2017)
31. Wang, J., Liu, Z., Wu, Y., Yuan, J.: Learning actionlet ensemble for 3d human action recognition. IEEE Trans. Pattern Anal. Mach. Intell. **36**(5), 914–927 (2013)
32. Vemulapalli, R., Arrate, F., Chellappa, R.: Human action recognition by representing 3d skeletons as points in a lie group. In: Proceedings of the IEEE Conference on Computer Vision and Pattern Recognition, pp. 588–595 (2014)
33. Qiu, H., Hou, B., Ren, B., Zhang, X.: Spatio-temporal tuples transformer for skeleton-based action recognition. arXiv preprint arXiv:2201.02849 (2022)
34. Fankhauser, P., Bloesch, M., Rodriguez, D., Kaestner, R., Hutter, M., Siegwart, R.: Kinect v2 for mobile robot navigation: Evaluation and modeling. In: 2015 international conference on advanced robotics (ICAR), pp. 388–394. IEEE (2015)
35. Liu, J., Shahroudy, A., Xu, D., Wang, G.: Spatio-temporal LSTM with trust gates for 3D human action recognition. In: Leibe, B., Matas, J., Sebe, N., Welling, M. (eds.) ECCV 2016. LNCS, vol. 9907, pp. 816–833. Springer, Cham (2016). https://doi.org/10.1007/978-3-319-46487-9_50

CoME: Collaborative Model Ensemble for Fast and Accurate Predictions

Lei Deng[1], Xinlin Gao[1], Yi Xiao[1], Sheng Chang[1], Xiaochun Cheng[2], and Xianchuan Yu[1(✉)]

[1] School of Artificial Intelligence, Beijing Normal University, Beijing 100875, China
dvs@mail.bnu.edu.cn , changsheng@mail.bnu.edu.cn,
yuxianchuan@163.com
[2] Department of Computer Science, Middlesex University, London, UK
xiaochun.cheng@swansea.ac.uk
https://www.bnu.edu.cn

Abstract. Ensemble learning, which combines multiple weak classifiers to form a strong classifier, has been shown to improve model accuracy and generalization. In the course of our research on convolutional neural networks (CNNs), we have discovered a novel model aggregation method called CoME, which accelerates model training speed, enhances model precision, and exhibits good interpretability. Starting from the relationship between convolutions and planar point classification problems, this paper explores the working mechanism of convolutions and their classification principles. We demonstrate how to leverage these principles to construct our ensemble model. Additionally, during the process of model simplification, we derive the Softmax function and gain new insights into the numerical values flowing through the model, referred to as logarithmic probability. Finally, we conduct experiments to validate the effectiveness of our model.

Keywords: Convolutional kernel · High-dimensional vector space classification · Interpretability · Gaussian probability density function · Ensemble learning

1 Introduction

The interpretability of neural networks has long been a challenging issue in the field of machine learning [18]. Our initial objective was to gain a deep understanding of the inner workings of neural networks. Taking convolutional neural networks as an example, we simplified a multi-layered, multi-convolutional-kernel network with thousands of trainable parameters into an ultra-simplified network consisting of just one layer with a 1×2 convolutional kernel and two trainable parameters. Through the study of this minimalist convolutional network, we discovered that the information produced by convolutional networks is

This research was funded by the National Natural Science Foundation of China, grant number 42172323.

more intricate and abundant than previously imagined. Often, our prior network designs failed to effectively harness this valuable information. Building on these findings in the realm of neural network interpretability research, we propose a novel model aggregation approach, which we term Collaborative Model Ensemble (CoME). CoME maximizes the utilization of valuable information derived from neural network outputs while maintaining strong interpretability.

Currently, there exist numerous classical ensemble learning models, broadly categorized into two groups. The first group primarily focuses on finding as many statistically independent classifiers as possible, while the second group concentrates on devising an effective means of combining multiple weak classifiers into a strong one. Representative methods from the first group include Bagging [5], which trains multiple diverse weak classifiers by repeatedly sampling the dataset with replacement. Boosting [1], on the other hand, emphasizes the boosting of misclassified samples from the previous model by increasing their weights, thereby enabling subsequent models to classify them correctly. Our approach falls into the second category, employing probabilistic techniques to effectively utilize the valuable information output by multiple models.

Existing methods in the second category, such as Stacking [17], introduce an additional fully connected layer to the output layer of all classifiers and subsequently train to obtain fusion weights for each model. However, the introduction of this fully connected layer adds a layer of non-interpretability and necessitates a new round of training to determine its parameters. Voting [10] solely relies on the class labels provided by classifiers, overlooking the critical confidence information provided by the classifiers. Averaging [13] represents a special case of Stacking when the fusion parameter is set to $\frac{1}{n}$, disregarding the differences between models. CoME maximizes the utilization of classifier output information, utilizing probabilistic methods to compute the parameters of the newly introduced network layer, thereby endowing it with strong interpretability. Consequently, CoME overcomes the limitations associated with the aforementioned methods.

The paper is structured as follows: 1. Establishing a connection between convolutional classification problems and classification problems of points on a two-dimensional plane. 2. Utilizing the classification problem of points in the plane to gain an intuitive understanding of convolutions. 3. Discovering model ensemble methods from the point classification problem. 4. Exploring the output patterns of convolutions and how our model leverages these patterns. 5. Introducing our proposed novel model and its simplification. 6. Conducting experiments and presenting the conclusions.

2 Methodology

2.1 Relationship Between Weighted Sum and Convolution

In this section, we will briefly explain how the weighted sum classification method works and its correspondence with convolutions.

Our exploration of the principles of CNNs began with the objective of understanding their underlying mechanisms [4,7]. Let's consider a binary classification task on a 3×3 grayscale image. By applying a 3×3 convolution without padding and bias, we obtain a single value as the result (as shown in Fig. 1a). This value can be used to classify the original image. If it exceeds a specified threshold, the sample is classified as positive; otherwise, it is classified as negative. By examining the convolution formula 1, we can understand how this works. However, why does this simple formula generate different magnitudes for samples from the two classes? Specifically, why do positive samples have larger values, while negative samples have smaller ones?

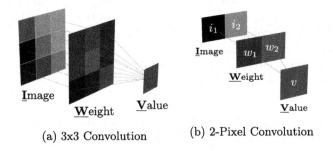

(a) 3x3 Convolution   (b) 2-Pixel Convolution

Fig. 1. Simplifying convolution from a 3×3 kernel to a 1×2 kernel for enhanced intuitive understanding of convolution's classification process. It was observed that convolution performs classification tasks based on the relative magnitudes of multiple pixels.

$$V = \sum_{m=1}^{3} \sum_{n=1}^{3} W[m,n] \times I[m,n] = \sum_{i=1}^{3 \times 3} W.flat[i] \times I.flat[i] \tag{1}$$

$$V = \sum_{i=1}^{1 \times 2} W.flat[i] \times I.flat[i] = w_1 \times i_1 + w_2 \times i_2 = v \tag{2}$$

The most commonly used convolutional kernel size is 3×3, which implies that neighboring 9 pixels are summed with weights. To simplify the situation and gain a better understanding of how the convolutional kernel achieves this, let's assume the image contains only two pixels (as illustrated in Fig. 1b). In this case, the convolution formula becomes remarkably simple (Eq. 2). This simplification facilitates the study of its underlying principles. Now, the problem shifts to how we can classify a two-dimensional vector. In fact, the original 3×3 convolutional kernel represents a 9-dimensional vector classification problem. According to the convolution formula 2, convolution performs classification by performing a weighted sum on the two values (i_1 and i_2). Therefore, the question becomes how to find the weights for this weighted sum, which are the convolutional kernel itself.

Table 1 presents a simple example of two-dimensional vector classification. All positive examples have features where the value of the first dimension is smaller than that of the second dimension, while all negative examples have features where the value of the second dimension is smaller than that of the first dimension. However, relying solely on one dimension is insufficient for classification. For instance, it appears that the second dimension's value for positive examples is greater than that of negative examples. However, in the third negative example, a counterexample emerges, with its value greater than all positive samples. Thus, how can we manually construct the convolutional kernel based on the relative magnitude of the two dimensions in positive and negative classes? $(-1, 1)$ is the simplest convolutional kernel that satisfies the requirements and can perfectly separate all positive and negative examples (as shown in the results column of Table 1). Here, we can simply choose 0 as the classification threshold. Through the above example, you can intuitively understand how the convolutional kernel performs classification. We can deduce that it accomplishes the task by considering the relative magnitudes of multiple elements, rather than relying solely on the magnitude of individual elements.

Table 1. A simple example of vector classification, where the convolution kernel $(-1, 1)$ perfectly achieves the classification task.

positive samples				negative samples			
i_1	i_2	v	result	i_1	i_2	v	result
1.0	2.0	1.00	>0	1.0	0.2	−0.80	<0
1.1	1.9	0.80	>0	1.1	−0.1	−1.20	<0
1.2	2.1	0.90	>0	3.1	2.2	−0.90	<0
1.3	1.8	0.50	>0	1.8	1.3	−0.50	<0

Mapping the Example in Table 1 to a coordinate axis, as shown in Fig. 2a, allows us to easily identify the decision boundary BC. Interestingly, the convolution kernel, represented by the vector $\overrightarrow{OA}$, is perpendicular to the decision boundary BC, as we will demonstrate. Figure 2a establishes a perfect correspondence between the classification problem of an image with only two pixels and the classification problem of points on a 2D plane. Thus, the convolution-based classification problem for images with more pixels can be directly associated with classification problems involving points in higher dimensions. Consequently, we can investigate how convolutions work by studying the simpler problem of classifying points on a two-dimensional plane.

With the help of the point classification problem on a two-dimensional plane, we can now explore more complex point classification problems (as shown in Fig. 2a). These complex problems often cannot be solved by manually constructing convolutional kernels based on observed numerical patterns. So, how can we utilize the classification problem of points on a plane to aid in constructing con-

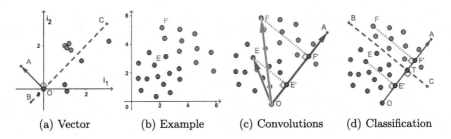

Fig. 2. (a) Coordinate axis representation of the previous example of vector classification, where $\overrightarrow{OA}$ represents the classification convolution kernel $(-1, 1)$. We observe that the decision boundary BC is perpendicular to $\overrightarrow{OA}$, which will be proven later. In (c), we demonstrate that the convolution result of point E is equal to the length of OE'. In (d), T represents the decision threshold, and the length of $E'T$ corresponds to the confidence of the classification.

volutional kernels? To continue our research, we need to first prove the following theorem.

Theorem 1. *In Fig. 2c, when the length of the convolutional kernel $\overrightarrow{OA}$ is 1, the convolution operation actually calculates the projection length of the sample point onto the convolutional kernel $\overrightarrow{OA}$.*

Proof. Let the convolutional kernel be $W.flat = [w_1, w_2]$, and consider an arbitrary point $E(x, y)$ on the plane. Let $\overrightarrow{OA} = (w_1, w_2)$ and $\overrightarrow{OE} = (x, y)$. Then, $\overrightarrow{OA} \cdot \overrightarrow{OE} = w_1 \times x + w_2 \times y = \sum_{i=1}^{1 \times 2} W.flat[i] \times E.flat[i] = CONV(E, W)$. Thus, $CONV(E, W) = \overrightarrow{OA} \cdot \overrightarrow{OE} = |\overrightarrow{OA}| \times |\overrightarrow{OE}| \times cos(\theta) = |\overrightarrow{OE}| \times cos(\theta)$, which is equal to the projection length of $\overrightarrow{OE}$ onto $\overrightarrow{OA}$, where $\theta = \angle AOE$.

To classify positive and negative examples, we only need to find a convolutional kernel vector $\overrightarrow{OA}$ that maximizes the projection length of positive samples and minimizes the projection length of negative samples. Specifically, positive samples should be concentrated towards the head of the vector, while negative samples should be concentrated towards the tail. The midpoint T of the vector can serve as the decision threshold. Sample points with projection lengths greater than T are classified as positive, while those with projection lengths less than T are classified as negative (as shown in Fig. 2d). By drawing the line BC through the decision threshold T and perpendicular to $\overrightarrow{OA}$, all points located above line BC will fall into the interval TA and be classified as positive samples, while all points below line BC will fall into the interval OT and be classified as negative samples (as shown in Fig. 2d). BC represents the decision boundary corresponding to the convolutional kernel $\overrightarrow{OA}$, and it is orthogonal to the kernel. For any sample point E on the plane, the projection point of E on the convolutional kernel $\overrightarrow{OA}$ is denoted as E', and the distance from E' to the decision threshold T is $E'T$, which represents the confidence. This confidence is a relative value that can exceed 1.

Through the above analysis, we establish a one-to-one correspondence between convolutional kernel classification problems and point classification problems on a plane. By studying the classification problem of points on a plane, we gain a clear understanding of how convolutional kernels work. They project the points to be classified in high-dimensional space onto the direction of the convolutional kernel vector, and determine the classification decision threshold based on the lengths and positions of the positive and negative sample projections, thereby achieving the classification task.

2.2   Dealing with More Complex Classification Scenarios

In Fig. 3a, D_1 and D_2 represent positive and negative examples, respectively. It is evident that we cannot find a perfect decision boundary BC to separate D_1 and D_2.

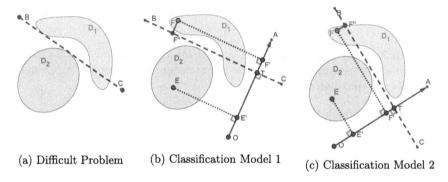

(a) Difficult Problem   (b) Classification Model 1   (c) Classification Model 2

Fig. 3. For a problem that is difficult to be perfectly classified, Model 1 and Model 2 provide completely opposite classification results for point F. However, by considering the confidences TF' provided by Model 1 and Model 2, we can correctly classify point F. But if there are three such models, how should we accurately utilize the confidence information?

Now, let's consider two classification models depicted in Fig. 3b and Fig. 3c. Regardless of how we choose the convolutional kernel $\overrightarrow{OA}$, there will always be a portion of the edge samples in D_1 misclassified as negative samples. Furthermore, for an edge sample F in D_1, it is classified as a positive sample in Fig. 3b and as a negative sample in Fig. 3c. Relying solely on the conflicting classification results of two models for the same point F does not allow us to determine whether F is a positive or negative sample. However, it appears that we have a way to obtain the correct class for F. In Fig. 3b, the confidence $F'T$ is greater than in Fig. 3c. Therefore, we can choose to trust the result with higher confidence. From the above analysis, we observe that by combining the results of models that have poor or even contradictory classification performance, we can still determine the correct class for F. But what if the situation becomes even more complex? If we have more than two models with poor classification performance, how can we effectively combine their results to make accurate judgments? Voting based on multiple models is a well-known approach, but voting essentially discards the valuable confidence information provided by the models' outputs. In the case of the conflicting results from only two models mentioned earlier, voting cannot make the correct judgment. We must find a way to leverage confidence information.

A simple example can illustrate this issue. Suppose you have an antique item and you consult five experts for evaluation. Four of the experts admit they are not very familiar with this type of antique, but based on their experience, they believe it is likely to be fake (meaning they are 60% confident in their conclusion). On the other hand, one expert is highly knowledgeable about this type of antique and firmly believes it is authentic (meaning they are 96% confident in their conclusion). The 96% authenticity conclusion from the expert who has extensive knowledge about this type of antique outweighs the combined conclusion of the other four experts who are less knowledgeable, giving a 60% counterfeit result. Hence, we can easily conclude that the antique is genuine. In the context of classification problems, when four models during training pay little attention to point F, naturally their classifications for the sample point F are uncertain and their conclusions have limited reference value. However, one model devoted considerable attention to point F during training and is highly confident in its classification result. Therefore, the classification result of this model holds greater reference value than the other four models. In such cases, where voting alone cannot yield the correct result, our proposed CoME method can provide accurate results. It is akin to how the truth often lies in the hands of a minority.

2.3   Model Ensemble

Based on the analysis above, the problem at hand now shifts to how to utilize the confidence information from multiple models to make collective judgments rather than relying solely on simple voting. This requires some knowledge of probability theory. By plotting the probability density curves of the convolution results for all points in regions D_1 and D_2, we can obtain the probability density curve for D_1 denoted as curve a and the probability density curve for D_2 denoted as curve b, as shown in Fig. 4a. And Fig. 4a represents the probability density curve of the convolution results for a specific two-dimensional input data. However, as the number of data samples and dimensions increase, according to the Central Limit Theorem [14], the probability density functions of convolution results for the same class will tend to approximate a normal distribution, as illustrated in Fig. 4b. In Fig. 4b, T represents the intersection point of the normal curves a and b, and its projection on the x-axis is denoted as T'. When the convolution result corresponds to T', the probabilities of the input samples being positive and negative are equal. To the left of T', the probability of the input samples being negative is higher, while to the right of T', the probability of the input samples being positive is higher. Therefore, the intersection point T can serve as the decision threshold between positive and negative samples, which is more reliable than manually specifying a threshold. When the convolution result is F, the probability of the input sample being positive is represented by the height of point F_a and denoted as P_a, and similarly, the probability of the input sample being negative is denoted as P_b. (Note: directly considering the function values of the probability density functions as probabilities is not correct, but they are proportional to the true probabilities, and their magnitudes do not affect the comparison of probabilities between two samples.) Therefore, the probability of the input sample being positive is given by: $\frac{P_a}{P_a+P_b}$, and the probability of the input sample being negative is given by: $\frac{P_b}{P_a+P_b}$.

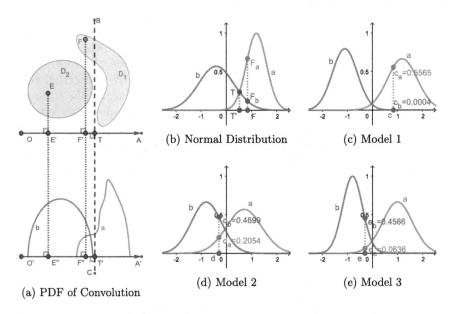

(a) PDF of Convolution

(b) Normal Distribution

(c) Model 1

(d) Model 2

(e) Model 3

Fig. 4. (a) Probability density function (PDF) representation of the computation result of convolution kernel $\overrightarrow{OA}$. (b) General case of PDF for convolution kernel output values, which follows a Gaussian distribution. The intersection point T, projected on the x-axis as T', represents the optimal decision boundary. Among the models 1, 2, and 3, two models consider the input as negative samples, while the other one considers it as a positive sample. However, utilizing probabilistic methods, we deduce that the probability of the input being a positive sample is 98.83%.

Let's assume we have three models, and their convolution results for positive and negative samples correspond to curves a and b in Fig. 4c, 4d, and 4e, respectively. The convolution results of these three models for a given sample are denoted as c, d, and e. We can calculate the probability of the input sample being positive as $P_a = c_a \times d_a \times e_a = 0.5565 \times 0.2054 \times 0.0636 = 7.269\,804\,36 \times 10^{-3}$, and the probability of it being negative as $P_b = c_b \times d_b \times e_b = 0.0004 \times 0.4699 \times 0.4566 = 8.582\,253\,6 \times 10^{-5}$. Therefore, the probability of the input sample being positive is $\frac{P_a}{P_a+P_b} = 98.83\%$, and the probability of it being negative is $\frac{P_b}{P_a+P_b} = 1.17\%$. Thus, the answer is positive. Despite the negative results from models 4d and 4e, their confidence levels are not high. Model 4c, on the other hand, provides a positive result with a high level of confidence because when the convolution result is c, there is a 0.5565 probability of it being a positive sample and only a 0.0004 probability of it being a negative sample, which is three orders of magnitude smaller than the positive probability. The voting mechanism is unable to utilize this additional information to make the correct judgment.

More generally, let's consider M classes and N models. We can calculate the probability of the input sample belonging to class j as $P_j = \prod_{i=1}^{N} p_{ij}, j \in [\![1, M]\!]$, where p_{ij} represents the probability output by model i for the sample as class j. The value of j that maximizes P_j corresponds to the model's classification result. During the training phase, the models only need to record the probability density curves for each class. During the prediction phase, we can use the probability density function (Eq. 3) as the activation function, multiply the activation results, and then normalize them to obtain the probabilities for each class. Here, μ_{ij} and σ_{ij} denote the mean and variance of the jth class output by model i, respectively. By setting $\lambda_{ij} = \frac{1}{\sigma_{ij}\sqrt{2\pi}}$ and $\varphi_{ij}(z) = -\frac{(z-\mu_{ij})^2}{2\sigma_{ij}^2}$, we can further simplify the probability formula P_j as shown in Eq. 4.

$$p_{ij} = \varepsilon_{ij}(z) = \frac{1}{\sigma_{ij}\sqrt{2\pi}}e^{-\frac{(z-\mu_{ij})^2}{2\sigma_{ij}^2}} = \lambda_{ij}e^{\varphi_{ij}(z)} \tag{3}$$

$$P_j = \prod_{i=1}^{N} p_{ij} = \prod_{i=1}^{N} \varepsilon_i(z) = \prod_{i=1}^{N} \lambda_{ij}e^{\varphi_{ij}(z)} = (\prod_{i=1}^{N} \lambda_{ij})e^{\sum_{i=1}^{N}\varphi_{ij}(z)} \tag{4}$$

At this point, it seems like we have solved our problem. However, that's not the case. The probability density function outputs results exponentially decreasing outside the 3-sigma range, and when multiple small floating-point numbers are multiplied continuously, it can result in underflow and lead to a result of zero. This prevents the models from calculating the correct results.

2.4 Model Simplification and New Insights

In this section, we will discuss how to improve the calculation process to address the issue of floating-point underflow and simplify the computations. In the previous chapters, we directly multiplied the values of the probability density function to obtain the probability P_j. However, this approach leads to the sum of probabilities for all classes not being equal to 1 because we treated the height values of the probability density function as probabilities instead of areas. Now, let's assume that the true probability of class j is P_j', while the probability calculated using the height values of the probability density function is P_j. There is a constant factor α that relates P_j and P_j', such that $P_j = \alpha P_j'$. Therefore, $\sum_{j=1}^{M} P_j = \sum_{j=1}^{M} \alpha P_j' = \alpha \sum_{j=1}^{M} P_j' = \alpha$. We can derive the true probability P_j' as shown in Eq. 5. Let's define $\varsigma_j(z) = \sum_{i=1}^{N} \varphi_{ij}(z)$, and then P_j' transforms into

Eq. 6. Remarkably, we have derived the Softmax activation function. Through this derivation, the calculation process is greatly simplified. We only need to pass the output z of node j in model i through a quadratic activation function $\varphi_{ij}(z)$, sum the activation results of corresponding nodes across all models using the function $\varsigma_j(z)$, and finally apply a Softmax activation function to obtain the probabilities for each class.

$$P'_j = \frac{P_j}{\alpha} = \frac{P_j}{\sum_{j=1}^{M} P_j} = \frac{(\prod_{i=1}^{N} \lambda_{ij}) e^{\sum_{i=1}^{N} \varphi_{ij}(z)}}{\sum_{j=1}^{M} (\prod_{i=1}^{N} \lambda_{ij}) e^{\sum_{i=1}^{N} \varphi_{ij}(z)}} = \frac{e^{\sum_{i=1}^{N} \varphi_{ij}(z)}}{\sum_{j=1}^{M} e^{\sum_{i=1}^{N} \varphi_{ij}(z)}} \quad (5)$$

$$P'_j = \frac{e^{\varsigma_j(z)}}{\sum_{j=1}^{M} e^{\varsigma_j(z)}} = Softmax(\varsigma_j(z)) \quad (6)$$

Through the above derivation, we have transformed the product form of probabilities shown in Eq. 4 into the additive form of probabilities represented by the function $\varsigma_j(z)$. This transformation occurs during the exponentiation step in the Softmax function. Consequently, the function $\varsigma_j(z)$ actually computes the addition of logarithmic probabilities (log-probabilities), and the addition of log-probabilities is ultimately transformed into multiplication of probabilities by the exponential function in Softmax. It is noteworthy that all the values flowing through the neural network are essentially logarithmic probabilities, and all the addition operations in the neural network are actually multiplication operations. The entire computation process effectively utilizes the Bayesian probability formula to calculate the probability of a higher-level feature occurrence.

From the deductions made above, we have gained new insights into neural networks: 1. The input value for each node corresponds to the log-probability of each sub-feature (e.g., eyes, nose, mouth). 2. The weighted summation operations in convolutional and fully connected layers assign weights to the probabilities of each sub-feature, while the exponential operation in Softmax transforms these weights into consideration scores for each sub-feature. 3. The summation operation, utilizing the log-probabilities of sub-features, calculates the log-probability of higher-level features (e.g., facial features). 4. Finally, the interplay of bias and ReLU layers zeroes out low-probability features, which are then effectively ignored through the subsequent exponential operation. 5. Ultimately, the node outputs the log-probability of a new higher-level feature, which, in turn, participates as a sub-feature in the calculation of other higher-level features. These operations iterate until we obtain the probability of the target feature (e.g., a person).

2.5   Final Model and Training Method

Based on the analysis conducted above, we have simplified the expensive and imprecise multiplication operations into simple and efficient addition operations. In this process, we have also derived the Softmax function and discovered that each node calculates the probability of a higher-level feature based on the previous layer's output using the Bayesian formula. Based on these findings, we can outline the training method for our final model, as depicted in Algorithm 1.

Algorithm 1: Training and Prediction Method of the CoME Model

---

Input: Number of models, denoted as m.

1 **for** $i \leftarrow 1$ **to** m **do**
2   Randomly initialize the model parameters.
3   Train model M_i using the normal training process.
4   **if** *model M_i uses Softmax as the activation function* **then**
5   Remove the Softmax layer to obtain the raw output, as illustrated in Fig. 5 (part M_1).
6   **else**
7   Take the logarithm of the model's output to restore the raw output, as shown in Fig. 5 (part M_n).
8   **end**
9   Calculate the mean and variance, denoted as μ_{ij} and σ_{ij}, respectively, for each raw output node j of model M_i, as shown in Fig. 5 (part A).
10   Save model M_i and the mean and variance information of the output nodes.
11 **end**
12 Load all models and their corresponding raw output mean and variance.
13 Feed the test data into model M_i to obtain the raw output.
14 Apply the activation function $\varphi_{ij}(z)$ to the raw output of model M_i to obtain the activation output y_i (log-probability).
15 Sum the corresponding nodes of the activation outputs y_i of each model using the function $\varsigma_j(z)$, yielding y, as shown in Fig. 5 (part y).
16 Apply the Softmax activation function to y to obtain the probabilities for each class.

---

3 Experiment and Results

To demonstrate the advantages of our method in terms of training speed and model accuracy, we conducted two experiments. The experimental network used a modified version of LeNet-5, similar to the model M_1 shown in Fig. 5, which was referenced from [6]. Our experimental results are consistent with the baseline results reported in that paper. To ensure fair and consistent comparisons, we set the random seed for all experiments to 1,907,350,387 (timestamp), and all experiments were conducted on the same machine with the same GPU.

We set the learning rate to 0.003, momentum to 0.8, and batch size to 60,000. For a training dataset of 60,000 samples, each epoch consisted of 10 batches, and the model's prediction accuracy was tested after each batch (0.1 epoch) to obtain the results shown in Table 2. In Table 2, "Acc." represents accuracy, "Base." represents the baseline model, and "Co.x" represents a combination model

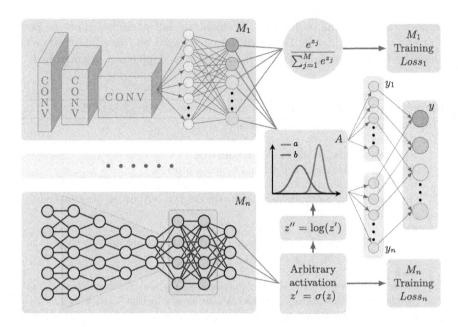

Fig. 5. CoME method for integrating output results from multiple network models with different types and structures, such as M_1 and M_n. All models require no additional adjustments during the training phase. After training, for models that use Softmax in the last layer, the Softmax layer is removed, while for models without Softmax, taking the logarithm of the output restores it to log-probability. Then, module A is used to calculate the probability distribution of each model's output for each class. Based on the distribution characteristics, the activation function for the prediction phase is computed, resulting in the activation results y_1 to y_n for models M_1 to M_n. The corresponding nodes in y_1 to y_n are summed to obtain y, which is passed through Softmax to obtain the probability for each class.

of x identical baseline models. The results in Table 2 indicate that our model achieves the same accuracy with less training epochs.

To demonstrate the effectiveness of our method, we conducted tests on diverse datasets, including *MNIST* [11], *Fashion-MNIST* [16], *CIFAR-10* [9], *SVHN* [12], *notMNIST*, *EMNIST* [3], *Kuzushiji-MNIST* [2], *Kannada-MNIST* [15], *MNIST-M* [8], *Quick, Draw!* [6] and *MNIST Variations*. We applied a standardized normalization process to these datasets to align them with the MNIST dataset. The specific processing steps were as follows: 1. Resizing images with resolutions other than 28×28 to the target resolution using the INTER_AREA interpolation algorithm. 2. Converting non-grayscale images to grayscale. 3. Selecting the first 60,000 samples for datasets larger than 60,000, or randomly sampling from the original dataset to reach 60,000 samples for datasets smaller than 60,000. 4. Selecting the first 10 classes for datasets with more than 10 classes. Although some of these datasets are not ideal for classification using such small baseline models, their inclusion allows us to clearly demonstrate the

Table 2. Minimum epochs required by different models to achieve corresponding accuracies, where a smaller value is better. The baseline model reaches 20% accuracy at 11.8 epochs, while Co.9 achieves 50% accuracy at 11.5 epochs.

Acc.	Base.	Co.2	Co.3	Co.4	Co.5	Co.6	Co.7	Co.8	Co.9	Co.10
0.20	11.8	8.6	7.4	6.9	5.8	4.7	5.0	4.5	4.9	**4.0**
0.30	17.2	12.3	10.5	9.9	8.2	7.0	7.2	6.6	6.9	**6.0**
0.40	23.0	15.9	13.7	13.3	11.0	9.4	9.5	8.6	9.0	**8.1**
0.50	31.8	20.6	17.5	17.1	14.2	12.3	12.2	11.2	11.5	**10.4**
0.60	47.0	27.4	23.1	22.3	18.2	16.3	16.1	14.9	15.1	**13.9**
0.70	70.3	40.2	32.8	32.4	25.9	23.2	22.9	21.2	20.7	**19.5**
0.80	118.6	68.8	61.4	61.7	48.9	43.1	44.6	38.8	35.6	**35.0**
0.90	297.2	234.7	208.8	218.7	190.2	166.6	**161.9**	166.8	171.5	171.6
0.95	988.8	809.1	788.6	812.2	790.5	730.8	706.3	716.5	**689.2**	706.5

Table 3. Minimum test set error rates achievable by different models on different datasets, smaller is better. For simple datasets, each sub-model possesses nearly identical classification abilities for the samples, resulting in limited improvement through integration. However, for challenging datasets, each sub-model has different classification abilities, creating a complementary relationship, leading to more significant improvements through integration. Gaussian probability density functions cannot perfectly fit the output distribution of sub-models, introducing some errors. The aggregation of multiple models amplifies this error, indicating that more models in aggregation do not necessarily yield better results.

Dataset	Base.	Co.2	Co.4	Co.6	Co.7	Co.8	Co.9	Co.10
MNIST	1.29	1.10	0.89	0.77	0.77	**0.76**	0.79	0.79
Fashion-MNIST	9.40	9.15	8.97	8.52	8.56	8.42	8.45	**8.37**
CIFAR-10	43.78	38.22	33.86	32.09	31.58	31.14	**31.07**	31.15
SVHN	14.22	11.29	10.25	9.65	9.62	9.52	9.46	**9.32**
notMNIST	5.12	4.71	4.25	3.98	**3.91**	3.97	3.96	3.93
EMNIST	1.18	1.25	1.16	1.06	0.99	**0.96**	0.97	0.97
Kuzushiji-MNIST	7.10	6.48	6.51	6.57	6.57	6.39	**5.40**	5.40
Kannada-MNIST	3.64	3.24	3.15	3.06	3.04	2.99	2.98	**2.97**
MNIST-M	13.18	11.29	10.43	9.99	9.61	9.56	**9.51**	9.53
Quick, Draw!	9.45	8.43	7.81	7.64	7.49	7.50	**7.12**	7.12
MNIST Variations	3.95	3.21	3.11	3.09	**2.96**	4.03	4.02	4.06

effectiveness of our method in improving test accuracy. Table 3 presents the test set error rates for 5,000 epochs on different datasets, with a learning rate of 0.01, momentum of 0.9, and batch size of 6,000.

From Table 2, it can be observed that the baseline model achieves only 20% accuracy after 11.8 epochs, whereas our Co.9 model reaches 50% prediction accuracy after 11.5 epochs by combining the predictions of 9 baseline models, each with 20% accuracy. This clearly demonstrates the effectiveness of our model, indicating that our method can combine multiple lower-accuracy models to obtain a higher-accuracy model. However, we also noticed that the advantage of our method in terms of speed is not very pronounced in the later stages of training. In the initial stages, the sub-models have not fully learned from the entire dataset, and each sub-model has a varying understanding of different samples in the dataset. In other words, each sub-model can confidently classify a small portion of the samples in the dataset. Although the individual sub-models correctly classify only a few samples, the union of these samples is substantial. This explains why combining 9 models with 20% accuracy results in a model with 50% accuracy, as the proverb goes, "Two heads are better than one". In the later stages, as the individual sub-models have almost learned all the samples in the dataset, and the samples learned by multiple sub-models are nearly identical. In other words, if one sub-model can classify a sample, the others can do so as well, and if it cannot, the others cannot either. Therefore, the union of samples does not increase significantly. This is the reason why our method becomes slower in the later stages of training.

From Table 3, it can be observed that the combination model with the lowest error rate does not necessarily have the highest number of sub-models. This indicates that more models in the combination do not necessarily lead to better performance. This can be attributed to the assumption made during the construction of the activation function, where we assumed that the raw output follows a Gaussian probability distribution. However, in reality, there are slight differences between the raw output and the Gaussian probability density function, introducing errors. The combination of multiple models amplifies these errors. When the accuracy gain achieved by combining multiple models cannot compensate for the combination loss, it results in a decrease in overall accuracy. However, we can mitigate this additional error by fitting a more accurate probability density function.

4   Conclusion

In summary, during our exploration of the underlying mechanisms of convolutional neural networks, we unexpectedly discovered an efficient model ensemble method known as CoME. CoME not only exhibits superior interpretability compared to Stacking but also makes better use of the valuable information provided by model outputs compared to Voting. During the model derivations, we revealed the equivalence between image convolution, vector dot product, and sample point projection. This led to conclusions regarding the orthogonality of convolutional kernels with decision boundaries and the relationship between confidence scores and projection distances. Based on this, we gained a more intuitive and profound understanding of the principles underlying image convolution. In the process of model simplification, we also unexpectedly arrived at the Softmax function, a remarkably elegant and unifying result. Building on this, we developed a new perspective on the numerical values flowing through neural networks: log-probability. Finally, our experiments confirmed the effectiveness of this novel approach.

In the future, we can consider employing this method for recursive model composition. By combining models generated by this approach as sub-models, we can construct deep neural networks. Importantly, the resulting network layers are sparse, and their parameters are computed, eliminating the need for further training.

References

1. Chen, T., Guestrin, C.: XGBoost: a scalable tree boosting system. In: Proceedings of the 22nd ACM SIGKDD International Conference on Knowledge Discovery and Data Mining, pp. 785–794 (2016)
2. Clanuwat, T., Bober-Irizar, M., Kitamoto, A., Lamb, A., Yamamoto, K., Ha, D.: Deep learning for classical Japanese literature. arXiv preprint arXiv:1812.01718 (2018)
3. Cohen, G., Afshar, S., Tapson, J., Van Schaik, A.: EMNIST: extending MNIST to handwritten letters. In: 2017 International Joint Conference on Neural Networks (IJCNN), pp. 2921–2926. IEEE (2017)
4. Cong, S., Zhou, Y.: A review of convolutional neural network architectures and their optimizations. Artif. Intell. Rev. **56**(3), 1905–1969 (2023)
5. Fernández-Delgado, M., Cernadas, E., Barro, S., Amorim, D.: Do we need hundreds of classifiers to solve real world classification problems? J. Mach. Learn. Res. **15**(1), 3133–3181 (2014)
6. Fernandez-Fernandez, R., Victores, J.G., Estevez, D., Balaguer, C.: Quick, stat!: a statistical analysis of the quick, draw! dataset. arXiv preprint arXiv:1907.06417 (2019)
7. Gambella, C., Ghaddar, B., Naoum-Sawaya, J.: Optimization problems for machine learning: a survey. Eur. J. Oper. Res. **290**(3), 807–828 (2021)
8. Ganin, Y., et al.: Domain-adversarial training of neural networks. J. Mach. Learn. Res. **17**(1), 2096-2030 (2016)
9. Krizhevsky, A., Hinton, G., et al.: Learning multiple layers of features from tiny images (2009)
10. Kuncheva, L.I.: Combining Pattern Classifiers: Methods and Algorithms. Wiley, Hoboken (2014)
11. LeCun, Y., Bottou, L., Bengio, Y., Haffner, P.: Gradient-based learning applied to document recognition. Proc. IEEE **86**(11), 2278–2324 (1998)
12. Netzer, Y., Wang, T., Coates, A., Bissacco, A., Wu, B., Ng, A.Y.: Reading digits in natural images with unsupervised feature learning (2011)
13. Opitz, D., Maclin, R.: Popular ensemble methods: an empirical study. J. Artif. Intell. Res. **11**, 169–198 (1999)

14. Petrov, V.V.: Sums of independent random variables. In: Sums of Independent Random Variables. De Gruyter (2022)
15. Prabhu, V.U.: Kannada-MNIST: a new handwritten digits dataset for the Kannada language. arXiv preprint arXiv:1908.01242 (2019)
16. Xiao, H., Rasul, K., Vollgraf, R.: Fashion-MNIST: a novel image dataset for benchmarking machine learning algorithms. arXiv preprint arXiv:1708.07747 (2017)
17. Zhang, C., Ma, Y.: Ensemble Machine Learning: Methods and Applications. Springer, New York (2012). https://doi.org/10.1007/978-1-4419-9326-7
18. Zhang, Y., Tiňo, P., Leonardis, A., Tang, K.: A survey on neural network interpretability. IEEE Trans. Emerg. Top. Comput. Intell. 5(5), 726–742 (2021)

Study on the Evolution of Public Opinion on Public Health Events

Yue Liu⬮, Yanmei Hu$^{(\boxtimes)}$⬮, and Xue Yue⬮

Chengdu University of Technology, Chengdu 610000, Sichuan, China
huym260@126.com

Abstract. It is very important to properly handle public emergencies, such as accident disasters, public health events and social security events, and understanding public opinion on public emergencies and its evolution is necessary to deal with the public emergencies. In this paper, we focus on nine public health events related to COVID-19, and explore the evolution of public opinion on these events. Specifically, we first collect information of public opinion on an event from Sina Weibo, including posts, comments. Based on the collected data, commenting networks are constructed. After that, we design a method to explore the evolution of public opinion on these events by observing and analyzing the evolution of commenting networks, including the changes in the number, emotions and topics of the comments. Further, we analyze the influence of emotion on the number and the topics of the comments. Finally, we obtain some observations that can help the emergency management departments understand the evolution of public opinion on public health events, and developing emergency plans to guide and control it.

Keywords: Social network analysis · Emotion analysis · Public emergencies · topic recognition

1 Introduction

Public emergencies include natural disasters, accidents, public health events, and social security events that occur suddenly. If a public emergency is not handled properly, it may have serious consequences and evolve into a crisis. In August 2021, news about pop star Wu Yifan's sex scandal went viral on the internet, causing horrific cyberbullying and public discussion [8]. During a public emergency, public opinion, e.g., views, comments, and emotions, can quickly spread among the crowd, which can have a significant impact on both societal stability and the management of the emergency event [29]. Therefore, understanding public opinion propagation patterns and their evolutions is necessary to handle public emergencies.

Social media, e.g., Sina Weibo, break the limitations of time and space and provide anonymity, making it convenient for people to get information and communicate with each other. Thus, more and more people are willing to express

Supported by the National Natural Science Foundation of China (No. 61802034), Sichuan Science and Technology Programs (Nos. 2021YFG0333 and 2022YFQ0017).

their opinions on public events through social media by behaviors including post-ing views, retweeting, giving thumbs up, and commenting on discussions related to the events [23]. These behaviors, which compose the main body of social media information, not only facilitate the propagation of information but also make it feasible to track public opinions on public events [20]. For example, we can prompt understand public emotion to public events from the behaviors of users who participate in discussions on the events. Based on understanding and tracking, we can further monitor the state, trend, and abnormal changes in pub-lic opinion, which can help the government make corresponding decisions and coordinating the emergency management of public events [4].

Until now, many studies have been performed on social media data, which can be essential to understanding people's opinions [19]. Over the past few years, lessons learned from disasters and emergencies suggest that social media tools may be essential for crisis response [22]. The existing studies provide us with valuable theoretical references, there are several things that can be improved:

First, they focused only on the descriptions of public opinion. For example, Kwon et al. used the earlier rumor studies as a theoretical framework for analyz-ing texts to shape public opinion but lack an exploration of how public opinion evolves [14]. And then, Cai et al. discussed the commonality of topic propagation and emotion propagation mechanisms under different types of emergencies and the relationship between topic propagation and emotion propagation through the forwarding network, but the influence of the comment network on the evolution of topic and emotion were ignored [6].

With the aim of solving these limitations and improving the understanding of public opinion on public events, we explore the evolution of comments on several public health events from two aspect: the number, and the emotions of comments. Moreover, we discuss the influence of emotion on the evolution of comments.

To finish the exploration, we propose the following two questions:

Question 1: What are the evolution of the number and the emotions of comments on the public events?

Question 2: What is the influence of emotion on the number and topics of comments?

To answer the above questions, we carry out the following work. First, we collect data from Sina Weibo on nine public health events related to COVID-19, including posts and comments. Second, we perform data preprocess including construct a commenting network and time slice for each event and filtering text content and wordsegmentation. Third, we design a method to analyze the evo-lution of the commenting network for each event by observing the changes in the number, the emotions and the topics of comments. Further, the influence of emotion on the number and the topics of the comments is also discussed. To identify the emotions of the comments, an ensemble method based on fastText, biLSTM, and BERT is developed. To identify the topics of comments, word2vec, TF-IDF, and K-means are applied.

The rest of this paper is organized as follows: Sect. 2 reviews the most related work, Sect. 3 outlines the methods, Sect. 4 discusses the results, and Sect. 5 concludes the work.

2 Related Work

In recent years, the rapid development of social media has enabled people to share or obtain information. Social media has gradually become an interactive communication channel that can quickly propagate information and receive feedback [1]. It is a low-cost and efficient method to use social media to collect and integrate various information related to an emergency [2,25]. Thus, social media has become the main source of data used to research public emergencies, and more and more related studies based on social media data have been witnessed. These studies can be classified into three categories: information gathering, disinformation detection, and public opinion analysis.

Information Gathering. During public emergencies, collecting information from bystanders and eyewitnesses is crucial for emergency management to obtain credible, first-hand information about the event's development [27]. For example, Alam et al. used social media images to assess the extent of damage during emergencies [2]. In addition, Eckhardt et al. employed textual information from Twitter messages to assess economic impact during disasters [10], and Yigitcanlar et al. analyzed media information to understand the influence of disasters on cities [26].

Disinformation Detection. Social media is a major source of information post-emergency, but it can also propagate false and harmful information, posing a challenge for detecting misinformation [7]. Pelen et al. developed mathematical models of vector-borne diseases to detect rumors on social media (Pelen, 2022). Pelen et al. have extended the classical modeling approach of rumor propagation to mathematical models of vector-borne diseases to detect the rumor on social media and explore their propagation patterns [21]. Dongsong et al. combined verbal and nonverbal behaviors on social media to identify false comments on the Web [28]. Maddock et al. explored the spread of different types of rumors online during crises through qualitative and visual analysis [17].

Public Opinion Analysis. Analyzing public opinion on social media is essential for understanding its propagation and ensuring online stability after an emergency. Li et al. conducted a study on the influence of emotional factors and influential users (with a lage number of followers) on the propagation of public opinion after disasters [15]. Luo et al. found the differences between different types of emotions in opinion propagation by analyzing the propagation characteristics and evolution pattern of online public opinion in crisis events [16]. Cai et al. focused on studying public health emergencies and revealed the laws of the formation and evolution of public opinion through data analysis on social media platforms [6]. In addition, An et al. constructed a topic and emotion communication map of microblogs on public events to visually explore the patterns of topic and emotion communication across different stages [3].

In summary, social media-based analysis of public emergencies has attracted the attention of a lot of scholars and has become a popular research topic. Our work falls into the line of public opinion analysis, but different from the previous studies, which almost focus on retweeting networks, we use comment networks to explore the evaluation of public opinions on several public events.

3   Methodology

To explore the evolution patterns of public emergencies around the questions raised in Sect. 1, we present a method in this section. See Fig. 1 for the framework of the method. It contains four steps: data collection, data preprocessing, data mining, and conjoint analysis. Data collection involves crawling information data about public events from social media, including discussions on the event (the posts related to the event and the corresponding comments). Data preprocess, e.g., time slice, constructed commenting network, filtering text content, and word segmentation, is then applied to the obtained data. After that, data mining technologies, e.g., clustering algorithms and deep neural networks are applied to the processed data to obtain the topics and emotions of comments. Finally, analysis is conducted based on these mining results to explore the answers to the raised questions. Next, we will describe each step of the method in detail.

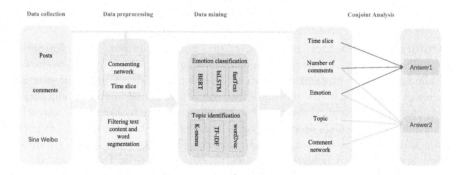

Fig. 1. The framework of the developed method

3.1   Data Collection and Preprocessing

Because our study focuses on public health events, we select events related to COVID-19 to explore the propagation rules of such events. Sina Weibo is one of the most popular social media platforms in China, has a daily active user base that reached 252 million by the end of March 2022 [11]. Thus, we take Sina Weibo as the data source and select nine COVID-19 related events that occurred between November 2021 and December 2021. More details of each selected event are shown in Table 1.

To collect the data related to the selected nine events, our first step is to search for popular topics using tags. Subsequently, we utilize web crawling techniques to collect posts and the corresponding comments involved in these topics.

Table 1. Statistic of microblog dataset

Events ID	Searched Hashtag	Original microblogs	Comments	Reposts	Time span
E1	This round of epidemic (Xi'an) has spread to 19 provinces	68	3478	1474	2021.11.04-2021.11.07
E2	The whole city of Xuzhou suspends offline teaching	63	4713	913	2021.11.26-2021.11.28
E3	A special case of a patient infecting thirteen patients appeared in Chengdu	148	5097	1759	2021.11.09-2021.11.12
E4	Advise Beijing citizens not to go out tomorrow unless necessary	439	6270	3313	2021.11.07-2021.11.09
E5	Xuzhou city-wide subway suspension	225	4981	2100	2021.11.25-2021.11.27
E6	Shanghai epidemic	651	18943	9390	2021.11.25-2021.11.30
E7	Do not open the package when you receive the express from this company in Hebei	76	3771	2227	2021.11.06-2021.11.09
E8	Chongqing epidemic	400	12926	4191	2021.11.02-2021.11.08
E9	Omicron	436	11243	8435	2021.11.29-2021.12.03

Once the event-related data is obtained, we preprocess it in the following manner. Firstly, we constructe a commenting network based on the posts and their corresponding comments. In the commenting network, each comment is represented as a node, and there is an edge from B to A if comment B is the reply to comment A. Subsequently, the data is divided into time slices based on each event. In order to clean the text of the posts and comments, we design regular expressions to remove HTML elements such as "//@ xxx" and "# xxx #", as well as punctuation and stop words.

3.2   Count the Number of Comments

The change in the number of comments on public emergencies on social media over time is an essential indicator of change in the heat of comments (i.e., the level of public interest in the event). To explore the changes in the number of comments for each event on social media over time, we begin by organizing all comments about the event based on their posting time; then, we count the number of comments in each interval, with an interval duration of one hour; after that, we draw a curve representing the number of comments in each interval; finally, according to the curve, we analyze the evolution pattern of the hotness of the comments on the event.

3.3   Topic Identification in Events

Topic identification is an effective approach for extracting meaningful information from social media data [24]. Methods for topic modeling have been well developed due to their widespread use in many text mining and natural language processing tasks. The advent of Word2vec, an efficient word embedding method that represents each word as a vector [18], topics can be identified using traditional clustering methods such as K-means. Here we follow this widely used method to identify topics in comments related to an event and describe the details as follows.

Firstly, we transform each comment into a vector by Word2vec because we want to cluster each comment into a single topic. Each comment related to an event is a short text that indicates the poster's opinion of this event, it is reasonable to cluster each comment into one topic. To transform each comment into a vector, we apply Word2vec to represent each word in the comment as a vector and take the mean vector to represent the comment. In addition, to reduce differences between text with different lengths, we control the length of each comment to be no more than l. For the comment with more than l words, we use the term frequency-inverse document frequency (TF-IDF) [39] to evaluate the importance of each word, and only keep the first l words of importance. In this paper, we set l to 20. Secondly, we apply K-means to cluster all the comments related to an event into different groups, and each group corresponds to a topic. For each topic, we also apply TF-IDF to evaluate the importance of each word in it; each topic can be described by the sorted words in descending order of importance.

3.4   Emotion Classification in Events

To classify the emotions of the comments, we developed an ensemble method based on three widely used emotion classification models, which are fastText [13], biLSTM [12] and BERT [9].

These three emotion classification models are constructed based on neural networks and require training on labeled data. As we know, large training sets generally produce good models. However, it is very time-consuming and unreliable to manually label a large number of texts. Thus, apply the following method. First, we randomly selected 2000 comments for each comment corresponding to the text and manually labeled each text with positive emotion or negative emotion. Second, we prepare a predefined dictionary including emotional words, adverbs of degree, and negative words, and each emotional word (adverb of degree) is associated with a value indicating its emotional value (degree value). The emotional words and the associated values are obtained from BosonNLP Chinese emotion vocabulary [5], and the adverbs of degree are manually marked, and the associated values are manually scored. Third, for an unlabeled text which is actually a sequence of words after preprocessing, we scan it and check each word encountered according to the predefined dictionary. Finally, to determine the emotion of the unlabeled text, i.e., positive emotion or negative emotion, we test the best threshold value of the emotional score using the manually labeled 2000 texts. (the best threshold value for positive emotion is 2 and negative emotion is -2, the accuracy on the manually labeled 2000 texts can achieve 85.7%). By aut labeling 9000 texts with this method, we obtain the training set for the three emotion classification models, i.e., fastText, biLSTM, and BERT.

After training the three models, on the training set obtained above, we integrate them to obtain an integrated model. Particularly, for a text t after preprocessing, the three models predict three labels for it, which are denoted as

$l_{fastText}$, l_{biLSTM}, and l_{BERT}, respectively; the final label for t, denoted as l_t, is decided by voting as follows:

$$l_t = \begin{cases} 0, & l_{fastText} + l_{biLSTM} + l_{BERT} \leq 1 \\ 1, & otherwise \end{cases} \tag{1}$$

Equation (1) means that at least two of the three models predict t as a positive emotion, it is taken as positively emotional t; otherwise, it is taken as a negatively emotional text. The test on the manually labeled 2000 texts shows that the ensemble model can obtain better accuracy (which is 89%) than the three single models (which is 86.6% for fastText, 86.5% for biLSTM, and 85.9% for BERT), and meets the requirements of the subsequent analysis.

4   Results and Discussions

4.1   The Evolutions of the Number, the Topics and the Emotions of Comments on the Public Events

The Evolutions of the Number of Comments. As shown in Fig. 2, we divide the duration of each event into time slices by hour, count the number of comments in each time slice, and draw them into a curve to represent the changing trend of the number of comments.

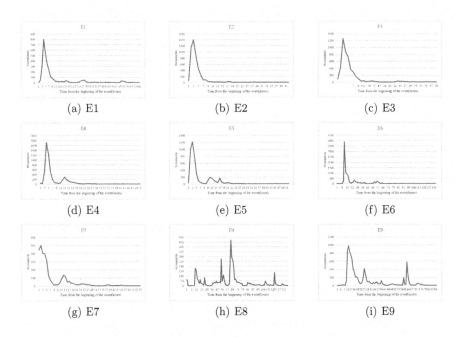

(a) E1   (b) E2   (c) E3

(d) E4   (e) E5   (f) E6

(g) E7   (h) E8   (i) E9

Fig. 2. The curve of the number of comments for each event over time

According to Fig. 2, the curves, which represent the change trends of the number of comments, can be classified into two categories. In the first category, there is only one peak located at the early time, and the number of comments rapidly declines after the peak and then fluctuates in a small range at a lower level. E1-E7 fall into this category, see Fig. 2(a)–(g). In the second category, there is a prominent peak with several small peaks, and E8 and E9 fall into this category (see Fig. 2(h) and (i)). Moreover, in the first category, the curve corresponding to E7 is a little different from others. Specifically, it starts from a large number of comments, while others start from very few comments. By analyzing the content of the event, we find that this difference is because E7 is about the outbreak caused by the express delivery of online purchases. During the pandemic, offline shopping leads to a higher risk of being infected due to crowd gathering, so many people choose to shop online, reducing infection because of rare contact with outsiders. However, the incident triggering E7 does not obey conventional wisdom. In addition, the incident was announced without specifying the item or the merchant, involving almost all the people that shopped online in the days before this incident occurred. Therefore, a lot of people were attracted to E7 in a short time.

There is also a slight rise after the peak in several curves in the first category, e.g., the curves corresponding to E4, E5, E6, and E7. By analyzing the timeline, we find that the peak of all the curves appears around 0:00 am, and the slight rise occurs between 6:00 am and 9:00 am, which is consistent with the sleep routine of many people in this era. Those people participate in the discussion before falling asleep and participate in the same discussion again after they wake up. The high consistency of the discussion content between the peak and the slight rise also provides strong evidence for this. For E8 and E9, which fall into the second category, we find that the occurrence of each peak is accompanied by a new message related to that event, which attracts people who care about the event to participate in the discussion again and causes an increase in the number of comments.

The Evolutions of the Emotions. To explore the evolution of public emotions on an event, we calculate the ratio of positive emotional comments to the total comments in each hour, starting from the beginning of the event. This ratio, denoted as R, is show in Fig. 3. In Fig. 3, the horizontal axis indicates the time (in hours) from the beginning of the event, while the vertical axis indicates R.

According to Fig. 3, we can find that R fluctuates heavily over time. This phenomenon implies that the participating users do not gather into positive or negative emotions, i.e., no consensus reaches on the emotion from a macro perspective. Moreover, by combining Fig. 2 and Fig. 3, we find that R is more stable during periods when a large number of comments are made, while it fluctuates relatively heavily when fewer people participate in the commnet. For example, the number of comments from the third to the seventh hour is large (see Fig. 2(a)), while R shows less fluctuation during this period compared to other periods (see Fig. 3(a)). Therefore, we believe that there is an adaptive

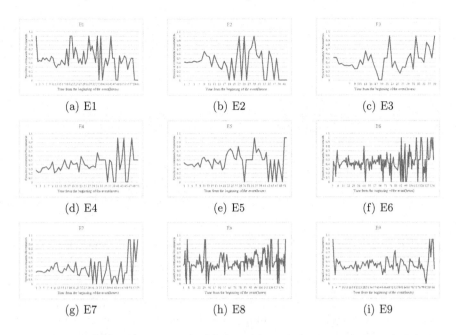

(a) E1   (b) E2   (c) E3

(d) E4   (e) E5   (f) E6

(g) E7   (h) E8   (i) E9

Fig. 3. The curve of R for each event over timee

equilibrium phenomenon on R when there is a large number of comments. In this case, positive and negative comments are relatively balanced, indicating intense arguments and disagreements among participants regarding the event.

Multiple small peaks may appear if new event-related messages are posted at different times; public emotions fluctuate significantly over time, but there is an adaptive equilibrium phenomenon when the number of comments is large.

Based on the discussions above, we can answer the question about the evolution of the number and emotions of comments on the public events (Question 1): 1) most events reach a prominent peak in about 4 h, and a slight rise may occur between 6:00 am and 9:00 am if the main peak appears around 0:00 am; 2) multiple small peaks may appear if new event-related messages are posted at different times; 3) public emotions fluctuate heavily over time, but there is an adaptive equilibrium phenomenon when the number of comments is large.

4.2   The Influence of Emotion on the Number and the Topics of Comments

The Influence of Emotion on the Number of Comments. For each event, we separately count the number of sub-comments for positive initial comments and negative initial comments, and show the average numbers of sub-comments for positive and negative initial comments are shown in Fig. 4.

According to Fig. 4, there are six events where negative initial comments have more sub-comments averagely, which are E2, E4, E5, E7, E8, and E9; and

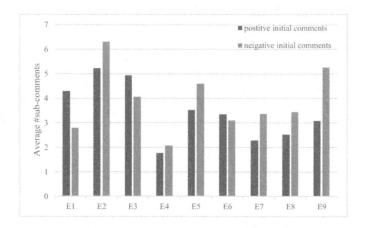

Fig. 4. The average numbers of sub-comments over positive initial comments and negative initial comments

in the remained events, i.e., E1, E3, and E6, positive initial comments have more sub-comments averagely. For E1 and E3, both events emphasize the high infectiousness of the virus and the feeling of helplessness. These factors are more likely to cause people negative emotions such as panic and despair, leading people to follow positive emotional comments. For E6, although positive initial comments have more sub-comments than negative initial comments, the difference is not significant. By analyzing the comments posted in E6, we found that the infected persons' locations included crowded places like hospitals and universities. The responses to the initial comments mainly asked for the status of the epidemic. Hence, the emotions expressed in the sub-comments were rarely influenced by the initial comment. In the remaining six events, it was found that people tended to experience emotional stress without a sense of hopelessness. In such cases, people are more likely to have negative emotions and prefer responding to negative emotional comments.

The Influence of Emotion on Topic Propagation

The Display of Topics. The topics of each event are shown in Table 2, where the keywords for each topic are also displayed (see the last column in Table 2). Moreover, we also summarize each topic based on the keywords, see the third column (i.e., the column of "Topic Summary") of Table 4. Take E1 as an example, there are four topics which are summarized as "People in the areas surrounding the outbreak express their concerns", "Accusing those who violate epidemic prevention regulations", "Hoping to overcome the epidemic as soon as possible", and "Question the effectiveness of vaccines", respectively (see the second row of Table 2).

According to Table 2, we can find that: 1) each event has at least one topic for comment and analysis of the event itself, such as the source of the epidemic or the tracing of infected individuals; 2) positive topics, such as showing support for

Table 2. Topics and keywords

Event	No	Topic Summary	keywords (Partial)
E1	T1	People in the areas surrounding the outbreak express their concerns	Hold on, Liaoning, surrounded, only remaining, safety, Jilin, sadness, encirclement, Yangtze River Delta, central, north China, west, in the gap
	T2	Accusing those who violate epidemic prevention regulations	Vaccine, abuse, play, concealment, country, Chengdu, isolation, epidemic prevention, Yinchuan, events, news, city, influence, life
	T3	Hoping to overcome the epidemic as soon as possible	Abuse, concealment, tourism, protection, infection, isolation, end, this wave, life, serious, source, early, work, defeat, concerted efforts, influence, past
	T4	Question the effectiveness of vaccines	Dalian, three injections, vaccination, Zhengzhou, diagnosis, make-up, Xingyang, managed, small shop, can't stand, travel group, train of thought, terror
E2	T1	Dissatisfaction with the local epidemic prevention policy	Shanghai, epidemic, vaccine, local people, one-size-fits-all, epidemic prevention, normal, suspension, scolding, refueling, spraying, government, outsiders, work
	T2	Encourage Xuzhou to get better quickly	Come on, epidemic situation, suspension of classes, response, hope, spray, support, case, serious, diagnosis, problem, rapid, control and resolute
	T3	Discuss the impact of the epidemic on students' study and life	Vaccine, epidemic, refueling, students, virus, normal, children, one size fits all, work, school, network
	T4	Criticizing irresponsible netizens	Cooperate, have the ability, ask you to take care of, pick matters, opinions, safety, hindrance, mouth, take care of, guarantee, willing, no
E3	T1	Discuss the role of nucleic acid detection and vaccine in epidemic prevention	Epidemic situation, nucleic acid, vaccine, case, concealment, mask, virus, infection, epidemic prevention, protection, wearing, detection, isolation
	T2	Discuss the source of the epidemic	Chongqing, case, medium and high risk, nucleic acid, isolation, concealment, going to, infection, epidemic, reporting, return, company, city
	T3	Talk about unfriendly comments about the epidemic on the Internet	Epidemic situation, Internet access, don't talk nonsense, voice, things, vaccine, everyday, subway, region, scold, COVID-19, conceal, fear
	T4	People hope the epidemic will not spread further to other regions	Wenjiang, pay attention to safety, be terrible, Qingyang District, celebrate the New Year this year, it's great, brave, poison king, it's hard to say,
E4	T1	The accusation notice does not consider the actual situation	Good night, bullshit, you raise me, tease, don't eat, open your mouth, don't hurry, shit, quilt, money, hot search
	T2	Discuss the impact of the weather in Beijing on people's lives	Community, takeout, Beijing, China, wearing armour, warning, short sleeve, subway, anti-skid, northeast, silent, go out, winter, snow
	T3	People are dissatisfied with the notice because they have to go out	Go out, count it or not, nothing, need it, don't go, Beijing, voluntary, mobile, nothing, don't understand, sure, must go, shit
	T4	Discuss the climate difference between the south and the north	Work, tomorrow, the boss, advice, do not go to work, Go out, short sleeve, Beijing, school, wear armour, air conditioning, snow, winter, don't look, wear, Guangdong, snow

(continued)

Table 2. (*continued*)

Event	No	Topic Summary	keywords (Partial)
E5	T1	Discuss the source of the epidemic	Xuzhou, isolation, Xuzhou people, McDonald's, Jiangsu, life, Nanjing, city, testing, condolence, Suzhou
	T2	Criticize netizens who speak ill on the Internet	Yancheng, laughing to death, commenting, slandering, killing, personal information, Weibo, Xuzhou, almost, determined
	T3	Discuss the impact of epidemic prevention policy on life	Cry, get bored early, amusement park, protection, New Year's Day, work, start again, quit, endless, vaccine,
	T4	Discuss the track of infected persons	Xuzhou, Suzhou, eat, that day, McDonald's, diagnosis, refueling, Jiangsu, Nanjing, influence, the whole country, Beijing, go home
	T5	Encouragement for the place where the epidemic occurred	Xuzhou, come on, report peace, Quanzhou, my grandma's home, too many people, feng shui treasure land, that night, hold on
E6	T1	Discuss the source of the epidemic	Shanghai, Southwest, Epidemic, Suzhou, Medical University, Robber, Mask, Europe and America, Beijing, Trade, Communist Youth League, Medical University
	T2	People express their fear of the virus	Terror, support, alumni, end, hamster, shit, report, sadness, help, accidental injury, wave after wave
	T3	People express their helplessness to the virus	Pay attention to safety, see, endless, come again, COVID-19, stop work, stop production, end, the world, closed, epidemic
	T4	People hope that the epidemic situation will get better soon	Engineering, stop, Chengyuan, mechanical engineering, alma mater, overcome the difficulties, hold on, win, work hard, hold on,
	T5	Discuss the track of infected persons	Shanghai, epidemic, Suzhou, nucleic acid, Beijing, isolation, mask, Disney, end, hospital, case, play, diagnosis
	T6	Discuss the current situation of the epidemic and the impact of the outbreak on the travel plan	Shanghai, epidemic, Suzhou, Beijing, tomorrow, isolation, nucleic acid, play, come back, Disney, end, transfer, case
E7	T1	I hope that the spread of information will attract more attention	Expand, thank you, release, Xiaoqiao Town, panic, flagship store, marketing, People's Daily, emergency, media, focus, official media, Hebei Province,
	T2	Criticize the incomplete information released by the media and create anxiety	Urgent, panic, comment, didn't say, can only, buy or not, People's Daily, focus, manufacturing, communication, official media, don't dismantle, manufacturer, epidemic prevention
	T3	People are worried about their express being polluted	Save lives, mix in, same batch, list, stop, one accurate, international, shipment, autumn clothes, hang, startled
E8	T1	People hope to return to normal life as soon as possible	epidemic situation, unsealing, nucleic acid, attention to safety, early recovery, going out, Chengdu, no mask, no suspension, over
	T2	Expressing concern for medical staff	Take care, key period, angel in white, staff, little angel, thank you, hug, baby, medical staff, doctor
	T3	Question the media's disclosure of the privacy of the diagnosed person	epidemic, nucleic acid, Chengdu, infection, track, company, journey, diagnosis, life, normal, Changzhou, isolation, scolding, work, announcement
	T4	Discuss the track of the confirmed person	Chongqing, Chengdu, nucleic acid, infection, epidemic situation, diagnosis, track, Changzhou, case, journey, abuse, detection, life, normal, concealment

(*continued*)

Table 2. (*continued*)

Event	No	Topic Summary	keywords (Partial)
E9	T1	Discuss the impact of the epidemic on life	Epidemic situation, New Year, virus, end, go home, Winter Olympics, hope, university, tourism, COVID-19, work, life, school closure
	T2	People hope that the epidemic will end soon	Epidemic situation, virus, end, COVID-19, mutation, hope, China, conceit, evolution, forever, disappear, roll
	T3	Worried that the Winter Olympics will accelerate the spread of the epidemic	Attention, Spring Festival, epidemic, transmission, Winter Olympics, virus, crying, next year, persistence, epidemic prevention, prosecution
	T4	Expressing frustration about the epidemic	Oh, my God, cry, take, save, save, end

local residents, are present in all events except E4. After checking the topics and comments in E4, we discovered that the negative comments primarily express dissatisfaction that the concern of the government on the event deviates from the needs of people's daily life. Therefore, we suggest that the emergency management department should consider people's living and work situations more carefully when addressing such events.

The Influence of Emotion on Topic Propagation. To analyze the correlation between the topic consistency of a comment with its sub-comments and the emotion of the comment, we evaluate the topic consistency between an initial comment and its sub-comments as follows:

$$T_{con} = T_s/T_a \tag{2}$$

where T_s is the number of sub-comments with the same topic as the initial comment, and T_a is the number of all sub-comments of the initial comment.

For each event, we separately calculate T_{con} with respect to positive initial comments and negative initial comment, and show the average T_{con} over positive initial comments and negative initial comments, respectively, in Fig. 5.

According to Fig. 5, there are seven events (i.e., E2, E4, E5, E6, E7, E8, and E9) where negative initial comments have a higher average T_{con}. This means that negative initial comments have a positive influence on topic propagation. However, in the remaining events, i.e., E1 and E3, positive initial comments have a higher average T_{con}. This is because both of them emphasize that the virus is highly infectious and people can do nothing about it, which is more likely to cause negative emotions such as panic and despair. In such case, people are willing to follow positively emotional comments and discuss similar topics. As for the other six events (i.e., E2, E4, E5, E6, E7, E8, and E9, where negative initial comments have an average T_{con}), they are about stopping offline teaching, not going out unless necessary, subway suspension, Shanghai epidemic, express delivery lead to the spread of the epidemic, Chongqing epidemic, Omicron, etc., resulting in people tend to be emotionally stressed but not hopeless. In such cases, people tend to respond to negative emotional comments and discuss similar topics.

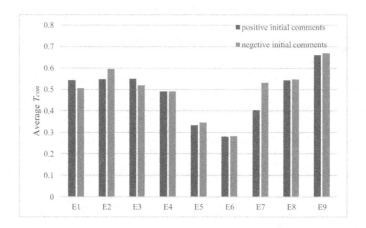

Fig. 5. Average T_{con} over positive initial comments and negative comments

Based on the discussions above, we can answer the question of the influence of emotion on the number and topics of comments (i.e., Question 2): 1) negative initial comments have more sub-comments on average, but for events where people feel powerless, positive initial comments have more sub-comments on average, probably because people tend to follow positive comments in such case; 2) negative initial comments have a positive influence on topic propagation, but for events where people feel powerless, positive initial comments are more conducive to topic propagation.

5 Conclusions

In this paper, we explore the evolution of public opinions on nine public health events related to COVID-19. Specifically, for each event, we first search for the related hot topics and crawl posts and their comments from Sina Weibo. Based on the collected data, we construct commenting networks for each event. After that, we design a method to explore the evolution of user opinions on events by observing and analyzing the evolution of commenting networks, including the changes in the number and emotions of the comments. Furthermore, we analyze the influence of emotions on the number and topics of the comments. Experimental results show that: 1) the number of comments on most events reaches a peak in about four hours, usually with only one peak; 2) public emotions fluctuates heavily over time, and there is an adaptive equilibrium phenomenon when the number of comments is high; 3) for most events, negative initial comments have more sub-comments averagely, and have a positive influence on the topic propagation; but for the events where people feel powerless, the observation is contrary; These observations can help emergency management departments in understanding the evolution of public opinions on public health events and developing effective emergency plans for guidance and control. For example, emergency management departments should pay attention to social media reactions within the first four hours after an event and focus on comments with negative emotions. Additionally, these observations can be applied to designing models that predict the development of public opinions following a public event.

There are some limitations to our study. Firstly, the observations are limited to a single type of events, i.e., public health events about COVID-19. Including different types of events can be introduced to obtain more generalizable results. Then, the methods used for emotion classification and topic identification in this paper require further improvement. Future work can address these limitations and enhance the accuracy and applicability of our findings.

References

1. Alalwan, A.A., Rana, N.P., Dwivedi, Y.K., Algharabat, R.: Social media in marketing: a review and analysis of the existing literature. Telematics Inform. **34**(7), 1177–1190 (2017). https://doi.org/10.1016/j.tele.2017.05.008
2. Alam, F., Ofli, F., Imran, M.: Processing social media images by combining human and machine computing during crises. Int. J. Hum.-Comput. Interact. **34**(4, SI), 311–327 (2018). https://doi.org/10.1080/10447318.2018.1427831
3. An, L., Zhou, W., Ou, M., Li, G., Yu, C., Wang, X.: Measuring and profiling the topical influence and sentiment contagion of public event stakeholders. Int. J. Inf. Manag. **58**, 102327 (2021). https://doi.org/10.1016/j.ijinfomgt.2021.102327
4. Bai, H., Yu, G.: A weibo-based approach to disaster informatics: incidents monitor in post-disaster situation via weibo text negative sentiment analysis. Nat. Hazards **83**(2), 1177–1196 (2016). https://doi.org/10.1007/s11069-016-2370-5
5. BosonNLP: Website (2014). https://finance.sina.com.cn/stock/usstock/c/2022-06-01/doc-imizirau6022250.shtml
6. Cai, M., Luo, H., Cui, Y.: A study on the topic-sentiment evolution and diffusion in time series of public opinion derived from emergencies. Complexity **2021** (2021). https://doi.org/10.1155/2021/2069010
7. Castillo, C., Mendoza, M., Poblete, B.: Predicting information credibility in time-sensitive social media. Internet Res. **23**(5), 560–588 (2013). https://doi.org/10.1108/IntR-05-2012-0095
8. Chen, M., Du, W.: The predicting public sentiment evolution on public emergencies under deep learning and internet of things. J. Supercomput. **79**(6), 6452–6470 (2023). https://doi.org/10.1007/s11227-022-04900-x
9. Devlin, J., Chang, M.W., Lee, K., Toutanova, K.: BERT: pre-training of deep bidirectional transformers for language understanding. In: Proceedings of the 2019 Conference of the North American Chapter of the Association for Computational Linguistics: Human Language Technologies, Volume 1 (Long and Short Papers), Minneapolis, Minnesota, pp. 4171–4186. Association for Computational Linguistics (2019). https://doi.org/10.18653/v1/N19-1423
10. Eckhardt, D., Leiras, A., Tavares Thome, A.M.: Using social media for economic disaster evaluation: a systematic literature review and real case application. Nat. Hazards Rev. **23**(1), 05021020 (2022). https://doi.org/10.1061/(ASCE)NH.1527-6996.0000539
11. Weibo released the financial report for the first quarter of 2022 (2022). https://finance.sina.com.cn/stock/usstock/c/2022-06-01/doc-imizirau6022250.shtml

12. Graves, A., Schmidhuber, J.: Framewise phoneme classification with bidirectional LSTM and other neural network architectures. Neural Netw. **18**(5–6), 602–610 (2005). https://doi.org/10.1016/j.neunet.2005.06.042
13. Joulin, A., Grave, E., Bojanowski, P., Mikolov, T.: Bag of tricks for efficient text classification. In: Proceedings of the 15th Conference of the European Chapter of the Association for Computational Linguistics: Volume 2, Short Papers, Valencia, Spain, pp. 427–431. Association for Computational Linguistics (2017)
14. Kwon, K.H., Bang, C.C., Egnoto, M., Rao, H.R.: Social media rumors as improvised public opinion: semantic network analyses of twitter discourses during Korean saber rattling 2013. Asian J. Commun. **26**(3), 201–222 (2016). https://doi.org/10.1080/01292986.2015.1130157
15. Li, L., Wang, Z., Zhang, Q., Wen, H.: Effect of anger, anxiety, and sadness on the propagation scale of social media posts after natural disasters. Inf. Process. Manag. **57**(6), 102313 (2020). https://doi.org/10.1016/j.ipm.2020.102313
16. Luo, H., Meng, X., Zhao, Y., Cai, M.: Exploring the impact of sentiment on multi-dimensional information dissemination using COVID-19 data in china. Comput. Hum. Behav. **144**, 107733 (2023). https://doi.org/10.1016/j.chb.2023.107733
17. Maddock, J., Starbird, K., Al-Hassani, H.J., Sandoval, D.E., Orand, M., Mason, R.M.: Characterizing online rumoring behavior using multi-dimensional signatures. In: Proceedings of the 18th ACM Conference on Computer Supported Cooperative Work & Social Computing, CSCW 2015, pp. 228–241. Association for Computing Machinery, New York (2015). https://doi.org/10.1145/2675133.2675280
18. Mikolov, T., Sutskever, I., Chen, K., Corrado, G., Dean, J.: Distributed representations of words and phrases and their compositionality (2013)
19. Oh, O., Agrawal, M., Rao, H.R.: Community intelligence and social media services: a rumor theoretic analysis of tweets during social crises. MIS Q. **37**(2), 407–120 (2013). https://doi.org/10.25300/MISQ/2013/37.2.05
20. Olteanu, A., Castillo, C., Diaz, F., Vieweg, S.: Crisislex: a lexicon for collecting and filtering microblogged communications in crises. In: Proceedings of the 8th International Conference on Weblogs and Social Media, ICWSM 2014, vol. 8, pp. 376–385 (2014). https://doi.org/10.1609/icwsm.v8i1.14538
21. Pelen, N.N., Golgeli, M.: Vector-borne disinformation during disasters and emergencies. Physica A Stat. Mech. Appl. **596**, 127157 (2022). https://doi.org/10.1016/j.physa.2022.127157
22. Simon, T., Goldberg, A., Adini, B.: Socializing in emergencies-a review of the use of social media in emergency situations. Int. J. Inf. Manag. **35**(5), 609–619 (2015). https://doi.org/10.1016/j.ijinfomgt.2015.07.001
23. Son, J., Lee, H.K., Jin, S., Lee, J.: Content features of tweets for effective communication during disasters: a media synchronicity theory perspective. Int. J. Inf. Manag. **45**, 56–68 (2019). https://doi.org/10.1016/j.ijinfomgt.2018.10.012
24. Stieglitz, S., Mirbabaie, M., Ross, B., Neuberger, C.: Social media analytics - challenges in topic discovery, data collection, and data preparation. Int. J. Inf. Manag. **39**, 156–168 (2018). https://doi.org/10.1016/j.ijinfomgt.2017.12.002
25. Yang, T., et al.: Social media big data mining and spatio-temporal analysis on public emotions for disaster mitigation. ISPRS Int. J. Geo-Inf. **8**(1), 29 (2019). https://doi.org/10.3390/ijgi8010029
26. Yigitcanlar, T., et al.: Detecting natural hazard-related disaster impacts with social media analytics: the case of Australian states and territories. Sustainability **14**(2), 810 (2022). https://doi.org/10.3390/su14020810

27. Zahra, K., Imran, M., Ostermann, F.O.: Automatic identification of eyewitness messages on twitter during disasters. Inf. Process. Manag. **57**(1), 102107 (2020). https://doi.org/10.1016/j.ipm.2019.102107
28. Zhang, D., Zhou, L., Kehoe, J.L., Kilic, I.Y.: What online reviewer behaviors really matter? Effects of verbal and nonverbal behaviors on detection of fake online reviews. J. Manag. Inf. Syst. **33**(2), 456–481 (2016). https://doi.org/10.1080/07421222.2016.1205907
29. Zhang, T., Cheng, C.: Temporal and spatial evolution and influencing factors of public sentiment in natural disasters-a case study of typhoon haiyan. ISPRS Int. J. Geo-Inf. **10**(5), 299 (2021). https://doi.org/10.3390/ijgi10050299

Enhance the Transferability from an Overfitting Perspective

Tong Wang, Zijiang Shan, Jie Guo$^{(\boxtimes)}$, and Wei Song

College of Information and Communication Engineering, Harbin Engineering University,
Harbin 150001, China
shawngj@hrbeu.edu.cn

Abstract. Deep neural networks perform best on a variety of collaborative computing tasks, but they are very susceptible to adversarial perturbations. Adversarial perturbations have been shown to be applicable in a variety of scenarios, and electronic data transmitted in the online world is highly vulnerable to adversarial examples. Adversarial attacks play a crucial role in robustness evaluation tests before deep neural networks are put to use. However, in the case where the attacker does not know the specific structure and parameters of the victim model, i.e., in the case of a black-box attack, the attacker can only deceive the victim model with a low success rate. The current black-box iterative attacks have two flaws. First, the iteration trajectories generated by existing attack methods lack diversity and adaptability. Second, insufficient efforts have been made to push adversarial examples towards incorrect classifications, which makes the adversarial examples not learn enough features of the wrong classification, resulting in lower transfer attack success rate. In this paper, we propose a scheme that can ameliorate these shortcomings. Our approach builds upon the Curls iteration, leveraging the Nesterov Accelerated Gradient method to accelerate gradient descent and introduce more diverse iteration trajectories. Additionally, to make the adversarial examples learn more features of the wrong classification, we further push the adversarial examples towards incorrect labels after successfully deceiving the model. Experimental results show that our scheme effectively enhances the transferability of generated adversarial examples across different network models.

Keywords: adversarial example · Nesterov Accelerated Gradient · Curls iteration

1 Introduction

Deep neural networks (DNNs) perform very well on challenging tasks such as image classification [1, 2] and semantic segmentation [3]. However, DNNs are extremely susceptible to small perturbations added to the inputs [4, 5]. Well-designed examples that look virtually indistinguishable from the original image can mislead models that have a very high discrimination success rate. This phenomenon, which may affect the completion of collaborative computing tasks and pose a security risk, was first proposed in [4]. What is worse, existing studies [5] show that adversarial examples can even transfer

© The Author(s), under exclusive license to Springer Nature Singapore Pte Ltd. 2024
Y. Sun et al. (Eds.): ChineseCSCW 2023, CCIS 2013, pp. 252–264, 2024.
https://doi.org/10.1007/978-981-99-9640-7_18

across models with different architectures and parameters, which means that attackers can use adversarial examples generated by substitute models to attack the target model. Research in adversarial attacks can help us enhance the robustness of our models [6] as well as improve existing training algorithms [5, 7].

Adversarial attacks can be classified into two categories based on the attacker's knowledge of the target model: white-box attacks and black-box attacks. White-box attacks require all the information about the victim model including architecture, parameter values, and so on. Those knowledge can be used to accurately calculate the gradient of the loss function of the input [8]. However, if the attacker doesn't know the details of the target model, white-box attacks can be completely unavailable. Contrary to the white-box attacks, black-box attacks can be operate without knowing the specific parameters of the model [9]. Black-box attacks can be roughly categorized into query-based attacks and transfer-based attacks [10]. Query-based attacks directly query the target model iteratively (potentially up to thousands of times) and elaborate adversarial examples based on the feedback from the model. However, in some scenarios, frequent use of similar image access models is likely to raise the alarm of the model owner and lead to their further action. In the cases where the number of model accesses is limited, transfer-based attacks may be a better option. The transferability of adversarial examples may be due to the fact that different DNN models obtained similar classification boundaries after training, so that adversarial examples designed for one DNN can also fool others. Transfer-based attacks require an alternative model whose parameter details are visible to the attacker. Attackers use white-box attack methods to generate adversarial examples on substitute models and exploit the transferability of these adversarial examples to attack the target model [8].

Transfer-based attacks can be categorized into iterative attacks and single-step attacks [11]. In the case of white-box attacks, single-step attacks have a lower success rate compared to iterative attacks. However, in a black-box setting, single-step attacks can achieve a higher success rate [12]. This may because iterative attacks are more prone to overfitting the specific features of the surrogate model and neglecting the common features, while single-step attacks only perform one gradient update and are more able to capture the common features of the model, not overly dependent on the model's details. Thus single-step attack producing adversarial examples with low white-box success rates but slightly better transferability [13].

After observing this phenomenon, enhancing the diversity of adversarial examples and avoiding their overfitting to specific networks seems to be a feasible point to enhance the transferability of adversarial examples. In this work, we propose a method to enhance the transferability of adversarial examples by increasing the diversity of iterative trajectories. Our work is inspired by [13] and [14]. In [13], the authors consider that monotonic gradient ascent is more likely to trap adversarial examples into local optimum of substitute model thus making it less likely that the adversarial examples will cross the classification boundary line of the target model Thus, they propose a method of first gradient rise to the apex and then gradient descent to increase trajectory diversity. According to [14] there are two main issues with iterative attacks: 1) During the iterative computational processing, the added perturbations is the accumulation of gradient in each iteration, which tends to overfit the substitute model. This leads to a lack of diversity of the generated perturbations, resulting in low transferability. 2) It is not sufficient to simply bring adversarial examples closer to the wrong classification without moving away from the original true classification.

We incorporate the Curls iteration and opinion of [14]. Unlike the original method, we use the Nesterov Accelerated Gradient method to implement gradient changes, which not only speeds up the convergence of the gradient, but also enhance the transferability by bringing more diverse iteration trajectories to adversarial examples. Once the model is successfully fooled, unlike other methods that stop iterative calculations, our method will continue to perform gradient ascent, pushing the adversarial example deep into the wrong classification. To further increase the diversity of the perturbations, we add Gaussian white noise to the examples during the iteration process.

2 Related Work

In this section, we briefly describe some of the existing adversarial attack and defense methods. Given a classifier $f(x) : x \rightarrow y$ that output y is the prediction label of the input x. The purpose of adversarial attacks is to construct perturbations that are small in magnitude but mislead the classifier when added to x. Adversarial attacks can be categorized into targeted and untargeted attacks based on the labels that the attacker expects the classifier to return after processing the adversarial examples.[15]. For a primeval input x with its true label y, a non-targeted adversarial example x' misdirects the classifier to $f(x') \neq y$. A targeted adversarial example tends to mislead the classifier to a specific attacker-specified label y'. In most studies, researchers use L_p norm as a limit on the size of the perturbations, where p could be 0, 1, 2, ∞. In this work, we use L_∞ norm to constrain the size of adversarial perturbations. Therefore, the constrained optimization problem can be formulated as:

$$\underset{\delta}{\arg max} J(x + \delta, y), \text{ s.t. } \|\delta\|_\infty \leq \epsilon \tag{1}$$

where J is often the cross-entropy loss.

2.1 Attack Methods

Fast Gradient Sign Method (FGSM). FGSM is a typical one-step attack method, that utilizes the gradient to create the adversarial example that maximizes the loss under the constraints [5]. The update equation is

$$x' = x + \alpha \cdot \text{sign}(\nabla_x J(x, y)) \tag{2}$$

where $\nabla_x J(x, y)$ is the gradient of the loss function.

Iterative Fast Gradient Sign Method (I-FGSM). I-FGSM is an improved version of FGSM [11]. FGSM only takes one step in the direction of gradient ascent, while I-FGSM takes small steps in the direction of gradient ascent, and recalculates the gradient after each update. Therefore, by increasing the iteration number and reducing the forward step size at each iteration, I-FGSM can construct more precise perturbations and achieve higher attack success rates while introducing smaller perturbations. I-FGSM can be expressed as:

$$x_0^* = x, x_{t+1}^* = x_t^* + \alpha \cdot \text{sign}(\nabla_x J(x_t^*, y)) \tag{3}$$

Previous studies [13] have demonstrated that I-FGSM has a higher white-box attack success rate than FGSM, but a lower transferability. This may be because iterative attacks are more likely to overfit the specific features of the substitute model and ignore its general features, while single-step attacks only perform one gradient update, which can capture the general features of the model more easily, without relying too much on the model's details.

Momentum Iterative Fast Gradient Sign Method (MI-FGSM). MI-FGSM [13] introduces momentum to make the update direction smoother, and momentum can also help to barrel poor local minima during the update process. The update procedure is formalized as:

$$\begin{aligned} g_{t+1} &= \mu \cdot g_t + \frac{\nabla_x J(x_t^{adv}, y^{true})}{\|\nabla_x J(x_t^{adv}, y^{true})\|_1} \\ x_{t+1}^{adv} &= \text{Clip}_x^\epsilon \{x_t^{adv} + \alpha \cdot \text{sign}(g_{t+1})\} \end{aligned} \tag{4}$$

Curls Iteration. Unlike other methods' gradient ascent schemes, Curls iterates along two trajectories, one gradient ascent and the other gradient descent followed by gradient ascent after reaching the local minimum of the class, which can increase the diversity of the iterative trajectories.

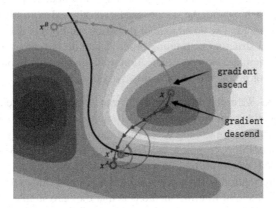

Fig. 1. Schematic of the Curls iteration trajectory

2.2 Defense Methods

Various defense methods have been proposed and their ideas can be divided into the following categories.

Adversarial Training. Adversarial training is a technique to enhance the robustness and generalization of DNN, by adding adversarial examples to the training dataset during model training. Adversarial examples are input samples that have been perturbed slightly, such that they can cause the model to produce erroneous outputs. The goal of adversarial training is to make the model adapt to both adversarial and clean data, and thus resist adversarial attacks. Adversarial training is an intrinsic defense strategy, it does not require modifying the model structure or the input preprocessing. However, adversarial training also has some limitations and issues, such as data generalization and overfitting. Therefore, in recent years, many researchers have explored and improved the methods of adversarial training and robust optimization from different perspectives.

There are two ways of adversarial training: one is straightforward but less efficient, which is to retrain the model with some adversarial examples that can deceive the model. The other is more efficient but more complicated, which is to dynamically generate adversarial examples in each training iteration, and mix them with the original inputs, then use an alternating objective function to optimize the model.

Detection Methods. Detection refer to judging whether an input is an adversarial example before the model receives it, and rejecting to process it if it is. Detection methods are usually based on some statistical features or heuristic rules, to distinguish adversarial examples from normal samples. For example, one can use gradient-based detection methods, which exploit the difference between the gradient information of adversarial examples and the gradient information normal inputs, to calculate a detection statistic. If the statistic exceeds a threshold, the sample can be recognized as an adversarial example, and discarded or marked. The advantage of detection methods is that they do not need to modify the model structure or training process, and do not affect the model performance on normal samples. However, detection methods may be bypassed by stronger adversarial attacks, or produce high false positive rates.

Filtering Methods. Refer to performing some transformations or preprocessing on the input sample before the model processes it, to eliminate or reduce the adversarial perturbation. Filtering methods are usually based on some image processing techniques, such as compression, smoothing, cropping, etc. For example, one can use JPEG compression as a filtering method, which utilizes the characteristic that JPEG algorithm loses some high-frequency information when compressing images, to remove the adversarial perturbation. The advantage of filtering methods is that they are simple to operate, and do not require additional training data or computational resources. However, filtering methods may lose some useful information, or fail to completely eliminate the adversarial perturbation.

3 Methodology

In this paper, we propose a methodology to accelerate Curls iteration with the Nesterov accelerated gradient. In order to move the adversarial examples further away from the classification dividing line and push it deeper into misclassification, we continue to perform gradient descent along the gradient direction of misclassification after successfully fooling the model. Also, to reduce the overfitting of adversarial examples to substitute networks, we introduce Gaussian noise into adversarial examples. In this section, we will describe the proposed algorithms in detail. We will begin by describing why and how the Nesterov accelerated gradient method is applied to Curls iterations Then introduce the opinion of [14], which considered pushing adversarial examples towards the valley of misclassification could bring more transferability. Finally, we have incorporated noise into the generated adversarial examples, aiming to address overfitting issues on the substitute network. This approach draws inspiration from the practice of adding noise to training samples during deep neural network training.

3.1 Nesterov Accelerated Gradient Hasten Curls Iteration

The process of generating adversarial examples is similar to the process of training neural networks. In the adversarial example generation stage, the attacked white box model can be regarded as the training data in the neural network training process. Adversarial examples can be viewed as parameters of the model. During the training process, the training parameters are continuously adjusted based on the output feedback of the model.

According to [13], increasing the diversity of adversarial example generation trajectories can increase the probability that an adversarial example crosses the classification boundary of different models. Thus, they proposed Curls iteration as a solution, which involves iterative updates to the image in two directions. The first direction is gradient ascent, while the second direction involves continuing updates along the direction of loss function descent, if the loss function hasn't reached the local minimum. Once the loss function approaches the local minimum, the update switches to the gradient ascent direction. Finally, the two images are compared and the one with smaller perturbation is retained. The update equation is:

$$x_0' = x, x_1' = Clip_{x,\varepsilon}\left\{x_0' - \alpha \cdot \nabla J_{sub}\left(x_0'\right)\right\} \tag{5}$$

$$g_{t+1} = \begin{cases} -\nabla J_{sub}\left(x_t'\right), J\left(x_t'\right) < J\left(x_{t-1}'\right), \\ \nabla J_{sub}\left(x_t'\right), J\left(x_t'\right) \geq J\left(x_{t-1}'\right), \end{cases} \tag{6}$$

$$x_{t+1}' = Clip_{X,\varepsilon}\left\{x_t' + \alpha \cdot g_{t+1}\right\} \tag{7}$$

However, the Curls iteration requires more time to calculate examples in two different directions simultaneously. Therefore, we introduced the NAG method to expedite gradient updates. Additionally, the NAG method also introduces greater diversity in the update trajectories. NAG (Nesterov Accelerated Gradient) method [16] is a variation of momentum method, which can speed up the gradient descent and reduces oscillations

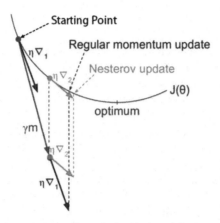

Fig. 2. Comparison of the NAG method with the original momentum method

near the extremes. As it is shown in the Fig. 1, NAG uses momentum prospectively which allows the NAG method to achieve gradient descent more quickly. The update equation for the NAG method is

$$v_{t+1} = \mu \cdot v_t + \nabla_{\theta_t} J(\theta_t - \alpha \cdot \mu \cdot v_t)$$
$$\theta_{t+1} = \theta_t - \alpha \cdot v_{t+1} \tag{8}$$

We integrated the NAG method into the Curls iterative attack(N-Curls), using the acceleration and momentum characteristics of the NAG method to construct a more powerful and faster adversarial attack, which we call the N-Curls iteration. Specifically, at each iteration, we use the NAG method to compute momentum and use it as the update direction. Start with $g_0 = 0$, the iterative update formula of adversarial example can be formalized as:

$$x_t^{nes} = x_t^{adv} + \alpha \cdot \mu \cdot g_t, \tag{9}$$

$$g_{t+1} = \begin{cases} \mu \cdot g_t - \frac{\nabla_x J(x_t^{nes}, y^{true})}{\|\nabla_x J(x_t^{nes}, y^{true})\|_1}, & J\left(x_t'\right) < J\left(x_{t-1}'\right), \\ \mu \cdot g_t + \frac{\nabla_x J(x_t^{nes}, y^{true})}{\|\nabla_x J(x_t^{nes}, y^{true})\|_1}, & J\left(x_t'\right) > J\left(x_{t-1}'\right) \end{cases} \tag{10}$$

$$x_{t+1}' = Clip_{X,\varepsilon}\left\{x_t' + \alpha \cdot g_{t+1}\right\} \tag{11}$$

where g_t denotes the calculated update direction in the iteration of round t, μ denotes the decay factor of g_t and ε represents the maximum acceptable disturbance.

3.2 Pushing Adversarial Examples Towards the Valley

According to the argument in [14], additional label information can be used in targeted black-box attacks to specifically push adversarial examples away from the original class, which can make the examples of targeted attacks obtain more transferability. This may be due to the differences in the classification boundaries between the target model and the substitute model in transfer attacks. The fact that an adversarial example crosses the boundary of the substitute model does not necessarily mean that it also crosses the boundary of the target model. Pushing the adversarial example moving towards misclassification after successfully fooling the substitute model is more probable to cause it to cross the boundary of the target model (Fig. 3).

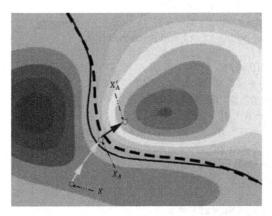

Fig. 3. The classification boundaries of substitute model and target model

As it is shown in Fig. 2, the solid line is the classification boundary of the substitute model, the dotted line is the classification boundary of the target model, X is the original image, X_A is the adversarial example, $X_{A'}$ is the adversarial example generated by further pushing X_A towards misclassification. It can be observed that although X_A successfully deceived the surrogate model, it did not cross the boundary of the target model. On the other hand, $X_{A'}$ can cause misclassification in the target model.

Therefore, after successfully fooling the substitute model, we convert the attack into a targeted attack, setting the target as the misclassified category. We continue to reduce the cross-entropy between the adversarial example and the misclassified category (Push towards the valley). With this initiative, the adversarial example moves further away from the original classification, and the adversarial example learns more features of misclassification. The update equation is:

$$x'_{t+1} = x'_t + \alpha \cdot g_t \tag{12}$$

$$g_t = -\nabla J_{sub}\left(x'_t, y_{wrong}\right) \tag{13}$$

3.3 Reduce Overfitting by Gaussian Noise

Algorithm 1:   Overall algorithm

Input: Substitute model Sub(x)
         Original picture x and its label y
         Perturbation limit ε
         Number of iterations T
         Variance of gaussian noise s
         Step size α
         The extra number of pushes P

Output: Adversarial example x'

1: Initialize starting points x_0^A, x_0^B and momentum g_0
2: for t = 1 to T do
        $\zeta_t^A, \zeta_t^B \sim N(0,s^2 I)$
        $x_t^A = x_{t-1}^A + \zeta_t^A, x_t^B = x_{t-1}^B + \zeta_t^B$
        Calculator g_t^A, g_t^B by NAG method
        $x_t^A = x_t^A + \alpha * g_t^A$
        $x_t^B = \begin{cases} x_t^B - \alpha * g_t^B, if\ unreach\ the\ extreme\ point \\ x_t^B + \alpha * g_t^B, if\ reached\ the\ extreme\ point \end{cases}$
        $x_t^A = Clip\ (x_t^A)$
        $x_t^B = Clip\ (x_t^B)$
   End for
   If Sub(x_t^A) $\neq$ y and Sub(x_t^B) $\neq$ y
      if $L_\infty(x_t^A) < L_\infty(x_t^B)$
            $x' = x_t^A$
      Else $x' = x_t^B$
      End if
   for p = 1 to P do
         $x' = x' + \alpha * g_p'$
   End for
Return x'

In the training process of neural networks, adding noise is often used to avoid overfitting. Previous research [17, 18] has shown that adding noise to the input data during the training of a neural network can significantly improve the generalization performance of the network. Noise can make the input space smoother, which is conducive to the learning of neural networks.

Based on the researches that noise can reduce overfitting in neural networks [19], we believe that noise may also reduce overfitting of adversarial examples on substitute models, thereby enhancing the transferability of adversarial examples. During the iterative attack process, the perturbation added is the accumulation of gradient momentum in each iteration, which results in high similarity of perturbations during the iteration [14]. Therefore, the diversity and adaptability of perturbation are insufficient, leading to low transferability. Adding Gaussian noise can effectively increase the diversity of adversarial examples and reduce overfitting of adversarial examples to substitute networks.

4 Experience

4.1 Setting

Dataset. All our experiments are performed on Stanford Dogs [20]. Randomly select 1000 images from the Stanford Dogs test set that can be correctly classified by the test model as the test dataset for the experiment.

Model. To synthesize and evaluate the advantages and disadvantages of different attack methods, we chose three different models for our experiments. Those are Inc-V3 [21], Inc-V4 [22] and ResNet50 [23].

Parameter. Our parameter settings are: step size $\alpha = 1$, the max number of iterations $T = 20$. The maximum perturbation of a single pixel is $\epsilon = 15$, a magnitude that remains imperceptible to human [24].The decay factor μ is set to be 0.9.

Baseline Algorithm. The comparison algorithms include FGSM, I-FGSM, and MI-FGSM. Denote our method as P-N-Curls.

Table 1. The success rate of different attack methods.

Model	Attack	Inc-V3	Inc-V4	ResNet50
Inc-V3	FGSM	58.9%*	22.4%	20.6%
	I-FGSM	99.7%*	11.9%	7.1%
	MI-FGSM	99.9%*	34.7%	28.5%
	P-N-Curls	99.9%*	38.1%	33.4%
Inc-V4	FGSM	28.3%	50.4%*	21.7%
	I-FGSM	20.6%	99.9%*	11.1%
	MI-FGSM	50.8%	99.9%*	31.3%
	P-N-Curls	52.5%	99.9%*	31.9%
ResNet50	FGSM	27.4%	20.3%	83.7%*
	I-FGSM	21.9%	16.2%	98.1%*
	MI-FGSM	52.7%	43.9%	98.7%*
	P-N-Curls	53.6%	48.7%	99.7%*

4.2 Transfer Attack

In Table 1, we present the success rates of attacking different models. The first column indicates the substitute models used for transfer attacks, and the second column records the attack methods employed. The blocks on the diagonal represent the results of white-box attacks, which have been marked with an asterisk (*). The remaining blocks record the success rates of the adversarial examples generated by the substitute model in fooling the model in the first row. As shown in Table 1, our approach achieves an attack success rate close to 100%, This indicates that our method can serve as a highly effective white-box attack technique.

It can be seen that the success rate of transfer attack success rate of the iterative method (I-FGSM) is lower than the single-step method(FGSM). We posit this is likely because the I-FGSM method overfits to the substitute model during the iterative computation process, resulting in a high success rate for white-box attacks but performs poorly in transfer attacks. On the other hand, the MI-FGSM method introduces momentum, which increases the diversity of the adversarial example generation trajectory, hence achieving a higher success rate for transfer attacks compared to I-FGSM. Our method, building upon the introduction of Nesterov accelerated gradient, further pushes the adversarial examples towards the valley of misclassification, resulting in better performance than MI-FGSM. Figure 4 shows the comparison of the image generated by our method with the original image, and it can be seen that the added perturbation is barely visible.

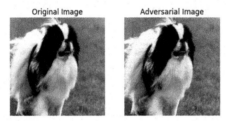

Fig. 4. The comparison between the generated image and the original image

4.3 Ablation Studies

In this section, we designed a series of ablation experiments to study the impact of NAG (N-Curls) and Push towards the valley (P-Curls) on the transferability. The experimental parameter settings are the same as in the previous section.

We have recorded the success rates of transfer attacks for the Curls method, P-Curls method, N-Curls method, and P-N-Curls method in Table 2. The first column of the table represents the substitute models used for the transfer attacks, while the second column indicates the attack methods employed. The blocks on the diagonal represent the results of white-box attacks, which have been marked with an asterisk (*).

From the results, it can be observed that both the NAG method and the push towards valley method increase the possibility that the adversarial example crosses the classification boundary. This aligns with the results obtained from our theoretical analysis, indicating that both increasing the diversity of adversarial sample iterative paths and further pushing adversarial samples towards misclassification can enhance their transfer attack capability. However, the improvement efficiency of these two methods is not the same. The NAG method can enhance the transferability of more effectively compared to the push towards valley method. This could be the fact that the push towards valley method employs ordinary gradient descent to generate adversarial examples, which significantly reduces the diversity in adversarial example generation. Furthermore, while the push towards valley method achieves more misclassification features when transferring adversarial examples in the direction of misclassification, it is also more influenced by the substitute model.

Table 2. Comparison of various enhanced Curls method

Model	Attack	Inc-V3	Inc-V4	ResNet50
Inc-V3	Curls	99.9%[*]	26.7%	19.6%
	P-Curls	99.9%[*]	29.2%	23.4%
	N-Curls	99.9%[*]	34.7%	28.5%
	P-N-Curls	99.9%[*]	38.1%	33.4%
Inc-V4	Curls	39.2%	99.9%[*]	21.7%
	P-Curls	47.3%	99.9%[*]	23.7%
	N-Curls	50.6%	99.9%[*]	27.3%
	P-N-Curls	52.5%	99.9%[*]	31.9%
ResNet50	Curls	43.5%	37.8%	98.1%[*]
	P-Curls	47.4%	41.6%	98.1%[*]
	N-Curls	51.3%	46.3%	99.2%[*]
	P-N-Curls	53.6%	48.7%	99.7%[*]

5   Conclusion

In this paper, we re-examine the transferability of adversarial examples from the perspective of overfitting to substitute models. We propose using the NAG method in conjunction with Curls iterations for gradient descent to enhance the diversity of paths in generating adversarial examples. Additionally, we suggest pushing the generated adversarial examples further towards the valley of misclassification after successfully attacking the substitute model, in order to increase transfer attack capabilities. A series of experiments were conducted to verify the effectiveness of the proposed methods and we explain why they work. Experimental results on Stanford Dogs demonstrate that compared to traditional iterative methods, our method generates images that are more likely to cross the classification borders of different models.

Acknowledgements. This article is supported by the National Natural Science Foundation of China (62372131).

References

1. Krizhevsky, A., Sutskever, I., Hinton, G.E.: Imagenet classification with deep convolutional neural networks. Commun. ACM **60**(6), 84–90 (2017)
2. Szegedy, C., Liu, W., Jia, Y., et al.: Going deeper with convolutions. In: Proceedings of the IEEE Conference on Computer Vision and Pattern Recognition, pp. 1–9 (2015)
3. Long, J., Shelhamer, E., Darrell, T.: Fully convolutional networks for semantic segmentation. In: Proceedings of the IEEE Conference on Computer Vision and Pattern Recognition, pp. 3431–3440 (2015)

4. Szegedy, C., Zaremba, W., Sutskever, I., et al.: Intriguing properties of neural networks. arXiv preprint arXiv:1312.6199 (2013)
5. Goodfellow, I.J., Shlens, J., Szegedy, C.: Explaining and Harnessing Adversarial Examples. International Conference on Learning Representations (2015)
6. Arnab, A., Miksik, O., Torr, P.H.S.: On the robustness of semantic segmentation models to adversarial attacks. In: Proceedings of the IEEE Conference on Computer Vision and Pattern Recognition, pp. 888–897 (2018)
7. Tramr, F., Kurakin, A., Papernot, N., et al.: Ensemble adversarial training: attacks and defenses. Int. Conf. Learn. Represent. 1, 2 (2018)
8. Ilyas, A., Santurkar, S., Tsipras, D., et al.: Adversarial examples are not bugs, they are features. In: Proceedings of the 33rd International Conference on Neural Information Processing Systems, pp. 125–136 (2019)
9. Papernot, N., McDaniel, P., Goodfellow, I., et al.: Practical black-box attacks against machine learning. In: Proceedings of the 2017 ACM on Asia Conference on Computer and Communications Security, pp. 506–519 (2017)
10. Li, X.C., Zhang, X.Y., Yin, F., et al.: F-mixup: attack CNNs from fourier perspective. In: 2020 25th International Conference on Pattern Recognition (ICPR), pp. 541–548. IEEE (2021)
11. Kurakin, A., Goodfellow, I.J., Bengio, S.: Adversarial examples in the physical world. In: Artificial Intelligence Safety and Security, pp. 99–112. Chapman and Hall/CRC (2018)
12. Kurakin, A., Goodfellow, I., Bengio, S.: Adversarial machine learning at scale. arXiv preprint arXiv:1611.01236 (2016)
13. Dong, Y., Liao, F., Pang, T., et al.: Boosting adversarial attacks with momentum. In: Proceedings of the IEEE Conference on Computer Vision and Pattern Recognition, pp. 9185–9193 (2018)
14. Li, M., Deng, C., Li, T., et al.: Towards transferable targeted attack. In: Proceedings of the IEEE/CVF Conference on Computer Vision and Pattern Recognition, pp. 641–649 (2020)
15. Pan, W.W., Wang, X.Y., Song, M.L., Chen, C.: Survey on generating adversarial examples. J. Softw. 31(1), 67–81 (2020)
16. Polyak, B.T.: Some methods of speeding up the convergence of iteration methods. USSR Comput. Math. Math. Phys. 4(5), 1–17 (1964)
17. Du, Y., Shao, W., Chai, Z., et al.: Synaptic 1/f noise injection for overfitting suppression in hardware neural networks. Neuromorph. Comput. Eng. 2(3), 034006 (2022)
18. Bejani, M.M., Ghatee, M.: A systematic review on overfitting control in shallow and deep neural networks. Artif. Intell. Rev. 54(8), 6391–6438 (2021)
19. Xie, Z., He, F., Fu, S., et al.: Artificial neural variability for deep learning: on overfitting, noise memorization, and catastrophic forgetting. Neural Comput. 33(8), 2163–2192 (2021)
20. Khosla, A., Jayadevaprakash, N., Yao, B., et al.: Novel dataset for fine-grained image categorization: stanford dogs. In: Proceedings of the CVPR Workshop on Fine-Grained Visual Categorization (FGVC). Citeseer, vol. 2, no. 1 (2011)
21. Szegedy, C., Vanhoucke, V., Ioffe, S., et al.: Rethinking the inception architecture for computer vision. In: Proceedings of the IEEE Conference on Computer Vision and Pattern Recognition, pp. 2818–2826 (2016)
22. Szegedy, C., Ioffe, S., Vanhoucke, V., et al.: Inception-v4, inception-resnet and the impact of residual connections on learning. Proc. AAAI Conf. Artif. Intell. 31(1) (2017)
23. He, K., Zhang, X., Ren, S., et al.: Deep residual learning for image recognition. In: Proceedings of the IEEE Conference on Computer Vision and Pattern Recognition, pp. 770–778 (2016)
24. Luo, Y., Boix, X., Roig, G., et al.: Foveation-based mechanisms alleviate adversarial examples. arXiv preprint arXiv:1511.06292 (2015)

CMGN: Cross-Modal Grounding Network for Temporal Sentence Retrieval in Video

Qun Zhang, Bin Jiang$^{(\boxtimes)}$, Bolin Zhang, and Chao Yang

College of Computer Science and Electronic Engineering, Hunan University,
Changsha 410082, Hunan, China
{zqlll,jiangbin,onlyou,yangchaoedu}@hnu.edu.cn

Abstract. Temporal sentence grounding in video (TSGV) focuses on identifying the most pertinent temporal segment within an untrimmed video, given a natural language query. Its principal aim is to ascertain and retrieve the specific moment that impeccably aligns with the given query. Although the existing methods have done much research in this field and achieved specific achievements, there are still problems of massive calculation and insufficient grounding. Our method mainly focuses on obtaining better video and query features performing cross-modal feature fusion better, and locating more accurately when dealing with this problem. We propose an efficient Cross-Modal Grounding Network (CMGN) to balance the amount of computation and localization accuracy. In our proposed structure, we obtain the local context information through a bidirectional Gated Recurrent Unit (GRU). We obtain the start and end boundary characteristics for a better video presentation. Then, the two-channel structure, divided into a start channel and an end channel, captures the temporal relationships among several video segments sharing common boundaries. To validate the effectiveness of our method, extensive experiments were conducted on two datasets.

Keywords: moment retrieval with nature language · Cross-modal retrieval · Multi-modal learning

1 Introduction

Video retrieval has become a vital issue in video understanding. The research based on this direction is mainly divided into two sub-directions: temporal sentence grounding and temporal action localization. The temporal action localization finally locates the given action queries in the video. This direction is limited to a closed set of actions; simple action classifications cannot describe complex situations in reality. Moment localization with natural language requires finding fragments described by a given natural language on untrimmed video. Unlike temporal action localization, it needs to process information across modalities, which is also a challenging task due to the complexity of natural language and video content. In order to obtain a richer representation of the video context,

Y. Sun et al. (Eds.): ChineseCSCW 2023, CCIS 2013, pp. 265–275, 2024.
https://doi.org/10.1007/978-981-99-9640-7_19

the work currently done is mainly divided into two parts: analyzing the local context and the global context. For example, given a query, "Takes now cooked eggs out of pan and onto plate," if you only analyze the current moment, you cannot judge whether the current moment is in line with the "cooked" of natural language description. So how to better integrate contextual information is vital to achieving video grounding. Existing approaches can be classified into moment-based and clip-based methods based on whether candidate moments are generated when processing video clips. The moment-based methods sample or enumerates the video first, then fuse the results with queries across modalities and scores the candidate moments according to the characteristics to achieve localization. However, the effect of the candidate moment-based approach has a strong dependence on the quality of the proposal at the candidate moment. This paper improves the quality of the proposal by allowing clips of any length in the video to be candidates through a dual-channel approach. This paper investigates the global and local context features of the video in order to obtain a comprehensive representation of video features. The main contributions are as follows:

(1) We propose a Cross-Modal Grounding Network (CMGN) that leverages global and local contextual features in video.
(2) We conducted experiments on the TACoS and ActivityNet datasets, and our results are competitive compared with the current methods on these datasets (Fig. 1).

Fig. 1. An example about temporal sentence grounding in an untrimmed video. TSGV aims to retrieve the most relevant moment in the video based on the given natural language sentence. In the accompanying figure, the correct query video moment is indicated by the green box. (Color figure online)

2   Related Work

TSGV is initially introduced in [1–3] to retrieve videos using natural language. Currently, there exist two primary approaches to solving this problem using strong supervised learning methods: proposal-based and proposal-free methods. Early proposal-based methods [1,2,4–7] can be further classified based on how proposals are generated, including sliding window-based methods, anchor-based methods and proposal generation methods. Gao et al. [1] first capture the video clips through the sliding windows to generate the candidate moment, then match the candidate moment with the queries, then score and rank to obtain the moment that matches the queries. However, this method cannot match the real moment perfectly. Anne et al. [2] allude to query characteristics and video suggestions in the public space, but the temporal information is easily ignored. Since the sliding window method will incur a high computational cost and need to recalculate the overlapping area, some methods [5,7–9] adopt the proposal generation method. The time attention weight is obtained by embedding the queries and interacting with visual features to obtain the time attention weight. The proposal generation strategy is weighted to improve the proposal generation strategy. This method solves the problem of proposal intensity, but there is still the problem that the context information may be ignored. The anchor-based approach produces candidate proposals of different sizes around the anchor point. Chen et al. [6] interact verbatim when generating proposals. Yuan et al. [7] and Zhang et al. [9] generate candidate proposals through time convolution modules. Zhang et al. [9] proposed a spares sampling strategy to remove redundant moments. Zhang et al. [10] obtain richer context by constructing a 2D map but ignores the multi-modal interaction part. Wang et al. [11] Generate time suggestion features, time content features, and time boundary features, then average pooling to obtain time features. Nevertheless, this approach is significantly constrained by the quality of proposals. This paper adopts the moment-based method for implementation and contributes to exploring the context characteristics of video, the feature fusion of video and sentences, and sentence encoding.

Recent research has made a lot of efforts to explore the contextual features of video, and currently, video processing is first used to extract features from videos, such as I3D [12] or C3D [13]. Gao et al. [1] only use max-pooling to obtain the moment features, which lacks the exploration of the video context features. Zhang et al. [5] use attention mechanism to obtain semantic dependencies.

Regarding feature fusion between video and sentences, a structured multi-level interaction module is used for structured moment interaction in SMIN [11]. Liu et al. [14] construct Cross-modal maps, and then cross-modal feature fusion is carried out by graph convolutional neural network. GAO et al. [8] directly perform addition or multiplication operations between video and sentence features to achieve cross-modal feature fusion in the feature fusion part of video and queries. Liu et al. [14] construct cross-modal graphs and then use graph convolutional neural networks for cross-modal feature fusion, but this processing significantly increased the computational amount of the network. Soldan et al. [15] understand the natural language localization of video as a problem of reading comprehension pairing and adopt a cross-graph attention-matching mechanism in the cross-modal fusion part. We followed the dual-channel approach in DCLN [16], which can obtain competitive results with low computational intensity.

3   Method

We first explain the problem of TSGV and then explain our method in detail from three modules: video encoding, natural language encoding, and video grounding in the following section (Fig. 2).

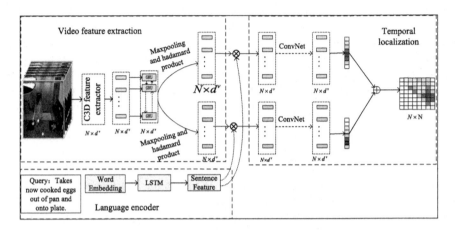

Fig. 2. The network architecture of Cross-Modal Grounding Network (CMGN). The network architecture of CMGN can be divided into video feature extraction, language encoder, and temporal localization. Video feature extraction generates the moment feature and then generates start and end channels. Language encoder implements natural language coding. Finally, the temporal localization part scores the candidate moments to realize localization.

3.1   Problem Formulation

The task involves determining the timestamps (t_s, t_e) of a specific video segment referring to the sentence. The query S contains l^s words, and we use w^i to represent the i-th word, so $S = \{w_i\}_{i=0}^{l^s-1}$. Video V consists of l^v frames. We use v_i to represent a frame, that is, $V = \{v_i\}_{i=0}^{l^v-1}$.

3.2   Language Encoder and Video Encoder

A natural language query is denoted as $S = \{w_i\}_{i=0}^{l^s-1}$. We use GloVe to encode words to obtain the vector sequence $q_i \in R^{d^Q}$. After that, we adopt LSTM to explore contextual semantic information of the subsequent result, denoted as $f^Q \in R^{d^Q}$.

A video has l^v consecutive frames, and we divide it into video segments of the length of each T-frame and then sample them at specific intervals, denoted as $V = \{v_i\}_{i=0}^{l^v-1}$. The sampled results were extracted using C3D [13]. A fully connected layer obtained the extracted frame features to obtain a compact visual feature. We followed the MCN [2] method to construct candidate moment features by pooling.

In order to make the moment features have richer context information, we use BiGRU [24] to aggregate local and context information.

$$h_i^f = GRU_q^f(v_i, h_{i-1}^f) \tag{1}$$

$$h_i^b = GRU_q^b(v_i, h_{i-1}^b) \tag{2}$$

$$f_i^v = [h_i^f : h_i^b] \tag{3}$$

The GRU_i^f and GRU_i^b represent the forward and backward GRU networks, respectively. The backward and forward hidden state at the i-th step are represented as h_i^f and h_i^b, corresponding to the backward and forward directions. By concatenating these two hidden states, denoted as f_i^v, we obtain the representation for the specific moment in the video. In this way, all candidate moments of the video are traversed, and the aggregation of local context information is achieved. When all the moment features of the video clip are traversed bidirectionally from front to back and back to front, we completed the context feature fusion of the video. Finally, we get the result of BiGRU denoted as $f^v \in R^{N \times d^v}$.

After aggregating the context characteristics, we obtain the boundary information of the video through maximum pooling. When obtaining boundary information, we use the DCLN [16] method to divide the video features into the start channel and end channel. For the start channel, we max-pool each moment feature with all features before that moment.

$$f_{a,N-1}^M = maxpool(f_a^V, f_{a+1}^V, \cdots, f_{N-1}^V) \odot f_a^V \tag{4}$$

where a denotes the index of the start channel. For the end channel, we use max-pooling for the features of each moment with all features after that moment.

$$f_{0,b}^M = maxpool(f_0^V, f_1^V, \cdots, f_b^V) \odot f_b^V \tag{5}$$

where b demotes the index of the end channel. Finally, we get the F_s^M and F_e^M as the start and end channel feature.

3.3   Moment Localization

In order to fuse the moment feature of the start and the end channel, we employ fully connected layers. We fuse the moment feature and sentence feature with Hadamard product. To ensure the stability of the fused feature representation, we apply ℓ_2 normalization.

$$F_s = ||(W_s^Q \times f^Q \times \mathbb{1}^T) \odot (W_s^M \odot F_s^M)||_F \tag{6}$$

$$F_e = ||(W_e^Q \times f^Q \times \mathbb{1}^T) \odot (W_e^M \odot F_e^M)||_F \tag{7}$$

where W_s^Q, W_s^M, W_e^Q and W_e^M are the learnable parameters, $\mathbb{1}^T$ is the transpose of an all-ones vector and $||\cdot||_F$ denotes Frobenius normalization. We build up the Dual Channel Localization Network over the dual channel feature maps F_s and F_e. This network is designed to improve the localization accuracy of the start and end boundaries. In order to get more context information, we will perform one-dimensional convolution of the obtained features, denoted as $\widetilde{F}_s$ and $\widetilde{F}_e$. Following the convolutional operation on the fused dual channel feature maps, we predict the matching scores for each candidate moment. To achieve this, we input $\widetilde{F}_s$ and $\widetilde{F}_e$ into a fully connected layer. Subsequently, we use sigmoid function to get the scores for the start channel and the end channel.

$$h_s = sigmoid(W_s \cdot \widetilde{F}_s) \tag{8}$$

$$h_e = sigmoid(W_e \cdot \widetilde{F}_e) \tag{9}$$

where W_s and W_e are the learnable parameters corresponding to the start channel and end channel, $h_s, h_e \in R^N$. As Fig. 2 illustrates, we extend the obtained scores h_s and h_e into $H_s \in R^{N \times N}$ and $H_e \in R^{N \times N}$. Then we add them to get the score map $H \in R^{N \times N}$, and reset the coordinate score of the start moment greater than the end moment to 0 to get the final score map. In this score plot, darker shades indicate larger predicted scores, with the maximum value representing the best match moment (Fig. 3).

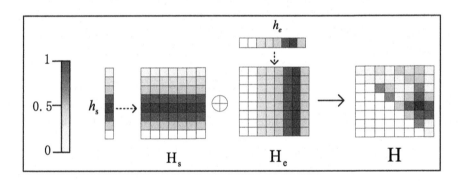

Fig. 3. The construction process of the score map.

3.4   Loss Function

The loss function for our model contain two parts: position regression loss and cross-entropy loss, and the total loss function is calculated as follows:

$$Loss_{total} = Loss_{Entro} + \alpha * Loss_{Loc} \tag{10}$$

$Loss_{Entro}$ denotes the cross-entropy loss function which is used to learn the confidence score for candidate moments. Based on the IoU metric, moments with higher scores are ranked with greater confidence. $Loss_{Loc}$ represents the regression loss function. Since the boundaries of the predefined candidate moments will be rough, the positioning shift of the candidates at the positive sample moment can be fine-tuned by the regression loss function. A hyperparameter α is introduced to balance two losses.

$Loss_{Entro}$. Firstly, we need to calculate the IoU of each candidate moment as a_i, and then scale a_i to the range of [0,1] to get u_i.

$$u_i = \frac{a_i - min(a)}{max(a) - min(a)} \tag{11}$$

where a represents the IoU vector of all candidate moments. The label is defined as follows,

$$y_i = \begin{cases} 0 & x < 0 \\ \frac{u_i - t_{m}in}{1 - t_{m}in} & u_i > t_{m}in \end{cases} \tag{12}$$

Finally, the obtained scaled IoU is used to calculate the cross-entropy loss.

$$Loss_{Entro} = \frac{1}{2N}(\sum_{i=1}^{2N} y_i + log h_i + (1 - y_i)log(1 - h_i)) \tag{13}$$

where h_i is the score of the moment.

$Loss_{Loc}$. We arrange y_i and h_i in descending order for each candidate moment, and the function is calculated as follows:

$$m_i = (y_i^{score} > t_{min}) \odot y_i^{score} \tag{14}$$

$$Loss_{Loc} = \frac{1}{2N}(|(y_i^{ranks} - h_i^{ranks}) \odot m_i|) \tag{15}$$

4   Experiment

4.1   Datasets

We evaluate the cross-modal video localization network proposed in this paper on two public datasets:

(1) TACoS [17]: This dataset comprises numerous culinary activities. It provides fine-grained activity labels with temporal positions and natural language descriptions with corresponding temporal locations for each video. The dataset consists of 127 videos along with 18,818 query statements.
(2) ActivityNet [18]: Each video contains a minimum of two real clips in this dataset, each paired with a real subtitle. The ActivityNet dataset includes 19,209 videos and 71,957 query statements.

4.2   Evaluation Metrics

In our evaluation, we employed the "Rank @ n, IoU = m" metric to ensure a fair comparison. Specifically, "Rank @ n, IoU = m" indicates that in the first n localized video moments, at least one cross-entropy (IoU) with the correct result is greater than m. In other words, it represents the percentage of query statements that successfully identify the correct result out of the total number of queries within the specified range of localized video moments.

4.3   Implementation Details

All the experiments were conducted utilizing pytorch framework and performed on an NVIDIA 3090 GPU card. The experiment applied the Adam optimizer during the optimization process. All hidden states in the model are sized to 512, and non-maximum suppression (NMS) is applied during inference.

Table 1. Performance comparison on TACoS (%). The best performing method and the second method are **bolded** and underlined, respectively.

Method	Rank@1, IoU = 0.1	Rank@1, IoU = 0.3	Rank@1, IoU = 0.5	Rank@5, IoU = 0.1	Rank@5, IoU = 0.3	Rank@5, IoU = 0.5
ACRN [4]	24.22	19.52	14.62	47.42	34.97	24.88
BPNet [19]	–	25.96	20.96	–	–	–
TGN [6]	41.87	21.77	18.90	53.40	39.06	31.02
CMIN [5]	32.48	24.64	18.05	62.13	38.46	27.02
2D-TAN [10]	47.59	37.29	25.32	70.31	57.81	45.04
FVMR [22]	53.12	41.48	29.12	78.12	64.53	50.00
CPNet [23]	–	42.61	29.29	–	–	–
DCLN [16]	65.16	44.96	28.72	82.40	66.13	51.91
VLG-Net [15]	57.21	45.46	**34.19**	81.80	**70.38**	**56.56**
Ours	**67.08**	**46.89**	30.17	**83.53**	68.08	52.39

4.4   Comparison to State-of-Art Methods

To assess the effectiveness of our proposed method for temporal sentence grounding, we conducted evaluations on two benchmark datasets. We compare it with state-of-the-art approaches, among which CTRL [1], ACRN [4], MCN [2] are based on sliding window, through different scales of sliding window to generate candidate moments. The use of large sliding windows imposes limitations and leaves significant room for improvement in terms of accuracy, and sliding window produces a lot of redundant calculations. BPNet [19] and QSPN [20] are proposal-based methods to acquire the attention weight by interacting the features of the query statement with the visual features, and then obtain the temporal attention weight, but there is still the problem of ignoring the context information. The 2D-Map-based methods 2D-TAN [10] and FVMR [22] can obtain the remote relationship of the video. VSLNet [21] does not generate candidate moments, but locates by predicting the probability that each video clip serving as the starting or ending position for the target moment. VLGNet [15] uses graph matching to obtain better candidate moments, so achieves better results when the IoU is 0.5. The performance is presented in Table 1 and Table 2. The model consistently achieves near-optimal or competitive results across all evaluated metrics, showcasing its efficacy.

Table 2. Performance comparison on ActivityNet Captions (%).

Method	Rank@1, IoU = 0.3	Rank@1, IoU = 0.5	Rank@1, IoU = 0.7	Rank@5, IoU = 0.3	Rank@5, IoU = 0.5	Rank@5, IoU = 0.7
CTR [1]	47.43	29.01	10.34	75.32	59.17	37.54
MCN [2]	39.35	21.36	6.43	68.12	53.23	29.70
BPNet [23]	58.98	42.07	24.69	–	–	–
QSPN [20]	52.13	33.26	13.43	77.72	62.39	40.78
TGN [6]	43.81	27.93	–	54.56	44.20	–
CMIN [5]	63.61	43.40	23.88	80.54	67.95	50.73
2D-TAN [10]	59.45	44.51	**26.54**	85.65	**77.13**	61.96
CPNet [23]	–	40.56	21.63	–	–	–
Ours	**66.69**	**45.45**	25.87	**85.82**	75.09	**63.62**

4.5 Ablation Studies

In order to assess the effectiveness of our proposed model, a comprehensive set of ablation experiments was conducted on the TACoS dataset. The objective was to evaluate the impact of video context information fusion on the model's performance. In Table 3, we show the results of the experiment of all ablation variants. From the observations, our method adopted in this paper to explore local context characteristics through BiGRU and max-pooling to explore global con-text characteristics is reasonable and effective. This is because when we understand the video content, we not only need to know the content of the current moment, but also need to combine the content of the context to make a judgment, BiGRU effectively combines the content of the local context, and the max-pooling can integrate the relationship of the global context.

Table 3. Ablation studies on the TACoS dataset (%).

Components		Rank@1, IoU=0.3	Rank@1, IoU = 0.5	Rank@1, IoU = 0.7	Rank@5, IoU = 0.3	Rank@5, IoU = 0.5	Rank@5, IoU = 0.7
GRU	Boundary						
✗	✗	62.96	40.16	23.12	80.38	62.18	44.56
✓	✗	63.16	44.31	27.54	81.28	62.71	46.29
✗	✓	65.68	44.86	27.82	82.75	65.93	52.19
✓	✓	67.08	46.89	30.17	83.53	68.08	52.39

5   Conclusion and Future Work

In our work, we propose a cross-modal video grounding network, which can better explore the temporal context relationship of video. Through experimental evaluations on two commonly used datasets, we demonstrate the competitive performance of our proposed method. In this paper, we only use the product method for cross-modal fusion, and we will investigate the localization of cross-modal by projecting the features of video and text modalities into a common subspace in the future.

Acknowledgements. This work was supported in part by National Natural Science Foundation of China under Grant 62072169, 62172156, Natural Science Foundation of Hunan Province under Grant 2021JJ30152.

References

1. Gao, J., Sun, C., Yang, Z., Nevatia, R.: TALL: temporal activity localization via language query. In: 2017 IEEE International Conference on Computer Vision (ICCV), pp. 5277–5285 (2017)
2. Anne Hendricks, L., Wang, O., Shechtman, E., Sivic, J., Darrell, T., Russell, B.: Localizing moments in video with natural language. In: IEEE International Conference on Computer Vision, pp. 5803–5812 (2017)
3. Dong, J., et al.: Dual encoding for video retrieval by text. IEEE Trans. Pattern Anal. Mach. Intell. **44**(8), 4065–4080 (2021)
4. Liu, M., Wang, X., Nie, L., et al.: Attentive moment retrieval in videos. In: 41nd International ACM SIGIR Conference on Research and Development in Information Retrieval (SIGIR), pp. 15–24 (2018)
5. Zhang, Z., Lin, Z., Zhao, Z., Xiao, Z.: Cross-modal interaction networks for query-based moment retrieval in videos. In: 42nd International ACM SIGIR Conference on Research and Development in Information Retrieval (SIGIR), pp. 655–664 (2019)
6. Chen, J., Chen, X., Ma, L., Jie, Z., Chua, T.S.: Temporally grounding natural sentence in video. In: 2018 Conference on Empirical Methods in Natural Language Processing (EMNLP), pp. 162–171 (2018)
7. Yuan, Y., Ma, L., Wang, J., Liu, W., Zhu, W.: Semantic conditioned dynamic modulation for temporal sentence grounding in videos. In: Advances in Neural Information Processing Systems (NIPS), pp. 534–544 (2019)
8. Wang, J., Ma, L., Jiang, W.: Temporally grounding language queries in videos by contextual boundary-aware prediction. In: AAAI Conference on Artificial Intelligence, vol. 34, no. 07, pp. 12168–12175 (2020)
9. Zhang, D., Dai, X., Wang, X., Wang, Y.F., Davis, L.S.: Man: moment alignment network for natural language moment retrieval via iterative graph adjustment. In: IEEE Conference on Computer Vision and Pattern Recognition (CVPR), pp. 1247–1257 (2019)
10. Zhang, S., Peng, H., Fu, J., Luo, J.: Learning 2d temporal adjacent networks for moment localization with natural language. In: AAAI Conference on Artificial Intelligence, vol. 34, no. 07 (2020)

11. Wang, H., Zha, Z.J., Li, L., Liu, D., Luo, J.: Structured multi-level interaction network for video moment localization via language query. In: IEEE/CVF Conference on Computer Vision and Pattern Recognition, pp. 7026–7035 (2021)

12. Carreira, J., Zisserman, A.: Quo vadis, action recognition? a new model and the kinetics dataset. In: IEEE Conference on Computer Vision and Pattern Recognition (CVPR), pp. 6299–6308 (2017)

13. Tran, D., Bourdev, L., Fergus, R., Torresani, L., Paluri, M.: Learning spatiotemporal features with 3D convolutional networks. In: 2015 IEEE International Conference on Computer Vision (ICCV), pp. 4489–4497 (2015)

14. Liu, D., Qu, X., Liu, X. Y., Dong, J., Zhou, P., Xu, Z.: Jointly cross- and self-modal graph attention network for query-based moment localization. In: 28th ACM International Conference on Multimedia, pp. 4070–4078 (2020)

15. Soldan, M., Xu, M., Qu, S., Tegner, J., Ghanem, B.: VLG-net: video-language graph matching network for video grounding. In: 2021 IEEE/CVF International Conference on Computer Vision Workshops (ICCVW), pp. 3217–3227 (2020)

16. Zhang, B., Jiang, B., Yang, C., Pang, L.: Dual-channel localization networks for moment retrieval with natural language. In: International Conference on Multimedia Retrieval (ICMR), pp. 351–359 (2022)

17. Regneri, M., Rohrbach, M., Wetzel, D., Thater, S., Schiele, B., Pinkal, M.: Grounding action descriptions in videos. Trans. Assoc. Comput. Linguist. 1, 25–36 (2013)

18. Krishna, R., Hata, K., Ren, F., Fei-Fei, L., Carlos Niebles, J.: Dense-captioning events in videos. In: Proceedings of the IEEE International Conference on Computer Vision, pp. 706–715 (2017)

19. Xiao, S., Chen, L., Zhang, S., Ji, W., Shao, J., Ye, L., Xiao, J.: Boundary proposal network for two-stage natural language video localization. In: AAAI Conference on Artificial Intelligence, vol. 35, no. 04, pp. 2986–2994 (2021)

20. Xu, H., He, K., Plummer, B.A., Sigal, L., Sclaroff, S., Saenko, K.: Multilevel language and vision integration for text-to-clip retrieval. In: Proceedings of the AAAI Conference on Artificial Intelligence, vol. 33, no. 01, pp. 9062–9069 (2019)

21. Zhang, H., Sun, A., Jing, W., Zhou, J.T.: Span-based localizing network for natural language video localization. In: The 58th Annual Meeting of the Association for Computational Linguistics (ACL), pp. 6543–6554 (2020)

22. Gao, J., Xu, C.: Fast video moment retrieval. In: IEEE/CVF International Conference on Computer Vision, pp. 1523–1532 (2021)

23. Li, K., Guo, D., Wang, M.: Proposal-free video grounding with contextual pyramid network. In: Proceedings of the AAAI Conference on Artificial Intelligence, vol. 35, no. 03, pp. 1902–1910 (2021)

24. Chung, J., Gulcehre, C., Cho, K., et al.: Empirical evaluation of gated recurrent neural networks on sequence modeling. arXiv preprint arXiv:1412.3555 (2014)

Fast Community Detection Based on Integration of Non-cooperative and Cooperative Game

Ling Wu[1,2(✉)], Mao Yuan[1,2], and Kun Guo[1,2,3]

[1] College of Computer and Data Science, Fuzhou University, Fuzhou 350108, China
[2] Fujian Key Laboratory of Network Computing and Intelligent Information,
Processing (Fuzhou University), Fuzhou 350108, China
{wuling1985,gukn}@fzu.edu.cn, ymao2023@sina.com
[3] Key Laboratory of Spatial Data Mining and Information Sharing, Ministry of
Education, Fuzhou 350108, China

Abstract. A clear game process helps to track community generation and evolution, so non-cooperative and cooperative games are applied to community detection. However, non-cooperative games focus on the competition between nodes, disregarding their cooperation. Solely considering individual perspectives often results in insufficient precision. Cooperative games consider the interests of both coalitions and individual. Nevertheless, involving a large number of participants in cooperative games can lead to high computational complexity and slow convergence. In this study, a fast community detection model called FCDG is proposed. It combines non-cooperative and cooperative games by exploring candidate communities and optimizing community merging. Firstly, a intimate core group identification strategy based on node mutual intimacy is designed to accelerate the convergence of candidate community detection using non-cooperative games and maximize individual benefits. Secondly, building upon of candidate community, a candidate community merging approach based on cooperative games is devised to achieve community optimal solution. The performance of FCDG is evaluated on both real-world and synthetic datasets. Experimental results demonstrate that FCDG effectively discovers community structure with higher accuracy and robustness compared to other baseline algorithms.

Keywords: community detection · game theory · node mutual intimacy · complex network

1 Introduction

Networks consist of nodes and edges that can represent a variety of individuals and relationships in the real world, and the application areas of complex networks currently include biology, epidemiology, sociology, transportation, and many other fields [1–6]. Studying the structure of networks allows researchers to better understand the deep relationships of networks, and they usually divide the network into several non-overlapping or overlapping components, i.e. community

Y. Sun et al. (Eds.): ChineseCSCW 2023, CCIS 2013, pp. 276–286, 2024.
https://doi.org/10.1007/978-981-99-9640-7_20

detection, where each community consists of a set of nodes and the relationships of these nodes of the same community are more complex than other node relationships [7]. Therefore, it's important to develop efficient methods to identify community structure. A large number of community detection algorithms have been proposed in the past two decades, including random walk-based methods, label propagation-based methods, modularity optimization-based methods, game theoretic-based methods.

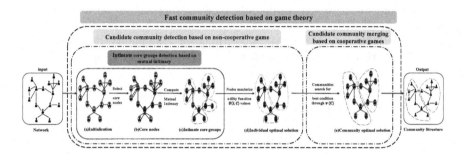

Fig. 1. Framework of FCDG

Fast community detection based on game theory(FCDG) is proposed in this paper. The framework of FCDG is shown in Fig. 1, it's a community detection model that integrates non-cooperative game first and then cooperative game. It includes the candidate community detection based on non-cooperative game as shown in Fig. 1(d) and the candidate community merging based on cooperative game as shown in Fig. 1(e). In addition, the FCDG incorporates the intimate core groups detection based on mutual intimacy into the candidate community detection based on non-cooperative game as shown in Fig. 1(a) to Fig. 1(c). The main contributions of this paper can be summarized as follows.

1. This paper proposes a community detection model FCDG that integrates non-cooperative game and cooperative game, FCDG adopts non-cooperative game first to achieve individual optimal solution, and then introduces cooperative game to achieve community optimal solution, which improves the accuracy of community detection and reduces the complexity of combining the two game methods.
2. FCDG introduces a strategy of candidate community detection based non-cooperative game. By combining the approach of intimate core groups detection based on mutual intimacy. FCDG effectively reduces the number of game iterations in non-cooperative game without sacrificing precision.
3. FCDG treats the candidate communities obtained from the non-cooperative game as game players and uses candidate community merging based on cooperative game to further optimize the community structure and improve the precision of community detection result.

4. FCDG's performance was evaluated on both real-world network datasets and synthetic network datasets, demonstrating its effectiveness with superior accuracy and robustness compared to other baseline algorithms.

2   Related Work

In 2010, Chen et al. [8] started to model community detection using game theory. After Chen's work, many community detection algorithms based on game theory were developed. Due to the availability of analyzing the formation process of community structure based on game theory, researchers have shown more interest in this topic. The game theoretic algorithms for community detction can be classified into three categories: non-cooperative game and cooperative game, combination of both. For more details, see [9].

3   FCDG Algorithm

3.1   The Framework of FCDG

As shown in Fig. 1, the framework of FCDG includes three steps, intimate core groups detection based on mutual intimacy, candidate community detection based on non-cooperative game and candidate community merging based on cooperative game. They will be explained in detail in Sect. 3.2, Sect. 3.3 and Sect. 3.4 respectively.

3.2   Intimate Core Groups Detection Based on Mutual Intimacy

In the real network, the more resources a individual has, the more important its role in the network is. Inspired by this phenomenon, FCDG takes the degree of nodes as the resources they have and recognizes the node with the largest degree compared to the neighbor as a hub, the node connecting the two hub nodes as a bridge. Because bridges are likely to connect the different communities and act as an interactive link between the different communities. Therefore, we take both the hub nodes and the bridge nodes as the core nodes as shown on the left in Fig. 2. On the basis of core nodes, we design an intimate core group detection method based on mutual intimacy, in order to quickly label nodes with basically correct labels.

Definition 1 (Adamic-Adar Index). [10] Suppose CN_{ij} is the set of common neighbors of node i and node j,d_k denotes the degree of the node k. Adamic-Adar Index is defined as Eq. (1).

$$AA_{ij} = \sum_{k \in CN_{ij}} \frac{1}{d_k} \tag{1}$$

Adamic-Adar Index is a common metric to describe the similarity relationship between nodes, and it is calculated based on the importance of neighboring nodes shared between nodes.

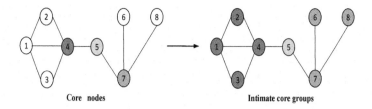

Fig. 2. Intimate core groups detection based on mutual intimacy

Definition 2 (Mutual Intimacy). The mutual intimacy between node i and node j is defined as Eq. (2).

$$MI_{ij} = AA_{ij} * \frac{d_i + d_j}{2} \qquad (2)$$

According to the guidance of mutual intimacy values, the nodes in the network are aggregated into different intimate core groups so as to avoid too many unnecessary decisions in the subsequent non-cooperative game.

Specifically at the beginning each node acts as a single community as shown in Fig. 1(a), and let other nodes join intimate core groups around the core nodes to form the initial community structure. The attraction between nodes is described by mutual intimacy, where each node is attracted to and joins the community that is most appealing to it. Briefly, node i selects itself as the initial label or selects the group in which its most intimate nodes are located based on the following conditions

$$C_{core\_i} = \begin{cases} c_i, d_i > \max(d_j), j \in N(i) \\ c_j \ with \max(MI_{ij}), d_i \leq \max(d_j), j \in N(i) \end{cases} \qquad (3)$$

where C_{core_i} represents the intimate core group to which node i belongs. If node i has the largest degree compared with the neighbors, node i still belongs to the original group c_i. If a neighbor node has the larger degree than node i, node i will join the community where its closest neighbor j is located, i.e.$c_j \ with \max(MI_{ij})$. In particular, if d_i is equal to 1 and has no common neighbors with other nodes, then it will join the community in which the unique neighbor is located. By traversing all nodes once, the node with more resources is more likely to attract other nodes to join the community it is in, thus forming many intimate core groups, as shown on the right in Fig. 2.

3.3 Candidate Community Detection Based on Non-cooperative Game

Before starting the non-cooperative game, the basic concepts of non-cooperative game theory are introduced. Given an undirected network $G = (V, E)$, detecting a community structure is finding a set of clusters $(C_1, C_2, ..., C_p)$, which can be expressed as follows, $\cup_{(1\leq i\leq p)}C_i = G$, and for non-overlapping communities $\forall i, j \in p, i \neq j, C_i \cap C_j = \emptyset$.

Definition 3 (Strategy Space). Given a player i, let s_i be the set of strategies of player i, $s_i \in (C_1, C_2, ..., C_p)$,in fact s_i is the community label to which node i belongs.

Definition 4 (Strategy Profile). The strategy profile of all player can be defined as $S = (s_1, s_2, ..., s_n)$, which is a vector containing the community labels of all players, where s_i represents the strategy of player i.

Definition 5 (Utility Function). The utility of player i is usually represented by the utility function u_i, each player has a corresponding utility function $(u_1, u_2, ..., u_n)$, and the utility function is the goal that each player pursues to maximize during the game, it should be noted that S_{-i} denotes the set of possible strategies of all players except player i, then the best response strategy $s_i' = \text{argmax}_{s_i \in [p]} u_i(s_i, S_{-i})$ where p represents the set of communities, In general, the concept of a community for a single node is considered meaningless. Therefore, the utility function of non-cooperative game is designed as follow.

$$U(i, C) = \sum_{\substack{i \neq j \\ j \in C}} MI_{ij} \tag{4}$$

After forming the intimate core group, the network has been initially divided, the utility of current initial communities needs to be calculated by Eq. (4) once before the non-cooperative game, non-cooperative game treats each node as a player with an initial label to get the candidate community at this stage, every player has the following operations:

- Switch (join a new community and leave current community)
- No operation

A node is randomly selected and this node visits only its neighboring communities, that is, the community C in which its neighboring nodes are located, instead of all communities. Since this is done after having basically clustered the nodes in the computing intimate core groups, it makes more sense to visit only the neighboring communities intuitively and theoretically. The node will try to join these neighboring communities C with the purpose of comparing the node's current payoff $U(i, c_i)$ and $U(i, C)$, if the utility of joining the community C is greater, the node will join this neighboring community. Each player tries to maximize its utility by choosing strategy multiple times until they can no longer improve their utility by unilaterally changing their strategies,at which point each player chooses its own best response strategy s_i', now a pure Nash equilibrium [11] state is reached. Actually pure Nash equilibrium is difficult to achieve, so researchers usually set the maximum number of iterations to terminate the game early within an acceptable range. In this study, due to the best results achieved after 20 rounds, the iteration will be set at 20.

3.4   Candidate Community Merging Based on Cooperative Game

Although the candidate communities obtained by non-cooperative games have obvious community structure, but it still has some unreasonably small clusters that do not have the typical characteristics of communities due to the non-cooperative game falling into individual optimal solution. One such case is the community in the red background as in Fig. 1(d). Therefore, FCDG adds the cooperative game to further optimize the community structure and obtain the community optimal solution.

By considering the candidate community as player in a cooperative game, the selected communities would try to cooperate with other communities to form coalition to improve the utility, and the game would continue until the merging operation cannot be performed, which indicates that the game has entered the equilibrium state of the coalition. The utility function of the coalition is defined as Eq. (5).

$$
v(C) = \begin{cases} -(\dfrac{e(C) - d(C)}{|E|})^2, e(C) = 0 \\ \dfrac{e(C) - d(C)}{e(C)} - (\dfrac{e(C)}{|E|})^2, e(C) > 0 \end{cases} \tag{5}
$$

where $e(C)$ is the number of connections within community C and $d(C)$ is the sum of the number of connected edges between community C and other communities, $|E|$ is the number of edges of network. In order to avoid the case where $e(C)$ is zero, Eq. (5) specifically deals with $e(C) = 0$. Similarly, before starting the cooperative game, the initial utility value of the current communities structure is calculated according to Eq. (5).

Definition 6 (The increment of utility of a coalition). Define $C_{ij} = C_i + C_j$ to denote the combined coalition C_i and C_j as the new coalition C_{ij}, then the increment of the coalition C_i utility should be $\Delta(C_{ij}, C_i) = v(C_{ij}) - v(C_i)$.

Inspired by the reality of the actual situation, cooperation does not only mean that the interests of both are enhanced, but that the overall benefits are enhanced. For example, in a match, if the members of a team all want to improve the team's score but no one is willing to play defense for the team, finally the team will lose the game. Thus cooperation condition would be modified to $\Delta(C_{ij}, C_i) + \Delta(C_{ij}, C_j) > 0$.

In each round, a community is randomly chosen to search for the most suitable coalition to merge with. If a suitable merging coalition is found, the two communities merge together. This process continues until no community is willing to merge with another community, indicating a stable state has been reached. Eventually, as shown in Fig. 1(e), community optimal solution is found.

4   Experiments

4.1   Datasets

Synthetic Networks. The well-known LFR model [12] will be used to create synthetic benchmark networks. Table 1 describes the parameters of the LFR model and the details of synthetic networks used in this study are shown in Table 2.

Table 1. Parameters of LFR

Parameter	Description
N	number of nodes
$\langle k \rangle$	average degree
k_{max}	maximum degree
C_{min}	minimum community size
C_{max}	maximum community size
μ	mixing parameter

Table 2. Synthetic networks

Network	Configuration
D1	N=1000, μ=0.1~0.8,$\langle k \rangle$=15,k_{max}=20,C_{min}=10,C_{max}=50
D2	N=1000,μ=0.1,$\langle k \rangle$=5~25,k_{max}=25,C_{min}=10,C_{max}=50
D3	N=2000~10000,μ=0.1,$\langle k \rangle$=25,k_{max}=50,C_{min}=10,C_{max}=50

Real-World Networks. The real-world networks used in this study are present in Table 3.

Table 3. Real-World networks

dataset	nodes	edges	$\langle k \rangle$	communities
Karate	34	78	4.5	2
Dolphin	62	159	5.1	2
Football	115	613	10.6	12
Polbooks	105	441	8.4	3
Polblogs	1490	17142	23.01	2

4.2 Baseline Algorithms and Evaluation Metrics

we choose LPA [13], Louvain [14], WT [15], Infomap [16], CDME [17], NashOverlap [18] as the benchmark algorithms and use NMI [19] and ARI [20] as evaluation metrics to check the performance of FCDG. Adjusting the overlap parameter α=1 of NashOverlap allows the algorithm to discover only non-overlapping communities. For other baseline algorithms with parameters, the default parameter settings are used.

4.3   Accuracy Experiment

Results on Synthetic Networks. Figure 3 shows the NMI and ARI results of the algorithms on the synthetic networks D1. It shows the performance of each algorithm for two different evaluation metrics on synthetic networks, with respect to Fig. 3(a) when the parameter μ is between 0.1 and 0.5.

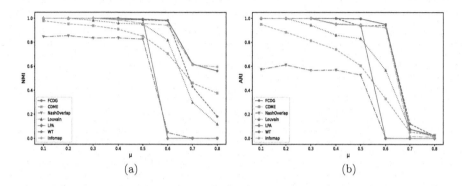

(a)   (b)

Fig. 3. NMI and ARI results on D1 when μ changes from 0.1 to 0.8

To evaluate the effectiveness of each comparison method on networks with different community densities, the mixing parameter μ will be fixed on 0.1 and changed the average degree parameter $\langle k \rangle$ from 5 to 25 to create synthetic benchmark networks D2.

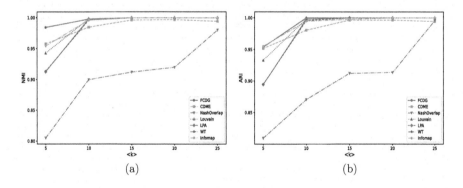

(a)   (b)

Fig. 4. NMI and ARI results on D2 when $\langle k \rangle$ changes from 5 to 25

Results on Real-World Networks. Table 4 presents the accuracy results of various baseline algorithms as well as FCDG for community detection on real-world networks, where the black font indicates the best results and the underlined numbers indicate the second best results. As can be seen, the FCDG algorithm performs very well on all of these real-world networks, with both NMI and ARI achieving four best results and one second-best result on all five datasets.

4.4 Ablation Experiment

In this section, we first demonstrate that computing intimate core groups has a significantly positive effect on accelerating the convergence of the non-cooperative game. Since combining mutual intimacy and non-cooperative game is consistent in accuracy with direct non-cooperative game, we demonstrate here that initial community formation and nodes with essentially correct community labels can effectively accelerate the convergence of non-cooperative game by comparing the total number of strategy choices made by participants. We set the total number of strategy choices made by participants as Numbers when the non-cooperative game reaches equilibrium. The mutual intimacy is abbreviated as MI, '-' indicates the removal of a specific strategy from FCDG.

Table 4. NMI and ARI results on real-world networks

dataset	metric	Louvain	LPA	WT	Infomap	CDME	NashOverlap	FCDG
Karate	NMI	0.6873	0.6949	0.5042	0.6995	**1.0000**	0.6050	**1.0000**
	ARI	0.5414	0.7026	0.3331	0.7022	**1.0000**	0.5732	**1.0000**
Dolphin	NMI	0.5162	0.5914	0.5373	0.5661	0.5354	0.4450	**0.8888**
	ARI	0.3431	0.4476	0.4167	0.3605	0.3753	0.2875	**0.9348**
Football	NMI	0.8903	0.8882	0.8874	**0.9242**	0.8701	0.8197	0.9060
	ARI	0.8069	0.7975	0.8154	**0.8967**	0.7699	0.6177	0.8321
Polbooks	NMI	0.5695	0.5030	0.5427	0.4935	0.5384	0.5832	**0.6012**
	ARI	0.6596	0.5097	0.6534	0.5361	0.6566	0.6551	**0.6679**
Polblogs	NMI	0.5335	0.5595	0.5346	0.2020	0.6643	0.7417	**0.7655**
	ARI	0.4990	0.5487	0.5052	0.0598	0.7115	0.8426	**0.8478**

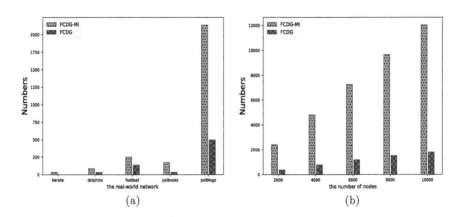

(a)   (b)

Fig. 5. The impact of initial community formation on non-cooperative game

In Fig. 5, we tested FCDG and FCDG-MI on real networks. The experimental results support the effectiveness of our formation of intimate core groups in accelerating the convergence of the non-cooperative game.

The effectiveness of the combination of mutual intimacy, non-cooperative game and cooperative game is then illustrated by the NMI performance of the algorithm on the real dataset. The cooperative game and non-cooperative game are abbreviated as CG and NCG respectively. In Fig. 6, FCDG-CG-NCG denotes the version using only mutual intimacy, FCDG-CG denotes the version only combining mutual intimacy and non-cooperative game, FCDG represents the version proposed in this paper. As shown in Fig. 6, FCDG demonstrates the best performance, followed by FCDG-CG, while FCDG-CG-NCG performs the worst. This ablation experiment result demonstrates the effectiveness of the proposed strategy combination.

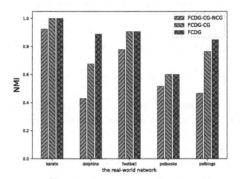

Fig. 6. The impact of proposed strategies on real-world networks

5   Conclusion

This study introduces a powerful algorithm called FCDG to accurately reveal the community structure in complex networks. FCDG is compared to several benchmark algorithms on synthetic and real-world networks, demonstrating superior performance in terms of both speed and quality of community detection. In future work, there are plans to extend FCDG to overlapping networks and dynamic networks.

References

1. Li, H.-J., Bu, Z., Li, A., Liu, Z., Shi, Y.: Fast and accurate mining the community structure: integrating center locating and membership optimization. IEEE Trans. Knowl. Data Eng. **28**(9), 2349–2362 (2016)
2. Hu, K., et al.: Predicting disease-related genes by path structure and community structure in protein-protein networks. J. Stat. Mech.: Theory Exp. **2018**(10), 100001 (2018)

3. Goltsev, A.V., Dorogovtsev, S.N., Oliveira, J.G., Mendes, J.F.: Localization and spreading of diseases in complex networks. Phys. Rev. Lett. **109**(12), 128702 (2012)
4. Li, H.-J., Daniels, J.J.: Social significance of community structure: statistical view. Phys. Rev. E **91**(1), 012801 (2015)
5. Xuan, Q., Zhang, Z.-Y., Fu, C., Hu, H.-X., Filkov, V.: Social synchrony on complex networks. IEEE Trans. Cybernet. **48**(5), 1420–1431 (2017)
6. Chong, P., Shuai, B.: Measure of hazardous materials transportation network invulnerability based on complex network. J. Central South Univ. **45**(5), 1715–1723 (2014)
7. Wang, Y., Cao, J., Bu, Z., Jiang, J., Chen, H.: Proximity-based group formation game model for community detection in social network. Knowl.-Based Syst. **214**, 106670 (2021)
8. Chen, W., Liu, Z., Sun, X., Wang, Y.: A game-theoretic framework to identify overlapping communities in social networks. Data Min. Knowl. Disc. **21**, 224–240 (2010)
9. Torkaman, A., Badie, K., Salajegheh, A., Bokaei, M.H., Ardestani, S.F.F.: A four-stage algorithm for community detection based on label propagation and game theory in social networks. AI **4**(1), 255–269 (2023)
10. Adamic, L.A., Adar, E.: Friends and neighbors on the web. Soc. Netw. **25**(3), 211–230 (2003)
11. Nash, J.F.: Equilibrium points in n-person games. Proc. Natl. Acad. Sci. **36**(1), 48–49 (1950)
12. Lancichinetti, A., Fortunato, S., Kertész, J.: Detecting the overlapping and hierarchical community structure in complex networks. New J. Phys. **11**(3), 033015 (2009)
13. Raghavan, U.N., Albert, R., Kumara, S.: Near linear time algorithm to detect community structures in large-scale networks. Phys. Rev. E **76**(3), 036106 (2007)
14. Blondel, V.D., Guillaume, J.-L., Lambiotte, R., Lefebvre, E.: Fast unfolding of communities in large networks. J. Stat. Mech: Theory Exp. **2008**(10), P10008 (2008)
15. Pons, P., Latapy, M.: Computing communities in large networks using random walks. In: Yolum, P., et al. (eds.) Computer and Information Sciences - ISCIS 2005. LNCS, vol. 3733, pp. 284–293. Springer, Heidelberg (2005). https://doi.org/10.1007/11569596_31
16. Rosvall, M., Bergstrom, C.T.: Maps of random walks on complex networks reveal community structure. Proc. Natl. Acad. Sci. **105**(4), 1118–1123 (2008)
17. Sun, Z., et al.: Community detection based on the matthew effect. Knowl.-Based Syst. **205**, 106256 (2020)
18. Arava, R.: Community detection using coordination games. Soc. Netw. Anal. Min. **8**(1), 65 (2018)
19. Strehl, A., Ghosh, J.: Cluster ensembles–a knowledge reuse framework for combining multiple partitions. J. Mach. Learn. Res. **3**, 583–617 (2002)
20. Rand, W.M.: Objective criteria for the evaluation of clustering methods. J. Am. Stat. Assoc. **66**(336), 846–850 (1971)

Professional Text Review Under Limited Sampling Constraints

Leiwen Yang[1], Tao Yang[1], Feng Yuan[2], and Yuqing Sun[1(✉)]

[1] School of Software, Shandong University, Jinan, China
`sun_yuqing@sdu.edu.cn`
[2] Shandong Shanda Oumasoft Co., Ltd., Jinan, China
`sdyuanf@sina.com`

Abstract. Text review is a task that determines whether the knowledge expression in a student answer is consistent with a given reference answer. In the professional scenarios, the number of labeled samples is limited, usually ranging from dozens to hundreds, which makes the text review task more challenging. This paper proposes a text review method based on data augmentation, which is performed by the combination of different positive and negative labeled samples. The review model infers the unlabeled samples, where the pseudo-labeled samples with the high confidences are selected for the subsequent training rounds. Experimental results in real national qualification exam datasets show that our method has improvement compared with the traditional method on the text review task under the limited sampling constraints.

Keywords: Text review · Limited sampling constraints · Data augmentation · Self-Training

1 Introduction

The subjective questions are commonly used in the professional examinations. Experts review the student answers by comparing their expressions with the reference answer from the point of knowledge. Expert reviewing is time-consuming and labor-intensive. Typically, we can get a limited quantity of expert reviewed samples so as to train the review model. Essentially student answers objectively reflect the different cognitive viewpoints and the text review task need infer the professional knowledge contained within the student answers. Thus this task is more complex than the traditional text inference.

In this paper, we propose a professional text review method based on data augmentation. We combine various labeled samples with different ratio for data

---

This work was supported by the National Nature Science Foundation of China, NSFC (62376138) and the Innovative Development Joint Fund Key Projects of Shandong NSF (ZR2022LZH007).
L. Yang and T. Yang—Equal contribution.

Y. Sun et al. (Eds.): ChineseCSCW 2023, CCIS 2013, pp. 287–295, 2024.
https://doi.org/10.1007/978-981-99-9640-7_21

augmentation. We adopt multiple rounds of self-training and obtain the pseudo-labeled samples with the confidences of predication by the review model infers unlabeled samples, where the selected pseudo-samples for the subsequent training rounds.

Experiments are conducted on the real national qualification exam datasets. The experimental results shown that the effectiveness of our method. By comparing with the traditional self-training methods, our proposed self-training model has the capability to mitigate the problem of error accumulation.

2   Related Work

2.1   Text Inference

Text inference involves deducing semantics and categorizing text into the predefined classes. The representative researches primarily based on the semantic similarity between text pair. For example, two texts are encoded separately and combined by the operations like Hadamard product to measure the similarity. Then the resulting semantic vector is fed into a classifier [1] to obtain the inference results [2,3]. The drawback of such methods lies in their independent encoding of two texts, which lacks the deep semantic interactions. Another way is to employ the attention mechanisms at the phrases, sentences, or syntax to obtain the alignment features of each text pair, which are fed into a classifier for inference [4]. For example, the pre-trained language model BERT [5] is used for text inference. Some methods introduce the external knowledge to assist inference. For example, zhang et al. combine the text semantic information with text rule information to enhance the performance [6], while Li et al. [7] introduce the supervised contrastive loss [8] on the interaction vectors of text pair to assist inference.

2.2   Low-Resource Learning

Low-resource learning refers to training model by a limited number of labeled samples. Prompt learning inserts the prompts and masks into the input text, it transforms the downstream tasks to predict the vocabulary in the masked spaces [9]. The MAML algorithm [10] uses a series of learning tasks to comprise the support and query sets for train the model. By addressing the problem of non-overlapping potential reasoning logic between texts [11], high-quality meta-learning tasks can be constructed. Self-training augments the training dataset with the pseudo-samples obtained by unlabeled samples [12]. Data augmentation is an important method to addressing low-resource issues. For example, the UDA [13] employs reverse translation on the unlabeled texts and synonym replacement techniques to perform data augmentation. By iteratively performing reverse translation on the unlabeled texts and using weighted averaging with sharpening [14], the soft labels are generated to optimize consistency between the unlabeled text and its copies. Utilize the idea of the virtual adversarial training [15], the KL divergence between the probability distributions of the original text and the perturbed text output is computed as a measure to evaluate the quality of augmented samples. Above methods solely focus on individual text and do not consider the complexity of semantic relationships between text pair.

3   Method

The overall framework of our method is illustrated in Fig. 1. It consists of three main components: data augmentation, model training, and pseudo-sample acquisition. Data augmentation is responsible for generating more samples for model training, while pseudo-sample acquisition process provides the high-quality samples for the self-training process. Each of these components are detailed below, separately.

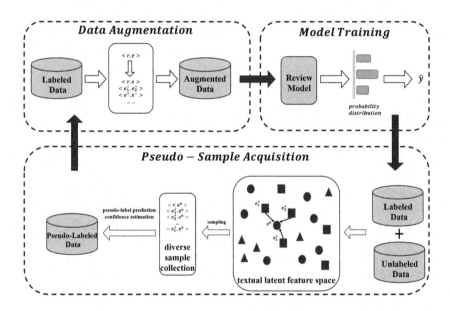

Fig. 1. The framework of professional text review based on data augmentation

3.1   Data Augmentation

The form of review sample is defined as a triplet $< r, e, y >$, where r, e, y represents the reference answer, student answer, label, respectively. Furthermore, we use e^+, e^-, and e^u represents the positive, negative, and unlabeled student answers, respectively.

Data Augmentation Based on Text Pair Construction. The traditional review methods involve the semantic reasoning only between r and e. Since the semantics of e^+ and r are similar, we construct the new meaningful text pairs for data augmentation by the following patterns, as shown in Table 1, where $\alpha, \beta, \gamma, \eta$ are the hyper-parameters and $\alpha + \beta + \gamma = 1$.

Table 1. Construction patterns for data augmentation.

Label	Description	Pattern	Proportion
positive	The text pair has consistent semantics.	$< r, e^+ >$	$\alpha * \eta$
		$< e_1^+, e_2^+ >$	$\alpha * (1 - \eta)$
negative	The text pair has inconsistent semantics.	$< r, e^- >$	$\beta * \eta$
		$< e^+, e^- >$	$\beta * (1 - \eta)$
neutral	The text pair has no inferential relationship.	$< r, e^* >$	$\gamma * \eta$
		$< e, e^* >$	$\gamma * (1 - \eta)$

3.2   Model Training

The text review model adopts an 'encoder + reasoner' architecture. The encoder employs BERT [5], and the reasoner utilizes a multi-layer perceptron (MLP) and the softmax function.

The texts r and e are concatenated with $[SEP]$ as the input for the encoder. After encoding, the $[CLS]$ token embedding, denoted as $\mathbf{x}$ (Eq. 1), is fed to the reasoner.It generates the probabilities for different classes (Eq. 2), where the classes $Y = \{1, 2, 3\}$ represent positive, negative, and neutral, respectively. We take the class with the highest probability as the review result (Eq. 3). The cross-entropy loss function is adopted as the objective function.

$$\mathbf{x} = \text{BERT}\,(r[SEP]e)_{[CLS]} \tag{1}$$

$$[p_1, p_2, p_3] = softmax(\text{MLP}(\mathbf{x})) \tag{2}$$

$$\hat{y} = \arg\max_{i \in Y} p_i \tag{3}$$

3.3   Self-training Process

We adopt τ-round self-training mode. M_t represents the model trained in the t-th round. The following section describes the details on how to acquire the pseudo-samples after training the model in each round.

Pseudo-sample Acquisition based on Multi-sample joint Reasoning.
First, we compute the TF-IDF vectors for all texts in the dataset. Then we
randomly choose an unlabeled student answer e^u, and select the kNN positive
samples for e^u forming a diverse sample collection E, which contains the $L-1$ e^+
and e^u. Next, we inference the sample in E using M_t, and vote inference results to
obtain the pseudo-label y^u for e^u. For the pseudo-sample (e^u, r, y^u). we calculate
the confidence b^u for it (Eq. 4,5), where $p_{l,i}$ represents the inference probability
being i in the l-th e^+. A larger value of b^u indicates higher confidence. Lastly,
we sample pseudo-samples of different class without replacement, following the
descending order of b^u. Then adds the sampled pseudo-samples to the training
set of the next round, resulting in the dataset D_{t+1}.

$$\delta_l = \min_{i \in C \wedge i \neq y^u} p_{l,y^u} - p_{l,i} \tag{4}$$

$$b^u = \sum_{l=1}^{L} \delta_l \tag{5}$$

4 Experiment

4.1 Datasets

To prevent data leakage, we uses a dataset different from the NQE (Section 4.2)
for professional text review. The NQE-30 dataset includes 15 questions from
the years 2018 to 2021, where each question set includes two sub-questions,
denoted by sq in the following discussion. Table 2 shows the statistics. Here, the
naming patten is *LetterNumber* like A1, A2, and etc., where the letters represent
the question number, and the digits represent the sub-question number. During
training, only a limited quantity of samples are extracted to simulate limited
sample constraints, and the labels are removed from the samples that are not
extracted to serve as unlabeled samples.

Table 2. Number of samples in the NQE-30 dataset (thousand)

Datasets	Label		Total	Datasets	Label		Total	Datasets	Label		Total
	Pos	Neg			Pos	Neg			Pos	Neg	
A1	5.5	23.7	29.2	F1	4.1	5.6	9.7	K1	29.5	17.8	47.3
A2	13.4	15.8	29.2	F2	8.2	1.5	9.7	K2	35.2	12.1	47.3
B1	4.0	25.0	29.0	G1	2.3	3.6	5.9	L1	20.7	27.4	48.1
B2	19.5	9.5	29.0	G2	2.9	3.0	5.9	L2	40.1	8.0	48.1
C1	3.8	49.5	53.3	H1	2.0	10.9	12.9	M1	5.4	41.9	47.3
C2	24.0	29.3	53.3	H2	7.8	5.1	12.9	M2	33.6	13.7	47.3
D1	14.0	34.0	48.0	I1	4.7	43.4	48.1	N1	7.8	42.9	50.7
D2	20.9	27.1	48.0	I2	42.7	5.4	48.1	N2	11.2	39.5	50.7
E1	1.0	12.7	13.7	J1	8.3	39.7	48.0	O1	10.0	12.8	22.8
E2	1.5	12.2	13.7	J2	34.8	13.2	48.0	O2	19.4	3.4	22.8

4.2   Comparative Methods

We mainly change the encoder (Section 3.2) for comparative experiments. Baseline employs BERT$_{base}$ [5] as the encoder. For comparison, RoBERTa$_{base}$ [16] and SBERT$_{base}$ [3] are also employed as encoder. To adapt the review model to the professional domain, we utilize the labeled data that covers a few years of the National Qualification Examination (NQE) for pre-training the model (NQEPT), which is employed as the encoder.

Below are variant models that utilize our proposed method. Models with the suffixes *-aug, *-ST, and *-MST represent the review model trained using data augmentation, traditional self-training and multi-sample joint reasoning for self-training, respectively.

4.3   Analysis of Experiments in Professional Text Review

To verify the performance of our method, we extract 50, 100, and 200 training samples for each sub-question in the NQE-30 dataset for experiments. The results are shown in Table 3.

Table 3. Method comparison on the NQE-30 dataset (Acc and Ma-F1 represents accuracy and macro F1, respectively)

Method		Number					
		50/sq		100/sq		200/sq	
		Acc	Ma-F1	Acc	Ma-F1	Acc	Ma-F1
BERT$_{base}$ (baseline)		93.30%	93.16	94.59%	94.48	96.00%	95.92
SBERT$_{base}$		89.39%	88.10	93.75%	93.61	95.76%	95.67
RoBERTa$_{base}$		93.16%	92.96	94.73%	94.60	95.72%	95.62
BERT$_{base}$-aug		94.19%	94.06	95.18%	95.07	96.10%	96.02
BERT$_{base}$-aug-MST	$\tau = 1$	94.40%	94.26	95.47%	95.38	**96.26%**	**96.17**
	$\tau = 2$	94.62%	94.49	**95.57%**	**95.47**	–	–
	$\tau = 3$	**94.65%**	**94.53**	–	–	–	–
NQEPT		94.60%	94.48	95.01%	94.91	96.03%	95.94
NQEPT-aug		95.03%	94.92	95.60%	95.51	96.34%	96.25
NQEPT-aug-MST	$\tau = 1$	**95.17%**	**95.08**	95.70%	95.60	**96.42%**	**96.33**
	$\tau = 2$	95.11%	95.02	**95.82%**	**95.73**	–	–
	$\tau = 3$	95.06%	94.97	–	–	–	–

The performances for all methods improve with the increasing size of training dataset. Comparing the results of BERT$_{base}$ with BERT$_{base}$-aug, we can see that the data augmentation method can achieve an accuracy improvement of 0.1% $\sim$ 0.89%. It is similar with the case of NQEPT with NQEPT-aug. Comparing the results of BERT$_{base}$-aug with BERT$_{base}$-aug-MST and NQEPT-aug with NQEPT-aug-MST, it can be seen that the self-training method based on multi-sample joint inference can achieve an accuracy improvement of 0.08% ∼ 0.46%. Almost every round of self-training is better than the results of the previous round of self-training. In addition, the review model using NQEPT as the encoder is better than the review model using BERT$_{base}$ as the encoder under the same conditions, proving that the professional knowledge learned from pre-training the review model has good transferability.

4.4 Analysis of Self-training Experiments

To verify the performance of our improved self-training method, we randomly extract 100 samples for each sub-question from the NQE-30 dataset. We also conduct the experiments to assess the impact of different inference sample numbers $L = \{3, 5, 7\}$. The results are shown in Table 4.

Table 4. The accuracy(Acc) of each self-training and error(Err) ratio of pseudo-label under the sample size of $100/sq$

Method		Round			
		1		2	
		Acc	Err	Acc	Err
BERT$_{base}$-ST		95.02%	2.82%	95.20%	3.32%
BERT$_{base}$-aug-MST	$L = 3$	95.50%	1.56%	94.49%	2.30%
	$L = 5$	95.48%	1.68%	95.54%	2.46%
	$L = 7$	95.47%	1.65%	95.57%	2.51%

In each round of self-training, both BERT$_{base}$-aug-MST and BERT$_{base}$-ST show the improvement in accuracy and exceed the 94.59% accuracy of BERT$_{base}$ under the same conditions. The accuracy of BERT$_{base}$-aug-MST always higher than BERT$_{base}$-ST. This proves that our self-training method is more effective than the traditional self-training methods, and indicates that single inference in traditional self-training methods is more likely to introduce bias.

In the two rounds of self-training, the error rate of pseudo-sample sampling of BERT$_{base}$-aug-MST is significantly lower than BERT$_{base}$-ST. Our method is better than traditional method, and achieves the best at $L = 3$. Although the inference sample number $L = \{5, 7\}$ has a relatively high error rate, its accuracy is still slightly higher than $L = 3$, which shows that the quality of pseudo-samples increases with the number of inference samples.

5 Conclusion

The paper proposes a text review method based on data augmentation, designed for the task of professional text review under limited sampling constraints.

We also propose the self-training strategy for training the model, where the high-confidence pseudo-samples are obtained for the next round of self-training. Experimental results demonstrate that the proposed data augmentation method and self-training strategy exhibit excellent performance on real professional datasets, which also satisfy the constraints of limited samples. For the future research, we would explore the relevant domain knowledge to enhance the understanding and reasoning the professional semantics of text.

References

1. Tai, K.S., Socher, R., Manning, C.D.: Improved semantic representations from tree-structured long short-term memory networks. In Proceedings of the 53rd Annual Meeting of the Association for Computational Linguistics and the 7th International Joint Conference on Natural Language Processing (Volume 1: Long Papers), pp. 1556–1566 (2015)
2. Conneau, A., Kiela, D., Schwenk, H., Barrault, L., Bordes, A.: Supervised learning of universal sentence representations from natural language inference data. In Proceedings of the 2017 Conference on Empirical Methods in Natural Language Processing, pp. 670–680. Association for Computational Linguistics (2017)
3. Reimers, N., Gurevych, I.: Sentence-BERT: sentence embeddings using Siamese BERT-networks. In Proceedings of the 2019 Conference on Empirical Methods in Natural Language Processing and the 9th International Joint Conference on Natural Language Processing (EMNLP-IJCNLP). Association for Computational Linguistics (2019)
4. Li, D., Liu, T., Pan, W., Liu, X., Sun, Y., Yuan, F.: Grading Chinese answers on specialty subjective questions. In: Sun, Y., Lu, T., Yu, Z., Fan, H., Gao, L. (eds.) ChineseCSCW 2019. CCIS, vol. 1042, pp. 670–682. Springer, Singapore (2019). https://doi.org/10.1007/978-981-15-1377-0_52
5. Devlin, J., Chang, M.-W., Lee, K., Toutanova, K.: BERT: pre-training of deep bidirectional transformers for language understanding. In Proceedings of NAACL-HLT, pp. 4171–4186 (2019)
6. Zhang, Z., et al.: Semantics-aware BERT for language understanding. In: Proceedings of the AAAI Conference on Artificial Intelligence, vol. 34, pp. 9628–9635 (2020)
7. Li, S., Hu, X., Lin, L., Wen, L.: Pair-level supervised contrastive learning for natural language inference. In: ICASSP 2022–2022 IEEE International Conference on Acoustics, Speech and Signal Processing (ICASSP), pp. 8237–8241. IEEE (2022)
8. Khosla, P., et al.: Supervised contrastive learning. Adv. Neural. Inf. Process. Syst. **33**, 18661–18673 (2020)
9. Schick, T., Schütze, H.: Exploiting cloze-questions for few-shot text classification and natural language inference. In: Proceedings of the 16th Conference of the European Chapter of the Association for Computational Linguistics: Main Volume, pp. 255–269 (2021)
10. Finn, C., Abbeel, P., Levine, S.: Model-agnostic meta-learning for fast adaptation of deep networks. In: International Conference on Machine Learning, pp. 1126–1135. PMLR (2017)
11. Murty, S., Hashimoto, T.B., Manning, C.D.: DReCa: a general task augmentation strategy for few-shot natural language inference. In: Proceedings of the 2021 Conference of the North American Chapter of the Association for Computational Linguistics: Human Language Technologies, pp. 1113–1125 (2021)

12. Pseudo-Label, D.-H.L.: The simple and efficient semi-supervised learning method for deep neural networks. In: ICML 2013 Workshop: Challenges in Representation Learning, pp. 1–6 (2013)
13. Xie, Q., Dai, Z., Hovy, E., Luong, T., Le, Q.: Unsupervised data augmentation for consistency training. Adv. Neural. Inf. Process. Syst. **33**, 6256–6268 (2020)
14. Chen, J., Yang, Z., Yang, D.: MixText: linguistically-informed interpolation of hidden space for semi-supervised text classification. In: Proceedings of the 58th Annual Meeting of the Association for Computational Linguistics, pp. 2147–2157 (2020)
15. Miyato, T., Dai, A.M., Goodfellow, I.: Adversarial training methods for semi-supervised text classification. In: International Conference on Learning Representations (2016)
16. Liu, Y., et al.: Roberta: a robustly optimized BERT pretraining approach. arXiv preprint arXiv:1907.11692 (2019)

Latent Diffusion Model-Based T2T-ViT for SAR Ship Classification

Yuhang Qi[1], Lu Wang[1,2(✉)], Kaiyu Li[1], Haodong Liu[1], and Chunhui Zhao[1,2]

[1] College of Information and Communication Engineering, Harbin Engineering University, Harbin, China
wanglu2019@hrbeu.edu.cn

[2] Key Laboratory of Advanced Marine Communication and Information Technology, Ministry of Industry and Information Technology, Harbin, China

Abstract. Recently, deep learning methods have been applied to ship classification in Synthetic Aperture Radar (SAR) images. However, because of the problem of imbalanced and insufficient samples in the SAR ship datasets, accurately identifying SAR ships still poses challenges. In this paper, we propose an improved T2T-ViT model based on the latent diffusion model, which expands the data set through image generation, and adds the SE attention mechanism to adjust the channel weight. To evaluate the effectiveness of the proposed method, training and experiments were conducted on the OpenSARShip 2.0 dataset. Our proposed model, in accordance with experimental results, achieves better recognition accuracy compared with existing models.

Keywords: Deep learning · Synthetic aperture radar · SAR ship classification

1 Introduction

The ocean occupies over 70% of the Earth's surface area, providing abundant natural resources for human development. Since the 21st century, with the result of the continuous development of maritime domain, human understanding of the ocean has been deepening, and the strategic value has also been continuously improving. Countries have gradually attached importance to the maintenance of marine rights and interests. As a major country with both land and sea resources, China has a coastline of 184000 km and a sea area of 3 million square kilometers. It faces six countries, including Malaysia, the Philippines, and South Korea, across the sea. Marine security is an important component of national security, and the security and harmony of coastal and coastal areas are closely related to China's basic interests and the development of the Chinese nation. Therefore, The development of the marine field is of great strategic significance to China.

This work was supported in part by the National Natural Science Foundation of China under Grant 62271162 and 61971153, and Natural Science Foundation of Heilongjiang Province (YQ2022E016).

Many researchers have made efforts to better recognize SAR ship targets. Ren *et al.* [1] proposed a method for detecting and classifying SAR image targets based on a multi-channel sparse representation classifier, which effectively improves the robustness and accuracy in complicated backgrounds. Yang *et al.* [2] proposed a SAR image target recognition method based on deep convolutional neural networks and demonstrated that deep convolutional neural networks in SAR image target recognition are superior to conventional machine learning algorithms. Guo *et al.* [3] proposed a method based on variational autoencoders and recurrent neural networks, which can effectively learn the feature representation of SAR ships and increase identification precision. However, in the absence of training data samples, the recognition effect of SAR ship targets is difficult to improve.

In this paper, an improved SAR ship image generation module is proposed based on the latent diffusion model to add to the classification model of the Tokens to Token Vision Transformer (T2T-ViT) [21] in view of the large amount of data required for the training of the Vision Transformer model in the aspect of target recognition, complete higher precision and more category recognition tasks.

This paper makes three significant contributions: Firstly, for the first time, we uses the VIsion Transformer (ViT) [19] framework as a feature extractor for SAR ship target classification, instead of using traditional CNN methods. Compared with traditional CNN methods, its performance is significantly better. Secondly, an image generation module has been added to the T2T-ViT model for expanding the SAR ship datasets. Finally, the SE [4] attention mechanism module was added to the model, which adaptively adjusts the weight of every characteristic, emphasizes important characteristic, and improves classification accuracy.

2   Proposed Model

The model is mainly composed of the latent diffusion model and the T2T-ViT model. The structure diagram of the proposed method is illustrated in Fig. 1. In order to meet the challenge of model performance, we combined the latent diffusion model with T2T-ViT to build a model for SAR ship classification. This model can further improve the classification performance of the model without increasing computational complexity. First, we preprocess the SAR ship datasets. Then we expand the datasets using latent diffusion model, transfer the newly obtained datasets to the pre trained T2T-ViT, complete Transfer learning and classify. Finally we can get the classification results.

2.1   Latent Diffusion Model

The framework structure of the latent diffusion model is illustrated in the upper part of Fig. 1. First, an AutoEncoder model that includes both an encoder and a decoder must be trained. In this manner, the image can be compressed using an encoder, then the potential representation space can be subjected to a diffusion operation, and finally the decoder can be used to restore the image to its original pixel space.

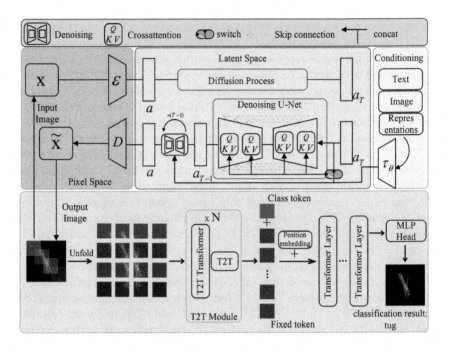

Fig. 1. The structure diagram of the proposed method.

Diffusion operation on the potential representation space follows a similar general pattern to the classic diffusion model. Time conditional U-Net [5] is the diffusion model's specific implementation that is in use.

The diffusion model is a statistical model created to gradually denoise the variables from the normal distribution in order to learn the data distribution $p(x)$. This process is equivalent to the inverse of a fixed Markov chain with a learning length of T. The best model for picture synthesis is a reweighted version of the $p(x)$-upper variational lower limit that takes denoising score matching into account. These models can be thought of as denoising autoencoders with equal weighted sequences $e_\theta(x_\theta, t)$, $\{1, ..., T\}$. They are trained to anticipate the input x_t that has been denoised, where x_t is the noisy input x. The corresponding objectives are as follows:

$$Loss_{DM} = \mathrm{E}_{x,e\sim\mathrm{N}(0,1),t}\left[\|\, e - e_\theta(x_t, t)\,\|_2^2\right], \qquad (1)$$

where t is uniformly sampled by $\{1, ..., T\}$.

We are now able to access an effective, low dimensional Potential space in which undetectable features are got thanks to the perceptual compression model made up of ε and D that we trained. This space is better suited for generative models based on likelihood than high-dimensional pixel space because it allows them to concentrate on the crucial semantic input and train in a far more effective, low-dimensional environment. We can employ our model's image-specific inductive bias, in contrast to earlier work on other models in extremely concentrated, discrete Potential space. It features the capability to construct the U-Net mostly from conv2D and concentrate the target on the most pertinent perceptual bits using reweighted boundaries, which are now read as

$$Loss_{LDM} = \mathrm{E}_{\varepsilon(x),e\sim N(0,1),t} \left[\| e - e_\theta(a_t, t) \|_2^2 \right], \tag{2}$$

The U-Net with a time condition serves as the neural backbone $e_\theta(o, t)$. We decipher the examples originate from $p(z)$ into the pixel space through D, and a_t can be effectively acquired from ε during training due to the fixed forward process.

The diffusion model can, in theory, model the conditional distribution in the form of $p(a|b)$, just as other varieties of generative models, with the aid of an automatic conditional denoising encoder $e_\theta(a_t, t, b)$. b manages the process of fusion, for example, the text information used in this paper.

The diffusion model is made into a more adaptable conditional image generator that is efficient for training models based on attention of different input modes by utilizing a cross attention [7] technique to improve its U-Net foundation. We develop a domain-specific encoder τ_θ that projects b onto the middle representation $\tau_\theta(b) \in R^{M \times d_\tau}$ and then maps it to the middle layer of U-Net by implementing a cross attention layer for attention to preprocess b (such as text information).

$$\mathrm{Attention}(Q, K, V) = soft \max(\frac{QK^T}{\sqrt{d}}) \cdot V, \tag{3}$$

where $Q = W_Q^{(i)} \cdot \varphi_i(a_t)$, $K = W_K^{(i)} \cdot \tau_\theta(b)$, $V = W_V^{(i)} \cdot \tau_\theta(b)$ [8].

Using image condition sets, we train the latent diffusion model by

$$Loss_{LDM} = \mathrm{E}_{\varepsilon(x),b,e\sim N(0,1),t} \left[\|e - e_\theta(a_t, t, \tau_\theta(b))\|_2^2 \right], \tag{4}$$

where τ_θ and e_θ are jointly optimized. This method is just as adaptable as τ_θ as it may be parameterized with certain domain parameters, like the Transformer when b is a text prompt.

2.2 T2T-ViT

Tokens to token Vision Transformers (T2T-ViT) [21] is a two-stage model that uses Transformers for image feature extraction and sequence modeling. Firstly, the input image is divided into different blocks and encoded through a set of nested Transformer encoders to generate a local perceptual image representation. Then, these local feature maps are fed into a global Transformer encoder to generate a global representation of the entire image. It can gradually mark images as tokens and has an effective backbone. The framework structure of the T2T-Vit is illustrated in Fig. 1.

By soft splitting and reshaping, the T2T module mixes together the eigenvalues and eigenvectors. Figure 2 provides an detailed representation of the T2T module.

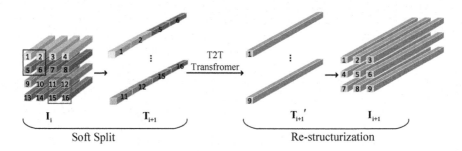

Fig. 2. The structure diagram of the T2T module.

We will employ a soft split method (SS) to tokenize the supplied input image $\mathbf{I_i}$:

$$\mathbf{T_{i+1}} = SS(\mathbf{I_i}). \tag{5}$$

Then, in order to get $\mathbf{T_{i+1}}'$, we will use a T2T transformer which includes MSA (multi-head self-attention) and MLP (multi-layer perceptron):

$$\mathbf{T_{i+1}}' = MLP(MSA(\mathbf{T_{i+1}})). \tag{6}$$

After, we will reshape these tokens obtained through a series of processing into images $\mathbf{I_{i+1}}$:

$$\mathbf{I_{i+1}} = Reshape(\mathbf{T_{i+1}}'). \tag{7}$$

By repeatedly performing the above reshaping and soft splitting, the T2T module can gradually reduce the length of the token and transform the spatial structure of the image.

2.3   SE Model

The SE module [4] boosts the expressive capacity and performance of the neural network by incorporating Squeeze and Excitation operations and dynamically learning the weights of each channel. This allows the network to effectively learn and utilize the correlations among feature channels. Figure 3 provides an detailed representation of the SE module.

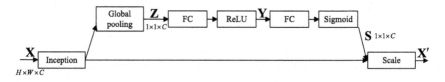

Fig. 3. The structure diagram of the SE model.

The input feature map is $\mathbf{X}$ with dimension $C \times H \times W$, where C denotes the number of channels, and H and W represent the height and width of the feature map, respectively. During the Squeeze operation, a global average pooling is performed on the feature map to transform it into a compressed feature vector, which is obtained by averaging the feature maps of each channel. The feature vector obtained after the pooling operation is denoted as $\mathbf{Z} \in R^C$, where $\mathbf{Z}_C$ represents the compressed feature of channel C.

In the Exit operation, we use a fully connected layer and nonlinear activation function to learn the weights of each channel to capture the relationships between channels. Assuming the parameters of the fully connected layer are $\mathbf{W}_1 \in R^{C/R \times C}$ and $\mathbf{W}_2 \in R^{C/R \times C}$, where C/R is the dimensionality reduction capability of the fully connected layer. Firstly, input the feature vector $\mathbf{Z}$ into a fully connected layer:

$$\mathbf{Y} = \delta\left(\mathbf{W}_1 \mathbf{Z}\right), \tag{8}$$

where δ represents the nonlinear activation function (ReLU). Then, input the output $\mathbf{Y}$ of the fully connected layer to another fully connected layer:

$$\mathbf{S} = \sigma\left(\mathbf{W}_2 \mathbf{Y}\right), \tag{9}$$

where σ represents the nonlinear activation function (Sigmoid). The final output $\mathbf{S}$ represents the weight vector of each channel.

Apply the learned weight vector $\mathbf{S}$ to each channel on the input feature map $\mathbf{X}$. For each channel, multiply its corresponding feature map $\mathbf{X}$ by the weight $\mathbf{S}$ to obtain a weighted feature map:

$$\mathbf{X}'_C = \mathbf{S}_C \times \mathbf{X}_C. \tag{10}$$

Finally, recombine all weighted feature maps to obtain the final output feature map $\mathbf{X}'$.

3   Experiment

3.1   Datasets and Evaluation Indicators

This paper's ship classification experiment uses the OpenSARShip 2.0 [6] public dataset, which primarily includes 5 Asian locations with a total of 17 different ship types.

We chose Accuracy (%) as the main index to quantify the classification effectiveness, choosing this metric similarly to the majority of target classification models [9–12]. The formula is as follows:

$$Accuracy = \frac{TP + TN}{TP + TN + FP + FN}, \tag{11}$$

where TP stands for true positivity, TN for true negativity, FP for false positivity, and FN for false negativity. This article also uses Precision (%), Recall (%), and F_1-score (%) to assess the performance of our model in classifying data.

3.2   Experimental Results and Analysis

Using the OpenSARShip 2.0 public dataset, three categories of ships with sufficient sample sizes were selected: Cargo, Fishing, and Tug. Each of the three categories of ships selected 320 pictures as the datasets

Using the proposed model, the existing datasets of images is expanded by adding the latent diffusion model, which is an image generation module, to the T2T-ViT model. Using the existing three categories of ship data as input, corresponding to the three language texts of SARCargo, SARFishing, and SARTug, ship images can be generated by inputting text information, as shown in Fig. 4.

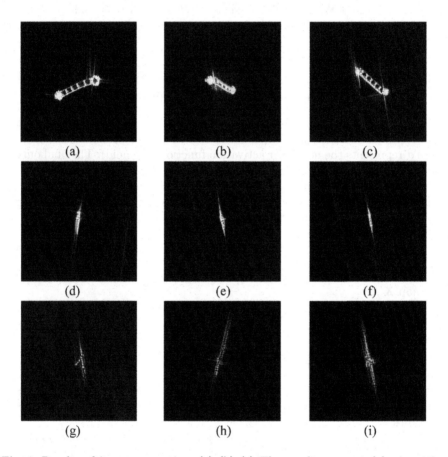

Fig. 4. Results of image generation. (a) (b) (c) The results generated by inputting SARCargo. (d) (e) (f) The results generated by inputting SARFishing. (g) (h) (i) The results generated by inputting SARTug.

From the above results, it can be seen that the generated images have reached the standard for datasets expansion in terms of resolution and clarity. After expanding the datasets of three categories of ship targets to 400 images, the datasets were divided into train set and test set in a 4:1 ratio. It was then input into the T2T-ViT model with SE attention mechanism for training, and the training results are as shown in Fig. 5.

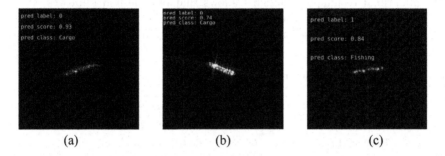

(a)   (b)   (c)

Fig. 5. Results of SAR ship classification.

The classification results of proposed method are shown in Table 1:

Table 1. Classification results of proposed method of three categories.

Ship Classes	Precision	Recall	F_1-score
Cargo	81.54	82.81	82.17
Fishing	68.42	60.94	64.46
Tug	66.18	72.58	69.23

The overall results of proposed method are shown in Table 2:

Table 2. The overall results of proposed method of the model.

Top-1 Acc	Precision	Recall	F_1-score
72.13	72.05	72.11	71.95

Through the above classification results, it can be found that the addition of the latent diffusion model to the image generation module has improved the recognition accuracy of three categories of ship SAR targets. To assess the effectiveness of the method, training was conducted on eight classic deep learning classification networks: LeNet [13], HorNet [14], TNT [15], MobileNet [16], DenseNet [17], Shufflenet [18], Vision Transformer [19], and SwinTransformer [20]. The comparison results with the proposed target classification method are shown in Table 3, where evaluation indicators represent their average values.

Through the comparison of the above results, it can be found that our proposed method achieves higher recognition performance compared to other traditional target classification methods. Table 1 shows the results, and the acquired accuracy (Acc) is 75.68%, outperforming other methods. A comparison with the suboptimal technique Shufflenet shows that our method improves Acc by 2.74%. In comparison to other methods, our method also shows considerable improvements in several secondary metrics that attain optimal performance.

Table 3. Comparison results of three categories of ship classification.

Model	Precision	Recall	F_1-score	Accuracy
LeNet [13]	58.07	64.03	62.21	64.24
HorNet [14]	64.53	63.61	63.89	63.83
TNT [15]	67.05	66.56	66.32	66.49
MobileNet [16]	60.16	65.64	63.01	65.84
DenseNet [17]	67.33	69.60	69.07	73.55
Shufflenet [18]	72.50	72.72	72.42	72.94
Vision Transformer [19]	65.34	64.93	64.89	64.89
SwinTransformer [20]	42.08	43.51	41.33	43.61
T2T-Vit [21]	72.05	72.11	71.95	72.13
Proposed method	**74.71**	**74.69**	**74.58**	**75.68**

4   Conclusion

This paper proposes an improved T2T-ViT model based on the latent diffusion model for SAR ship classification. This method adds an image generation module to the T2T-ViT model for data sample expansion to make up for the imbalance and insufficiency of the SAR ship data set samples. At the same time, an SE attention mechanism module was added to the model to highlight key features by adjusting channel weights. According to the results of three classification experiments performed on the OpenSARShip 2.0 dataset, this method performs better than other methods for classifying SAR ships, and all evaluation indicators have been improved to a certain extent.

References

1. Ren, H., Yu, X., Zou, L., Xhou, Y., Wang, X.: Joint supervised dictionary and classifier learning for multi-view SAR image classification. IEEE Access **7**, 165127–165142 (2019)
2. Yang, T., Zhu, J., Liu, J.: SAR image target detection and recognition based on deep network. In: SAR in Big Data Era, pp. 1–4 (2019)

3. Guo, D., Chen, B., Zheng, M., Liu, H.: SAR automatic target recognition based on supervised deep variational autoencoding model. IEEE Trans. Aeros. Electron. Syst. **57**(6), 4313–4328 (2019)
4. Hu, J., Shen, L., Sun, G.: Squeeze-and-excitation networks. In: IEEE/CVF Conference on Computer Vision and Pattern Recognition, pp. 7132–7141 (2018)
5. Ronneberger, O., Fischer, P., Brox, T.: U-net: convolutional networks for biomedical image segmentation. In: Navab, N., Hornegger, J., Wells, W.M., Frangi, A.F. (eds.) MICCAI 2015. LNCS, vol. 9351, pp. 234–241. Springer, Cham (2015). https://doi.org/10.1007/978-3-319-24574-4_28
6. Li, B., et al.: OpenSARShip 2.0: a large-volume dataset for deeper interpretation of ship targets in sentinel-1 imagery. In: Big Data Era: Models, Methods and Applications, pp. 1–5 (2017)
7. Vaswani, A., et al.: Attention is all you need. In: Neural Information Processing Systems, pp. 5998–6008 (2017)
8. Jaegle, A., et al.: Perceiver: general perception with iterative attention. In: Proceedings of the 38th International Conference on Machine Learning, vol. 139, pp. 4651–4664 (2021)
9. He, J., Wang, Y., Liu, H.: Ship classification in medium-resolution SAR images via densely connected triplet CNNs integrating fisher discrimination regularized metric learning. IEEE Trans. Geosci. Remote Sens. **59**(4), 3022–3039 (1998)
10. Xu, Y., Lang, H.: Ship classification in SAR images with geometric transfer metric learning. IEEE Trans. Geosci. Remote Sens. **59**(8), 6799–6813 (2021)
11. Xiong, G., Xi, Y., Chen, D., Yu, W.: Dual-polarization SAR ship target recognition based on mini hourglass region extraction and dual-channel efficient fusion network. IEEE Access **9**, 29078–29089 (2021)
12. Wang, C., et al.: Semisupervised learning-based SAR ATR via self-consistent augmentation. IEEE Trans. Geosci. Remote Sens. **59**(6), 4862–4873 (2021)
13. Lecun, Y., Bottou, L., Bengio, Y., Haffner, P.: Gradient-based learning applied to document recognition. Proc. IEEE **86**(11), 2278–2324 (1998)
14. Veerapaneni, S.-K., Biros, G.: A high-order solver for the heat equation in 1D domains with moving boundaries. Siam J. Sci. Comput. **29**, 2581–2606 (2007)
15. Han, K., et al.: Transformer in transformer. In: Neural Information Processing Systems, pp. 15908–15919 (2021)
16. Howard, A.-G., et al.: MobileNets: efficient convolutional neural networks for mobile vision applications. In: IEEE/CVF Conference on Computer Vision and Pattern Recognition, pp. 432–445 (2017)
17. Huang, G., Liu, Z., Laurens, V., Weinberger, K.: Densely connected convolutional networks. In: IEEE/CVF Conference on Computer Vision and Pattern Recognition, pp. 2261–2269 (2016)
18. Zhang, X., Zhou, X., Lin, M., Sun, J.,: ShuffleNet: an extremely efficient convolutional neural network for mobile devices. In: IEEE/CVF Conference on Computer Vision and Pattern Recognition, pp. 6848–6856 (2016)
19. Dosovitskiy, A., Beyer, L., Kolesnikov, A., Weissenborn, D., Houlsby, N.: An image is worth 16×16 words: transformers for image recognition at scale. In: International Conference on Learning Representations, pp. 1–22 (2021)
20. Liu, Z., et al.: Swin transformer: hierarchical vision transformer using shifted windows. In: IEEE/CVF Conference on Computer Vision and Pattern Recognition, pp. 9992–10002 (2021)
21. Yuan, L., et al.: Tokens-to-Token ViT: training vision transformers from scratch on ImageNet. In: IEEE/CVF Conference on Computer Vision and Pattern Recognition, pp. 538–547 (2021)

Domain-Specific Collaborative Applications

An Empirical Study on the Urgent Self-admitted Technical Debt

Chengyi Lin, Bo Jiang[(⊠)], Qiao Huang, and Ye Wang

School of Computer and Information Engineering, Zhejiang Gongshang University,
Hangzhou 310018, China
nancybjiang@zjgsu.edu.cn

Abstract. Technical Debt (TD) refers to the phenomenon of taking shortcuts to achieve short-term gains at the cost of higher maintenance effort in the future. While Self-Admitted Technical Debt (SATD) is the TD that has been documented in code comments. Due to its impact on software quality, SATD that is of more long-term interest should be prioritized for removal. However, most current research infers the priority of SATD removal from self-defined features, and lacks a systematic understanding of it. In this paper, we define "urgent SATD", as the SATD that have a high priority for removal. We conduct an empirical study on nearly 6500 SATD in two popular open-source projects to examine the distribution and features of "urgent SATD" with other SATD. We found that only a small fraction of removed SATD is urgent SATD (4%–16%), and urgent SATD has significant differences from other SATD in terms of text features and code size features, indicating that it has more complex text descriptions and related-code.

Keywords: Self-Admitted Technical Debt · Technical Debt Prioritization · Sofrware Maintenance

1 Introduction

Technical debt generally refers to development practices that sacrifice long-term gains for the sake of achieving short-term goals [1]. And the Self-Admitted Technical Debt specifically refers to those TD instances that developers intentionally identify within commit messages, issue tracking systems, or source code.

Due to the suboptimal implementations resulting from SATD will undermining software's maintainability and robustness, it might appear intuitive that all instances of SATD should be promptly removed [2, 3]. However, the practicalities of software development, encompassing business logic, developer preferences, and available resources, dictate that it's not feasible to address all SATD in a single effort. Consequently, prioritizing the removal of SATD becomes a crucial task, yet current research in this area remains insufficient. Current studies rely solely on author-defined features to judge the priority of SATD removal, such as the number of issues associated with SATD-related code [4], keywords about emergency or emotions in comments [5]. They are not clear about the high-priority SATD in the real project, and only observe whether the project has removed SATD with their own predicted outcomes within a certain number of commits.

© The Author(s), under exclusive license to Springer Nature Singapore Pte Ltd. 2024
Y. Sun et al. (Eds.): ChineseCSCW 2023, CCIS 2013, pp. 309–320, 2024.
https://doi.org/10.1007/978-981-99-9640-7_23

Hence, in this paper we propose the concept of "urgent SATD" to refer to the SATD with a high priority for removal. To obtain results more in line with the real development process and easier for developers to understand, we reconstruct the database at the version-level to detect SATD removal, rather than at commit-level or date-level as in previous research. And we explore the specific distribution and features of urgent SATD. In particular, we examine the following questions:

RQ 1: *What is the specific distribution of urgent SATD in the open-source software projects?* In this research question, we first investigate how prevalent the urgent SATD is in open source systems. Then, we observe whether the distribution of urgent SATD is uniform on the scale of versions.

RQ 2: *What are the significant features of the urgent SATD?* Having confirmed the existence of the urgent SATD in RQ1, we calculate the differences between it and other SATD that will help us better describe it.

In summary, we make the following key contributions in this paper:

- We construct a dataset of SATD introductions and removals using release versions of open source software.
- We investigate the specific distribution of urgent SATD.
- We explored what significant features urgent SATD has compared to other SATD.

The remainder of this paper is organised as follows. Section 2 presents our research methodology and Sect. 3 presents our findings for each research question. Next, Sect. 4 reviews the related work. Finally, Sect. 5 discusses the limitations of our study and Sect. 6 concludes the paper.

2   Case Study Setup

The primary objective of our research is to investigate the distribution and features of SATD with high-priority for removal. For these purpose, we have defined "urgent SATD", which represents the SATD that well be removed in the next release version of the software. Urgent SATD has the highest priority for removal. This indicates that these SATD instances require immediate refactoring due to the business requirements or maintenance needs of the upcoming release version.

Two widely popular open-source projects from GitHub were selected as our data sources. We then use SATD detector [6] to detect SATD from source code comments. Once SATD has been detected, we mark the version and file in which it appears for our subsequent research. We use SourceMeter[1] to compute various object-oriented (OO) metrics as features of urgent SATD, such as CBO, DIT, and LCOM. We then analyze the data obtained from the above to derive the results. Figure 1 shows an overview of our approach, and the following subsections detail each of the steps.

2.1   Project Selection

We select projects written in the JAVA and used Git as their version control system. The former is selected specifically because it is compatible with our ASA Tools, and

---

[1] https://www.sourcemeter.com.

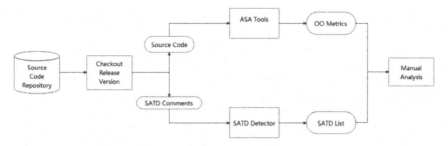

Fig. 1. Steps of empirical study on open source projects

the latter is picked due to its ability to provide a more extensive variety of release and candidate versions, which enhances our dataset. In addition, we carefully chose projects that possess extensive and meaningful comments due to the significant reliance on source code comments for SATD identification. Considering our interest in studying the dynamics of SATD (both its introduction and removal), we specifically focus on projects with high activity levels. Our project selection includes Ant, a Java-based build tool, and Jruby, which is an implementation of Ruby on the JVM, and we start analyzing the selected projects at the beginning.

Table 1 provides details about the two projects used in our study. Including project names, popularity (Stars), development scale (Contributors, Forks), and the number of release versions analyzed in our study.

Table 1. Overview of the projects selected

Project	Stars	Contributors	Forks	Versions
Ant	367	68	410	83
JRuby	3,691	420	928	147

2.2 Release Version Collection

Previous studies have primarily analyzed SATD removal at the commit-level [4, 8], or have focused solely on SATD survival time without considering iterative development [7]. However, both approaches present certain limitations. In actual open-source project development, a large-scale project may have tens of thousands of commits, or even more, with minimal differences between each commit. By manually examining the last 100 commits in the Ant project, we find that most commits modified only two to five files, with changes limited to a few dozen lines of code. Furthermore, the time intervals between these commits were often quite short, sometimes spanning only a few hours. These findings indicate that analyzing projects at the level of individual commits would lead to a significant waste of storage space and analysis time. Moreover, it would prevent us from observing the long-term iterative nature of software development. Similarly, focusing solely on the survival time of the SATD also hinder the comprehensive understanding of software iterations over a longer period of time. This approach fails to capture the broader context and evolution of the software system. Therefore, we adopt a different approach at the version-level, to address these limitations and provides a more comprehensive perspective on the analysis of SATD in open-source projects.

To determine the commits corresponding to release versions, we use the Tag feature available on GitHub. Tags are used to mark a specific version of the codebase within a repository [9]. Unlike branches, tags represent static versions that cannot be modified. By assigning a tag to a particular commit in the codebase, it becomes easier to locate, trace, and utilize that version of the code in the future. In large-scale open-source projects, tags are commonly used to indicate the version number of the software. It is important to note that not all tagged commits are our target for analysis.

From a complete list of tags in a project, we select tags according to the following rules:

- **Explicitly indicate release versions in tag.** It helps to exclude the commits that have been tagged for other purposes, such as marking special merges (commit 3b370ea in Ant) or documentation (commit d464069 in Ant).
- **Release Candidate (RC) versions.** Unlike beta versions, RC versions rarely introduce new features and focus primarily on bug fixes. They typically go through several iterations before reaching the final release version (e.g. 1.3.5, 1.4.0 RC1, 1.4.0 RC2, 1.4.0). So we consider the tagged RC versions, unless their interval with the previous version is too short.

Based on these selection criteria, we also need to exclude some versions:

- **Versions with short update intervals.** We exclude versions that have an interval of less than three days with the previous release version. Short update times imply that developers did not have enough time to make substantial additions or changes to the code. Consequently, these versions cannot be considered as normal iterations in the software development process.
- **One branch for pallel updates.** In both projects, we observed that at a specific point in time, two different versions emerged and received synchronous updates. One version contained significant updates and new features, while the other version retained most of the original functionality. As the versions iterated, the differences between them amplified and their underlying foundations diverged. As shown in Fig. 2, we present an example from the Ant project where two different branch versions emerged. We therefore select one branch for continuous tracking of version updates, as it provides sufficient insight into the evolving nature of the software.

2.3   SATD Removal Identification

In the previous steps, we chose the projects on GitHub and filtered the release versions of interest, along with their respective commit ID. After pulling the corresponding code, we use heuristic rules to extract comments from the code.

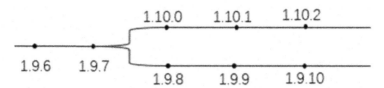

Fig. 2. An example of version forks in Ant project

After collecting the release versions by aforementioned steps, we pull the corresponding code and extract comments from the code to identify the SATD. We use SATD Detector [6], an automatic tool which is stable and has good precision on SATD identification, to accomplish this task.

To avoid false positive SATD instances, we exclude the following types of comments:

- **Commented-out source code.** If a SATD instance appears within a commented-out code block, we will exclude it. Because being commented out indicates that it is no longer needed and will be deleted along with the commented code block instantly.
- **Javadoc comments.** They are also excluded from the analysis because they can easily be misjudged as SATD when describing the function of a code block does, but they rarely mention self-admitted technical debt.

We can obtained a list of SATD for each release version after that, then, we define the first occurrence of SATD in a version as its introduction, and its disappearance in a version as its removal to get the lifespan of a SATD instance.

2.4 Feature Extraction

In the literature, indicators such as object-oriented (OO) metrics, code smells, issues from ASA tools, and software quality metrics from quality assessment tools have been widely used to monitor and quantify TD and software maintainability [11, 12]. For instance, in the context of OO programming, metric sets like the Chidamber and Kemerer (C&K) metrics enable the characterization of code size, complexity, coupling, and cohesion, among other factors [13]. The C&K metrics have been extensively studied and employed due to their ability to predict maintainability and maintenance effort, which are closely linked to TD [14, 15].

In this paper, We applied SourceMeter, a static source code analysis tool, which allowed us to obtain Object-Oriented (OO) metrics at class-level in addition to the C&K metrics. We use OO metrics as features to describe SATD, which can comprehensively describe the SATD comments and the context code.

3 Case Study Results

We hope to improve developers' understanding of urgent SATD, so as to help them manage SATD and improve software quality. To achieve this, we investigate the distribution and features of urgent SATD in software projects and utilize real version updates to observe the survival of SATD to provide more comprehensible results. For each research question, we provide detailed explanations of the motivation, approach, and results.

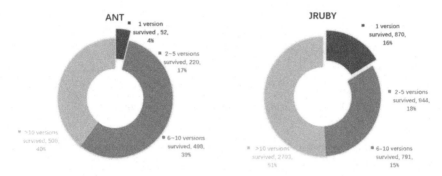

Fig. 3. The number of surviving versions of all removed SATD

3.1 What is the Specific Distribution of "Urgent SATD"?

Motivation. To assist developers in managing TD, we need to know the exact surviving versions of all removed SATD in order to reflect the development process in another way. Also find out if there is any SATD will be deleted immediately to provide a data foundation for subsequent research.

Approach. We first calculated the proportion of urgent SATD among all SATD in two open-source projects, as shown in Fig. 3. SATD that survives for only one version is considered urgent SATD. We then calculated the distribution of urgent SATD in each release version in detail, the results are shown in Fig. 4.

Results. Figure 3 shows the value and proportion of SATD surviving different numbers of versions. The Ant project has a total number of 1279 removed SATD and the Jruby project has 5308. "1 version survived" represents urgent SATD, as can be seen, In the Ant project, there were 52 urgent SATD, accounting for 4% of the total number of removed SATD. Although this is a relatively small number, it reflects the need or habit of software developers to refactor imperfect code immediately. In the Jruby project, there were 870 urgent SATD, accounting for 16% of the total number of removed SATD. This is a considerable number, further proving that some SATD need to be prioritized.

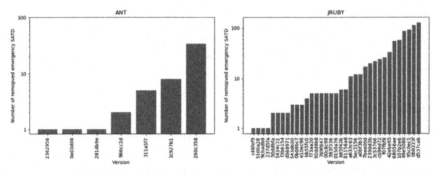

Fig. 4. The number of removed urgent SATD in each version

At the same time, we believe that the difference between the two may be related to the size of the project. Developers in large projects are more aware of debt management and are more likely to carry out standardized development operations [16]. Another point worth noting in the figure is that SATD that survives for only 2–5 version has similar proportions in two projects (17% in Ant and 18% in Jruby), indicating that some specific SATD is removed in short-term version updates. Although our definition excludes it from the scope of urgent SATD, it is still a relatively timely debt repayment in actual development, while 2–5 release versions correspond to an interval of about 60 to 150 days, which is consistent with the research of Maldonado et al. [7]. At the same time, however, over 60% of SATD survives for 6 versions or more and were not removed in the short term.

Figure 4 shows the number of urgent SATD removed in each version. For the sake of clarity, we exclude versions where the number of urgent SATD removed was zero from figure. In the two projects, proportion of these excluded versions was 90% in Ant and 76% in Jruby. Figure 4 shows the remaining versions, we can see that there is a huge gap between the different versions. Ideally, each version would remove an average number of urgent SATD, which would indicate that developers' TD management is very effective and can greatly improve software quality. However, as shown in the figure, this situation indicates that a few versions have removed a large number of urgent SATD, probably due to large-scale code refactoring.

Answer to RQ 1. In practical projects, only a small fraction of SATD (4% in Ant and 16% in Jruby) are removed immediately. Another portion of SATD that are removed in the short term (i.e., within 2-5 versions) accounts for 16%-17% of the total number of SATD removed. This indicates that there is indeed a proportion of SATD that needs to be repaid immediately. However, urgent SATD is not evenly distributed across versions, which means that debt is not well managed.

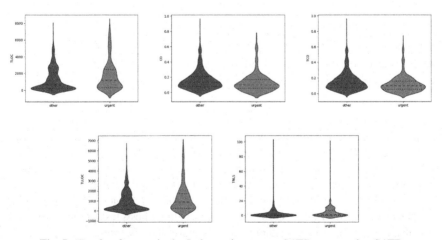

Fig. 5. Top five features in the Jruby project urgent SATD versus other SATD

3.2 What Are the Significant Features of "Urgent SATD"?

Motivation. Although there are studies on the priority of SATD removal [4, 5, 17], the results given are either not proven by the project [4, 17] or not further explained [5]. As the first study on urgent SATD, our goal is to understand its code features and how it differs from other SATD.

Approach. Since the Jruby project has more abundant urgent SATD and other types of SATD, as well as a more typical update iteration process, we chose to analyze this question on the Jruby project, while the data source is introduced in Sect. 2.4.

We first compare the distribution of features between urgent SATD and other SATD, using violin plots with quartile lines for easy comparison.

Secondly, because the features are not normally distributed, we apply the Mann–Whitney U test [18] with a 95% confidence level to test the statistical difference between the them, which verifies whether a difference exists.

Finally, we use Cliff's delta to test the practical significance of the features. The value of Cliff's delta (denoted by d) ranges from -1 to $+1$: a positive d implies that the value of the feature is often larger in urgent SATD than in other SATD, while a negative d implies the opposite. We convert the d values into qualitative magnitudes based on the following thresholds, as suggested by Hess and Kromrey [19]:

$$\text{Effect size } = \begin{cases} \text{Negligible,} & |d| \leq 0.147 \\ \text{Small,} & 0.147 < |d| \leq 0.33 \\ \text{Medium,} & 0.33 < |d| \leq 0.47 \\ \text{Large,} & 0.474 < |d| \leq 1 \end{cases} \tag{1}$$

Table 2. Definitions of the top five features of most practical importance

Metric name	Category	Abbreviation
Comment Density	Documentation metrics	CD
Total Comment Density	Documentation metrics	TCD
Total Logical Lines of Code	Size metrics	TLLOC
Total Number of Local Setters	Size metrics	TNLS
Total Lines of Code	Size metrics	TLOC

Results. We selected the top five features with the highest d values in the Cliff's delta test. Their definitions are in Table 2, which shows that they belong only to the Size metrics and Document metrics categories. It indicates that the code and documents associated with urgent SATD are more complex than other SATD, so developers increase their deletion priority. Figure 5 shows the distribution of these five features in urgent SATD and other SATD, while Table 3 shows their results in hypothesis testing and Cliff's delta experiments. It can be seen that although these features have differences between urgent SATD and other SATD, they are not very significant.

Table 3. Results of top five features on Mann whitney test and Cliff's Delta test in Jruby project

Feature	p value	d value	Significant
TCD	<0.0001	0.187	Small
TNLS	<0.0001	0.180	Small
CD	<0.0001	0.172	Small
TLLOC	<0.0001	0.171	Small
TLOC	<0.0001	0.164	Small

Answer to RQ 2. We heva used Cliff's delta test to identify the five features that are most practically significant for urgent SATD. They are CD, TCD, TLOC, TLLOC, and TNLS. They belong to the Document metrics and Size metrics categories. This indicates that urgent SATD are associated with more complex documents and source code.

---

4 Related Works

Comments within the source code serve as the primary method for developers to document and indicate the intentional insertion of Technical Debt. As such, recent studies have outlined strategies for identifying, understanding, and managing SATD [1, 8]. Various strategies are used to identify SATD, including the use of Textual Patterns [8], Natural Language Processing [20], and Composite Classification [6].

Previous research on the priority of TD removal has been from the perspective of TD management, analyzing the evolution and interest of TD to maximize the benefits of TD removal. For instance, Alfayez et al. use a Multi-objective Evolutionary Algorithm (MOEA) to indicate which TD items should be repaid to maximize the value of a repayment activity within a specific cost constraint [21], Ribeiro et al. also use a multiple decision criteria to decide when to pay debt items off [22].

The first to explicitly study the priority of SATD removal was Mensah et al. using textual identifiers to point out SATD tasks [4]. They use keywords to classify different types of SATD, and judge the importance and urgency of tasks according to the different results of the classification. Mensah et al. additionally consider the source code and the possible existing problems presented by to prioritize [5]. They combine priority terms and issues associated with each SATD instance in the source code to calculate a score and prioritize according to it. However, it does not dig deep enough into the features related to the source code. The only feature it takes into account is the number of issues contained in the source code, which doesn't describe the code in a comprehensive and detailed way. So the conclusions it drawns from it are one-sided.

5   Threats to Validity

5.1   Internal Validity

Our internal threats come mainly from the dataset construction stage. One comes from the SATD detector we use to identify SATD. Although it achieved an f1-score of 0.737 in the SATD identification task on eight large open-source projects, there are still some potentially erroneous results. We have tried our best to avoid this situation in the paper, but we cannot guarantee that all SATD instances used for analysis are true positives.

Similarly, when extracting OO (Object-Oriented) metrics, the tools we use (SourceMeter) may introduce threats. Although there are established rules and formulas for calculating each metric, the limitations within the tools may not allow for the complete and accurate recognition and computation of all metrics.

Another threat comes from the judgement of SATD removal. Previous studies have raised doubts about the actual removal of SATD [10]. Situations may arise where the source code has been changed or the issue has been resolved, bug the SATD instance remains. Conversely, the SATD instance may has been removed without any changes to the source code, meaning that the issue persists. These scenarios pose a threat to the validity of this study. Furthermore, SATD may be removed due to file deletion, in which case such instances are excluded from the dataset used.

5.2   External Validity

Threats to external validity concern the generalization of our results. Our research only analyzed two open-source projects of different scales and fields and only counted a total of 6,500 SATD and 218 release versions. Compared to open-source software, the quality of the development process in closed-source software is heavily driven by commercial objectives. Factors such as competition among various product lines, market pressures, and personnel changes significantly influence the development process. These aspects are unpredictable and distinct from open-source software. Therefore, our results may not be representative of other software projects.

6   Conclusion and Future Work

Removing SATD instantly has long-term benefits for debt management and project maintenance. To gain a more comprehensive understanding of the SATD that need to be removed in a high priority, we conducted a study on two Github open source projects with different development scales and popularity. We found that a small proportion (4%–16%) of SATD will be removed in the next version, which we call urgent SATD, and another proportion (16%–17%) will also be removed in the short term (i.e. in 2 to 5 versions). In further research on urgent SATD, we found that Document metrics and Size metrics have a greater impact on them. Specifically, urgent SATD is associated with more complex documents and source code.

In future research, we will explore whether features other than code features, such as developer or project characteristics, influence the immediate deletion of SATD and develop automated models to predict which SATD will be removed immediately, in order to help developers manage technical debt better.

References

1. Potdar, A., Shihab, E.: An exploratory study on self-admitted technical debt. In: 2014 IEEE International Conference on Software Maintenance and Evolution, ICSME, pp. 91–100. IEEE, Victoria (2014)
2. Kamei, Y., Maldonado, E.S., Shihab, E., et al.: Using analytics to quantify interest of self-admitted technical debt. QuASoQ-TDA 2016, pp. 68–71, Hamilton (2016)
3. Wehaibi, S., Shihab, E., Guerrouj, L.: Examining the impact of selfadmitted technical debt on software quality. In: IEEE 23rd International Conference on Software Analysis, Evolution, and Reengineering 2016, SANER, vol. 1, pp.179–188. IEEE, Osaka (2016)
4. de Lima, B.S., Garcia, R.E., Eler, D.M.: Toward prioritization of self-admitted technical debt: an approach to support decision to payment. Software Qual. J. **30**(3), 729–755 (2022)
5. Mensah, S., Keung, J., Svajlenko, J., et al.: On the value of a prioritization scheme for resolving self-admitted technical debt. J. Syst. Softw.Softw. **135**, 37–54 (2018)
6. Liu, Z., Huang, Q., Xia, X., et al.: SATD detector: a text-mining-based self-admitted technical debt detection tool. In: Proceedings of the 40th International Conference on Software Engineering: Companion Proceeedings, pp. 9–12. ACM, Gothenburg (2018)
7. Maldonado, E.D.S., Abdalkareem, R., Shihab, E., et al.: An empirical study on the removal of self-admitted technical debt. In: IEEE International Conference on Software Maintenance and Evolution 2017, ICSME, pp. 238–248. IEEE, Shanghai (2017)
8. Bavota, G., Russo, B.: A large-scale empirical study on self-admitted technical debt. In: Proceedings of the 13th International Conference on Mining Software Repositories, MSR, pp. 315–326. ACM, Austin (2016)
9. Cosentino, V., Luis, J., Cabot, J.: Findings from GitHub: methods, datasets and limitations. In: Proceedings of the 13th International Conference on Mining Software Repositories, MSR, pp. 137–141. ACM, Austin (2016)
10. Zampetti, F., Serebrenik, A., Di Penta, M.: Was self-admitted technical debt removal a real removal? an in-depth perspective. In: Proceedings of the 15th International Conference on Mining Software Repositories, MSR, pp. 526–536. ACM, Gothenburg (2016)
11. Seaman, C., Guo, Y.: Measuring and monitoring technical debt. In: Advances in Computers, vol. 82, pp. 25–46. Elsevier (2011)
12. Hamzehloui, M.S., Sahibuddin, S., Salah, K.: A systematic mapping study on technical debt. In: Proceedings 3rd International Conference of Reliable Information and Communication Technology, pp. 1–12. IEEE, Kuala Lumpur (2018)
13. Chidamber, S.R., Kemerer, C.F.: A metrics suite for object oriented design. IEEE Trans. Softw. Eng.Softw. Eng. **20**(6), 476–493 (1994)
14. Alves, N.S.R., Mendes, T.S., de Mendonça, M.G., et al.: Identification and management of technical debt: a systematic mapping study. Inf. Softw. Technol. Softw. Technol. **70**, 100–121 (2016)
15. Palomba, F., Bavota, G., Di Penta, M., et al.: On the diffuseness and the impact on maintainability of code smells: a large scale empirical investigation. In: Proceedings of the 40th International Conference on Software Engineering, p. 482. ACM, New York (2018)
16. Pantiuchina, J., Lin, B., Zampetti, F., et al.: Why do developers reject refactorings in open-source projects? ACM Trans. Softw. Eng. Methodol. **31**(2), 1–23 (2021)
17. Tsoukalas, D., Siavvas, M., Kehagias, D., et al.: A practical approach for technical debt prioritization based on class-level forecasting. J. Softw. Evol. Process, e2564 (2023)
18. Mann, H.B., Whitney, D.R.: On a test of whether one of two random variables is stochastically larger than the other. Ann. Math. Stat., 50–60 (1947)
19. Hess, M.R., Kromrey, J.D.: Robust confidence intervals for effect sizes: a comparative study of Cohen'sd and Cliff's delta under non-normality and heterogeneous variances. In: Annual Meeting of the American Educational Research Association, vol. 1 (2004)

20. da Silva, M.E., Shihab, E., Tsantalis, N.: Using natural language processing to automatically detect self-admitted technical debt. IEEE Trans. Software Eng. **43**(11), 1044–1062 (2017)
21. Alfayez, R., Boehm, B.: Technical debt prioritization: a search-based approach. In: IEEE 19th International Conference on Software Quality, Reliability and Security 2019, QRS, pp. 434–445. IEEE, Sofia (2019)
22. Ribeiro, L.F., Alves, N.S.R., Neto, M.G.D.M., et al.: A strategy based on multiple decision criteria to support technical debt management. In: 43rd Euromicro Conference on Software Engineering and Advanced Applications 2017, SEAA, pp. 334–341. IEEE, Vienna (2017)

Modular Joint Training for Speech-Driven 3D Facial Animation

Xinran Cao[1], Jia Zhu[2(✉)], Changfan Pan[1], Changqin Huang[2], Jianyang Shi[2], and Xin Liu[2]

[1] School of Computer Science and Technology, Zhejiang Normal University, Jinhua, China
[2] College of Education, Zhejiang Normal University, Jinhua, China
jiazhu@zjnu.edu.cn

Abstract. Speech-driven 3D facial animation is still an intensive field of research, with some persistent challenges. These difficulties arise from the intricate nature of achieving facial realism and the scarcity of audio-visual data. Previous studies have mainly focused on learning phoneme-level features from brief audio segments, which often lead to suboptimal lip movements. To capture the nuances of facial expressions, such as eyebrow-raising or lip curling, our proposed solution builds upon the autoregressive model of the Transformer, which can generate realistic facial movements based on previous frames and introduces a modular face separation model, which can separately control the upper face and lips, to enhance the quality of voice-driven 3D facial animation. This novel modular separation technique divides the facial mesh into two parts: the upper face and the lips, using our uniquely designed mask. Such an approach not only significantly improves facial animation synthesis but also lays the foundation for future research and application in this domain.

Keywords: Facial generation · Speech-driven · Modular separation

1 Instruction

In the realm of visual technology, speech-driven 3D facial animation is a challenging research problem that has attracted much attention in recent years. High-quality 3D facial animation plays a key role in applications such as virtual reality, making movies, game scenes, and news. The successful execution of 3D facial animations requires high levels of naturalness and relevance, especially for lip synchronization. Numerous studies have evaluated 3D facial animations through image and video data. However, considering the fact that the human visual system is constantly attuned to recognize minute details in facial movements and expressions, poorly coordinated or unsynchronized facial animations can inadvertently cause distraction and discomfort for the users. Therefore, there exists an urgent requirement to elevate the accuracy of facial animations with the aim of enhancing user immersion and overall user experience.

High-quality facial animation is intrinsically tied to audio support, despite these two components residing in separate feature spaces. However, creating realistic and synchronized facial animation from audio input is a challenging task that requires a deep understanding of the relationship between speech and facial expressions. To better establish a dependent relationship between audio and facial animation, the majority of recent technologies have turned to deep learning to address this challenge [3,14,18]. By training on extensive speech and mesh data, these methods have produced highly realistic facial animations. Notably, Karras T and colleagues [12] have successfully derived facial animation from the audio input, even inferring emotional state from long-term audio contexts. However, the performance of these methods tends to falter when faced with test data significantly divergent from the training data. To depict more realistic three-dimensional facial expressions and movements, high-quality vision-based motion capture must be performed on users to acquire the necessary training data. Recently, due to the scarcity of 3D audiovisual data, the FaceFormer [10] has emerged, integrating self-supervised pre-trained speech representations and encoding long-term audio contexts to autoregressively predict 3D facial mesh animations.

Fan et al. [10] proposed pre-trained speech representations to enhance speech-driven 3D facial animation with limited data, but they could not reconstruct the upper and lower facial regions independently and precisely. To address this issue, we introduce our modular face separation model, which treats the upper and lower faces as independent, resulting in more realistic animations. Our model uses a distinct loss function that trains the model to restore facial features precisely during the reconstruction process. This approach helps to distinguish facial movements between the lower and upper regions, avoiding overly smooth results. Figure 1 shows the face sequence generated by this model.

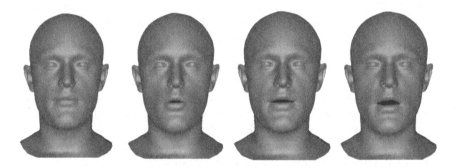

Fig. 1. Example grid for VOCASET subjects.

The main contributions of this paper are as follows:

1. Our approach introduces a modular face separation model built on top of the Transformer decoder, which allows independent training of each separate

region, enabling independent expression of each facial region and ensuring highly precise lip movements.

2. Our approach leverages a unique cross-modal loss function to train the model, which can effectively reconstruct the upper facial and mouth regions independently of the audio input. This is achieved by introducing masks tailored to specific facial areas, which enhance the precision of reconstruction.

3. We are committed to establishing a benchmark for future Speech-driven 3D facial animation tasks by ensuring the complete usability of our code, covering elements like data processing, metrics, and model training.

2   Related Work

The research on speech-driven facial animation generation in computer vision has attracted much attention [15] and remains a challenging task. Speech-driven facial animation generates a character's facial expression based on an input voice sequence synchronized with the voice content. The development of facial animation in recent years, from the generation model based on viseme sequence [7,9] to 2D head animation [1,2,5,16] to 3D facial animation [12,13].

In the earlier research, facial animation synthesis based on viseme sequence was an important method. De Martino et al. [6] proposed identifying phonetic context-dependent visemes that can drive facial animation by clustering all pronunciation objects of the same segment in different phonetic contexts. The model proposed by Edwards P et al. [7] automatically generates expressive lip-sync facial animations from input audio and speech transcripts. Viseme-based synthesis methods are favored in commercial applications, and especially it is in the field of virtual reality and other fields.

The extension [11,19] of faces from 2D to 3D is also a hot topic. While most of the literature is about studying the generation of 2D facial animations, we focus more on animating 3D models. The X2Face model proposed by Wiles O et al. [20] is based on a given 2D source face through a large amount of video data for full self-supervision, using the driving frame, audio data, or specified pose vectors to control the facial changes of the source face. Most voice-driven 3D facial animation generation needs to design a specific model and extract audio and facial features to map out facial animation. Eskimez S et al. [8] utilize a long short-term memory (LSTM) network trained on video data to extract facial features. After training, the method can generate speech drivers from unseen speakers and the acoustic speech of utterances. Karras T et al. [12] 's model learns a voice-driven 3D facial mesh from 3–5 minutes of data from each participant. Then the emotional state of the facial expression is continuously adjusted to its model to obtain the generated facial mesh grid. The lip-sync and facial expression fidelity of the model needs to be further improved, and the model's generalization ability needs to be considered so that it can be applied to new facial features and speech input. Our work focuses more on training high-resolution audio mesh matching data and independent animation of the entire facial mesh, which is innovative in the current study. In speech-driven 3D facial animation, ensuring accurate lip movement requires alignment between audio and facial motion.

Furthermore, to animate entire faces, we need to account for the long-term audio context. FaceFormer [10] utilizes the Transformer architecture to capture the long-term audio context and produce consistent animations over time. However, this approach may over-smooth the facial motion because it directly predicts the facial movement from the audio. This can lead to uncertainty and ambiguity, especially when the audiovisual data are highly unpredictable. It thus necessitates a more nuanced approach to address these challenges. Our proposed method can accurately reconstruct facial features while training. Furthermore, it ensures that the model solely relies on the provided audio input for precise reconstruction of the mouth region.

3 Methods

Animating a neutral facial mesh to match a speech signal is challenging, as there are many possible facial animations for the same speech. This ambiguity reduces the effectiveness of cross-modal learning and causes the loss of average and subtle movements. We propose a method that uses a Transformer model with multi-head attention to capture contextual information effectively. Then, we process the lower and upper halves of the generated facial motion sequence separately. This segmentation helps us understand and control the facial animation generation process better, and reduces the ambiguity effect. We use a specific loss function to train the model for the segmented upper and lower motion sequences. The loss function guides the model to learn accurate face reconstruction and synchronize the mouth region generation with the audio input, resulting in accurate mouth shape matching.

Our goal is to overcome the ambiguity problem in generating continuous 3D facial motions from long speech sequences, by using the above strategies.

3.1   Training Module for 3D Facial Motion

To better extract speech characteristics and generate motion sequences, our audio encoder utilizes the state-of-the-art self-supervised pre-training speech model, wav2vec 2.0. It comprises an audio feature extractor and a multi-layered Transformer encoder. The model is able to extract speech features from raw waveforms and transform these features into context-aware speech representations $A_{1:T}$ through a multi-layer transformer encoder. Besides the audio encoder, our proposed cross-modal decoder contains a multi-layer transformer decoder with a self-attention mechanism. This cross-modal decoder combines and embeds past facial motion sequences with styles via:

$$Z'_{1:T-1} = P_\theta \left(Z_{1:T-1} \right) + \frac{s}{\|s\|_1}, \tag{1}$$

where P_θ represents a linear projection layer, and $Z_{1:t-1}$ denotes the past facial movements. The variable $s = [s_0, ..., s_n]$ denotes the individual identities of distinct speakers. The variable $s = [s_0, ..., s_n]$ denotes the individual identities of distinct speakers. s_0 refers to the identity of the first speaker, s_1 to the second, and so on, until s_n, which represents the identity of the nth speaker. Figure 2 shows the overall architecture of our model.

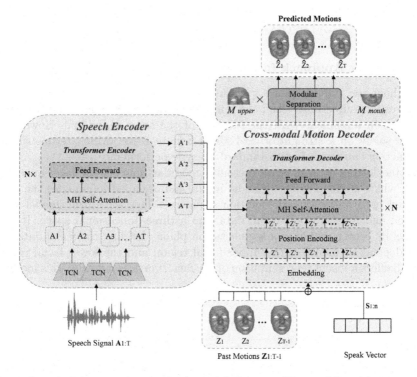

Fig. 2. Speech-driven motion synthesis model diagram. The model architecture takes speech sequence $A_{1:T}$, facial motion sequence $Z_{1:T-1}$, and style vector $S_{1:n}$ as input. It incorporates a multi-head self-attention mechanism to process longer input sequences and employs a unique facial region segmentation technique, dividing the face into upper and lower sections to generate refined facial animation.

We integrate style embeddings and compute contextual representations with weights to find the interrelation of frames in previous facial motions. We label the time-encoded facial motion representation sequence as $[Z_1, ..., Z_{t-1}]$, which is subsequently subjected to a linear projection onto the query Q^Z, key K^Z, and value V^Z vectors. This process is executed via H parallel operations, leveraging scaled dot-product attention. Further enhancement is achieved by a forward projection utilizing the W^Z parameter matrix:

$$MH\left(Q^Z, K^Z, V^Z\right) = (head_1 \| \cdots \| head_H) W^Z,$$
$$where\ head_i = Att(Q_i^Z, K_i^Z, V_i^Z)$$

(2)

We utilize a transformer decoder outfitted with self-attention to learn the relationships between individual frames within the context of previous facial motion sequences. Further, we align audio and motion modalities using cross-modal attention. The newly predicted motion, denoted as $\hat{Z}_{1:t}$, serves to update the past motion to $Z_{1:t-1}$. This recursive procedure can be formally expressed as follows:

$$\hat{Z}_{1:t} = D_{\text{motions}} \left(E_{\text{audio}} \left(A_{1:T} \right), Z_{1:t-1}, s \right). \tag{3}$$

3.2 Modular Approach to Facial Separation

Throughout the training phase, the authenticity of the generated facial motion sequences is assured only when the template grid, speech signal, and utterance signal are in alignment with the identity of the same individual. However, a reliance solely on a straightforward Mean Square Error (MSE) reconstruction loss function can result in substandard lip-sync performance.

To tackle this challenge, we present a modular upper-lower face separation model, which is independent of audio input, and designed to enhance the accuracy and naturalness of facial motion sequences. This separation model maps denoised and filtered point cloud data into a three-dimensional space. It then employs its center vector as a segmentation plane, dividing the facial data into two independent modules: the upper facial region and the lower facial region. Figure 3 offers a visual representation of the facial vertices following this modular separation.

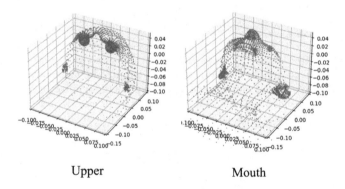

Upper   Mouth

Fig. 3. Visualization of facial vertices following modular segmentation.

The upper facial region incorporates features such as eyebrows and eyes, which are crucial for expressing emotions and conveying non-verbal cues. On the other hand, the lower facial region includes elements such as lips and chin, which are essential for speech and other vocal expressions. Each module operates independently, facilitating a more precise creation of motion sequences for distinct facial regions. This separation enhances not only the accuracy of our facial animations but also contributes to their naturalness by enabling each facial region to articulate independently, mirroring real-life facial movements.

3.3   Cross-Modal Loss in Animated Speech Synthesis

To facilitate individual training for each module, we propose an innovative cross-modal loss function specifically crafted to independently train the upper and lower regions of the face. The loss function, explicitly defined for the upper facial region, is expressed as follows:

$$\mathcal{L}_{upper} = \sum_{t=1}^{T}\sum_{v=1}^{V} \mathcal{M}_v^{(\text{upper})}\left(\|\hat{Z}_{t,v} - Z_{t,v}\|^2\right) \tag{4}$$

where $M_v^{(\text{upper})}$ represents the upper facial mask, conferring high weights to the upper vertices. This weighting system helps the model reconstruct the upper face accurately and independently. Training the model involves using the sequences $[\hat{Z}_1, ..., \hat{Z}_t]$ and the respective ground truth $[Z_1, ..., Z_{t-1}]$.Similarly, we define the loss function for the lower face as follows. $M_v^{(\text{mouth})}$ is the mask for the lower face, giving high weights to the mouth vertices. These high weights are crucial for precise reconstruction of the model's lower face, which is very important for realistic speech movements:

$$\mathcal{L}_{mouth} = \sum_{t=1}^{T}\sum_{v=1}^{V} \mathcal{M}_v^{(\text{mouth})}\left(\|\hat{Z}_{t,v} - Z_{t,v}\|^2\right) \tag{5}$$

We have discovered that the additive training of these two terms performs effectively in practice, notably reducing the overall error in face vertex positioning. The ultimate loss function that we optimize is represented as:

$$\mathcal{L} = \mathcal{L}_{upper} + \mathcal{L}_{mouth} \tag{6}$$

This innovative dual approach enables the model to gain a comprehensive understanding of the different features and motion patterns of the upper and lower facial regions. It allows us to deliver high-quality, realistic facial animations that closely correlate to natural, real-world facial movement, improving the overall efficacy and realism of our models.

4   Experiments Results

4.1   Dataset

The current research on 3D facial mesh datasets is limited by the small number of available datasets. We use the publicly available 3D dataset VOCASET [4] to train and test our model. The dataset consists of spoken English audio-3D scan pairs. The VOCASET dataset has 255 distinct sentences, some of which are shared among subjects.

The dataset comprises 480 pairs of audio-4D scans, capturing facial motion sequences from 12 subjects, including six females and six males. Each sequence has a frame rate of 60 and lasts for 3 to 5 s. The 3D facial mesh for each person utilizes the FLAME topology model, consisting of 5023 3D vertices. The VOCASET dataset has 255 unique sentences. All participants shared five sentences. Three to five participants spoke each of the other 15 sentences in the dataset, making a total of 50 unique sentences.

Additionally, there were 20 sentences that were spoken by only one or two participants, resulting in a total of 200 unique sentences. This means that each sentence has varying degrees of sharing, with some sentences being unique and spoken by individual participants. To ensure a fair comparison, we utilize the same division for training (VOCA-Train), validation (VOCA-Val), and testing (VOCA-Test) datasets. By using such a dataset and split, we are able to conduct comprehensive and accurate experiments to verify the effectiveness and reliability of our model in generating continuous 3D facial motions. These data are informative and broad in coverage, providing a solid basis for our findings.

4.2   Audio-driven Evaluation

Lip-sync Evaluation. We refer to the lip-sync metric used in MeshTalk [17] to evaluate the quality of lip movements. This metric calculates the lip error per frame by considering the maximum deviation of the lip vertices. We compute the error by comparing predicted and processed 3D face geometry data. As illustrated in Table 1, our method consistently achieves a lower per-frame lip error on average. We employ these metrics to quantitatively assess the precision and consistency of lip movements, thereby facilitating the objective evaluation of our models.

Table 1. Comparison of lip-sync errors

Methods	Lip Vertex Error($\times 10^{-4} mm$)
FaceFormer	3.66
FaceFormer + Our face separation	3.63
Ours	3.31

To gain a comprehensive perspective of the overall performance across the entire test set, we undertake a thorough evaluation process, computing the averages across ten groups. This robust evaluation strategy enables us to graphically visualize the quality of lip motion across different sequences while facilitating comparisons between our proposed technique and other established methodologies. By presenting these computed averages, we offer an objective evaluation of our model's performance and establish a benchmark against prior research findings. Such results are vital to corroborating the reliability and validity of our model and offering insights for its future enhancements and subsequent investigations. The results of which are illustrated in Fig. 4.

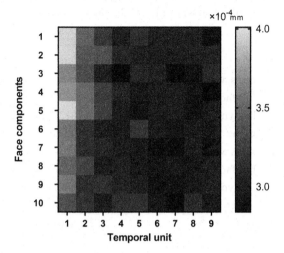

Fig. 4. A comprehensive evaluation of the overall performance of the entire test set by computing the mean.

Perceptual Evaluation. We conducted a user study wherein we showcased our method along with the VOCA and tracked ground-truth facial videos to 93 participants. These participants were tasked to evaluate three distinct categories: a full-face comparison, a lip-sync comparison, and an upper-face comparison. In the lip-sync comparison task, only the region around the nose and the area surrounding the lips was displayed. Conversely, in the upper-face comparison task, only the region above the nose was presented.

In each subtask, a specific number of clip pairs are assessed. Each clip showcases a sentence spoken by a participant from the test set. Participants have the freedom to select their preferred facial animation or deem our motion sequences as compared to the alternatives.

When compared to VOCA, our method consistently performs equally well or better in the full-face animation and lip-sync scenarios. Despite a slight deviation in lip motion, participants have shown a strong preference for our method, with our approach outperforming or matching VOCA in a significant number of cases. Notably, our method is favored over VOCA in most instances, with only a few cases where the two approaches are viewed as comparable.

The majority of participants found the ground truth to have a superior performance over the tracked ground truth. However, in a noteworthy proportion of instances, our method was rated as equally good, and only in a certain fraction was it ranked below the tracked ground truth. This highlights that our method delivers commendably satisfactory results, even when compared to the ground truth. The varied support rate results are summarized in Table 2.

Qualitative Evaluation. By decoupling identities from facial movements, we have effectively produced animations for an array of adult faces. To demonstrate the versatility of our model, we meticulously handpicked, aligned, and normal-

Table 2. User study results on VOCASET

	favorablity		
	competitor	equal	ours
ours vs. VOCA			
full-face	29.6%	12.4%	58%
lip sync	23.75%	25%	51.25%
upper face	30%	13.75%	56.25%
ours vs. Ground truth			
full-face	71.875%	15.625%	12.5%
lip sync	68.75%	6.25%	25%
upper face	65.625%	12.5%	21.875%

ized poses from multiple neutral scans within the dataset, thereby exposing a significant variety in facial structures. In Fig. 5, we present two static templates on the left, animated by audio sequences, side-by-side with selected frames from the VOCA animation.

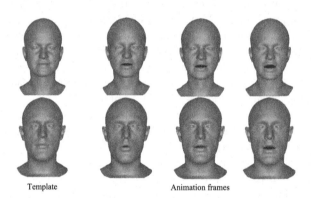

Template   Animation frames

Fig. 5. The figure shows a theme template selected from VOCASET on the left, driven by an audio input to three randomly selected animation frames on the right.

An example of an audio-propelled animation rendered via our methodology is portrayed in the figure. In this exemplification, the contours of the lips are synchronized with each subject's speech, spawning a chronicle of predicted facial maneuvers. These instances encapsulate an array of facial animation sequences, providing visually clear proof of our study's outcomes and underlining our strides in speech-propelled facial animation synthesis. Via these demonstrations, our aspiration is to manifest the practicality and real-world implementation of our technique to readers, as well as its adaptability and dependability when utilized on the VOCASET dataset.

This approach necessitates substantial amounts of fine grid data for the training phase, making the evaluation of its time complexity a challenging task. Addressing this issue, and thereby enhancing the efficiency of the training process, stands as a future objective.

4.3   Ablation Study

To investigate the role of upper face and lip masks in facial animation synthesis, we conducted a sequence of ablation experiments. These studies are meticulously designed to examine the influence of upper face and lip masks on the end results, particularly their effects on lip synchronization and facial expression generation. Throughout these ablation experiments, we preserve the consistency of training data and network architecture. The distinctive aspect of these tests is that only the upper face and lip masks are integrated into the loss function for computing the full-face error.

From the comparative experimental results in Table 3, we observe that the model with upper face and lip masks achieves better performance in lip synchronization and facial expression synthesis. This is because the combination of the upper face and lip masks can better guide the model to focus on the movement of the lip area and accurately reconstruct the details of the upper face. Among them, the upper face mask can help the model to focus on learning the movements and expressions of the upper face area, thereby improving the fidelity and expressiveness of facial animation. Lip masks better capture the shape and movement of lips for more accurate lip-syncing.

Table 3. Comparison of lip-sync errors

Methods	Full-face Vertex Error($\times 10^{-4} mm$)
Alter.(mouth)	6.85
Alter.(upper)	4.06
Alter.(upper+mouth)	3.37

5   Discussion and Conclusion

In this study, we introduce a transformer-based autoregressive architecture for generating speech-driven 3D facial animation sequences and achieving upper and lower face separation. The encoder leverages a pre-trained speech model to efficiently capture audio context dependencies. The decoder employs a multi-head attention module designed to ensure cross-modal alignment and enhance generalization to longer sequences. Our model employs a specific loss function for upper and lower face separation independent of audio input and is trained with different masks to prevent overly smoothed results and ensure highly accurate lip motion representation. This design can effectively improve the quality and realism of facial animation.

However, the overall perceptual quality is still lower than the ground truth. The limitation of the matching of audio-visual data is the main reason. As future work, an interesting direction is to guide the generation of 3D facial animation by exploiting prior knowledge from available large-scale videos of talking heads. In addition, the design and optimization strategies of the upper face and lip masks can be further explored to improve the effect of facial animation synthesis. This includes research exploring different masking forms, adjusting mask weights, and introducing more contextual information. Through these efforts, we can further improve the realism and naturalness of facial animation synthesis and advance the development of facial synthesis technology.

Acknowledgments. This work was supported by the Key Research and Development Program of Zhejiang Province (No. 2021C03141), the National Natural Science Foundation of China under Grant (62077015), the Natural Science Foundation of Zhejiang Province under Grant (LY23F020010) and the Key Laboratory of Intelligent Education Technology and Application of Zhejiang Province, Zhejiang Normal University, Zhejiang, China.

References

1. Alghamdi, M.M., Wang, H., Bulpitt, A.J., Hogg, D.C.: Talking head from speech audio using a pre-trained image generator. In: Proceedings of the 30th ACM International Conference on Multimedia, pp. 5228–5236 (2022)
2. Chen, L., et al.: Talking-head generation with rhythmic head motion. In: Vedaldi, A., Bischof, H., Brox, T., Frahm, J.-M. (eds.) ECCV 2020. LNCS, vol. 12354, pp. 35–51. Springer, Cham (2020). https://doi.org/10.1007/978-3-030-58545-7_3
3. Chen, L., Maddox, R.K., Duan, Z., Xu, C.: Hierarchical cross-modal talking face generation with dynamic pixel-wise loss. In: Proceedings of the IEEE/CVF Conference on Computer Vision and Pattern Recognition, pp. 7832–7841 (2019)
4. Cudeiro, D., Bolkart, T., Laidlaw, C., Ranjan, A., Black, M.J.: Capture, learning, and synthesis of 3d speaking styles. In: Proceedings of the IEEE/CVF Conference on Computer Vision and Pattern Recognition, pp. 10101–10111 (2019)
5. Das, D., Biswas, S., Sinha, S., Bhowmick, B.: Speech-driven facial animation using cascaded GANs for learning of motion and texture. In: Vedaldi, A., Bischof, H., Brox, T., Frahm, J.-M. (eds.) ECCV 2020. LNCS, vol. 12375, pp. 408–424. Springer, Cham (2020). https://doi.org/10.1007/978-3-030-58577-8_25
6. De Martino, J.M., Magalhães, L.P., Violaro, F.: Facial animation based on context-dependent visemes. Comput. Graph. **30**(6), 971–980 (2006)
7. Edwards, P., Landreth, C., Fiume, E., Singh, K.: Jali: an animator-centric viseme model for expressive lip synchronization. ACM Trans. Graph. (TOG) **35**(4), 1–11 (2016)
8. Eskimez, S.E., Maddox, R.K., Xu, C., Duan, Z.: Generating talking face landmarks from speech. In: Deville, Y., Gannot, S., Mason, R., Plumbley, M.D., Ward, D. (eds.) LVA/ICA 2018. LNCS, vol. 10891, pp. 372–381. Springer, Cham (2018). https://doi.org/10.1007/978-3-319-93764-9_35

9. Ezzat, T., Poggio, T.: Miketalk: A talking facial display based on morphing visemes. In: Proceedings Computer Animation 1998 (Cat. No. 98EX169), pp. 96–102. IEEE (1998)
10. Fan, Y., Lin, Z., Saito, J., Wang, W., Komura, T.: FaceFormer: speech-driven 3d facial animation with transformers. In: Proceedings of the IEEE/CVF Conference on Computer Vision and Pattern Recognition, pp. 18770–18780 (2022)
11. Garrido, P., et al.: Reconstruction of personalized 3d face rigs from monocular video. ACM Trans. Graph. (TOG) **35**(3), 1–15 (2016)
12. Karras, T., Aila, T., Laine, S., Herva, A., Lehtinen, J.: Audio-driven facial animation by joint end-to-end learning of pose and emotion. ACM Trans. Graph. (TOG) **36**(4), 1–12 (2017)
13. Liu, Y., Xu, F., Chai, J., Tong, X., Wang, L., Huo, Q.: Video-audio driven real-time facial animation. ACM Trans. Graph. (TOG) **34**(6), 1–10 (2015)
14. Mittal, G., Wang, B.: Animating face using disentangled audio representations. In: Proceedings of the IEEE/CVF Winter Conference on Applications of Computer Vision, pp. 3290–3298 (2020)
15. Parke, F.I., Waters, K.: Computer Facial Animation. CRC Press, Boca Raton (2008)
16. Prajwal, K., Mukhopadhyay, R., Namboodiri, V.P., Jawahar, C.: A lip sync expert is all you need for speech to lip generation in the wild. In: Proceedings of the 28th ACM International Conference on Multimedia, pp. 484–492 (2020)
17. Richard, A., Zollhöfer, M., Wen, Y., De la Torre, F., Sheikh, Y.: Meshtalk: 3d face animation from speech using cross-modality disentanglement. In: Proceedings of the IEEE/CVF International Conference on Computer Vision, pp. 1173–1182 (2021)
18. Suwajanakorn, S., Seitz, S.M., Kemelmacher-Shlizerman, I.: Synthesizing Obama: learning lip sync from audio. ACM Trans. Graph. (ToG) **36**(4), 1–13 (2017)
19. Wang, L., Han, W., Soong, F.K.: High quality lip-sync animation for 3d photo-realistic talking head. In: 2012 IEEE International Conference on Acoustics, Speech and Signal Processing (ICASSP), pp. 4529–4532. IEEE (2012)
20. Wiles, O., Koepke, A.S., Zisserman, A.: X2Face: a network for controlling face generation using images, audio, and pose codes. In: Ferrari, V., Hebert, M., Sminchisescu, C., Weiss, Y. (eds.) ECCV 2018. LNCS, vol. 11217, pp. 690–706. Springer, Cham (2018). https://doi.org/10.1007/978-3-030-01261-8_41

Extracting Structural Knowledge for Professional Text Inference

Tianyu Xia[1], Jian Wang[1], Tianyuan Liu[1], Hailan Jiang[2], and Yuqing Sun[1(✉)]

[1] School of Software, Shandong University, Jinan, China
937885834@qq.com, wangjian026@126.com, zodiacg@foxmail.com,
sun_yuqing@sdu.edu.cn
[2] Shandong Polytechnic, Jinan, China
1792@sdp.edu.cn

Abstract. Grading subjective questions of specialty text is a kind of text inference task. Since there are many specialty terms and concepts, it is difficult to judge the knowledge contained in a text as the usual way on inferring a general text. In this paper, we propose a specialty text inference model by extracting the structural knowledge from text. We first propose a knowledge graph construction method for the extraction of knowledge from specialty texts. By combining the constructed knowledge features with the text semantic features, we design the specialty text inference model. Finally, we use real datasets from a national professional exam to validate the soundness of the knowledge graph construction method and the performance of the inference model. The experiments under different training set sizes and network structures are also conducted to detailly analyze the design of our method. The experimental results show the effectiveness and practicality of our approach.

Keywords: Specialty Text · Structural Knowledge · Text Inference

1 Introduction

The specialty text inference task is the analysis and reasoning of specialty texts according to the given reference text, which is widely used the subjective questions, medical diagnosis, legal case analysis. Since there are many specialty terms and concepts, it is difficult to judge the knowledge contained in a text as the usual way on inferring a general text.

To solve this problem, the large pre-trained language models are used in the inference task. Since training these models are mostly on the general corpus, they are often not applicable for the specialty text. Researches indicate that fine-tuning large pre-trained language models with domain-specific datasets can enhance the performance [15]. In recent years, researchers have applied the above

This work was supported by the National Nature Science Foundation of China, NSFC (62376138) and the Innovative Development Joint Fund Key Projects of Shandong NSF (ZR2022LZH007).

methods to the automatic grading of subjective questions and achieved good results [10]. But most of the existing methods focus on the text semantics without considering the knowledge in an explicit way [9].

In this paper, we propose a specialty text inference method based on structural knowledge extraction. Firstly, we propose a knowledge graph construction method for specialty texts, enabling structural extraction of knowledge. The knowledge graph consists of specialty elements like terms, entities, and important general words, along with their relationships. This kind of knowledge graph represents the key point of specialty knowledge in text in an understandable way that is used for the subsequent text inference.

Secondly, we design a specialty text inference model based on structural knowledge extraction, called KnowSTI. We construct the knowledge features and semantic features of the text. And then we use the consistency loss function to train the model, which combines these two features for text inference. Additionally, the graph provides an explainable way for the inference results.

The rest of this paper is organized as follows. Section 2 introduces related works. Section 3 introduces the knowledge graph construction method. We present the details of our model in Sect. 4. We validate our model on real datasets and analyze the experimental results in Sect. 5. Section 6 summaries this paper and presents the future work.

2 Related Work

2.1 Specialty Text Inference

The large pre-trained language models are used in the inference task [7,12]. Since training these models are mostly on the general corpus, they are often not applicable for the specialty text. Lee et al. [8] found these model are difficult to estimate their performance on datasets containing biomedical texts, they created BioBERT from BERT pre-trained on a biomedical corpus.

Data augmentation is a technique for specialty text inference. It extends datasets to improve the model performance of large pre-trained language models on specialty texts. Classical data enhancement techniques include methods such as EDA [18], back translation [14], mixup [20]and text generation [11]. Ding et al. [2] studied how to infer patient condition from the description text with the mixup data augmentation method. Lun et al. [13] utilized the BERT pre-trained language model to review subjective questions and experimented with various data enhancement methods to boost model performance. On the same task, Li et al. [10] employed back-translation for data enhancement. However, these methods lack an inferential basis for the results, leading to untrusted outcomes in practical scenarios and impacting model usability.

2.2 Knowledge Extraction on Specialty Text

Knowledge extraction includes named entity recognition (NER) and relation extraction (RE). For specialty scenarios, pre-trained models for NER need adaptation. Jia et al. [6] used a language model as a concomitant task for NER in a new specialized domain using multi-task learning. Wu et al. [19] introduced the LTN model to reuse knowledge from a general NER task without refactoring. Many methods also use remotely supervised technique to address the lack of training data. Gu et al. [4] used the Comparative Toxicogenomics Database (CTD) for remote supervision, while Di et al. [1] optimized relational mention representation by selecting suitable knowledge bases and associated texts.

Researchers have also explored the open relation extraction task, aiming to extract relations without predefined types. Some methods extract features from entity pairs and then identify inter-entity relations through clustering [5,17]. There are also supervised methods which use labeled data with predefined relations to guide extraction in unsupervised data [3,21]. While the proposed technique overcomes the limitation of undefined relation extraction, its performance still requires improvement and may not be suitable for real scenarios.

3   Constructing the Knowledge Graph from Text

We propose the concept *knowledge graph* to describe the knowledge contained in a specialty text. For a given the student text $X = x_1 x_2 \ldots x_{|X|}$, the knowledge graph is denoted by $G_X = (V_X, E_X)$, where the node set $V_X = \{v_1, v_2, \ldots v_{k_X}\}$ refer to the specialty elements in the text, k_X is the total number of nodes, and $E_X = \{(v_i, v_j) \,|\, v_i, v_j \in V_X\}$ is the edge set. The proposed structural knowledge extraction method is shown in Fig. 1. The details are given below.

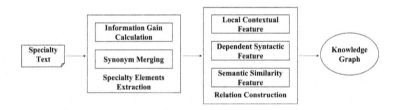

Fig. 1. A Knowledge Graph Construction Method for Specialty Texts

3.1   Expert Rule Based Specialty Elements Extraction

We choose the specific terms, entities, and important general words as the specialty elements, which are essential for understanding the specialty text and constructing the knowledge graph. Since information gain (IG for short) is often used to measure the importance of features, we use IG to calculate the importance of specialty elements. Let $H(C)$ denote the overall entropy of the predicated score. $H(C|T)$ denotes the conditional entropy, given the presence or absence of T: For word T, the information gain $IG(T)$ is computed as follow.

$$IG(T) = H(C) - H(C|T) \tag{1}$$

For the purpose of synonym merging, the information gain value $IG\left(T'\right)$ of a synonymous specialty element T is factored into the information gain value $IG(T)$ of the word T in calculating the information gain:

$$IG(T) = \sum_{T' \in V_T} IG\left(T'\right) \qquad (2)$$

where V_T denotes the set of synonymous specialty elements of the word T. Finally, the information gain values $IG(T)$ that have completed the synonym merging are sorted. The elements N_{ig} with the highest $IG(T)$ value constitute the specialty element table. These elements constitute as the set of nodes of the knowledge graph $V_X = \{v_1, v_2, \ldots v_{k_X}\}$, k_X is the total number of specialty elements in the professional text, based on which we to extract the specialty elements in text X.

3.2 Relation Construction Based on Multi-information Fusion

To obtain structural knowledge representation, we combine the local contextual features, dependent syntactic features, and semantic similarity features of the two specialty elements in the specialty text as the weights of their relation.

The local contextual feature $d_{ij}^c = 1$ is defined as the concurrence of two specialty elements v_i and v_j within a given widow c_n, which is used to capture the short-distance interactions. $d_{ij}^c = 0$ for otherwise.

The dependency syntactic feature d_{ij}^n focuses on the dependency relation between two specialty elements. We use stanza to parse an input sentence to a dependency syntax tree. If there is a parent-child relation between specialty elements v_i and v_j, $d_{ij}^{n_1} = 1$; otherwise, it is 0.

In order to better utilize the inter-lexical dependency information contained in the dependency syntax tree, we also consider the indirect associations $d_{ij}^{n_2}$ between two specialty elements, including the following three cases:

$$d_{ij}^{n_2} = \begin{cases} 1, \text{There is a grandchild relationship between } v_i \text{ and } v_j \\ 1, v_i \text{ and } v_j \text{are brother nodes} \\ 0, \text{otherwise} \end{cases} \qquad (3)$$

The two features $d_{ij}^{n_1}$ and $d_{ij}^{n_2}$ consist of the syntactic feature d_{ij}^n:

$$d_{ij}^n = \left[d_{ij}^{n_1} : d_{ij}^{n_2}\right] \qquad (4)$$

We use BERT, a pre-trained language model, to encode the text X into a sequence of vectors $\mathbf{C} = [\mathbf{c}1, \mathbf{c}2, \ldots, \mathbf{cn}]$, where each element v_i corresponds to vector c_i. The semantic similarity feature d_{ij}^s is computed as the cosine value between vectors c_i and c_j:

$$d_{ij}^s = cos\left(\mathbf{c_i}, \mathbf{c_j}\right) = \frac{\mathbf{c_i} \bullet \mathbf{c_j}}{|\mathbf{c_i}| \times |\mathbf{c_j}|} \qquad (5)$$

Then the above features are combined for an edge e_{ij}, namely the local context features d_{ij}^c, the syntactic features d_{ij}^n, and the semantic similarity features d_{ij}^s for the specialty elements v_i and v_j in X:

$$\mathbf{d_{ij}} = \left[d_{ij}^c, d_{ij}^n, d_{ij}^s \right] \tag{6}$$

The weight e_{ij} of the relation between specialty elements v_i and v_j in the adjacency matrix is computed by multiplying these vectors with the weight vector $\mathbf{w} = [\alpha_p, \beta_p, \gamma_p]$ for information fusion. The parameter matrix w is trained in the subsequent task. The relation between the specialty elements in text X forms the edges in the knowledge graph $E_X = \{(v_i, v_j) \, | v_i, v_j \in V_X \}$.

$$e_{ij} = \mathbf{w}^T \bullet \mathbf{d_{ij}} = \alpha_p d_{ij}^c + \beta_p d_{ij}^n + \gamma_p d_{ij}^s \tag{7}$$

4 Structural Knowledge Based Specialty Text Inference

We propose a lightweight specialty text inference model based on structural knowledge. The specialty text inference task involves a subjective question Q, candidate text X, and reference answer text R. We extract knowledge graphs G_X and G_R using the model and make inferential scores $y \in S$ for X. S is the set of inference results with $|S|$ possible scores. G_X serves as the knowledge that explains the inferred results.

4.1 Model

We propose KnowSTI, a specialty text inference model based on structural knowledge extraction. The model takes candidates' texts and reference answer as inputs and outputs the inference results, as shown in Fig. 2.

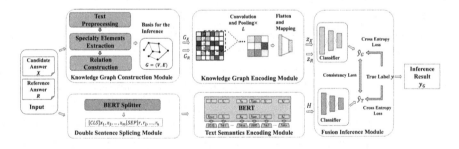

Fig. 2. Structural Knowledge Based Specialty Text Inference

4.2   Knowledge Graph Self-encoder

A knowledge graph is formed as an adjacency matrix A_X. We use a convolutional neural network with L layers for encoding A_X as the vector z_X. Let $M^0 = A_X$ and M^l denotes the representation matrix of the lth hidden layer. Formally,

$$M^l = MaxPooling\left(Conv2D\left(M^{l-1}, K^{l-1}\right)\right) \tag{8}$$

Then the *Flatten* operation is applied to M_L and then M_L is downscaled using a multilayer perceptron to obtain the vector z_X for G_X:

$$\mathbf{z_X} = MLP_{enc}\left(Flatten\left(M_L\right)\right) \tag{9}$$

The decoder is MLP network that accepts z_X as input and outputs the graph matrix $\hat{A}_X$:

$$\hat{A}_X = MLP_{dec}\left(\mathbf{z_X}\right) \tag{10}$$

The mean square error between $\hat{A}_X$ and A_X is used as a loss function to train the encoder:

$$J = \frac{1}{N^2}\left\|\hat{A}_X - A_X\right\|_2^2 \tag{11}$$

4.3   Structural Knowledge and Semantics Based Text Inference

We use BERT to encode $X = x_1, x_2 \ldots x_m$ and the reference answer $R = r_1, r_2 \ldots r_n$, i.e. $H = BERT\left(R \oplus X\right)_{\{CLS\}}$. To consider both differences and similarities, we introduce the feature differences $|\mathbf{z_X} - \mathbf{z_R}|$ and feature correlation $\mathbf{z_X} \otimes \mathbf{z_R}$. Here, $\otimes$ denotes the outer product of two vectors, reflecting their similarity and interaction, and $\oplus$ denotes the splicing operation on the vectors. The knowledge feature Z is obtained after splicing:

$$\mathbf{Z} = \mathbf{z_X} \oplus \mathbf{z_R} \oplus |\mathbf{z_X} - \mathbf{z_R}| \oplus (\mathbf{z_X} \otimes \mathbf{z_R}) \tag{12}$$

Then the knowledge-based classifier MLP_G yields a probability distribution of inferred outcomes $\hat{y}_G$. The loss function MLP_G is cross entropy.

$$\hat{y}_G = softmax\left(MLP_G\left(\mathbf{Z}\right)\right) \tag{13}$$

$$J_1 = -\sum_{i=1}^{|S|} y_i log\left(\hat{y}_{G,i}\right) \tag{14}$$

where $|S|$ is the number of inferred outcome categories, and $\hat{y}_{G,i}$ is the probability for category i.

By using the text semantic features, the inference probability distribution $\hat{y}_T$ is obtained by the text semantics-based classifier MLP_T:

$$\hat{y}_T = softmax\left(MLP_T\left(\mathbf{H}\right)\right) \tag{15}$$

$$J_2 = -\sum_{i=1}^{|S|} y_i log\left(\hat{y}_{T,i}\right) \tag{16}$$

Then KL divergence is used to constrain these two classifiers, aiming for a consistent results:

$$J_{con} = KL\left(\hat{y}_G \,\|\hat{y}_T\right) \tag{17}$$

Finally, the loss function is defined as:

$$L = \alpha_l J_1 + \beta_l J_2 + \left(1 - \alpha_l - \beta_l\right) J_{con} \tag{18}$$

where α_l and β_l are hyper-parameters. Besides, the Knowledge graph can be regarded as the interpreter for the inferred results, where the nodes and edges in the graph present the important words and relations.

5 Experiment

5.1 Dataset and Evaluation

We adopt eight subjective question datasets, which are selected from a national professional qualification examination. Each dataset includes the question title, reference answer, examinee's answer text, and corresponding score. The data is divided into training, validation, and test sets with ratios of 70%, 20% and 10%, respectively. To assess the model performance with varying training set sizes, training sets of 5% and 1% of the dataset are also constructed to simulate limited samples, as shown in Table 1. In the experiments, the accuracy is used as the overall evaluation metric.

Table 1. Amount of data in different settings

Category	Dataset							
	I	II	III	IV	V	VI	VII	VIII
70%training set	11104	11002	11084	11009	4199	9916	9764	9935
5%training set	793	786	792	786	300	708	698	710
1%training set	159	157	158	157	60	142	140	142
Test set	3173	3144	3167	3146	1200	2834	2790	2839
Validation set	1587	1572	1584	1573	600	1417	1396	1420
Total	15864	15718	15835	15728	5999	14167	13950	14194

5.2   Comparison Models

As grading subjective questions is a kind of text inference task, we choose several text inference models for comparison.

- **Base-BERT** [7]: Text is encoded with the pre-trained language model BERT and the encoding result is forwarded to a classifier.
- **Base-RoBERTa** [12]: Text is encoded with the pre-trained language model RoBERTa, followed by a classifier for grading.
- **LR+** [15]: The pre-trained BERT model is enhanced by fine-tuning it on textbooks as a specialty corpus. It encodes the text and reference answer, with a classifier for predicting the scores.
- **Conv-GRNN** [16]: The model encodes examinee text sentences using a convolutional neural network at the vocabulary level, generating document vectors with GRU at the sentence level for classification.
- **KnowSTI**: The model proposed in this paper.

5.3   Setting

In the knowledge graph construction process, the specialty element table size is selected from $\{30, 50, 100, 200\}$. Semantic similarity feature is calculated with BERT-base. The word window's size is set 2 and 7. The initial value for $\mathbf{W_e}$ is $[0.15, 0.15, 0.25, 0.25, 0.2]$. The knowledge graph encoder uses a 3 layer CNN with convolution kernel sizes of 5, 2 and 3, respectively, while the pooling kernel sizes are all set 2. The encoding vector dimension size is 800 and the decoder is a 2-layer MLP. The specialty text classifier uses a two-layer MLP with a hidden layer vector dimension of 1000. The RoBERTa-wmm pre-training language model is used for semantic encoding.

During training, the model uses a learning rate of 4e-4, a batch size of 32, and AdamW as the optimizer. The model has about 950K trainable parameters. In the use phase, the number of parameter in the model is about 650K, making it faster and more efficient compared to natural language models with billions of parameters. This approach can be trained and tested on a single Nvidia GeForce RTX 2080Ti, making it suitable for closed grading scenarios. Therefore, this model is highly applicable in real scenarios.

5.4   Comparison Results

We compare our method with baselines and the results on different sizes of training sets are shown in Table 2, Table 3, and Table 4, where 1%, 5%, and 70% denote the proportion of the training set to the total sample size.

The results show that our model consistently outperforms comparison methods, highlighting its effectiveness. LR+ slightly improves over the original BERT model, indicating the impact of parameter fine-tuning. Our method consistently outperforms LR+, showcasing knowledge graph-based specialty text inference's value. Requiring less training data and a smaller model size than pre-trained language models, our method is more practical.

Table 2. Accuracy of each model on the 70% training set

Model	Dataset							
	I	II	III	IV	V	VI	VII	VIII
Conv-GRNN	89.17%	83.82%	89.38%	89.54%	90.22%	86.39%	87.32%	89.28%
Base-BERT	95.19%	93.64%	90.51%	90.38%	93.81%	93.21%	91.43%	93.53%
Base-RoBERTa	96.87%	94.76%	94.75%	91.24%	94.97%	95.44%	94.00%	95.88%
LR+	96.03%	96.45%	96.66%	95.09%	96.54%	95.53%	94.63%	96.22%
KnowSTI	**97.28%**	**96.87%**	**97.92%**	**95.47%**	**97.07%**	**95.68%**	**96.83%**	**97.06%**

Table 3. Accuracy of each model on the 5% training set

Model	Dataset							
	I	II	III	IV	V	VI	VII	VIII
Conv-GRNN	83.40%	80.51%	88.74%	84.20%	89.97%	85.49%	86.50%	84.84%
Base-BERT	85.85%	82.97%	90.25%	86.54%	89.96%	90.57%	88.27%	89.44%
Base-RoBERTa	96.05%	94.36%	95.11%	89.89%	92.34%	91.00%	90.66%	90.38%
LR+	**96.79%**	93.00%	96.31%	91.09%	**96.03%**	94.89%	**93.55%**	91.24%
KnowSTI	96.51%	**94.46%**	**96.82%**	**93.90%**	94.57%	**95.04%**	92.83%	**93.06%**

Table 4. Accuracy of each model on the 1% training set

Model	Dataset							
	I	II	III	IV	V	VI	VII	VIII
Conv-GRNN	81.59%	80.65%	87.67%	84.03%	88.12%	84.61%	85.94%	82.51%
Base-BERT	90.50%	86.72%	91.90%	84.48%	85.71%	90.15%	83.95%	87.90%
Base-RoBERTa	92.27%	89.87%	93.00%	87.77%	84.80%	90.46%	84.00%	86.91%
LR+	**92.40%**	91.39%	**94.16%**	92.38%	91.15%	90.85%	90.13%	88.57%
KnowSTI	92.28%	**92.24%**	93.88%	**93.30%**	**92.69%**	**92.37%**	**91.55%**	**89.95%**

In real grading scenarios, training data is limited. We test our method's robustness by comparing it with others across different training set sizes. Our model achieves over 95% accuracy with a 70% training set and around 90% accuracy with 1% or 5% training sets. Notably, as shown in Table 3, our model attains over 95% accuracy for datasets I, III, and VI with a 5% training set, illustrating its capacity to excel with limited data.

5.5   Results of Ablation Experiments

This section conducts an in-depth analysis of the model's structure and performance, evaluating the contribution of each module. The experiments include three variants of our method:

- **Without reference answer**: The model takes only the student text as input, and during inference, it relies only on the encoded text for inference.
- **Without knowledge graph encoding**: The model uses only the semantic encoding of the text for inference.

Table 5. Model ablation experiments on specialty subjective datasets

Model structure	Dataset							
	I	II	III	IV	V	VI	VII	VIII
No reference answer	90.00%	92.64%	89.75%	87.71%	86.19%	91.53%	94.63%	94.44%
No KG encoding	96.88%	96.19%	97.32%	95.25%	96.81%	94.29%	95.98%	96.93%
No semantic encoding	97.15%	96.23%	97.80%	95.00%	97.00%	95.15%	96.80%	96.85%
KnowSTI	**97.28%**	**96.87%**	**97.92%**	**95.47%**	**97.07%**	**95.68%**	**96.83%**	**97.06%**

- **Without semantic encoding**: The model utilizes only knowledge graph encoding for inference.

The results in Table 5 show that omitting any module reduces the performance. The proposed model *KnowSTI* outperforms the cases without knowledge graph encoding or text semantic encoding module. Thus fusing structural knowledge and text semantics enhances the performance. Especially, omitting reference answers notably degrades the performance, which illustrates that the reference answer helps model understand the text.

5.6   Analysis on Knowledge Graph Construction Methods

In order to illustrate the effectiveness of the knowledge graph construction method, we have experimentally verified the role of each step in the knowledge graph construction method.

Impact of the Size of Specialty Element Table. As the nodes of knowledge graph are based on the element table, we explore how the size of specialty element table impacts the performance. The results in Table 6 show that the moderate number of specialty elements are desired. The performance approaches the best at above 50 for most datasets. It is necessary to select the based on data characteristics.

Table 6. Performance with different sizes of specialty element tables

Size	Dataset							
	I	II	III	IV	V	VI	VII	VIII
30	96.34%	93.63%	95.37%	93.71%	96.94%	95.53%	94.63%	96.96%
50	**97.28%**	**96.87%**	97.92%	**95.47%**	97.07%	**95.68%**	96.83%	97.06%
100	97.10%	93.56%	**98.00%**	94.81%	97.49%	95.31%	**97.05%**	97.14%
200	94.56%	93.74%	95.19%	94.00%	**97.57%**	95.44%	96.81%	**97.33%**

The Method on Constructing Element Relation. Then we assess how the parameters on constructing the relations of knowledge graph influence the model performance, namely d_{ij}^c, d_{ij}^n, and d_{ij}^s. Specifically, we construct specialty text knowledge graphs using one or two features to establish relations among elements. The specialty text inference model is then trained and tested on these graphs to gauge feature contributions.

In Table 7, combining all three features performs best in our method. Among these, the syntactic features are very important as it effectively captures both the syntactic and semantic information. Besides, combining syntactic and semantic similarity features also enhance knowledge graph construction. These results show the importance of long-distance dependencies among specialty elements.

Table 7. Performance with different relation construction features

Type	Dataset							
	I	II	III	IV	V	VI	VII	VIII
c	91.33%	89.14%	92.25%	91.89%	92.59%	90.54%	92.58%	91.00%
n	94.73%	92.06%	91.88%	92.61%	95.51%	90.48%	94.52%	96.52%
s	91.89%	90.87%	93.96%	92.54%	93.99%	92.36%	92.31%	94.81%
cn	95.41%	92.42%	95.15%	94.91%	95.87%	93.57%	94.69%	96.79%
cs	93.02%	90.91%	94.28%	93.85%	94.44%	94.16%	93.12%	95.50%
ns	94.85%	93.53%	96.51%	95.04%	96.12%	94.58%	95.44%	96.42%
cns	**97.28%**	**96.87%**	**97.92%**	**95.47%**	**97.07%**	**95.68%**	**96.83%**	**97.06%**

The Effect of Synonym Merging on Extracting Specialty Elements. We examine the effect of synonym merging on model performance during specialty elements extraction by creating knowledge graphs with and without this process. The results in Table 8 indicate a significant performance drop, particularly in dataset I, where the absence of synonym merging leads to a potential 10% decrease. In professional exams, the expressions vary from candidate to candidate. Synonym merging unifies synonymous elements under one node, enhancing both accuracy and recall in specialty element extraction.

Table 8. Comparison of model performances with/without synonym merging

Synonym merging	Dataset							
	I	II	III	IV	V	VI	VII	VIII
w/o	87.32%	89.64%	96.75%	90.19%	93.46%	86.86%	91.33%	90.35%
w	**97.28%**	**96.87%**	**97.92%**	**95.47%**	**97.07%**	**95.68%**	**96.83%**	**97.06%**

Distribution Analysis of Specialty Elements Under Different Training Set Sizes. To examine the effect of training set size on constructing specialty elements tables through information gain, a dataset was randomly selected. Information gain was calculated under various training set proportions, and the 50 words with the highest IG in the 70% proportion training set are selected. Scatter points of different colors indicate information gain across different scaled datasets. The Fig. 3 highlights a consistent trend in information gain values between words across various datasets, with minor variations in individual values. This method of selecting specialty elements based on information gain maintains stability regardless of training set size, ensuring a consistent table construction process.

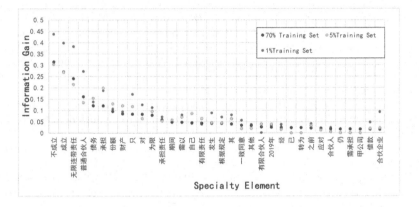

Fig. 3. Information gain values of specialty elements under different training set sizes

6   Conclusion

For the task of grading subjective questions in professional examinations, we propose a structural knowledge based specialty text inference model. We first design a knowledge graph construction method to extract structural knowledge from the specialty text, based on which the specialty text inference model is designed with the hybrid loss functions. We verify our model on real datasets from a national professional exam with different training set sizes. The ablation experiments are conducted to verify the validity of the components of the model. We also design a series of experiments to show the effectiveness of our knowledge graph construction method. In the future, we are planning to generate reusable knowledge when grading, which will enable model to provide feedback to the user, increasing the practicality of the automatic grading.

References

1. Di, S., Shen, Y., Chen, L.: Relation extraction via domain-aware transfer learning. In: Proceedings of the 25th ACM SIGKDD International Conference on Knowledge Discovery & Data Mining, pp. 1348–1357 (2019)

2. Ding, X., Lybarger, K., Tauscher, J., Cohen, T.: Improving classification of infrequent cognitive distortions: domain-specific model vs. data augmentation. In: Proceedings of the 2022 Conference of the North American Chapter of the Association for Computational Linguistics: Human Language Technologies: Student Research Workshop, pp. 68–75 (2022)

3. Duan, B., Wang, S., Liu, X., Xu, Y.: Cluster-aware pseudo-labeling for supervised open relation extraction. In: Proceedings of the 29th International Conference on Computational Linguistics, pp. 1834–1841 (2022)

4. Gu, J., Sun, F., Qian, L., Zhou, G.: Chemical-induced disease relation extraction via attention-based distant supervision. BMC Bioinform. **20**, 1–14 (2019)

5. Hu, X., Zhang, C., Xu, Y., Wen, L., Yu, P.S.: Selfore: self-supervised relational feature learning for open relation extraction. arXiv preprint arXiv:2004.02438 (2020)

6. Jia, C., Liang, X., Zhang, Y.: Cross-domain NER using cross-domain language modeling. In: Proceedings of the 57th Annual Meeting of the Association for Computational Linguistics, pp. 2464–2474 (2019)

7. Devlin, J., Chang, M.W., Lee, K., Toutanova, K.: Bert: pre-training of deep bidirectional transformers for language understanding. In: Proceedings of NAACL-HLT, vol. 1, p. 2 (2019)

8. Lee, J., et al.: Biobert: a pre-trained biomedical language representation model for biomedical text mining. Bioinformatics **36**(4), 1234–1240 (2020)

9. Li, D., Liu, T., Pan, W., Liu, X., Sun, Y., Yuan, F.: Grading Chinese answers on specialty subjective questions. In: Sun, Y., Lu, T., Yu, Z., Fan, H., Gao, L. (eds.) ChineseCSCW 2019. CCIS, vol. 1042, pp. 670–682. Springer, Singapore (2019). https://doi.org/10.1007/978-981-15-1377-0_52

10. Li, Z., Tomar, Y., Passonneau, R.J.: A semantic feature-wise transformation relation network for automatic short answer grading. In: Proceedings of the 2021 Conference on Empirical Methods in Natural Language Processing, pp. 6030–6040 (2021)

11. Liu, D., et al.: Tell me how to ask again: question data augmentation with controllable rewriting in continuous space. In: Proceedings of the 2020 Conference on Empirical Methods in Natural Language Processing (EMNLP), pp. 5798–5810 (2020)

12. Liu, Y., et al.: Roberta: a robustly optimized bert pretraining approach. arXiv preprint arXiv:1907.11692 (2019)

13. Lun, J., Zhu, J., Tang, Y., Yang, M.: Multiple data augmentation strategies for improving performance on automatic short answer scoring. In: Proceedings of the AAAI Conference on Artificial Intelligence, vol. 34, pp. 13389–13396 (2020)

14. Sennrich, R., Haddow, B., Birch, A.: Improving neural machine translation models with monolingual data. In: Proceedings of the 54th Annual Meeting of the Association for Computational Linguistics (Volume 1: Long Papers), pp. 86–96 (2016)

15. Sung, C., Dhamecha, T., Saha, S., Ma, T., Reddy, V., Arora, R.: Pre-training bert on domain resources for short answer grading. In: Proceedings of the 2019 Conference on Empirical Methods in Natural Language Processing and the 9th International Joint Conference on Natural Language Processing (EMNLP-IJCNLP), pp. 6071–6075 (2019)

16. Tang, D., Qin, B., Liu, T.: Document modeling with gated recurrent neural network for sentiment classification. In: Proceedings of the 2015 Conference on Empirical Methods in Natural Language Processing, pp. 1422–1432 (2015)

17. Tran, T.T., Le, P., Ananiadou, S.: Revisiting unsupervised relation extraction. In: Proceedings of the 58th Annual Meeting of the Association for Computational Linguistics, pp. 7498–7505 (2020)

18. Wei, J., Zou, K.: EDA: easy data augmentation techniques for boosting performance on text classification tasks. In: Proceedings of the 2019 Conference on Empirical Methods in Natural Language Processing and the 9th International Joint Conference on Natural Language Processing (EMNLP-IJCNLP), pp. 6382–6388 (2019)

19. Wu, J., Liu, T., Sun, Y., Gong, B.: A light transfer model for Chinese named entity recognition for specialty domain. In: Sun, Y., Liu, D., Liao, H., Fan, H., Gao, L. (eds.) ChineseCSCW 2020. CCIS, vol. 1330, pp. 530–541. Springer, Singapore (2021). https://doi.org/10.1007/978-981-16-2540-4_38

20. Zhang, H., Cisse, M., Dauphin, Y.N., Lopez-Paz, D.: mixup: beyond empirical risk minimization. arXiv preprint arXiv:1710.09412 (2017)

21. Zhao, J., Gui, T., Zhang, Q., Zhou, Y.: A relation-oriented clustering method for open relation extraction. In: Proceedings of the 2021 Conference on Empirical Methods in Natural Language Processing, pp. 9707–9718 (2021)

Card Mini Program Design
and Implementation Based on SCHOLAT
Social Network

Guoqiang Liu[1], Junming Zhou[1], Yu Weng[1], Lu Yu[1], and Chengzhe Yuan[2(✉)]

[1] School of Computer Science and Technology, South China Normal University,
Guangzhou, Guangdong, China
[2] School of Electronic and Information, Guangdong Polytechnic Normal University,
Guangzhou, Guangdong, China
ycz@gpnu.edu.cn

Abstract. SCHOLAT is an academic social network service website designed and built specifically for scholars, learners, and course instructors. This article mainly designs and implements a SCHOLAT Card Mini Program based on the SCHOLAT social network and WeChat mini program framework, which implements functions such as viewing, collecting, and sharing SCHOLAT cards in WeChat, enabling SCHOLAT users to quickly exchange business cards and other social behaviors on the WeChat platform. Meanwhile, due to the inclusion of the "Think Tank" module in the SCHOLAT Card Mini Program, the SCHOLAT Think Tank high-quality user API is used to quickly implement scholar recommendation and scholar search functions. The SCHOLAT Card Mini Program serves as the port of SCHOLAT in the WeChat community. It can be quickly used and shared through the vast user community of WeChat, achieving the goal of attracting users and expanding SCHOLAT's popularity. This system serves as an extension of SCHOLAT, which is an online system in "SCHOLAT+".

Keywords: WeChat mini program · SCHOLAT · Social network

1 Introduction

SCHOLAT [15] (www.scholat.com) is an academic social network service website designed and constructed specifically for scholars, learners, and course instructors, aiming to promote communication and cooperation among scientific researchers, strengthen cooperation and social interaction among academic communities around academic and learning discourse. SCHOLAT provides services such as scholar social networks [13], academic information management, literature retrieval, course management, and scholar communication. In addition to social networking functions, SCHOLAT also integrates various modules to encourage collaboration and interactive discussions, such as chatting, email, events, news posts, etc. At present, SCHOLAT has more than 100,000 active users, most of whom are teachers and students from universities.

Exchanging business cards is an effective way to make friends and introduce oneself quickly in formal social occasions. One nature of business card exchanges is that when two persons exchange business cards, it is very likely that they are meeting each other for the first time [3]. Business cards generally contain personal information such as name, occupation, work unit, contact information, etc. With the rapid development of computer technology, most of the computing resources, environments of computing, and online application services have been moved to a computing environment based on mobile [2]. Nowadays, electronic business cards have become increasingly popular, and the behavior of exchanging business cards has become more and more convenient. WeChat [12], as a national-level application in China, has a very large user base. Therefore, this article designs and develops a scholar business card mini program called "SCHOLAT Card", which is based on the SCHOLAT social network and WeChat mini program framework, achieving functions such as viewing, collecting, and sharing business cards in the WeChat community. This system serves as an extension of SCHOLAT, which has already been online in "SCHOLAT+". As shown in Fig. 1 is the SCHOLAT card of Professor Tang, the founder of SCHOLAT.

Fig. 1. Professor Tang's SCHOLAT card

The rest of this article is organized as follows. Section 2 introduces the relevant work of the SCHOLAT Card Mini Program. Section 3 introduces the recommendation algorithm model used by the SCHOLAT main website, and the process of the mini program obtaining the recommendation list through the SCHOLAT API. Section 4 provides the system design and implementation of the mini program. Finally the conclusion is drawn in Sect. 5.

2   Related Work

2.1   WeChat Mini Program

WeChat mini program [6] is a kind of application that can be used without downloading and installing which is base on WeChat application. It realizes the application "At your fingertips" dream, user scan or search can open the application [17]. WeChat mini program is a new way to connect users and services, which can be easily accessed and disseminated within WeChat. On January 17, 2022, the Aladdin Research Institute released the "2021 White Paper on the Development of Mini Program Internet" data, which showed that the number of mini programs in the entire network has exceeded 7 million, with mini program developers has exceeded 3 million and the mini program DAUs has exceeded 450 million. Not only that, the average daily usage has increased by 32 percent year-on-year, while active mini programs have increased by 41 percents. The WeChat DevTools provides a simple and efficient application development framework with rich components and APIs. Through the WeChat DevTools, mini programs can be quickly developed, and then quickly used and shared through the vast user community of WeChat.

2.2   Front-End Framework Technology

The view layer of the WeChat mini program framework is written by WXML and WXSS, and is displayed by components. It reflects the data of the logic layer into the view, and sends the events of the view layer to the logic layer at the same time. In front-end development [5], we used Vant mobile terminal component library. Vant is an open-source mobile Vue [8] component library which is suitable for mobile H5 pages. It has features such as lightweight and customizable.

2.3   Backend Framework Technology

In this part, we use Python Flask framework technology [9], which is mainly responsible for providing SCHOLAT card generation. In addition, the SCHOLAT Card Mini Program is docked with the SCHOLAT main website, using high-quality user APIs from the SCHOLAT Think Tank, which can quickly implement scholar recommendation and scholar search functions.

2.4   VGNAE Module

Variational Graph Normalized AutoEncoders(VGNAE). Link prediction is one of the key problems for graph-structured data. VGNAE utilizes L_2 -normalization for link prediction, and it performs better embedding in the problem of isolated node exports compared to other models such as GAEs and VGAE [1,7].

3   Module Design

The homepage of the SCHOLAT Card Mini Program is the "Think Tank" page, which contains scholar recommendation and scholar search functions. When the user is in a non-login state, the mini program cannot obtain the recommendation list in the SCHOLAT main website cache. At this time, the scholars in the recommendation list are randomly recommended by SCHOLAT active users. After the user logging in with a SCHOLAT account, the mini program will use the SCHOLAT Think Tank API to obtain the recommendation scholar list in the SCHOLAT main website cache based on the user ID. This chapter mainly introduces the recommendation system [4] model used in SCHOLAT.

3.1   Model Introduction

VGNAE model is a link prediction model [1,11]. The system converts the predicted user node pairs and their corresponding user feature information into a format acceptable to the model and inputs it into the model. Next, the model performs link prediction based on the input user data. Finally, the model will return the probability of all node pairs having edges as the result of user recommendations.

VGNAE model mainly consists of two parts: an encoder and a decoder. The encoder maps the input graph network structure and node features into the latent space. Then, the decoder solves the latent space information and reduces the latent space information to the graph network information, which contains the prediction result of the node pair to be predicted [16].

A graph G can be represented as $G = (V, E, X)$ where V is a set of vertices, $E \subset V \times V$ is a set of edges, and X is a feature matrix of V . $N(v)$ denotes a set of neighbors of $v \in V$, $n = |V|$ denotes the number of vertices, and $A \in R^{n \times n}$ is an adjacency matrix of G [1]. Let z_v be a vector that is an embedding of a node v. Define $Z = [z_1, z_2, \ldots, z_n]^T$ is a node embedding matrix.

VGNAE encoder takes a simple inference model with the following equation:

$$q(Z|X, A) = \prod_{i=1}^{n} q(z_i|X, A) \quad with \quad q(z_i|X, A) = N(z_i|\mu_i, diag(\sigma_i^2)) \quad (1)$$

where $\mu = [\mu_1, \mu_2, \ldots, \mu_n]^T = GNCN(X, A, c)$ is the matrix of mean vectors μ_i; similarly $log\sigma = [log\sigma_1, log\sigma_2, \ldots, log\sigma_n]^T = GCN(X, A)$.

And the decoder's inference equation as follows:

$$p(A|Z) = \prod_{i=1}^{n} \prod_{j=1}^{n} p(A_{ij}|z_i, z_j) \quad with \quad p(A_{ij} = 1|Z) = \sigma(z_i^T z_j) \tag{2}$$

For VGNAE, optimization is made by maximizing a tractable variational lower bound (ELBO) [14] as follows:

$$L_{ELBO} = E_{q(Z|X,A)}[logp(A|Z)] - KL(q(Z|X,A)||p(Z)) \tag{3}$$

where $KL(q||p) = \sum_j Q_j log(\frac{Q_i}{P_i})$ is the Kullback-Leibler divergence [10] between q and p. Finally we use a Gaussian prior $p(Z) = \prod_{i=1}^{n} N(z_i|0, 1)$.

3.2 Process Introduction

Step 1. Build Matrix. The first step is to find the users who need to be predicted. The system first constructs a list of recommended users for the users who are requesting recommendation, which is composed of the users' K-Hop neighbors on the social network graph. The recommended users list is consists of two smaller lists: S and D. Each element of S represents the user ID of the requesting recommendation, while each element of D represents the user ID of the user to be recommended [16]. These two lists form a sparse adjacency matrix, which is input into the model as edge information. At the same time, the system constructs a feature matrix of all user features to be predicted.

Step 2. Model Inference. The model uses an encoder to encode the input edge information and feature information, then maps them into the latent space. Afterwards, the model will use a decoder to transform the latent space into a prediction result matrix that has the same dimension as the sparse adjacency matrix. The values in the result matrix are distributed between 0 and 1, which indicates the probability of links existence between the corresponding node pairs. The model outputs the prediction results as a list that corresponds to each sparse adjacency matrix in the input list [16].

Step 3. Result Processing. The system will sort the predicted results, then selects the top 100 pairs of nodes which has the highest probability as the recommendation results. The final prediction results will be saved in the recommendation cache file.

4　System Design and Implementation

The SCHOLAT Card Mini Program can be roughly divided into three parts based on its functions, namely the "Registration and Login" module, the "Think Tank" module, and the "SCHOLAT Card" module. The following will be divided into three sections for introduction.

4.1   Registration and Login

The user who uses the SCHOLAT Card Mini Program for the first time belongs to non login users. The user interface is shown in Fig. 2, which includes the "Me" page in Fig. 2(a) and the "Registration" page in Fig. 2(b). It should be noted that the SCHOLAT Card Mini Program uses SCHOLAT account to login instead of WeChat account. Only part of the functions of the mini program can be used in non login state. Meanwhile, due to the inability to access the cache of SCHOLAT social networks and recommendation lists when not logged in, the scholars in the recommendation list are randomly recommended by SCHOLAT active users.

(a) Me Page   (b) Registration Page

Fig. 2. Example of relevant pages in non login status

After logging in with the SCHOLAT account, users can use all the functions of the SCHOLAT Card Mini Program and will obtain personalized scholar recommendation lists from SCHOLAT based on their user ID to the "Think Tank" page. At the same time, they will also obtain the their follow list in SCHOLAT to the "Card Favorite" page. The user view in login status is shown in the following Fig. 3, which includes the "Card Favorites" page in Fig. 3(a) and the "Me" page in Fig. 3(b).

(a) Card Favorites Page   (b) Me Page

Fig. 3. Example of relevant pages in login status

The "Registration and Login" module flowchart is shown in Fig. 4.

4.2   Think Tank

The "Think Tank" module of the SCHOLAT Card Mini Program is located on the homepage of the mini program as shown in Fig. 5. This module mainly including scholar recommendation function and scholar search function. The API of

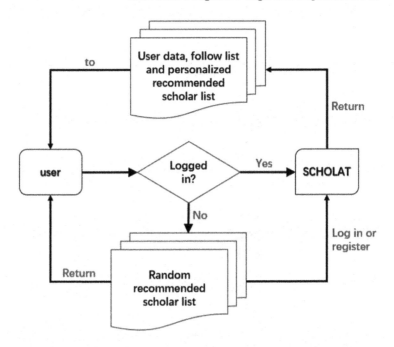

Fig. 4. The "Registration and Login" function flowchart

the SCHOLAT main website Think Tank is used to obtain the recommendation scholar list. In a non logged in state, a randomly recommendation scholar list will be presented. After logging in with a SCHOLAT account, the personalized recommendation scholar list for that user in the SCHOLAT main website cache will be obtained based on their user ID. The model and algorithm of the recommendation system in SCHOLAT main website have been introduced in Sect. 3.

4.3 SCHOLAT Card

The main functions of the "SCHOLAT Card" module of the mini program include viewing and following SCHOLAT cards, as well as sharing SCHOLAT cards to friends and group chats through the WeChat application.

Card Viewing Function. After logging in, users can view their SCHOLAT card information on the "Me" page, including name, professional title, work unit, email, phone number, address, etc., as shown in the Fig. 3(b). At the same time, they can also directly access their SCHOLAT homepage and SCHOLAT Zone. By clicking on the "Think Tank" page's recommend scholars, searching for scholars, or clicking on someone else's shared SCHOLAT card, we can view others SCHOLAT card and obtain information about the scholar. For example, Fig. 1 shows the SCHOLAT card of SCHOLAT founder, Professor Tang. Also, when

Fig. 5. Example of "Think Tank" Page

viewing someone else's SCHOLAT card, we can also perform more operations, such as visiting the their SCHOLAT homepage, saving the SCHOLAT card to your phone address book, sharing the SCHOLAT card to your WeChat friends, following the scholar, and so on. It should be noted that users using the "Follow" function will be synchronized to SCHOLAT's main website "Follow" function. The further introduction of this function will be placed in the next section.

Follow Function. The "Card Favorites" page is interconnected with the user's follow list in SCHOLAT main website. After logging in to the SCHOLAT Mini Program using a SCHOLAT account, the user will automatically obtain the follow list in SCHOLAT and add it to the "Card Favorites" page, which is shown in Fig. 3(a). Also, when users use the "Follow" function to collect other's SCHOLAT cards in the mini program, they will also synchronously follow the scholar in SCHOLAT main website. The followed scholar will also receive the information about being followed in their SCHOLAT Zone. Then the system will record the user's following behavior and remove the followed scholar from the recommendation list. The flowchart of "Follow" function is shown in Fig. 6.

Sharing Function. WeChat mini program relies on the large WeChat community which can quickly be shared with WeChat friends. The SCHOLAT Card Mini Program supports users to share their or others' SCHOLAT cards, and the

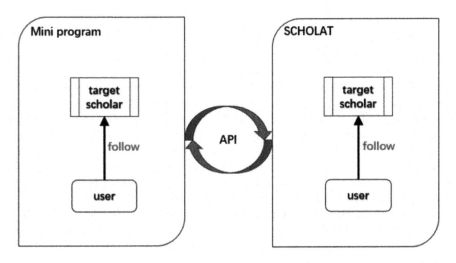

Fig. 6. The "Follow" function flowchart

specific implementation effect is shown in Fig. 7. When sharing the SCHOLAT cards, a "business card" style image will be generated, which contains the relevant information of the scholar such as name, professional title, work unit, email, address, phone number, SCHOLAT website, etc. If the scholar's work unit is a certain university, the university emblem watermark will be added to the image, which can enhance the uniqueness of SCHOLAT card.

Fig. 7. Example of sharing Professor Tang's Scholar Card in Wechat

5   Conclusion

This article first briefly introduces SCHOLAT and the behavior of exchanging business cards in social activities. Based on this, an electronic business card system called SCHOLAT Card Mini Program was designed, allowing SCHOLAT users to quickly view, collect, and share SCHOLAT cards in the WeChat community. The "Think Tank" module in the mini program uses the SCHOLAT Think Tank main website API to implement scholar recommendation and scholar search functions. Due to the use of SCHOLAT's Recommendation Scholar List API, this article also introduces the recommendation algorithm implemented based on the VGNAE model in SCHOLAT main website. Finally, the functions and implementation effects of the system were introduced, also the system has been launched on the WeChat platform. As a port of SCHOLAT on WeChat, SCHOLAT Card Mini Program can rely on WeChat's huge user community to achieve rapid use and sharing, and achieve the purpose of attracting users and expanding SCHOLAT's popularity.

In the future work, the SCHOLAT Card Mini Program will continue to be updated and iterated, adding more modules and features, improving the UI interface, and providing users with a better experience.

Acknowledgements. Our works were supported by the National Natural Science Foundation of China (No. U1811263)

References

1. Ahn, S.J., Kim, M.: Variational graph normalized autoencoders. In: Proceedings of the 30th ACM International Conference on Information & Knowledge Management, pp. 2827–2831 (2021)
2. Center, S.: Design of mobile application service of e-business card and NFC. Int. J. Multimed. Ubiquit. Eng. **9**(3), 403–414 (2014)
3. Dahbura, J.N.M., Komatsu, S., Nishida, T., Mele, A.: A structural model of business card exchange networks. arXiv preprint arXiv:2105.12704 (2021)
4. Das, D., Sahoo, L., Datta, S.: A survey on recommendation system. Int. J. Comput. Appl. **160**(7), 6–10 (2017)
5. Edkins, A., Geraldi, J., Morris, P., Smith, A.: Exploring the front-end of project management. Eng. Proj. Org. J. **3**(2), 71–85 (2013)
6. Hao, L., Wan, F., Ma, N., Wang, Y.: Analysis of the development of WeChat mini program. In: Journal of Physics: Conference Series, vol. 1087, p. 062040. IOP Publishing (2018)
7. Kipf, T.N., Welling, M.: Variational graph auto-encoders. arXiv preprint arXiv:1611.07308 (2016)
8. Li, N., Zhang, B.: The research on single page application front-end development based on VUE. In: Journal of Physics: Conference Series, vol. 1883, p. 012030. IOP Publishing (2021)
9. Lokhande, P., Aslam, F., Hawa, N., Munir, J., Gulamgaus, M.: Efficient way of web development using python and flask (2015)

10. Lopes, A.O., Mengue, J.K.: On information gain, Kullback-Leibler divergence, entropy production and the involution kernel. arXiv preprint arXiv:2003.02030 (2020)
11. Lü, L., Zhou, T.: Link prediction in complex networks: a survey. Phys. A **390**(6), 1150–1170 (2011)
12. Montag, C., Becker, B., Gan, C.: The multipurpose application WeChat: a review on recent research. Front. Psychol. **9**, 2247 (2018)
13. Stringhini, G., Kruegel, C., Vigna, G.: Detecting spammers on social networks. In: Proceedings of the 26th Annual Computer Security Applications Conference, pp. 1–9 (2010)
14. Sutter, T.M., Daunhawer, I., Vogt, J.E.: Generalized multimodal ELBO. arXiv preprint arXiv:2105.02470 (2021)
15. Tang, F., Zhu, J., He, C., Fu, C., He, J., Tang, Y.: SCHOLAT: an innovative academic information service platform. In: Cheema, M.A., Zhang, W., Chang, L. (eds.) ADC 2016. LNCS, vol. 9877, pp. 453–456. Springer, Cham (2016). https://doi.org/10.1007/978-3-319-46922-5_38
16. Weng, Y., Yu, W., Lin, R., Tang, Y., He, C.: ScholarRec: a user recommendation system for academic social network. In: Sun, Y., et al. (eds.) Computer Supported Cooperative Work and Social Computing: 17th CCF Conference, Chinese CSCW 2022, vol. 1681, pp. 28–41. Springer, Singapore (2023). https://doi.org/10.1007/978-981-99-2356-4_3
17. Zhao, L.: Application analysis of visual design elements of WeChat mini program. In: Journal of Physics: Conference Series, vol. 1345, p. 062045. IOP Publishing (2019)

A Traffic Flow Prediction Based Task Offloading Method in Vehicular Edge Computing

Liqiong Xie, Long Chen$^{(\boxtimes)}$, Xiaoping Li, and Shuang Wang

School of Computer Science and Engineering, Key Laboratory of Computer Network and Information Integration, Ministry of Education, Southeast University, Nanjing 211189, China
chen_long@seu.edu.cn

Abstract. Vehicular Edge Computing (VEC) emerges as a promising paradigm by deploying computation and storage resources on edge servers located in close proximity to vehicles, such as roadside units or base stations. This proximity enables VEC to provide abundant resources and low-latency services, catering to the computational needs of vehicles. However, the dynamic nature of traffic flow presents new challenges in terms of task offloading decisions and resource allocation within VEC environments. This paper addresses the task offloading problem in VEC systems, considering the impact of dynamic traffic flow. To address this problem, we formulate an integer programming model that captures the essence of the studied scenario. To devise an efficient solution, we propose a novel traffic flow prediction-based heuristic algorithm (TFPVTO). TFPVTO incorporates different rules and strategies to generate an optimal offloading task sequence, make informed offloading decisions, and allocate resources effectively. To assess the performance of the proposed algorithm, we utilize a real-world traffic flow dataset. In order to fine-tune and optimize the algorithm's components, we employ a multi-factor analysis of variance (ANOVA) technique. The proposed TFPVTO algorithm is then rigorously compared against other state-of-the-art algorithms, namely TAVF, MONSA, and RANDOM. Through extensive experiments and statistical analysis, we demonstrate the effectiveness and efficiency of the proposed algorithm in terms of task offloading performance.

Keywords: vehicular edge computing · traffic flow prediction · task offloading · resource allocation

1 Introduction

Emerging applications in the era of the Internet of Vehicles (IoV), such as path planning, and autonomous driving, require low-latency access to powerful computation resources. Vehicular edge computing is a promising technology by deploying servers at the Internet edge. In essence, the computing paradigm where vehicular applications offload their latency-sensitive tasks to nearby edge

Y. Sun et al. (Eds.): ChineseCSCW 2023, CCIS 2013, pp. 360–374, 2024.
https://doi.org/10.1007/978-981-99-9640-7_27

servers can greatly extend the capacity of vehicles and enlarge the coverage of cloud computing.

However, traditional edge computing network architectures cannot be directly applied to the Internet of Vehicle (IoV) due to the dynamic and high-speed flow of vehicles [5,8]. Compared with traditional edge computing, task offloading in vehicular edge computing presents some unique challenges and requirements. Firstly, the dynamic changes in traffic flow on the road need to be considered since the traffic flow in a certain area reflects the number of service requests for task offloading in that area, and the number of service requests varies with changes in traffic flow. For example, areas with heavy traffic flow have more vehicles and produce more service requests than areas with light traffic flow, resulting in higher loads on edge nodes in congested areas, or even overloading. In contrast, edge nodes in sparsely populated areas have lower loads and resources that are not fully utilized. Therefore, dynamic traffic flow has a direct impact on task offloading and resource allocation, and task offloading decisions need to be adjusted based on real-time traffic conditions. If traffic congestion occurs on a road segment, network load may increase, which may cause unreasonable task offloading and long waiting times for tasks, affecting user experience. By taking traffic flow into account during task offloading, such as offloading tasks from congested road segments to less loaded edge nodes to achieve load balancing, it is possible to reduce waiting times for tasks and alleviate the pressure on overloaded service nodes, thereby efficiently completing tasks. Besides, the computing power and storage capacity of edge devices in the connected car network is limited, requiring a flexible and efficient resource allocation approach to meet the needs of different tasks. Compared to heavyweight virtual machines (VM), using container-based virtualization technology for computation offloading is more suitable for the connected car network. Containers have the advantages of fast startup time, less hardware overhead, and secure resource isolation, providing high flexibility in platform management and improving the task execution efficiency of MEC servers.

Therefore, in the problem studied in this article, dynamic traffic flow should be taken into consideration. Container-based virtualization technology is introduced to facilitate edge computing task execution. The optimization problem of task offloading and resource allocation in a heterogeneous environment is studied. The tasks to be offloaded are independent, computationally intensive, and delay-sensitive tasks generated by vehicles on the road, including task input data size, computational resource requirements, and other attributes. Resources include local resources of heterogeneous MEC servers and vehicle terminals. Vehicle properties, task properties, and MEC server conditions are all factors that need to be considered when optimizing the problem. Based on existing connected vehicular edge computing systems, in the case of limited resources of heterogeneous MEC servers, the problem of task offloading and resource allocation in the vehicular edge computing environment is studied, and heterogeneous tasks are offloaded to suitable edge nodes for execution, with reasonable resource allocation plans made for the tasks.

The remainder of this paper is organized as follows. Section 2 presents the system overview and system model of our work. The traffic flow prediction-based task offloading algorithm is proposed in Sect. 3. Numerical results are given in Sect. 4, followed by the conclusion in Sect. 5.

2   System Model and Problem Formulation

As illustrated in Fig. 1, we consider a heterogeneous vehicular edge computing scenario. A set of RSUs equipped with edge servers, denoted by $\mathcal{E} = \{1, ..., e, ..., E\}$. The RSU is responsible for collecting user service demands, traffic conditions, and other information and has a certain communication coverage range. The coverage range between RSUs may overlap, and a vehicle may be covered by one or more RSUs. An MEC server $e \in \mathcal{E}$ is characterized by a quadruple $e = (R_e, f_e, u_e, \mathbf{L}_e)$, where R_e is the transmission rate for V2I (Vehicle-to-Infrastructure) communication, f_e represents the processing ability of the MEC server e, u_e is the communication range of the RSU, and $\mathbf{L}_e$ represents the location of the RSU. The MEC servers are heterogeneous, and each server has multiple container images that can be used for task execution after startup. The set of containers on MEC server e is denoted as $\mathcal{S}_e = \{1, ..., s, ..., S\}$, where the containers are heterogeneous with different startup time θ_s and computing capabilities, and f_s represents the computing capability of container $s \in S_e$.

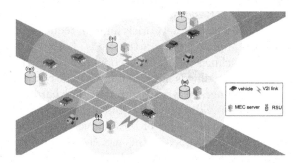

Fig. 1. Model diagram of vehicular edge computing system in dynamic traffic flow scenarios

The task model considered in this article is independent tasks with high resource demands generated by user vehicles, which are sensitive to delays. For tasks that cannot be processed by the vehicle terminal, they need to be offloaded to the edge layer for computation. The time period is divided into a set of discrete time slots denoted as $\mathcal{T} = \{1, ..., t, ..., T\}$, where t is the number of the time slot. In time slot t, the set of vehicles is represented as $\mathcal{V} = \{1, ..., v, ..., V\}$, where each vehicle v is represented by a tuple (vs_v, vd_v) indicating its driving speed and direction, and its current location is $\mathbf{L}_v$. Each vehicle $v \in \mathcal{V}$ generates one task, denoted as $k_v \in K_t$, where K_t represents the set of tasks generated in time slot t, and k can be used as shorthand for a task. Following scenarios presented in references [7,12], it is assumed that tasks in time slot t are generated simultaneously, with generation time starting at 0. A task k is characterized by a triplet (d_k, c_k, t_k^{max}), representing data size, computing resource demand, and deadline constraint respectively. The distance between vehicle v and edge node e is denoted as $dist_{v,e}$. Reliable communication between user vehicles and corresponding edge nodes is achieved through Vehicle-to-Infrastructure (V2I) connections. MEC servers provide computing resources for users, and tasks are offloaded to the MEC server for execution through RSU transmission. Tasks can be offloaded directly to the currently accessed MEC server for computation, or through collaborative transmission between RSUs, offloaded to an unaccessed MEC server for computation.

Table 1. Main Symbols Used in This Paper

Notation	Description
$\mathcal{T}$	the set of discrete time slots $\mathcal{T} = \{1, ..., t, ..., T\}$
$\mathcal{E}$	the set of MEC servers, $\mathcal{E} = \{1, ..., e, ..., E\}$, $e = (R_e, c_e, u_e, \mathbf{L}_e)$
R_e	the V2I uplink transmission rate of service node$e$
f_e	the total computing capacity of MEC server
$\mathcal{V}$	the set of vehicles $\mathcal{V} = \{1, ..., v, ..., V\}$, vehicle v is represented by a tuple $v = (vs_v, vd_v)$
K_t	the set of tasks generated in time slot t
k_v	the task generated by vehicle v in time slot t, which can be abbreviated as k, $k_v \in K_t$, where $k_v = (d_k, c_k, t_k^{max})$
d_k	the input data size of taskk_v
c_k	the computing resource demand of task k_v
t_k^{max}	the deadline of task k_v
$\mathcal{V}_e^t$	the set of vehicles covered by MEC server e in time slot t
K_e^t	the set of tasks generated by the vehicles covered by MEC server e in time slot t, $K_e^t = \{k_v | v \in \mathcal{V}_e^t\}$
$K_{q_e}^t$	the set of tasks offloaded to MEC server e in time slot t
$\mathcal{E}_v^{candi}$	the set of candidate offloading nodes for the tasks generated by vehicle v
$\mathcal{S}_e$	the set of containers on MEC server e, $\mathcal{S}_e = \{1, ..., s, ..., S\}$
θ_s	the instance startup time required for container s

The objective (equation (1)) is to minimize the average completion time of all tasks in a certain period. The time period T is divided into discrete time slots $\{1, ..., t, ...T\}$, and the offloading decision is made for the task set K_t generated in each time slot t. The average task completion time is calculated as the total completion time of all tasks in T time slots divided by the total number of tasks in T time slots.

$$\min \overline{T} = \frac{\sum_{t=1}^{T} T_t}{\sum_{t=1}^{T} |K_t|} \tag{1}$$

3   Proposed Approaches

3.1   Traffic Flow Prediction Model

Task offloading in edge computing for connected vehicles has a close relationship with traffic flow. Traffic flow can reflect the task requests and traffic load of the edge computing system. Traffic flow prediction can provide important assistance for the computing offloading decision-making of the edge computing system, thereby improving its performance and efficiency. Based on traffic flow prediction information, the system can decide where tasks should be offloaded, either to an edge node or processed locally. For example, if it is predicted that there will be a large traffic flow on a certain road segment and relatively less traffic on adjacent segments, the system can choose to offload more tasks to the MEC servers on that particular segment to reduce the load on congested road segments' edge nodes. This can also utilize idle computing resources to achieve load balancing and improve response time, thus reducing task completion time. Therefore, traffic flow prediction information can assist the vehicular edge computing system in making wiser computing offloading decisions, improving the system's performance, and enhancing user experience.

Long Short-Term Memory (LSTM) is a special type of recurrent neural network structure that is widely used in sequence data processing problems. It can capture the inherent characteristics of long-term dependencies in time series data and has been successfully applied to predict a range of time series data, including traffic flow, achieving impressive results [9]. In this chapter, we modify the LSTM network based on the extension of the recurrent neural network (RNN) to adapt it to our system model. We use the LSTM model to extract the temporal features of traffic flow data for prediction. Algorithm 1 presents the basic framework of the LSTM prediction model. The following sections will describe the LSTM model in detail, including its input, output, model structure, and loss function.

(1) Input

At the time t, the traffic flow passing through the RSU where the MEC server e is located is defined as tf_e^t. TF_e^t records the historical traffic flow sequence passing through the RSU where the MEC server e is located from time $(t - th + 1)$ to $(t - \Delta t + 1)$ and at time t, where th is the historical time range, and Δt is the historical time step. Therefore, we have:

$$TF_e^t = \{tf_e^{t-th+1}, ..., tf_e^{(t-\Delta t+1)}, ..., tf_e^t\} \quad (2)$$

(2) Output

The output of the LSTM network, which represents the predicted information, is denoted as Y_e^t and can be expressed as:

$$Y_e^t = \{tf_e^{t+1}, ...tf_e^{t+t_p}\} \quad (3)$$

Here, t_p is the prediction time range or the number of time steps to be predicted.

Based on historical traffic flow information in the t period, the traffic flow information for the next t_p periods can be obtained using the following formula:

$$TF_e^t \underset{f}{\rightarrow} Y_e^t \tag{4}$$

Here, f represents the traffic flow prediction model. This chapter uses the LSTM model as the traffic flow prediction model f. Then the output result is de-normalized, and the normalized data is restored to the original data form for subsequent use.

(3) Model Structure The specific structure of an LSTM network is shown in Fig. 2. At each time step t, there is a memory cell state C_t and a hidden state h_t. The LSTM network controls the memory cell state through gate mechanisms. First, the forget gate determines which information to discard from the cell state. It processes the input by looking at the information from h_{t-1} and X_t, and outputs a vector between 0 and 1, representing which information to keep or discard from the previous cell state C_{t-1}. Second, the input gate decides which new information to add to the cell state. This process has two steps: first, it decides which information to update through the input gate using h_{t-1} and X_t, and then it obtains a new candidate cell state information $C_{t'}$ through a tanh layer using h_{t-1} and X_t, which may be used to update the cell state information and output i_t and $C_{t'}$. Then, some of the old cell state information that was selected by the forget gate is added to some of the new candidate cell state information selected by the input gate, resulting in a new cell state C_t. Finally, after updating the cell state with the output gate, the network determines which state features to output using h_{t-1} and X_t, obtains a judgment condition through the sigmoid layer of the output gate, and uses a tanh layer to obtain a vector of values between -1 and 1 for the cell state. The vector is multiplied by the judgment condition to obtain the final output h_t [10]. This chapter designs an LSTM model with an input layer, LSTM layer, and output layer for predicting future traffic flow.

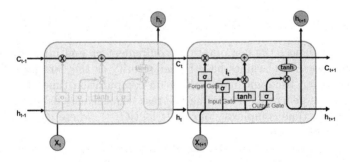

Fig. 2. LSTM model structure [1]

(4) Loss Function Using Mean Square Error (MSE) as the loss function for prediction training, we obtain the error formula between the predicted value $\hat{y}_i$ and the true value y_i.

$$L(\theta^{st}) = \frac{\sum\limits_{i=1}^{N} (y_i - \hat{y}_i)^2}{N} \tag{5}$$

Here, θ^{st} represents the set of model parameters.

3.2   Traffic Flow Prediction Based Vehicular Task Offloading

The adaptive learning rate algorithm Adam is used to adaptively adjust the learning rate based on the gradient information of the model parameters, thereby optimizing the model parameters. This prevents significant oscillations in the loss function during updates and further accelerates the convergence speed of the model.

$$\theta^{st} \leftarrow \theta^{st} - \frac{\eta}{\sqrt{G + \epsilon}} \odot \nabla L(\theta^{st}) \tag{6}$$

Here, G is the cumulative sum of the square of gradients, ϵ is a very small constant, and $\odot$ denotes element-wise multiplication. Repeat the above process until the maximum iteration number or precision threshold is reached, and finally find the parameter set $L(\theta^{st})$ that minimizes $L(\theta^{st})$.

The optimization objective of the problem studied in this chapter is to minimize the average completion time of system tasks within a period of time T. From a system perspective, by minimizing the average completion time of tasks in the vehicular edge computing system, the tasks can be completed as quickly as possible, improving user experience and satisfaction. The input of the algorithm proposed in this chapter includes the task set K, the vehicle set $\mathcal{V}$, the edge node set $\mathcal{E}$, and the historical traffic flow data set TF. The output is the average completion time of tasks, denoted as $\overline{T}$.

For offloading task sequence generation, we use the Minimum Ratio of Data Size and Computation (MRDSC) rule. This rule considers both the data volume and computation requirements of tasks. The ratio RDC is calculated as follows:

$$RDC_k(\%) = \frac{c_k}{\lambda d_k} \times 100\% \tag{7}$$

Where λ balances the computation requirement c_k and input data size d_k. Tasks with lower RDC values have higher priority as they are less affected by data transmission time and more reliant on computation time. The offloading task sequence is generated by sorting the task sequence Q_1 using the quicksort algorithm, with time complexity of $O(|Q_1| \log(|Q_1|))$, where $|Q_1|$ is the number of tasks to be offloaded.

For offloading decision, we use the Maximum Average Computing Capacity First (ACCF) rule, This rule uses traffic flow prediction information as auxiliary information and considers both future and current request numbers. The task is assigned to the server with the maximum average computing capacity, allowing

---

Algorithm 1: TFPVTO (Traffic Flow Prediction based Vehicular Task Offloading)

Input: Time slots set $\mathcal{T}$; Tasks set K; Vehicles set $\mathcal{V}$; Edge node set $\mathcal{E}$; Traffic flow dataset TF

Output: Average task completion time $\overline{T}$

1 **begin**
2 | **foreach** $t \in \mathcal{T}$ **do**
3 | | $Y^t \leftarrow \emptyset$
4 | | /*Future traffic flow Y^t of each edge node is predicted using historical traffic flow information TF */
5 | | **foreach** $e \in \mathcal{E}$ **do**
6 | | | $Y_e^t \underset{f}{\leftarrow} TF_e^t$; /* Using model f based on TF_e^t to predict future traffic flow */
7 | | | $Y^t \leftarrow (Y^t \cup Y_e^t)$;
8 | | /* Divide the task set K_t into local computing sequence $\mathcal{Q}_0$ and edge computing sequence $\mathcal{Q}_1$ */
9 | | $\mathcal{Q}_0, \mathcal{Q}_1 \leftarrow$ Call offloading task sequence generation algorithm;
10 | | **while** $\mathcal{Q}_1 \neq \emptyset$ **do**
11 | | | $k \leftarrow$ head task of queue $\mathcal{Q}_1$;
12 | | | /* Assign specific service node e_k^{target} for task k based on predicted traffic flow information Y^t */
13 | | | Call offloading decision algorithm to select the offloading node for task k;
14 | | **foreach** $e \in \mathcal{E}$ **do**
15 | | | Call RA algorithm to perform task-container matching for edge node e;
16 | Calculate the average completion time $\overline{T}$ of the task set K using Equation 1;
17 | **return** $\overline{T}$;

---

the task to be executed on a server with greater processing capacity and fewer tasks, resulting in faster completion speed.

$$\overline{f_e^t} = \frac{f_e}{|K_{q_e}^t| + \gamma_1 |K_e^{t+1}|} \tag{8}$$

Here, γ_1 is used to balance the impact of future and current requests on task loads, because the impact of future request volume on task load is relatively small compared to current request volume.

After the offloading decision is made, specific service nodes have already been allocated for task execution. As shown in Algorithm 1, this process is divided into two sub-steps. The first step involves generating a task scheduling sequence to determine the priority of tasks during the resource allocation phase. The second step is task scheduling, which involves matching container resources to the tasks in the scheduling sequence after they have been allocated resources.

For task scheduling sequence generation, we use the Minimum Estimated Completion Time First (MECT) rule, we sort tasks by considering their transmission resource requirements and computing resource demand. Tasks with smaller resource demands are assigned containers first to ensure sufficient container resource utilization. Tasks with larger resource demands take longer to execute and are assigned later to reduce the waiting time for smaller tasks.

For task-container matching, we use the Minimum Weight Perfect Matching Algorithm (MWPM). Improvement on the solution to the maximum-weighted perfect matching problem based on the weighted bipartite graph is proposed in [2] by introducing an algorithm for minimum-weighted perfect matching. The weighted bipartite graph has two sets of vertices, A and B, with each edge connecting a vertex from A to a vertex in B. Each edge has a weight value, and the bipartite graph $G = (V, E)$ is fully weighted and balanced such that $|A| = |B| = \frac{1}{2}|V|$. In this chapter, the two sets of vertices represent the sequence of tasks awaiting processing on a server and the list of containers available for use. The weight is determined by the estimated completion time ECT for a task on a specific container. In each batch, a number of tasks equal to the number of available containers are selected from the task sequence. These tasks are then connected to their corresponding containers to form a weighted bipartite graph, which is subsequently matched using the Algorithm 1 to achieve one-to-one matching between tasks and containers. The algorithm is based on the KM (Kuhn-Munkres Algorithm) algorithm [3] to solve the minimum-weighted perfect matching problem on the weighted bipartite graph. In Algorithm 1, an edge is defined as a tight edge if it satisfies the following conditions:

$$lx(a) + ly(b) = w(a, b) \tag{9}$$

where $lx(a)$ and $ly(b)$ are the label values of sets A and B respectively. The pseudo-code for this strategy is shown in Algorithm 1. The average time complexity of the algorithm is $O(\frac{|K_{qe}|}{|S_e|} \times |S_e|^3)$.

4   Experiment and Analysis

Extensive simulations are carried out to evaluate the performance of our algorithm and validate the superiority of our algorithm in comparison with other reference algorithms.

4.1   Simulation Parameter Setting and Comparison Scheme

The dataset used in this experiment is derived from real traffic data in the suburbs of Chicago. This data was collected between June 5th and July 18th, 2019, through 100 network cameras covering the traffic flow data set of Lake County, Illinois suburbs called STREETS [4]. The data was sampled every 5 min from each of the 100 cameras, resulting in a total of 28,800 samples collected per day. The dataset includes information about camera views represented as $(ID, \mathbf{L}, d)$

denoting camera identification, location, and description, and processed traffic flow data $(ID, time, flow)$ collected by the cameras, representing camera identification, time and traffic flow. Using Equation (10), all traffic flow on road segment R during the time interval τ can be calculated:

$$M_R(\tau) = \sum_{(time, ID, \mathbf{L}, flow) \in D} f_{time \in \tau \wedge \mathbf{L} \in R}(flow) \tag{10}$$

$$f_{time \in \tau \wedge \mathbf{L} \in R}(flow) = \begin{cases} 0 \\ flow \end{cases} \tag{11}$$

Here, D represents all traffic information in the dataset, and $f_{time \in \tau \wedge \mathbf{L} \in R}(flow)$ is a judicial function. The value of the function is the recorded flow value $flow$ when the recorded time $time$ falls within the time interval τ and the location $\mathbf{L}$ is within the area of road segment R, otherwise it is 0. Firstly, the dataset was preprocessed, and the location of one intersection was selected as the research area. Traffic flow data from 8 directions on 4 road segments at the intersection were collected for experimentation. The road is depicted in Fig. 3. The processed dataset is in the format of a triple (t, id, f), where t represents time, id represents the road segment identifier, and f represents the traffic flow passing through during the time period t. During the experiment, traffic flow data from the first 35 d (10,080 sampling intervals) of received data was used for model training, and data from the following 3 d (864 sampling intervals) were used as test samples.

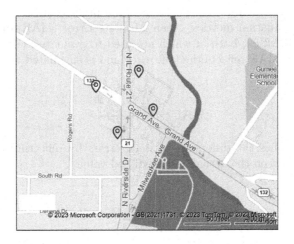

Fig. 3. Deployment diagram of RSU in the Grand Avenue, Gurnee, Illinois, USA

The paper sets the total number of vehicles passing through a given section to be one of the values $\{60, 70, 80, 90, 100\}$. To verify the influence of task data size on algorithm performance, four different task data size values are selected from $\{[300, 500], [500, 700], [700, 1000], [1000, 1500]\}$ (KB). To test the effect of resource allocation on algorithm performance, four different container values are selected, $\{5, 10, 15, 20\}$. The experimental parameter settings refer to reference [11], and the specific settings are shown in Table 2. For each of the five vehicle values, four task data size interval values, and four container values, ten instances are generated, resulting in a total of 800 random instances. In the parameter calibration stage, there are three values for OTSS, OD, TSS, and TCM each, resulting in a total of $3 \times 3 \times 3 \times 3 \times 800 = 64800$ experiments, which determine the optimal combination through experimental results. In the algorithm comparison experiment, the values of the number of vehicles, task data size, container values, and instance numbers are the same as those in the parameter calibration stage, and there are 800 instances in total for the algorithm comparison experiment.

Table 2. Default Parameter Settings in the Simulations

Parameter	Value
Number of MEC servers	4
Input data size of tasks	$\{[300, 500], [500, 700], [700, 1000], [1000, 1500]\}$ KB
Computation requirement of tasks	$[0.4, 1.0] (\times 10^9)$ CPU cycles
CPU computing capacity of on-board terminal	$[0.5, 0.8]$ GHz
CPU computing capacity of MEC servers	$[1.0, 3.0]$ GHz
V2I transmission power	$[12, 15]$ Mbps

To verify the accuracy of the traffic flow prediction model, this chapter employs two evaluation metrics: Mean Absolute Error (MAE) and Root Mean Square Error (RMSE), both of which are used to evaluate the results of traffic flow prediction. MAE reflects the true error and is calculated as follows:

$$MAE = \frac{\sum\limits_{i=1}^{N} |y_i^* - y_i|}{N} \qquad (12)$$

RMSE amplifies the difference between errors by reflecting the root mean square error between the actual and predicted values:

$$RMSE = \sqrt{\frac{1}{N} \sum_{i=1}^{N} (y_i^* - y_i)^2} \qquad (13)$$

Here, N refers to the number of samples, y^* denotes the predicted value, and y denotes the true value.

To verify the performance of the algorithm, the Relative Percentage Deviation (RPD) evaluation metric is used to compare the performance of different algorithms. RPD is used to analyze the performance of the algorithm and is calculated as follows:

$$RPD(\%) = \frac{\overline{T} - \overline{T^*}}{\overline{T^*}} \times 100\% \tag{14}$$

$\overline{T}$ represents the average completion time of tasks obtained during a certain period when the algorithm is executed, while $\overline{T^*}$ represents the optimal solution obtained by all algorithms when executing tasks in the same environment, i.e., the minimum average completion time of tasks. The experimental results of algorithm performance comparison are analyzed using the analysis of variance (ANOVA) technique with multiple factors.

4.2 Algorithm Comparison

In order to verify the performance of the TFPVTO algorithm, the following algorithms are selected for performance comparison:

(1) TAVF (Task Allocation in Vehicular Fogs) [6]: Sorts tasks in ascending order and provides higher processing priority to small tasks to reduce the waiting time of tasks in the pending task queue. Based on a heuristic rule of mini-mizing expected completion time, the algorithm assigns tasks to the service node with the shortest completion time.
(2) MONSA (Mobile Offloading Nodes Selection Algorithm) [11]: The algorithm evaluates the optional service nodes for tasks based on computing resources and transmission rate, and then selects the edge node with the highest evalu-ation value as the offloading node. This algorithm does not consider resource allocation issues, so it chooses the earliest completion time strategy for task scheduling.
(3) RANDOM algorithm: This algorithm randomly selects the offloading node for tasks, including executing locally or selecting from optional nodes for offloading.

As shown in Fig. 4, this is a comparison of algorithms under four different data ranges: [300,500]KB, [500,700]KB, [700,1000]KB, and [1000,1500]KB, as the number of vehicles changes. From Fig. 4a, it can be observed that as the number of vehicles increases, the RPD value of the TFPVTO algorithm remains stable, while the RPD values of the other three comparative algorithms decrease. Among them, the RPD values of the TAVF and MONSA algorithms are smaller than that of the RANDOM algorithm. This is because the RANDOM algorithm randomly chooses to execute locally or unload to the edge for execution. Due to weak local computing power, the task completion time is longer. When making the unloading decision, the MONSA algorithm only considers the resource sit-uation but ignores the server's workload, and the server selection leans towards servers with high processing capabilities, causing the server to become over-loaded and the task waiting time to increase. Therefore, compared to the TAVF algorithm, the performance of the MONSA algorithm is poor. As the number

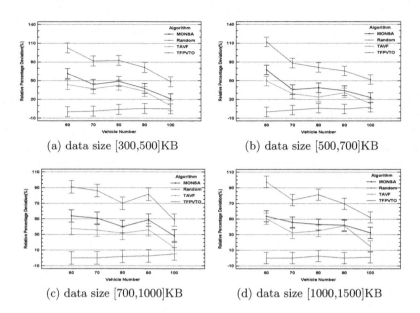

(a) data size [300,500]KB   (b) data size [500,700]KB

(c) data size [700,1000]KB   (d) data size [1000,1500]KB

Fig. 4. RPD value under different number of vehicles for different data size range of the task with 95% Tukey HSD confidence intervals

of vehicles increases, the performance gap between the three comparative algorithms and the TFPVTO algorithm shrinks. This is because as the number of vehicles increases, the request volume between each server also increases. Due to differences in traffic flow on the roads, overloaded servers may occur on congested roads, leading to increased waiting times for tasks. To address this, tasks could be unloaded to MEC servers located on sparsely populated road segments using load balancing techniques. This can reduce task waiting times, better utilize system resources, and improve overall system performance. However, as the number of vehicles increases, all servers may be busy, and resources become a scheduling bottleneck, resulting in an increase in task response time and a reduction in optimization space for unloading decisions. Therefore, as different algorithms make unloading decisions, the difference in average task completion time decreases and the differences between RPD values also become smaller. As a result, the performance gap between algorithms gradually narrows.

As shown in Fig. 4a, 4b, 4c, and 4d, as the task data size increases, the transmission time of the tasks increases, which in turn leads to an increase in the average task completion time for the RANDOM, MONSA, and TAVF algorithms, resulting in a reduction of the RPD differences between them. However, as the task data size value increases, the RPD value of the TFPVTO algorithm gradually decreases overall, and its performance advantage becomes increasingly apparent. The reason is that the TFPVTO algorithm takes into account both the computational resource requirements and the transmission resource requirements of tasks when making unloading decisions, while the TAVF algorithm does not consider the amount of task data and the MONSA algorithm does not consider task requirements. In the case of the RANDOM algorithm, some tasks are randomly unloaded to edge servers for execution, which results in longer transmission times and longer task completion times as task data sizes increase.

The RANDOM algorithm randomly selects whether to execute tasks locally or on edge servers. Although this saves transmission time, the execution time of tasks is long due to limited local resources in vehicles. The MONSA algorithm considers both communication and computational resources but does not take into account server load conditions and container startup times. This results in resource-rich servers being overloaded with too many pending tasks, leading to longer task queue waiting times and longer average task completion times. The TAVF algorithm prioritizes small tasks, reducing task waiting times while also taking into account server processing capabilities. It matches tasks with the smallest completion times to containers but does not consider resource competition between tasks and the impact of transmission time on task completion time. For some large tasks with limited candidate nodes and tight available resources, they can only be passively assigned to later selected unloading nodes, resulting in long execution times. In contrast, the TFPVTO algorithm comprehensively considers task attributes, server resources, and dynamically changing traffic flow conditions when creating an unloading sequence. It makes decisions based on both computational resource requirements and transmission resource requirements for tasks, allowing tasks with more candidate nodes to be adjusted accordingly. When making unloading decisions, it considers both server load conditions and resource situations. It also prioritizes small tasks during task scheduling to reduce waiting times while balancing container startup and queue times. It solves the task-container matching problem using a bipartite graph approach, obtaining better matching solutions, and resulting in superior algorithm performance compared to other algorithms.

5   Conclusion

In this paper, we focused on the design of vehicular edge computing task offloading strategy in order to improve resource utilization and enhance user experience. The problem of exploiting traffic flow prediction information for task offloading in VEC networks was studied to minimize the average completion time of tasks over a period of time. Different from existing work, the offloading decisions were made by taking into account dynamic traffic flow. Based on future traffic flow prediction information, a heuristic solution is proposed for task offloading and scheduling. It takes into account the number of task requests, task properties, and resource availability of service nodes. The simulation results showed that the proposed traffic flow prediction-based offloading scheme significantly improves the average completion time of task performance compared to state-of-the-art schemes. For future work, we will investigate high-speed mobility of vehicles can be taken into consideration, and dynamic traffic flow and task offloading issues in scenarios with high-speed moving vehicles can both be considered.

References

1. Gers, F.A., Schmidhuber, J., Cummins, F.: Learning to forget: continual prediction with LSTM. In: Ninth International Conference on Artificial Neural Networks ICANN, vol. 2, pp. 850–855 (1999)
2. Korula, N.: Maximum weight matching in bipartite graphs (2010)
3. Munkres, J.R.: Algorithms for the assignment and transportation problems. J. Soc. Ind. Appl. Math. **10**, 196–210 (1957)
4. Corey Snyder and Minh Do. STREETS: a novel camera network dataset for traffic flow. In: Advances in Neural Information Processing Systems, pp. 10242–10253 (2019)
5. Song, X., Guo, Y., Li, N., Zhang, L.: Online traffic flow prediction for edge computing-enhanced autonomous and connected vehicles. IEEE Trans. Veh. Technol. **70**(3), 2101–2111 (2021)
6. Tang, C., Wei, X., Zhu, C., Wang, Y., Jia, W.: Mobile vehicles as fog nodes for latency optimization in smart cities. IEEE Trans. Veh. Technol. **69**(9), 9364–9375 (2020)
7. Wen, Y., Zhang, W., Luo, H.: Energy-optimal mobile application execution: taming resource-poor mobile devices with cloud clones. In: Proceedings of the IEEE INFOCOM, pp. 2716–2720. IEEE (2012)
8. Xu, X., Fang, Z., Qi, L., Zhang, X., He, Q., Zhou, X.: TripRes: traffic flow prediction driven resource reservation for multimedia IoV with edge computing. ACM Trans. Multimedia Comput. Commun. Appl. (TOMM) **17**(2), 41:1-41:21 (2021)
9. Yang, B., Sun, S., Li, J., Lin, X., Tian, Y.: Traffic flow prediction using LSTM with feature enhancement. Neurocomputing **332**, 320–327 (2019)
10. Yong, Yu., Si, X., Changhua, H., Zhang, J.: A review of recurrent neural networks: LSTM cells and network architectures. Neural Comput. **31**(7), 1235–1270 (2019)
11. Zhang, R., et al.: Task offloading with task classification and offloading nodes selection for MEC-enabled IoV. ACM Trans. Internet Technol. (TOIT) **22**(2), 51:1-51:24 (2022)
12. Zhang, Y., Chen, X., Chen, Y., Li, Z., Huang, J.: Cost efficient scheduling for delay-sensitive tasks in edge computing system. In: 2018 IEEE International Conference on Services Computing (SCC), pp. 73–80. IEEE (2018)

A Prediction-Based Fuzzy Method for Multi-objective Microservice Workflows Scheduling

Jingwen Xu, Long Chen$^{(\boxtimes)}$, Xiaoping Li, and Shuang Wang

School of Computer Science and Engineering, Key Laboratory of Computer Network and Information Integration, Ministry of Education, Southeast University, Nanjing 211189, China
chen_long@seu.edu.cn

Abstract. Microservice workflows are widely used in real-time mobile computing scenarios such as face recognition and speech recognition. The key challenge is to develop efficient, stable, and robust algorithms capable of handling uncertain and fuzzy workflow tasks. In this paper, we consider the real-time microservice workflow fuzzy scheduling problem under VM-Container two-tier resources. A novel model based on triangle fuzzy numbers is formulated. The model encompasses two metrics: cost and degree of satisfaction. In response, this paper proposes an ARIMA prediction-based workflow fuzzy scheduling method (PFSM), comprising five key components: prediction of workflow arrival number, predistribution of task sub-deadlines, ordering of the task pool, task scheduling strategy, and resource management. To assess the performance of the proposed algorithms, several comparison algorithms are selected for analysis, and their performance differences are evaluated using ANOVA. The experimental results demonstrate the significant superiority of the proposed algorithms over the other compared algorithms in terms of overall performance.

Keywords: Microservice · Muti-Objective · Workflow · Fuzzy scheduling

1 Introduction

With the explosive rise of the Mobile Internet, especially the popularity of mobile terminals, real-time applications and systems such as face recognition, voice recognition, and surveillance video analysis have emerged. On the other hand, traditional monolithic applications can no longer meet the exponentially growing user traffic demand. Microservices, as a new application development paradigm, shortens the development lifecycle with its fine-grained, loosely coupled, and flexible architecture [1], and speeds up the maintenance and update process. Major global application service providers such as Netflix, Google, Amazon, etc. are starting to adopt the microservices architecture paradigm as a solution [2].

Y. Sun et al. (Eds.): ChineseCSCW 2023, CCIS 2013, pp. 375–389, 2024.
https://doi.org/10.1007/978-981-99-9640-7_28

In the context of the significant attention to both real-time and microservice applications, it is of great research value and practical significance to construct scheduling policies and allocate resources for real-time microservice application tasks deployed in the cloud.

Unlike traditional workflows that are deployed to virtual machines for execution on IaaS, such as Amazon Elastic Compute Cloud (Amazon EC2) [3] offered by Amazon. Microservices applications typically choose lightweight, more flexible, and scalable containers as resources. This is because each fine-grained microservice task typically requires far fewer compute resources than the virtual machine specification, and its loosely coupled nature means that it needs to run in a separate process. Using VMs would result in a significant waste of resources if resource isolation was guaranteed for each task at the same time. Therefore containers are a better resource choice for microservices and are more conducive to modular development and deployment of large applications and elastic scaling.

Compared to previous research on microservice applications [4–6] and real-time applications [7–9] of the study mainly focuses on a certain environment, this paper focuses on the uncertain arrival time and execution time of the workflow in the cloud, which is more in line with the real system environment. Fuzzy is one of the effective methods to deal with uncertainty [10,11]. The specific strategy is to use fuzzy numbers to represent the uncertain parameters and increase the quality of the final scheduling policy by prediction and pre-assignment before the actual scheduling. Forecasting models based on ARIMA (Autoregressive Integrated Moving Average model) were previously mostly used in economics and natural sciences [12,13], and in recent years, they have been gradually applied to the load of resources in the cloud [14,15] and task execution time (QoS) prediction, which is mainly applied to the prediction of uncertain arrival time in this paper.

The scheduling problem of workflows in the cloud has long been shown to be an NP-Hard problem [16], and considering uncertainty makes the problem more complex. Zhu. et al. [17] have previously studied the fuzzy scheduling problem for linear multi-stage jobs, and in the problem considered in this paper, the significantly increased number of tasks in microservice workflows and more complex bias order relationships will bring greater challenges: (i) During the scheduling process, the uncertainty of arrival and execution time of each task, and the complex features of workflow partial order relation make the deviation generated by the fuzzy workflow arrival time and container execution time accumulate gradually, resulting in more uncertainty for later scheduled tasks. (ii) The conflict between rental cost and satisfaction is challenging. Workflows arriving in real-time have tighter deadlines, and when the number of arriving workflows increases, the rental cost will rise if more instances are chosen to meet user demand; if delays are tolerated without renting more instance resources, user satisfaction will decrease.

The rest of the paper is organized as follows. Section 2 gives a review of the related works. The considered problem is described and modeled in Sect. 3. Section 4 presents the proposed algorithm framework and its major components.

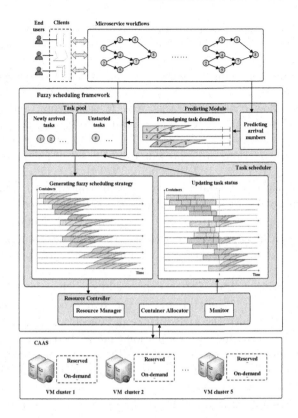

Fig. 1. Real-time Microservice application Workflow Fuzzy Scheduling Framework.

Thorough experiments are performed to evaluate the proposal and to compare algorithms in Sect. 5, followed by conclusions and future research in Sect. 6.

2 Problem Description

This paper considers microservice real-time applications that are deployed to the cloud platform for computation and data processing, etc. A real-time microservice application workflow fuzzy scheduling framework is proposed as shown in Fig. 1.

The execution time of a task is uncertain and can only be estimated from historical data as well as from expert experience. In this paper, the relevant uncertain parameters are described using triangular fuzzy numbers. A triangular fuzzy number $\tilde{x}$ is defined as $\tilde{x} = (x^{min}, x^{most}, x^{max})$, $x^{min} \leq x^{most} \leq r^{max}$. x^{min} is the minimum value, x^{max} is the maximum value and x^{most} is the most probable value.

The workflow for end-user submission of real-time microservice applications, modeled similarly to the traditional workflow model, can be represented by a directed acyclic graph (DAG). ε is the scheduling period width. $N(t)$ is the number of workflows arriving at time t, T is the total time of Q scheduling periods, and $WS = \{W_1, W_2, \ldots, W_{N(T)}\}$ represents the set of all arriving workflows. Each workflow contains μ tasks, and K task types, and the set of all task types is $\mathbb{K}$, $\mathbb{K} = \{0, \ldots, K\}$. The arrival time of workflow W_j is a_j and the set of all tasks is $T_j = \{t_{j,1}^1, \ldots, t_{j,\mu}^k\}$. The data dependencies between tasks and component invocations are represented by the set of partial order relations $E = \{(t_{j,i}^k, t_{j,i'}^{k'}) | t_{j,i}^k \in T_j, t_{j,i'}^{k'} \in T_j, j = 0, \ldots, N(T)\}$. $G = (T_j, E)$ is the topology of the workflow. Since all workflows have the same topology, $\forall j \in \{1, \ldots, N(T)\}$, G is the same, only the task size on each node is different. $pred(t_{j,i}^k)$ denotes the set of all direct predecessor tasks of $t_{j,i}^k$, and $succ(t_{j,i}^k)$ denotes the set of all direct successor tasks of $t_{j,i}^k$. $t_{j,i}^k$ must wait until all predecessor tasks have been executed and its data and runtime environment are ready before it can start execution.

The fuzzy execution time of $t_{j,i}^k$ is expressed using the triangular fuzzy number as $\tilde{p}_{j,i} = (p_{j,i}^{min}, p_{j,i}^{most}, p_{j,i}^{max})$. $p_{j,i}$ is the real execution time of $t_{j,i}^k$ and $p_{j,i}^{min} \leq p_{j,i} \leq p_{j,i}^{max}$. Since the arrival time and execution time of the workflow are uncertain, the start time and completion time of the task are also uncertain, and the same is represented by the triangular fuzzy number. The fuzzy start time of $t_{j,i}^k$ is $\tilde{b}_{j,i}$ and the fuzzy completion time is $\tilde{f}_{j,i}$. The real start and completion times corresponding to the two are $b_{j,i}$ and $f_{j,i}$. Since the network fluctuation in the cloud is small, $d_j^{i,i'}$ represents the data transmission time between $t_{j,i}^k$ and $t_{j,i'}^{k'}$ with fixed bandwidth and certain task size. Each workflow W_j is based on the SLA to assign due date. Since the task execution time is uncertain, a binary fuzzy number is used to represent the due date $\tilde{D}_j = (D_j^1, D_j^2), D_j^1 < D_j^2$. Combined with the real completion time $f_{j,\mu}$.

The resource model used in this paper is Amazon Elastic Container Service [19], and the charging method is EC2 startup model [20], which has no additional cost, and users only need to pay according to the configuration of the virtual machine and the length of the rental, rather than using the container as the charging unit. The rental method is a mix of Reserved Instances and On-demand Instances. Reserved Instance is a monthly or annual payment model, compared to On-demand rental, the cost will be more discounted and can be deployed in advance according to the type of task on the reserved instance of the corresponding dependency library and environment. The disadvantage is that users need to rent a longer period of time, and also need to pay the corresponding fees when not in use. On-demand rental is for the case that the reserved instance resources are not enough, and new instances are rented according to the demand of the current task, and the resources are released after the use is completed, usually based on the real usage time, usually by hourly charging, less than one hour rounded up, the disadvantage is that the unit price is higher.

According to the microservice workflow characteristics in this paper, all tasks are executed in containers deployed on a set of virtual machine clusters. The

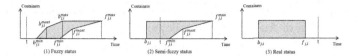

Fig. 2. Task execution status.

virtual machines in each cluster are used to execute the same type of tasks, including the containers deployed on them, and also have the same environment, dependency libraries, etc., to be able to save container configuration and startup time. $\mathbb{R}^k$ and $\mathbb{O}^k$ represent clusters of reserved VMs for tasks of type k and clusters of on-demand VMs, where the VMs are represented by $v_m^k \in \mathbb{R}^k \cup \mathbb{O}^k$ and $c_{j,i}^k$ represents the container assigned to task $t_{j,i}^k$. In this paper, we consider the scenario of heterogeneous resources, where different virtual machines have different configurations of available resources (mainly including CPU, RAM, etc.), and $\mathbb{L}_m^k$ represents all the available resources of v_m^k. The occupied resources on the v_m^k at t are represented by $L_m^k(t)$ at t, and the resources required for $t_{j,i}^k$ are $L_{j,i}^k$. The rental cost of VMs varies for different configurations. ψ_R^k represents the unit price of reserved VMs in $\mathbb{R}^k$, ψ_O^k the unit price of on-demand VMs, and u is the unit of rental time for on-demand VMs.

For the task $t_{j,i}^k$, the quaternion $s_{j,i}^k(t) = (\tilde{b}_{j,i}, \tilde{f}_{j,i}, v_{j,i}^k, c_{j,i}^k)$ can be used to represent the status of this task at t, executed in the container $c_{j,i}^k$ on the virtual machine $v_{j,i}^k$. If the task is executed on a reserved VM, $v_{j,i}^k \in \mathbb{R}^k$. As the task is scheduled periodically, the fuzzy status gradually changes to certain status as the task executes. When the task does not start, i.e., $t < b_{j,i}^{min}$, the task execution state is $s_{j,i}^k(t) = (\tilde{b}_{j,i}, \tilde{f}_{j,i}, v_{j,i}^k, c_{j,i}^k)$; when the task starts but does not complete, i.e., $s_{j,i}^{max} b_{j,i}^{max} \leq t < f_{j,i}^{min}$, the task execution status is $s_{j,i}^k(t) = (b_{j,i}, \tilde{f}_{j,i}, v_{j,i}^k, c_{j,i}^k)$; when the task is completed, i.e., $t \geq f_{j,i}^{max}$, $s_{j,i}^k(t) = (b_{j,i}, f_{j,i}, v_{j,i}^k, c_{j,i}^k)$. Figure 2 depicts the transition of the above task execution status.

Equation (1) represents the optimization objective considered in this paper, i.e., user satisfaction per unit rental cost. Making the two as a ratio can effectively make the two conflicting objectives consistent and does not bring in redundant parameters, and the calculation is simple and less time-consuming, which is suitable for the scheduling problem of real-time application tasks. The higher the value, the higher the user satisfaction and the lower the rental cost, indicating a better current scheduling strategy.

$$\max \frac{S(T)}{P(T)} \tag{1}$$

3   Proposed Algorithms

A prediction-based fuzzy scheduling method is proposed and consists of five main parts: prediction module, resource occupancy update, task deadline division, ready task collection and sorting, and fuzzy scheduling strategy generation. The algorithm is shown in Algorithm 1 as follows:

Each period q starts at $t = q \times \varepsilon$ (Line 2). The number of workflows arriving in the next period $N(t + \varepsilon)'$ is predicted by the established ARIMA model, and the arrival time of these workflows is set as the start time of the next period and is used as the arrival time of workflows to start scheduling (Line 3–4). For all predicted workflows, pre-divide sub deadlines and set the initial status of tasks (Lines 5–8).

$WS(t)$ is all the workflows arriving at the current moment and put into WS (Line 9–10). Update the task execution of the incomplete workflows and put all the ready tasks into the $taskPool$ (Lines 11–12).

Iterate through all tasks in the task pool and take out the task with the highest priority. Generate a feasible scheduling strategy $\pi_{j,i}(t)$ according to the resources, and add the set of scheduling strategies $\pi(t)$ of all schedulable tasks in the current period (Line 13–16). If all predecessors of this task's successor task $t_{j,s}^{k'}$ have been completed or assigned resources, it is added to the $taskPool$ as a new ready task. Until the task pool is empty, end the scheduling for the period (Lines 17–18).

Calculate user satisfaction and the total rental cost (Lines 19–20).

Algorithm 1. Prediction-based Fuzzy Scheduling Method(PFSM).

1: **for**$(q = 1$ to $Q)$
2:     $t = q \times \varepsilon$;
3:     $N(t + \varepsilon)'$ ←Number of workflow arrivals in the next period;
4:     $WS(t + \varepsilon)' \leftarrow \{W_{j+1}, \ldots, WS_{j+N(t+\varepsilon)'}\}$;
5:     **foreach**$(W_{j'} \in WS(t + \varepsilon)')$
6:         $a_j' \leftarrow t + \varepsilon$;
7:         Pre-divide sub-deadline of $W_{j'}$;
8:         Preset task initial status;
9:     $WS(t) \leftarrow \{W_{j-N(t)}, \ldots, W_j\}$;
10:    $WS \leftarrow WS \cup WS(t)$;
11:    Update resource occupancy and task execution in WS;
12:    $taskPool$ ←All ready tasks in WS;
13:    **while**$(taskPool$ is not empty)
14:        $t_{j,i}^k \leftarrow$ top priority tasks;
15:        Generate fuzzy scheduling strategy $\pi_{j,i}^k(t)$ for $t_{j,i}^k$;
16:        $\pi \leftarrow \pi(t) \cup \pi$;
17:        **if**$(t_{j,i'}^{k'} \in succ(t_{j,i}^k)$ is ready$)$
18:            $t_{j,i'}^{k'} \rightarrow taskPool$;
19: $T \leftarrow Q \times \varepsilon$;
20: Calculate $S(T), P(T)$;
21: **return**$(S(T), P(T))$

3.1   Prediction Module

It is necessary to obtain the time series, i.e. the historical data of the number of workflow arrivals. The first step mainly includes white noise verification and smoothness verification. The ARIMA model can be used for predictive analysis only if it is a smooth, non-white noise series. The main method of the smoothness test is ADF verification. If the time series is not smooth, the test is repeated by differencing until a smooth series is obtained. The main method of the white noise test is the LB test, when the test significance level is less than 0.05, it is not a white noise series and valid information can be extracted. After obtaining a smooth non-white noise series to determine the order of the model, that is, to determine the value of (p, q). This can be determined by observing the characteristics of ACF (autocorrelation) and PACF (partial autocorrelation) plots, or by enumerating the (p, q) values and calculating the corresponding AIC (chi-squared information criterion) and BIC (Bayesian information criterion) to determine the appropriate order and model parameters. The details of the calculation are given in Eq. (2) and (3).

$$AIC = 2k - 2ln(L) \qquad (2)$$
$$BIC = ln(n)k - 2ln(L) \qquad (3)$$

Based on the ARIMA model, the number of workflows arriving in the next period is predicted at the beginning of each period, and then sub-deadline are pre-divided for each corresponding workflow.

3.2   Resource Management Methods

In this paper, we use the form of a two-dimensional cross-time-slot link list to manage resources at both VM-container levels. Each time slot is represented by a quadruple $(cid, L, [\tilde{x}, \tilde{y}], status)$. cid is the container number to which the time slot belongs, containing the VM number, and can uniquely position a container instance. L represents the resource occupation size of the container to which the time slot belongs. $\tilde{x}$ represents the start time of the time slot, $\tilde{y}$ represents the end time of the time slot, $status$ is the status of the time slot, the initial status is uncertain when the execution of the task represented by the time slot is completed, the status will change to certain along with the task execution.

Each container instance deployed on a virtual machine maintains a time slice linked list for each instance, concatenating all its time slots in time order, including idle time slots and occupied time slots. The initial time slot of that container is idle and of length $[0, +\infty]$. A cluster of VMs with execution task type k consists of two parts: reserved VMs and on-demand VMs. $\mathbb{R}^k$ and $\mathbb{O}^k$ each maintain an $Idlelink$ that manages all free and available time slots in the cluster so that they are sorted in ascending order of start time. The advantage of this method is that when scheduling tasks to assign resources, it is easy to find feasible free time slots and to quickly occupy, insert, change, and delete operations.

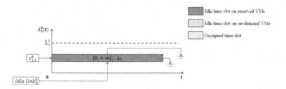

Fig. 3. Resource initialization.

The start and end times of all time slot links may be uncertain and are uniformly represented as rectangles in the figure for easier representation and observation. The length is the length of the time slot, and the width is the size of the resources occupied by the container to which the time slot belongs. The initial status of the VM cluster $\mathbb{R}^k \cup \mathbb{O}^k$ is shown in Fig. 3. The figure shows the reserved rented VM instances in $\mathbb{R}^k$, and the free time slots initialized before the tasks are assigned after renting VMs for time slots with smooth traffic to execute tasks. After the microservice tasks are gradually assigned with corresponding resources and scheduled to be executed in containers deployed on VMs.

When a task needs to be scheduled to execute on a container resource and occupy a free time slot, it will not fully occupy the current idle time slot but will generate a smaller idle time slot. For $t_{j,i}^k$ to be assigned a and an occupiable idle time slot $slot = (cid, L, [\tilde{a}, \tilde{b}], \text{``}IDLE\text{''})$, the following four scenarios may arise:

1. If $\tilde{a} = \tilde{b}_{j,i}^k$ and $\tilde{f}_{j,i}^k = \tilde{b}$. Change the status of this time slot to occupied and remove it from the $Idlelink^k$. No extra free time slice is generated.
2. If $\tilde{a} = \tilde{b}_{j,i}^k$ and $\tilde{f}_{j,i}^k < \tilde{b}$. The idle time slot is split into two time slots. The former status is changed to occupied and removed from $Idlelink^k$ to execute $t_{j,i}^k$. The latter one is the latest generated idle time slot $(cid, L, [\tilde{f}_{j,i}^k, \tilde{b}], \text{``}IDLE\text{''})$, added to $Idlelink^k$.
3. If $\tilde{a} < \tilde{b}_{j,i}^k$ and $\tilde{f}_{j,i}^k = \tilde{b}$. A new idle time slot fragment $(cid, L, [\tilde{a}, \tilde{b}_{j,i}^k], \text{``}IDLE\text{''})$ is generated at the front end of the time slot using $\tilde{b}_{j,i}^k$ as the boundary. Add it to $Idlelink^k$ and remove the time slot used to execute $t_{j,i}^k$ from it.
4. If $\tilde{a} < \tilde{b}_{j,i}^k$ and $\tilde{f}_{j,i}^k < \tilde{b}$. The task occupies the middle position of this idle time slot, generating one idle time slot fragment $(cid, L, [\tilde{a}, \tilde{b}_{j,i}^k], \text{``}IDLE\text{''})$ and $(cid, L, [\tilde{f}_{j,i}^k, \tilde{b}], \text{``}IDLE\text{''})$. Add both to $Idlelink^k$, and set the time slot in the original idle time slot to occupied status and remove it.

The task will release the resources after the real execution is completed, and the idle time slot may also be generated after the release. If there are other idle time slots before and after this time slot and the fuzzy start/end times of the time slots are contiguous, the merge operation is required.

3.3   Task Sub-deadline Division

Each workflow W_j has a fuzzy due date $\tilde{D}_j = (D_j^1, D_j^2)$, and if the due date for workflow is assigned to each task so that each task can be completed within the sub deadline as much as possible, the whole workflow can guarantee its deadline requirement. Using $\widetilde{EST}_{j,i}^k$, $\widetilde{LST}_{j,i}^k$, $\widetilde{EFT}_{j,i}^k$ and $\widetilde{LFT}_{j,i}^k$ to represent the earliest start time, the latest start time, the earliest completion time, and the latest completion time of $t_{j,i}^k$. According to the DAG partial order relationship of the workflow, the $\widetilde{EST}_{j,i}^k$ and $\widetilde{LST}_{j,i}^k$ can be calculated.

$$\widetilde{EFT}_{j,i}^k = \widetilde{EST}_{j,i}^k + p_{j,i}^k \tag{4}$$

$$\widetilde{LFT}_{j,i}^k = \widetilde{LST}_{j,i}^k + p_{j,i}^k \tag{5}$$

$$\widetilde{EST}_{j,i}^k = \begin{cases} a_j, & t_{j,i}^k \in T_{entry} \\ \max\limits_{t_{j,p}^{k'} \in pred(t_{j,i}^k)} \{\widetilde{EFT}_{j,p}^{k'} + d_j^{p,i}\}, & t_{j,i}^k \notin T_{entry} \end{cases} \tag{6}$$

$$\widetilde{LST}_{j,i}^k = \begin{cases} \tilde{D}_j - \tilde{p}_{j,i}^k, & t_{j,i}^k \in T_{exit} \\ \min\limits_{t_{j,s}^{k'} \in succ(t_{j,i}^k)} \{\widetilde{LST}_{j,s}^{k'} - d_j^{i,s} - \tilde{p}_{j,i}^k\}, & t_{j,i}^k \notin T_{exit} \end{cases} \tag{7}$$

T_{entry} is the set of tasks in G that do not have a direct predecessor task, and T_{exit} is the set of tasks that do not have a direct successor task. Tasks cannot be executed earlier than the earliest start time, while if the latest start time is exceeded, user satisfaction will be significantly affected.

Define the relaxation time of the task $t_{j,i}^k$ as the interval $[\widetilde{EST}_{j,i}^k, \widetilde{LST}_{j,i}^k]$. If the slack time is divided according to a certain policy and assigned to each task, it makes the deadline division of tasks more uniform and reasonable compared to using $\widetilde{LFT}_{j,i}^k$ as task sub-deadlines, which is more beneficial to microservice workflows with complex partial-order relational structures.

This paper proposes the Execution-time Proportion Distribution based division methods Method. The length of the workflow critical path CL_j is calculated by the Eq. (8). The slack time is assigned according to the ratio of the fuzzy execution time of each task in the workflow to the critical path length.

$$\tilde{CL}_j = \max_{t_{j,i}^k \in T_{exit}} \{\widetilde{EST}_{j,i}^k + \tilde{p}_{j,i}^k\} - a_j \tag{8}$$

$$\tilde{sd}_{j,i}^k = \widetilde{EST}_{j,i}^k + \frac{\widetilde{EFT}_{j,i}^k - a_j}{\tilde{CL}_j} \times (\tilde{D}_j - a_j) \tag{9}$$

3.4   Task Pool Management

Task Collection Strategy. The task pool contains all ready tasks, which are defined as tasks for which all predecessor tasks have been assigned resources in the current period. The initial ready tasks in the task pool for each period consist of two main parts: all the tasks in T_{entry} that newly arrive in the workflow, and the ready tasks on the cloud platform that are executing the workflow at the current moment. This paper uses the min-heap to implement the functions related to task pooling. The advantages are fast lookup, the top of the heap can automatically keep the highest priority tasks, low time complexity, and suitability for periodic scheduling of real-time workflows.

Task Sequencing Strategy. The ready tasks in the task pool are arranged in a certain order according to their priority and are scheduled for resource assignment in this order. Therefore, the scheduling order of the tasks greatly affects the quality of the solutions obtained by the scheduling algorithm. In this paper, we use the earliest start time of the task. Tasks are ordered according to their earliest start time $\widetilde{EST}_{j,i}^{k}$ in ascending order from early to late.

3.5   Task Scheduling Method

The Algorithm 2 shows the fuzzy scheduling strategy for real-time microservice workflows for each period based on PFSM.

At the current moment t iterates through all the ready tasks in the task pool and generates a fuzzy pre-scheduling strategy $\tilde{\pi}(t)$ for each task in order of priority in the task pool.

For the task $t_{j,i}^{k}$ with the highest priority in the task pool, it is first necessary to judge whether its $\widetilde{EST}_{j,i}^{k}$ exceeds the start time of the next period. If it does, the task is unlikely to start execution in the current period. Considering the uncertainty of the task execution time, the task will be kept in the task pool and judged again in the next period. If the current task with the highest priority $\widetilde{EST}_{j,i}^{k} > t + \varepsilon$ continues to iterate through the other ready tasks in the task pool in order of priority.

If the current task $\widetilde{EST}_{j,i}^{k} > \widetilde{LST}_{j,i}^{k}$, i.e., the task will definitely be overdue, no new VM instance is rented for it, and only the earliest available idle time slot is selected for it on all currently rented VMs. The purpose is to sacrifice a certain amount of user satisfaction to ensure that the rental cost does not increase excessively due to task overruns. If the current task can be executed normally, different scheduling schemes need to be generated and the results compared based on the currently available rented VMs and the rented new VMs, and finally stored in the current time total scheduling strategy $\tilde{\pi}(t)$. Until all the tasks in the task pool have been traversed, return $\tilde{\pi}(t)$.

Algorithm 2. Generate task fuzzy scheduling strategy

1: **while**($taskPool \neq \phi$)
2:     $t_{j,i}^k \leftarrow$ Top priority task;
3:     $resPlan \leftarrow null$;
4:     **if**($\widetilde{EST}_{j,i}^k > t + \varepsilon$)
5:         continue;
6:     **if**($\widetilde{EST}_{j,i}^k > \widetilde{LST}_{j,i}^k$)
7:         $plan \leftarrow$ Assign $t_{j,i}^k$ to the feasible time slot with
8:         the earliest start time in the rented resources;
9:         $resPlan \leftarrow plan$;
10:    **else**
11:        $plan1 \leftarrow$ Assign $t_{j,i}^k$ to the first feasible time slot
12:        on the reserved VM;
13:        $plan2 \leftarrow$ Assign $t_{j,i}^k$ to the first feasible time slot
14:        of a rented on-demand VM;
15:        **if**($plan1! = null$ && $plan2! = null$)
16:            **if**($\widetilde{EST}_{j,i}^k$ of plan1 $< \widetilde{EST}_{j,i}^k$ of plan2)
17:                $resPlan \leftarrow plan1$;
18:            **else**
19:                **if**($t < plan2$)
20:                    $plan3 \leftarrow$ Assign $t_{j,i}^k$ to the first feasible
21:                    time slot of a new rented on-demand;
22:                    $resPlan \leftarrow plan3$;
23:                **else**
24:                    $resPlan \leftarrow plan2$;
25:        **else**
26:            $resPlan \leftarrow plan \neq null$;
27:        $\tilde{\pi}(t) \leftarrow \tilde{\pi}(t) \cup resPlan$;
28: **return**($\tilde{\pi}(t)$)

4   Computational Experiments

In the proposed PFSM there are several proposed variants for some of its components. We first calibrate these components and select the best combination for solving the considered problem. Then the calibrated algorithm is compared with the existing and highly related algorithms. All tested algorithms are coded in Java and run on an Intel(R) Core(TM) i5-9500 CPU with 16 GBytes of RAM.

Considering the actual situation of the short execution time of microservice tasks, this paper uses simulation experiments with scientific workflows Montage [17]. For the same application, the requests issued by each user should have the same partial order relationship when described as multi-workflow in the cloud platform, but with different task sizes in the workflows.

Reference [17] sets the parameters needed for the experiments in this paper, as shown in Table 1. $N(T)$ is the number of workflows contained in each test case. μ is the number of tasks contained in each workflow in the current use case. Referring to the actual workflow template, $\mu \in \{25, 50, 100, 200, 300\}$ for

Table 1. Experimental parameters

Parameter	Value
$N(T)$	100
μ	$\{25(30), 50, 100, 200, 300\}$
ρ	$\{0, 1, 2, 3\}$
e	$\{0.1, 0.2, 0.3\}$
df	$\{2.0, 3.0, 4.0, 5.0, 6.0, 7.0, 8.0\}$
θ	$\{0.5, 1.0, 1.5\}$

Montage workflows. Each number of tasks generates workflows with different partial order relations. The arrival time density parameter ρ controls the arrival time interval of the generated workflows. The larger the ρ, the smaller the workflow arrival interval and the more workflows arrive per period.

This paper uses Amazon ECS [19] as a resource model. The instance configuration and pricing are shown in Table 2.

Table 2. AWS EC2 instance configuration and price

Instance	vCPUs	Mem(GiB)	On-demand price($/h)
a1.large	2	4	0.051
a1.xlarge	4	8	0.102
a1.2xlarge	8	16	0.204
a1.4xlarge	16	32	0.408

4.1 Algorithm Comparison

The optimal combination of components for PFSM in a random data set is obtained by parameter calibration. In this paper, the PFSM is compared with the ROSA (unceRtainty-aware Online Scheduling Algorithm) and FDES (Fuzzy Dynamic Event Scheduling) [17] proposed in the existing work.

Since ROSA and FDES are based on the IaaS single-tier VM model, their task scheduling methods and charging strategies are different from those of container resources. To better compare with PFSM, use the same parameters to set up the reserved VM instance part for them and extend the resource model to two tiers.

Montage. As shown in Fig. 4. For different numbers of tasks, the RPD values of PFSM are lower and better when the number of tasks is smaller. At $\mu = 25$, the RPD value of the worst ROSA is twice that of PFSM. As the number of tasks rises, the RPD values of all three algorithms increase and the gap becomes smaller. The gap between the three is smallest when the number of tasks $\mu = 300$.

With different arrival time densities, all three algorithms perform relatively smoothly, PFSM is the best, FDES is the second and ROSA is the worst. The main reason is that the PFSM algorithm adds a prediction module, which predicts the number of workflow arrivals based on historical data, effectively avoiding the situation of untimely task scheduling caused by a sudden increase in workflow density.

As e increases, PFSM and FDES have the same upward trend, but the RPD value of PFSM is smaller and slower, which has better robustness compared to FDES. The value has less impact on ROSA, mainly because the three use different ways of describing the uncertain parameters; PFSM and FDES both use triangular fuzzy number representation, and FDES is randomly generated based on α quantile. The performance of PFSM is the best in all cases, and the difference is obvious, indicating that the algorithm is suitable for different task execution times.

As df increases, the RPD values all show a decreasing trend, indicating that a more relaxed deadline will yield better results. The PFSM has the most significant decreasing trend, while ROSA is less affected by df, but the overall results are worse.

All three algorithms show an increasing trend in RPD values for different reserved instance factors. ROSA is smoother, while PFSM and FDES have similar upward trends, but PFSM has better overall results. This indicates that for Montage, renting fewer reserved VM instances in advance can result in less rental cost while satisfying user satisfaction. Because the charge time for reserved instances is the total time for scheduling, renting too many may result in a significant increase in rental costs.

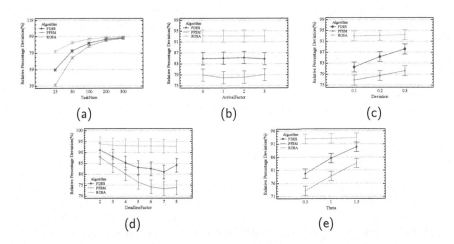

Fig. 4. Interactions between instance parameters and the compared algorithms with 95.0% Tukey HSD intervals for the instances with Montage workflow.

In conclusion, for the Montage instance, the overall effect of PFSM has better results than the other two algorithms in different cases and the difference is significant.

5   Conclusion

This paper studies the fuzzy scheduling problem of real-time microservice workflows under container resources. Based on the existing fuzzy scheduling framework, a fuzzy scheduling framework including a prediction module is proposed. Establish the corresponding mathematical model based on triangular fuzzy numbers.

Considering the fuzzy scheduling problem of real-time microservice workflows under VM-container two-tier resources, a VM-container resource management method based on a two-dimensional cross-time slot link list is proposed, which can better utilize the fragmented idle time and rapidly insert and delete time slots when the resources are occupied and released.

Proposes an ARIMA prediction-based workflow fuzzy scheduling method (PFSM). The algorithm mainly includes 1) Prediction module. The number of workflow arrivals is predicted and three different strategies are proposed to pre-divide sub-deadlines into tasks; 2) Ready task sequencing. The task pool is implemented using a min-heap, and four ready-task sequencing strategies are proposed by combining the characteristics of the ready tasks; 3) Resource management. Updating resource execution, a two-level resource management approach based on a two-dimensional cross-linked list. 4) Generating fuzzy scheduling strategies. Scheduling policies are generated periodically for the ready tasks in the task pool.

To validate the performance of the proposed algorithm, use the ANOVA analysis technique to calibrate the algorithm parameters and select the optimal combination of algorithm components. The experimental results show that the proposed algorithm PFSM significantly outperforms other comparison algorithms under different parameter settings.

References

1. Lewis, J., Fowler, M.: Microservices (2023). http://martinfowler.com/articles/microservices.html
2. O'Connor, R.V., Elger, P., Clarke, P.M.: Continuous software engineering-a microservices architecture perspective. J. Softw. Evol. Process **29**(11), e1866 (2017)
3. Amazon: Amazon EC2 container service (2023). https://aws.amazon.com/ec2
4. Bhamare, D., Samaka, M., Erbad, A., Jain, R., Gupta, L., Chan, H.A.: Multi-objective scheduling of micro-services for optimal service function chains. In: 2017 IEEE International Conference on Communications (ICC), pp. 1–6 (2017)
5. Zhou, R., Li, Z., Wu, C.: Scheduling frameworks for cloud container services. IEEE/ACM Trans. Netw. **26**(1), 436–450 (2018)

6. Hu, Y., Zhou, H., de Laat, C., Zhao, Z.: Concurrent container scheduling on heterogeneous clusters with multi-resource constraints. Futur. Gener. Comput. Syst. **102**, 562–573 (2020)
7. Stavrinides, G.L., Karatza, H.D.: An energy-efficient, QoS-aware and cost-effective scheduling approach for real-time workflow applications in cloud computing systems utilizing DVFS and approximate computations. Futur. Gener. Comput. Syst. **96**, 216–226 (2019)
8. Ma, X., Xu, H., Gao, H., Bian, M.: Real-time multiple-workflow scheduling in cloud environments. IEEE Trans. Netw. Serv. Manage. **18**(4), 4002–4018 (2021)
9. Meng, S., et al.: Security-aware dynamic scheduling for real-time optimization in cloud-based industrial applications. IEEE Trans. Industr. Inf. **17**(6), 4219–4228 (2021)
10. Liu, N., Zhu, M., Wu, N.: A co-evolutionary algorithm for uncertain scheduling in cloud manufacturing. In: 2021 13th International Conference on Wireless Communications and Signal Processing (WCSP), pp. 1–5 (2021)
11. Yousefli, A.: A fuzzy ant colony approach to fully fuzzy resource constrained project scheduling problem. Ind. Eng. Manag. Syst. **16**(3), 307–315 (2017)
12. Youness, J., Driss, M.: An arima model for modeling and forecasting the dynamic of univariate time series: the case of Moroccan inflation rate. In: 2022 International Conference on Intelligent Systems and Computer Vision (ISCV), pp. 1–5 (2022)
13. Abu Amra, I.A.S., Maghari, A.Y.A.: Forecasting groundwater production and rain amounts using ARIMA-hybrid ARIMA: case study of Deir El-Balah City in GAZA. In: 2018 International Conference on Promising Electronic Technologies (ICPET), pp. 135–140 (2018)
14. Gao, P., Wan, R., Wang, C., Cheng, Y.: Container load prediction algorithm based on ARIMA model and BP neural network. In: 2022 IEEE 6th Advanced Information Technology, Electronic and Automation Control Conference (IAEAC), pp. 334–337 (2022)
15. Xie, Y., et al.: Real-time prediction of docker container resource load based on a hybrid model of ARIMA and triple exponential smoothing. IEEE Trans. Cloud Comput. **10**(2), 1386–1401 (2022)
16. Abrishami, S., Naghibzadeh, M., Epema, D.H.: Deadline-constrained workflow scheduling algorithms for infrastructure as a service clouds. Future Gener. Comput. Syst. **29**(1), 158–169 (2013). https://www.sciencedirect.com/science/article/pii/S0167739X12001008
17. Zhu, J., Li, X., Ruiz, R., Li, W., Huang, H., Zomaya, A.Y.: Scheduling periodical multi-stage jobs with fuzziness to elastic cloud resources. IEEE Trans. Parallel Distrib. Syst. **31**(12), 2819–2833 (2020)
18. Arabnejad, V., Bubendorfer, K., Ng, B.: Dynamic multi-workflow scheduling: a deadline and cost-aware approach for commercial clouds. Futur. Gener. Comput. Syst. **100**, 98–108 (2019)
19. AWS: Amazon elastic container service (2023). https://aws.amazon.com/ecs
20. AWS: Amazon elastic container service pricing (2023). https://aws.amazon.com/ecs/pricing

Smart Contract Generation Supporting Multi-instance for Inter-Organizational Process Collaboration

Shangqing Feng[1], Chang Jia[1], Maolin Pan[2], and Yang Yu[2(✉)]

[1] School of Computer Science and Engineering, Sun Yat-sen University, Guangzhou, China
{fengshq5,jiach}@mail2.sysu.edu.cn
[2] School of Software Engineering, Sun Yat-sen University, Zhuhai, China
{panml,yuy}@mail.sysu.edu.cn

Abstract. Blockchain can help to maintain trusted Inter-Organizational Process Collaboration (IOPC) among parties or organizations. The key to such studies is to translate the IOPC models into smart contracts, the executable programs in the blockchain. There are some smart contract generation solutions for IOPC. However, most of them don't support multi-instance, which is an important feature of IOPC. The proposed method is designed to fill the research gap. One core of our method is that it sums up multi-instance elements of BPMN collaboration diagram and use Communicating Sequential Programs (CSP#) to formalize them. This formalization focuses on interactions, helps to get precise process execution semantics and makes model verification feasible, avoiding flawed models being translated. The other core is a translation technique based on syntax trees to generate smart contracts from CSP# models. The method is implemented and evaluated in terms of features and cost.

Keywords: Inter-Organizational Process Collaboration · Multiple instance · BPMN · Verification · Smart Contract

1 Introduction

With the development of economic globalization, inter-organizational process collaboration (IOPC) has become more and more common. Because the participants[1] of IOPC are from different parties or organizations, the traditional centralized IOPC cannot prevent participants from cheating, resulting in a lack of trust [1]. Blockchain technology emerging in recent years provides an idea to solve this problem. As a decentralized distributed ledger, blockchain can establish trusted data sharing among the organizations and make sure the process execution records are tamper-proof [2,3]. The core and premise of blockchain-based IOPC is to translate IOPC models (e.g., written in BPMN) to smart contracts.

---

[1] In this paper, a participant is a representative of an organization. And sometimes, it refers to an organization.

Y. Sun et al. (Eds.): ChineseCSCW 2023, CCIS 2013, pp. 390–405, 2024.
https://doi.org/10.1007/978-981-99-9640-7_29

Some solutions for smart contract generation are provided as a part of tools such as Caterpillar [3], Lorikeet [4] and ChorChain [5]. Some are proposed for specific goals such as cost optimization [1, 6] and dealing with time-dependent events [7]. However, most of them don't provide support for multi-instance, which is an important feature of IOPC. Multi-instance means that some tasks in a business process need to be executed by several participants in parallel, or that multiple participants execute the same process (but different instances) within the same period. It is frequent in IOPC. For example, when reviewing a paper, multiple participants play the role of *Reviewer* to do the same tasks independently in the same period. In this context, existing solutions no longer work. In order to expand the scope of application, it is necessary for blockchain-based IOPC to support multi-instance. In other words, it is important to propose a smart contract generation method that supports multi-instance IOPC.

To achieve the goal of transforming multi-instance IOPC models to smart contracts, there are some challenges: 1) Different from the ordinary elements, multi-instance elements require new processing logic. For example, a multi-instance task can have multiple instances, each of which is similar to an ordinary task. But every instance is considered part of the task and must conform to the constraints imposed on the task. 2) There are many multi-instance elements and their meanings vary in detail. These elements should be distinguished and translated to different contract code. 3) To avoid flawed models being translated and deployed, an approach to verify the models in advance is needed. Multi-instance complicates the execution of IOPC. The more complex the situation, the more likely the model contains flaws (like deadlock in the control flow). This will make the generated contract flawed, too. Once deployed, it may cause huge loss.

Some studies can help us resolve these challenges. [8] has provided a Backus-Naur Form (BNF) syntax of BPMN collaboration structure. Based on the BNF syntax, [9] uses Communicating Sequential Programs (CSP#) [10], which supports interaction description and verification well, to formalize a part of elements in BPMN collaborations. In this paper, we summarize the interaction elements in BPMN collaborations to cover most of the multi-instance IOPC. Then, we extend the CSP# formalization in [9] to support all of the elements, so that we can verify multi-instance IOPC. To get the final contract, a technique based on syntax trees is developed to generate smart contracts from CSP# models.

To sum up, the major contributions of this paper are: 1) We provide a summary of interaction elements in BPMN collaborations involving multi-instance, a CSP# formalization for the elements, and a soundness definition of CSP# models in this context. These help to verify multi-instance IOPC from interactions perspective. 2) We develop a translation technique to generate smart contracts from CSP# models. This technique captures the logic order of the CSP# processes based on syntax trees and generate smart contract code for each atomic CSP# process. 3) We propose a low code method that supports model verification and automatic smart contract generation for multi-instance IOPC. The method takes a BPMN collaboration model as input. It first transforms the collaboration model to a CSP# model, then verifies the CSP# with the soundness definition and an existing CSP# analysis tool. Finally, it generates smart contract code based on the CSP# model.

The rest of this paper is organized as follows: Sect. 2 reviews the related work. Section 3 lists the summarized interaction elements and shows a running example to illustrate the context. The detail of the proposed contract generation method is described in Sect. 4. Section 5 holds evaluation, followed by conclusion and future work in Sect. 6.

2   Related Work

2.1   Research on Smart Contract Generation Related to IOPC

Recent research related to blockchain-based IOPC and smart contract generation has focused on providing a business process management system, or reducing the cost of smart contracts. Most of the work does not support multi-instance.

Weber et al. [2] presented the first blockchain-based approach and implementation to address the lack of trust in IOPC, in which a translator was designed to derive a smart contract from a BPMN choreography model. It generates smart contract code according to the patterns of choreography elements. But due to the lack of model verification, if there are flaws in the choreography, it is possible that the contract is unsuitable to be deployed.

After that, García et al. [6] proposed a method to optimize the cost for executing business processes on top of blockchain. The method translates the BPMN process model into a Petri Net, and generates a smart contract in Solidity based on the reduced Petri Net. A similar approach was introduced by Nakamura et al. in [1]. The difference is that [1] used the BPMN process model with multiple lanes to model IOPC and used state charts for optimization work.

López-Pintado et al. [3] introduced a completely blockchain-based BPMS execution engine named Caterpillar, whose compiler is based on the translator of [2]. Tonga Naha et al. [7] extended Caterpillar to support time-dependent events and inclusive gateways

The methods proposed in [1,3,6] and [7] focus on dealing with BPMN process diagrams. They require the IOPC to be modelled as a BPMN process diagram, like a process within an organization. However, different from the process within an organization, what is important for IOPC is the interaction (i.e. exchange of messages) among the participants/organizations, which indicate how multiple participants/organizations cooperate to achieve the shared goal [8]. While the BPMN process diagram has no advantages in describing these. In other words, these methods don't support two important features of IOPC—multi-instance and interaction description.

Note that, in [3], all the participants share the same workflow engine—blockchain, and execute the whole process (including the inner tasks) on blockchain. It increases the burden of blockchain and decreases the efficiency of IOPC execution. In addition, execution details of inner tasks are exposed on the blockchain, which leads to privacy issues. We prefer the design proposed in [11], in which each participant executes his/her own process (including the inner tasks) in his/her own BPMS. Only when a participant needs to interact with others, the BPMS interacts with the Blockchain environment, which provides a tamper-proof record for the interactive messages and business data. This design helps to not only protect the privacy of inner tasks and data, but also reduce the burden of blockchain and improve the efficiency of blockchain-based IOPC. Our smart contract generation method is designed for this context.

2.2   Research on Multi-instance of Business Process

Corradini et al. [8] provided a formal semantics for BPMN collaborations including multiple instances of paticipants and developed an visualization tool called MIDA to help to check multi-instance collaboration models. The latest development about MIDA can be seen in [12]. Muzi et al. [13] formalised the execution semantics of service interaction patterns to remove ambiguity in BPMN collaboration. [13] was based on [8], and the formalization concerned multiple instances of tasks and processes.

Xiong et al. [9] developed a formal approach and framework to support the conformance between BPMN multi-instance choreography and collaboration. The formalization is based on the BNF syntax inspired by [8] and structured CSP# processes.

3   BPMN Collaboration Elements Involving Interactions

Inspired by [9] and [13], we summarize the BPMN collaboration elements (as listed in Table 1) from the perspective of message interactions.

Table 1. BPMN collaboration elements related to interactions.

Element Category	Element	Abbreviation
(Ordinary) Tasks	Send Task	ST or sndTask
	Receive Task	RT or rcvTask
Multi-instance Tasks (MTs)	Parallel Multi-instance Send Task	PMST
	Parallel Multi-instance Receive Task	PMRT
	Sequential Multi-instance Send Task	SMST
	Sequential Multi-instance Receive Task	SMRT
	Time-bounded Parallel Multi-instance Send Task	TPMST
	Time-bounded Parallel Multi-instance Receive Task	TPMRT
	Time-bounded Sequential Multi-instance Send Task	TSMST
	Time-bounded Sequential Multi-instance Receive Task	TSMRT
Processes	(Ordinary) Process	P
	Parallel Multi-instance Process	PMP
Gateways	Exclusive Gateway	EG
	Parallel Gateway	PG
	EventBased Gateway	EBG

In a process, message exchanges are carried out through "tasks", which consists of Send Task (ST) and Receive Task (RT). As for Multi-instance Task (MT), there are Sequential Multi-instance Send Task (SMST), Parallel Multi-instance Send Task (PMST), Sequential Multi-instance Receive Task (SMRT) and Parallel Multi-instance Receive Task (PMRT) [9]. To get the precise execution semantics, in this paper, every MT is assigned an attribute-*InstanceNum*, which indicates how many instances the task will have in the IOPC. Besides, MTs can be time-bounded (like TSMST, TPMST, TSMRT and TPMRT in Table 1), which means they can only execute in a period of time. Similarly, they are extended with new attributes - *MessageNum* and *Duration*. *Duration* specifies the time window, and *MessageNum* means that once enough messages are received in the period, the task will also stop.

A process can also be multi-instance, and the instances are executed without interfering with each other. In other words, they run in parallel. So it can be called a Parallel Multi-instance Process (PMP). From the perspective of the whole IOPC, the tasks in a PMP are all MTs. Gateways are also included in this paper because they affect the logic order of interactions in IOPC. Exclusive Gateway (EG) means choices. Only one of the tasks linked by a EG can be executed. While Parallel Gateway (PG) is opposite. All tasks linked by a PG can be executed at the same time. EventBased Gateway (EBG) is similar to EG, the difference is that the task to be executed depends on the occurrence of the captured external events or message reception [9].

Figure 1 shows an IOPC scenario adapted from [8]. It focuses on the interactions and removes the inner tasks of the participants.

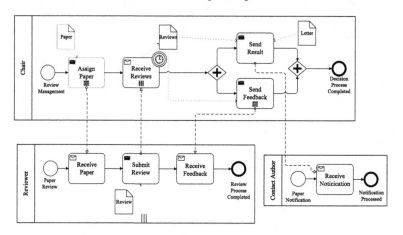

Fig. 1. BPMN collaboration diagram of paper review scenario.

In this collaboration, *Program Committee Chair* (short for *Chair*) assigns a paper to multiple (e.g., 5) *Reviewers*, who are required to review the paper and submit reviews in a certain period of time (e.g., a month). If a specified number (e.g., 3) of reviews are received, *Chair* stops receiving reviews, makes evaluation and decides to accept or reject the paper. The result will be sent to the (*Contact*) *Author*, and relevant *Reviewers* will get the feedback. If submitted reviews in the period are not enough, this paper reviewing fails. *Chair* will send the result and feedback to inform the *Reviewers* and *Author* that there are not enough reviews to evaluate the paper.

The task *Assign Paper* is a SMST because the paper will be sent to multiple reviewers sequentially, so is *Send Feedback*. *Receive Reviews* is a time-bounded PMRT. It means that *Chair* wants to receive *MessageNum* reviews within *Duration*. The process of *Reviewer* is a PMP. Because multiple reviewers do the paper review work in the same period.

It is possible for this IOPC to encounter a deadlock. For example, *Chair* wants to receive 3 reviews, but the *InstanceNum* of *Reviewer* is set to 2 or *Submit Review* is marked as a Receive Task.

To implement the collaboration above in blockchain, the collaboration model needs to be translated to a smart contract which contains precise semantics. Besides, to avoid the loss caused by deployment of a flawed model, it is necessary to verify the model in advance.

4 Smart Contract Generation from BPMN to Solidity

This section details our smart contract generation method. There are three phases to generate smart contracts. First, it transforms a BPMN collaboration model to CSP#. Then it verifies the soundness of the CSP# model with an available analysis tool. Finally, it generates smart contract code for every task.

4.1 Transformation Form BPMN to CSP# Model

[9] has provided a CSP# formalization for the MTs without time boundaries. In this paper, we extend it to support the time-bounded MTs and PMP. Table 2 shows a part of our formalization rules.

Table 2. A CSP# formalization for core collaboration model elements.

Elements	BPMN Syntax	CSP#
Tasks	sndTask(M)	ch!m ->Skip;
	rcvTask(M)	ch?m ->Skip;
	PMST(sndTask,n)	|||i:{1..n}@(sndTask)
	PMRT(rcvTask,n)	|||i:{1..n}@(rcvTask)
	SMST(sndTask,n)	if(i<n){sndTask; SMST(i+1)}
	SMRT(rcvTask,n)	if(i<n){rcvTask; SMRT(i+1)}
	TPMST(PMST,msgNum)	pcase{PMST(msgNum)}
	TPMRT(PMRT,msgNum)	pcase{PMRT(msgNum)}
	TSMST(SMST,msgNum)	pcase{SMST(msgNum)}
	TSMRT(SMRT,msgNum)	pcase{SMRT(msgNum)}
Gateways	EG(T1,T2...Tn)	(T1 [] T2 []...[] Tn);
	PG(T1,T2...Tn)	(T1 || T2 || ... || Tn);
	EBG(T1,T2...Tn)	(T1 [*] T2 [*]...[*] Tn);

In Table 2, M refers to the message flow that can be describe as (sender, receiver, m), where m is a message; And n refers to the instance number of the MT. The feature of the formalization is that every task for message interaction is described as a csp# process sending a message through a channel (e.g. *ch!m*, where "ch" means a message channel, and "!" means sending) or receiving a message from a channel (e.g. *ch?m*, where "?" means receiving). And for MTs without time boundaries, they are described as csp# processes running in parallel (e.g., |||i:{1..n}@(sndTask), where "|||i:{1..n}" means that n csp# processes run in parallel) or sequentially (e.g., if(i<n){rcvTask; SMRT(i+1)}).

Time-bounded MTs are special, we use Probability CSP# (PCSP#) [14] to formalize them. We refuse to use CSP# with time-extension. Because our early trial shows it will cause too large searching space to finish model verification. So we find the alternative - PCSP#, which supports probability assignment for the CSP# processes. For time-bounded MTs, the number of task instances executed within the specific period (*Duration*) is indeterminate (randomly between 1 and *MessageNum*). With PCSP#, we can remove the time attribute *Duration*, describe all the cases and assign each case an execution probability so that model verification can be completed quickly. And when generating smart contract, we recover the attribute and generate code according to its original semantics. Take *Receive Reviews* in Fig. 1 as an example. There are 3 possible execution results for this TPMRT: *Chair* receives 1, 2 or 3 reviews in a month. Each case can be taken as a PMRT. So this TPMRT can be taken as a composition of 3 PMRTs with execution probabilities, which can be described with PCSP#.

According to Table 2, we can get the CSP# processes for every participant in Fig. 1, as shown in Code 1.1. To support the automatic transformation from BPMN collaboration model to CSP#, we develop a transformation algorithm, part of which is shown in Algorithm 1. It first parses the BPMN collaboration model (line 1), then generates csp# code for message definitions and channel definitions (line 2). Finally, it generates csp# code for each participant process according to Table 2 (line 3–7).

Code 1.1. CSP# processes for Paper Review collaboration.

```
1   AssignPaper(i) = if (i< 5){   //SMST(AssignPaper,InsNum=5)
2       PaperChannel!AssignPaper−>Skip;
3       AssignPaper(i+1)};
4   ReceiveReviews() = pcase {  //pcase{PMST(MsgNum=3)}
5           1: ReviewChannel?ReceiveReviews−>Skip
6           1: ||| i:{0..1} @ReviewChannel?ReceiveReviews−>Skip
7           1: ||| i:{0..2} @ReviewChannel?ReceiveReviews−>Skip};
8   SendFeedback(i) = if (i< 5){  //SMST(SendFeedback,InsNum=5)
9       FeedbackChannel!Feedback−>Skip;
10      SendFeedback(i+1)};
11  Chair() = AssignPaper(0);ReceiveReviews();(ResultChannel!SendResult−>Skip ||
            SendFeedBack(0));
12  Reviewer() = |||i:{0..4}@(  //PMP(process, InsNum=5)
13  PaperChannel?AssignPaper−>Skip; ReviewChannel!ReceiveReviews−>Skip);
```

Algorithm 1: A part of Transfomation Algorithm

Input: *BPMN collaboration model in XML*
Output: *CSPCode*
1 *BPMNodes, MsgFlow, SeqFlow = ParseBPMNModel();* // parsing the BPMN
    collaboration model, getting the elements related to interactions
    // generating the code that defines msgs and msg channels
2 *CSPCode += CodeForMsgAndChDef(Msgflow);*
    // get the id for each participant process
3 *participantProcesses = getParticipantProcessID(BPMNodes);*
4 **for** *p in participantProcesses* **do**
       // generating the csp# code for each participant
5 | *element = getStartEvent(p, BPMNodes);* // get the start event for *p*
6 | **while** *element != null* **do**
7 | | *CSPCode +=* CodeForProc(p,element,BPMNodes);// generate code
      | | according to Table 2

8 **return** *CSPCode;*

4.2   Model Verification

We verify the collaboration model by verifying the corresponding CSP# model. In this paper, we mainly verify the soundness because it is fundamental for IOPC. A multi-instance IOPC is sound if all participant processes are terminable, deadlock-free and all the tasks are reachable. The formal definition is:

$\forall$ *participant* $\in P$: deadlockfree(*participant*) $\land <>$ ($\forall$ *participant* $\in P$: *participant* reaches *end*)

where *deadlockfree, nonterminating* and *reaches* are CSP# based attribute assertions, *end* is a given conditional proposition.

With the definition, it is easy to check the soundness of the CSP model with existing CSP# analysis tools like PAT [10].

4.3   Contract Generation from CSP# Model to Solidity

When the CSP# model passes the soundness verification, it is time to generate the smart contract, which takes three steps.

Step 1: Preliminary Association Relationships Extraction. First, we abstract the interaction logic of the CSP# processes. This is based on the syntax trees of the CSP# processes. The syntax trees are obtained with the help of antlr4 [15], which helps us to get precise semantics of the CSP# processes. Figure 2 shows an example. In Fig. 2, leaf nodes form the CSP processes, and the content of a non-leaf-node is the composition of all the related leaf-nodes, which is always a composite CSP# process.

We define 6 association relationships to describe the interaction logic. They are *Init, End, Next, And, Xor* and *Enable*:

Init and *End* describe the relationships between a CSP# parent process and some (but not all) of its child processes, where a parent (child) process is a CSP# process represented by a parent (child) node in the syntax tree. *Init[P]=C[]*

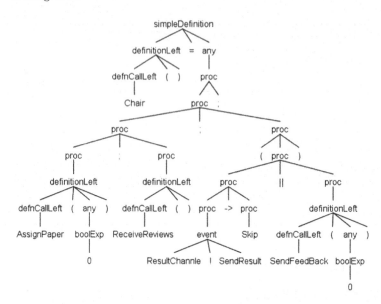

Fig. 2. A part of syntax trees of Chair.

means that if process P begins, then it will start the processes in $C[]$. $End[C]=P$ means that if C ends its execution, then it will end P's execution.

Next describes the sequential logic between the CSP# processes within a participant. $Next[A]=B[]$ means that if process A ends its execution, then processes in $B[]$ can start its execution.

And describes the relationship among the CSP# processes in a parallel gateway. $And[A]=B[]$ means that process A and processes in $B[]$ can be executed in parallel, and only when all of them completes, the task after the parallel gateway can start.

Xor describes the relationship among the CSP# processes in an exclusive gateway. $Xor[A]=B[]$ means that if process A starts its execution, then all the processes in $B[]$ can not start any more.

Enable describes the relationship related to message interactions. If A is a CSP# process to send a message, and B is a CSP# process to receive the message, then $Enable[A]=B$. It means that only when a message has be sent, it can be received.

A traversal algorithm is developed to capture the association relationships with the syntax trees, part of which is shown in Algorithm 2. It traverses the syntax trees and records the relationships according to the content of the nodes.

Figure 3 shows a part of relationships of *Chair*. It can be observed that it contains too many intermediate composite CSP# processes to be suitable as input for smart contract generation. So simplification is needed.

Algorithm 2: A part of Relationship Traversal Algorithm

Input: *Syntax tree node with subtrees*
// Traverse the node with (3 or more) subtrees
// *Node.LeftS*: process composed of leaf nodes of the left subtree
// *Node.RightS*: process composed of leaf nodes of the right subtree
// *Name*: identifier of a defined process

1 **if** *VisitPME(Node)* **then** // meet a parallel multi-instance task or process
2 | get *InsNum, MsgNum* (if exists) and *TaskContent*;
3 | add *TaskContent* to *Init[Node]*;
4 | add *Node* to *End[TaskContent]*;

5 **if** *VisitSME(Node)* **then** // meet a sequential multi-instance task or process
6 | get *InsNum, MsgNum*(if exists) and *TaskContent*;
7 | add *TaskContent* to *Init[Node]*;
8 | add *Node* to *End[TaskContent]*;

9 **if** *VisitTME(Node)* **then** // meet a time-bounded multi-instance task
10 | get *InsNum, MsgNum*(if exists), *Duration* and *TaskContent*;
11 | add *TaskContent* to *Init[Node]*;
12 | add *Node* to *End[TaskContent]*;

13 **return** *Next, End, Init, And, Xor*;

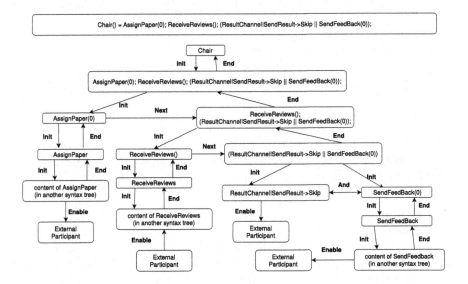

Fig. 3. A part of the relationships of *Chair*.

Step 2: Reduced Association Relationship Extraction. Relationships in Step 1 are defined to take all nodes in the syntax trees into consideration to cover the whole interaction logic order. However, due to the non-leaf nodes, the state transitions are too complex and redundant. So we take some measures to reduce them. The principle is to focus on the leaf nodes, that is **atomic** CSP# processes like *ResultChannel!SendResult ->Skip*.

Here we define three new relationships to achieve our reduction: *Activate, Inactivate, Parallel*. They are similar to the *Next, Xor* and *And* in Step 1. The

difference is that they only focus on the atomic csp# processes. We develop a
Reduction Algorithm, as shown in Algorithm 3, to get the new relationships. It
removes the redundant state transitions caused by the non-leaf nodes. Finally,
Activate, Inactivate, Parallel and *Enable* are enough to describe the logic order
of interactions.

Algorithm 3: A part of Relationship Reduction Algorithm

Input: *CSP# procs of the participants* and *Relationships: Init, End, Next, And, Xor*
1   **for** *ap in AtomicProcesses* **do**
        // find a composite csp# proc *nxtCP* with *End* [] and *Next* []
2 | *nxtCP=FindNextCompositeProc*(ap);
3 | **for** *child in Init[nxtCP]* **do** // find atomic processes in *Init* [*nxtCP*].
4 | | *nxtAP = FindAtomicProcesses(child);* // with the help of Init[]
5 | └   add *nxtAP* to *Activate*[*ap*];

6   **for** *xorp in ExclusiveGatewayProcesses* **do** // *xorp* is a composite csp# proc that
        contains all atomic procs in a EG.
        // find the first atomic processes in every outgoing path
7 | *FirstFAPGroup, SecondFAPGroup =FindFisrtAtomicProcesses*(*Xor*[*xorp*]);
8 | **for** *ap in FirstAPGroup* **do**
9 | └   add *SecondAPGroup* to *Inactivate*[*ap*];
10 | **for** *ap in SecondAPGroup* **do**
11 | └   add *FirstAPGroup* to *Inactivate*[*ap*];

12 **return** *Activate,Inactivate, Parallel*;

Figure 4 shows the reduced relationships of participant *Chair*. It includes
atomic CSP# processes on multiple syntax trees related to *Chair* and removes all
the composite processes, making state transitions simpler. Each multi-instance
task in Fig. 4 is annotated with its type and the extended attributes.

Step 3: Smart Contract Generation. After step 1 and step 2, our smart
contract generation method generates functions for every atomic CSP# process
(that is every interaction task in the collaboration model) with a template. The
functions form the main content of the contract and control the execution of the
collaborative process in specific order, which we capture above through *Activate,
Inactivate, Parallel* and *Enable*. These functions are generated to handle external
requests. With different templates, we can generate different code, which makes
it convenient to customize the smart contracts. An example of contract code
generated with our method can be seen in this repository[2].

Algorithm 4 shows a brief processing logic for a function related to a sequential
multi-instance task. It first checks whether the task is waiting for execution (line 1) and whether it meets the execution requirements (line 3). Then it
behaves according to the type of the task (line 4–5), such as sending a message,
and increasing the *count* that indicates how many instances the MT has now.
When the MT has its first instance, it prevents the related tasks in *Inactivate*

---

[2] https://github.com/fsqHub/SCG4mIOPC.

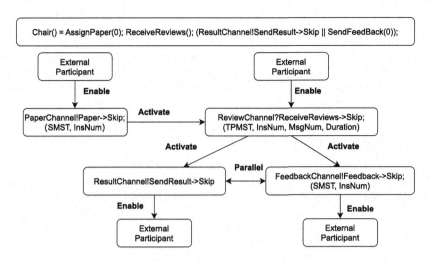

Fig. 4. Reduced relationships of *Chair*.

to execute (line 7). If the MT has enough instances, it completes its execution (line 8–9) and makes the next tasks waiting to be executed (line 10).

Algorithm 4: A part of ExternalRequest Algorithm

Input: *CSP# atomic proc*
1 **if** *State(proc) is not Waiting* **then**
2   **return** false;
3 **if** *proc is (Time-bound) SMT (and timestamp < proc.ddl)* **then**
4   *ExecuteTask(proc)*;
5   *proc*.count ++; // count refers to the number of the task instances
6 **if** *count == 1 and Inactivate[proc] exists* **then**
7   *InactivateProcs(Inactivate[proc])*;
8 **if** *(count == InsNum) or (proc is time-bounded and count == proc.MsgNum)* **then**
    // enough instances
9   *StopTask(proc)*;
10   *ActivateProc(Activate[],proc)*;// Activate the next procs

---

For ordinary tasks, the processing is similar and simpler: sending or receiving a message according to the type of the task when the execution requirements are met, preventing the corresponding tasks in *Inactivate[]* from being executed and making the tasks in *Activate[]* wait to be executed.

For parallel multi-instance tasks, the processing is also similar. The key is to control the synchronization of *count*. And for a PMP, every instance of it belongs to different participants. Assigned unique ids, the PMP instances can be taken as different ordinary processes. So the tasks of each PMP instance can be processed as ordinary tasks in ordinary processes.

5   Evaluation

This section we evaluate our smart contract generation method. First, we compare the features of our method with ones of related work. Second, we setup an experiment to test the model verification ability of our method and the cost of the generated contracts.

5.1   Comparison with Related Method

Table 3 shows the features of our method and methods in literature [2], [6] and [1]. The major contribution of our work is that we support all multi-instance elements introduced in Sect. 3, while others don't support any of them.

Table 3. Features Comparison with Related Methods.

Features	Our method	[2]	[6]	[1]
Begin with	BPMN collaboration model	BPMN choreography model	BPMN process model	BPMN process model (with lanes)
Interaction description	Yes	Yes	No	No
Formal intermediate	CSP#	No	Petri Net	State Chart
Model Verification Included	Yes	No	No	No
Cost Optimization	No	No	Yes	Yes
Multi-instance Support	All elements mentioned	None (but can be extended)	none	none

Method in [2] is a classic one in smart contract generation. It supports and focuses on the interactions among the participants of IOPC. But it doesn't include any model verification measures, which makes the generated smart contract possibly flawed, resulting in loss for unexpected process execution.

[6] and [1] use similar steps to generate smart contracts and have the same goal - optimize the cost of smart contract. Both of them translate a process model to a formal intermediate. For [6], it is Petri Net. And for [1], it is state chart. This makes model verification possible. However, none of BPMN process model, Petri Net or state chart can provide support for description and verification of interactions in IOPC without any extension, which are important and reflect how participants cooperate to achieve the collaboration. And if they are extended, extra work for properties validation and tool development is needed. Our choice of BPMN collaboration model and CSP# helps us avoid this. It is convenient to abstract interaction information from a collaboration diagram and describe the interactions with CSP#. Because there is no additional property extension, model verification can be done with existing analysis tools.

To conclude, our method supports all the multi-instance elements mentioned, description of interactions in IOPC, and model verification from interactions perspective.

5.2   Experiment

We collect 4 cases of multi-instance IOPC: Paper Review (PR), Order Fulfilment (OF), Cake Preparation (CP) and Supply Chain (SC) from [8,12,13] and [9] respectively. These cases are adapted so that they can pass our model verification and cover all of the multi-instance elements without time boundaries and a part of time-bounded elements. It is acceptable. Because in this experiment, the cost depends on the contract content and the number of executions of each function. For comparison with other methods, the only acceptable variable is the contract content. This makes time boundaries not important.

Model Verification. Before cost evaluation, to test the model verification ability of our method, 5 copies of each case are made and modified to cause control flow deadlocks. These modifications can be changes in task types or process types, changes in attribute values, or deletions of elements. For example, in Fig. 1, if *Chair* wants to receive 3 reviews, we can set the *InstanceNum* of *Reviewer* to 2 or change the type of *Submit Review* to Receive Task to cause a deadlock. Then these flawed models are transformed to CSP# models according to Table 2 and verified. Unsurprisingly, none of them passes the verification.

Cost Evaluation. Only support for interaction description and model verification is not convincing enough. The contracts are used to executed in blockchain, and the cost is an important indicator for users.

We generate smart contracts for the four cases with our method (labelled as A) and test the gas cost to complete the IOPC. There are two comparison groups. One (labelled as B) generates contracts with the method extended from [2]. The other (labelled as C) generates contracts manually based on the idea of [1]. The instance numbers of each multi-instance elements in each case are consistent in three groups. We use Ganache[3] with 10 nodes to simulate Ethereum. The contract compiler is Solc 0.8.19. Table 4 shows the result.

Table 4. Gas Cost Comparison

Case	Cost Item	our method (A)	B	C
PR	Total Cost	1382242	1417043	1039798
	Compared with C	133%	136%	100%
OF	Total Cost	1300899	1147732	1037978
	Compared with C	125%	111%	100%
CP	Total Cost	1701442	1459754	1268307
	Compared with C	134%	115%	100%
SC	Total Cost	2724285	2502170	1929297
	Compared with C	142%	130%	100%

In general, our method has the highest cost, while C has the lowest cost. It is within our expectation. As automatic methods, A and B need to handle

---

[3] https://trufflesuite.com/ganache/.

more variables and state transitions than C, leading to more gas cost for contract initialization and execution. And compared with B, our method consumes (12%-19%) more gas, especially when there are many multi-instance elements. This is the shortcoming of our method because of our lack of optimization. However, our method provides model verification before contract generation to avoid the unexpected implementation and execution of IOPC, which always costs more. In this context, 12%-19% of extra gas cost is acceptable.

6   Conclusion

This paper proposes a method to support model verification and smart contract generation for multi-instance IOPC. We focus on the elements related to interactions in multi-instance IOPC. Thus we make use of CSP#, which supports formal description of interactions well, to formalize the semantics of BPMN collaboration, making model verification feasible. After the formalization, we generate the smart contract based on the syntax trees of CSP# processes. Compared with other research, our method supports all of the multi-instance elements we have mentioned, and model verification from interactions perspective. Both of the features are important. One expands the applicability and utility of blockchain-based IOPC. The other prevents models with flaws from being translated into smart contracts, avoiding the loss of unexpected execution of IOPC.

As the experiment shows, our method costs more gas. In the future, we will optimize the generation to reduce the cost. Besides, it is planned to expand the CSP# formalization to support more elements like inclusive gateway. Also, support for user-defined properties verification for IOPC with CSP# is another future goal.

Acknowledgments. This work is supported by the NSFC-Guangdong Joint Fund Project under Grant Nos. U1911205, U20A6003; the National Natural Science Foundation of China (NSFC) under Grant No. 61972427; the Research Foundation of Science and Technology Plan Project in Guangdong Province under Grant No. 2020A0505100030.

References

1. Nakamura, H., Miyamoto, K., Kudo, M.: Inter-organizational business processes managed by blockchain. In: Hacid, H., Cellary, W., Wang, H., Paik, H.-Y., Zhou, R. (eds.) WISE 2018. LNCS, vol. 11233, pp. 3–17. Springer, Cham (2018). https://doi.org/10.1007/978-3-030-02922-7_1
2. Weber, I., Xu, X., Riveret, R., Governatori, G., Ponomarev, A., Mendling, J.: Untrusted business process monitoring and execution using blockchain. In: La Rosa, M., Loos, P., Pastor, O. (eds.) BPM 2016. LNCS, vol. 9850, pp. 329–347. Springer, Cham (2016). https://doi.org/10.1007/978-3-319-45348-4_19
3. Lòpez-Pintado, O., García-Bañuelos, L., Dumas, M., Weber, I., Ponomarev, A.: Caterpillar: a business process execution engine on the Ethereum blockchain. Softw. Pract. Exp. **49**(7), 1162–1193 (2019)

4. Tran, A.B., Lu, Q., Weber, I.: Lorikeet: a model-driven engineering tool for blockchain-based business process execution and asset management. In: BPM (Dissertation/Demos/Industry), pp. 56–60 (2018)

5. Corradini, F., Marcelletti, A., Morichetta, A., Polini, A., Re, B., Tiezzi, F.: Engineering trustable choreography-based systems using blockchain. In: Hung, C., Cerný, T., Shin, D., Bechini, A. (eds.) SAC 2020, pp. 1470–1479. ACM (2020). https://doi.org/10.1145/3341105.3373988

6. García-Bañuelos, L., Ponomarev, A., Dumas, M., Weber, I.: Optimized execution of business processes on blockchain. In: Carmona, J., Engels, G., Kumar, A. (eds.) BPM 2017. LNCS, vol. 10445, pp. 130–146. Springer, Cham (2017). https://doi.org/10.1007/978-3-319-65000-5_8

7. Tonga Naha, R., Zhang, K.: Pupa: smart contracts for BPMN with time-dependent events and inclusive gateways. In: Marrella, A., et al. (eds.) BPM 2022. LNBIP, vol. 459, pp. 21–35. Springer, Cham (2022). https://doi.org/10.1007/978-3-031-16168-1_2

8. Corradini, F., Muzi, C., Re, B., Rossi, L., Tiezzi, F.: Animating multiple instances in BPMN collaborations: from formal semantics to tool support. In: Weske, M., Montali, M., Weber, I., vom Brocke, J. (eds.) BPM 2018. LNCS, vol. 11080, pp. 83–101. Springer, Cham (2018). https://doi.org/10.1007/978-3-319-98648-7_6

9. Xiong, T., Pan, M., Yu, Y., Lou, D.: Conformance between Choreography and Collaboration in BPMN involving multi-instance participants. Int. J. Pattern Recognit. Artif Intell. **36**(07), 2259013 (2022)

10. Sun, J., Liu, Y., Dong, J.S., Pang, J.: PAT: towards flexible verification under fairness. In: Bouajjani, A., Maler, O. (eds.) CAV 2009. LNCS, vol. 5643, pp. 709–714. Springer, Heidelberg (2009). https://doi.org/10.1007/978-3-642-02658-4_59

11. Tang, X., Yu, Y., Wu, J., Pan, M.: Business process interoperability service framework based on blockchain. Comput. Integr. Manuf. Syst. **27**(9), 2508 (2021)

12. Corradini, F., Muzi, C., Re, B., Rossi, L., Tiezzi, F.: Formalising and animating multiple instances in BPMN collaborations. Inf. Syst. **103**, 101459 (2022)

13. Muzi, C., Pufahl, L., Rossi, L., Weske, M., Tiezzi, F.: Formalising BPMN service interaction patterns. In: Buchmann, R.A., Karagiannis, D., Kirikova, M. (eds.) PoEM 2018. LNBIP, vol. 335, pp. 3–20. Springer, Cham (2018). https://doi.org/10.1007/978-3-030-02302-7_1

14. Morgan, C., McIver, A., Seidel, K., et al.: Refinement-oriented probability for CSP. Form. Asp. Comput. **8**, 617–647 (1996). https://doi.org/10.1007/BF01213492

15. Parr, T.J., Quong, R.W.: ANTLR: a predicated-LL(k) parser generator. Softw. Pract. Exp. **25**(7), 789–810 (1995)

Arterial Traffic Optimization Algorithm Based on Deep Reinforcement Learning and Green Wave Coordination Control in Complex Lane Queuing Conditions

Tong Wang, Songming Liu⬝, Liwei Chen$^{(\boxtimes)}$, Min Ouyang, Shan Gao, and Yingxue Zhang

Harbin Engineering University, Harbin 150001, China
chenliwei@hrbeu.edu.cn

Abstract. With the development of transportation, the traditional traffic signal systems being unable to provide dynamic and flexible timing schemes for urban arterial road traffic in complex lane queuing conditions. In the control of arterial traffic, to solve the problem that vehicles queuing in turning lanes of branch road and then congesting the arterial road, this paper proposed an arterial traffic optimization algorithm based on deep reinforcement learning (DRL) and green wave coordination control in complex lane queuing conditions. The proposed algorithm provides a detailed division of the arterial roads and analyzed the mutual influence between vehicles inside the roads, combines DRL algorithm with the MAXBAND algorithm to optimize the signal period, phase sequence and green signal ratio of arterial roads, creates a new reward function for Deep Q Network (DQN) algorithm for multi-agent coordination. The algorithm was validated in SUMO simulation environment. The simulation results prove that the algorithm can flexibly perform signal timing and is more effective than traditional algorithms.

Keywords: Deep Reinforcement Learning · Green Wave Coordination Control · Arterial Traffic · Vehicle Infrastructure Cooperative System

1 Introduction

Traffic congestion is an important issue that urgently needs to be solved in the field of transportation intelligence and collaborative computing. Researching traffic control algorithms for arterial roads and improve the efficiency of transportation facilities has become an important topic in urban transportation systems. Complex lanes refer to exclusive lanes with left-turn, straight-going and right-turn lanes for each road in city's arterial roads. Besides, complex lane consists of two traffic lanes in opposite directions to form a two-way lane. Traffic lights allocate right-of-way to traffic flow according to established rules. However, in complex lane conditions, left turning vehicles may conflict with straight vehicles. When the flow of turning vehicles is high, turning vehicles cannot be cleared in a timely manner, forming a queue on the straight lane. In this kind of scenario, the interference with arterial traffic flow is significant, reducing the capacity of the arterial roads.

Y. Sun et al. (Eds.): ChineseCSCW 2023, CCIS 2013, pp. 406–421, 2024.
https://doi.org/10.1007/978-981-99-9640-7_30

Traditional arterial road control strategies include fixed parameter algorithms such as the MAXBAND, MULTIBAND, TRANSYT [1], etc. However, predetermined parameters cannot adapt to the high dynamic nature of traffic flow. In order to make the control system automatically adjust the strategy according to the current state, scholars have combined intelligent algorithms with traditional green wave algorithms. Shen [2] proposed a new bidirectional green wave intelligent control strategy based on the decomposition and coordination theory in systems engineering to address the bidirectional coordination control problem of traffic arteries that classical traffic control methods cannot effectively solve. Zheng [3] proposed an adaptive evolution green wave strategy. The study introduces evolution strategies into green wave system to avoid traffic situations where action sequences are too long and reward delays occur. Xavier [4] adjusted the MAXBAND model and proposed a hybrid heuristic traffic light coordination method based on the MAXBAND. Oblakova [5] analyzed the green waves at the intersection series and optimized the parameters in green wave system by using genetic algorithm. Yin [6] improved the traditional green wave coordination control algorithm by using fuzzy algorithm and genetic algorithm to optimize the green wave period and signal timing. However, the existing research lacks analysis of queue delays caused by turning vehicles in multi-lane conditions and modeling in complex lane conditions. These are all issues that still need to be studied in detail for traffic control on arterial roads.

In recent years, deep reinforcement learning (DRL) technology has developed rapidly, including classic algorithms such as Deep Q Network (DQN) [7]. DRL technology has been widely used in practical scenarios such as UAV communication [8], automatic driving [9], traffic prediction [10], etc. In this paper, we combined DRL with green wave coordination control and did the following work: We provided a detailed division of arterial roads and analyzed the mutual influence between vehicles inside the roads; optimized traffic control on arterial roads from multiple perspectives such as period, phase difference, and green signal ratio; created a new reward function for DQN in the framework of traffic control; proposed an arterial traffic optimization algorithm considering queuing characteristics by combining green wave coordination control and DQN. Finally, we verified the proposed algorithm in SUMO [11] simulation environment. The results prove that the proposed algorithm can effectively reduce the waiting delay of road vehicles, and its performance is better than fixed time algorithm and non-coordinated DQN algorithm.

2 Analysis of Complex Arterial Traffic

2.1 Vehicle Arriving Distribution Model

This paper divides the roads in arterial road model into two categories: branch road and main road, as shown in Fig. 1. Branch roads refer to a road that is not connected to other intersections in the arterial traffic coordinated control system. Main roads refer to the roads between target intersections. Assuming the road is composed of intersection 1, intersection 2... Intersection n, represented by $I(n), i \in [1, n]$. The east-west direction is the coordinated direction of the arterial road. The distance between intersection $I(i-1)$ and intersection $I(n)$ is represented by $L_{i-1,i}$. To describe the formation of congestion on the arterial road, the road and road lanes are numbered.

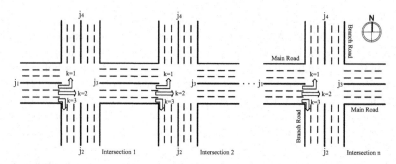

Fig. 1. The schematic diagram of road classification and road lanes.

The traffic flow of the branch road comes from outside the arterial traffic coordination and control system, and it can be considered that its arrival distribution is random. Therefore, the arrival distribution of traffic flow on branch roads is the same as that of isolated signalized intersections.

The arrival pattern of vehicles on arterial road is influenced by the vehicle travel time, the dispersion characteristics of road traffic flow, the upstream vehicle departure pattern and the upstream traffic control scheme. As shown in Fig. 2, assume the west side is upstream and the east side is downstream, the arriving vehicles at downstream intersection $I(i)$ consist of three parts: the straight traffic flow from west, the left turn traffic flow from north, and the right turn traffic flow from south at upstream intersection $I(i-1)$.

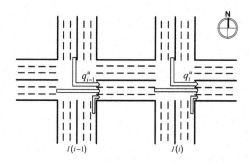

Fig. 2. The traffic flow between adjacent intersections.

According to Fig. 2, the relationship between the departure pattern of the upstream intersection and the arrival pattern of the downstream intersection is:

$$P_i^a(T) = \int_0^T q_{i-1,i}^a(t)dt = \int_{-tr_{i-1,i}}^{T-tr_{i-1,i}} q_{i-1}^u(t)dt \tag{1}$$

In the formula, $P_i^a(T)$ is the number of vehicles arriving at $I(i)$ during the time period $[0, T]$. $q_{i-1,i}^a(t)$ represents the arriving traffic flow at downstream intersection $I(i)$, $q_{i-1}^u(t)$ represents the traffic flow leaving from the upstream intersection $I(i-1)$.

$r_{i-1,i}$ represents the red light time from $I(i-1)$ to $I(i)$. The number of vehicles arriving at the downstream intersection during the time period $[0, T]$ is roughly equal to the number of vehicles departing from the upstream intersection during the time period $[-tr_{i-1,i}, T - tr_{i-1,i}]$. Considering that the right turning traffic flow is not controlled by signals, the departure rate of the right turning traffic flow is equal to the arrival rate. After obtaining the arrival patterns of traffic flow in each branch direction, overlay them to obtain the arrival patterns of the lanes. The expression for the traffic flow leaving the intersection $I(i)$ is as follows:

$$q_i^u(t) = \begin{cases} s_{i,1,2} + q_{i,2,3}, 0 \le t < t_1 \\ q_{i,1}^a(t) + q_{i,2,3}, t_1 \le t < t_2 \\ q_{i,2,3}, t_2 \le t < t_3 \\ s_{i,4,1} + q_{i,2,3}, t_3 \le t < t_4 \\ q_{i,4,1} + q_{i,2,3}, t_4 \le t < C \end{cases} \tag{2}$$

$$t_1 = \frac{q_{i,1,2} \times r_{i,1,2}}{s_{i,1,2} - q_{i,1,2}} \tag{3}$$

$$t_2 = g_{i,1,2} \tag{4}$$

$$t_3 = r_{i,4,1} \tag{5}$$

$$t_4 = \frac{q_{i,4,1} \times r_{i,4,1}}{s_{i,4,1} - q_{i,4,1}} + r_{i,4,1} \tag{6}$$

On lane k of road j at intersection i, $s_{i,j,k}$ represents saturated traffic speed, $q_{i,j,k}$ represents average arrival rate, $r_{i,j,k}$ represents red light time, $g_{i,j,k}$ represents green light time.

2.2 Vehicle Delay

This paper uses the HCM 2010 delay model [12] to calculate the delay of branch roads. For the arterial road, the total delay of vehicles consists of uniform delay, initial queue delay, and remain queue delay. Uniform delay refers to the vehicle arrival delay when the vehicle arrival state is uniform and stable under ideal conditions. The initial queue delay refers to the additional delay caused by the initial waiting vehicles left in the previous signal period to the subsequent vehicles. The remain queue delay refers to the delay caused by the remaining waiting vehicles to subsequent vehicles after the end of the signal period. The formula for calculating the total delay D is as follows:

$$D_{i,j,k} = d_{i,j,k}^1 + d_{i,j,k}^2 + d_{i,j,k}^3 \tag{7}$$

On lane k of road j at intersection i, $D_{i,j,k}$ represents the total delay, $d_{i,j,k}^1$ represents the uniform delay, $d_{i,j,k}^2$ represents the initial queue delay, $d_{i,j,k}^3$ represents the remain queue delay.

Vehicle Delay Under Undersaturated Flow. According to HCM 2010, under unsaturated traffic flow, the sum of initial queuing vehicles' number and arriving vehicles' number in each period is less than the number of vehicles that can be released within a green light duration at saturated flow rate. As shown in Fig. 3(a), under undersaturated flow, the initial vehicle queue and arriving vehicles can leave the intersection before the green light ends, and there is no remaining queue at the end of the period.

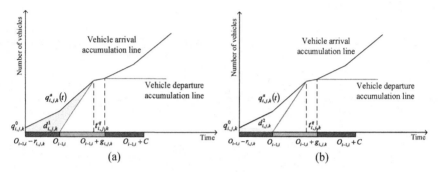

Fig. 3. Vehicle delay under undersaturated traffic flow. (a) Uniform delay. (b) Initial queue delay.

The queuing dissipation time $t^q_{i,j,k}$ is the intersection point of vehicle arrival accumulation line and vehicle departure accumulation line. The formula for calculating $t^q_{i,j,k}$ is as follows:

$$q^0_{i,j,k} + \int_{O_{i-1,i}-r_{i,j,k}}^{t^q_{i,j,k}} q^a_{i,j,k}(t)dt = s_{i,j,k} \times \left(t^q_{i,j,k} - O_{i-1,i}\right) \tag{8}$$

In the formula, $q^0_{i,j,k}$ represents the number of vehicles queuing at the beginning of the period, $q^a_{i,j,k}(t)$ represents the arrival flow of entrance lane, $s_{i,j,k}$ represents the saturated flow of entrance lane, $O_{i-1,i}$ represents the phase difference between $I(i-1)$ and $I(i)$. The uniform delay $d^1_{i,j,k}$ under undersaturated traffic flow is calculated as follows:

$$
\begin{aligned}
d^1_{i,j,k} = \int_{O_{i-1,i}-r_{i,j,k}}^{t^q_{i,j,k}} \int_{O_{i-1,i}-r_{i,j,k}}^{u} q^a_{i,j,k}(t)dtdu + q^0_{i,j,k} \\
\times \left(t^q_{i,j,k} - (O_{i-1,i} - r_{i,j,k})\right) - \frac{s_{i,j,k} \times \left(t^q_{i,j,k}\right)^2}{2}
\end{aligned}
\tag{9}
$$

As shown in Fig. 3(b), under undersaturated traffic, the initial queue can be cleared before the green light ends. The initial queue delay is calculated as follows:

$$d^2_{i,j,k} = r_{i,j,k} \times q^0_{i,j,k} + \frac{\left(q^0_{i,j,k}\right)^2}{2 \times s_{i,j,k}} \tag{10}$$

Under undersaturated traffic flow, there is no remaining queue, so the remain queue delay $d^3_{i,j,k}$ is 0.

Vehicle Delay Under Supersaturated Flow. Under supersaturated traffic flow, when the sum of the initial queue and arriving vehicles at the beginning of a signal period is greater than the capacity of the entrance road, a remain queue is generated. The uniform delay under supersaturated traffic flow is shown in Fig. 4(a).

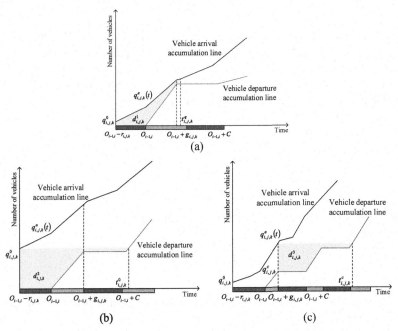

Fig. 4. Vehicle delay under supersaturated traffic flow. (a) Uniform delay. (b) Initial queue delay. (c) Remain queue delay.

In this condition, the uniform delay is calculated as follows:

$$d_{i,j,k}^1 = \int_{O_{i-1,i}-r_{i,j,k}}^{O_{i-1,i}+g_{i,j,k}} \int_{O_{i-1,i}-r_{i,j,k}}^{u} q_{i,j,k}^a(t)dtdu + q_{i,j,k}^0 \times C - \frac{s_{i,j,k} \times (g_{i,j,k})^2}{2} \quad (11)$$

Usually, the initial queue can be cleared before the green light ends. But in supersaturation condition, the initial queue is too large and the vehicle queue cannot be completely cleared in one period, as shown in Fig. 4(b). Therefore, when calculating the delay of initial queue, not only the delay to the current period, but also the delay to the future period must be considered. Assuming that the initial queue can be completely cleared in the μ th period, then the calculation formula for the delay caused by the initial queue in the x th period is:

$$d_{i,j,k}^2(x) = \begin{cases} \left[q_{i,j,k}^0 - (x-1) \times s_{i,j,k} \times g_{i,j,k} \right] \times C - \frac{g_{i,j,k} \times (s_{i,j,k})^2}{2}, x = 1, 2, ..., \mu - 1 \\ r_{i,j,k} \times \mathrm{mod}\left(q_{i,j,k}^0, s_{i,j,k} \times g_{i,j,k} \right) + \frac{\left[\mathrm{mod}\left(q_{i,j,k}^0, s_{i,j,k} \times g_{i,j,k} \right) \right]^2}{2 \times s_{i,j,k}}, x = \mu \end{cases}$$

$$(12)$$

The total delay of the initial queue is:

$$d_{i,j,k}^2 = \sum_{x=1}^{\mu} d_{i,j,k}^2(x) \tag{13}$$

The remain queue delay under supersaturated traffic flow is shown in Fig. 4(c). The delay of the remaining queue also needs to consider its impact on the future period. $q_{i,j,k}^c$ represents the number of stranded vehicles at the end of the period. Assuming that the remaining queues can be completed in the η th period, then the delay generated by the remaining queues in the γ th period is calculated as follows:

$$d_i^3(y) = \begin{cases} \left[q_{i,j,k}^c - (y-1) \times s_{i,j,k} \times g_{i,j,k} \right] \times C - \frac{g_{i,j,k} \times (s_{i,j,k})^2}{2}, & x = 1, 2, ..., \eta - 1 \\ r_{i,j,k} \times \mathrm{mod}\left(q_{i,j,k}^c, s_{i,j,k} \times g_{i,j,k} \right) + \frac{\left[\mathrm{mod}\left(q_{i,j,k}^c, s_{i,j,k} \times g_{i,j,k} \right) \right]^2}{2 \times s_{i,j,k}}, & x = \eta \end{cases} \tag{14}$$

The total delay for the remaining queues is calculated as follows:

$$d_i^3 = \sum_{y=1}^{\eta} d_i^3(y) \tag{15}$$

In summary, the total delay of the road is the sum of the delays of each lane, and the calculation formula is as follows:

$$D_{i,j} = \sum_{k} D_{i,j,k} \tag{16}$$

3　The Proposed Algorithm

3.1　General Framework

The algorithm proposed in this paper analyzes the traffic control process of arterial roads in complex lane queuing conditions. The algorithm uses the MAXBAND algorithm to calculate the parameters such as the period and phase difference of the signal lights, and models the constraints of the MAXBAND as a mixed integer linear programming problem for solution [13]. A new reward function is created to DQN algorithm to dynamically optimize the green signal ratio of the signal light. The flowchart of the algorithm proposed in this paper is shown in Fig. 5.

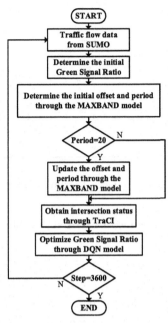

Fig. 5. Flow chart of arterial traffic optimization algorithm in complex lane queuing conditions combining deep reinforcement learning and green wave coordination control.

3.2 The MAXBAND Model

The MAXBAND model aims to obtain the widest up direction and down direction green wave bands through the green wave time-distance diagram under the condition of given part of the control parameters [14]. It optimizes the intersection phase difference and green light time in the arterial road signal control system, using a mixed integer programming model to obtain the optimal solution. Green wave time-distance diagram of the MAXBAND model is shown in Fig. 6. It shows the time-distance relationship when adjacent intersections on an arterial road coordinate with each other to produce green wave belts.

The parameters in Fig. 6 are defined as follows: b and $\bar{b}$ represent the bandwidth of the green wave in down direction and up direction; r_i and $\bar{r}_i$ represent the time of red light in down direction and up direction at $I(i)$; $t_{i-1,i}$ and $\bar{t}_{i,i-1}$ represent the travel time for vehicles down and up between $I(i)$ and $I(i-1)$; ω_i and $\bar{\omega}_i$ represent the interval time between the right (left) side of the red light phase and the left (right) side of the green wave band at $I(i)$; Δ_i represents the time interval between the midpoint of red light of $I(i)$ in down direction and up direction; $\varphi_{i,i-1}$ and $\bar{\varphi}_{i-1,i}$ represent the time interval between the midpoint of red light phase at $I(i-1)$ and $I(i)$ in down direction and up

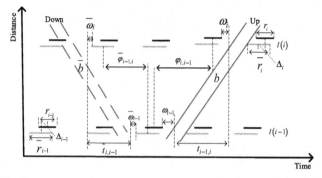

Fig. 6. Green wave time-distance diagram of the MAXBAND model.

direction. The basic expression of the MAXBAND model is shown in formula (17).

$$F = \max(b)$$

$$st. \begin{cases} b = \overline{b} \\ \omega_i + b \le 1 - r_i; \overline{\omega}_i + \overline{b} \le 1 - \overline{r}_i \ i = 1, 2, ..., n \\ 0.5(r_i + \overline{r}_i) + \omega_i + \overline{\omega}_i + \Delta_{i-1} - \Delta_i \\ \quad = 0.5(r_{i-1} + \overline{r}_{i-1}) + \omega_{i-1} + \overline{\omega}_{i-1} + t_{i-1,i} + \overline{t}_{i,i-1} + \lambda C \ i = 2, 3, ..., n \\ b, \overline{b}, \omega_i, \overline{\omega}_i \ge 0 \ i = 1, 2, ..., n \\ \lambda \in Z \end{cases} \quad (17)$$

The algorithm uses the open source solver Gurobi [15] to solve the integer linear programming problems involved in the MAXBAND model. The output is the phase difference and period.

3.3 Multi-agent Cooperation in Reinforcement Learning Framework

The algorithm in this paper models the traffic control problem under the framework of DRL, which makes up for the shortcomings of the MAXBAND algorithm that cannot adapt to short-term changes in complex traffic flows. For each agent, in addition to paying attention to the local state and reward, the state and reward information of adjacent agents should also be included in the calculation of its own Q value, and finally reach the global optimal solution. The multi-agent collaboration model in this paper is shown in Fig. 7.

3.4 Combined State Representation Based on Road Pheromone

In terms of traffic control, a common approach to state representation is to form a feature-based value vector. Considering the cooperation between agents, this paper uses matrix M_i to represent the combined state, which is defined as follows:

$$M_i = [s_i, s_1, s_2, ..., s_k]^T = \begin{bmatrix} x_i & lane_1^i & c_1^i & lane_2^i & c_2^i & a_1 \\ x_1 & lane_1^1 & c_1^1 & lane_2^2 & c_2^2 & a_2 \\ \vdots & \vdots & \vdots & \vdots & \vdots & \vdots \\ x_k & lane_1^k & c_1^k & lane_2^k & c_2^k & a_k \end{bmatrix} \quad (18)$$

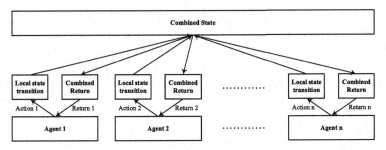

Fig. 7. The interacting mechanism between multi-agent and environment.

In the matrix, s_k represents the local state information of the k th agent, x_k represents the average discrete level of congestion in different lanes of the k th agent, $\left(lane_1^k, c_1^k\right)$ represents the most congested lane and its congestion status in the k th agent, $\left(lane_2^k, c_2^k\right)$ represents the second congested lane and its congestion status in the k th agent, a_k represents the decision of the k th agent in the last round. According to the level of road congestion, select the two most congested intersections from the four intersections for coordination. Each agent needs to discretize the congestion level according to the number of road vehicles, and take the road congestion level as the state. This paper sets three congestion levels. The division for congestion degree is shown in formula (19), and the selection of the threshold depends on the number of vehicles in the actual scene. This paper set $\delta_0 = 5$, $\delta_1 = 10$. N represents the number of road vehicles. 0 means that the road congestion is low, 1 means that the road is in a medium congestion state, and 2 means that the road congestion is high.

$$x = \begin{cases} 0, N \leq \delta_0 \\ 1, \delta_0 \leq N \leq \delta_1 \\ 2, N \geq \delta_1 \end{cases} \tag{19}$$

Common road feature vectors only focus on vehicle information, ignoring the importance of roads for environmental feature extraction. In this paper, the local state of agent takes into account the difference of each lane, and calculates the road pheromone by lane. The pheromone formula is as follows:

$$\rho_{realtime,i} = \frac{N_{vehicle,i}}{L_{edge,i}} \tag{20}$$

In the formula, $\rho_{realtime,i}$ represents the road pheromone of lane i, $L_{edge,i}$ represents the lane length ahead the intersection, $N_{vehicle,i}$ represents the number of vehicles in lane, $i = 1, 2, 3$.

3.5 Action Space

In most traffic control problems, the action set is usually discrete, which helps to reduce the action space [16] by orders of magnitude. In the current algorithmic model of traffic lights controlled by reinforcement learning, the main action space is the binary action choice of keeping the same phase or changing the phase. It may cause the sudden braking and driving of vehicles traveling on the actual road, causing great potential safety hazards [17]. In this paper, in order to reflect the flexibility of the algorithm, the reinforcement learning action is set to adjust the duration of the green light phase. Since the phase sequence is fixed, this paper sets the action to the adjustment amount of the green light time $\{-2, 0, 2\}$ (seconds). In addition, the sum of the straight-going and turning time adjustments at the intersection is guaranteed to be zero to ensure that the period does not change.

3.6   Combined Reward Function

Rewards represent the guidance of the environment on agent actions. After receiving the feedback, the agent adjusts the strategy to complete the learning process of interaction with the environment. In traffic control, the ultimate goal is to minimize the waiting time of all vehicles [18] and quickly alleviate road congestion. Aiming at the difficulty of determining the target reward of multi-agents, this paper proposes a reward function. The reward function is divided into two parts, one is local reward and the other is neighbor reward. Each agent should not only consider its own actions and rewards, but also comprehensively consider the behavior of other agents. The agents interact with each other, and the strategies are coordinated with each other to make the current optimal decision. The reward function is as follows:

$$R = \beta r_i + (1 - \beta) \sum_{j \in N_i} \frac{r_j}{d_{ij}} \tag{21}$$

$$r = \Delta \hat{\rho}_{realtime} = \sum_{a,b \in \{1,2,3\}} \left(\frac{\left(\rho_{realtime,a} \right)^2}{\sum_b \rho_{realtime,b}} \right) \tag{22}$$

In the formula, r represents local reward; β represents weighting parameter, the value range is [0, 1]; $d_{i,j}$ represents the distance between intersection i and j. Considering the operability of the simulation and the research goals, this paper defines the local reward as the change of pheromone, calculates the change of road pheromone by lane, and increases the weight of each lane.

4   Simulation and Analysis

4.1   Configuration of Simulation Environment

The simulation uses the Python-SUMO platform. In the simulation, the mixed integer optimization model is used to optimize the period and phase difference every 20 signal periods; DQN algorithm is used to optimize the green signal ratio once per signal period. The weight value β of the reward function is 0.4. The agent parameter configuration is shown in the Table 1.

In the simulation, the arterial road is set with two-way, six-lane and four-intersection to simulate the real complex condition. Each road is divided into three lanes: straight-going, left-turning and right-turning lanes. The distance between adjacent intersections

Table 1. Agent parameter settings.

Parameter	Parameter setting
Deep Neural Network	[24, 24, 24, 2]
Actor Critic Network	[24, 2], [24, 24, 1]
Learning Rate lr	0.001
Activation Function	ReLu
Initial Exploration Rate	1
Final Exploration Rate	0.01
Attenuation Factor	0.99
Loss Function	MSE
Optimizer	AdamOptimizer
Batchsize	8

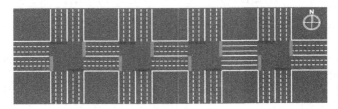

Fig. 8. The arterial traffic simulation scene.

is 500 m. The paper adopts a two-phase signal light control mode. The simulation scene is shown in Fig. 8.

In order to verify the performance of the algorithm, four cases are set up in the simulation. The traffic flow of main road and branch road are different. The specific simulation parameters settings are shown in Table 2.

Table 2. Specific simulation parameters in different cases.

	Main road traffic flow (veh/h)	Branch road traffic flow (veh/h)
Case 1	2000	500
Case 2	2000	1000
Case 3	2000	1500
Case 4	2000	2000

4.2 Result Analysis

In the above simulation environment, the algorithm proposed in this paper is compared with fixed time algorithm and non-coordinated DQN algorithm. Train the model until it converges, each episode takes 3600 s. The average waiting delay of each algorithm under different traffic flow cases is shown in Fig. 9.

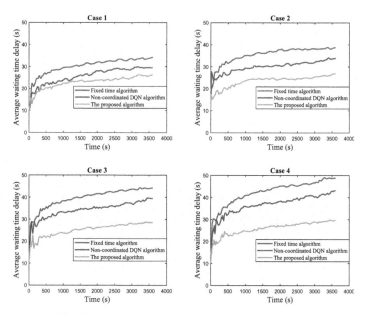

Fig. 9. Average waiting time delay in different cases.

It can be seen from Fig. 9 that the algorithm proposed in this paper performs well in every condition. Compared with the other algorithm, it has a more stable performance. In order to verify the control effect of the model, statistical analysis was carried out on the vehicle queue length in the four cases. In the four different traffic flow cases, the average queue length of each algorithm changes with training iterations as shown in Fig. 10.

For the simulation results of average waiting time, in case 1, the proposed algorithm shows a 22.94% enhancement over fixed time algorithm, and a 10.64% improvement over non-coordinated DQN algorithm. In case 2, improvements of 30.52% and 20.62% are respectively achieved. Case 3 demonstrates enhancements of 35.42% and 27.51%. In case 4, improvements of 38.76% and 31.07% are observed, respectively (Table 3).

Regarding the results of vehicle queue length, in case 1, the proposed algorithm shows a 19.73% enhancement over fixed time algorithm, and a 7.63% improvement over non-coordinated DQN algorithm. In case 2, improvements of 21.45% and 9.07% are respectively achieved. Case 3 demonstrates enhancements of 22.69% and 11.87%. In case 4, improvements of 23.88% and 13.75% are observed, respectively.

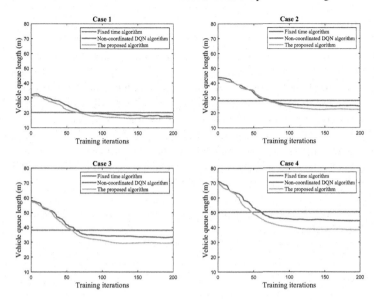

Fig. 10. Vehicle queue length in different cases.

Table 3. The performance of each algorithm in different cases.

Case	Algorithm	Average waiting time delay (s)	Vehicle queue length (m)
1	Fixed time algorithm	34.22	20.22
	Non-coordinated DQN	29.51	17.57
	The proposed algorithm	26.37	16.23
2	Fixed time algorithm	38.73	28.21
	Non-coordinated DQN	33.90	24.37
	The proposed algorithm	26.91	22.16
3	Fixed time algorithm	44.24	38.13
	Non-coordinated DQN	39.41	33.45
	The proposed algorithm	28.57	29.48
4	Fixed time algorithm	48.81	50.34
	Non-coordinated DQN	43.36	44.43
	The proposed algorithm	29.89	38.32

The simulation results show that the proposed algorithm can reduce the queue length and average waiting time delay of road vehicles, and improve the fluency of urban multi-intersection traffic. Besides, the control effect of the proposed algorithm is better when the traffic flow of branch roads is high.

5 Conclusion

This paper focuses on solving the problem that vehicles queuing in turning lanes of branch road and then congesting the arterial road. We proposed an arterial traffic optimization algorithm based on deep reinforcement learning and green wave coordination control in complex lane queuing conditions. When the traffic flow in branch road is large, it can effectively reduce the average waiting time delay of road vehicles and the length of vehicle queuing. On the other hand, the experiments of the algorithm proposed in this paper are all based on the SUMO simulation platform, without traffic data or experiments in actual road scenarios. In the next stage, we will further conduct research based on real-world scenarios and real-world data.

Acknowledgments. This work is supported by the National Natural Science Foundation of China under Grant No. 62372131.

References

1. Little, J.: The synchronization of traffic signals by mixed-integer linear programming. Oper. Res. **14**(4), 568–594 (1966)
2. Shen, G.: Urban traffic trunk two-direction green wave intelligent control strategy and its application. In: 6th World Congress on Intelligent Control and Automation, pp. 8563–8567. IEEE, Dalian (2006)
3. Zheng, Y., Ma, D., Jin, F., Zhao, Z.: ES-band: a novel approach to coordinate green wave system with adaptation evolutionary strategies. In: 2nd ACM SIGSPATIAL International Workshop on GeoSpatial Simulation, pp. 36–39. ACM, Chicago (2019)
4. Cabezas, X., García, S., Salas, S.: A hybrid heuristic approach for traffic light synchronization based on the MAXBAND. Soft Comput. Lett. **1**, 100001 (2019)
5. Oblakova, A., Hanbali, A., Boucherie, R., Ommeren, J.: Green wave analysis in a tandem of traffic-light intersections. Memorandum Faculty of Mathematical Sciences University of Twente (2017)
6. Yin, M.: Multi-junction traffic light optimization during holiday based on improved green wave band control. J. Phys. Conf. Ser. **1486**(7), 072012 (2020)
7. Mnih, V., Kavukcuoglu, K., Silver, D., et al.: Human-level control through deep reinforcement learning. Nature **518**(7540), 529–533 (2015)
8. Liu, C., Chen, Z., Tang, J., Xu, J., Piao, C.: Energy-efficient UAV control for effective and fair communication coverage: a deep reinforcement learning approach. IEEE J. Sel. Areas Commun. **36**(9), 2059–2070 (2018)
9. Wu, Y., Liao, S., Liu, X., Li, Z., Lu, R.: Deep reinforcement learning on autonomous driving policy with auxiliary critic network. IEEE Trans. Neural Netw. Learn. Syst., 1–11 (2021)
10. Monireh, A., Ana, B.: Hierarchical traffic signal optimization using reinforcement learning and traffic prediction with long-short term memory. Expert Syst. Appl. **171**, 114580 (2021)
11. Hay, R.T.: SUMO: a history of modification. Mol. Cell **18**(1), 1–12 (2005)
12. Ghanim, M.S., Shaaban, K., Allawi, S.: Operational performance of signalized intersections: HCM and microsimulation comparison. In: 2022 Intermountain Engineering, Technology and Computing (IETC), pp. 1–6. IEEE, Orem (2022)
13. Buşoniu, L., Babuška, R., De Schutter, B.: Multi-agent reinforcement learning: an overview. In: Innovations in Multi-Agent Systems and Applications-1, vol. 310, pp. 183–221. Springer, Heidelberg (2010). https://doi.org/10.1007/978-3-642-14435-6_7

14. Little, J., Kelson, M., Gartner, N.: MAXBAND: a versatile program for setting signals on arteries and triangular networks. Transp. Res. Rec. J. Transp. Res. Board **795**, 40–46 (1981)
15. Pedroso, J P.: Optimization with Gurobi and python. INESC Porto and Universidade do Porto, Porto, Portugal, 1 (2011)
16. Prashanth, L.A., Bhatnagar, S.: Reinforcement learning with function approximation for traffic signal control. IEEE Trans. Intell. Transp. Syst. **12**(2), 412–421 (2010)
17. Noaeen, M., Naik, A., Goodman, L., et al.: Reinforcement learning in urban network traffic signal control: a systematic literature review. Expert Syst. Appl. **199**, 116830 (2022)
18. Hawi, R., Okeyo, G., Kimwele, M.: Techniques for smart traffic control: an in-depth. Int. J. Comput. Appl. Technol. Res. **4**(7), 566–573 (2015)

Multi-robots Formation and Obstacle Avoidance Algorithm Based on Leader-Follower and Artificial Potential Field Method

Zhenrui Liu$^{(\boxtimes)}$, Wancheng Li, Beiming Li, Shan Gao, Min Ouyang, and Tong Wang

Harbin Engineering University, Harbin 150001, China
liuzhenrui@hrbeu.edu.cn

Abstract. Multi-robots collaborative has important application prospects in fields such as military, medical, transportation, security patrols, rescue and disaster relief. Robots keep formation and obstacle avoidance are two of the core technologies in the application of multi robot cooperative system. This paper designs and implements a distributed robots formation and obstacle avoidance system based on the combination of fuzzy cascade PID and improved artificial potential field. This paper also designs a model of 2D lidar used to judge obstacles. It ensures the stability of multi robot formation through cascade fuzzy PID, When multi-robots system encountering obstacles, Combine with the cascade fuzzy PID and the improved artificial potential field algorithm, the multi-robots can complete obstacle avoidance while ensuring the formation. Finally, experiments were conducted on multi-robots physical platform, and the results showed that the algorithm can ensure formation during robot movement and avoid obstacles when moving in the scenario with massive obstacles.

Keywords: Mult-robots · Leader-follower · Fuzzy cascade PID · Artificial Potential Field

1 Introduction

Single robot systems are usually limited to simplifying tasks in small scenes, with drawbacks such as large volume, low reliability, complex structure, and high cost of sensor processors. Multi robots systems have lower hardware performance Compared with single robot systems. The greater advantages of multi-robots lie in the efficiency in facing complex tasks, the robustness in handling unexpected faults and external disturbances, and the scalability and flexibility of clusters. Formation obstacle avoidance control belongs to the category of robot group behavior coordination and is the core foundation of future complex mult-robots systems. Now it has been preliminarily applied, such as collaborative transportation of large goods, security patrols, cluster encirclement, fire search and rescue, unmanned aerial vehicle group operations, and so on. However, most of the current research in this field is still in the simulation and verification stage. In practical engineering, the external interference, vibration noise, communication delay, and environmental accidents faced by robot clusters pose enormous challenges

© The Author(s), under exclusive license to Springer Nature Singapore Pte Ltd. 2024
Y. Sun et al. (Eds.): ChineseCSCW 2023, CCIS 2013, pp. 422–437, 2024.
https://doi.org/10.1007/978-981-99-9640-7_31

to the application implementation. The improvement of its accuracy and robustness has been one of the goals of multi robot human technology research in recent years. Multi robot formation control requires the implementation and maintenance of a predefined formation mode, allowing multiple robots to collaborate to complete a given task. In unknown environments, it is not only necessary to have effective formation control algorithms and collaborative obstacle avoidance algorithms to ensure the completion of team collaborative tasks, but also for robots to perceive the surrounding environmental information.

At present, the main methods for controlling the formation of multiple mobile robots include: leader-follower method, virtual structure method, behavior based method, etc. The leader-follower method is widely used due to its simplicity and scalability. The leader-follower method was first proposed by Cruz and is currently the most common formation control method. Its basic principle is that the leader follows the control instructions, while the follower takes the leader as the benchmark and maintains the formation through real-time distance and angle with the leader. The formation strategy is simple and easy to implement, but the leader determines the overall movement trend of the robot formation, overly relying on the leader, lacking information feedback in the formation, and low control accuracy. Koo T J et al. [1] combined the traditional leader-follower method with linearized feedback method, by establishing the expected relative positions of the leader and follower in advance, and then stabilizing each follower at their respective expected positions through linearized feedback, thereby achieving a stable formation during driving. Xu Jianxin [2] combines the leader-follower method with the consistency algorithm to establish a differential robot motion model, transforming the trajectory tracking problem of the formation into a point stabilization problem of the tracking error model. For measurement errors, the sliding film control is used for processing.

Desai et al. [3] divided the multi robot formation control problem into three sub problems: robot control, trajectory tracking, and formation control. Multi-robots formation control is achieved by controlling the relative angle and distance between follower and leader. Sun Yujiao et al. [4] established a mathematical model of wheeled robots under non holonomic constraints, and then transformed the navigation following model into a local coordinate system error model through global coordinate transformation. Wu Juncheng et al. [5] proposed a multi robot formation control algorithm that does not require global coordinates to address the problem of multi-robots struggling to maintain a certain formation to reach a predetermined target in uncertain environments. Some researchers have proposed using the Lyapunov method to derive the global stability of the system, but the positioning error between the leader and follower is bounded and cannot converge to zero.

Although significant progress has been made in the navigation following formation control of multiple robots, research on obstacle avoidance algorithms needs to be strengthened in the design of formation control. The artificial potential field method has the characteristics of simple structure and good real-time performance, and is widely used in multi robot formation. Kowdiki et al. [6] proposed a hybrid formation control technology based on the navigation following method, and used the artificial potential field method for path planning of the navigation intelligent agent to maintain stable control of the entire formation. However, the artificial potential field method also has shortcomings. Sang Lei et al. [7] pointed out that the artificial potential field method is prone to falling into local minima and slow feedback response in open-loop control; There is limited research on the current research methods for multi robot formation in dynamic scenarios, especially on how to maintain stable formation, real-time obstacle avoidance, and formation feedback.

This article is based on the leader-follower method for formation control, combining fuzzy cascade PID control with APF to ensure the stability of the formation and real-time obstacle avoidance. By using sensors carried by robots to autonomously perceive and obtain information about obstacles in the environment, an improved artificial potential field method is proposed to avoid falling into local minima in dynamic scenes. Finally, the feasibility was verified through software simulation and validated on a ROS based multi-robots experimental platform.

2   Formation Strategy and Controller Design

2.1   Formation Strategy

In the leader-follower method, the follower take the leader as the reference to determine the relative position according to the fixed included Angle θ and distance l to form a formation, that is, the coordinate value (x, y) in the current leader coordinate system [10]. The target point of the formation is given based on the coordinate system of the leader. Each follower cannot get the azimuth information of the target point directly from this coordinate system, and must convert it to its own coordinate system for processing. It is assumed that the current leader is robot1, robot2 and robot3 are followers, {map} is the map coordinate system (Fig. 1).

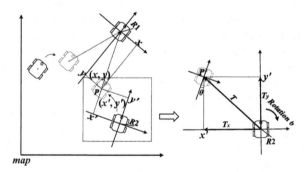

Fig. 1. Schematic diagram of formation strategy for pilot-following method

The chassis coordinate system of robot1 gives the coordinate P of the target point of robot2's formation (x, y). If robot2 wants to track point P, it needs to convert the coordinate value of the coordinate to the coordinate (x',y') under its chassis coordinate system {R2}. The two transformation relations are fused to obtain the direct transformation relation between {R1} and {R2}, which is represented by the translation vector $T_{r1\text{-}r2}$ and the quaternion $Q_{r1\text{-}r2}$ Suppose:

$$\mathbf{T_{r1-r2}} = \begin{bmatrix} x_{12} \\ y_{12} \\ 0 \end{bmatrix} \tag{1}$$

$$\mathbf{Q_{r1-r2}} = \begin{bmatrix} q_0 \\ q_1 \\ q_2 \\ q_3 \end{bmatrix} \tag{2}$$

Obtain the Angle between the two coordinate systems by α:

$$\alpha = \arctan\left(2*(q_0*q_3 - q_1*q_2), 1 - 2*\left(q_2{}^2 + q_3{}^2\right)\right) \tag{3}$$

Then we get the coordinates (x', y')

$$\begin{bmatrix} x' \\ y' \end{bmatrix} = \begin{bmatrix} \cos\alpha & -\sin\alpha \\ \sin\alpha & \cos\alpha \end{bmatrix}\begin{bmatrix} x \\ y \end{bmatrix} + \begin{bmatrix} -x_{12} \\ -y_{12} \end{bmatrix} \tag{4}$$

2.2   Fuzzy Cascade PID Formation Controller Design

Formation control algorithm position-velocity cascade PID loop is used for formation control, in which the pose of virtual robot is taken as the expected vector, the real-time pose of the robot is taken as the measurement feedback, and the output generated by the pose error input to the PID operation of the position loop is taken as one of the input of the speed ring. In order to maintain the consistency of the speed of the following robot and the virtual robot, the real-time speed of the virtual robot is taken as the expected input of the speed PID, and then the speed error is obtained by the feedback operation with the real-time speed of the following robot. After the operation of the speed PID, the final control input of the robot is obtained [8]. The core aim lof fuzzy PID is to dynamically adjust PID parameters through fuzzy control, avoid manual inaccurate tuning, and optimize PID parameters in the whole control process so as to improve control performance.

The control frame is shown in Fig. 2. The input of the fuzzy controller is error $e(t)$ and the rate of error change $e_c(t)$, and the output is K_p, K_i and K_d. Fuzzy PID can adaptively adjust PID parameters through fuzzy reasoning, reduce the workload of robot cluster parameter tuning, and continuously optimize the parameters during the control process, greatly improving the dynamic performance of the control system [9].

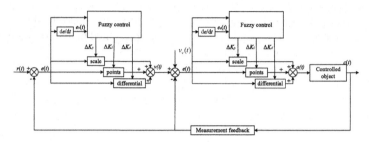

Fig. 2. Fuzzy position-velocity ring cascade PID structure

3 Artificial Potential Field Algorithm

3.1 Traditional APF Algorithm

The traditional Artificial Potential Field method (APF) is a path planning algorithm imitating the potential field. The target point has a gravitational pull on the robot, while the obstacle has a repulsive force on the robot. As shown in Fig. 3, along the combined force direction of the gravitational force and all the repulsive forces in the environment, Finally, the robot moves from the starting point with higher potential energy to the target point with lower potential energy [11].

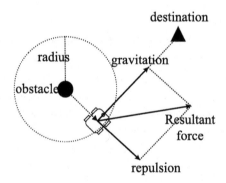

Fig. 3. APF principle

The artificial potential field consists of two parts: the gravitational field and the repulsive field:

$$U(q) = U_{attr}(q) + U_{rep}(q) \tag{5}$$

$U_{attr}(q)$ is the gravitational potential energy of the robot at point q;
$U_{req}(q)$ is the repulsive potential energy of the robot at the point;
$U(q)$ is the total potential energy of the robot at point q;
The gravitational field function and gravity of the robot at point q are:

$$U_{attr}(q) = \frac{1}{2}\lambda\rho^2(q, q_{goal}) \tag{6}$$

$$\rho(q, q_{goal}) = \left\| q - q_{goll} \right\|_2 \tag{7}$$

$$F_{attr}(q) = -\nabla U_{attr}(q) = -\lambda\rho(q, q_{goal}) \tag{8}$$

$$\nabla U_{attr} = \lambda\rho(q, q_{goal}) \tag{9}$$

where, λ is the gravitational coefficient; $\rho(q, q_{goal})$ is the distance between two points q and q_{goal}; $F_{attr\,(q)}$ is the robot's gravitational force at point q; The repulsive force field and repulsive force of the robot at point q are:

$$U_{rep}(q) = \begin{cases} \frac{1}{2}\eta(\frac{1}{\rho(q,q_{obst})} - \frac{1}{l_{thres}})^2 & \rho(q, q_{obst}) \leqslant l_{thres} \\ 0 & \rho(q, q_{obst}) > l_{thres} \end{cases} \tag{10}$$

$$F_{rep}(q) = -\nabla U_{rep}(q) = \begin{cases} -\eta(\frac{1}{\rho(q,q_{obst})} - \frac{1}{l_{thres}})\nabla\rho(q, q_{obst}) & \rho(q, q_{obst}) \leqslant l_{thres} \\ 0 & \rho(q, q_{obst}) > l_{thres} \end{cases} \tag{11}$$

where, l_{thres} is the influence range of the obstacle; q_{obst} is the current obstacle coordinate; The resultant force received by the robot at q point is:

$$F(q) = F_{attr}(q) + F_{rep}(q) \tag{12}$$

When there are multiple obstacles around the robot, the resultant force is the sum of multiple repulsion forces and gravitation forces:

$$F(q) = F_{attr}(q) + \sum_{i=0}^{N-1} F_{rep-i}(q) \tag{13}$$

The traditional APF algorithm has the following defects:

(1) Fall into local optimal solutions. For the dense concave obstacle area, the repulsive force of the robot may be balanced with the resultant force, and the robot wobbles in a small range in place and cannot escape.

(2) The target point is unreachable. When there is an obstacle near the target point, the repulsive force will be greater than the gravitational force, causing the robot to never reach the target point.

3.2 2D APF Convex Obstacle Model of LiDAR

At present, the research on APF algorithm focuses on simulation experiments, in which the obstacle model is simplified into centroid and influence radius model, while the physical robot senses the surrounding environment through LiDAR, and the observed data is the obstacle point cloud data. The deployment of APF algorithm needs to complete the conversion of the point cloud data to the obstacle [centroid, influence radius] in the environment. Secondly, considering that APF has the problem that the robot is trapped in the local optimal and cannot escape in the dense concave obstacle area, a 2D LiDAR scanning method of convex obstacle model is proposed in this section.

As shown in Fig. 4, if there is an obstacle in the robot detection range l, the measured distance value of laser data will be less than l, and this part of the point cloud is the obstacle point cloud. The algorithm will segment the obstacle point cloud to identify the obstacle outline. In the process of segmentation, it is necessary to determine the segmentation distance. When the distance between the contour of the obstacle is less than the diameter of the robot d, the robot cannot pass between the two obstacles, which does not meet the requirement of the segmentation distance, and the two obstacles will be merged into a whole obstacle. This processing method can also effectively deal with the measurement noise of laser point cloud data, and prevent the obstacle segmentation error caused by noise, which leads to the joint force mutation of the robot during operation and thus makes the robot jitter.

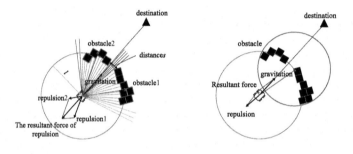

(a) Obstacle profile detection　　　　(b) Obstacle model building

Fig. 4. Obstacle model

After detecting the outline of the obstacle, the robot will build the center of mass and radius circle model of the obstacle. Particle O is selected as the obstacle centroid q on the ring with radius of detection range l, and the selection condition is that the distance r between the centroid and the boundary of both sides of the obstacle contour is equal. The solid circle with this particle as the center of the circle and r as the radius is the obstacle model. The subsequent repulsion force calculation is based on this model. The calculation method of obstacle radius r and centroid coordinates (x_q, y_q) is as follows:

$$\begin{cases} x_q^2 + y_q^2 = l^2 \\ (x_q - x_1)^2 + (y_q - y_1)^2 = (x_q - x_2)^2 + (y_q - y_2)^2 \\ r = \sqrt{(x_q - x_1)^2 + (y_q - y_1)^2} \end{cases} \tag{14}$$

where (x_1, y_1) and (x_2, y_2) are the coordinates of the two boundary points of the obstacle contour respectively, l is the probe radius of the robot.

This model can solve the local minimum problem of the traditional APF algorithm to some extent. For the densely concave region, as shown in Fig. 4 (a), the robot is trapped in the concave region formed by two obstacles and cannot escape because the repulsive force is equal to the gravitational force to form a local stable state. As shown in Fig. 4

(b), the obstacle model established is convex and circular, and the robot will not enter the concave area at all. The repulsive forces and gravitational forces cannot reach the stable state, and the robot will bypass the obstacle along the side of the obstacle.

The convex model ensures that the robot will not enter the concave obstacle area through which it is impossible to pass if the obstacle interval s is less than the robot diameter d. However, when the obstacle interval $s > d$, the two obstacles will still be modeled separately to form the concave obstacle area. The difference is that there must be space between the obstacles for the robot to pass. By improving the potential field function, the robot can pass smoothly.

3.3 Potential Field Function Improvement

Because the traditional artificial potential field method has problems of local optimal and unreachable target point, the potential field function needs to be reconstructed.

The improved repulsion field function is as follows:

$$
\begin{cases}
U_{rep}(q) = \begin{cases} \frac{1}{2}\eta(\frac{1}{\rho(q,q_{obst})-r_{obst}} - \frac{1}{l_{thres}})^2 \rho(q, q_{goal}) & \rho(q, q_{obst}) \leqslant l_{thres} \\ 0 & \rho(q, q_{obst}) > l_{thres} \end{cases} \\
l_{thres} > r_{obst} + r_{robot}
\end{cases}
\tag{15}
$$

The repulsive force on the robot at q point is simplified as follows:

$$
\begin{cases}
F_{rep}(q) = \begin{cases} -\nabla\rho(q, q_{obst})(F_1 + F_2) & \rho(q, q_{obst}) \leqslant l_{thres} \\ 0 & \rho(q, q_{obst}) > l_{thres} \end{cases} \\
F_1 = \eta\frac{\rho(q,q_{goal})}{[\rho(q,q_{obst})-r_{obst}]^2}(\frac{1}{\rho(q,q_{obst})-r_{obst}]} - \frac{1}{l_{thres}}) \\
F_2 = \eta\frac{1}{2}(\frac{1}{\rho(q,q_{obst})-r_{obst}} - \frac{1}{l_{thres}})^2
\end{cases}
\tag{16}
$$

where r_{obst} is the radius of obstacle in obstacle model, r_{robot} is the radius of robot, l_{thres} is the influence radius of the obstacle, which must be greater than the sum of r_{obst} and r_{robot} to ensure the safety of driving. $\rho(q, q_{goal})$ is the distance between two points of q and q_{goal}, $F_{rep}(q)$ is the repulsive force on the robot at point q; $U_{rep}(q)$ is the repulsive potential energy of the robot at point q.

The repulsion coefficient η is determined by debugging. The denominator $\rho(q, q_{obst})$ $-r_{obst}$ in $U_{rep}(q)$ will make the potential energy tend to infinity when the distance between the robot and the centroid of the obstacle approaches the radius of the obstacle, and the repulsion $F_{rep}(q)$ of the obstacle on the robot will also tend to infinity to prevent collision.

Secondly, the $\rho(q, q_{goal})$ factor is added to make the repulsion potential energy decrease as the robot approaches the target point so as to avoid the unreachable problem caused by repulsion preventing the robot from approaching the target point. The decrease trend is of the first order, which is weaker than the increase trend of repulsion potential energy towards infinity when the robot approaches the obstacle. It will not affect the collision protection function of the repulsion force.

The improved gravitational field function and gravity function are as follows:

$$
U_{attr}(q) = \frac{1}{2}(1 + \frac{K}{\gamma})\lambda\rho^2(q, q_{goal})
\tag{17}
$$

$$F_{attr}(q) = -\lambda(1 + \frac{K}{\gamma})\rho(q, q_{goal}) \tag{18}$$

Among them, the gravitational coefficient λ is determined by engineering debugging, and the actual value is 2.55. K is the number of times that the robot jitter occurs when it is trapped in the local optimum, which is updated in real time by the jitter detection unit. γ is the step coefficient. When the robot is trapped in the local optimal, the increasing of K will lead to the increasing gravitational force, which will destroy the local optimal equilibrium condition by strengthening the attractive effect of the target point on the robot. If $\gamma = 20$, the gravitational force will increase by 50% after 10 times of jitter, and γ determines the speed at which the robot escapes from the local optimal condition. In the actual experiment, under the premise of 50 Hz control frequency, $\gamma = 23$ is the optimal system state.

The principle of jitter detection is: The design of joint force and robot displacement detection window stores the latest 1 s robot joint force data and the displacement vector during each control cycle. Under the premise that the robot is subjected to repulsion and gravity at the same time, the jitter detection mechanism is opened, real-time statistics are made on the changes in the direction of the robot joint force and the changes in the direction and size of the displacement, and the 360° azimuth is divided into 20 equal parts. If there are more than 5 different situations in the direction of resultant force in the resultant force window and they are distributed in more than 2 quadrants, when the same situation occurs in the displacement direction of the displacement window, it is judged to be trapped in a local optimal situation, and K is added 1 for each subsequent occurrence, and it gradually returns to 0 after it deviates from the local optimal situation.

The traditional APF algorithm by increasing the gravitational effect in the local optimal may only cause the robot to constantly fall into the concave obstacle region or even cause collision, because there may be no narrow path for the robot to pass through in this region. However, the obstacle model proposed in this paper has a point cloud segmentation distance determination. If there is no path larger than the robot diameter in the concave obstacle region, the region will be divided into a convex circular obstacle model, and the robot will not fall into the region from the beginning. Conversely, if the local optimal situation occurs, the robot will not fall into the region. Then there must be a path with a width greater than the diameter of the robot in the concave area, and the robot will gradually escape along this path by increasing the gravitational action.

The improved algorithm is simulated by Matlab software. As shown in Fig. 5, the target point is surrounded by obstacles, red marks the normal trajectory of the robot, and blue marks the jitter trajectory. It can be seen from Eqs. 11 and 11 that the closer the traditional artificial potential field algorithm gets to the target point, the stronger the repulsive force is, the weaker the gravitational force is. As a result, when the robot is about to reach the target point, the repulsive effect is greater than the attracting effect and it cannot move forward. As can be seen from Formula 14 of the improved algorithm, when the repulsion is close to the target point, the repulsion will weaken simultaneously, and the robot can reach the target point normally.

As shown in Fig. 6, there are two concave obstacle areas in the map. There is a passable gap larger than the diameter of the robot in the first area at the lower left corner, while there is no large gap in the second area. Since the robot before improvement is

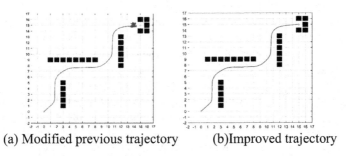

(a) Modified previous trajectory   (b)Improved trajectory

Fig. 5. Improvement of unreachable target point problem

trapped in the local optimal in the first region, the robot still cannot escape despite the existence of a passable path. After the improved algorithm falls into local optimal jitter for several times, it can be seen from Eq. 17 that the gravity gradually increases and the robot escapes from the first region. For the second concave region with no passable path, the robot regards it as a large convex obstacle model and makes obvious avoidance behavior to it. Instead of entering the second region, the robot successfully reaches the target point.

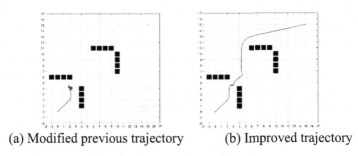

(a) Modified previous trajectory   (b) Improved trajectory

Fig. 6. Locally optimal defect improvement

4 Obstacle Avoidance Control Algorithm of Formation Based on PID and APF Fusion

In most studies of formation based on APF, the real-time control of formation is directly carried out by APF algorithm. At this time, the target point of formation is the robot target point in APF algorithm. As the leader moves, the target point of each robot formation moves accordingly, and the robots tend to the target due to gravitational pull and avoid obstacles along the way through repulsion. APF pays more attention to obstacle avoidance, and the maintenance of formation is an open-loop control, which can only obtain the direction of the path, but cannot strictly maintain the formation. PID is a closed-loop control for error. The algorithm adjusts the control output in reverse according to the error size, error rate of change and error integral, so that the size, change rate and integral of the formation error can approach 0. The error itself strictly converges to 0. Therefore, PID can better form the formation without obstacles.

The closed-loop formation control of PID can achieve strict formation maintenance. However, it does not have obstacle avoidance function, so it is necessary to combine APF algorithm to provide obstacle avoidance ability for the current formation algorithm.

As shown in Fig. 7, in the leader-follower mode, each follower has the corresponding formation target point in the team. When the robot is near the influence range of the obstacle, it is affected by the gravitational and repulsive forces, and the direction of the resultant force is calculated at this time. An obstacle avoidance displacement offset is applied to the original formation target point in the direction of the resultant force received by the robot, and a new formation target point away from the obstacle is obtained. The offset size T is calculated as follows:

$$T = \begin{cases} \delta F & r_{obst-min} + r_{robot} < \rho(q_{goal}', q_{obst-min}) \leqslant T_{max} \\ r_{obst-min} + r_{robot} - \rho(q_{goal}, q_{obst-min}) & \rho(q_{goal}', q_{obst-min}) \leqslant r_{obst-min} + r_{robot} \\ T_{max} & \rho(q_{goal}', q_{obst-min}) > T_{max} \end{cases}$$

(19)

$$T = \begin{cases} \delta F & r_{obst-min} + r_{robot} < \rho(q_{goal}', q_{obst-min}) \leqslant T_{max} \\ r_{obst-min} + r_{robot} - \rho(q_{goal}, q_{obst-min}) & \rho(q_{goal}', q_{obst-min}) \leqslant r_{obst-min} + r_{robot} \\ T_{max} & \rho(q_{goal}', q_{obst-min}) > T_{max} \end{cases}$$

(20)

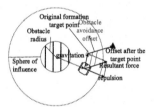

Fig. 7. Obstacle avoidance offset principle

where, δ is the offset coefficient and F is the resultant force size; $r_{obst-min}$ is the radius of the nearest obstacle, and r_{robot} is the radius of the robot; $\rho(q_{goal}', q_{obst-min})$ indicates the distance between the target point and the nearest obstacle after migration. T_{max} indicates the maximum offset value, which is determined after debugging.

5 Experimental Test and Analysis

In this section, the proposed algorithm is tested and the results are analyzed on the real machine platform of McNamum Wheel robots. The multi-robots system is based on FreeRTOS, Linux, ROS software development environment and real-time control of hardware platforms such as STM32 and Raspberry PI 4B. It communication is carried out through local area network, and experiments such as formation and maintenance of robot cluster formation and obstacle avoidance are carried out to test the performance of the algorithm in this paper.

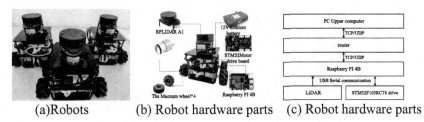

(a)Robots   (b) Robot hardware parts   (c) Robot hardware parts

Fig. 8. Robot hardware

As shown in Fig. 8(a), the main body size of the robot is 12 cm long, 14 cm wide and 16 cm high, the chassis of the driving wheel is 23 cm long and 15 cm wide, and the weight is 2.36 kg. The robot components and system hardware frame are respectively shown in Fig. 8(b) and 8(c). The experimental scenario is a rectangular experimental field with a length of 5.0 m and a width of 4.0 m. The paper box enclosure scheme is adopted, and there is no gap around the environment, and the layout of internal obstacles varies with the experiment content. The experimental field used in this experiment is shown in Fig. 9.

APF and fuzzy PID formation control were respectively conducted in triangular formation. The experimental environment is shown in Fig. 9(a). The Z-axis heading Angle error is multiplied by 0.25 and then the plot is drawn. Figure 9(a)(b) Fuzzy PID formation keeping error is much smaller than APF algorithm.

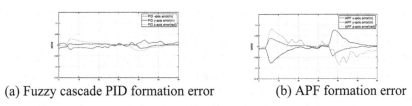

(a) Fuzzy cascade PID formation error   (b) APF formation error

Fig. 9. Robot hardware

The trajectory of the robot in the field is shown in Fig. 10 (b). The trajectory of the leader robot1 walking a rounded rectangle is shown in the red line in the figure, the trajectory of robot2 is green, and the trajectory of robot3 is blue. In this experiment, the maximum X-axis formation error amplitude of robot2 is 0.048 m, the maximum Y-axis formation error value is 0.03 m and the maximum Z-axis formation error value is 0.04 rad. The maximum X-axis formation error of robot3 is 0.026 m, the maximum Y-axis formation error is 0.019 m, and the maximum Z-axis formation error is 0.045 rad. In summary, the error values of the robot speed curve are controlled within 0.05, and the error rate is 10.8% at the formation interval of 0.5 m.

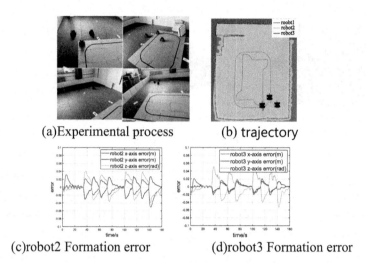

(a)Experimental process   (b) trajectory

(c)robot2 Formation error   (d)robot3 Formation error

Fig. 10. Triangular formation rectangular trajectory experiment

As shown in Fig. 11(a), the horizontal obstacle formation is set up with a length of 0.5 m, a width of 0.1 m and a height of 0.4 m, and the space between the two obstacles is 0.8 m. In the face of large obstructions, the robot can still normally avoid obstacles and restore the formation. During the experiment, the maximum error amplitude of robot2x and Y-axis formation is 0.043 m, and the maximum error amplitude of Z-axis formation is 0.01 rad, and the maximum error amplitude of robot3 Xand Y-axis formation is 0.05 m, and the maximum error amplitude of Z-axis formation is 0.02 rad.

In the artificial potential field algorithm, there are overlapping holes in the area of obstacle potential energy influence, resulting in chaotic potential energy distribution in the environment, and the robot cannot walk out of the obstacle area in this case. This experiment verifies whether the formation obstacle avoidance algorithm proposed in this paper can cope with the complex environment. As shown in Fig. 12, obstacles in the field vary in size, the distance between obstacles is 0.5 m to 1 m, and the formation distance between robot formation is 0.5 m. As shown in Fig. 12, in the multi-obstacle area, the robot formation can smoothly pass through the obstacle area while maintaining the formation as much as possible, and restore the original formation after passing.

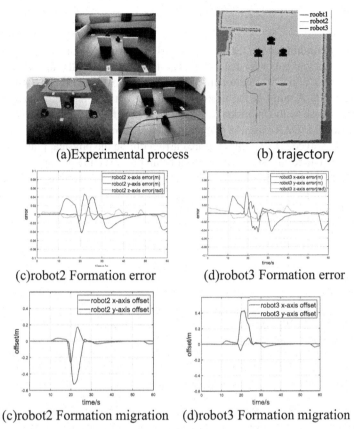

(a)Experimental process   (b) trajectory

(c)robot2 Formation error   (d)robot3 Formation error

(c)robot2 Formation migration   (d)robot3 Formation migration

Fig. 11. Obstacle avoidance by horizontal obstacle formation

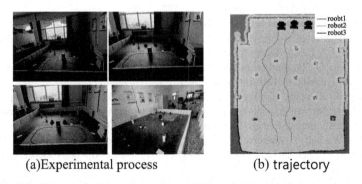

(a)Experimental process   (b) trajectory

Fig. 12. Obstacle avoidance experiment of formation in complex obstacle area

6 Conclusion

In this paper, a combination of fuzzy cascade PID and artificial potential field is designed to avoid obstacles in robot formation. 1) The fuzzy cascade PID algorithm is used to solve the problem of poor formation maintenance in formation method based on artificial potential field. 2) Aiming at the problems of local optimal and unreachable target in obstacle avoidance with traditional artificial potential field method, the reconstructed two-dimensional LiDAR obstacle judgment model and modified potential field function are effectively solved. 3) Experiments are carried out on the physical platform of multi-robots system. The results show that the algorithm proposed in this paper can effectively maintain formation and can effectively avoid obstacles under various scenarios.

Acknowledgments. This work is supported by the National Natural Science Foundation of China under Grant No.62372131.

References

1. Koo, T.J., Shahruz, S.M.: Formation of a group of unmanned aerial vehicles (UAVs). In: Proceedings of the 2001 American Control Conference (Cat. No. 01CH37148), vol. 1, pp. 69–74. IEEE (2001)
2. Xu, J.: Research on mobile robot formation control based on consistency algorithm. Wuhan University of Technology (2020). https://doi.org/10.27381/d.cnki.gwlgu.2020.000162
3. Desai, J.P., Ostrowski, J.P., Kumar, V.: Modeling and control of formations of nonholonomic mobile robots. IEEE Trans. Robot. Autom. **17**(6), 905–908 (2001)
4. Sun, Y., Yang, H., Yu, M.: Research on finite time consistency control of multi robot systems based on navigation following. Complex Syst. Complexity Sci. **17**(04), 66–72+84 (2020). https://doi.org/10.13306/j.1672-3813.2020.04.008 [Desai, 2001 #112]
5. Wu, J., Xiao, Y., Huo, J.: Formation control of multiple robots in uncertain environments research. Comput. Appl. Res. **38**(4), 1123–1127 (2021)
6. Kowdiki, K.H., Barai, R.K., Bhattacharya, S.: A hybrid system simulation for formation control of wheeled mobile robots: an application of artificial potential field and kinematic controller. Int. J. Eng. Technol. Sci. Res. **4**(11), 247–258 (2017)
7. Lei, S., Lv, Q.: Formation and obstacle avoidance of multiple robots based on artificial potential field method. Lett. Inf. Syst. Eng. (3), 139–142, 145 (2020)
8. Ruifang, S., Xiaolong, Z., Wenkai, L., Xiaoquan, X.: Speed feedback and incomplete differential PID control of pneumatic proportional position system. Electron. Sci. Technol. **33**(04), 65–70 (2020). https://doi.org/10.16180/j.cnki.issn1007-7820.2020.04.012
9. Shuyan, W., Shi, Y., Zhongxu, F.: Research on control methods based on fuzzy PID controllers. Mech. Sci. Technol. **30**(01), 166–172 (2011). https://doi.org/10.13433/j.cnki.1003-8728.2011.01.035
10. Li, X., Xiao, J.: Robot formation control in leader-follower motion using direct Lyapunov method. Int. J. Intell. Control Syst. **10**(3), 244–250 (2005)

11. Li, Y., Tian, B., Yang, Y., Li, C.: Path planning of robot based on artificial potential field method. In: 2022 IEEE 6th Information Technology and Mechatronics Engineering Conference (ITOEC), Chongqing, China, pp. 91–94 (2022). https://doi.org/10.1109/ITOEC53115.2022.9734712
12. He, N., Su, Y., Guo, J., Fan, X., Liu, Z., Wang, B.: Dynamic path planning of mobile robot based on artificial potential field. In: 2020 International Conference on Intelligent Computing and Human-Computer Interaction (ICHCI), Sanya, China, pp. 259–264 (2020). https://doi.org/10.1109/ICHCI51889.2020.00063

A Multi-stage Network with Self-attention for Tooth Instance Segmentation

Yongcun Zhang, Zhiming Luo$^{(\boxtimes)}$, and Shaozi Li

Department of Artificial Intelligence, Xiamen University, Xiamen 361005, China
{zhiming.luo,szlig}@xmu.edu.cn

Abstract. Automatic and accurate instance segmentation of teeth from 3D Cone-Beam Computer Tomography (CBCT) images is crucial for dental diagnose. Although Convolutional Neural Networks (CNNs) are widely used for tooth instance segmentation, the limitations of CNNs in capturing global image information can impact model performance. Recently, Transformer models leveraging the Self-Attention mechanism have exhibited exceptional capabilities in modeling global relationships in images. In this paper, we propose a fully automated tooth instance segmentation model utilizing the Self-Attention mechanism. The model is primarily based on the Self-Attention UNETR++ network and consists of three stages. In the first stage, a V-Net is employed to identify the region of interest (ROI) containing the teeth. In the second stage, a multitask UNETR++ network is utilized to extract the centroid and skeleton of the teeth. In the third stage, another multitask UNETR++ is employed to simultaneously learn the tooth mask and boundary, leading to accurate tooth instance segmentation. Experimental results on a dataset consisting of 98 CBCT images demonstrate the efficacy of our method. It achieves a Dice score of 95.1% and reduces the average surface distance (ASD) to 0.14 mm.

Keywords: Tooth segmentation · Self-Attention · CBCT image

1 Introduction

Currently, there is an increasing demand for dental health. Dental health issues mainly include dental diseases, dental implants, orthodontics. Although the growing number of patients seeking dental diagnoses contributed to the rapid development of the dental healthcare market, there is a significant shortage of dentists per million population, which poses a substantial burden on dentists. In clinical diagnosis, Cone Beam Computer Tomography (CBCT) is widely utilized for acquiring high-resolution 3D images of teeth, thereby offering accurate representations of dental crowns, roots, and bones. Additionally, CBCT offers the advantages of low Radiation exposure and short scanning time. On the other hand, the voxel information in CBCT images is highly complex, necessitating extensive manual segmentation to extract vital information. Therefore, this process becomes time-consuming and labor-intensive for clinicians and researchers.

© The Author(s), under exclusive license to Springer Nature Singapore Pte Ltd. 2024
Y. Sun et al. (Eds.): ChineseCSCW 2023, CCIS 2013, pp. 438–450, 2024.
https://doi.org/10.1007/978-981-99-9640-7_32

Thus, the development of digital dentistry and fully automated tooth segmentation methods is crucial for tooth analysis from 3D CBCT scans.

Computer vision technology has found widespread applications in the field of medical imaging. Driven by computer vision technology, digital oral cavity is rapidly developing. Automatic tooth segmentation is a primary step for tooth image analysis, and has attracted more and more research attention. Existing tooth instance segmentation methods can be categorized into two types: traditional methods and deep learning-based methods. Traditional methods, such as level set [1,14,15,20], graph cut [18,21], and template fitting [2,29]. However, these method rely on manually designed features, which are highly sensitive to complex dental situations, requiring tedious manual initialization and correction. They often lead to suboptimal segmentation performance in complicated cases. Deep learning methods, on the other hand, are known for their automatic feature extraction, strong adaptability, and high accuracy. They have been widely adopted in medical image segmentation.

Deep learning-based tooth instance segmentation methods [7–12,19,22,31] generally achieve better performance than traditional methods. However, nearly all deep learning-based methods rely on convolutional neural networks (CNNs) to extract features from CBCT images and achieve tooth detection and segmentation. None of these methods introduce attention mechanisms. CNNs' limitations in obtaining global image information to some extent lower the model's performance. Overcoming these limitations and improving the performance of tooth segmentation models pose challenging tasks. The widespread application of Transformers [5,13,25,33] indicates that Self-Attention can effectively obtain global information of images. This makes the model based on the Self-Attention mechanism have certain advantages in the field of image segmentation. In recent years, several outstanding neural networks using Self-Attention mechanisms [4,6,16,32,34] have emerged in the medical image segmentation field. Therefore, this paper aims to construct a fully automatic tooth instance segmentation method incorporating Self-Attention mechanisms.

Inspired by the above work, we propose a fully automated tooth instance segmentation model that utilizes the Self-Attention mechanism. The model has three stages: First, we use V-Net [24] to extract tooth ROI. Next, we use a multi-task UNETR++ network [28] to predict the centroids and skeletons of teeth. This step localizes teeth, detects tooth shapes, and represents teeth. Finally, we further segment teeth within the tooth ROIs using the multi-task UNETR++ network. By combining the centroids and skeletons of teeth, we achieve tooth instance segmentation. To evaluate the performance of our method, our fully automatic tooth segmentation achieved a Dice similarity coefficient of 95.1% and an Average Surface Distance of 0.14mm in tooth segmentation.

In summary, the main contribution of this study are as follows:

1. We propose a multi-stage model that is capable of fully automatic tooth instance segmentation on input 3D CBCT images.

2. By introducing a self attention mechanism, we have effectively improved the segmentation accuracy of our model which surpasses the performance of other comparative models.
3. By using multitasking learning, we successfully reduced the error in tooth surface segmentation while maintaining a high level of mask segmentation accuracy.
4. By evaluating our model with other CNN based models through experiments, we have demonstrated that introducing self attention mechanism can improve the performance of tooth segmentation models.

2   Related Work

Tooth Segmentation Based on Deep Learning. Inspired by 3D Mask R-CNN [17], Cui et al. [11] introduced ToothNet, an automatic tooth instance segmentation method in CBCT images. ToothNet employs 3D Region Proposal Network (RPN) [26] for tooth detection, recognition, and segmentation. Chung et al. [8] proposed the PATRCNN+TSNet method, which addressing metal artifacts in CBCT images using pose-aware techniques. Chen et al. [7] presented 3D FCN+MWT, a method that combines deep learning and traditional methods. They utilized a multi-task 3D fully convolutional network (FCN) to simultaneously predict tooth masks and surfaces. They then employed marker-controlled watershed transform (MWT) for tooth recognition and segmentation. Wu et al. [31] incorporated a center-sensitive mechanism into their method to guide tooth localization, thus avoiding the computational burden of numerous anchors generated by RPN in 3D CBCT images. Additionally, they employed DenseASPP-UNet for tooth segmentation and added boundary loss to reduce prediction errors on tooth boundaries. Jang et al. [19] proposed PanoramicNet, a novel tooth instance segmentation method. This method first expands the 3D tooth image into a 2D Panorama by calculating the dental arch curve. Then, it detects the teeth on the 2D Panorama images and completes instance segmentation by combining the 2D and 3D results. To address the diverse and complex tooth morphologies and reduce computational complexity, Cui et al. [12] extended their previous work [11] and introduced Hierarchical Morphology-Guided Network (HMGNet). The HMGNet utilizes tooth centroids to represent tooth positions and introduced tooth skeletons to depict the tooth's morphological structure, which can significantly enhance tooth segmentation accuracy in complex cases.

Self-attention. The Self-Attention mechanism calculates the similarities between different positions in the input sequence, assigns weights to each position, and then uses these weights to compute the output for each position. Specifically, given an input sequence X, it first performs linear transformations to obtain three matrices Q, K, V. Next, it calculates the similarity matrix QK^T by taking the dot product of each row vector in matrix Q and matrix K. Finally,

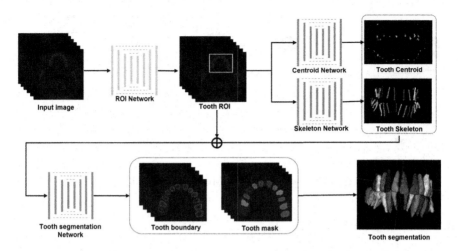

Fig. 1. The overall architecture of our method for fully automatic tooth instance segmentation.

these similarities are normalized into a probability distribution using the softmax function. The result is multiplied with matrix V to obtain the Self-Attention representation [30]:

$$\text{Attention}(Q, K, V) = \text{softmax}\left(\frac{QK^T}{\sqrt{d_k}}\right) \times V, \tag{1}$$

where d_k represents the dimension of the key vector for stabilizing the learning process. Self-Attention allows the model to capture long-range dependencies and global information from the input sequence, which can lead to improved performance in various tasks. In this paper, we introduce the Self-Attention mechanism in tooth instance segmentation for improving the accuracy.

3   Method

The overall architecture of our method for fully automatic tooth instance segmentation is shown in Fig. 1, which mainly consists of three stages. In the first stage, V-Net [24] is employed for coarse binary segmentation of teeth to obtain the teeth Region of Interest (ROI). In the second stage, a muti-task UNETR++ is used to extract teeth centroids and skeletons. These provide a rough representation of the morphological structure of teeth. The third stage involves utilizing an another muti-task UNETR++ for tooth segmentation with the guidance of the tooth skeleton. This stage simultaneously generates teeth masks and boundaries.

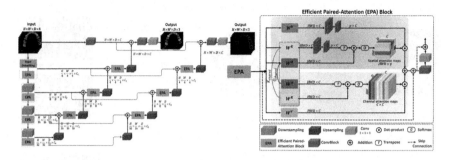

Fig. 2. The architecture of Multi-task UNETR++.

3.1 Multi-task UNETR++

In this paper, the multi-task UNETR++ is employed as the backbone network for tooth instance segmentation. As depicted in Fig. 2, the network follows a hierarchical Encoder-Decoder structure. To process the input 3D image, it is first converted into 3D patches using Patch Embedding [13]. Given an input image $X \in R^{H \times W \times D}$, it is partitioned into patches of resolution (P_h, P_w, P_d), resulting in feature maps of size $\frac{H}{P_h} \times \frac{W}{P_w} \times \frac{D}{P_d} \times C$. Throughout the experiments, a patch size of $(4, 4, 4)$ is utilized. The designed multi-task UNETR++ introduces an additional decoder for the achieving the multi-tasks, such as tooth mask segmentation and tooth boundary estimation. Both decoders use skip connections to obtain feature maps from the encoder at each layer.

The core design of UNETR++ is the Efficient Pairwise Attention (EPA) blocks. It can effectively learn spatial and channel features through a pair of interdependent branches based on spatial and channel attention [28]. According to Eq. 1, spatial and channel attention can be calculated:

$$A_s = Attention(Q_{shared}, K_{spatial}, V_{spatial})$$
$$A_c = Attention(Q_{shared}, K_{shared}, V_{channel}) \tag{2}$$

In the spatial attention, $V_{spatial}(HWD \times C)$ and $K_{shared}(HWD \times C)$ are linearly projected into low-dimensional matrices $V_{spatial}(p \times C)$ and $K_{spatial}(p \times C)$, respectively. To facilitate communication between the branches of spatial and channel attention, the weights of the query and key mapping functions are shared, achieving Paired-Attention. This operation also reduces the total number of network parameters. Finally, the spatial attention map and channel attention map are fused through convolutional operations:

$$X = Conv_1(Conv_3(A_s + A_c)). \tag{3}$$

The $Conv3$ represents a convolutional block with a $3 \times 3 \times 3$ kernel size, while $Conv1$ represents a convolutional block with a $1 \times 1 \times 1$ kernel size.

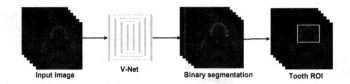

Fig. 3. Computing the ROI of teeth from 3D CBCT image.

3.2 Obtaining ROI of Teeth

The first step for the input 3D CBCT image is to obtain the Region of Interest (ROI) containing teeth. This step can reduce the computational workload for the subsequent tooth centroid and skeleton extraction phase, as well as the segmentation phase. Moreover, it has the potential to improving the overall segmentation accuracy. The specific pipeline of this step is illustrated in Fig. 3. V-Net is used to perform binary segmentation of the image (without distinguishing individual teeth), resulting in the tooth's foreground region. Then, the tooth ROI can be computed from this foreground region.

In order to accurately compute the ROI, the loss function used for training in this step is the combination of the Dice loss and the Cross-Entropy loss.

$$L_{s1} = L_{seg} = \alpha \cdot L_{dice} + (1 - \alpha) \cdot L_{ce}, \tag{4}$$

where

$$L_{dice} = 1 - \frac{2 \sum_{i=1}^{N} p_i q_i + \epsilon}{\sum_{i=1}^{N} p_i^2 + \sum_{i=1}^{N} q_i^2 + \epsilon}, \tag{5}$$

$$L_{ce} = -\frac{1}{N} \sum_{i=1}^{N} \left(q_i \log\left(p_i\right) + (1 - q_i) \log\left(1 - p_i\right) \right). \tag{6}$$

Here, p_i represents the value of the i-th voxel in the predicted result, q_i represents the value of the i-th voxel in the ground truth label, and ϵ is a very small number used to prevent division by zero.

3.3 Extraction of Teeth Centroids and Skeletons

The tooth centroid helps determine the tooth's position and instantiate its label, while the tooth skeleton provides an approximate representation of the tooth's morphological structure. By combining the centroid and skeleton information, they can provide guidance for the tooth instance segmentation. The process of this step is illustrated in Fig. 4.

The 3D image is processed by two UNETR++ sub-networks, each containing two decoders. One decoder predicts the binary segmentation map, while the other predicts the 3D offset map. The centroid offset map represents the offset between each voxel and its corresponding tooth centroid, while the skeleton offset is the offset between each voxel and the nearest point on the tooth skeleton.

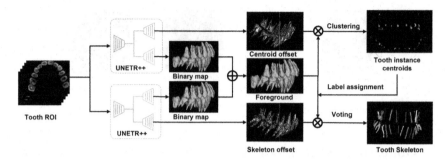

Fig. 4. Extract the centroid and skeleton of teeth

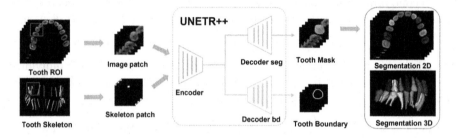

Fig. 5. Complete instance segmentation of teeth

By adding the tooth centroid offset vector to the current foreground voxel coordinates, the tooth centroid density map is obtained. After obtaining the tooth centroid density map, a clustering method [27] is applied to cluster the tooth centroid density map to get tooth instance centroid labels. These labels are then mapped onto the tooth foreground, resulting in instance-level tooth foreground images. Similarly, by using the tooth foreground and skeleton offset vector maps together in the clustering operation, the final instance-level teeth skeleton labels are obtained.

In this step, the loss function considers both the tooth mask segmentation and the tooth centroid or skeleton parts,

$$L_{s2} = L_{seg} + L_{cs}, \tag{7}$$

where L_{seg} represents the loss for tooth mask segmentation, which combines Dice loss and Cross-Entropy loss. L_{cs} represents the loss for tooth centroid or skeleton, using L1 Loss.

3.4   Tooth Instance Segmentation

The final step for tooth instance segmentation is illustrated in Fig. 5. After obtaining the tooth ROI and tooth skeleton, each individual tooth can be cropped around its centroid. The cropped tooth, along with its skeleton, is then concatenated and used as the input to the multi-task UNETR++ model. The model's output simultaneously predicts tooth masks and tooth boundaries, aiming to maintain accurate tooth segmentation while minimizing errors in tooth surface segmentation.

The loss function for individual tooth segmentation considers both tooth mask segmentation (L_{seg}) and tooth boundary segmentation (L_b):

$$L_{s3} = \lambda L_{seg} + \mu L_b. \tag{8}$$

Here, L_{seg} represents the loss for tooth mask segmentation, which combines Dice loss and Cross-Entropy loss. L_b represents the loss for tooth boundary segmentation, using L2 Loss. In the experiments, $\lambda = 0.6$ and $\mu = 0.1$.

4   Experiments

4.1   Experimental Setup

Dataset. We evaluate the performance of our method on the tooth dataset from [9]. This dataset consists of 100 three-dimensional CBCT images of teeth. After excluding two cases where the tooth images did not match the corresponding annotation labels, we were left with 98 valid data cases. Throughout the experiments, the complete dataset was randomly split into 70 cases for training, 8 samples for validation, and 20 samples for testing.

Data Preprocessing. First, we normalize each CBCT image to the range [0, 1]. The specific data preprocessing at different stages is as follows. (1) Obtaining tooth ROI: Due to the limitations of GPU memory, the input tooth CBCT images are randomly cropped to a size of $256 \times 256 \times 256$. (2) Extracting tooth centroids and skeletons: The tooth centroid uses the center of the tooth label. The distance-transform-based algorithm is used to obtain the tooth skeleton [23], which iteratively removes voxels from the binary mask until the skeleton is extracted. After that, the tooth image, tooth label, and tooth skeleton are randomly cropped to a size of $128 \times 128 \times 128$ for training. (3) Tooth instance segmentation: The tooth boundaries are computed by the Canny edge detection algorithm [3] on each 2D CT slice of the 3D CBCT image.

Implementation Details. The experiments were conducted using the PyTorch framework and a GeForce RTX 3090 GPU. The batch sizes for the three stages are 1, 1, and 4. The initial learning rates are set to 0.001, 0.001, and 0.0001 for the three stages. A polynomial learning rate decay strategy is used, which continuously decreases the learning rate during training. The Adam optimizer with a weight decay of 0.0001 is used for optimization. The number of iterations for the three stages are set as 30k, 60k, and 50k, respectively.

Evaluation Metrics. In this study, multiple metrics are used to assess the accuracy and surface error of the segmentation model, including Dice similarity coefficient (DSC), Jaccard Index, Average Surface Distance (ASD), Sensitivity (Sen), and Hausdorff distance (HD).

Table 1. Comparison of segmentation accuracy with other models.

Models	DSC(%)	Jaccard(%)	ASD (mm)	HD(mm)
MWTNet [7]	89.6 ± 1.2	82.5 ± 1.7	0.36 ± 0.14	4.82 ± 1.68
ToothNet [11]	91.9 ± 1.3	84.2 ± 1.8	0.30 ± 0.11	2.82 ± 1.02
CGDNet [31]	93.9 ± 0.9	89.2 ± 0.7	0.27 ± 0.03	1.99 ± 0.78
HMGNet [12]	94.8 ± 0.4	89.1 ± 0.9	0.18 ± 0.02	1.52 ± 0.28
Ours	**95.1 ± 0.3**	**90.8 ± 0.5**	**0.13 ± 0.02**	**1.39 ± 0.24**

4.2   Experimental Results

Comparison with Other Methods. In order to validate the segmentation performance of the proposed fully automatic tooth segmentation model based on UNETR++, we conducted comparison experiments with state-of-the-art (SOTA) methods for tooth instance segmentation based on CNN. These methods include MWTNet [7] based on 3D-FCN, ToothNet [11] based on 3D RPN, CGDNet [31] which utilizes tooth center guidance and DenseASPP-UNet, as well as HMGNet [12] based on tooth center and skeleton guidance, and V-Net.

In Table 1, we can see that our model can achieve a Dice Similarity Coefficient (DSC) of 95.1% and a Jaccard index (Jaccard) of 90.8%. These values are higher than other comparison methods, which indicates that our model performs the best in terms of accuracy for tooth segmentation. Additionally, our model also shows the smallest values of Average Surface Distance (ASD) and Hausdorff Distance (HD), which are 0.14 mm and 1.39 mm, respectively. These results prove that the proposed fully automatic tooth instance segmentation method based on UNETR++ not only exhibits higher overall similarity in tooth segmentation, but also performs better in tooth edge segmentation.

To summarize, the tooth segmentation model based on UNETR++ proposed in this study outperforms existing tooth instance segmentation models. This is attributed to the introduction of Self-Attention, which allows the model to easily capture the global information from 3D CBCT images. Additionally, tooth centroids and tooth skeletons contribute to the coarse description of teeth and help improve the accuracy of our model. And the high segmentation accuracy achieved for both tooth masks and tooth edges proves that multi-task learning has shown significant effectiveness.

Ablation Experiment. To better investigate the effectiveness of the proposed UNETR++-based tooth instance segmentation model, we conducted ablation experiments while keeping all other experimental conditions the same. In these experiments, the main backbone networks for all three stages were replaced with V-Net as a baseline, and then UNETR++ was used in the second and third stages and compared with the original model. The results are shown in Table 2.

Table 2 shows that using UNETR++ in both the second and third stages led to improvements in the model's performance. Replacing the network for tooth

Table 2. The performance of replacing the UNETR++ with V-Net.

Models	DSC(%)	Jaccard(%)	ASD(mm)	Sen(%)
VNet(s1,s2,s3)	93.7	88.2	0.21	95.8
VNet(s1,s3) + UNETR++(s2)	93.9	88.6	0.18	**96.6**
VNet(s1,s2) + UNETR++(s3)	94.8	90.1	0.13	94.9
VNet(s1) + UNETR++(s2,s3)(Proposed)	**95.1**	**90.8**	**0.13**	96.1

centroid and skeleton extraction with multi-task UNETR++ in the second stage resulted in a 0.2% increase in DSC and a 0.3 mm reduction in ASD. In the third stage, replacing the network for tooth segmentation with multi-task UNETR++ led to a 1.1% increase in DSC and a 0.8 mm reduction in ASD. Lastly, replacing the backbone networks for both the second and third stages with multi-task UNETR++ resulted in a 1.4% increase in DSC and a 0.8 mm reduction in ASD.

These results indicate that the utilization of the UNETR++ network with Self-Attention mechanism in this study significantly improved the tooth segmentation performance compared to the V-Net based CNN tooth segmentation model. This is because in 3D CBCT images, the morphology and positions of teeth are quite complex, and the images themselves contain massive amounts of information. Therefore, obtaining the global information of the images can help improve the model's performance. The introduction of the Self-Attention mechanism in UNETR++ allows for the effective capture of the global information from 3D CBCT images. The EPA (Efficient Pairwise Attention) blocks play a key role in this process.

5   Conclusion and Future Work

In this paper, we investigate a tooth segmentation method for 3D CBCT images. We use UNETR++ as the backbone network due to its low parameter count, low computational requirements, and state-of-the-art performance in medical image segmentation. We establish a fully automated tooth instance segmentation approach. It begins by obtaining the tooth's Region of Interest (ROI) using V-Net. Subsequently, it represents the tooth's morphological structure coarsely by predicting tooth centroids and tooth skeletons. These centroids and skeletons are then used to guide the tooth instance segmentation process. As a result, the fully automated tooth instance segmentation method developed in this paper outperforms other tooth segmentation methods in terms of both tooth instance segmentation accuracy and tooth boundary segmentation error on CBCT images. This also indicates that using a network with Self-Attention mechanisms can achieve excellent segmentation results in tooth segmentation.

Although our method can outperform other comparison methods, some limitations still exist in this research: (1) Despite UNETR++ being a lightweight model with fewer parameters and computational requirements, the training time is still longer than that of simple CNN networks. (2) The model requires multiple steps to provide guidance for the final segmentation, which necessitates training multiple networks independently for each step. Future work can be focused on the following directions: (1) Researching even lighter segmentation networks or performing data preprocessing to speed up the training process. (2) Refining the model to combine tasks such as obtaining tooth ROI, tooth centroids, tooth skeletons, and tooth masks into a single stage, achieving tooth instance segmentation in a one-stage process. By addressing these limitations and exploring new approaches, the tooth segmentation method can be further improved and applied more effectively in clinical settings.

References

1. Akhoondali, H., Zoroofi, R., Shirani, G.: Rapid automatic segmentation and visualization of teeth in CT-scan data. J. Appl. Sci. **9**(11), 2031–2044 (2009)
2. Barone, S., Paoli, A., Razionale, A.V.: Ct segmentation of dental shapes by anatomy-driven reformation imaging and b-spline modelling. Int. J. Numer. Method. Biomed. Eng. **32**(6), e02747 (2016)
3. Canny, J.: A computational approach to edge detection. IEEE Trans. Pattern Anal. Mach. Intell. **PAMI-8**(6), 679–698 (1986)
4. Cao, H., et al.: Swin-UNet: Unet-like pure transformer for medical image segmentation. In: Karlinsky, L., Michaeli, T., Nishino, K. (eds.) ECCV 2022. LNCS, vol. 13803, pp. 205–218. Springer, Cham (2022). https://doi.org/10.1007/978-3-031-25066-8_9
5. Carion, N., Massa, F., Synnaeve, G., Usunier, N., Kirillov, A., Zagoruyko, S.: End-to-end object detection with transformers. In: Vedaldi, A., Bischof, H., Brox, T., Frahm, J.-M. (eds.) ECCV 2020. LNCS, vol. 12346, pp. 213–229. Springer, Cham (2020). https://doi.org/10.1007/978-3-030-58452-8_13
6. Chen, J., et al.: Transunet: transformers make strong encoders for medical image segmentation. arXiv preprint arXiv:2102.04306 (2021)
7. Chen, Y., et al.: Automatic segmentation of individual tooth in dental CBCT images from tooth surface map by a multi-task FCN. IEEE Access **8**, 97296–97309 (2020)
8. Chung, M., et al.: Pose-aware instance segmentation framework from cone beam CT images for tooth segmentation. Comput. Biol. Med. **120**, 103720 (2020)
9. Cui, Z., et al.: A fully automatic AI system for tooth and alveolar bone segmentation from cone-beam CT images. Nat. Commun. **13**(1), 2096 (2022)
10. Cui, Z., et al.: Tsegnet: an efficient and accurate tooth segmentation network on 3D dental model. Med. Image Anal. **69**, 101949 (2021)
11. Cui, Z., Li, C., Wang, W.: Toothnet: automatic tooth instance segmentation and identification from cone beam CT images. In: Proceedings of the IEEE/CVF Conference on Computer Vision and Pattern Recognition, pp. 6368–6377 (2019)
12. Cui, Z., et al.: Hierarchical morphology-guided tooth instance segmentation from CBCT images. In: Feragen, A., Sommer, S., Schnabel, J., Nielsen, M. (eds.) IPMI 2021. LNCS, vol. 12729, pp. 150–162. Springer, Cham (2021). https://doi.org/10.1007/978-3-030-78191-0_12
13. Dosovitskiy, A., et al.: An image is worth 16x16 words: transformers for image recognition at scale. arXiv preprint arXiv:2010.11929 (2020)
14. Gan, Y., Xia, Z., Xiong, J., Zhao, Q., Hu, Y., Zhang, J.: Toward accurate tooth segmentation from computed tomography images using a hybrid level set model. Med. Phys. **42**(1), 14–27 (2015)

15. Gao, H., Chae, O.: Individual tooth segmentation from CT images using level set method with shape and intensity prior. Pattern Recogn. **43**(7), 2406–2417 (2010)

16. Hatamizadeh, A., Nath, V., Tang, Y., Yang, D., Roth, H.R., Xu, D.: Swin UNETR: swin transformers for semantic segmentation of brain tumors in MRI images. In: Crimi, A., Bakas, S. (eds.) BrainLes 2021. LNCS, vol. 12962, pp. 272–284. Springer, Cham (2021). https://doi.org/10.1007/978-3-031-08999-2_22

17. He, K., Gkioxari, G., Dollár, P., Girshick, R.: Mask R-CNN. In: Proceedings of the IEEE International Conference on Computer Vision, pp. 2961–2969 (2017)

18. Hiew, L., Ong, S., Foong, K.W., Weng, C.: Tooth segmentation from cone-beam CT using graph cut. In: Proceedings of the Second APSIPA Annual Summit and Conference, pp. 272–275. ASC, Singapore (2010)

19. Jang, T.J., Kim, K.C., Cho, H.C., Seo, J.K.: A fully automated method for 3D individual tooth identification and segmentation in dental CBCT. IEEE Trans. Pattern Anal. Mach. Intell. **44**(10), 6562–6568 (2021)

20. Ji, D.X., Ong, S.H., Foong, K.W.C.: A level-set based approach for anterior teeth segmentation in cone beam computed tomography images. Comput. Biol. Med. **50**, 116–128 (2014)

21. Keustermans, J., Vandermeulen, D., Suetens, P.: Integrating statistical shape models into a graph cut framework for tooth segmentation. In: Wang, F., Shen, D., Yan, P., Suzuki, K. (eds.) MLMI 2012. LNCS, vol. 7588, pp. 242–249. Springer, Heidelberg (2012). https://doi.org/10.1007/978-3-642-35428-1_30

22. Lahoud, P., et al.: Artificial intelligence for fast and accurate 3-dimensional tooth segmentation on cone-beam computed tomography. J. Endod. **47**(5), 827–835 (2021)

23. Lee, T.C., Kashyap, R.L., Chu, C.N.: Building skeleton models via 3-D medial surface axis thinning algorithms. CVGIP Graph. Models Image Process. **56**(6), 462–478 (1994)

24. Milletari, F., Navab, N., Ahmadi, S.A.: V-net: fully convolutional neural networks for volumetric medical image segmentation. In: 2016 Fourth International Conference on 3D Vision (3DV), pp. 565–571. IEEE (2016)

25. Radford, A., et al.: Learning transferable visual models from natural language supervision. In: International Conference on Machine Learning, pp. 8748–8763. PMLR (2021)

26. Ren, S., He, K., Girshick, R., Sun, J.: Faster R-CNN: towards real-time object detection with region proposal networks. In: Advances in Neural Information Processing Systems, vol. 28 (2015)

27. Rodriguez, A., Laio, A.: Clustering by fast search and find of density peaks. Science **344**(6191), 1492–1496 (2014)

28. Shaker, A., Maaz, M., Rasheed, H., Khan, S., Yang, M.H., Khan, F.S.: UNETR++: delving into efficient and accurate 3D medical image segmentation. arXiv preprint arXiv:2212.04497 (2022)

29. Strbac, G.D., Schnappauf, A., Giannis, K., Bertl, M.H., Moritz, A., Ulm, C.: Guided autotransplantation of teeth: a novel method using virtually planned 3-dimensional templates. J. Endod. **42**(12), 1844–1850 (2016)

30. Vaswani, A., et al.: Attention is all you need. In: Advances in Neural Information Processing Systems, vol. 30 (2017)

31. Wu, X., Chen, H., Huang, Y., Guo, H., Qiu, T., Wang, L.: Center-sensitive and boundary-aware tooth instance segmentation and classification from cone-beam ct. In: 2020 IEEE 17th International Symposium on Biomedical Imaging (ISBI), pp. 939–942. IEEE (2020)

32. Xie, E., Wang, W., Yu, Z., Anandkumar, A., Alvarez, J.M., Luo, P.: Segformer: simple and efficient design for semantic segmentation with transformers. Adv. Neural. Inf. Process. Syst. **34**, 12077–12090 (2021)
33. Zheng, S., et al.: Rethinking semantic segmentation from a sequence-to-sequence perspective with transformers. In: Proceedings of the IEEE/CVF Conference on Computer Vision and Pattern Recognition, pp. 6881–6890 (2021)
34. Zhou, H.Y., Guo, J., Zhang, Y., Yu, L., Wang, L., Yu, Y.: nnFormer: interleaved transformer for volumetric segmentation. arXiv preprint arXiv:2109.03201 (2021)

Fault Tolerance Aware Virtual Machine Scheduling Algorithm in Cloud Data Center Environment

Heyang Xu[✉], Sen Xu, and Naixuan Guo

School of Information Engineering, Yancheng Institute of Technology, Yancheng, China
xuheyang124@126.com

Abstract. Virtual machine (VM) scheduling is a complex problem in cloud environments, especially when reliability is considered. However, most of existing related works ignore the influence of this point. Therefore, this paper deeply explores fault tolerance aware VM scheduling (FTVS) and proposes an optimization model with multiple objectives and quality of service (QoS) constraints. Then, according to the characteristics of computing nodes (CNs) in CDC, a cost efficiency factor model of CN is defined and a heuristic algorithm based on best fit method is then proposed. Finally, to evaluate the efficiency and feasibility of the algorithm and models of this work, we use both simulation data sets and real-life cloud data center cluster data sets to conduct experiments. Experimental results show that the developed algorithm can improve successful execution rate of users' VM requests and increase their overall satisfactions about cloud services.

Keywords: Fault Tolerance · VM Scheduling · QoS

1 Introduction

Cloud computing convenient users to achieve universal, on-demand and easily access to various shared resources (e.g. servers, networks, storage and applications) through Internet and provides them with a pay-as-you-go model for charging the rented resources [1]. Nowadays, more and more information technology (IT) companies offer varieties of cloud services. They have built multiple datacenters in different places, which can provide their users with powerful service capabilities. With the rapid development of virtualization, cloud users, including individuals, enterprises or other organizations, are more and more inclined to choose to rent resources or services from cloud providers to complete their own business. By renting cloud services, users can reduce the IT operating costs and improve the operating efficiency of enterprises [2].

The heterogeneity of servers and complexity of internal structures bring challenges to daily operation and maintenance of cloud data centers and also give rise to a great increase in the possibility of failure of computing nodes (servers, VMs and so on)[3]. When impacted by external factors or internal factors, failures of computing nodes in cloud data centers are no longer accidents [4]. At the same time, a failure of a server may result in that all VMs deployed on it are unavailable [5]. Once a computing node fails, if any appropriate fault tolerance technology is not adopted, their customers' businesses will be resumed on other alternative servers or be terminated instantly, which will greatly decrease the satisfaction of cloud users. Therefore, cloud providers usually adopt recovery technologies (such as rollback, checkpoint) in their daily operation and maintenance of data centers to improve service reliability. This will evoke another concern that the recovering processes of failed nodes take a certain amount of time. Thus, it will unavoidably influence the performances (such as prolonging the actual execution time, increasing the cost and so on) of the running services.

The VM scheduling problem in cloud data centers refers to how to assign suitable computing nodes to VM service demand submitted by users under some constraints so that certain performance goals can be optimized. When service reliability is considered, the scheduling problem refers to FTVS. It not only needs to optimize different performance targets, but also to consider the impact of reliability factors on scheduling performance. Existing VM scheduling algorithms mostly consider the CPU, memory and network requirements of VMs to optimize some favorite objectives, while ignoring the impact of reliability factors on scheduling performance. Thus, the proposed methods can not accurately reflect the actual situation of cloud data centers.

Therefore, this paper analyzes the randomness influences of CNs' failures and recoveries. An actual service time model of a user's service request is established and future the users' cost model of executing their service requests is also derive. Therefore, this paper investigates the problem of FTVS by establishing a multiple objectives optimization model, which minimizes the cost of user execution service requests and improves the execution success rate of user services as much as possible. According to the characteristics of the computing nodes, a cost efficiency (CE) factor model is defined. Then, we propose a greedy-based best fit (GBF) algorithm whose kernel is to schedule each VM request to the CN with the minimum CE value. Finally, the results demonstrate that with the increase of failure rate, the actual execution times of users' businesses gradually increase. While with the increase of the recovery rate, the actual execution times decrease gradually and the execution success rate significantly increases.

2 Problem Description and Optimization Model

2.1 Description of the Studied Problem

A cloud data center is comprised by thousands of multifaceted computing nodes (or physical servers). Generally, we use $\mathbf{CN} = \{CN_1, CN_2, ..., CN_m\}$ to represent the $m(m \geq 1)$ computing nodes that make up the cloud data center and $CN_j(1 \leq j \leq m)$ represents the jth CN, represented by $CN_j = (Core_j, Mem_j, s_j, p_j, \lambda_j, \mu_j)$[6–8]. Among them, the CPU and memory capacity of CN_j are expressed as $Core_j$ and Mem_j respectively. s_j represents each CPU core's operational efficiency whose index is MIPS; p_j represents the price per CPU core of CN. λ_j and μ_j indicate the failure and recovery rate of CN_j, respectively.

Cloud users always expect their services to be executed quickly and obtain the expected QoS at a low cost. Therefore, this paper considers two QoS constraints that users are more concerned about, namely the deadline for VM completion and the execution budget. A VM request may require multiple tasks to be performed and all tasks within the identical VM request are supposed to be carried out simultaneously on the same CN [9, 10]. Generally, we use $\mathbf{VM} = \{VM_1, VM_2, ..., VM_n\}$ ($n \geq 1$) to indicate the total VM requests that customers submit to the data center. Let $VM_i = (K_i, WL_i, mem_i, subt_i, B_i, D_i)$ represents the ith VM request [7, 11], in which K_i is the quantity of jobs included in VM_i and also represents the quantity of CPU cores required by VM_i. $WL_i = \{wl_{ik} | 1 \leq k \leq K_i\}$ denotes workloads of the jobs of VM_i, where wl_{ik} is the workload required to be completed by the kth job of VM_i. $Subt_i$ represents the time at which VM_i was submitted to the datacenter. VM_i's execution budget and deadline are expressed as B_i and D_i respectively. The former denotes that the user expects the cost of executing VM_i to be no more than the budget and the latter is similar.

Therefore, the studied FTVS is following: given the collections of m CNs that constitute the cloud data center $\mathbf{CN} = \{CN_1, CN_2,..., CN_m\}$ and n VM requests $\mathbf{VM} = \{VM_1, VM_2, ..., VM_n\}$, the FTVS problem is how to allocate VMs to appropriate CNs considering physical server failures and failure recoveries.

2.2 Optimization Model

Let τ_{ikj} represent the time to execute the k-th task of the VM_i on CN_j in a ideal case (regardless of node failure and recovery), thus:

$$\tau_{ijk} = wl_{ik}/s_j. \tag{1}$$

In real cloud data center environments, CNs may fail when running users' applications and failure recovery requires a certain process, which inevitably affects the performance indicators, such as task execution time. We supposes that all failures in the cloud data center can be monitored and after a certain repair process, they can be restored to the original running state and continue to execute users' businesses. Suppose that failures on CN_j follow a Poisson process with parameter $\lambda_j (\lambda_j \geq 0)$ and node failure events are independent of each other. Let $N_j(\tau_{ikj})$ represent the total quantity of failures on CN_j within the time interval τ_{ikj}. The probability of $N_j(\tau_{ikj}) = M$ ($M = 0,1,2,...$) can be given by

$$\Pr\{N_j(\tau_{ikj}) = M\} = \frac{(\lambda_j \tau_{ikj})^M}{M!} e^{-\lambda_j \tau_{ikj}}. \tag{2}$$

Obviously, the expectation of $N_j(\tau_{ikj})$ is

$$E[N_j(\tau_{ikj})] = \lambda_j \tau_{ikj}. \tag{3}$$

Once a computing node fails, the repair process is started immediately. The repair time of each failure is also independent of each other. Suppose that the failure recovery time of the computing node CN_j follows a negative exponential distribution with the parameter $\mu_j(\mu_j \geq 0)$. $RT_j(\tau_{ikj})$ represents the total recovery time of failures on the computing node CN_j within the time interval τ_{ikj} and $RT_j^{(M)}$ represents the Mth ($M = 0,1,2,...$) recovery time of the failure happened on CN_j. Thus, the total recovery time

$RT_j(\tau_{ikj})$ of CN_j in $(0, \tau_{ikj}]$ can be obtained:

$$RT_j(\tau_{ikj}) = \sum_{M=1}^{N_j(\tau_{ikj})} RT_j^{(M)}. \tag{4}$$

AT_{ikj} represents the actual running time (AT) of VM_i's kth job executing on CN_j, which can be expressed by:

$$AT_{ikj} = \tau_{ikj} + RT_j(\tau_{ikj}). \tag{5}$$

Obviously, the expectation of AT_{ikj} is:

$$E[AT_{ikj}] = \frac{(\mu_j + \lambda_j)\tau_{ikj}}{\mu_j}. \tag{6}$$

AE_{ij} represents the actual execution expenditure (AE) of VM_i on CN_j, which can be expressed as the product of the quantity of CPU cores of CN_j occupied by VM_i, the execution time of VM_i and the unit price of CPU cores of CN_j

$$AE_{ij} = K_i \cdot \max_{1 \le k \le Ki}(AT_{ikj}) \cdot p_j. \tag{7}$$

Among them, K_i represents the quantity of tasks included in VM_i, which is the quantity of CPU cores that VM_i needs to occupy on CN_j; $\max_{1 \le k \le K_i} \max_{1 \le k \le Ki}(AT_{ikj})$ indicates the maximum actual completion time of VM_i's K_i tasks executed on CN_j.

Let x_{ij} represent whether VM_i is scheduled to CN_j: if VM_i is assigned to CN_j for execution, it must satisfy Eq. (8) and Eq. (9), which means that CN_j can perform the workload required by VM_i before the deadline D_i and the execution cost is not higher than VM_i's budget B_i. In this situation, $x_{ij} = 1$; otherwise, $x_{ij} = 0$. Obviously, the scheduling matrix $\mathbf{X}$ is a 0–1 matrix.

$$wt_{ij} + \max_{1 \le k \le Ki}(AT_{ikj}) \le D_i. \tag{8}$$

$$AE_{ij} \le B_i. \tag{9}$$

Equation (8) indicates that completion time of VM_i on CN_j is less than its deadline. It limits that the actual completion time of VM_i on CN_j is no more than the deadline. Equation (9) limits that the actual cost of VM_i on CN_j is no more than its budgeted amount.

Let TE represent total cost of executing n VM requests and it can be given by:

$$TE = \sum_{i=1}^{n} \sum_{j=1}^{m} x_{ij} \cdot AE_{ij} \tag{10}$$

Substituting Eq. (7) into Eq. (10), we can obtained:

$$TE = \sum_{i=1}^{n} \sum_{j=1}^{m} x_{ij} \cdot \left[K_i \cdot \max_{1 \le k \le K_i} (AT_{ikj}) \cdot p_j \right] \tag{11}$$

Obviously, the expectation of TE is

$$E[TE] = \sum_{i=1}^{n} \sum_{j=1}^{m} x_{ij} \cdot \left[K_i \cdot E[\max_{1 \le k \le K_i} (AT_{ikj})] \cdot p_j \right] \tag{12}$$

Let φ_i indicate whether VM_i is successfully executed: If VM request VM_i can be successfully executed by CN_j, it must satisfy Eq. (8) and Eq. (9), which means that CN_j can perform the workload required by VM_i before the deadline D_i and the execution cost is not higher than VM_i's budget B_i. φ_i can be calculated by

$$\varphi_i = \sum_{j=1}^{m} x_{ij}. \tag{13}$$

Let θ indicate the rate of all successfully completed VM requests, which is.

$$\theta = \frac{1}{n} \cdot \sum_{i=1}^{n} \varphi_i \times 100\%. \tag{14}$$

The studied FTVS can be modeled as following.

$$\text{Min } TE = \sum_{i=1}^{n} \sum_{j=1}^{m} x_{ij} \cdot \left[K_i \cdot \max_{1 \le k \le K_i} (AT_{ikj}) \cdot p_j \right] \tag{I}$$

$$\text{Max } \theta = \frac{1}{n} \sum_{i=1}^{n} \phi_i \tag{II}$$

Constraints:

1) For arbitrary i and j, $x_{ij} \in \{0,1\}$;
2) For an arbitrary i, $\sum_{j=1}^{m} x_{ij} \le 1$ $\sum_{j=1}^{m} x_{ij} \le 1$ 1;
3) For an arbitrary j, $\sum_{i=1}^{n} x_{ij} \cdot K_i \le Core_j$ and $\sum_{i=1}^{n} x_{ij} \cdot mem_i \le Mem_j$;
4) For an arbitrary i, if $x_{ij} = 1$, then VM_i and CN_j must satisfy formulas (8) and (9).

Constraint 1) specifies the range of values for the decision variable x_{ij} and the second specifies that each VM request can't be divisible and can only be assigned to a single CN. Constraint 3) gives the capability limit of computing node CN_j's CPU core and memory; Constraint 4) ensures that if VM_i is assigned to CN_j, then CN_j must meet the deadline and budget requirements.

3 Greedy-Based Best Fit (GBF) Algorithm

For an arbitrary VM_i, CN_j is a candidate node for VM_i only if CN_j's available resources can meet the resource requirements of VM_i and at the same time it can complete the workloads of VM_i's tasks within the deadline and budget constraints. The set of all candidate nodes of VM_i is called the candidate node set of VM_i, represented by CNS_i.

If there is only a few quantity of candidate nodes in CNS_i, it means that the QoS requested by VM_i are tight or VM_i requires a large quantity of resources and few CNs can fulfill VM_i's constraints. In order to upgrade the success rate of VM requests executions, VM requests with a small quantity of candidate nodes should be executed first. Therefore, the proposed GBF algorithm is based on this point and adopts greedy strategy to preferentially schedule the VM request with a minimum quantity of candidate nodes.

For an arbitrary CN_j, its cost efficiency, denoted by CE_j, is mainly affected by its own parameters, namely s_j, p_j, λ_j and μ_j. If CN_j is often failed down, thus VMs allocated on it may undergo a long execution time and will inevitably enlarge the cost of users. Similarly, if CN_j's CPU cores are more expensive, it will also enlarge the cost of users for performing VM requests. Conversely, the faster its speed, the shorter the time it takes to complete the VM requests. For the same reason, the cost efficiency of CN_j is directly proportional to the processing speed and recovery rate of that node and inversely proportional to its price and failure rate, which can be given by Eq. (15). It can be easily found that the higher the cost efficiency of a node, the lower the expense of executing VM requests.

$$CE_j = \mu_j s_j / \lambda_j. \tag{15}$$

Based on the above definitions and analysis, the main ideas of the proposed GBF algorithm contains two points. First, it preferentially schedules the VM request with minimum quantity of candidate nodes to upgrade the success rate of VM requests execution. Second, it preferentially schedules the VM requests to the node whose CE factor is largest, which can decrease customers' cost.

Algorithm 1: GBF algorithm
Input: VM set **VM**=$\{VM_1,VM_2,...,VM_n\}$ and CN set **CN**=$\{CN_1, CN_2, ..., CN_m\}$;
Output: matrix X=$(x_{ij})_{n\times m}$.
1 set **X=0** and all CNS empty, set all VMs' status as "*unscheduled*";
2 sort all CN by the values of CE factor by descending order, such as CN_1', CN_2', ..., CN_m' ;
3 **for** an arbitrary *unscheduled* $VM_i \in$ **VM**
4 **for** an arbitrary $CN_j'(1\leq j\leq m)$
5 **if** CN_j' can satisfy VM_i's requirements
6    $CNS_i = CNS_i \cup CN_j'$;
7 if $CNS_i = \Phi$
8 set the status of VM_i to *failed scheduling*;
9 else if $|CNS_i|=1$
10 schedule VM_i to its candidate node （supposing that is CN_j'）;
11 change resource capacities of CN_j';
12 set $x_{ij}=1$;
13 set the status of the VM_i to "*scheduled*";
14while there exists *unscheduled* VM in **VM**
15 for all unscheduled VMs, find the VM with the fewest elements in the candidate nodes set（supposing that is VM_i） ;
16 schedule VM_i to the node（supposing that is CN_j'）whose CE factor is lowest;
17 change resource capacities of CN_j';
18 set $x_{ij}=1$;
19 set the status of the VM_i to "*scheduled*";
20 return **X**;

4 Experiments and Performance Evaluation

We conduct experimental verification by comparing the results of FCFS [12], GDPS [9] and MBFD [7] algorithms.

4.1 Simulation Data Configuration

The experimental environment of this article is: CORE i7 2.4 GHz, 8 GB RAM, Win 10 system, and the development language used is DEV-C++.

The CNs in experiments contain six parameters, which are randomly generated by different uniform distributions. The variable $Core_j$ is randomly generated from $\{2, 4, 8, 16\}$. The processing speed of the CPU core is evenly distributed in the [100, 200], with an average speed of 150 MIPS. The CPU core cost of CNs falls within the interval [0.35, 1], which ensures that faster CNs require higher execution costs than slower ones when execute the same VM requests. The memory size is randomly generated within the set of $\{4$ GB, 8 GB, 16 GB, 32 GB. The variables λ_j and μ_j are uniformly generated within the ranges of [0.01, 0.1] and [0.05, 0.15], respectively.

In the simulation data set, the arrival times of all VMs are in (0, 100)s. The memory size is randomly generated in the set of $\{1$ GB, 2 GB, 3 GB, 4 GB$\}$ by a uniform distribution. The quantity of tasks included in each VM request is randomly generated within the interval [1, 7] and the variable wl_{ik} is generated in { 100000, 120000, 140000, 160000,..., 500000}. The deadline constraint of a VM request has a linear relationship with the average running time of its maximum workload of its tasks, randomly fluctuating by 10%. The budget for each VM request is set to its actual execution time multiplied by the quantity of tasks with a random float within 10%.

4.2 Performance Metrics

This paper adopts the following four metrics to conduct comparative analysis: 1) θ, which is the second optimization goals. 2) Average Expenditure (AE). 3) Average Completion Time (ACT). 4) Overall Satisfaction of Users (OSU): Generally speaking, cloud users expect that business can be executed as rapidly as possible while paying the lowest cost. Let us_i represent the user satisfaction of VM_i. Consequently, it is usually affected by whether VM_i is successfully executed (φ_i), actual execution cost of VM_i ($Acost_i$) and actual completion time ($Atime_i$), thus:

$$us_i = \varphi_i[\alpha(B_i - Acost_i)/B_i + \beta(D_i - Atime_i)/D_i], \qquad (16)$$

in which α and β represent the preference coefficients of cloud users for business execution costs and response time, respectively. In this paper, we treat execution cost and response time as two equally important goals, so both α and β are set as 0.5 in the experiment. The OSU is the sum of the satisfaction of all users:

$$OSU = \sum_{i=1}^{n} us_i. \qquad (17)$$

4.3 Experimental Analysis

Experiment 1. First, the recovery rates of all CNs are fixed as 0.1. Table 1 shows the results obtained by GBF algorithm when failure rates (FR) changes in the range of [0.01, 0.1]. It can be seen that the values of θ and OSU gradually decrease as the failure rates increase and the values of AE and ACT gradually increase. The four metrics all become worse with the growth of failure rate because the recovery process of each failure will take a certain amount of time and it unavoidably prolongs the execution time of user services and increase service execution costs. Thus, it will destroy users' QoS constraints and eventually decrease users' satisfaction.

Second, the failure rates of all CNs are fixed to 0.05. The results obtained by GBF algorithm when recovery rate (RR) changes in the range of [0.05, 0.14] are shown in Table 2. As it is shown, the values of θ and OSU gradually increase and the values of AE and ACT gradually decrease with recovery rates' increasing. The four performance indicators all become better because the growth of CNs' recovery rates will reduce the recovery time of each failure and thus decrease the execution time of customers' businesses and reduce service execution costs. This situation can improve the success rate of users' businesses and improve the overall satisfaction of users.

Table 1. Results obtained by GBF with the increasing of failure rates.

FR	θ	AE	ACT	OSU
0.01	100%	2.22	0.84	102.11
0.03	100%	2.63	0.99	84.64
0.05	100%	3.02	1.11	68.10
0.07	100%	3.44	1.24	51.86
0.09	97%	3.90	1.37	33.45
0.1	72%	3.70	1.56	17.08

Table 2. Results obtained by GBF with the increasing of recovery rates

RR	θ	AE	ACT	OSU
0.05	71.5%	3.70	1.56	17.08
0.07	100%	3.48	1.26	50.13
0.09	100%	3.14	1.15	63.62
0.11	100%	2.94	1.10	70.57
0.13	100%	2.80	1.05	77.24
0.14	100%	2.74	1.03	79.64

Consequently, although fault tolerance technology can improve service reliability of cloud services, it indeed influences the performances of VM scheduling and it is necessary to conduct in-depth research and analysis on this point.

Experiment 2. In this experiment, the scheduling performances of FCFS, GDPS, MBFD and GBF algorithms are compared and Table 3 lists the obtained results. As shown in the table, the success rate of users' businesses obtained by GBF algorithm is largest, which is 12.05%, 4.88% and 4.25% larger than other ones because GBF algorithm firstly schedules the VM with stricter QoS constraints or high resource requirements and there may be few candidate nodes that can meet these VM requests. Giving these VM requests with higher priority can increase the probability of being successfully executed. In the meantime, the average cost of executing VM requests by GBF algorithm is low and the average completion time is also short. Finally, in terms of overall users' satisfaction, the GBF algorithm is improved by 20.1%, 10.7% and 8.7% compared to other algorithms because it takes the impacts of the failure rates into consideration comprehensively, recovery rates, processing speeds and resource prices of the CNs (Eq. (15)).

Table 3. Obtained results on fault tolerance aware cloud datacenters.

Metrics	FCFS	GDPS	MBFD	GBF
θ	82.3%	89.47%	90.1%	**94.35%**
AE	2.87	**2.78**	2.81	2.79
ACT	1.23	1.23	**1.19**	1.21
OSU	57.69	62.58	63.74	**69.26**

5   Conclusion

Based on the stochastic of computing nodes' failures and recoveries, two random models are established for the actual completion time and actual execution cost of VM request. Then, we propose a heuristic algorithm based on best fit method. At last, the simulated results prove the feasibility of the contributions. As a future work, we will take into account the situation that VM requests will fail and can't be restored.

Acknowledgement. This work is partially supported by the National Natural Science Foundation of China (No. 62076215), the Natural Science Foundation of the Jiangsu Higher Education Institutions (No. 21KJD520006), the Future Network Scientific Research Fund Project (No. FNSRFP-2021-YB-46) and the Funding for School-Level Research Projects of Yancheng Institute of Technology (No. xjr2021047).

References

1. Armbrust, M., Fox, A., Griffith, R., et al.: A view of cloud computing. Commun. ACM **53**(4), 50–58 (2010)
2. Liu, X., Cheng B., Yue, Y., et al.: Traffic-aware and reliability-guaranteed virtual machine placement optimization in cloud datacenters. In: 12th IEEE International Conference on Cloud Computing (CLOUD). IEEE (2019)
3. Xu, L., Lv, M., Li, Z., et al.: PDL: a data layout towards fast failure recovery for erasure-coded distributed storage systems. In: 39th IEEE Conference on Computer Communications (INFOCOM2020). IEEE (2020)
4. Luo, L., Meng, S., Qiu, X., et al.: Improving failure tolerance in large-scale cloud computing systems. IEEE Trans. Reliab. **68**(2), 620–632 (2019)
5. Liu, X., Cheng, B., Yue, Y., et al.: Enhancing availability of traffic-aware virtual cluster allocation in cloud datacenters. In: IEEE International Conference on Services Computing. IEEE (2019)
6. Wei, L., Foh, C., He, B., et al.: Towards efficient resource allocation for heterogeneous workloads in IaaS clouds. IEEE Trans. Cloud Comput. **6**(1), 264–275 (2018)
7. Xu, H., Cheng, P., Liu, Y.: A fault tolerance aware virtual machine scheduling algorithm in cloud computing. Int. J. Performabil. Eng. **15**(11), 2990–2997 (2019)
8. Yu, L., Chen, L., Cai, Z., et al.: Stochastic load balancing for virtual resource management in datacenters. IEEE Trans. Cloud Comput. **8**(2), 459–472 (2020)
9. Xu, H., Liu, Y., Wei, W., et al.: Incentive-aware virtual machine scheduling in cloud computing. J. Supercomput. **74**(7), 3016–3038 (2018)

10. Sun, P., Dai, Y., Qiu, X.: Optimal scheduling and management on correlating reliability, performance, and energy consumption for multi-agent cloud systems. IEEE Trans. Reliab. **66**(2), 547–558 (2017)

11. Sotiriadis, S., Bessis, N., Buyya, R.: Self managed virtual machine scheduling in cloud systems. Inf. Sci. **433–434**, 381–400 (2018)

12. Wang, D., Dai, W., Zhang, C., Shi, X., Jin, H.: TPS: an efficient VM scheduling algorithm for HPC applications in cloud. In: Man Ho Allen, A., Castiglione, A., Choo, K.-K.R., Palmieri, F., Li, K.-C. (eds.) GPC 2017. LNCS, vol. 10232, pp. 152–164. Springer, Cham (2017). https://doi.org/10.1007/978-3-319-57186-7_13

Personalized Learning Made Simple: A Deep Knowledge Tracing Model for Individual Cognitive Development

Xin Liu[1], Jia Zhu[1(✉)], Changfan Pan[2], Changqin Huang[1], Yu Song[3], and Xinran Cao[2]

[1] College of Education, Zhejiang Normal University, Jinhua, China
jiazhu@zjnu.edu.cn
[2] School of Computer Science and Technology, Zhejiang Normal University, Jinhua, China
[3] School of Education, South China Normal University, Guangzhou, China

Abstract. Knowledge tracing is the fundamental technology for constructing learner models that dynamically estimate and predict a learner's knowledge state. While current research on knowledge tracing has improved the predictive capacity of the model by investigating the relationship between learners and problem concepts, these models become static after training. This limits their ability to adapt to the varying developmental stages of learners due to human diversity. Drawing inspiration from the synaptic plasticity that grants lifelong learning capabilities to the biological brain, this study incorporates plasticity weights into the Transformer architecture. This leads to the proposal of a deep knowledge tracing model designed to adapt to individual learner development. Moreover, it demonstrates significant performance improvements compared to the baseline model.

Keywords: Knowledge tracing · Transformer · Plasticity weights

1 Introduction

In 1994, Corbett et al. introduced Bayesian Knowledge Tracing (BKT) [5], a method that employs a binary group to denote a student's comprehension state - whether they have mastered a knowledge point. This approach leverages the Hidden Markov Model (HMM) to track alterations in students' knowledge states dynamically and predicts the likelihood of students grasping knowledge points. In recent years, numerous researchers have attracted the attention of deep learning due to its full feature extraction capabilities and its independence from manually labeled data. Piech et al. [14], in 2015, pioneered the application of deep learning to the domain of knowledge tracing. They proposed a classic model based on Recurrent Neural Network (RNN), denoted as the Deep Knowledge Tracing model (DKT) [9]. Despite the trade-off in interpretability, DKT and its refined versions deliver leading-edge performance across an extensive array of benchmark datasets.

Y. Sun et al. (Eds.): ChineseCSCW 2023, CCIS 2013, pp. 462–472, 2024.
https://doi.org/10.1007/978-981-99-9640-7_34

However, this model and its variants utilize identical parameters in subsequent training processes, leading to a significant challenge: according to Piaget's theory of cognitive development [7], children exhibit individual differences in learning as they develop, and different learners possess distinct cognitive characteristics. Instruction should be aligned with students' cognitive levels. Training a model with the same parameters does not adapt to a learner's cognitive development, instead, it fails to track the learner's progress in later stages.

Contrasting with neural networks that have fixed parameters post-training, the biological brain possesses the capacity for continuous learning. This ability grants humans adaptability to their environment, with the acquisition of lifelong learning primarily hinging on remarkable neural plasticity. This plasticity predominantly involves activities between neurons [4]. The synaptic plasticity of these neurons principally aligns with Hebbian theory, positing that if neuron 'A' persistently stimulates neuron 'B,' metabolic alterations will occur between the two cells, thereby fortifying the synaptic connection between neuron 'A' and 'B' [6]. However, neuronal activation exceeding zero results in computational instability. As a countermeasure, the BCM theory is proposed, grounded in Hebbian theory, to regulate the strength of synaptic connections.

This paper presents a knowledge tracing model designed to adapt to the cognitive development of individual learners. Building on the foundation of the DKT model, we introduce the Transformer model and incorporate response time data to adjust the model's attention weight calculations. This integration better considers the influence of temporal characteristics on prediction outcomes. Our model introduces plastic weights into the feed-forward neural network, consistently updating them with input and output parameters. It trains independent parameters according to different learners, elucidating how learners comprehend specific knowledge points and related concepts over time. This approach is better suited to adapt to learners' cognitive development. The primary contributions of this paper are encapsulated in the following three points:

1) We introduce plasticity weights into the encoder and decoder of the Transformer model. These weights allow for parameter modifications based on the model's input and output, making it more adaptive to a learner's personal knowledge trajectory. This enhancement has also been empirically validated. Plasticity weights tailor the learning model more accurately to each learner's cognitive development, bridging the gap between artificial and biological learning mechanisms and yielding a more personalized and effective educational tool.

2) We implement the BCM theory instead of the Hebbian theory for updating plastic weights, which brings about higher stability in the computation of these weights. The BCM theory, which uses multiplicative weight updates, offers a more robust and reliable framework for neural plasticity, ensuring better learning consistency within our model.

3) We incorporate Piaget's theory of cognitive development in education to examine learners' cognitive progression. In the experiment, we compare our model against existing knowledge tracing models. The results obtained are

good, demonstrating our approach's effectiveness in capturing learners' cognitive development in a more nuanced and individualized manner.

2   Related Work

Our related work is mainly divided into: knowledge tracing, Piaget's cognitive development theory, and synaptic plasticity. The details are as follows:

2.1   Knowledge Tracing

Bayesian Knowledge Tracing [17] and Additive Factor Model (AFM) are two representative models in traditional machine learning methods. They have been widely used in intelligent teaching systems to assess the knowledge level of learners [16]. The BKT model is interpretable in the case of predicting students' answers to questions. The BKTC model extends the BKT model by combining knowledge points and exercises. Qiu et al. [15] added a knowledge forgetting feature to the model, Agarwal et al. [1] used recency weight instead of learning rate to further refine the state of binary knowledge to make the update of learning level estimation smoother for 21 states. The researchers later found a model in psychometric theory that can solve BKT-related problems, namely the Additive Factor Model (AFM). AFM considers the influence of two variables, the number of practice attempts and the learning rate, on the learner's knowledge state. Researchers have also extended AFM with parameter constraints [2], error factors [12], and emotional factors.

2.2   Piaget's Theory of Cognitive Development

Piaget's theory was that as the brain matures and children experience the world through action, they go through four broad stages of thinking. Each stage is qualitatively different and better suited to understanding the world. The four cognitive stages are: the sensorimotor stage, preoperational stage, concrete operational stage, and formal operational stage [13]. One of the essential meanings of Piaget's theory is that the instruction should be adapted to the development level of the learner. Teaching content should be in line with learners' development. [8]. Piaget uses four concepts to explain cognitive development: schema, assimilation, adaptation, and balance. Schema helps learners explain and understand the world as they acquire knowledge [10], assimilation is using existing schema to fit new stimuli into existing cognition, and adaptation is modifying or creating new schema to adjust to new stimuli. Balance is how individuals achieve harmony through assimilation and adaptation. Based on this theory, we know that knowledge tracing models need to change their parameters constantly to meet students' cognitive development.

2.3   Synaptic Plasticity

Synaptic plasticity refers to the variability and adjustability of synaptic connections between neurons, and is one of the basic mechanisms of learning and memory in the brain. Basic forms of synaptic plasticity include long-term potentiation (LTP) and long-term depression (LTD). Synaptic plasticity enables neurons to adapt to environmental changes and learning tasks by adjusting the strength and efficiency of their connections, resulting in flexibility and adaptability of brain function. When we learn new knowledge or skills, the connections between related neurons change, forming new synaptic connections or strengthening existing ones. This long-term synaptic plasticity forms the basis of memory in the nervous system, allowing us to remember past experiences and acquire new information.

3   Method

3.1   Problem Definition

The Knowledge Tracing (KT) problem involves sequential analysis, where the sequence of previous questions answered by the learner is utilized to predict their mastery of specific knowledge points. We represent the learner's knowledge mastery using binary pairs(q_i, r_i), where q_i denotes the question being attempted or solved by the learner, and r_i represents their response, indicating whether it is correct or incorrect. An incorrect response is denoted by 0, while a correct response is indicated by 1. The ultimate objective is to estimate whether the learner will correctly answer the next knowledge question q_{i+1}.

3.2   Models of Synaptic Plasticity

The process of human cognitive development involves the activity of the nerve cells in the brain. Synaptic plasticity refers to the connections between nerve cells where synapses are strengthened or weakened in response to their activity which is thought to play a role in the brain's ability to integrate fleeting experiences into lasting memory traces for more than a century [3]. The Hebbian theory describes its primary mechanism: neuron N_i repeatedly stimulates neuron N_j, and metabolic changes will occur between the two cells, thereby strengthening the synapse between the connection between neuron N_i and neuron N_j. Its mathematical formula is expressed as follows:

$$N^{pos} = \sum_{i=1}^{n} w_i N_i^{pre}$$
$$\Delta w_i = \mu N_i^{pre} N^{pos}, \quad i = 1, \dots, n \tag{1}$$

Δw_i represents the change between two synapses, N_i^{pre} represents the activity of the pre-synaptic neuron, and N_j^{pos} represents the activity of the post-synaptic neuron.

However, in practical scenarios, the firing rate between two neurons often exceeds zero. Under the mechanism of Hebbian theory, synaptic connections can only continue to strengthen but not weaken, leading to a potential runaway computational effect. Thus, the need arises for the BCM theory, which introduces a mechanism to adjust and set a modulation threshold according to the rise or fall in activity between two neurons. The rules are as follows:

$$\Delta w_i = \frac{\mu N^{\text{pos}} \left(N^{\text{pos}} - \theta(m)\right) N_i^{\text{pre}}}{\theta(m)} \tag{2}$$

$\theta(m)$ means to adjust the threshold; as the value of the post-synaptic neuron changes, it is allowed to increase $(N_{pos} > \theta(m))$ or decrease $(N_{pos} < \theta(m))$.

3.3   Concept Interaction Mapping

We added a concept interaction mapping layer to better predict learners' mastery of the concepts corresponding to the knowledge points. First, create a concept interaction mapping matrix W and a concept embedding matrix C, and use e_i to represent the high-dimensional vector of the problem that involves concept interactions. The calculation formula for their interaction is as follows:

$$e_i = softmax(W_i)C \tag{3}$$

W_i represents the i-th row of the matrix W, which indicates the weights of each interaction. These weights are normalized using the softmax function. The advantage of this method is that, for the established model, it adopts an approach that can continue to evolve with continuous input and output even after training. These adaptable weights enable the model to tailor different parameters for each learner, accommodating individual differences without requiring additional inputs [11].

3.4   Plastic Weights in Transformer

In this model, the calculation of the plastic weight participates in the calculation of the feedforward neural network. The two neurons are connected by the traditional weight $(W_{i,j}^s)$ and the plastic weight $(W_{i,j}^p)$, the role of the plastic weight here is to continuously increase or decrease according to the activity between the two neurons.

$$N_j = \sigma \left(\sum_{i \in \text{ inputs}} \left(w_{i,j}^s N_i + \beta_j w_{i,j}^p N_i\right) \right) \tag{4}$$

N_i represents the nerve cell activity of the current layer, N_j represents the activity of nerve cells in the next layer, β_j represents the coefficient of the plastic weight $W_{i,j}^p$, and the neurons in the next layer have the same value of β_j.

To dynamically update the plastic weight of the model, we use the BCM theory mentioned above to formulate rules and provide a sliding threshold to adjust the size of the plastic weight to prevent the calculation from getting out of control.

$$w_{i,j}^p = w_{i,j}^p + \frac{\eta \left(N_j \left(N_j - \theta(m) \right) N_i \right)}{\theta(m)} \tag{5}$$

$\eta \epsilon \left(0, 1 \right)$ adjusts the change of the plastic weight, $\theta \left(m \right)$ represents the modification threshold, adjusts the plastic weight, and is defined as a post-synaptic neuron mean absolute value of the activity.

$$\theta(m) = E \left[\|N_j\| \right] \tag{6}$$

when $N_i > \theta \left(m \right)$, and N_i is positive, the plastic weight between neuron N_i and neuron N_j will increase, when N_i is negative, the plastic weight between neuron N_i and neuron N_j will decrease, when $N_j < \theta \left(m \right)$, the result is opposite.

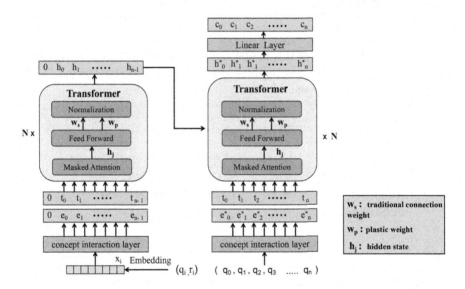

Fig. 1. Framework of the Knowledge Tracing Model Adapted to Individual Cognitive Development

As illustrated in Fig. 1, the model framework represents a simplified version of the transformer model, with the encoder on the left and the decoder on the right. The student's question sequence (q_i, r_i) passes through an embedding layer to produce the interaction sequence x_i. The concept interaction layer generates the sequence $(0, e_0, e_1, ..., e_{n-1})$, which, along with the time sequence t_i, is fed into the transformer model to generate the hidden state of the student, denoted as h_i. Moving to the decoding phase, the hidden state h_i from the encoder, the sequence e_{i+1} output by the concept interaction layer, and the time series t_{i+1} are combined to generate the following hidden state denoted as h_{i+1}^*.

3.5   Loss Function

All trainable parameters are optimized by minimizing the binary cross-entropy loss of the true response c_{i+1} and the predicted probability p_{i+1}. Where L represents the loss function, c_{i+1} is the real label, and p_{i+1} is the prediction result of the model.

In the formula, the first term, $-c_{i+1}\log(p_{i+1})$, indicates that when the actual label is 1, a smaller loss is desired when the model's prediction p_{i+1} is closer to 1. The second term, $-(1 - c_{i+1})\log(c_{i+1})$, signifies that when the actual label is 0, a smaller loss is expected when the model's prediction p_{i+1} is closer to 0.

$$L = -\sum_i c_{i+1}\log(p_{i+1}) + (1 - c_{i+1})\log(1 - p_{i+1}) \qquad (7)$$

4   Experiments

4.1   Dataset

To verify the effectiveness of this model, we performed five-fold cross-validation validation using three datasets publicly available in knowledge tracing. Table 1 is a specific description of the datasets.

Table 1. Dataset statistics

Datasets	Interactions	Students	Records	Concept
ASSISTments2017	943K	1709	942816	102
STATICS	190K	333	189297	81
ASSISTments2015	709K	19840	708631	100

4.2   Experimental Results

Overall Performance. Table 2 presents a comparison of our model's performance against classic knowledge tracing models. As observable from the table, our proposed model outperforms the other models. Notably, our model exhibits the most remarkable performance on the STATICS dataset, improving by 21.2%, 19.1%, 17.6%, and 16.4% over DKT, DKVMN, SAKT, and CKT, respectively. Our model also demonstrates impressive performance on the ASSISTments2017 dataset, showing an increase of 20.4%, 13.2%, 19.7%, and 7.6% respectively, and exhibits slight improvements on the ASSISTments2015 dataset. This comparison underscores that our plasticity-focused model, designed to adapt to individual cognitive development, consistently outperforms non-plastic models, such as DKT.

Table 2. Performance comparison between models

Dataset	AUC				
	DKT	DKVMN	SAKT	CKT	MODEL
ASSISTments2017	0.644	0.685	0.648	0.721	0.776
STATICS	0.790	0.804	0.814	0.823	0.958
ASSISTments2015	0.719	0.723	0.732	0.734	0.736

Table 3. Experimental result data

Standard	Dataset	With-BCM	Without-BCM
AUC	ASSISTments2017	0.7768	0.7759
	STATICS	0.9584	0.9580
	ASSISTments2015	0.7361	0.7302
ACC	ASSISTments2017	0.7264	0.7257
	STATICS	0.9694	0.9680
	ASSISTments2015	0.7353	0.7351
RMSE	ASSISTments2017	0.4249	0.4254
	STATICS	0.1546	0.1538
	ASSISTments2015	0.4289	0.4253

Ablation Experiment. Ablation experiments are often used to study and evaluate the performance of algorithms, models, or systems. This type of experimentation evaluates the impact on overall system performance by selectively removing or disabling certain parts of the system. Table 3 compares this model's performance with and without plastic weights. The model's performance will be improved with the addition of plastic weights. We can see that the model's performance after adding plastic weights will be improved compared to without adding them.

Adapt to the Individual Development of Learners. Pi Yejie's 'cognitive development' theory expounds in detail on the four stages of children's cognitive development and has a positive guiding role in modern education and teaching development. We should pay attention to students' differences and respect their differentiated development in education. Regarding educational roles, we should emphasize putting students at the center of teaching and giving full play to their subjective initiative. Regarding teaching content, we should respect the laws of students' physical and mental development and adapt to the development of student's cognitive stage. In the teaching process, we should not break the existing cognitive balance of students to help students establish a new balance. In the proposed model for adapting to individual cognitive development, we provide a mechanism of assimilation and adaptation, enabling learners to integrate new knowledge points into existing schemas during the learning process and commu-

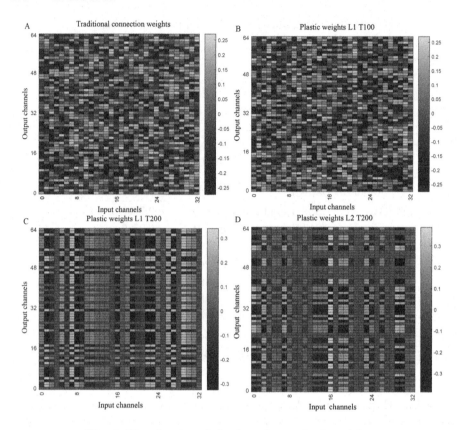

Fig. 2. Visualization of plastic and non-plastic weights

nicate with new topics by adapting to and changing the existing schema. This approach helps students achieve cognitive equilibrium, facilitating balanced and unbalanced cognitive transformations and developments.

Figure 2 mainly visualizes the change in traditional weight and plastic weight, where A represents the change in traditional weight, and B-D represents the change in plastic weight. B represents the change of plasticity weight after the user completes 100 sets of exercises, and C represents the change of plasticity weight after the user completes 200. Note that this is the same user. The D represents another learning weighted plastic weight after that person has completed two hundred sets of exercises. We can see that the plastic weights are constantly changing as the learners continue to learn, which means that the model can continuously adapt to the cognitive development of different learners.

5   Conclusions and Future Work

In this paper, we propose a deep knowledge tracing model for individual cognitive development. This model aims to track the knowledge individuals acquire in cognitive development and carry out personalized knowledge shaping and adaptive adjustment according to the individual's learning ability and needs. The model uses the individual's learning history and behavioral data to model and track the individual's cognitive state and knowledge level through machine learning and data analysis methods. In the future, we plan to improve further and expand this plastic knowledge tracing model that adapts to the cognitive development of individuals.

Acknowledgements. This work was supported by the Key Research and Development Program of Zhejiang Province (No. 2021C03141), the National Natural Science Foundation of China under Grant (62077015), the Natural Science Foundation of Zhejiang Province under Grant (LY23F020010) and the Key Laboratory of Intelligent Education Technology and Application of Zhejiang Province, Zhejiang Normal University, Zhejiang, China.

References

1. Agarwal, D., Baker, R.S., Muraleedharan, A.: Dynamic knowledge tracing through data driven recency weights. International Educational Data Mining Society (2020)
2. Cen, H.: Generalized learning factors analysis: improving cognitive models with machine learning. Carnegie Mellon University (2009)
3. Citri, A., Malenka, R.C.: Synaptic plasticity: multiple forms, functions, and mechanisms. Neuropsychopharmacology **33**(1), 18–41 (2008)
4. Cooper, L.N., Bear, M.F.: The BCM theory of synapse modification at 30: interaction of theory with experiment. Nat. Rev. Neurosci. **13**(11), 798–810 (2012)
5. Corbett, A.T., Anderson, J.R.: Knowledge tracing: modeling the acquisition of procedural knowledge. User Model. User-Adap. Inter. **4**, 253–278 (1994)
6. Hebb, D.O.: The Organization of Behavior: A Neuropsychological Theory. Psychology press (2005)
7. Huitt, W., Hummel, J.: Piaget's theory of cognitive development. Educ. Psychol. Interact. **3**(2), 1–5 (2003)
8. Kuhn, D.: The application of Piaget's theory of cognitive development to education. Harv. Educ. Rev. **49**(3), 340–360 (1979)
9. LeCun, Y., Bengio, Y., Hinton, G.: Deep learning. Nature **521**(7553), 436–444 (2015)
10. Lefa, B.: The Piaget theory of cognitive development: an educational implications. Educ. Psychol. **1**(1), 1–8 (2014)
11. Li, Z., Yu, S., Lu, Y., Chen, P.: Plastic gating network: adapting to personal development and individual differences in knowledge tracing. Inf. Sci. **624**, 761–776 (2023)
12. MacLellan, C.J., Liu, R., Koedinger, K.R.: Accounting for slipping and other false negatives in logistic models of student learning. International Educational Data Mining Society (2015)
13. Piaget, J.: Piaget's theory of cognitive development. Child. Cogn. Dev. Essent. Read. **2**, 33–47 (2000)
14. Piech, C., et al.: Deep knowledge tracing. In: Advances in Neural Information Processing Systems, vol. 28 (2015)
15. Qiu, Y., Qi, Y., Lu, H., Pardos, Z.A., Heffernan, N.T.: Does time matter? modeling the effect of time with Bayesian knowledge tracing. In: EDM, pp. 139–148 (2011)

16. Rowe, J., Lester, J.: Modeling user knowledge with dynamic Bayesian networks in interactive narrative environments. In: Proceedings of the AAAI Conference on Artificial Intelligence and Interactive Digital Entertainment, vol. 6, pp. 57–62 (2010)

17. Yudelson, M.V., Koedinger, K.R., Gordon, G.J.: Individualized Bayesian knowledge tracing models. In: Lane, H.C., Yacef, K., Mostow, J., Pavlik, P. (eds.) AIED 2013. LNCS (LNAI), vol. 7926, pp. 171–180. Springer, Heidelberg (2013). https:// doi.org/10.1007/978-3-642-39112-5_18

Vehicle Edge Computing Network Service Migration Strategy Based on Multi-agent Reinforcement Learning

Zhongli Chen[1,2], Jichang Chen[1], and Taoshen Li[1,2(✉)]

[1] School of Information Engineering, Nanning University, 8 Longting Road, Nanning, China
19920091@gxu.edu.cn
[2] School of Computer, Electronics and Information, Guangxi University, 100 Daxue Road, Nanning, China

Abstract. In order to address the decision-making problem in vehicular edge computing networks, this paper presented a vehicle edge computing service migration strategy based on multi-agent deep learning. This strategy employs the multi-agent deep deterministic policy gradient algorithm, enabling vehicles to learn from incomplete system information and make distributed online migration decisions with only partial observations. Users collaborate and compete to achieve common goals, making the system more flexible and enhancing the overall benefits and stability. Simulation results using real datasets demonstrate that the proposed strategy converges rapidly and exhibits superior performance, robustness, and stability in scenarios with varying numbers of users and task arrival rates compared to other benchmark strategies.

Keywords: Vehicular Edge Computing Networks · Multi-agent Reinforcement Learning · Service Migration Decision-making · Multi-Agent Deep Deterministic Policy Gradient

1 Introduction

With the development of sensor technology and wireless communication technology, autonomous vehicle can make intelligent driving decisions using advanced computing power and decision-making system [1]. Intelligent vehicles need to process a large amount of data in a very short time [2]. Mobile edge computing (MEC) can provide efficient data processing, storage and computing capabilities for vehicles, enabling autonomous vehicle to make faster and more accurate decisions and provide a better user experience. In practical applications, however, due to the high-speed mobility of vehicles, the limited geographical coverage of MEC servers, it is easy to cause service interruption, hot spot service congestion, and other problems [3]. How to efficiently select the appropriate server for service migration according to the real-time location of the vehicle, the service demand of the vehicle and the status of the server has become a key problem to be solved in the vehicle edge computing network.

At present, there are many researches on mobile edge computing network dynamic service migration strategy. [4] presented a mobility aware transfer strategy, which modeled optimization problems as mixed integer nonlinear problems and was solved by using Lyapunov methods. [5] studied the joint optimization problem of service deployment and request routing decisions, and proposed an online service migration algorithm. In [6], the authors turned service migration into a multi-dimensional Knapsack problem, and proposed a coordination mechanism that can determine the best destination and time point for service migration and base station handover. [7] presented CLA-PSO service migration strategy based on particle swarm optimization algorithm. [8] developed a migration strategy based on deep Q-learning to realize active service migration. [9] proposed a fast transfer reinforcement learning method which combines transfer learning and reinforcement learning.

Due to the high-speed mobility of the vehicle and the service limitations of the edge server, unreasonable service migration strategies will lead to long service interruption time and service delay. To solve the above problems, this paper proposes a service migration strategy based on the multi-agent deep deterministic policy gradient (MADDPG) algorithm, which enables vehicles to make appropriate service migration decisions based on observed information, and can better handle competition and cooperation relationships, improving the flexibility and profitability of system.

2 System Model

2.1 Network Model

Consider a typical edge computing scenario of vehicle movement (as shown in Fig. 1). Multiple vehicles $(V_1, V_2,...,V_N)$ move in the geographical area covered by a group of MEC servers $(S_1, S_2,...,S_M)$. Each server is connected to a corresponding base station and other servers through a stable data link. Due to the different task requirements of different vehicles, MEC servers will provide independent services for vehicle operation. We refer to the MEC server running vehicle services as a work node, and the MEC server directly connected to the vehicle as a local node. Vehicles can indirectly access their services through multi-hop communication. To ensure satisfactory delay for users, it is assumed that suitable MEC servers can be selected for migration based on the dynamic changes in vehicle location and MEC network.

2.2 Communication Model

We use slicing mode to describe time as a set of discrete time slots. The user's location and server status change at the beginning of each time slot. When the vehicle changes position, its computing task is offloaded to the service node. In a time slot, the system's delay mainly consists of service migration delay, computing delay and transmission delay.

(1) Service migration delay

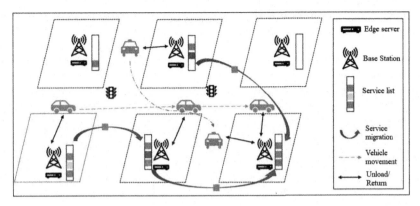

Fig. 1. Multi-vehicle system model

In the process of migrating services from the source node to the target node, the original node first seals the services, then transmits the services to the target node through the data link between MEC servers, and finally starts the services by the target node. The calculation formula for service migration delay D_t^{mig} is as follows:

$$D_t^{mig} = D_t^{freeze} + D_t^{st} \cdot H_i^{mig} + D_t^{restart} \tag{1}$$

where, D_t^{freeze} devotes the time required for the source node to seal the service, D_t^{st} devotes the time required for one hop of service transmission, H_i^{mig} devotes the time required for the destination node to start the service, and $D_t^{restart}$ devotes the number of hops from the source node to the destination node.

(2) Computing delay

Computing delay refers to the time consumed by the work node server to process vehicle tasks. Assuming that the computing resources of the server are equally shared, the calculation delay D_t^{com} can be expressed as:

$$D_t^{com} = (W_t^m + C_t^n)/F^m \tag{2}$$

where, C_t^n is the number of CPU cycles required for the computing task, W_t^m is the workload of the work node, and F^m is the computing power of the server.

(3) Transmission delay

When the vehicle unloads the task, it first transmits the task data to the communication local node m_{local}, and the transmission delay can be expressed as:

$$D_t^{local-trams} = Data_t^n/Rate_t^{local} \tag{3}$$

where, $Data_t^n$ devotes the data volume of the vehicle unloading task, and $Rate_t^{local}$ devotes the upload rate of the vehicle to the local node.

When the work node is inconsistent with the local node, the local node needs to transmit task data to the work node through the interconnection link between MEC servers. The transmission delay can be expressed as:

$$D_t^{local-reans} = \begin{cases} 0, & ifH_t^{mec} = 0 \\ Data_t^n/Rate_t^{mec}, & ifH_t^{mec} \neq 0 \end{cases} \tag{4}$$

where, $Rate_t^{mec}$ is the data link rate between MEC servers, H_t^{mec} is the number of network hops from the working node to the local node. When $H_t^{mec} = 0$, it indicates that the working node and the local node are the same MEC server. Because the result of returned after MEC calculation is usually only a small amount of data, we ignore the computing delay. Therefore, the transmission delay of the system can be expressed as:

$$D_t^{trans} = D_t^{mig} + D_t^{local-trans} \tag{5}$$

2.3 Optimization Objectives

The optimization goal of this paper is to minimize the system delay and provide users with the optimal service migration decision $\{a_1,a_2,\ldots,a_T\}$ in the vehicle edge computing network with dynamic changes in vehicle location and network. Assuming S is a set of MEC servers, the optimization problem can be expressed as:

$$\min_{a_1,a_2,\ldots,a_T} \sum_{t=1}^{T} \sum_{n=1}^{N} D_t^{mig} D_t^{com} D_t^{trans} \tag{6}$$

$$s.t. \ a_T \in S$$

The difficulty in achieving the above optimization goals lies in the high-speed mobility of users and the inability to fully access system information. Therefore, we propose a service migration strategy based on multi-agent reinforcement learning, which users can independently make effective migration decisions according to some observed information.

3 Our Service Migration Strategy

3.1 Service Migration Mode

We model the service migration decision problem as a multi-agent partially observable Markov decision process(POMDP) model [10],which each intelligent agent corresponds to a vehicle user. The POMDP model is represented by a tuple (O, S, A, P, R, Ω), where O devotes the observation space of the agent, S devotes the state space of the environment, A devotes the action space of the agent, P devotes the state transition probability matrix, R devotes the reward function, and Ω devotes the observation Stochastic matrix. The S, P, and Ω cannot be directly obtained here, and the intelligent agent can only receive observation information and rewards in continuous interaction with the environment, attempting to learn and infer hidden information. O and R in the POMDP model of vehicle edge computing service migration are defined as follows:

- O represents the information that can be observed from the user's perspective:

$$o_t = (L_t, Data_t, Rate_t, C_t) \tag{7}$$

where, L_t denotes the geographic location of the user, $Data_t$ denotes the data volume of the user's computing task, $Rate_t$ denotes the data upload rate, and C_t denotes the number of CPU cycles required for the user's computing task.

- In the POMDP model, the reward function R is set to the negative sum of migration delay, communication delay, and calculation delay:

$$R = - \left(D_t^{mig} + D_t^{com} + D_t^{trans} \right) \tag{8}$$

The POMDP problem is a decision-making problem with incomplete information, where agents are unable to accurately observe the environment's state. Traditional decision theory and optimization methods cannot effectively solve the POMDP problem. Reinforcement learning (RL) is an incomplete machine learning method. It can learn effective decision-making strategies through trial and error in the interaction process between agents and the environment without prior knowledge, which is suitable for solving POMDP problems.

3.2 MADDPG Algorithm for Vehicle Edge Computing Network Service Migration

The MADDPG algorithm is a deep reinforcement learning method designed for multi-agent environment [11]. For complex multi-agent scenarios, we propose a MADDPG algorithm for network service migration of vehicle edge computing. The design idea of the algorithm is to combine deep learning and reinforcement learning methods to achieve collaboration and competition between vehicles in a multi-vehicle environment. In the travel process, vehicles can flexibly handle dynamic interactions according to their observed information, which is more stable and reliable in the face of complex scenes, and improves the flexibility and overall benefits of multi vehicle edge computing networks.The network structure of the algorithm is shown in Fig. 2. The algorithm describes each agent as two types of neural networks: Critic network and Actor network. The Critic network is responsible for processing the global information, evaluating the joint state and action value in the Multi-agent system, helping agents understand the behavior of other agents in the system, and making decisions based on the global information. The Actor network focuses on local observation information and is responsible for generating appropriate actions. The characteristic of MADDPG algorithm is that it adopts centralized training and distributed execution strategies. During the training phase, all agents share global information and conduct centralized training, which is beneficial for agents to understand the strategies and actions of other agents. During the execution phase, the agent only uses its own local observation information to make decisions. In the algorithm, each agent is composed of four neural networks: Actor current network θ_i^π, Critic current network θ_i^Q, Actor target network $\theta_i^{\pi'}$, and Critic target network $\theta_i^{Q'}$. The target network is introduced for stable training to alleviate training instability and overestimation issues.During the training process, the Critic network uses the target network to evaluate the value of joint states and actions, and fits the joint state action value function $Q_i(o,a)$.

In addition, the Critic network uses the target network to modify the policy of the actor network. During the execution process, the trained Actor network selects the optimal action $a_i = (o_i, \theta_i^\pi)$ according to local observations and obtains the cumulative reward value $J_i(\theta)$ of the agent i, which is represented as follows:

$$J_i(\theta) = E_{a_i \sim \pi(o_i, \theta_i^\pi)} \left(\sum \gamma r_i \right) \tag{9}$$

where, $\gamma \in (0,1)$ is a reward discount coefficient, and a smaller γ indicates a higher expectation of long-term rewards; θ is the set of network parameters for each agent; E represents the expected value of cumulative rewards, and the goal of an intelligent agent is to obtain as many average rewards as possible through learning.

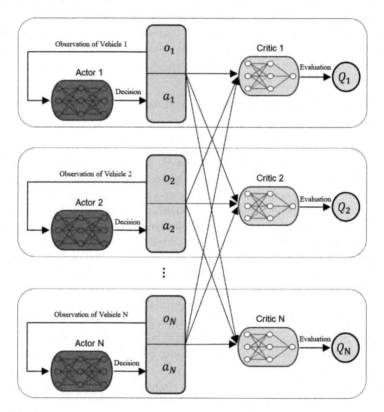

Fig. 2. Network structure of MADDPG algorithm for MEC service migration

Actor current network updates parameters through a gradient rise algorithm, and its gradient calculation formula is:

$$\nabla_{\theta_i^\pi} J = E[\nabla_{\theta_i^\pi} \pi(o_i, \theta_i^\pi) \cdot \nabla_{a_i} Q_i(o, a, \theta_{a_i}^Q)|_{a_i=\pi(o_i,\theta_i^\pi)}] \tag{10}$$

where, $\nabla_{a_i} Q_i(o, a, \theta_{a_i}^Q)|_{a_i=\pi(o_i,\theta_i^\pi)}]$ deotes the observation of the agent i in the current time slot and corresponding action state value.

Critic current network minimizes the mean squared error (MSE) through the gradient descent method, and then updates the network parameters. The calculation formula of loss function is:

$$y_i = r_i + \gamma Q_i(o', a', \theta_i^{Q'})|_{a_{i'}=\pi(s_{i'},\theta_i^{\pi'})} \tag{11}$$

$$L\left(\theta_i^Q\right) = E\left[y_i - Q_i\left(o, a, \theta_i^Q\right)\right]^2 \tag{12}$$

where, y_i is the target Q value; $Q_i(o', a', \theta_i^{Q'})|_{a_{i'}=\pi(s_{i'},\theta_i^{\pi'})}$ is the target Q value of the agent calculated by the Critic target network, which takes the state and action of the next state agent, as well as the actions of other agents, as inputs. The a' is next action, and o' is next observation.

In the algorithm, parameter updates for the Actor target network and the Critical target network are completed using soft updates. During each update, only a small portion of the target network parameters are updated to reduce jitter and oscillation during the training process. The method of soft update is as follows:

$$\theta_i^{Q'} \leftarrow \tau\theta_i^Q + (1 - \tau)\theta_i^{Q'} \tag{13}$$

$$\theta_i^{\pi'} \leftarrow \tau\theta_i^\pi + (1 - \tau)\theta_i^{\pi'} \tag{14}$$

where, τ is the soft update coefficient, $0 < \tau < 1$.

In order to address the correlation between training samples and the instability of sample probability distribution,the our algorithm adopts an experience replay strategy. The algorithm first stores the training samples generated by executing actions into the experience replay buffer pool. Then, during the training of the network, a data batch is uniformly extracted from the experience replay buffer pool as the training samples for each round of training. The probability of selecting new and old samples is equal. The size of the experience replay buffer is called the experience replay buffer pool size and the batch size extracted in each round is called the sampling size. The algorithm training process evaluates the quality of training results through the generated states and corresponding reward functions, so its training and testing use the same environmental settings.

The MADDPG algorithm for MEC service migration are described below:

Algorithm 1: MADDPG algorithm for vehicle edge computing network

1: For each agent i, initialize the Critic network $Q_i(o_i,a_i,\theta_i^Q)$ and Actor network $\pi(o_i,\theta_i^\pi)$ with random parameters θ_i^Q and θ_i^π

2 : initialize target network $\theta_i^{Q'}=\theta_i^Q$, $\theta_i^{\pi'}=\theta_i^\pi$.

3 : initialize experience replay buffer pool D and its volume M.

4 : **for** $episode = 1,2,...,K$ **do**

5 :   initialize local observation o

6 :   **for** $t = 1,2,...,T$ **do**

7 :   For each agent, select action $a_i=\pi(o_i,\theta_i^\pi)+\varepsilon,$, where ε is exploring noise.

8 :   Perform action $\{a_1,a_2,...,a_N\}$ and observe reward $\{r_1,r_2,...,r_N\}$ and new local observation o'.

9 :   Store tuple D($o,\{a_1,a_2,...,a_N\},\{r_1,r_2,...,r_N\},o'$) in experience replay buffer pool

10 :   Set local observation $o=o'$.

11 :   Randomly extract B tuples from the experience replay buffer pool D.

12 :   **for** each agent i **do**

13 :   According to equation (13), update Critic network Q_i by minimizing the loss function $L(\theta_i^Q)$.

14 :   By using equation (11), gradient update Actor networks π_i.

15 :   According to equation (14) and (15), update the target network by using soft update coefficient τ.

16 :   **end for**

17 :   **end for**

18: **end for**

4   Simulation Experiments and Performance Analysis

To make the simulation experiment closer to the actual scene, this paper uses the GPS track data set of taxis in Chengdu, China, to simulate the driving track of vehicles in the vehicle edge computing network. The experimental area selects a square area with a side length of 8km in the center of Chengdu urban area, and 4277 vehicle trajectories belonging to the region in the data set. Each trajectory last for 300min, and the position of the vehicle is recorded every 3min. We evenly place 64 MEC servers in this area, which each server covers an area of 1 square kilometer and a computing power F is 128GHz. During the experiment, the upload rate $Rate_t^{local}$ of the vehicle to the local node is set to 50Mbps, and the data link rate $Rate_t^{mec}$ between MEC servers is set to 500Mbps. The D_t^{freeze} and $D_t^{restart}$ are randomly taken in the [0.05, 0.2], and D_t^{st} is taken in [1.0, 3.0], and the hop count H_t^{mig} from the source node to the destination node is the Taxicab geometry between the two nodes. Within each time slot, the vehicle offloads all computing tasks to server, which a data volume of each task is taken in [0.2, 10] MB, and computing data per bit required [200, 120000] CPU cycles.

In the experiment, 4277 trajectories are divided into 3000 training data and 1277 validation data. During training and testing, n trajectories are randomly selected each time to form a user group. Three other service migration strategies are used as comparative strategies: (1) Random migration strategy which randomly selects MEC servers for migration each time; (2) Nearest migration strategy which selects the MEC server closest to the user for migration each time; (3) DQN based service migration strategy (DQN) [12].

The first experiment is to analyze the convergence of the algorithm.Set the number of users $n = 100$, and the arrival rate of user tasks $\lambda = 5$. The experimental results are shown in Fig. 3. After about 90 rounds, the algorithm gradually converges. The experimental results demonstrate that proposed algorithm is convergent and effective.

The second experiment verifies the effectiveness of our algorithm by comparing the performance of four strategies on real datasets. Experimental comparison results are shown in Fig. 4. It can be seen that the proposed algorithm performs the best among all algorithms, and can make better decisions when only partial observations are obtained.

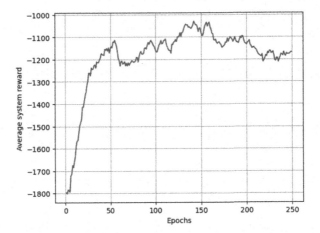

Fig. 3. Convergence analysis of the proposed algorithm

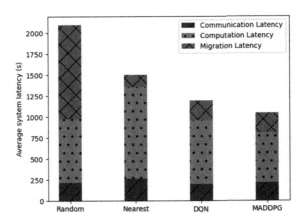

Fig. 4. Performance comparison of service migration strategies

The third experiment is to compare and analyze the adaptability of four algorithms when dealing with different numbers of users, with the number of users $n = 100, 120,$

140, 160, 180, and 200, respectively. Experimental results as shown in Fig. 5 show that the average system delay of four algorithms increases with the increase of the user's number. However, the proposed algorithm maintains its performance advantages over the other three algorithms, indicating that the proposed algorithm has relatively stable performance and can more effectively adapt to the increase in user numbers.

The fourth experiment is a performance comparison experiment of four algorithms under different task arrival rates. In the experiment, the task arrival rates are set to 1, 3, 5, 7, 9, and 11, respectively. From the experimental results as shown in Fig. 6, it can be seen that as the task arrival rate increases, the average system delay of all algorithms gradually increases. However, the proposed algorithm grows relatively slowly and remains lower than the level of other strategies, indicating that the proposed algorithm can better adapt to the increase in task arrival rate, and has good robustness.

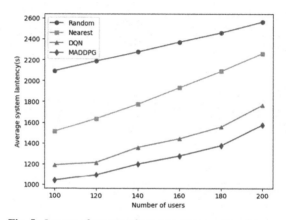

Fig. 5. Impact of user numbers on average system latency

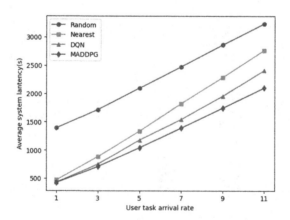

Fig. 6. Impact of user task arrival rate on average system latency

5 Conclusions

This paper proposes a vehicle edge computing service migration strategy based on multi-agent deep learning. This strategy models the service migration problem as a partially observable Markov decision process, and applies the MADDPG algorithm to enable vehicles to make appropriate distributed online migration decisions based on observed incomplete information during driving, properly handling competition and cooperation relationships, and improving system flexibility and overall profitability. The comparison results of simulation experiments have verified the convergence and effectiveness of the proposed strategy. However, in practical applications, other factors may also need to be considered, such as channel interference, dynamic network environment, etc. Future research can further consider these factors to improve the practicality of the algorithm.

Acknowledgment. These works were supported by the National Natural Science Foundation of China (No. 62062008,61762010).

References

1. Lv, P., Li, K., Xu, J., Li, T.S., Chen, N.J.: Cooperative sensing information transmission load optimization for automated vehicles. Chin. J. Comput. **44**, 1984–1997 (2021). https://doi.org/10.11897/SP.J.1016.2021.01984 (in Chinese)
2. Lv, P., Xu, J., Li, T.S., Xu, W.B.: Survey on edge computing technology for autonomous driving. J. Commun. **42**, 190–208 (2021). https://doi.org/10.11959/j.issn.1000-436x.2021045. (inChinese)
3. Yuan, Q., Li, J., Zhou, H., Lin, T., Luo, G., Shen, X.: A joint service migration and mobility optimization approach for vehicular edge computing. IEEE Trans. Veh. Technol. **69**, 9041–9052 (2020). https://doi.org/10.1109/TVT.2020.2999617
4. Wu, D.P., Lv, J., Li, Z.S., Wang, R.: Mobility aware edge service migration strategy. J. Commun. **41**, 1–13 (2020). https://doi.org/10.11959/j.issn.1000-436x.2020085. (inChinese)
5. Chen, X., et al.: Dynamic service migration and request routing for microservice in multicell mobile-edge computing. IEEE Internet of Things J. **9**, 13126–13143 (2022). https://doi.org/10.1109/JIOT.2022.3140183
6. Ngo, M.V., Luo, T., Hoang, H.T., Tony Quek, Q.S.: Coordinated container migration and base station handover in mobile edge computing. In: 2020 IEEE Global Communications Conference, pp. 1–6. IEEE Press, Taipei (2020). https://doi.org/10.1109/GLOBECOM42002.2020.9322368
7. Velrajan, S., Ceronmani, S.V.: QoS-aware service migration in multi-access edge compute using closed-loop adaptive particle swarm optimization algorithm. J. Network Syst. Manage. **31**, 17–36 (2023). https://doi.org/10.1007/s10922-022-09707-y
8. Abouaomar, A., Mlika, Z., Filali, A., Cherkaoui, S., Kobbane, A.: A deep reinforcement learning approach for service migration in mec-enabled vehicular networks. In: 2021 IEEE 46th Conference on Local Computer Networks, pp. 273–280. IEEE Press, Edmonton, AB (2021). https://doi.org/10.1109/LCN52139.2021.9524882
9. Peng, Y., et al.: Computing and communication cost-aware service migration enabled by transfer reinforcement learning for dynamic vehicular edge computing networks. IEEE Trans. Mob. Comput. **41**, 1–12 (2022). https://doi.org/10.1109/TMC.2022.3225239

10. Feriani, A., Hossain, E.: Single and multi-agent deep reinforcement learning for AI-enabled wireless networks: a tutorial. IEEE Commun. Surv. Tutor. **23**, 1226–1252 (2021). https://doi.org/10.1109/COMST.2021.3063822
11. Lowe, R., Wu, Y., Tamar, A., Harb, J., Abbeel, P., Mordatch, I.: Multi-agent actor-critic for mixed cooperative-competitive environments. In: 31st Annual Conference on Neural Information Processing Systems, pp. 6380–6391. MIT Press, Long Beach, CA (2017)
12. Arulkumaran, K., Deisenroth, M.P., Brundage, M., Bharath, A.A.: Deep reinforcement learning: a brief survey. IEEE Signal Process. Mag. **34**(6), 26–38 (2017). https://doi.org/10.1109/MSP.2017.2743240

A Lightweight Dual Branch Fusion Network for Single Image Deraining

Xin Wang⬛, Yangyang Zhang⬛, Hongxiang Liu⬛, and Chen Lyu$^{(\boxtimes)}$⬛

Shandong Normal University, Jinan 250014, China
lvchen@sdnu.edu.cn

Abstract. Transformers have shown promise in high-level vision tasks, but their direct application to low-level vision can lead to artifacts and high computational costs. To strike a balance between image quality and computational efficiency, this paper introduces a lightweight dual branch fusion network for single image deraining, termed LDFNet. LDFNet's encoder simultaneously uses CNN and Transformer, adeptly grasping global dependencies and detailed spatial nuances. To effectively fuse features from different branches, we propose Dual Branch Feature Fusion (DBFF) to continuously fuse intermediate features from two independent branches to complement each other and extract rich features to guide image reconstruction. For a streamlined network, the CNN branch employs Ghost to minimize feature map redundancy and cut down convolutional calculations. Meanwhile, the Transformer branch leverages recursive procedures and shares weights among its blocks, deepening the network but using less GPU resources and model parameters. Inside the encoder-decoder network, reuse encoder features using Gated Skip Connection (GC) to prevent over-decoding. Benchmark dataset tests indicate that LDFNet delivers commendable results, trimming down network parameters by 31%.

Keywords: Transformer · Convolutional neural network · Fusion · Lightweight neural network · Single image deraining

1 Introduction

Single image deraining presents a notably challenging issue. Initial studies emphasized understanding the structure of the background and rain layers, formulating constraints to refine the model's solution space [1–3]. In recent years, CNN-based methods for learning generalized priors have performed well and gradually replaced traditional image deraining methods [4–9]. However, the nature of convolutional local perceptual fields cannot model long-range pixels, and the fixed static weights prevent the network from flexibly adapting to the input. Transformer [10–13] which is not constrained by local connectivity, allows the network to learn long dependencies of the input image, which also makes Transformer naturally adapted to capture texture details in single image deraining. Vision Transformer [14] uses patches for image computation, and the recovered image introduces boundary artifacts around the patches, which affects the

© The Author(s), under exclusive license to Springer Nature Singapore Pte Ltd. 2024
Y. Sun et al. (Eds.): ChineseCSCW 2023, CCIS 2013, pp. 485–495, 2024.
https://doi.org/10.1007/978-981-99-9640-7_36

image quality. Vision Transformer shows a new way of thinking about single image deraining, and it is worth exploring how to use Transformer efficiently to get the best out of it. Enhancing the efficiency of global context modeling in single image deraining, while preserving intricate details, remains a sought-after improvement.

We found several problems with applying Transformer to single image deraining methods: 1) Transformer lacks inductive bias and the network converges slowly; 2) the excellent performance of Transformer usually comes at the cost of complexity and computational burden, making the algorithm difficult to deploy to resource-constrained real-world application devices; 3) relying solely on Transformer for single image deraining can lead to boundary issues and overlooks the potential benefits of blending CNN and Transformer features.

In response to these challenges, we've crafted a lightweight dual-branch fusion network for single image deraining, known as LDFNet.

More precisely, our key contributions include:

- We introduce LDFNet, a streamlined dual-branch fusion network tailored for single image deraining. This network synergizes the strengths of CNN's local feature extraction with the Transformer's ability to harness long-range dependencies, adeptly capturing both intricate spatial nuances and overarching semantic contexts.
- We propose Dual Branch Feature Fusion (DBFF), where different branches extract complementary features on demand to obtain rich features for image reconstruction, and the fusion module fuses features from different branches to obtain better features and makes full use of intermediate features to assist model training.
- For computational efficiency, we incorporate Ghost's enhanced channel attention block into the CNN branch and embed recursive functions within the Transformer segment. To minimize feature redundancy and repurpose encoder attributes, we suggest the Gated Skip Connection (GC) approach.

2   Related Work

Conventional techniques predominantly rely on manually crafted features and priors to characterize rain patterns. Li et al. [1] employs a Gaussian Mixture Model (GMM) as a preliminary model to differentiate between rain patterns and the background in the rain removal process. Kang et al. [15]proposes segmenting the image into low and high-frequency components and utilizing dictionary learning to eliminate rain patterns in the high-frequency sections. While satisfactory results are seen in certain situations, the prior-based method leans heavily on specific priors, potentially making it less effective in real-world settings with varied and intricate rain patterns. Consequently, conventional techniques may have constrained adaptability.

Lately, numerous deep learning-driven approaches have been introduced for single image deraining, marking substantial advancements in the field. For instance, Jiang et al. [7] introduced a multi-scale network that operates from coarse to fine levels for the purpose of eradicating rain patterns. Fu et al. [16] employed a basic CNN followed by an in-depth ResNet to eliminate rain patterns.

Recently, the Vision Transformer [14] has been applied to image restoration tasks, demonstrating impressive results owing to its robust modeling potential. Chen et al. [10] initially utilized the conventional Transformer with multiple heads and tails for various low-level vision challenges. Liang et al. [12] introduced a model that merges CNN and Transformer, grounded in the Swin Transformer framework, demonstrating outstanding results with retained computational efficiency. Wang et al. [17] developed a U-structured Transformer for image restoration, drawing inspiration from the Swin Transformer.

3   Method

3.1   Network Architecture

As illustrated in Fig. 1, the LDFNet we introduced comprises a dual-branch encoder-decoder primary network along with Gated Skip Connections (GC).

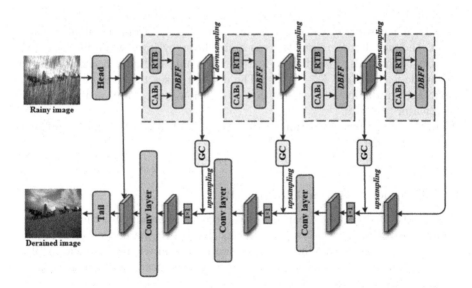

Fig. 1. The architecture of the proposed LDFNet.

For a provided rainy image $I \in \mathbb{R}^{H \times W \times C}$, H_{SF} is initially employed to derive shallow feature $F_0 \in \mathbb{R}^{H \times W \times C}$:

$$F_0 = H_{SF}(I) \tag{1}$$

where $H \times W$ is the spatial dimension and C is the number of channels. H_{SF} is used as the shallow feature extraction module, a 3×3 convolutional layer is employed to capture low-level features, preserving intricate textures.

Following the U-shaped structure, the extracted shallow features F_0 enter the dual-branch encoder-decoder network with Gated Skip Connection (GC) to obtain the deep features $F_D \in \mathbb{R}^{H \times W \times C}$:

$$F_D = H_{DF}(F_0) \tag{2}$$

Here, H_{DF} represents the primary dual-branch encoder-decoder network functioning as the deep feature extraction module. The derived features, F_i, from every layer are directed into the encoder-decoder network's dual branches. F_i enters the CNN branch and uses Channel Attention Block (CAB) to extract the image local features F_i^C; after F_i enters the Transformer branch, it is downsampled 2 times and sent to the recursive Transformer block to extract the image global features F_i^T. After obtaining the features extracted from two different branches, the two are fed into Dual Branch Feature Fusion(DBFF) to obtain the fused features $F_i^{'}$:

$$F_i^{'} = DSFF(F_i^C, F_i^T), \quad i = 1, 2, ..., N \tag{3}$$

$F_i^{'}$ gets the next layer of input features F_{i+1} after downsampling to the desired dimension according to the encoder structure. Starting from the high-resolution input, the encoder decreases the space size layer by layer while increasing the number of channels. The shallow feature F_0 is obtained after 4 encoding layers to encode feature $F_E \in \mathbb{R}^{\frac{H}{8} \times \frac{W}{8} \times 8C}$. The decoder takes the coded feature F_E as input and gradually recovers the high-resolution representation to obtain the deep feature $F_D \in \mathbb{R}^{H \times W \times C}$.

In the image reconstruction module H_{IR}, a 3×3 convolution is applied to produce the final image.

$$\hat{I} = H_{IR}(F_D + F_0) \tag{4}$$

3.2   Channel Attention Block(CAB)

In a well-trained network, feature maps are usually redundant, thus ensuring a comprehensive understanding of the data. To reduce the burden of redundant features on the network, Ghost convolution is used in Channel Attention Block for redundant feature maps obtained using a simple linear transformation. Ghost convolution generates the feature maps in two steps, the first part is a regular convolution with reduced number of channels, and the second part uses simple linear transformation to generate the remaining channels. Fig. 2 illustrates that each CAB is composed of two Ghost modules, followed by a ReLU activation and a SE-Net built upon the Ghost module.

3.3   Recursive Transformer Block(RTB)

Using recursive structures between Transformer blocks enables parameter sharing while increasing network depth and reducing memory consumption. As shown

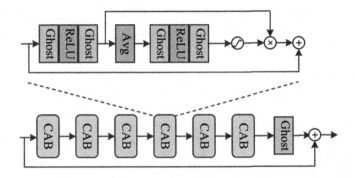

Fig. 2. Channel Attention Module(CAB).

in Fig. 3, Recursive Transformer Block can be represented as:

$$RTB = TB_L^{\circlearrowleft}(F_{in}) \tag{5}$$

where TB is two tandem Transformer blocks, $\circlearrowleft$ represents recursive operations, and each RTB recurses L times.

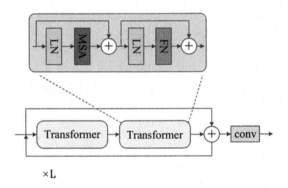

Fig. 3. Recursive Transformer block(RTB).

3.4 Dual Branch Feature Fusion(DBFF)

To effectively combine the features of CNN and Transformer, we use (as shown in Fig. 4) Dual Branch Feature Fusion module (DBFF), which combines the self-attention mechanism and the multimodal fusion mechanism. The dual attention mechanism effectively captures useful spatial and channel information, allows only useful information features to be passed further, and uses spatial attention and channel attention for the CNN branch and Transformer branch, respectively, to achieve feature reproduction calibration.

For a given i^{th} CNN branch feature F_i^C and i^{th} Transformer branch feature F_i^T, DBFF first fuses the two directly at a fine grain to obtain the fused feature F_i^{CT}.

$$F_i^{CT} = ReLU(conv(F_i^C)) \odot ReLU(conv(F_i^T)) \tag{6}$$

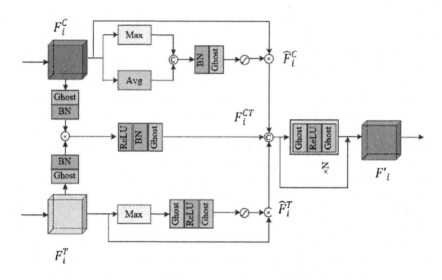

Fig. 4. Dual Branch Feature Fusion(DBFF).

Global averaging and maximum pooling operations are performed on F_i^C to capture the spatial correlation of features in CNN branches, while enhancing local details and suppressing noise.

$$\hat{F_i^C} = SpatialAttn(F_i^C) \tag{7}$$

Using channel attention for F_i^T to further mine feature contextual information enhances the global information of Transformer.

$$\hat{F_i^T} = ChannelAttn(F_i^T) \tag{8}$$

After getting the above 3 features, DBFF concats them together into a 3-layer residual block to further fuse the features, and finally the feature $F_i^{'}$ effectively captures the global and local contextual information.

$$F_i^{'} = RB_3(RB_2(RB_1(concat(F_i^{CT}, \hat{F_i^C}, \hat{F_i^T})))) \tag{9}$$

3.5 Gated Skip Connection (GC)

If the features are directly passed from encoder to decoder, redundant information may interfere with the decoding stage. As shown in Fig. 5, this paper uses

Gated Skip Connection (GC) to transfer the features encoded by each encoder layer into two parallel paths, and after one of the paths is nonlinearly activated by GELU, the two paths are multiplied by elements to obtain F_i^E. After splicing F_i^E with F_i^D at this point, the number of channels is then adjusted using 1×1 convolution.

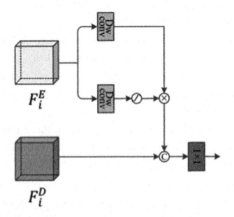

Fig. 5. Gated Skip Connection (GC).

3.6 Loss Function

In this paper, we use a mixed loss function, including $\mathcal{L}_1$ and $\mathcal{L}_{SSIM}$:

$$\mathcal{L}_1 = \frac{1}{N} \sum_{i=1}^{N} ||\hat{I} - GT|| \tag{10}$$

$$\mathcal{L}_{SSIM} = 1 - SSIM(\hat{I}, GT) \tag{11}$$

Combining the two loss weights, the final loss function can be expressed as:

$$\mathcal{L} = \mathcal{L}_1 + \lambda \mathcal{L}_{SSIM} \tag{12}$$

4   Experiment

4.1   Implementation Details

Datasets. In our tests, the effectiveness of our approach is verified using five synthetic datasets: Test100 [18], Test2800 [16], Rain100L [19], Rain100H [19], and Test1200 [20].

Setting. We augmented the training dataset by horizontally flipping and rotating images at 90°, 180°, and 270° angles. Regarding training specifics, our paper's network incorporates four encoder-decoder levels. The Transformer blocks count from level-1 to level-4 is as follows: [2,3,3,4]. Every level has 2 recursions, and attention headers count is [1,2,2,4]. The channels distribution is [48,96,192,384], and each CNN block consists of 6 concatenated CAB blocks. Training employed 256×256 patches, a batch size of 16, and spanned 4×10^{-5} iterations. The Adam optimizer is used with an initial learning rate of 2×10^{-4} that gradually reduces to 1×10^{-6}, leveraging the cosine annealing approach. All experiments utilized the Pytorch platform on four Nvidia RTX 3090 GPUs.

4.2   Comparision with the State-of-the-Art Methods

Qualitative Results. In Fig. 6, we show the example of LDFNet with state-of-the-art methods on Rain100L. Compared to other methods, LDFNet can remove rain patterns and restore clean backgrounds more effectively.

Fig. 6. Comparison with state-of-the-art methods on Rain100L.

Quantitative Results. To demonstrate the effectiveness of LDFNet, we tested the deraining results on the synthetic datasets using PSNR and SSIM as shown in Table 1. LDFNet improved PSNR by 0.05~0.12 dB and SSIM by 0.003~0.004 dB on the synthetic dataset.

4.3   Ablation Study

Study on DBFF. For the two-branch design of the network, various architectural choices are tried in this paper. First, a single-branch network with only a Transformer is compared with a single-branch network with only a CNN branch.

Table 1. Average PSNR and SSIM metrics on five synthetic datasets.

Methods	Test100		Rain100H		Rain100L		Test2800		Test1200	
	PSNR	SSIM	PSNR	SSIM	PSNR	SSIM	PSNR	SSIM	PSNR	SSIM
DerainNet [16]	22.77	0.810	14.92	0.592	27.03	0.884	24.31	0.861	23.38	0.835
DIDMDN [20]	22.56	0.818	17.35	0.524	25.23	0.741	28.13	0.867	29.65	0.901
RESCAN [21]	25.00	0.835	26.36	0.786	29.80	0.881	31.29	0.904	30.51	0.882
PreNet [5]	24.81	0.851	26.77	0.858	32.44	0.950	31.75	0.916	31.36	0.911
MSPFN [7]	27.50	0.876	28.66	0.860	32.40	0.933	32.82	0.930	32.39	0.916
MPRNet [8]	30.27	0.897	30.41	0.890	36.40	0.965	33.64	0.938	32.91	0.916
HiNet [22]	30.29	0.906	30.65	0.894	37.28	0.970	33.91	**0.941**	33.05	0.919
Ours	**30.36**	**0.909**	**30.71**	**0.897**	**37.53**	**0.974**	**33.95**	**0.941**	**33.17**	**0.923**

Next, this paper uses a two-branch network, which can be classified as no fusion, one-way fusion, and two-way fusion. Among them, the two-branch network without fusion block is poor, which is because the features are too separated. And the performance is improved when the intermediate features are fused unidirectionally, but the information flows unidirectionally and lacks information exchange. Finally, intermediate bidirectional fusion is chosen as the architecture of the two-branch fusion block.

Study on Recursive. Specifically, good deraining results can be achieved in this paper using only 2.64M. In this paper, the recursive design is discussed for ablation experiments, that is, the number of recursions. The following Table 2 lists the PSNR on Rain100L for different recurrence counts.

Table 2. PSNR on Rain100L for different number of recursions.

Number of recursions	PSNR(dB)
1	6.726
2	37.53
3	35.18
4	25.78

Study on Lightweight Network. This subsection conducts ablation experiments on the effect of each component of the network on the model parameters, and the superiority of the proposed module selection design for model lightweighting is known from in Table 3. For each model this paper is trained in Rain100L from scratch and the corresponding PSNR is given.

Table 3. Ablation experiments about various architectural design related to the proposed method.

component	Params (MB)	PSNR (dB)
CNN	0.578	34.36
CNN(without Ghost)	0.593	34.19
Transformer	10.47	35.44
Transformer(without recursive)	22.73	34.78
CNN+Transformer	2.64	37.53
CNN+Transformer(without GC)	2.69	37.21
CNN +Transformer(without Ghost)	2.71	37.33
CNN +Transformer(without recursive)	5.14	37.19

5   Conclusion

In this paper, we propose a lightweight dual branch fusion network for single image deraining(LDFNet) that effectively combines the complementary features of CNN and Transformer using DBFF. To achieve a lightweight network, Ghost is introduced in the CNN branch to reduce redundant features, and recursive shared parameters are introduced in the Transformer. In addition to this, this paper also uses Gated Skip Connection to reuse encoder features to prevent over-decoding. We hope that the work in this paper brings some inspiration for feature extraction of single image deraining.

References

1. Li, Y., Tan, R.T., Guo, X., Lu, J., Brown, M.S.: Rain streak removal using layer priors. In: Proceedings of the IEEE Conference on Computer Vision and Pattern Recognition, pp. 2736–2744 (2016)
2. Luo, Y., Xu, Y., Ji, H.: Removing rain from a single image via discriminative sparse coding. In: Proceedings of the IEEE International Conference on Computer Vision, pp. 3397–3405 (2015)
3. Chen, Y.-L., Hsu, C.-T.: A generalized low-rank appearance model for spatio-temporally correlated rain streaks. In: Proceedings of the IEEE International Conference on Computer Vision, pp. 1968–1975 (2013)
4. Wei, W., Meng, D., Zhao, Q., Xu, Z., Wu, Y.: Semi-supervised transfer learning for image rain removal. In: Proceedings of the IEEE/CVF Conference on Computer Vision and Pattern Recognition, pp. 3877–3886 (2019)
5. Ren, D., Zuo, W., Hu, Q., Zhu, P., Meng, D.: Progressive image deraining networks: A better and simpler baseline. In: Proceedings of the IEEE/CVF Conference on Computer Vision and Pattern Recognition, pp. 3937–3946 (2019)
6. Yasarla, R., Patel, V.M.: Uncertainty guided multi-scale residual learning-using a cycle spinning CNN for single image de-raining. In: Proceedings of the IEEE/CVF Conference on Computer Vision and Pattern Recognition, pp. 8405–8414 (2019)

7. Jiang, K., et al.: Multi-scale progressive fusion network for single image deraining. In: Proceedings of the IEEE/CVF Conference on Computer Vision and Pattern Recognition, pp. 8346–8355 (2020)
8. Zamir, S.W., et al.: Multi-stage progressive image restoration. In: Proceedings of the IEEE/CVF Conference on Computer Vision and Pattern Recognition, pp. 14 821–14 831 (2021)
9. Tu, Z., et al.: Maxim: multi-axis MLP for image processing. In: Proceedings of the IEEE/CVF Conference on Computer Vision and Pattern Recognition, pp. 5769–5780 (2022)
10. Chen, H., et al.: Pre-trained image processing transformer. In: Proceedings of the IEEE/CVF Conference on Computer Vision and Pattern Recognition, pp. 12 299–12 310 (2021)
11. Zamir, S.W., Arora, A., Khan, S., Hayat, M., Khan, F.S., Yang, M.-H.: Restormer: efficient transformer for high-resolution image restoration. In: Proceedings of the IEEE/CVF Conference on Computer Vision and Pattern Recognition, pp. 5728–5739 (2022)
12. Liang, J., Cao, J., Sun, G., Zhang, K., Van Gool, L., Timofte, R.: SwinIR: image restoration using Swin transformer. In: Proceedings of the IEEE/CVF International Conference on Computer Vision, pp. 1833–1844 (2021)
13. Wang, Z., Cun, X., Bao, J., Zhou, W., Liu, J., Li, H.: Uformer: a general u-shaped transformer for image restoration. In: Proceedings of the IEEE/CVF Conference on Computer Vision and Pattern Recognition, pp. 17 683–17 693 (2022)
14. Dosovitskiy, A., et al.: An image is worth 16×16 words: Transformers for image recognition at scale. arXiv preprint arXiv:2010.11929 (2020)
15. Kang, L.-W., Lin, C.-W., Fu, Y.-H.: Automatic single-image-based rain streaks removal via image decomposition. IEEE Trans. Image Process. **21**(4), 1742–1755 (2011)
16. Fu, X., Huang, J., Ding, X., Liao, Y., Paisley, J.: Clearing the skies: a deep network architecture for single-image rain removal. IEEE Trans. Image Process. **26**(6), 2944–2956 (2017)
17. Wang, Z., Cun, X., Bao, J., Zhou, W., Liu, J., Li, H.U.: A general u-shaped transformer for image restoration. In: Proceedings of the IEEE/CVF Conference on Computer Vision and Pattern Recognition, New Orleans, LA, USA, pp. 19–24 (2022)
18. Zhang, H., Sindagi, V., Patel, V.M.: Image de-raining using a conditional generative adversarial network. IEEE Trans. Circuits Syst. Video Technol. **30**(11), 3943–3956 (2019)
19. Yang, W., Tan, R.T., Feng, J., Liu, J., Guo, Z., Yan, S.: Deep joint rain detection and removal from a single image. In: Proceedings of the IEEE Conference on Computer Vision and Pattern Recognition, pp. 1357–1366 (2017)
20. Zhang, H., Patel, V.M.: Density-aware single image de-raining using a multi-stream dense network. In: Proceedings of the IEEE Conference on Computer Vision and Pattern Recognition, pp. 695–704 (2018)
21. Li, X., Wu, J., Lin, Z., Liu, H., Zha, H.: Recurrent squeeze-and-excitation context aggregation net for single image deraining. In: Ferrari, V., Hebert, M., Sminchisescu, C., Weiss, Y. (eds.) ECCV 2018. LNCS, vol. 11211, pp. 262–277. Springer, Cham (2018). https://doi.org/10.1007/978-3-030-01234-2_16
22. Chen, L., Lu, X., Zhang, J., Chu, X., Chen, C.: HINet: half instance normalization network for image restoration. In: Proceedings of the IEEE/CVF Conference on Computer Vision and Pattern Recognition, pp. 182–192 (2021)

3D Object Detection Method Based on LiDAR Point Cloud Data

Shufan Wang, Zeqiu Chen, Shulin Sun, Jiayao Li, and Ruizhi Sun[✉]

College of Information and Electrical Engineering, China Agricultural University, Beijing 100083, China
{wsf,chenzq,sunshulin,lijiayao,sunruizhi}@cau.edu.cn

Abstract. With the development of autonomous driving technology, the agricultural field is also developing in the direction of intelligence and automation, and the automated operation of agricultural machinery has become an inevitable trend. Among them, the application of LIDAR-based three-dimensional object detection technology is receiving more and more attention in the field of agricultural production. In this paper, we explore the 3D detection technology of agricultural machines based on LiDAR point cloud data during the driving process of unmanned agricultural machines. A 3D object detection method based on LiDAR point cloud data is proposed to detect 3D objects (i.e., tractors) in unmanned farm surroundings. First, the Euclidean clustering algorithm is used to cluster point cloud data of the region of interest to generate non-ground point cloud. Then, the Ensemble of shape Function is introduced to extract point cloud cluster characteristics. Finally, the support vector machine classifier optimized by genetic algorithm is constructed to detect 3D objects for unmanned farming machine operation. The experimental results show that the method can achieve object detection in 3D object detection at a faster speed and provide support for downstream path planning and road obstacle avoidance for autonomous driving.

Keywords: Unmanned farm machinery · Object detection · Point cloud · Cluster · Classification

1 Introduction

The application of driverless technology in agriculture not only helps to significantly improve the farming environment, but also helps to save a great deal of physical labor and promotes the modernization, informatization and autonomy of agriculture. However, improving the efficiency of farming operations also brings certain risks. Agricultural machinery has many safety hazards. In order to ensure the safety of farm machineries and pedestrians, during the driving process of unmanned farm machinery, more attention must be paid to the surrounding environment, including people, farm machineries and other obstacles, etc.

Lidar is an active sensor with high accuracy of 3D spatial measurement, strong anti-interference capability, independent of light, and has been widely used for environment sensing in autonomous vehicle driving. There are deep learning and clustering methods for obstacle detection based on LiDAR. Currently, numerous researchers based on the KITTI dataset [1] use PointNet [2], PointNet + + [3], PointRCNN (PV-RCNN) [4], PointVoxel-RCNN (PV-RCNN) [5], PointNetVLAD [6], SE-SSD [7]. Although deep learning methods have advantages such as good fitting ability, they also have disadvantages such as low training efficiency and high hardware requirements. As a result, some scholars have also used clustering methods to process LiDAR point cloud data. To this end, in response to the application requirements for safety in common working scenarios of agricultural machinery, this paper explores the combination of point cloud clustering algorithms and support vector machines with the aim to achieve accurate detection of tractors in the above scenarios. We take the detection of pedestrians and other operating agricultural machinery as an example, which can be a technical reference for improving the safety of agricultural machinery driving and operation.

2   Establishment of the Dataset

Some relatively well-established datasets have been established in the field of autonomous driving, such as the KITTI. However, in practical applications, it has been found that the data diversity of the current dataset is limited and greatly influenced by the objective environment. To increase the accuracy of object detection and test the application effect of the proposed algorithm in real farmland scenarios, this paper builds a real farmland scenario obstacle detection dataset based on a John Deere JD1204 tractor built with LiDAR, and collects environmental data from fields, field machine paths and real working scenarios of farmland in Miyun District Agricultural Machinery Cooperative in Beijing. The dataset is built in three steps. Firstly, point cloud data are collected based on a LIDAR equipped tractor. Secondly, the point cloud data are annotated by using image and point cloud annotation tools. And finally the dataset for target detection is created.

By enough representative data, a dataset of agricultural machine operation scenes that can be used for 3D obstacle detection is constructed, with a total of 1450 sets of point cloud data. This dataset can lay a solid foundation for subsequent unmanned agricultural machine object detection and promote the development of unmanned agricultural machines.

2.1   Collection Device

The data acquisition unit is mounted on the JD1204 tractor and consists mainly of the VLP-16 LiDAR, the combined GNSS/IMU navigation system, the FLIR camera and the Nuvo-810GC IPC. The LiDAR, camera and GNSS/IMU are jointly calibrated. The LIDAR is mounted on the front tractor mount and the data is collected at a tractor height of 2.7 m and h of 0.89 m. The VLP-16 LIDAR has a point cloud data acquisition frequency of 10 Hz and can acquire 288,000 data points per second [8] meets the requirements for tractor point cloud data acquisition.

2.2   Region of Interest Determination

The area of interest is a rectangle (a $\times$ b $\times$ c) and is the smallest area that the LIDAR should scan in the longitudinal, lateral and vertical directions, objects outside the area of interest can be disregarded. The area of interest is determined by considering the following three dimensions:

(1) in the longitudinal direction, the braking distance and safety reserve distance between the runway and farmland are crucial;
(2) in the transverse direction, the tractor in the adjacent lane in the machine road and the adjacent operating strip in the farmland should be considered;
(3) in the vertical direction, the height of the tractor should be considered.

Based on this, the length of the rectangular body is determined to be 15 m, using two times this value as a reference distance. In the horizontal direction, the width of the rectangular body is determined to be three times the width, i.e. 15 m, by referring to the maximum width of common implements in Beijing (generally less than 5 m).

3 Object Detection Process

The object detection process based on LiDAR data is shown in Fig. 1. The detection process consists of four main modules: point cloud data acquisition module, point cloud data pre-processing module, clustering analysis module and object detection module.

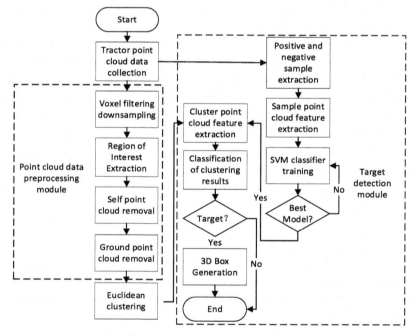

Fig. 1. Detection process of tractor

3.1   Point Cloud Data Acquisition Module

LiDAR point cloud data was collected from the front, side and rear of the tractor in common working scenarios of agricultural machinery (Fig. 2).

(a) Garage scenes   **(b) Mechanized road scenes**   **(c) Farmland scenes**

Fig. 2. Point cloud data acquisition of tractors' shape in working scene

3.2   Point Cloud Data Pre-Processing Module

Point cloud data pre-processing is the basis for tractor detection. The Voxel Grid voxel filtering method was used to down-sampling, then the LIDAR was used to delineate the area of interest and extract the point cloud data, and to remove the point cloud data from the data acquisition tractor itself, and finally the Random Sampling Consistency (RANSAC) method [9] was used to remove the ground point cloud data.

3.3   Cluster Analysis Module

The main clustering algorithms include DBSCAN [10], K-means Euclid's clustering algorithm [8]. Among them, DBSCAN algorithm consumes a lot of memory resources and requires a high performance processor for large scale data. K-means algorithm is difficult to achieve the real-time requirement in the case of more complex scenes. The tractor has a large shape and its point cloud data has obvious neighborhood relationship compared with the point cloud data of other objects. Therefore, this paper uses the Euclidean clustering algorithm based on the distance criterion, combined with the KD-Tree nearest neighbor query algorithm [11], to perform nearest neighbor search for closely spaced point clouds, which can achieve the effects of aggregating point clouds of different objects separately and reducing the clustering time.

3.4   Tractor Detection Module

In addition to the tractor, the clustering results also contain other objects, such as trees and walls, which have different point cloud features, so the point cloud features of the tractor and other objects are extracted for classification and detection. In the process of extracting tractor point cloud features, the method used in this article is the Ensemble of shape Functions (ESF) [12].

The point cloud features of the tractor have small samples and high dimensional patterns, so the point cloud clusters are trained by using Support Vector Machine (SVM)

[13] and therefore the Gaussian function is chosen as the kernel function of the SVM. To train the model, point cloud clusters of tractors and other objects are keyed from the original point cloud data, and the ESF features of the point cloud clusters are extracted and fed into the SVM model as positive and negative samples respectively.

Once tractor identification is complete, bounding boxes need to be added to the tractor point cloud clusters to determine whether adjacent tractors are in collision. To do this, the point cloud clusters are defined along the x and y axes [14], generating bounding boxes for better prediction accuracy.

4   Results and Analysis

The proposed method was verified on a computer with an Intel i7–8595 processor and 12 GB of RAM on an Ubuntu system, based on C + +.

4.1   Point Cloud Pre-Processing

Point Cloud Down-Sampling. The number of points before filtering was 19,690 and after filtering was 5,807, a reduction of approximately 70%. Thus, the Voxel Grid voxel filtering method can preserve key features while saving significant computational resources (Fig. 3).

(a) Original point cloud   (b) Point cloud after down-sampling

Fig. 3. Comparison of point cloud before and after down-sampling

Define the Area of Interest. Figure 4 shows the results of the point cloud data extraction for the area of interest. The point cloud data include the tractor and other objects and the number of point clouds is further reduced to 1,253, a reduction of approximately 78%. The average time for point cloud down-sampling and region of interest extraction was 1 ms per frame. Extracting the point cloud from the region of interest allows the computational resources to be focused on the area of greatest interest to the tractor, which will greatly reduce the workload and complexity of subsequent point cloud processing.

Ground Division. The region of interest in Fig. 4 contains ground point clouds which are classified as noise in the obstacle point cloud clustering. Figure 5 shows the results of

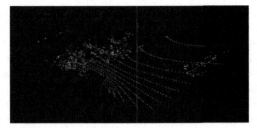

Fig. 4. Extracting results of point cloud for region of interest

using RANSAC to remove the ground point cloud in the region of interest. 605 ground points are removed, leaving 648 non-ground points, with a removal rate of nearly 50% and an average time of 30 ms per frame.

Fig. 5. Results of removing the influence of ground point clouds

4.2 Clustering

The clustering results are shown in Fig. 6, where the point cloud clusters of three tractors and seven other objects in the region of interest are clustered. The average clustering time per cluster is reduced from 0.207 ms to 0.125 ms with the KD-Tree nearest neighbor search algorithm, so Euclidean clustering performs well in terms of real-time and robustness for full scene obstacle point cloud clustering.

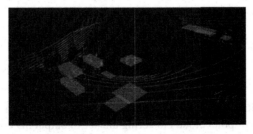

Fig. 6. Result of clustering

4.3   Object Detection

Classification Results. SVM uses the Gaussian function as the kernel function for training. When the penalty factor c and the parameter g of the Gaussian function are adjusted, over fitting is easy to occur. Therefore, multiple optimization algorithms are used for comparative experiments on SVM optimization, and ten-fold cross-validation is conducted for the optimization parameter value function provided by the SVM class to train the optimal model.

The optimization algorithm Particle Swarm Optimization (PSO), Genetic Algorithm (GA), Sparrow Search Algorithm (SSA) and Firefly Algorithm (FA) are selected to optimize the parameter selection of SVM. Besides, three representative datasets of UCI are used for training and testing verification. The data features have similarities and differences, making it easier to compare the control variables, as shown in Fig. 1.

Table 1. Test data set

Dataset	Data type	Type of property	Number of instances	Number of attributes
Glass	Diversity	Real numbers	214	9
Wine	Diversity	Integers, Real numbers	178	13
Shuttle	Diversity	Integer	14500	9

Through comparison experiments, the classification accuracy of PSO, GA, SSA and FA for SVM optimization was obtained. It can be seen from Table 1, the SVM optimized by GA has a higher accuracy of 91.18%, and the high correct rate lays the foundation for the subsequent accurate detection of tractors and generation of 3D frames (Table 2).

Table 2. Accuracy of the four optimization algorithms

Standard datasets	PSO-SVM accuracy/%	GA-SVM accuracy/%	SSA-SVM accuracy/%	FA-SVM accuracy/%
Glass	70.5	79.6	77.3	84.1
Wine	97.1	94.3	94.3	88.6
Shuttle	99.7	99.7	99.8	99.8
Average accuracy rate	89.1	91.2	90.4	90.8

Tractor Test Results. After completing the tractor identification, a 3D border needs to be added to the tractor point cloud clustering cluster to output 3D coordinates based on the LiDAR coordinate system.

(1) Garage Scene

The tractors in the garage are of many types and closely spaced, the results of the inspection are shown in Fig. 7 and the coordinates of the four tractors are shown in Table 3. Some of the tractors have incomplete point clouds as they are obscured or only parts of the bodies are within the area of interest, so the generated 3D boxes only contain parts of the scanned point cloud.

Fig. 7. Detection results of tractors in garage

Table 3. Coordinates of tractors in the garage(m)

Number	Min.x	Min.y	Min.z	Max.x	Max.y	Max.z
1	0.05	2.30	−0.53	1.34	4.40	1.17
2	1.94	4.22	−0.09	3.82	5.44	1.53
3	4.15	0.18	−0.57	7.88	2.13	2.08
4	4.78	2.86	0.99	6.02	6.15	2.06

(2) Machine Path Scene

Figure 8 shows the point cloud data from the data collection tractor driving over the tractor path for two tractors, the coordinates of the two tractors are shown in Table 4. Due to the distance between the two tractors, the farthest tractor can only be scanned, but a 3D frame containing part of the tractor point cloud can still be generated.

(3) Farmland Scenes

Figure 9 shows the point cloud data of a data collection tractor from a farm field with one tractor on the left and one on the right, and the coordinates of the two tractors are shown in Table 5.

In the farmland, the braking distance of the tractor is much smaller than the braking distance of the machine path. In Table 5, the LIDAR detects the tractor ahead at a distance of approximately 13 m. The average single frame data processing time is 110 ms. Thus,

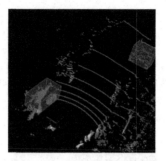

Fig. 8. Detection results of tractors on farm road

Table 4. Coordinates of tractors on farm road(m)

Number	Min.x	Min.y	Min.z	Max.x	Max.y	Max.z
1	0.21	1.92	−0.67	4.00	3.58	0.63
2	12.64	−2.01	−0.23	13.79	0.13	1.71

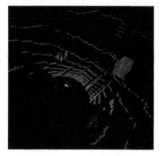

(a) Right-hand tractor   (b) Tractor on the left

Fig. 9. Detection results of tractors in field

the tractor has sufficient time to take safety measures after detecting the tractor in the area of interest ahead.

Table 5. Coordinate of tractors in field (m)

Number	Min.x	Min.y	Min.z	Max.x	Max.y	Max.z
1	9.02	−4.89	0.17	13.33	−3.09	1.98
2	2.35	3.43	−0.51	6.50	5.33	1.63

In the garage, the accuracy rate is 88.9%, but the tractors in the garage are closely spaced and heavily obscured, making them susceptible to false detection and a lower recall rate of 86.0%. The recall rate is 95.2% on the farm tracks, but the tracks contained obstacles such as trucks and carts, which are more similar to the tractor point cloud features and prone to false detection, resulting in a relatively low accuracy rate of 86.8%. In the farmland, the environment is simpler, there are only obstacles such as pedestrians, farm machinery and crops. There are fewer types of obstacles, and the point cloud features vary greatly between each obstacle, so it is easy to detect. The accuracy rate and the recall rate are 94.4% and 96.2% respectively in the farmland scenes, which are better than the garage and the machine road scenes.

This shows that the tractor detection method based on LiDAR data has a high accuracy rate in all three different scenarios. Compared to the vehicle detection in the urban road scenario, the detection accuracy of this method has been improved. Of course, there are differences between the farmland scenario and the urban scenario, as well as the accuracy rate can not be fully and directly judged as to the merits of the method (Table 6).

Table 6. Evaluation of experimental results

Collection scenes	Correct inspection/vehicle	Error detection/vehicle	Missing inspection/vehicle	Accuracy rate/%	Recall rate/%
Garages	692	86	113	88.9	86.0
Mechanized Roads	178	27	9	86.8	95.2
Farmland	102	6	4	94.4	96.2

5   Conclusion

For the application needs of agricultural machinery detection in common working scenarios such as garages, machine paths and farmlands for unmanned and autonomous operations, this paper explores a tractor detection method based on LIDAR data and clustering algorithms, taking tractors as an example.

(1) According to the tractor driving and operating characteristics, braking distance and safety reserve distance, the LIDAR area of interest is determined to be 15 m long × 15 m wide × 5 m high.

(2) Use the Euclidean clustering algorithm based on KD-Tree to cluster non-ground point cloud clusters in the region of interest. According to the external features of the tractor, the point cloud clustering features are extracted by using the set of shape geometry functions, and the point cloud clusters are classified by using the SVM method to finally generate a 3D frame of the tractor.

(3) The object detection and coordinate output of LIDAR for tractors in common working scenarios of agricultural machinery were achieved. Based on the continuous multi-frame point cloud dataset, the detection accuracies of the tractor in the garage, farm track and farm field are 88.9%, 86.8% and 94.4% respectively, and the recall

rates are 86.0%, 95.2% and 96.2%, respectively, with an average single-frame data processing time of 110 ms. Compared with the vehicle detection in urban road scenarios, the detection accuracy of this method is improved.

3D object detection is an important part of the perception system in the unmanned field and is of great significance for subsequent autonomous driving tasks such as path planning and road obstacle avoidance.

References

1. Geiger, A., Lenz, P., Urtasun, R.: Are we ready for autonomous driving? The KITTI vision benchmark suite. In: Proceedings of the IEEE Conference on Computer Vision and Pattern Recognition (CVPR), pp. 3354–3361. IEEE Computer Society Press, Los Alamitos (2012)
2. Charles, R.Q., Su, H., Kaichun, M., et al.: PointNet: deep learning on point sets for 3D classification and segmentation. In: Proceedings of the IEEE International Conference on Computer Vision and Pattern Recognition (CVPR), pp. 77–85. IEEE Computer Society Press, Los Alamitos (2017)
3. Qi, C.R., Yi, L., Su, H., et al.: PointNet++: deep hierarchical feature learning on point sets in a metric space. In: Proceedings of the IEEE/CVF Conference on Computer Vision and Pattern Recognition (CVPR), pp. 5099–5108 (2017)
4. Shi, S.S., Wang, X.G., Li, H.S.: PointRCNN: 3D object proposal generation and detection from point cloud. In: Proceedings of the IEEE/CVF Conference on Computer Vision and Pattern Recognition (CVPR), pp. 770–779. IEEE Computer Society Press, Los Alamitos (2019)
5. Shi, S., Guo, C., Jiang, L., et al.: PV-RCNN: point-voxel feature set abstraction for 3D object detection. In: Proceedings of the IEEE/CVF Conference on Computer Vision and Pattern Recognition (CVPR), pp. 10529–10538 (2020)
6. Uy, M.A., Lee, G.H.: PointNetVLAD: deep point cloud based retrieval for large- scale place recognition. In: IEEE/CVF Conference on Computer Vision and Pattern Recognition (CVPR), pp. 4470–4479 (2018)
7. Zheng, W., Tang, W., Jiang, L., et al.: SE-SSD: self-ensembling single-stage object detector from point cloud. In: Proceedings of the IEEE/CVF Conference on Computer Vision and Pattern Recognition (CVPR), pp. 14494–14503 (2021)
8. Meng Di, L.I., Sheng Ping, J., Hong Ping, W.: A RANSAC-based stable plane fitting method of point clouds. Sci. Surveying Mapp. (2015). (in Chinese)
9. Dong, K., Xiao-Yuan, W., Ya-Qi, L., et al.: Vehicle target identification algorithm based on point cloud of vehicle 32-line laser lidar. Sci. Technol. Eng. (2018). (in Chinese)
10. Xiangyang, C., Yang, Y., Yunfei, X.: Measurement of point cloud data segmentation based on euclidean clustering algorithm. Bull. Surveying Mapp. (2017). (in Chinese)
11. Jingjing, F., Li, W., Wenbo, C., et al.: Research on pedestrian recognition in cross-country environment based on KDTree and euclidean clustering. Automot. Eng. (2019). (in Chinese)
12. Wohlkinger, W., Vincze, M.: Ensemble of shape functions for 3D object classification. In: Proceedings of the IEEE Conference on Robotics and Biomimetics (2011)
13. Guyon, I., Weston, J., Barnhill, S., et al.: Gene selection for cancer classification using support vector machines. Mach. Learn. **46**(1–3), 389–422 (2002)
14. Rusong, L.: Research on multi-feature fusion recognition algorithm based on minimum euclidean distance between samples. Comput. Digit. Eng. (2023). (in Chinese)

Collaborative Computer Vision and Cloud Platform for Gastrointestinal Polyp Detection

Diankui Li[1], Zhenyu Wang[1], Yude Chen[1(✉)], and Liang Wu[2]

[1] Jiamusi University, Jiamusi, China
jmscyd@126.com

[2] Department of Gastroenterology, Chaoyang Central Hospital, Beijing, China

Abstract. Gastric cancer is a common malignant tumor in the world. Regular endoscopic examination and timely removal of precancerous polyps in early patients can significantly reduce mortality. A real-time detection model for gastrointestinal polyps based on the improved YOLOv7 algorithm is proposed to address the issues of unclear early symptoms, small target size, high missed and misdiagnosis rates of gastric cancer. Firstly, a comprehensive and intuitive endoscopic polyp image dataset was constructed by collecting publicly available gastrointestinal polyp image data; Then, based on the YOLOv7 algorithm, the CBAM attention mechanism is introduced to improve the algorithm's feature extraction ability in complex situations, and the WIoU bounding box regression loss function is used to improve the positioning accuracy of the target bounding box. The experimental results show that the improved model accuracy has increased from 88.8% to 92.5%, and the average accuracy has increased from 91.25% to 92.16%, which can better meet the real-time accuracy and speed requirements of endoscopic examination. Finally, deploying the trained model to the cloud service platform can provide free testing services to the public conveniently and flexibly.

Keyword: Object Detection · Endoscopic Polyp · Cloud Service

1 Introduction

Gastric cancer is a common malignant tumor in the world. Every year, there are about 1.03 million new cases of cancer, and the incidence rate ranks sixth in the world. In addition, an average of approximately 780000 people died from type 3 cancer every year, with the mortality rate ranking second in the world. China is a high-risk area for the onset of gastric cancer, with approximately 430000 new cases and approximately 300000 deaths from gastric cancer every year. Even worse, the prognosis of gastric cancer is relatively poor, with a survival rate of only 30% within 5 years after onset. However, patients with early gastric cancer can be basically cured through clinical treatment. However, the early symptoms of this type of tumor are not obvious, and the onset is mostly implicit. Most patients only show obvious symptoms in the middle to late stages.

So far, the pathogenesis of gastric cancer is not fully understood. In clinical practice, the preferred method for diagnosing gastric cancer is endoscopy, which is also the best

Y. Sun et al. (Eds.): ChineseCSCW 2023, CCIS 2013, pp. 507–514, 2024.
https://doi.org/10.1007/978-981-99-9640-7_38

screening method. Under endoscopy, the shape of early cancer can appear as small polyp like protrusions or depressions, but some lesions are flush with the mucosa and difficult to identify. In addition, the detection effect is constrained by various objective factors, Moreover, during the endoscopic examination process, endoscopists need to maintain a high level of attention, but as the examination time increases, it can lead to excessive fatigue among endoscopists, leading to an increase in misdiagnosis and missed diagnosis rates. Moreover, due to significant differences in the distribution proportion of gastroen-terologists and endoscopic resource allocation in different regions of China, the level of gastrointestinal diseases varies, and the average misdiagnosis rate for endoscopic polyp detection is about 20% [4]. In recent years, with the development of artificial intelligence technology in the field of medical imaging, many computer-aided detection systems have emerged and achieved good detection results in their application directions. Therefore, it is necessary to construct an objective diagnostic system that can automatically detect and recognize gastrointestinal polyps to assist endoscopists.

Deep learning technology can automatically extract relevant imaging features [5], effectively avoiding human perception bias, and has excellent performance in the field of computer vision. Object detection is one of the important research directions in the field of computer vision. Its main task is to find all the desired targets in the input image based on the user's interest in target information, and classify and label the categories and positions of the targets. It is an image segmentation based on target position and statistical features. The YOLOv7 [6] algorithm is currently one of the most advanced object detection algorithms, which can support high-resolution images and various types of targets. It has better adaptability and strong generalization ability, and has strong robustness in transfer learning. So, this article proposes an improved YOLOv7 algorithm that combines the attention mechanism of Convolutional Block Attention Module (CBAM) [7] and replaces the original CIoU [8] loss function with the Wise IoU (WIoU) [9] bounding box loss function to construct an objective diagnostic assistance system that can automatically detect and recognize gastrointestinal polyp detection.

2   YOLOv7 Algorithm and Improvement

2.1   YOLOv7 Algorithm

The current popular object detection algorithms are mainly divided into two categories: two-stage algorithms such as R-CNN [10], Fast R-CNN [11], Fast R-CNN [12], and one-stage algorithms such as YOLO series and SSD [13] series. Among them, the YOLOv7 algorithm uses a single convolutional neural network for detection. Its training and prediction are end-to-end, simple and fast. And based on the global information of the image for prediction, it has strong generalization ability. It is currently a relatively balanced algorithm in terms of model accuracy and inference performance, which can be applied to real-time systems.

2.2   CBAM Attention Mechanism

The CBAM attention mechanism is a simple and effective feedforward neural network attention mechanism module proposed by Sanghyun Woo et al. in 2018. It is currently the most popular attention network model that combines channel and space. Its core is to apply channel attention module and spatial attention module to process the input feature layer separately to improve the performance of the model. The CAM module acts on the channel dimension, enhancing the network's modeling ability for channel features by learning how to select the most important channel in the input image. On the other hand, the SAM module plays a role in the spatial dimension by learning how to combine spatial and channel features, thereby further improving the performance of the network. Compared with other attention network models, CBAM attention mechanism has been widely applied due to its advantages of simple network structure, strong universality, high computational efficiency, and good performance.

2.3 WIoU Loss Function

In the target detection task, the Loss function of boundary box regression (BBR) is crucial to the target detection task, and excellent Loss function can bring significant performance improvement to the model. Focal EIoU [24] was proposed to solve the BBR balance problem between samples with good quality and poor quality, but because of its static focusing mechanism, the potential of the nonmonotone static focusing mechanism has not been fully utilized. Based on this idea, Zhangjia Tong et al. proposed a Loss function WIoU based on IoU. In the simulation experiment, this Loss function has lower error than the most advanced SIoU [25] Loss function. Compared with other loss functions, the WIoU loss function can help the model better understand and distinguish different categories, thereby improving overall performance.

3 Production of Gastrointestinal Polyp Dataset

The number of training datasets in target detection tasks has a significant impact on the results. More data means that more samples can be used for training, thereby reducing the risk of overfitting and improving the model's generalization ability. However, due to limitations in medical ethics, ethical standards, and other factors, the publicly available dataset of gastrointestinal polyps is relatively limited and chaotic, and some publicly available polyp image data lack screening and labeling information from professional endoscopists. Therefore, in order to ensure the training quality and practical application value of the model, this article constructs a widely sourced and rich endoscopic polyp dataset by collecting public datasets on the Internet. Including CVC-ClinicDB [26], CVC ConlonDB [27], ETIS AribPolypDB [28], Kavsir [29], LDPolypVideos [30], etc.

4 Experiment and Result Analysis

4.1 Experimental Environment

The training tasks of all models in this article are conducted on a hardware configuration of Intel (R) Core (TM) i7-10870H CPU @ 2.20GHz × On a high-performance cloud server with a 16 core CPU processor and NAVIDIA GeForce RTX 3060 Laptop GPU. Some other relevant software information and model training parameter information are shown in Table 1:

Table 1. Relevant software version and model parameter information.

Name	Version	Parameter	Value
Cuda	11.6	Optimizer	Adam
Cudnn	11.3	Learning rate	0.001
System	Windows 11	Images Size	640 × 640
Pytorch	1.13.0	Weight decay	0.0005

4.2 Model Evaluation Indicators

For target detection tasks, precision, recall, and mean average precision are generally used as evaluation indicators for the model. Among them, Precision is a main evaluation indicator, mainly used to measure the percentage of correctly predicted targets. High accuracy can reduce the probability of false detection, and its calculation formula is shown in formula (1):

$$\Pr ecision = \frac{TP}{TP + FP} \tag{1}$$

Among them, TP represents true positive, which is the number of positive targets correctly recognized by the model, while FP represents false positive, which is the number of positive targets incorrectly recognized by the model.

In the field of medical lesion detection, Recall is the most concerned evaluation indicator, which refers to the ratio of the number of samples that can be correctly predicted as positive samples to the actual number of positive samples. Its calculation formula is shown in formula (2):

$$\mathrm{Re}call = \frac{TP}{TP + FN} \tag{2}$$

Among them, FN represents the number of negative samples erroneously determined as positive.

F1 score is an improvement on two simple evaluation indicators, accuracy and recall, defined as the harmonic average of accuracy and recall. Its calculation formula is shown in formula (3):

$$F1 = \frac{2 \times \Pr ecision \times \mathrm{Re}call}{\Pr ecision + \mathrm{Re}call} \tag{3}$$

After obtaining the two simple evaluation indicators of model accuracy and recall, by determining the confidence threshold of the target score, the accuracy and recall of each type of target in each image of the validation set can be calculated at various confidence levels that meet the conditions. A P-R curve can be drawn, where the area below the P-R curve represents the average accuracy (AP). By averaging all image samples, the final AP standard values for this type of target can be obtained, and then averaging all categories of APs to obtain average accuracy. The response calculation formula is formula (4) (N represents the number of categories):

$$mAP = \frac{\sum\limits_{k=1}^{N} AP(k)}{N} \tag{4}$$

4.3 Experimental Results and Analysis

To verify the impact of different numbers of datasets on experimental results. This article selects different data from different datasets and conducts comparative experiments on the improved YOLOv7 algorithm. The final experimental results are shown in Table 2.

Table 2. Experimental results for different numbers of datasets.

Datasets	Precision	Recall	F1-score	mAP.5
CVC-ClinicDB	90.03%	80.42%	84.95%	85.91%
CVC-ConlonDB	89.02%	82.12%	85.43%	86.23%
ETISAribPolypDB	88.31%	83.23%	85.69%	85.98%
Kavsir	88.74%	83.68%	86.13%	88.75%
LDPolypVideos	88.69%	82.96%	85.72%	89.94%
Our Built Dataset	92.58%	83.95%	88.05%	92.16%

From Table 2, it can be seen that our built dataset, in terms of accuracy, recall, F1 score, and mAP. 5 evaluation indicators, is superior to its individual dataset. Therefore, the more datasets there are, the better the performance of the model, the stronger its generalization ability, stability, and adaptability to various scenarios.

The experimental results and analysis were conducted to explore the impact of different improvement modules on the YOLOv7 algorithm. This article also conducted ablation experiments, and the evaluation indicators are shown in Table 3.

Table 3. Ablation experiment.

Model	Precision	Recall	F1-score	mAP.5
YOLOv7	88.80%	84.12%	86.39%	91.25%
CBAM	91.02%	84.12%	87.42%	90.82%
WIoU	89.31%	86.23%	87.73%	91.53%
CBAM + WIoU	92.58%	83.95%	88.05%	92.16%

Table 3 shows that after adding CBAM attention mechanism network to the backbone network of YOLOv7 algorithm, its Precision has increased by 2.2 percentage points, indicating that CBAM attention mechanism can enhance the feature extraction ability of YOLOv7. After the Loss function of the WIoU bounding box replaces the original Loss function of the CIoU bounding box of YOLOv7, Precision increases by 0.5 percentage points, Recall increases by 2.11 percentage points, and mAP. 5 increases by 0.28 percentage points, which proves that the WIoU Loss function has stronger generalization ability than the CIoU Loss function. After adding CBAM attention mechanism and WIoU bounding box Loss function, Precision increased by 3.78 percentage points and mAP. 5 increased by 0.91 percentage points. The final experimental results indicate that the improved method proposed in this article has a promoting effect on the YoloV7 algorithm.

5   Cloud Platform Construction

Gastrointestinal polyp is a common disease of the digestive system. If it is not detected and treated in time, it may develop into gastrointestinal cancer, posing a great threat to human health. A cloud platform is a service platform that provides computing, network, and storage capabilities based on hardware and software resources. Due to its advantages such as elastic resource allocation, security and reliability, high performance and scalability, flexibility, and cost savings, it has been widely applied. Based on these advantages of the cloud platform, a gastrointestinal polyp detection cloud platform has been constructed. Users can quickly obtain detection results by uploading images detected by endoscopy, and the detection results will mark the position of polyps in the image in detail. Compared with traditional endoscopic polyp detection, it not only reduces the workload of doctors, but also improves the efficiency of detection, and can provide services to the required population more flexibly.

6   Conclusions and Prospects

This article proposes an improved YOLOv7 algorithm that detects gastrointestinal polyps in real-time through a self-built gastrointestinal polyp image dataset and deploys it on a cloud platform to better serve patients. The experimental results of model improvement indicate that the improved algorithm can better meet the requirements for real-time accuracy and speed in the endoscopic examination process. Next, we will conduct comparative experiments using other different attention mechanisms and the loss function of bounding boxes to find the best combination and further improve the performance of the algorithm.

Acknowledgment. This work was supported by the Basic Research Business Fee Basic Research Project of Heilongjiang Provincial Department of Education 2021-KYYWF-0577.

References

1. Bray, F., Ferlay, J., Soerjomataram, I., Siegel, R.L., Torre, L.A., Jemal, A.: Global cancer statistics 2018: GLOBOCAN estimates of incidence and mortality worldwide for 36 cancers in 185 countries. CA Cancer J. Clin. **68**(6):394–424 (2018). https://doi.org/10.3322/caac.21492. Epub 2018 Sep 12. Erratum in: CA Cancer J Clin. 2020 Jul; 70(4):313. PMID: 30207593
2. Wanqing, C., Kexin, S., Rongshou, Z., et al.: Cancer incidence and mortality in China, 2014. Chin. J. Cancer Res. **30**(1), 1–12 (2018)
3. Global surveillance of trends in cancer survival 2000–14(CONCORD -3): analysis of individual records for 37513025 patients diagnosed with one of 18 cancers from 322 population -based registries in 71 countries. The Lancet **391**(10125), 1023–1075 (2018)
4. Rustagi, T.: Quality indicators for colonoscopy and the risk of interval cancer. NEngl. J. Med. **363**(14), 1372 (2010). author reply 1373. 1056/NEJMc1006842
5. LeCun, Y., Bengio, Y., Hinton, G.: Deep learning. Nature **521**(7553), 436–444 (2015). https://doi.org/10.1038/nature14539
6. Wang, C.Y, Bochkovskiy, A., Liao, H.Y.M.: YOLOv7: trainable bag-of-freebies sets new state-of-the-art for real-time object detectors. arXiv preprint arXiv:2207.02696, (2022)
7. Woo, S., Park, J., Lee, J.Y., et al.: CBAM: convolutional block attention module. In: Proceedings of the European Conference on Computer Vision (ECCV), pp. 3–19 (2018)
8. Zheng, Z., Wang, P., Liu, W., et al.: Distance-IoU loss: faster and better learning for bounding box regression. In: Proceedings of the AAAI Conference on Artificial Intelligence, vol. 34, no. 07, pp. 12993–13000 (2020)
9. Tong, Z., Chen, Y., Xu, Z., et al.: Wise-IoU: bounding box regression loss with dynamic focusing mechanism. arXiv preprint arXiv:2301.10051 (2023)
10. Girshick, R., Donahue, J., Darrell, T., et al.: Rich feature hierarchies for accurate object detection and semantic segmentation. In: Proceedings of the IEEE Conference on Computer Vision and Pattern Recognition, pp. 580–587 (2014)
11. Girshick, R.: Fast R-CNN. In: Proceedings of the IEEE International Conference on Computer Vision, pp. 1440–1448 (2015)
12. Ren, S., He, K., Girshick, R., et al.: Faster R-CNN: towards real-time object detection with region proposal networks. In: Advances in Neural Information Processing Systems, vol. 28 (2015)
13. Liu, W., et al.: SSD: single shot multibox detector. In: Leibe, B., Matas, J., Sebe, N., Welling, M. (eds.) Computer Vision – ECCV 2016. ECCV 2016. Lecture Notes in Computer Science, vol. 9905, pp. 21-37. Springer, Cham (2016). https://doi.org/10.1007/978-3-319-46448-0_2
14. Zhang, X., Zeng, H., Guo, S., et al.: Efficient long-range attention network for image super-resolution. In: Computer Vision–ECCV 2022: 17th European Conference, Tel Aviv, Israel, October 23–27, 2022, Proceedings, Part XVII, pp. 649-667. Springer, Cham (2022). https://doi.org/10.1007/978-3-031-19790-1_39
15. Hou, Q., Zhou, D., Feng, J.: Coordinate attention for efficient mobile network design. In: Proceedings of the IEEE/CVF Conference on Computer Vision and Pattern Recognition, pp. 13713–13722 (2021)
16. Qin, Z., Zhang, P., Wu, F., et al.: FcaNet: frequency channel attention networks. In: Proceedings of the IEEE/CVF International Conference on Computer Vision, pp. 783–792 (2021)
17. Wang, Q., Wu, B., Zhu, P., et al.: ECA-Net: efficient channel attention for deep convolutional neural networks. In: Proceedings of the IEEE/CVF Conference on Computer Vision and Pattern Recognition, pp. 11534–11542 (2020)
18. Park, J., Woo, S., Lee, J.Y., et al.: BAM: bottleneck attention module. arXiv preprint arXiv: 1807.06514 (2018)

19. Fu, J., Liu, J., Tian, H., et al.: Dual attention network for scene segmentation. In: Proceedings of the IEEE/CVF Conference on Computer Vision and Pattern Recognition, pp. 3146–3154 (2019)
20. Wang, X., Girshick, R., Gupta, A., et al.: Non-local neural networks. In: Proceedings of the IEEE Conference on Computer Vision and Pattern Recognition, pp. 7794–7803 (2018)
21. Li, X., Wang, W., Hu, X., et al.: Selective kernel networks. In: Proceedings of the IEEE/CVF Conference on Computer Vision and Pattern Recognition, pp. 510–519 (2019)
22. Zhang, H., Goodfellow, I., Metaxas, D., et al.: Self-attention generative adversarial networks. In: International Conference on Machine Learning, pp. 7354–7363. PMLR (2019)
23. Cao, Y., Xu, J., Lin, S., et al.: Global context networks. IEEE Trans. Pattern Anal. Mach. Intell. (2020)
24. Zhang, Y.F., Ren, W., Zhang, Z., et al.: Focal and efficient IOU loss for accurate bounding box regression. Neurocomputing **506**, 146–157 (2022)
25. Gevorg yan, Z.: SIoU loss: more powerful learning for bounding box regression. arXiv preprint arXiv:2205.12740 (2022)
26. Jorge Bernal, F., Sánchez, J., Fernández-Esparrach, G., Gil, D., Rodríguez, C., Vilariño, F.: WM-DOVA maps for accurate polyp highlighting in colonoscopy: validation vs. saliency maps from physicians. Comput. Med. Imaging Graph. **43**, 99–111 (2015). https://doi.org/10.1016/j.compmedimag.2015.02.007
27. Tajbakhsh, N., Gurudu, S.R., Liang, J.: Automated polyp detection in colonoscopy videos using shape and context information. IEEE Trans. Med. Imaging **35**(2), 630–644 (2015)
28. Silva, J., Histace, A., Romain, O., et al.: Toward embedded detection of polyps in wce images for early diagnosis of colorectal cancer. Int. J. Comput. Assist. Radiol. Surg. **9**, 283–293 (2014)
29. Borgli, H., Thambawita, V., Smedsrud, P.H., et al.: HyperKvasir, a comprehensive multi-class image and video dataset for gastrointestinal endoscopy. Sci. Data **7**(1), 283 (2020)
30. Ma, Y., Chen, X., Cheng, K., et al.: LDPolypVideo benchmark: a large-scale colonoscopy video dataset of diverse polyps. In: Medical Image Computing and Computer Assisted Intervention–MICCAI 2021: 24th International Conference, Strasbourg, France, September 27–October 1, 2021, Proceedings, Part V 24, pp. 387–396. Springer, Cham (2021). https://doi.org/10.1007/978-3-030-87240-3_37

An Intelligent Teaching Evaluation System Integrating Emotional Computing and Cloud Platform

Diankui Li[1], Yan Chen[2], and Yude Chen[1(✉)]

[1] School of Information and Electronic Technology, Jiamusi University, Jiamusi 154000, Heilongjiang, China
jmscyd@126.com
[2] School of Educational Science, Jiamusi University, Jiamusi 154000, Heilongjiang, China

Abstract. The teaching evaluation of classroom teaching is an indispensable and important link, which provides teaching feedback information for teachers. In the current teaching evaluation of course teaching, it mainly pays attention to the achievement of learners' knowledge goals and teachers' performance, and ignores the content of teachers' emotion in classroom teaching activities. In this study, an intelligent teaching evaluation system was constructed to integrate emotion computing and cloud platform technology to analyze and evaluate the middle school classroom teaching behavior by analyzing teachers' emotions. Firstly, the Stm32 microcontroller with 4G module is used to collect images or video data of teachers' facial expressions. Then, the convolutional neural network model is established, and the model is trained and tested, and the convolutional neural network model is used for feature extraction and classification to achieve the effect of teachers' emotion analysis. Finally, the trained model is deployed on the cloud platform to make real-time identification of multiple nodes and realize teachers' emotion analysis in classroom teaching. The system combines emotional computing and cloud computing technology, which is a beneficial attempt to apply modern technology in the field of education.

Keywords: Emotional computing · Cloud platform · teaching evaluation · Convolutional neural network

1 Research Background

With the development of artificial intelligence technology, people began to explore how to apply it in the field of education, especially in teaching evaluation. It can be seen that in the new era of the background, continuing to improve the education and teaching evaluation, and using advanced means to gradually improve the current teaching evaluation methods, has become an important direction of research in the field of education in China.

This work was supported by Basic Research Business Fee Basic Research Project of Heilongjiang Provincial Department of Education (No. 2021-KYYWF-0577)

Therefore, this study proposes an intelligent classroom teaching evaluation method that integrates emotional computing and cloud platform, and constructs an intelligent evaluation system for middle school classroom based on facial expression recognition technology, which can better understand teachers' emotional expression, improve the teaching effect, and provide more practical teaching feedback for middle school teachers.

2 Development Status

2.1 Development Status of Classroom Teaching Evaluation

With the deepening of the educational reform, the classroom teaching evaluation, as an important means to improve the teaching quality, has attracted more and more extensive attention. Teaching evaluation plays an important role in the process of talent training. In recent years, due to the influence of multiple intelligence theory and constructivism, the methods, orientation and content of traditional evaluation are all changing according to the demand. The specific changes are as described in Table 1.

Table 1. Changes in the evaluation methods.

	Traditional evaluation	Modern evaluation
Method	Questionnaire survey method, observation method, interview method, and portfolio evaluation method	Artificial intelligence technology is combined with education, and advanced information technology means are used to achieve teaching evaluation
Orientation	Pay attention to the screening and selection, mainly is the summative evaluation	Emphasize the diversified comprehensive evaluation system and pay attention to the process evaluation
Content	Attach importance to the mastery of students 'knowledge and teachers' teaching performance	While paying attention to the development of students, pay attention to the development of teachers

2.2 The Development Status of Emotional Computing

With the rapid development of artificial intelligence technology, emotional computing has become a research field with much attention.

At present, the common emotional computing is mainly based on facial expression, voice, text, human posture and other directions. Psychologist Mehrabian showed that emotional expression = 7% words + 38% sounds + 55% facial expression [1].

Teacher's Facial Expressions in Class. Teachers' facial expressions can affect students' learning effect and education quality. For the division of facial expression in the classroom, this paper draws a lot of existing research results, and adopts the method of questionnaire survey, to a junior high school five classes, a total of 230 students to "teachers in the classroom teaching facial expression" this problem, finally given in the classroom teaching environment teachers the most common five teaching emotional state, respectively, happy, calm, anger, disgust and sad. The details are shown in Fig. 1.

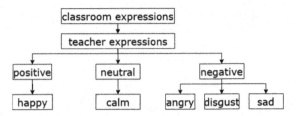

Fig. 1. Teacher expression classification.

2.3 Research Status of Auxiliary Teaching Evaluation in Expression Recognition

Appearance recognition technology has wide application prospects in education field, especially in teaching evaluation.

Foreign Research. For example, Behzad et al. [2] proposed using a bounded residual gradient network for expression recognition. At the same time, since 2013, the expression recognition competitions such as FER2013 [3] and EmotiW [4] have collected relatively sufficient training data from challenging real scenes, and deep learning has gradually become the mainstream technology in the field of expression recognition.

Domestic Research. Compared with foreign countries, there are few research studies on emotional computing in education. In 2017, Gao Xinxin used the expression recognition technology to evaluate the teachers' teaching ability from the emotion dimension, and established a teacher's emotional model based on the emotion dimension theory.

3 System Architecture

3.1 System Composition Module

The intelligent evaluation system of middle school classroom teaching which integrates emotion computing and cloud platform is mainly divided into three modules: data collection, facial expression recognition and cloud services. As shown in Fig. 2.

Data Collection. This system uses a Stm32 microcontroller with a camera and 4G module to capture images or videos during classroom teaching and automatically upload them to a cloud server for storage. In each classroom that needs to be evaluated, cameras and other devices should be installed to point the camera at the teacher's face and collect facial expression data, which can realize multi-directional, multi-angle and multi-state image acquisition.

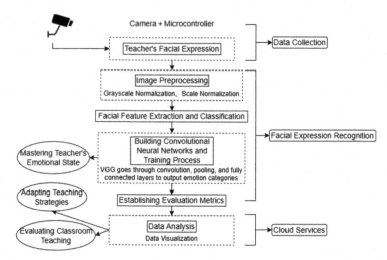

Fig. 2. An intelligent teaching evaluation system integrating emotional computing and cloud platform.

Facial Expression Recognition. AI technology is used to detect the facial expression images of teachers collected from the camera, and the detected images should be further analyzed and processed.

Cloud Services. Cloud services refers to the emotion analysis of teachers' facial expression data in real time and generating summary reports.The generation and application of cloud computing provide the construction basis for the design of open computer control system based on cloud services.

The intelligent evaluation system of middle school classroom teaching behavior, which integrates emotion computing and cloud platform, can intelligently evaluate teachers' facial expressions based on the collected data, face detection and emotion analysis results. The evaluation results can be fed back to the teachers to help them improve their teaching methods and improve their teaching quality.

3.2   Training Datasets

The training data set of this system mainly comes from two parts. On the one hand, it is the existing public facial expression data set at home and abroad; on the other hand, the facial expression data set of middle school classroom teachers is collected for the experimental subjects, so as to train the model and improve the recognition rate of facial expressions.

The public data set selected by this system is the data set fer2013 of the face recognition contest in Kaggle in 2013. It contains 28709 training set images (Training), 3589 public test set images (PublicTest), and 3589 private test set images (PrivateTest), each with 4848 size gray images.

The main processes are as follows: first, preprocess the training set; second, train the deep convolutional neural network to recognize the face expression (train); third, use the trained model to identify the face expression emotion (predict).

The Training Set was Preprocessed. In the process of sorting the data, each expression data is a csv file, which does not directly give the picture, but the pixel value. Therefore, we need to read these numerical data and store them as image data after transformation. After processing, the expression data is mainly composed of seven categories: anger, disgust, fear, happy, sad, surprise and neutral. According to the classification of teachers' facial expressions in the classroom, it was further improved based on the data set fer2013 to get the required classification of facial expressions, namely, happy, calm, angry, disgust and sad, and the model was trained and tested.

Training Model. In the process of training, the training requires a lot of time and energy, and it is easy to be affected by the network and other factors. Therefore, this study uses Tencent Cloud server to train the model. Tencent Cloud server is convenient to operate, provides various operation modes such as console, facilitates users to conduct model training and debugging, and the network performance is stable, providing high-speed and stable network connection, which can improve the efficiency of model training.

Identify the Expressions and Emotions in the Face. Different faces can be identified through the trained model to recognize the teacher's facial expressions Expression, and further analyze the corresponding emotional states.

3.3 Teacher's Facial Expression Recognition Algorithm

To achieve the best effect of recognizing teachers' facial expressions, this paper selects the more popular classification algorithms at present. Nowadays, there are various types of emotion recognition algorithms, such as Chen et al. using deep convolutional neural networks to recognize emotions [5], Li et al. using convolutional neural network features and support vector machines (SVM) to recognize facial expressions [6], etc., they have all achieved fairly good recognition results in tests on public datasets.

With the development of neural networks, deep learning models have designed different network structures and learning algorithms according to the characteristics of data and task requirements. These models have certain advantages in emotional data processing, and can automatically extract features from raw data, identify and classify emotional information, so as to realize emotional computing.

At present, the most popular network structures are: deep neural network (DNN), convolutional neural network (CNN), recurrent neural network (RNN), and generative adversarial network (GAN). They are analyzed in comparison, as shown in Table 2.

Common convolutional neural network structures include AlexNet [7], VGGNet [8], GoogLeNet [9], etc. Among them, VGG was proposed by the Computer vision Group of University College London. The VGG network structure contains multiple convolution layers, pooling layers, and fully connected layers, which are usually used for image classification tasks.

The convolutional layer is the basic operation and the core structure of the convolutional neural network. It retains the spatial features of the human image, mainly

Table 2. Comparative analysis of the different network structures.

Network structure	Feature	Primary mission	Scope of application
DNN	Composition of multiple hidden layers	Feature extraction	Classification, regression, and other tasks
RNN	Cycle layer composition	Feature extraction	Sequence data
GAN	Generators and discriminators are against learning	Generate adversarial samples	Generate realistic sample images
CNN	Convolution, pooling, and fully connected layers	Feature extraction	Images, audio, video and other two-dimensional data

composed of convolution kernel, which is responsible for the extraction of image features. The fully connected layer acts as a "classifier" in the entire convolutional neural network. The pooling layer is an important step in selecting the important features and squeezing the information of the original features layer, which is an important step in the convolutional neural network.

In recent years, the convolutional neural network has made a breakthrough in the field of emotional image processing, but due to direct training their convolutional neural network is relatively complex, the training emotion model is not accurate and reliable, so adopted the pre training good convolutional neural network model on the target emotional data set, to achieve the purpose of detecting teachers facial expression emotional characteristics. In this study, the feature extraction of facial expressions was based on convolutional neural network model, initialized convolutional neural network trained on Fer2013 data set, and VGG convolutional neural network was selected as the deep learning neural network of emotion computing. VGG was operated through convolution, pooling and full connection, and finally output the predicted emotion category.

In emotion computing, VGG networks can be used in image emotion classification tasks. Specifically, this paper replaces the last layer of the VGG network with a specific layer for emotion classification, using softmax to output the probability distribution of emotion categories (e. g., joy, sadness, anger, etc.). During the training process, the input image is transmitted to the VGG Network, to calculate the emotional probability distribution of the images. Then, the deviation between the result and the actual labels is predicted by the cross-entropy loss function, and the network parameters are updated by the back-propagation algorithm.

The formula of softmax is

$$\text{soft} \max(xi) = \frac{\exp(xi)}{\sum_j \exp(xj)} \tag{1}$$

4   Conclusion

This system serves as the main device for image or video acquisition based on the Stm32 microcontroller, aiming to conduct emotional analysis on teachers' facial expressions in the classroom through facial recognition. Specifically, the VGG16 convolutional neural network algorithm is adopted for facial expression recognition, and it's deployed to the cloud platform to provide cloud services, eventually realizing teacher expression analysis on the platform and providing an emotion-based teaching evaluation report. By adopting this intelligent evaluation method, teachers can gain a better understanding of their own emotional expressions, improve their teaching, and enhance their teaching effectiveness. The evaluation further expands and provides more practical teaching feedback for middle school teachers. This evaluation can compensate for the emotional shortcomings of teachers in existing teaching evaluations in practice. It's a beneficial attempt to apply smart evaluations to teaching evaluations, which promotes educational reform, and also supplements existing evaluation methods. It can serve as a useful reference for the reform of classroom teaching evaluation.

References

1. Mehrabian, A.: Communication without words. Commun. Theory **6**(07), 193–200 (2008)
2. Hasani, B., Negi, P.S., Mahoor, M.H.: Bounded residual gradient networks (breg-net) for facial affect computing. In: 2019 14th IEEE International Conference on Automatic Face & Gesture Recognition (FG 2019), pp. 1–7. Lille, France. IEEE(2019)
3. Carrier, P.-L., Courville, A., Goodfellow, I.J., Mirza, M., Bengio, Y.: FER-2013 face database. Universit de Montral (2013)
4. Dhall, A., Goecke, R., Joshi, J., et al.: Emotion recognition in the wild challenge 2013. In: Proceedings of the 15th ACM on International Conference on Multimodal Interaction, pp. 509–516 (2013)
5. Chen, J.Y., Xu, R.Y., Liu, L.Y.: Deep peak-neutral difference feature for facial expression recognition. Multimedia Tools Appl. **77**(22), 29871–29887 (2018)
6. Li, M., Xu, H., Huang, X.C., et al.: Facial expression recognition with identity and emotion joint learning. IEEE Trans. Affect. Comput. **12**(2), 544–550 (2021)
7. Krizhevsky, A., Sutskever, I., Hinton, G.E., et al.: ImageNet classification with deep convolutional neural networks. In: Advances in Neural Information Processing Systems, pp. 1097–1105 (2012)
8. Simonyan, K., Zisserman, A.: Very deep convolutional networks for large-scale image recognition. arXiv preprint arXiv:14091556 (2014)
9. Szegedy, C., Liu, W., Jia, Y.: Going deeper with convolutions. In: Proceedings of the IEEE Conference on Computer Vision and Pattern Recognition, pp. 1–9 (2015)

Deep Learning-Based Fastener Counting Method and Localization Correction Method

Jun Guo[1], Xiao Yang[1]([✉]), Jie Lan[1], JianWei Zou[2], and FeiLong Chen[2]

[1] Northeastern University, Shenyang, China
shawy.chn@outlook.com
[2] Electrical Engineering Company of China Railway No. 9 Group Co., Ltd., Shenyang, China

Abstract. Low accuracy and wear are common issues with single photoelectric encoders in track positioning. A deep learning-based method for clip detection, counting, and positioning correction can effectively improve the accuracy of the photoelectric encoder. In this paper, we propose a subway track clip detection model based on MobileNetV3-YOLOv5s, a clip counting and positioning model based on DeepSort, and a fusion correction model for positioning data. Finally, through comparative experiments, we validate that our adopted method achieves higher positioning accuracy and stronger reliability.

Keywords: DeepSort · MobileNetV3 · Track fastener detection

1 Introduction

High-precision localization problems for moving objects are commonly addressed using GPS positioning systems [1]. However, traditional indoor positioning methods are not suitable for underground environments [2]. The use of photoelectric encoders solves the issue of indoor positioning in tunnels, but underground environments pose challenges due to numerous obstacles and difficulties in installing other positioning facilities [3]. Therefore, an effective solution can be achieved by combining deep learning and sensors.

Currently, object detection algorithms are broadly categorized into two types. The first type is two-stage algorithms, which generate candidate regions and employ CNN for classification, such as Mask RCNN [4], Fast RCNN [5], Faster RCNN [6], etc. These algorithms achieve high detection accuracy but are slow, making them unsuitable for track point detection. The second type is one-stage algorithms, which directly apply algorithms to input images, outputting the class and location of objects, such as YOLO [7], SSD [8], etc. These algorithms have significantly faster detection speeds compared to the first type.

In this paper, we propose a deep learning-based method for fastener detection, counting, and positioning correction. Rail clips on the track are identified and counted using an improved DeepSort [9] model based on MobileNetV3 [10] and YOLOv5 [11]. The track position is then calculated based on the number of clips, and the photoelectric encoder is utilized for track positioning. The positioning data from both sources are fused and corrected, resulting in accurate and reliable track positioning.

Y. Sun et al. (Eds.): ChineseCSCW 2023, CCIS 2013, pp. 522–532, 2024.
https://doi.org/10.1007/978-981-99-9640-7_40

2 Detection and Tracking Models

2.1 Subway Track Clip Detection Model Based on MobileNetV3-YOLOv5s

To improve the accuracy and detection speed of rail clip recognition, this paper employs the YOLOv5s network model. However, the model's large number of parameters leads to slower detection speed. To address this issue, the backbone network C3 in the model is replaced with a lightweight network called MobileNetV3 small. This modification aims to enhance the detection speed and frame rate of rail clips while maintaining the model's accuracy. The structure of the MobileNetV3 small network is shown in Table 1.

Table 1. Overall structure of MobileNetV3 small network

Input	Operator	exp-size	#out	SE	NL	s
$224^2 \times 3$	Conv2d,3×3	–	16	–	HS	2
$112^2 \times 16$	bneck,3×3	16	16	Y	RE	2
$56^2 \times 16$	bneck,3×3	72	24	–	RE	2
$28^2 \times 24$	bneck,3×3	88	24	–	RE	1
$14^2 \times 40$	bneck,5×5	96	40	Y	HS	2
$14^2 \times 40$	bneck,5×5	240	40	Y	HS	1
$14^2 \times 40$	bneck,5×5	240	40	Y	HS	1
$14^2 \times 48$	bneck,5×5	120	48	Y	HS	1
$14^2 \times 48$	bneck,5×5	144	48	Y	HS	1
$7^2 \times 96$	bneck,5×5	288	96	Y	HS	2
$7^2 \times 96$	bneck,5×5	576	96	Y	HS	1
$7^2 \times 96$	bneck,5×5	576	96	Y	HS	1
$7^2 \times 576$	Conv2d,1×1	–	576	Y	HS	1
$7^2 \times 576$	Pool,1×1	–	–	–	–	1
$1^2 \times 576$	Conv2d 1×1, NBN	–	1024	–	HS	1
$1^2 \times 1024$	Conv2d 1×1, NBN	–	k	–	–	1

The Table 1 presents the size changes of each layer in the MobileNetV3 small network in the "Input" column. The "Operator" column represents the block structure that each feature layer is about to undergo. "exp size" and "#out" respectively denote the channel size after the channel expansion in the bneck and the channel size of the feature layer input to the bneck. The fifth column, "SE," indicates whether attention mechanisms are introduced at this layer. The sixth column, "NL," represents the type of activation function used. "RE" stands for the Rectified Linear Unit (ReLU) function. The seventh column, "s," denotes the stride used in each block structure. "HS" represents the h-swish activation function, which is composed of common operators. Its calculation formula is as follows:

$$h - swish[x] = x\frac{RELU6(X + 3)}{6} \tag{1}$$

The expression "RELU6 = min(RELU, 6)" denotes the usage of the Rectified Linear Unit 6 (ReLU6) function, which caps the output of the ReLU function at 6.

MobileNetV3 small improves its model performance and robustness by incorporating attention mechanisms into the network architecture, in addition to optimizing the loss function. The main idea behind this approach is to allocate different weights among different parts of the input data to reflect their importance in model decision-making. The core concept of the attention mechanism is illustrated in Fig. 1.

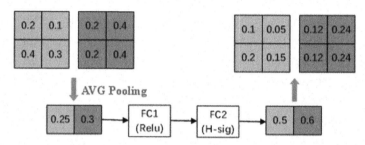

Fig. 1. Overall structure of MobileNetV3 small network.

The specific steps of the aforementioned process are as follows:

1. Perform global average pooling on the feature map, resulting in a one-dimensional vector with a length equal to the number of channels in the feature map.
2. Feed the globally average-pooled feature map into two fully connected layers. The output channel size of the first fully connected layer is 1/4 of the original input feature map's channel size, while the output channel size of the second fully connected layer is the same as the original input feature map's channel size. The ReLU and hard_sigmoid activation functions are used.
3. After passing through the two fully connected layers, obtain a vector consisting of "channel" elements, where each element represents a weight for each channel. Multiply the weights with the corresponding elements in the original feature map to obtain a new feature map.

These steps describe the process of applying attention mechanism to the feature map, where the weights obtained from the fully connected layers are used to emphasize or suppress certain features in the original feature map.

2.2 Clip Counting and Localization Model Based on DeepSort

By employing the DeepSort algorithm, it is possible to track and count railway clips while calculating the current position of each clip on the track. The flowchart of the clip counting and localization method based on DeepSort is shown in Fig. 2.

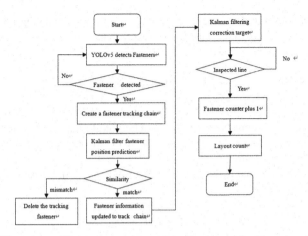

Fig. 2. Flow chart of fastener counting and positioning method based on DeepSort

The DeepSort algorithm suffers from issues such as slow detection speed and vulnerability to target loss when encountering occlusions. These drawbacks arise from the original DeepSort algorithm's use of IOU cascaded matching for object tracking in videos. The IOU (Intersection over Union) as a loss function does not consider the overlap pattern or the distance when there is no overlap, leading to suboptimal matching performance. The calculation formula for the IOU loss is as follows:

$$IOU = \frac{A \cap B}{A \cup B} \tag{2}$$

In order to address the aforementioned issues, this paper proposes the utilization of the SIOU (Spatial IOU) loss as a replacement for the IOU loss during the cascaded matching process. This aims to resolve the problem of incorrect assignment of clip IDs due to occlusion, which affects the accuracy of localization. The SIOU loss consists of four components: angle cost, distance cost, shape cost, and IOU cost.

The angle cost (Angle Cost) is calculated using the following formula:

$$A = 1 - 2 \times sin^2\left(\arcsin\left(\frac{c_h}{\delta}\right) - \frac{\pi}{4}\right) \tag{3}$$

The distance loss calculation formula is as follows, where 'ch' represents the height difference between the detection box and the predicted box, and 'δ' represents the distance between the center points of the two boxes.

$$\Delta = \sum_{t=x,y}\left(1 - e^{-\gamma \rho t}\right) = 2 - e^{-\gamma \rho x} - e^{-\gamma \rho y} \tag{4}$$

$$\rho x = \left(\frac{b_{cx}^{gt} - b_{cx}}{c_w}\right)^2, \rho y = \left(\frac{b_{cy}^{gt} - b_{cy}}{c_h}\right)^2, \gamma = 2 - A$$

where b_cx^gt and b_cy^gt represent the center coordinates of the ground truth bounding box, and b_cx and b_cy represent the center coordinates of the predicted bounding box.

c_w and c_h denote the width and height of the minimum enclosing rectangle of the ground truth and predicted bounding boxes, respectively.

The calculation formula for the shape cost is as follows:

$$\Omega = (1 - e^{-W_w})^{\theta} + (1 - e^{-W_h})^{\theta} \tag{5}$$

where w_w = (|w - w^gt|) / max(w, w^gt) and w_h = (|h - h^gt|) / max(h, h^gt), where (w, h) and (w^gt, h^gt) represent the width and height of the predicted and ground truth bounding boxes, respectively. θ is a parameter that controls the degree of emphasis on the shape cost, ranging from 2 to 6.

Taking all the components into account, the final calculation formula for the SIOU loss is as follows:

$$\text{SIOU} = 1 - IOU + \frac{\Delta + \Omega}{2} \tag{6}$$

2.3 Data Fusion and Correction Methods for Localization

By fusing and correcting the track position obtained from clip counting with the track position obtained from optical encoder distance measurements, the errors generated during the track localization process can be reduced. To address the issue of encoder wheel wear during locomotion, the clip counting method can also be used for correction. The distance measurement principle of the optical encoder can be represented by the following formula:

$$S = \frac{T_{sum}}{T}\pi d = (1 + (d - D)/D)S_r \tag{7}$$

where S represents the travel distance measured by the optical encoder, Tsum represents the cumulative pulse count recorded by the optical encoder during locomotion, T represents the pulses generated by the optical encoder in one revolution, and d represents the measured wheel diameter of the encoder.

To address the aforementioned issue, an approximate correction method based on clip counting can be employed. Assuming the distance between adjacent clips is L and the number of pulses generated by the optical encoder between adjacent clips is n, the corrected wheel diameter D of the encoder can be calculated using the following formula:

$$D = \frac{TL}{n\pi} \tag{8}$$

To address situations such as obstacle occlusion and missing clips, reverse correction using the optical encoder positioning can be employed. Assuming the standard distance between adjacent clips is L = 600 mm with an error tolerance of ±20 mm, a threshold value (Th) can be set. When the recorded travel distance (SL) by the encoder satisfies the condition SL < 600 + 20 + Th, it indicates that there is a missing clip, and clip counting compensation is required.

Clip counting compensation primarily determines the number of missed clips based on the relationship between the recorded travel distance by the encoder and the clip counting results. The number of missed clips can be calculated using the following formula:

$$m \approx \left[\frac{S_L}{L} \right] - 1 \tag{9}$$

In the above equation, m represents the number of missed clips, SL denotes the recorded difference in mileage between adjacent clips, and L represents the standard distance between adjacent clips.

3   Analysis of Experimental Results

3.1   Evaluation and Analysis of the Lightweight MobileNetV3-YOLOv5s Model

Figure 3 depicts the relationship between the three loss functions of the MobileNetV3-YOLOv5s model after 300 training iterations. During the training process, both the box_loss and obj_loss values consistently decrease and eventually stabilize around 0.02. This trend indicates an enhancement in the model's ability to accurately localize objects and predict their confidence levels, resulting in a significant improvement in overall performance.

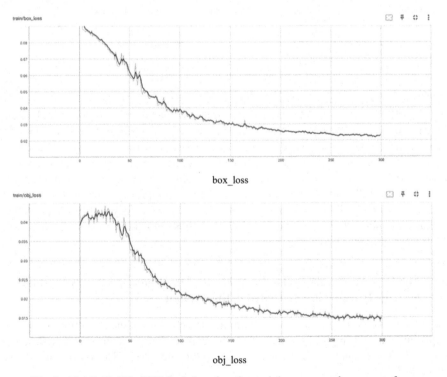

box_loss

obj_loss

Fig. 3. MobileNetV3 - YOLOv5s loss function training process change waveform

To further validate the detection performance of our proposed model, Fig. 5 presents the corresponding PR curve and the curve showing the variation of F1 score with confidence thresholds, comparing our model with the original model. From the graph, it can be observed that the AP (Average Precision) value of the original model is 0.977, while our proposed model achieves an AP value of 0.971. This indicates that our model performs nearly on par with the original model in terms of accuracy. Figures 5(b) and 5(d) depict the F1 scores of the original model and our proposed model, respectively, as they vary with confidence thresholds. It can be observed that there is a slight decrease in the F1 score compared to the original model.

According to Table 2, it can be observed that the MobileNetV3-YOLOv5s model used in this chapter exhibits comparable accuracy to the original model, with no significant decrease. However, the proposed model achieves a parameter count and floating-point operations of approximately 0.71 and 0.68 times that of the original model, respectively. Additionally, the model size is approximately 0.74 times that of the original model. Through optimization, our proposed model successfully reduces the parameter count and complexity while maintaining the detection accuracy. This leads to improved operational efficiency and speed, as well as enhanced applicability and flexibility.

Table 2. Model parameter comparison.

Algorithm	Average Precision(AP) /%	Params	FLOPs/G	Model Size /M
MobileNetV3-YOLOv5s	97.1	5024100	11.3	10.3
YOLOv5s	97.7	7063542	16.5	14

The MobileNetV3-YOLOv5s model used in this chapter exhibits comparable accuracy to the original model, with no significant decrease. However, the proposed model achieves a parameter count and floating-point operations of approximately 0.71 and 0.68 times that of the original model, respectively. Additionally, the model size is approximately 0.74 times that of the original model. Through optimization, our proposed model successfully reduces the parameter count and complexity while maintaining the detection accuracy. This leads to improved operational efficiency and speed, as well as enhanced applicability and flexibility. Figure 4 illustrates the detection results of the MobileNetV3-YOLOv5s algorithm.

3.2 The Experimental Results and Analysis of the Improved DeepSort Model for Clip Tracking are Presented in this Section

To validate the performance of the clip multi-object tracking method proposed in this paper in practical application scenarios, the collected video data was tested, and a comparison was made with the original DeepSort algorithm. The results are shown in Table 3.

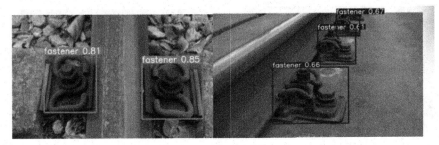

Fig. 4. PR curve and F1 curve of MobileNetV3-YOLOv5s

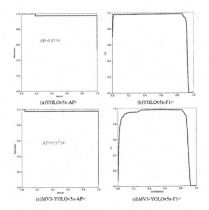

(a)YOLOv5s-AP

(b)YOLOv5s-F1

(c)MV3-YOLOv5s-AP

(d)MV3-YOLOv5s-F1

Fig. 5. MobileNetV3-YOLOv5s detection rendering

Table 3. Comparison of Algorithm Effects

algorithm	average tracking accuracy/%	average tracking precision /%	ID_switch
Improve DeepSort	69.6	59.3	16
DeepSort	66.2	55.6	28

The improved DeepSort multi-object tracking method in this paper outperforms the original algorithm, with increased average accuracy and multi-object tracking precision, and a reduced number of target ID switches. The improved algorithm enables accurate and fast tracking of multiple clip objects in real-world track environments. A visualization result of one of the tracked clips is shown in Fig. 6.

In Fig. 6, the yellow and blue lines represent the detection lines for the clips. When a clip drives from the yellow line to the blue line, the downward clip counter is incremented. Similarly, when a clip drives from the blue line to the yellow line, the upward clip counter is incremented. By observing Fig. 6 (b), it can be observed that the original DeepSort algorithm had missed detections in clip detection. Through the improvement of the feature extraction and classification model in the DeepSort algorithm, this paper

 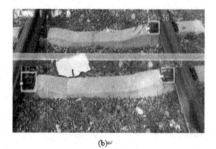

(a)   (b)

Fig. 6. Comparison of detection performance between improved Deepsort algorithm and original algorithm (Color figure online)

successfully detects the missed clips from the original algorithm. This demonstrates that the improved algorithm has good monitoring and tracking capabilities, thereby enhancing the accuracy of clip detection.

3.3 Localization Experimental Results and Analysis

To validate the accuracy of the fused localization results, experiments were conducted to measure the cumulative error generated by the encoder during the travel process. In the experiments, the encoder's travel distance was set to 20.00 m, and 8 sets of results were recorded for each specified distance. The experimental results are presented in Table 4.

Table4. Encoder positioning results when the preset travel distance is 4 m

Experimental Group	Preset Distance (m)	Actual Ditance (m)	Moving Deviation (%)
1	20.00	15.88	0.75%
2	20.00	15.68	2.00%
3	20.00	15.76	1.50%
4	20.00	15.72	1.75%
5	20.00	15.92	0.50%
6	20.00	15.80	1.25%
7	20.00	15.92	0.50%
8	20.00	15.92	0.50%

The experimental results show that during the travel process, the fused localization error is relatively small, enabling accurate tracking of the vehicle's motion state.

Figure 7 presents a comparison of experimental results between standalone positioning using the optical encoder and the fused localization correction incorporating the count of fasteners, under the conditions of a travel time of 150 s and a travel speed

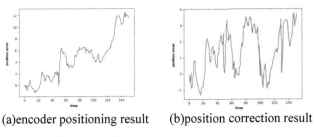

(a)encoder positioning result   (b)position correction result

Fig. 7. Positioning error comparison chart

of 5 km/h. From the figure, it can be observed that when using the optical encoder for standalone positioning, the short-term error can reach up to approximately 13 cm. However, after incorporating the fastener count correction with an error threshold set to 6 cm, the positioning error is effectively controlled to around 4 cm. This demonstrates that the proposed localization correction method in this study achieves high positioning accuracy and can be applied to practical track positioning environments.

4   Conclusion

We propose a deep learning-based method for fastener counting and localization, and validate it through experiments using data collected from subway tunnels. In the future, we aim to apply this method to a wider range of scenarios, such as other transportation facilities and industrial fields, to enhance the accuracy and reliability of localization. Additionally, we plan to further optimize the algorithm to handle more complex environmental conditions and explore integration with other localization techniques to achieve a more comprehensive localization solution.

References

1. Werner, M.: Indoor Location-Based Services: Prerequisites and Foundations. Springer, Cham (2014). https://doi.org/10.1007/978-3-319-10699-1
2. Hengjun, Z., Hanbiao, Q.: Research on the mine personnel localization algorithm based on the background of week signal. Int. J. Smart Home **10**(7), 47–56 (2016)
3. Pang, M., Shen, G., Yang, X., et al.: Achieving reliable underground positioning with visible light. IEEE Trans. Instrum. Meas. **71**, 1–15 (2022)
4. He, K., et al.: Mask R-CNN. In: Proceedings of the IEEE International Conference on Computer Vision (2017)
5. Girshick, R.: Fast R-CNN. In: Proceedings of the IEEE International Conference on Computer Vision (2015)
6. Ren, S., et al.: Faster R-CNN: towards real-time object detection with region proposal networks. In: Advances in Neural Information Processing Systems, vol. 28 (2015)
7. Redmon, J., et al.: You only look once: unified, real-time object detection. In: Proceedings of the IEEE Conference on Computer Vision and Pattern Recognition (2016)
8. Liu, W., et al.: SSD: single shot multibox detector. In: Leibe, B., Matas, J., Sebe, N., Welling, M. (eds.) Computer Vision–ECCV 2016, Part I 14. LNCS, vol. 9905, pp. 21–37. Springer, Cham (2016). https://doi.org/10.1007/978-3-319-46448-0_2

9. Wojke, N., Bewley, A., Paulus, D.: Simple online and realtime tracking with a deep association metric. In: 2017 IEEE International Conference on Image Processing (ICIP). IEEE (2017)

10. Howard, A., et al.: Searching for mobilenetv3. In: Proceedings of the IEEE/CVF International Conference on Computer Vision (2019)

11. Jocher, G., et al.: ultralytics/yolov5: v5. 0-YOLOv5-P6 1280 models, AWS, Supervise. ly and YouTube integrations. Zenodo (2021)

Design and Simulation of Cooperative Communication Networks for Wireless Sensors in Underwater Environments

Shan Gao[1], Honglin Lu[1], Linhan Wang[2(✉)], and Min OuYang[1]

[1] Harbin Engineering University, Harbin 150000, China
{gaoshan08,oym}@hrbeu.edu.cn
[2] Harbin Institute of Technology, Harbin 150000, China
2022111626@stu.hit.edu.cn

Abstract. The underwater communication environment is complex and change-able, with special requirements for delay and packet loss rate. This paper proposes a cluster-based cooperative sensor network with switchable topology, MAC layer protocol, and routing protocol for underwater environments. Through the dynamic selection of cluster heads and cluster members, and the reasonable setting of the topology structure, the sensors in the network can cooperate in communication and aggregate information to the sink node. The protocol and cluster head nodes are dynamically adjusted according to the network conditions, and the MAC protocol and routing protocol are dynamically switched to ensure that all nodes in the network can successfully cooperate in communication. At the same time, nodes can switch states to ensure the robustness and network life of the entire network.

Keywords: Underwater environment · dynamic clustering · protocol selection · node state switching

1 Introduction

In recent years, with the growth of population and the development of society, land resources can no longer meet people's needs, and the vast ocean and its rich resources have become the focus of people's attention and research. The ocean covers an area of about 360 million square kilometers, accounting for about 71% of the earth's surface area, with an average depth of about 3795 m. However, at present, human research and development of the ocean is only about 5%, and the abundant mineral resources, biological resources, ocean current energy and other resources in the ocean are beyond what humans can obtain or far less than on land. For a country, territorial waters involve many influencing factors such as national security, resource acquisition, economic construction, etc., which are indispensable for a country and affect the important foundation of national development and people's livelihood construction.

But at the same time, the ocean also harbors many risks. Disasters such as tsunamis, submarine volcanic eruptions, ocean current movements and so on pose serious threats to coastal areas and sailing vessels. The special environment of the seabed also increases

© The Author(s), under exclusive license to Springer Nature Singapore Pte Ltd. 2024
Y. Sun et al. (Eds.): ChineseCSCW 2023, CCIS 2013, pp. 533–543, 2024.
https://doi.org/10.1007/978-981-99-9640-7_41

the difficulty of people's research and development of the ocean. The high pressure, cold and dark environment of the seabed makes scientific research work difficult to proceed smoothly. Only with the help of auxiliary equipment can people detect the complex and variable environment of the seabed.

For this reason, underwater wireless sensor network (UWSN) [1] technology has attracted the attention of researchers. Underwater wireless sensor networks mainly consist of underwater sensor nodes, surface or land receiving control nodes. Underwater sensor nodes are responsible for information collection, transmission and completion of specific tasks; surface or land control nodes are responsible for receiving, summarizing and analyzing data returned by underwater nodes and performing data analysis and network coordination management. Underwater wireless sensor network nodes themselves have characteristics such as limited energy, complex communication environment, variable topology structure and so on.

In underwater environments, sound waves are usually used for information transmission. Electromagnetic waves have different propagation characteristics in water and air, and will be severely interfered with and attenuated in water. I. I. Smolyaninov et al. [2] achieved a transmission distance of more than 7 m along a sandy seabed using a 50 MHz radio signal through experiments, which cannot meet people's needs in practical engineering. Sound waves are the most widely used long-distance transmission method in underwater environments, which can usually achieve communication requirements of several kilometers or more.

This is crucial for scenarios where underwater sensor network nodes are sparsely deployed. But at the same time, the propagation speed of sound waves in water is much slower than that of electromagnetic waves in air. The speed of electromagnetic waves in air can reach the speed of light, but the propagation speed of sound waves in water is only about 1500 m/s. This leads to high delay and low bandwidth of underwater acoustic communication. The transmission distance of systems with 1–10 km is about 10 kHz; The bandwidth of underwater acoustic communication systems with transmission distance of 0.1–1 km is 20–50 kHz [1]. These characteristics pose higher requirements for communication system design.

2 Related Work

Resource constraints are a major issue that wireless sensor networks must face, especially in special environments such as underwater where it is difficult to replenish energy using conventional methods. Therefore, reducing energy consumption during operation and extending the working time of the network as much as possible has become the main design direction.

In response to the above problem, clustering communication technology has received attention from researchers. Clustering communication technology can be roughly divided into two categories: the first is the classic routing protocol based on LEACH, and the other is the clustering routing protocol based on swarm intelligence optimization algorithms [4].

2.1 Classic Clustering Routing Protocol Based on LEACH

Heinzelman [5] et al. first proposed the Low Energy Adaptive Clustering Hierarchy (LEACH) routing protocol. By setting various indicators including the cluster head ratio, the number of nodes, and the probability threshold related to the current network round, a random number is generated to determine the relationship with the probability threshold, and thus determine whether the node can become a cluster head. At the same time, all nodes can become cluster heads in the next cycle through cluster head rotation. In this protocol, the cluster head transmits data directly to the base station using single-hop, but this will cause cluster heads far from the base station to consume a lot of energy.

To avoid low-energy nodes acting as cluster heads, Behera [6] et al. proposed adding residual energy and optimal cluster head number factors to the probability threshold, and proposed a Residual-based Low Energy Adaptive Clustering Hierarchy (RLEACH) routing protocol. This protocol will prioritize the selection of high residual energy nodes as cluster heads, thus extending the first node death time (First Node Dead, FND) to a certain extent, which is conducive to improving the overall life of the network. However, this protocol ignores the uniformity of cluster head location distribution and load balancing, making it difficult to effectively reduce network energy consumption and extend the last node death time (Last Node Dead, LND).

Sabet and Naji [4] (2016) proposed a Multi-Level Routing Aware Clustering (MLRC) protocol. In this protocol, the base station first sends a message to the nodes to start the competition for the cluster head. Nodes with residual energy above the threshold participate in the competition as cluster head candidates. They broadcast specific information to their neighbors, and based on this information, each node calculates the value of the proposed algorithm function and compares it with the values of its neighbors. If a node has the highest value, it becomes the new cluster head.

2.2 Clustering Routing Protocol Based on Swarm Intelligence Optimization Algorithms

Dai Jianyong [7] et al. introduced an inertial weight factor and an adaptive step size factor to the position update of the firefly optimization algorithm to accelerate the search accuracy and convergence speed of the firefly optimization algorithm, and combined with the BP neural network and comprehensively considered factors such as cluster head density, cluster head distance, and position to optimize node clustering and cluster head election. By constructing an uneven clustering method (the closer to the base station, the smaller the cluster size), the problem of uneven energy consumption is alleviated. However, the training of neural networks and the iteration of firefly algorithms bring huge network resources, and there are defects such as long training time and low accuracy.

Wu Xiao Nian [8] improved the position update formula of the classical particle swarm algorithm by introducing adaptive learning factors and inertial weights. They set a cluster head selection fitness function related to the remaining energy of the node and the position balance factor, mainly iterated with the cooperation information between particles, and selected the cluster head according to the remaining energy and distribution of the node, so that the most suitable node was elected. At the same time, a hybrid inter-cluster communication method of single-hop and multi-hop was proposed based on the difference in distance between the cluster head and the base station, realizing balanced energy consumption between nodes. However, this scheme did not consider the energy hotspot problem, which easily led to two adjacent cluster heads undertaking too many forwarding tasks and quickly dying, reducing the energy utilization rate of nodes.

2.3 Main Contributions of This Paper

This study designs and simulates wireless sensor networks based on the requirements of realistic underwater projects, using the required functions and indicators of the project as the benchmark. The design includes cluster nodes that can dynamically switch routing and MAC layer protocols, and a coordinated communication network with cluster head rotation. The following are the main contributions:

1. In order to achieve long-term underwater operation, according to work requirements, nodes have states such as hibernation, wake-up, and cluster head rotation.
2. The network is divided into three clusters for communication, and the cluster heads can rotate. In an ideal situation, all nodes have the opportunity to be elected as cluster head nodes.
3. Wireless sensor networks will switch routing protocols and MAC layer protocols according to the state during operation (packet loss rate, delay) to ensure the overall communication quality of the network.
4. For the underwater environment, using the NS3 platform, multiple topology structures are designed and verified according to the transmission distance and quality requirements of the project, and comparative experiments are carried out. The best topology structure is selected based on the results.

3   Proposed Design of Underwater Sensor Network

3.1   Construction of Simulation Platform and Parameter Setting

The simulation platform used in this paper is the NS-3 platform. NS-3 is a discrete-time network simulator [9]. Although both NS-3 and its predecessor NS-2 are written in C++, NS-3 is not a simple extension of NS-2, but a brand new network simulator. NS-3 supports both C++ and Python programming languages. By abstracting concepts such as nodes and channels in real networks into various C++ classes, the continuous behavior in the physical world is abstracted into a series of discrete events [10]. NS-3 provides an underwater acoustic communication module UAN (underwater acoustic network) to implement real underwater network scenarios, providing channels, physical layers, MAC layers, sensor acoustic modulation energy models, node energy models, environmental noise, etc. in the underwater environment, so that network simulation can be highly consistent with real scenarios.

The simulation environment of this paper is the underwater environment where the nodes are arranged in different topological structures in a fixed state as mentioned in the previous chapter. The Sink node is independent of other nodes and is located at the coordinate (0,0). The topological structure is designed by us. In order to reflect the effects of different topologies and meet the project requirements, the experimental part of this paper will be based on various regular graphics. Before each simulation, different topology files are selected for configuration, and finally, the performance of the network under different topological structures is statistically analyzed. In the underwater wireless sensor network designed in this paper, the underwater nodes themselves will not move actively, and will only move slowly in the horizontal direction due to ocean currents, so it is ignored. The nodes are deployed by us according to the set topological structure and know their own position information, so the multipath effect caused by reflection and the Doppler frequency shift phenomenon caused by relative fast movement between nodes are also ignored. The specific simulation parameters are shown in the following Table 1:

Table 1. Simulation parameter setting.

Parameter type	Parameter value
Underwater sound propagation speed	1500 m/s
Nodes Communication distance	6000 m
Number of nodes	28
Packet Size	600 byts
Number of cluster heads	3
Initial wake-up nodes ratio	80%
MAC layer protocol	Broadcast/Aloha
Routing protocol	VBF
Number of Sink nodes	1

3.2 Evaluation Index

This paper evaluates network performance using average delay, packet loss rate, and delivery rate as indicators [11,12]. Average packet delay (APD) refers to the average time it takes for a data packet to be transmitted from the source node to the destination node and can be expressed by the following formula:

$$APD = \frac{\sum\limits_{p_i \in P} T_{p_i}}{N_{recv}} \qquad (1)$$

where T_{p_i} represents the time it takes for a data packet to be generated from the source node to the destination node, and N_{recv} represents the total number of data packets received by the destination node.

Packet Loss Ratio (PLR) refers to the ratio of the total number of discarded data packets to the total number of data packets sent by the network and can be expressed by the following formula:

$$PLR = \frac{N_{loss}}{N_{send}} \qquad (2)$$

where N_{loss} represents the total number of discarded data packets and N_{send} represents the total number of data packets sent by the source node.

Packet delivery ratio (PDR) refers to the ratio of the total number of data packets received by the destination node to the total number of data packets generated by the source node and is expressed as:

$$PDR = \frac{N_{recv}}{N_{send}} \qquad (3)$$

3.3 Proposed Clustering and Cluster Head Selection Method

This paper proposes a method of dividing the entire sensor network into three regions by angle, and selecting suitable nodes as cluster heads in each region through an algorithm. The cluster heads must be able to communicate with all member nodes while ensuring that they can communicate with each other. This paper is based on a real underwater network project, which requires that the node communication range can cover a larger communication range with relatively fewer nodes within a diameter of 6000 m. Therefore, our node deployment is carried out within a circular sea area, and various topological deployment methods are compared. Our node deployment shape is a regular graphic. In order to allow the cluster head nodes to cover more member nodes, we chose to divide the area around the Sink node into three regions by angle, each covering 120°.

The routing and MAC protocols will change as the network performance changes during operation. In the underwater environment, ocean currents and the life activities of aquatic animals can affect the working status of sensor nodes, such as position offset or node damage that cannot work. The Sink node will monitor the network status. When the average packet loss rate of the network reaches the set threshold (10%), the routing protocol and MAC protocol will switch.

Nodes have three states: wake-up, sleep, and self-test. During the initialization process of the network, only 80% of the nodes are in the wake-up state. Nodes will switch states as needed. The selection of cluster heads and the method of protocol switching are shown in the following Table 2:

Table 2. Simple algorithm diagram.

Algorithm Cluster head selection
Input: The number of clusters: nCluster, and the location of sink node
Output: The node number that becomes the cluster head: node_status[] = CLUSTER_HEAD;
Step 1: Select nodes
1: **if** node_status[] != WAKE_UP return ture
2: **if** Dis>5500 return true
3:**then** return false
Step 1: Select Clusterheads
4: **if:** nCluster < 3
5: **make** tmp = r->GetInteger(0, nNodes-1)
6: **Select** the nodes in Step 1
7: assert(node_status[tmp] == WAKE_UP)
8: node_status[tmp] = CLUSTER_HEAD
9: **Then** reassign the head for each node

3.4 Experimental Results and Analysis

The underwater wireless sensor network designed in this paper will switch MAC protocols according to the set packet loss rate and delay threshold. For the convenience of statistics, the two protocols are compared separately. First, when using the Broadcast MAC protocol, under different topological structures, the experimental results are shown in the following figure:

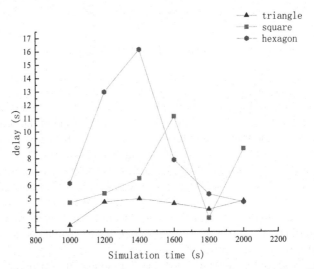

Fig. 1. Delay schematic diagram of different topological structures under Broad MAC protocol

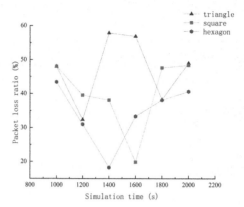

Fig. 2. Packet loss ratio schematic diagram of different topological structures under Broad MACprotocol

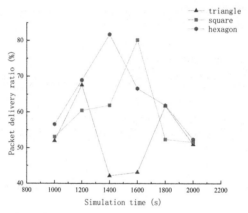

Fig. 3. Delivery ratio schematic diagram of different topological structures under Broad MAC protocol

As can be seen from Fig. 1, the triangular topological distribution of nodes has the best effect, with the delay stable within 3–5 s; the overall delay of the square topology is higher than that of the triangle and lower than that of the hexagon; the overall delay of the hexagonal topology is high, with an average value of 8–9 s. Figure 2 is a packet loss rate statistics chart. From the chart, it can be seen that the performance of all three topologies is not good and the packet loss rate is relatively high. The hexagonal topology distribution has a relatively good effect, but the packet loss rate is also on average at 35%. Figure 3 is a delivery rate statistics chart. Overall, the delivery rate of hexagonal topological distribution is higher than that of square and triangular distributions, and the triangular distribution has the worst effect.

Next are the experimental results of different topological distributions when using the Aloha MAC protocol:

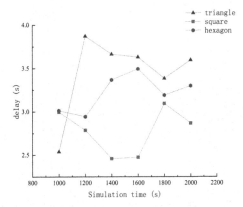

Fig. 4. Delay schematic diagram of different topological structures under Aloha MAC protocol

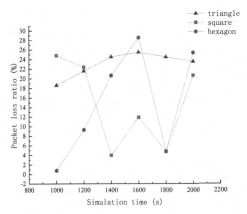

Fig. 5. Packet loss ratio schematic diagram of different topological structures under Aloha MAC protocol

As can be seen from Fig. 4, the overall delay of the square distribution is relatively low, and the overall delay is within 3 s. The triangular distribution has the worst effect but the average is also controlled at around 3 s. Figure 5 is a packet loss rate statistics chart. The triangular distribution has the worst effect with an average value of 23%. In the square and hexagonal distribution charts, due to obvious fluctuations in errors, but the calculated average values of the two are not much different, respectively 15.3% and 14.8%, both better than the triangular distribution. Figure 6 is a delivery rate statistics chart.

It can be seen that the delivery rate of triangular distribution is relatively low, but the average delivery rate is also above 76%. The average delivery rates of square and hexagonal distributions are 84.6% and 85%, respectively, with a small difference.

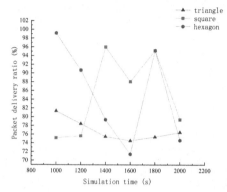

Fig. 6. Packet delivery ratio schematic diagram of different topological structures under Aloha MAC protocol

4 Conclusion and Future Work

From the experimental results in the previous section, it can be seen that whether it is delay, packet loss rate or delivery rate, using the Aloha protocol is generally better than the Broadcast MAC protocol. In the experiment, square and hexagonal distributions often have large fluctuations in network performance, but the overall effect is better than triangular topological distribution. In the future, the currently used VBF routing protocol [13,14] will be optimized to further reduce delay and packet loss rate.

Acknowledgement. This work is supported by Heilongjiang Provincial Natural Science Foundation of China (No. YQ2023F014).

References

1. Su, Y., et al.: Review of security for underwater wireless sensor networks. J. Electron. Inf. Technol. **45**(3), 1121–1133 (2023). https://doi.org/10.11999/JEIT211576
2. Smolyaninov, I., Balzano, Q., Kozyrev, A.B.: Surface electromagnetic waves at sea-water-air and seawater-seafloor interfaces. IEEE Open J. Anten. Propag. **4**, 51–59 (2023). https://doi.org/10.1109/OJAP.2022.3231885
3. Borowski, B.: Characterization of a very shallow water acoustic communication channel, OCEANS,: Biloxi. MS, USA, pp. 1–10 (2009). https://doi.org/10.23919/OCEANS.2009.5422360
4. Rayenizadeh, M., Rafsanjani, M.K., Saeid, A.B.: Cluster head selection using hesitant fuzzy and firefly algorithm in wireless sensor networks. Evolv. Syst. **13**, 65–84 (2022). https://doi.org/10.1007/s12530-021-09405-1
5. Heinzelman, W.B., Chandrakasan, A.P., Balakrishnan, H.: An application-specific protocol architecture for wireless microsensor networks. IEEE Trans. Wirel. Commun. **1**(4), 660–670 (2002)
6. Behera, T.M., Mohapatra, S.K., Samal, U.C., et al.: Residual energy-based cluster-head selection in WSNs for IoT application. IEEE Internet Things J. **6**(3), 5132–5139 (2019)

7. Jianyong, D., Xianhong, D., Bin, W., Henghao, W.: WSNs clustering routing protocol based on improved Firefly optimized neural network. J. Beijing Univ. Posts Telecommun. **43**(3), 131–137 (2020)
8. Wu, X., Zhang, C., Zhang, R., Sun, Y.: Clustering routing protocol based on improved particle swarm optimization algorithm in WSN. J. Commun. **40**(12), 114–123 (2019)
9. Chunguang, M., Jiansheng, Y.: Basics and applications of ns-3 network simulator. People's Post and Telecommunications Publishing House (2014)
10. Zhou, D.: Open source network simulator ns-3 architecture and practice. Machinery Industry Press (2019)
11. Yuan, Y., Liu, M., Zhuo, X., Wei, Y., Tu, X., Qu, F.: A Q-learning-based hierarchical routing protocol with unequal clustering for underwater acoustic sensor networks. IEEE Sensors J. **23**(6), 6312–6325 (2023). https://doi.org/10.1109/JSEN.2022.3232614
12. Chenthil, T.R., Jesu Jayarin, P.: An energy-aware multilayer clustering-based butterfly optimization routing for underwater wireless sensor networks. Wireless Pers. Commun. **122**, 3105–3125 (2022). https://doi.org/10.1007/s11277-021-09042-6
13. Maulana, H., Prihandono, M.A., Elfa, A.S., Harwahyu, R., Sari, R.F.: Analysis of VBF and DBR performance in environmental monitoring system using aquasim at NS-3. In: 2019 International Conference on Informatics, Multimedia, Cyber and Information System (ICIMCIS), Jakarta, Indonesia, pp. 17–22 (2019). https://doi.org/10.1109/ICIMCIS48181.2019.8985348
14. Wu, Z., Liu, M., Zhang, S.: RV-SFAMA-MA: RTS-VBF algorithm used in a slotted-based MAC protocol for underwater acoustic networks with an acknowledgement scheduling algorithm. In: 40th Chinese Control Conference (CCC). Shanghai, China, pp. 5714–5720 (2021). https://doi.org/10.23919/CCC52363.2021.9550631

Author Index

Printed in the United States
by Baker & Taylor Publisher Services